D0205480

THE LEAMINGTON ITALIAN COMMUNITY

The Leamington Italian Community

Ethnicity and Identity in Canada

WALTER TEMELINI

Published for the
Leamington Roma Club
by
McGill-Queen's University Press
Montreal & Kingston • London • Chicago

LONDON PUBLIC LIBRARY

© McGill-Queen's University Press 2019

ISBN 978-0-7735-5469-6 (cloth)
ISBN 978-0-7735-5585-3 (ePDF)
ISBN 978-0-7735-5586-0 (ePUB)

Legal deposit second quarter 2019
Bibliothèque nationale du Québec

Printed in Canada on acid-free paper that is 100% ancient forest free
(100% post-consumer recycled), processed chlorine free

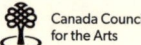

Funded by the Government of Canada / Financé par le gouvernement du Canada | Canadä | Canada Council for the Arts / Conseil des arts du Canada

We acknowledge the support of the Canada Council for the Arts, which last year invested $153 million to bring the arts to Canadians throughout the country.

Nous remercions le Conseil des arts du Canada de son soutien. L'an dernier, le Conseil a investi 153 millions de dollars pour mettre de l'art dans la vie des Canadiennes et des Canadiens de tout le pays.

Library and Archives Canada Cataloguing in Publication

Title: The Leamington Italian community : ethnicity and identity in Canada /
Walter Temelini.
Names: Temelini, Walter, 1939– author.
Description: Includes bibliographical references and index.
Identifiers: Canadiana (print) 20190060476 | Canadiana (ebook) 20190060530
 | ISBN 9780773554696 (hardcover) | ISBN 9780773555853 (PDF) | ISBN
 9780773555860 (ePUB)
Subjects: LCSH: Italians—Ontario—Leamington—History. | LCSH: Italians—Ontario—
 Leamington—Social life and customs. | LCSH: Italians—Ontario—Leamington—Ethnic
 identity. | CSH: Italian Canadians—Ontario—Leamington—History | Italian Canadians—
 Ontario—Leamington—Social life and customs | Italian Canadians—Ontario—
 Leamington—Ethnic identity
Classification: LCC FC3099.L4 Z75 2019 | DDC 305.85/1071331—dc23

This book was typeset in 10.5/13 Sabon.

To my sons Mark, Michael, Leonard

Nescire autem quid ante quam natus sis acciderit, id est semper esse puerum. Quid enim est aetas hominis, nisi ea memoria rerum veterum cum superiorum aetate contexitur?
To be ignorant of what occurred before you were born is to remain always a child. For what is the worth of human life, unless it is woven into the life of our ancestors by the records of history?

Cicero

This book is dedicated in memory of the generations of brave men and women who left their treasured homeland in search of a better life. The opportunities granted us through their sacrifice are endless. Thank you.

We also acknowledge the original committee that realized the importance and value of documenting their stories. Many generations to come will appreciate and celebrate the bravery of their ancestors because this book outlines the journey that led them from Italia to Canada.

Contents

Foreword

The desire for a better life led eight men living in Villa Canale, a small hillside village in Italy, on a journey that eventually landed them in Leamington, Ontario, Canada, a small rural community that offered the one thing that Villa Canale did not. Opportunity! It was here in Leamington where these men planted their roots and laid the foundation for future generations to prosper.

Life was not easy, but the promise and hope for a successful life helped them persevere. And although they came with very little, they quickly discovered that hard work and determination were the keys to the success they so deeply longed for. They worked at hard and arduous jobs that no one else wanted. When speaking to these early immigrants or their children, the word often used to describe those times is *sacrifice*. They sacrificed so much for a better life, and it eventually paid off. They took financial risks and purchased parcels of land. It was more than they could have imagined. To an immigrant, the true definition of success is ownership of land, regardless of its size. To have their own home for their family? The dream!

They came to Canada with very little, but hard work and determination helped them succeed and prosper. They needed only the opportunity to succeed, and they did! These attributes were lessons that each generation have inherited and passed along and what have brought each generation further ahead than the last. Although we live more luxuriously than our ancestors, the concept of working hard, saving your money, and reinvesting those savings are principles that many of our Italian businessmen and women adhere to today, and it is what ensures their continued success.

Although Leamington still remains a largely agricultural community, it would have been impossible for those early immigrants to imagine what farming in 2018 would look like. In the earlier years, many farms supplied H.J. Heinz Canada with bountiful loads of tomatoes grown as outdoor crops, as well as other fruits and vegetables, but tomatoes remained the largest crop grown in Leamington. So many, in fact, that Leamington became known as the tomato capital of Canada. As time passed though, more and more farmers transitioned from growing outdoor crops to growing tomatoes, peppers, and cucumbers in greenhouses. Acreage back then was small compared to today. In 2018, there is an estimated 2,800 acres of greenhouses with the latest technology in Leamington and surrounding area. New expansions/developments are consistently on the rise. Crops grown in today's greenhouses are still traditionally tomatoes, cucumbers, and peppers, but the varieties grown are numerous. Long gone are the days of growing the popular beefsteak tomato! Tomatoes come in all shapes, sizes, and colours and are packaged and sold accordingly. Crops have also grown to include strawberries, eggplant, runner beans, and medicinal marijuana – something I am certain those early immigrants would never have imagined!

It is important to make note of H.J. Heinz Company in Leamington. Not only did many immigrants grow for Heinz, but many were also employed by the factory. These were good paying jobs that offered excellent benefit packages and the security of lucrative retirement packages. Unfortunately, after 105 years in Leamington, H.J. Heinz Company closed their doors in 2014, leaving many with uncertain futures. It was a devastating blow to the town, but Leamington, like those early settlers, persevered. The 2.1 million-square-foot facility reopened later that same year as Highbury Canco Corporation, a new food processing plant, which is slowly rebuilding a solid footprint within the community. Its wages do not compare to those paid by Heinz, but they do offer a promising start. and the legend of the Tomato Capital of Canada continues.

In addition to the ownership of property, and perhaps even more satisfying for those early immigrants and their families, was the ability to give their children a solid education, something they were not afforded. Many of the elders in our community will tell you that the school building was almost always the nicest building in every small town or village, including Villa Canale. Education was valued and so, as soon as they could afford to have their children attend school instead of work, these early immigrants did so. It was their dream to have their offspring finish elementary school and possibly secondary school, but a post-secondary education must have seemed too far-fetched to even wish for in those early years. In 2018, however, the value of an education still holds true amongst Italian families, and those young men seeking a better life would be thrilled to see that many of their descendants have become successful business people, nurses, doctors, lawyers, engineers, accountants, certified tradespeople, writers, educators, and so much more. The dream of a better life has been redefined, but one thing remains true. It is redefined with the hope that, as it was so many years ago, the next generation will do better than the previous one.

Leamington today remains a culturally diverse community with a large Italian population. It is possibly the greatest gift these eight men gave to us all. Roots. Leamington is home. A town where many generations before us have raised their families and built their lives, and it is also a town where future generations will continue to raise their families and build their lives. As a community, we celebrate and practise our Italian traditions, perhaps in a different and more modern way, but we do celebrate them. We celebrate them because we were taught to cherish these traditions, and we, in turn, teach our children to treasure them as well. It is a gift and a blessing.

The Roma Club of Leamington is still looked upon as cultural hub, a place to gather and celebrate our Italian culture and heritage. Many weddings, baptisms, communions, and other family milestones have been celebrated at this Italian club. St Michael's Festival continues to be celebrated every fall, as does the Members' Banquet every spring. Although it does have its challenges, the Roma Club continues to be an Italian legacy to this town, started by young men and their families in the hopes that a lasting cultural heritage would remain in this small town called Leamington.

Younger generations have often wondered what it would have been like for those eight men who travelled to unknown lands in search of a better life. They did not know the people they would encounter or speak their language. They came with very little in their wooden trunks that they transported across the world with them, but they carried big hopes and dreams in their hearts. The generations that followed them owe them a huge debt of gratitude. To say thank you seems so little, yet we do thank them for their bravery and everything that we have been granted because of it.

Lily DiCiocco
Leamington Roma Club

Preface

The study of even a small section of a Canadian ethnocultural group, such as the Leamington (Ontario) Italian community, has far-reaching historical, sociological, and human implications. The preparatory research and investigation, however sporadic, uncertain, or incomplete, always produces an abundance of material and documentation that will remain invaluable. The lists of names, places, and occupations, and the stories of displacement and disorientation, hard work, adjustment, and achievement can be tedious and overwhelming. But they provide a sound statistical base for the in-depth understanding of the growth of the community, and thereby even reveal some of its distinctive characteristics. They are also a base for other studies, including, as in this case, literary works.

This type of study, though limited, offers an opportunity to further explore the nature and meaning of emigration/immigration or migration in general. It may even make clearer its demographic and socio-economic effects on the country of origin and the country of destination or, more specifically, on the receiving communities, which increasingly become ethnoculturally diverse or multicultural, and on those *paesi* (villages) that were often depopulated or robbed of their "best young people." (The bulk of Italian migrant workers in Canada at the beginning of the twentieth century were young men.) The study of a limited area and of a small community illustrates the history of both countries. It can also fill a gap in the patchy history of emigration. According to some scholars (e.g., Rosoli, Harney), the data or statistics on migration, especially for the earlier period, are often unavailable, complex, inconsistent or unreliable. Thus, the study of such a community or group can help clarify, corroborate, or even reshape general trends established by historians for longer periods of migration.

Beyond the statistics, facts, and charts, there is the human story – individual and collective. In the simple and direct accounts of the first protagonists of this human migration the whole story of the uprooting and resettlement unfolds. Often it is not so much the order or accuracy of the events that is important as the urgency to relate the experience. At times they are cautious, as if some unfortunate consequence might befall them in exposing too much. But reserved or enthusiastically spontaneous, they reveal a wide range of emotions, always manifesting a natural awareness and fullness of humanity. In some cases, though as many as sixty years have gone by, the memory of those youthful experiences remains vivid. The feelings emerge as intense as in the age that produced them: dissatisfaction and rebellion ("I did not wish to play music for Mussolini"); impetuousness tempered by an innate wisdom; determination balanced by aspirations and a staid sense of humour ("We didn't find the streets paved with gold, but we did find jobs").

Their tales today may seem disconnected, lacking in structure and syntax. Yet the salient events are described fully and clearly. Even after such a long time, the mother tongue often re-emerges intact and exact, reaching at times poetic qualities and painfully moving tones: "We fell into the hands of the *contrabbandieri dell'emigrazione* [merchants of emigration]," a clear reference to the practices, well documented by historians, of the agents who recruited and exploited emigrants-immigrants. Their stories highlight unpleasant events and sentiments that moulded their dreams, hopes, and struggles, that guided these men toward the land of opportunity. All are part of the legacy of those, aptly and perceptively defined, unschooled but not unintelligent first immigrants.[1]

In the interviews with three generations of Leamington Italians, one can see the not so simple world of these proud "new Canadians" come alive. We become spectators to the birth and evolution of a small community: initially insignificant, but gradually developing and progressing while retaining its distinct features; almost imperceptibly undergoing integration to eventually become a significant part of the larger community, of Canadian society, still different from it in many ways, but very much Canadian. We witness the life of a community from its almost fortuitous beginnings to its ethnic maturity.

The beginning of this long and subtle transformation is often marked by culture shock, the social and psychological displacement into an unfamiliar environment. The linguistic and economic hardships are aggravated by anxiety and nostalgia, sometimes accompanied by ill feelings toward the homeland ("Italy never gave me anything"; "I forgot Italy the day I arrived"). The struggle for survival may often lead to success, but the assimilation of new ways of life and lifestyles may also revive dogged efforts to remain attached to the good old ways and values. The inevitable clash between the two modes of life and thinking may continue through the years; on the other hand, a degree of synthesis of the two lifestyles may result, along with self-fulfilment, a sense of pride, and a greater role in society. Then their impact on the whole community becomes increasingly visible through constant interaction in the workplace and through their new social and commercial enterprises. In three generations, this impact has not been limited to just the social and economic spheres but also involved the political and cultural milieu. It is a pattern followed by all immigrant communities.

But as the study will show, the Italian-Canadian community in the southernmost part of Canada does present unique features: it is a community composed mostly of immigrants from the southern part of Italy; it is the only surviving rural and largely agricultural Italian community in Canada, one that has remained relatively close-knit (see chapter 1, "A Unique Italian-Canadian Community").

The compactness is the result of the other two aspects of their interaction: the common Southern Italian origins and their shared experience in rural Southwest Ontario. Their common origins are particularly manifested in the regional, socio-cultural, and linguistic affinities, as well as in the family ties of most settlers from the 1920s to the 1970s, and especially of the handful of pioneer families and founders of the community. Their common origins were reinforced by their shared experience in a well-defined, rural area and in farming or farm-related activities. Farming or the farm was, above all and from the beginning, the pivotal point of each family, group of families, and community, particularly because by 1946 most of the 1920s pioneer families (twelve of the fourteen that settled in the Leamington area) had become owners of a farm, often with a greenhouse plant. The farm was not only the centre of life and work in the pre–Second World War, formative years of the community but also a base for the massive postwar sponsorship (chain migration, employment, settlement) of the new immigrants, mostly relatives. The farm was subsequently a springboard for further expansion or other ventures (see chapters 7, 8, 9).

The compactness has remained relatively firm through the decades, in spite of increasing occupational and generational differentiation or the ordinary disrupting forces of modern life. The close-knit, almost monolithic nature of the community was especially visible in their political behaviour, their continuous support of one political party. More recently, this compactness has manifested in a new awareness and community spirit at work within the larger Canadian society.

After decades of self-effacing hard work and silent building, the community has become more conscious of itself and of its role in the economic growth and transformation of the region (specifically from a tobacco- to a produce-growing area, especially through their modern greenhouse complexes). No doubt influenced by the changes in the Canadian social and political climate throughout the 1970s, they quickly responded to the new policy of multiculturalism: the policy, the philosophy, the program that encourages all ethnocultural groups in Canada to rediscover their roots and traditions in order to assess the contribution of each group to the Canadian mosaic, or, according to the widely publicized official slogan, to "celebrate and share" this heritage with other Canadians. Multiculturalism offered a new Canadian opportunity. They grasped this opportunity as new Canadians to show other Canadians not only their commitment to Canada but also the work and contribution to this country by their parents and grandparents, by the pioneers of their community.

The response was the creation of the Leamington Roma Club Italian Historical Book Committee, a group composed of a cross-section of the community. The project found support and encouragement among most members of the club and community, and the collection of material, contacts, and interviews was entrusted to the equally committed younger people of the community, many of them descendants of the pioneers. This aspect in itself seems to distinguish the Leamington Italian community. It appears that whatever form of *campanilismo*, that particularly Italian parochialism or blind attachment to one's own hometown or region that may have survived, and still prevailing in other Italian communities (including nearby Windsor), was put aside in Leamington for a common, more durable goal (see chapter 1). The study also makes an attempt to define this new awareness of themselves, of their contribution through the years: to seek out the essence of their Italian ethnicity and place it within the Leamington and Canadian multicultural context (i.e., intergroup relations). Finally, the hope is that the study, as an outcome of their own project, will also be a humble monument to the vision and energy of the entire community, especially its founders.

Walter Temelini

Acknowledgments

This volume owes its existence to the Italian-Canadian community in the Leamington area (Southeast Essex County). The Leamington Roma Club introduced the idea of a book through its Italian Historical Book Committee and provided leadership and part of the funds for its realization. Most of the Italian families participated in the project. Three groups of Leamington Italian-Canadian student-researchers, in spite of many obstacles, conducted much of the preparatory work, taped most of the oral testimonies, and prepared written reports, particularly Nino Ricci's *Radici,* which often served as a general outline; and all along two community leaders supervised the project and provided the author with substantial additional documentation: Gino DiMenna and Gino Pannunzio.

Invaluable assistance also came from many sources. The author is especially indebted to Nevi Rusich (executive director, Windsor Italo-Canadian Culture Centre – wiccc) and to Rita Bison (managing editor of *La Gazzetta,* Windsor-Detroit Italian weekly) for their ongoing collaboration in researching early Italian settlement in Southwest Ontario, collecting and collating data and statistics, compiling the first draft, and to Vanessa Shields, Kayla Marsh, and David Sandor for their subsequent editorial work. Sonia Giovanatto and Flora Cozzetto were, though briefly, efficient research assistants. Keith Ouellette (Land Registry Office for the County of Essex in Windsor) and Shirley Lehn (Mersea Township Office in Leamington) kindly obtained many of the deeds of land and/or records relating to the early farm purchases by Leamington-area Italians. Their most generous assistance, while helping to greatly reduce time and costs, provided the study with the necessary documentary evidence for early farm ownership, the base of the development of this farming community.

For their contributions, the author is very grateful to: Fr Lino Santi (pastor, St Angela Merici Church, Windsor) and Fr Ugo Rossi (Italian priest at St Michael's Church, Leamington), for facilitating access to their parish records; the late John Hughes (former Windsor chief of police) and Douglas Brombal (Ottawa), for documents pertaining to the 1940 suspension of Constable Nero (Nereo) Brombal; Bob Gault (curator of the Canadiana and Auto Museum, LaSalle, Ontario), for sharing his knowledge about early vehicles and auto-related products; Fernando Busico and Luciano Iarusso (both of Windsor), and Anthony Gori and Gino Ingratta (both of Leamington), for use of their personal library holdings (books, newspapers, videos, photos, and other material); Walter Cunial (Windsor photographer), for reproducing old photos and documents; Alfio Golini (former director of the Italian-language program at CHYR Radio, Leamington) and Joseph Raffa (London, Ontario, teacher, poet, musician), for helping identify Italian popular songs; Albert Pecoraro, Tamara Murray, Michael Bortolin, and other former University of Windsor students of Italian or multicultural studies, including my sons Mark, Michael, and Leonard, for helping to find library material and newspaper articles; Angela Urbano (Kingsville), for the many clarifications regarding families and farms in her area; and Luigi Mastronardi (Agnone, Italy) for his communication about Villa Canale.

Heartfelt thanks also to all those who readily communicated specific and sometimes delicate information about their families and/or other Italian families or groups in the Southwest Great Lakes area: Steve Aiuto (Windsor Sicilians); Emanuele Calamita (Windsor, Essex County Apulians); Paul Marra (Amherstburg, Ontario); Judge Velma Meconi (Belle River, Ontario); the Peralta families (Leamington/Detroit); Sid Spano family (Leamington); John Rossi (Windsor, Bernachi family), and Nicola Valentino (Windsor).

I would like also to honour the memory of Ana Besné and Emma Ferry who, as part of the University of Windsor Department of Classical and Modern Languages, Literatures, and Civilizations, helped me give shape to the very difficult first typewritten manuscript.

Gratitude is owed as well to others who helped revise and refine the product: the very professional staff at the University of Windsor Word Processing Centre; readers of the manuscript, in the Leamington area (particularly Marius Ingratta, Reno Melatti, and Gino Pannunzio) and in other parts of Canada; Professor Charles Fantazzi, University of Windsor, and especially Professor D.H. Akenson, editor, McGill-Queen's University Press, for his suggestions and encouragement.

The support of the following is acknowledged: the Government of Ontario through the Ministry of Culture and Communications; Employment and Immigration Canada: Young Canada Works Program; and the Secretary of State.

THE LEAMINGTON ITALIAN COMMUNITY

The "Oral History Method": Advantages and Disadvantages

The project to produce a history of the Leamington Italian community came into being as an activity of the Leamington Roma Club in the late 1970s. Its newly formed Historical Book Committee "wished to provide a living testament to the experiences of the Italian immigrants in their area, both for present and future generations, and ... produce a volume of history which would shed light on the nature of the immigrant experience in Canada."[1] The work was to be based on the information collected by interviewing all the Italian families that settled in the area from the 1920s to the 1970s; particularly by recording the testimonies of the few surviving members of the 1920s pioneer groups, both men and women, and their children (see appendices A, B).

It was deemed best to begin with the earliest immigrants, not just for the sake of chronology, which "would allow us to see more clearly the developing patterns," but particularly for the invaluable general information that the pioneers would provide, as well as out of respect for the founders of the community. There was also a sense of urgency, an anxiety, that a further delay would result in a great loss and sorrow for family and community: the death of one of them also meant the disappearance of another irreplaceable part of their heritage.[2]

Over 430 families participated in the project: about 78 per cent of the approximately 550 families (or about 2,000 individuals) that formed the community or settled in the area (appendix A). While focused on the town of Leamington and Mersea Township, where most of the Italians resided, the study included also the nearby localities of Ruthven, Kingsville, Essex Town, Cottam, Blytheswood, and Wheatley (including Harrow in Colchester South Township). The research or collection of information covered most of the southeast quarter of Essex County, an area of about 450 square kilometres consisting of Gosfield South, Gosfield North, and Mersea Townships.

The interviews and gathering of information, carried out mostly by university students hired by the club during the summers of 1979 to 1981, produced a vast amount of material: 376 cassettes containing the interviews themselves and eight binders of written summaries of the recorded interviews; as well as two "Master Binders" with other pertinent information including family documents (mostly in photocopy) – photos, passports, tickets, identity cards, and army discharge papers; and a card catalogue of families, each containing basic biographical data of both husband and wife: date and place of birth; date and port of entry into Canada; means of travel and name of ship (if applicable); residence before immigration and/or place of origin; date of settlement in Leamington (if different from date of entry), as well as date of marriage, children, and occupation before and after immigration. A master list of family names was also formed to serve as a cross-reference (appendix A). They were all useful tools in the reconstruction of each personal experience and collective story.

Nevertheless, part of the difficulties in writing the book stemmed directly from this very process of taking testimony. As Robert F. Harney outlined in his *Oral Testimony and Ethnic Studies* and as the Leamington students also described in their own reports, the problems inherent in this method of collecting information relate to both mechanical/technical and human factors: the limited knowledge or improper use of the equipment (tape recorder) and the inadequate experience in the interviewing technique.[3] In our case, the effect was confusion: recorded interviews and written summaries lacked logical and chronological sequence; consequently the writer had to spend inordinate time in sifting through the maze of information to give some form and role to their testimonies.

At times attempts to overcome some complications created others. Two students were usually present at an interview: one to ask questions and operate the tape recorder, the other to write down the salient points of the interview (and though disconnected, the notes proved useful when the tapes were defective, or the only source when recording was not permitted). Two students working together may have helped alleviate the interviewers' initial awkwardness and self-consciousness, but it also extended the period of interviews over three summers, causing fragmented or contradicting views of "developing patterns." Together, they may have complemented each other's questioning, ensuring, in their view, that the interviews were thorough; nevertheless, it produced unnecessary repetitions.

Following the written questionnaire too closely was found to be too mechanical, too formal, blocking spontaneity, even intimidating, especially to those interviewed, thus causing prolonged gaps in the conversation. The question sheet was eventually abandoned for a more informal, conversational method of interviewing. However, the results were mixed: a very spontaneous and informal flow of information, but a great deal of rambling later caused further aggravation.

Similarly, the tape recorder was an endless source of frustration. Though the large majority of participants consented to have their remarks recorded, many were uncomfortable. Some may even have tailored their response for the tape recorder. A few even admitted afterwards that they were not being totally honest because of the tape recorder, or went on to provide a wealth of information that they were reluctant to release while the recorder was on. As the summer progressed, the students were able to create a more relaxed atmosphere conducive to more effective interviewing. But their newly acquired techniques could not be carried over to the following summer. Each group of students had to go through the same process of rapid training, often by discovering and resolving the problems themselves.

Some difficulties derived from circumstances particular to this project: the interviews were carried out in three separate stages and by three different groups of students, inevitably resulting in repetition, overlapping, and time wasted in revisions. The lack of continuity and delays, partly due to limited funds, even though supplemented by government grants, were also cause of some frustration to all involved: sponsoring group and granting agencies as well as researchers and writer. The project as a whole was also made more difficult by the fact that no study on Italian immigration had ever been done for this general area.

Breaking new ground, however exciting, presented its own problems: the first step was to identify the Italian families in the area and compile a comprehensive list of them. The names were gathered by consulting club membership lists and records, which went back only to the 1960s, the telephone directory, for the current residents, and older members of the community for the earlier settlers – all useful sources but not always reliable for their limitations, uncertainties, or contradictions (often due to unclear recollections). Continuous screening and revisions were required, especially to verify some names that appeared Italian but were not, or vice versa (and some may have been omitted from the project also for this reason). Other records – church, school, cemetery, Registry Office – were also consulted, but were often inaccessible or unavailable, another obstacle in this type of study.[4]

Nevertheless, the commitment to the project remained firm. What the young interviewers-researchers lacked in experience, they made up in resourcefulness, initiative, and motivation. After all, they were dealing with their own community, with a part of their heritage and of themselves. Their thoroughness, teamwork, and readiness to incorporate suggestions and to learn always spurred them on, guiding them even on unfamiliar terrain. And the experience had immediate benefits: the project, some said, provided them with important, marketable skills. Above all they collected a body of valuable information and supplied a base to achieve the objectives of the Historical Book Committee and of the community as a whole.[5]

What the students collected was more than facts. An attempt was made "to establish a personal life history of each immigrant," and that often involved prying "into [the] personal opinions, feelings, moralities, and philosophies" of each one of them. But as a result, in the students' words, the interviews came to be "a combination of fact and feeling, of the objective and subjective aspects of each Italian's life. In this way, we were able to establish the nature of the Italian immigrant and the effect of the immigrant experience." To a great extent the interviews did present what the students claimed; and perhaps part of the confusion also present in them may be explained by "a combination of fact and feeling."[6]

Through their direct experience, the students recognized basic aspects of the "oral history" method: "Undoubtedly the best source for the study of the cluster of motives which led to the decision to migrate and for recording the details of the crossing is the immigrant himself ... Even the severest critics of oral history admit that the method works best for gathering impressions, opinions, and attitudes rather than determining fact ... Flesh and blood, the nuance and inflection of a tape recorded reminiscence, complicate historical analysis, but obviously enrich it as well."[7] The students' work, interviews, and reports, particularly *Radici*, together served as a starting point and as a guideline for the "volume of history" and an invented story of their grandparents' or parents' "immigrant experience in Canada."

LITERATURE AND HISTORICAL ANALYSIS
OR THE INTERDISCIPLINARY METHOD

The history or story of the Leamington Italian community was at first intended to be based mainly on the oral testimonies of the protagonists themselves. The wish of the sponsoring committee and community was that their stories – most often related in a fragmented, disconnected, repetitious, and dramatic manner – be integrated into an informative and entertaining whole. While agreeing on a more "popular" mode of presentation (also favoured, it seemed, by the government agency co-funding the project), I tried to steer the committee away from a narration of self-aggrandizement, and to abate the tendency, inherent also in the passionate testimonies, toward idealization. But it was clear that what was desired was not an "academic" or "scholarly" book.

I was not expected to engage in other research, but I could not completely divest myself from my academic training. The committee was made aware that, by incorporating historical, sociological, and literary references and/or evidence, the protagonists' acts, words, and feelings would be placed within a larger historical and human context, and thus have a more universal dimension, an ampler meaning. Thereby, the book would also have a scholarly frame. It was therefore agreed that an attempt would be made to strike a balance between the "local" and "academic" history format.

The idea of seeking a balance, however, was not simply a sudden response to circumstantial exigencies. It was to be primarily a conscious application of long-standing theory and practice: the interdisciplinary approach. The French historian Fernand Braudel, for example, connected history to all human sciences: "History is the science of man as long as it incorporates all the sciences of man ... You cannot advance unless you bring together all the human sciences, like an orchestra." More than "interdisciplinary study," Braudel favoured what he called "generalized promiscuity ... Let us mix all the sciences, including the traditional ones such as philosophy and philology."[8]

Nancy S. Struever has analyzed the relation of language and historical consciousness from ancient times to the Italian Renaissance. "Language theories and techniques," she wrote, "have great resonance in historical theory and practice: the structure of language relates to the structure of knowledge and thus to the definition of historical reality." Struever investigated, above all, the "[triangular] relationship" of history with other disciplines and human activities, including the "connection of rhetoric, poetic, and history ... Thus eloquence, and therefore rhetoric, is an essential, not accidental, part of history."[9]

As a student of literature and of the Renaissance, I am guided by the principle that literature informs history as much as history informs literature: "The Renaissance, at its dawning," wrote Eugenio Garin, "places itself under the sign of philology, by philology intending [that] vast and clear and critical consciousness of human activity ... that same attitude [toward reality which is also a method] that gives life and direction even to the new scientific research."[10] According to Francesco Tateo, "The new spirit with which the [humanists] carried on this [philological] activity, that is [their] conviction of restoring the past in its integrity and in its historical reality, makes humanistic philology the foundation of the modern historical consciousness." A "noteworthy indication of [Leonardo] Bruni's historical and literary conception [is his] assertion [that] the translator [of ancient texts] is substantially equivalent to the historian, because both do not do other than a literary work of transcription, the latter of facts, the former of someone else's words."[11] Briefly, in the words of Erwin Panofsky, "The humanist ... is, fundamentally, an historian."[12]

In the 1980s Umberto Eco, theorist of language and communication and author of *The Name of the Rose*, showed that both the invented and the recognizable characters and/or events, in the historical novel, "[serve] to make history, what happened, more comprehensible ... they tell us things about [a particular era or situation] that history books have never told us so clearly."[13] That literature and history are mutually enriching is exemplified by the representation of the world of the Middle Ages in Eco's novel or by the transformation of an ethnocultural reality in Nino Ricci's first novel, *Lives of the Saints*. The interrelation of literature and history benefits both and improves effectiveness of representation. See chapter 15, "*Lives of the Saints*: A Legacy and a Goal for All Canadians."

Nevertheless, the promiscuous approach may generate reactions or objections: one may concern the classification of this study, which may lead one to ask, Is it history? sociology? literature? In fact, it incorporates all three. And the observation may even be taken as a compliment. Still, a particular category of scholarship or methodology is not the sole criterion for judging a work more or less academic, scholarly or scientific. Besides, why does a work need to be classified at all? Scholarship is not diminished by what does not conveniently fit into a specific, preestablished mould. It is not fair or scholarly to treat as unworthy what cannot be pigeonholed or compartmentalized, be it methods of inquiry or truths reached! It seems that this mode of thinking and acting is a cause and defect of today's fragmentary education, of the split between the humanities and the sciences, between academia and society or community, or even of regional and cultural fragmentation in our present world.

"This obsession with methodology," wrote Robert E. Proctor, "affects all the disciplines of modern universities," producing a type of scholarship (e.g., "the vogue for 'quantitative reasoning' in the social sciences") that has "lost touch with morally significant issues ... This obsession with methodological fads, while it may keep a good number of specialized journals and university presses in business ... simply does not address the problem of what ... we should be teaching our students, unless we're content to argue ... that the essence of education is exposure to different methodologies and disciplinary perspectives."

Proctor found an answer in the "*studia humanitatis* [which] began, in part, as a revolt against this obsession with the techniques of ratiocination ... The early humanists [unhappy] with a primarily technical approach to education and to life ... encouraged instead the study of classical poetry, rhetoric, moral philosophy, and history." Proctor's global approach to learning and resulting global view of the self and of humanity ("a cultural and historical experience")[14] does not differ from Marshall McLuhan's response to the inadequacy, in our global-sized village, of specialized erudition or skills, of our mechanistic, fragmentary and piecemeal education: particularly his emphasis on the need for "intense sensitivity to the interrelation and interprocess of the whole," for "interrelating every human experience," and "for over-all consideration of human unity."[15]

The method followed in this study reflects those views, and for a purpose. Empirical and intuitive writings, of both Canadians and Italians, have been interwoven in order to provide an ampler vision of the complex psychological motives and socio-economic causes for the particular and general migration phenomenon. The method is not new; it has been used to explain this vast phenomenon by historians and cultural anthropologists in Canada and Italy, witness Robert F. Harney (Toronto) and Cesare Pitto (University of Calabria).[16]

The literary references or parallels in the study are not simply a reflection of my field of specialization – language and literature; in fact, their main purpose is to enhance and illustrate the effects of emigration. Literature is, after all, a particular use of language; and language, wrote Mario Pei, "is the indispensable vehicle of all human knowledge ... the basic foundation of all human cooperation," and therefore "the study of language is a social science to the highest degree." Language, according to Pei, is "all-pervasive ... Its functions are as numerous as the fields in which human ingenuity operates." Literature is also by its very nature all-inclusive because it incorporates language and life (form and content). Since, as Pei again states, "all forms of human activity hinge on the use of language,"[17] then history, sociology, and literature are fully interrelated. Fittingly, a Canadian writer showed how the properties of language and literature benefit multicultural Canada, thus all diverse societies. Since "literature comes from life-events, [through] literature [one] can look at the values, attitudes and beliefs of people and see what there is in common, what would help toward unity and better understanding." Literature fosters awareness of different cultures and different social levels, and above all an "attitude of belonging."[18] Clearly, literary works are effective in exploring and explaining the human condition. As a human art and science, literature integrates historical or sociological analysis.

The method used in this study can be further illustrated by considering three related issues. The first pertains to a view of history, historiography, historical inquiry, or even epistemology in general. It centres on a contrast between the empirical, "scientific" method and the intuitive, "humanistic" approach in the interpretation of reality, in the acquisition of knowledge, in seeking truth, wisdom, or simply understanding. I see history as a "humanity," without considering it less or more valid as a "social science." Its two modes have complementary roles: it is "a tool for understanding man," in Braudel's words, or to make men wise, according to Francis Bacon. For Cicero and the humanist Leonardo Bruni, history is a "fundamentally literary activity" and a "*magistra vitae*" – a teacher of life. Lessons can be drawn from history as from literature: "History," states Braudel, "if it is to be valuable, must be integrated into the other sciences. And the human sciences, for their part, must take the historical dimension into account. Sociologists, anthropologists, and the like have not concerned themselves enough with the historical perspective ... The present can be explained only by the past – and the relatively distant past at that."

The two aspects of history favour a multi-dimensional outlook, or our need for "horizons of significance," especially "the speech of deep diversity."[19] Such a view of history promotes the indispensability of global awareness in a time of unprecedented "interaction and interdependence of nations and peoples of the world ... All of us confront political and economic relationships [that] demand that we approach history from a global perspective," and "global" refers to both world and multidisciplinary.[20] History needs to be viewed, therefore, as a human science in its widest sense, incorporating aspects and methods of both the social sciences and the humanities; it has to follow what Garin called "that human *art* that fuses science and poetry,"[21] that is, the best literary and language arts and sciences: philology, rhetoric, and literature.

The correlation, scientific-positivist perspective derived from Auguste Comte's theories, appears too restrictive. It may even suggest a bias, an unscientific premise and judgment, even a contradiction. A nineteenth-century philosophy or system cannot be considered more scientific or more contemporary than a method that emphasizes the whole human being and human values, that fuses science and art and is based on a vast intellectual, spiritual, and cultural movement that spread from Italy throughout Europe (in the fourteenth to sixteenth centuries), as the Renaissance and humanism have been described![22] Isn't it a personal choice or fashionable trend to favour Comte's theories over the definition of history or method of inquiry as presented or practised, let us say, by Renaissance humanists such as Salutati, Bruni, or Poliziano,[23] or by such a philosopher as Giambattista Vico,[24] or historians such as Struever or Braudel?

"All ideologies [science included] must be seen in perspective," wrote Paul Feyerabend. "One must not take them too seriously. One must read them like fairytales which have lots of interesting things to say but which also contain wicked lies." Science or the scientific method, once "an instrument of liberation and enlightenment ... has now become as oppressive as the ideologies it had once to fight ... Science has become rigid, a reverence-demanding dogma. For example consider the role of science in education ... There is no attempt to waken the critical abilities of the pupil so that he may be able to see things in perspective. At the universities the situation is even worse, for indoctrination is here carried out in a much more systematic manner." Feyerabend questions especially the claim "that science has finally found the correct *method* for achieving results," and the "answer ... that science works by collecting facts and inferring theories from them ... is unsatisfactory as theories never *follow* from facts in the strict logical sense." In essence, Feyerabend's "criticism of modern science is that it inhibits freedom of thought."[25] In light of such arguments, the scientific or positivist perspective can hardly be the exclusive means to investigate life or to assess scholarship.

The more inclusive interdisciplinary or humanistic approach provides greater flexibility of mind and method, at least another perspective, especially in the practice or the "study of history," which, Braudel says, "is ever-changing"; and "a particular history must be incorporated into the whole." In this study, an attempt was made to incorporate the modes and findings of other disciplines, not only for the desired ampler perspective but for other more specific reasons. In dealing with emigration, immigration, or migration, empirical data are not always available, and when they are, their interpretations greatly vary. In other words, the truth cannot always be represented by scientifically verified facts. As Braudel again makes clear, "A historian cannot ... write like a novelist ... attempts [have to be made] to force history as far as possible into a scientific framework ... statistics [and] figures are useful in posing questions or preventing the questions from being poorly framed." But, Braudel adds, "I am not saying that statistics are the long and short of history."

In exploring a particular reality, or in dealing with what Braudel calls "a slowly moving history – [such as the] migrations of people, new nations, war" (in our case migration of Italians, new communities as well as war), it is often necessary to resort to other means in order to define or give form to that reality. Some historians have engaged in "interpreting mental states, as they relate to history – or psychohistory." Other scholars have stressed the investigation of a well-defined event, community, village, or family – microhistory; others still have employed the interdisciplinary approach, which includes related literary works.[26]

Helen Nader sketched "a synthesis of the [historical] research of the past twenty-five years to demonstrate how quickly and thoroughly the old European world was transformed by the encounter within Columbus's lifetime," particularly "the speed and extent of the transformation ... In these new historical studies, it is the American reality – its weather, peoples, and ecology – that is forcing the end of the old world." Thus, in the section "Proposal for a New Approach to the History of the Encounter" Nader describes the changes that took place before and after 1492; and in conclusion she again states that "America imposed its own needs, its own criteria. It was this American imperative that ended the old world." And quite revealing is Nader's closing section, "Implications for Future Research," where she writes, "The real story is no longer one of monarchy or the hierarchy of government. The action is at the micro level, the level of local history. The demands come from the environment, from the interactions of natives and Europeans, from the new world that was being created year by year."[27]

Equally indicative is Walter D. Mignolo's research (1992) on the "semiotic interactions between different writing systems during the colonial expansion," after the encounter between the mainly written or Latin alphabet-based European Renaissance culture and the mainly oral or pictogram/ideogram-based Mesoamerican and Amerindian cultures. "In the past," Mignolo concludes, "literary scholarship tended to focus on the European sources of colonial culture ... while specialists in pre-Columbian cultures focused on the reconstruction of Amerindian cultures. What I have tried to suggest is that there is ample evidence that the darker side of the Renaissance is being explored by a new generation of scholars who have moved from literary scholarship to the human sciences and art history, as well as by social scientists and art historians who have engaged themselves in a productive dialogue with literary scholars." Clearly, in any human endeavour that confronts the complex human condition – past or present – it is not only possible but also more productive to transcend the boundaries of a particular science, especially in the "human science" of history. Again Braudel states, "There is only one history: global history. A material history is a partial history ... You cannot advance unless you bring together all the human sciences, like an orchestra."[28]

The second issue, closely linked to the first, relates to a concept of historiographical tradition dating back several hundred years and still considered valid among contemporary scholars, as evidenced by Braudel, Struever, and Proctor. Their historical scholarship or methods have earned an honoured place among authorities in historical scholarship in the last fifty years. They have renewed a valid historiographical strand that all scholars need to take into account. Struever, quoting Petrarch, writes, "The historian must balance the exigencies of his freedom of creation with the exigencies of the evidence which is available." Again, according to Struever, the Renaissance humanists viewed "aesthetic form as value and power ... speech [literature, poetry] as expression of personality, and ordinary language as exploration of reality." And this view, states Struever, dates back to Thucydides: "Faced with the impossibility of communicating 'what really was,' Thucydides justifies his invention of speeches ... [He] explains that he has designed his speeches (which of course were never delivered as he wrote them), to reflect the imperfect record of what was said but also the demands of the circumstances which had surrounded their delivery and impelled a particular reaction ... His speeches are thus closer to reality – the ambiance of human action and opinion – than the necessarily faulty attempts at factual reporting." Quoting Roland Barthes, Struever points out also that rhetoric has not only been "characterized ... as the 'august forbear' of contemporary Structuralism," but also that rhetoric's "historical role has generally been underestimated or discredited for ideological reasons."[29]

Thus we come to the third issue: the role of the literary references in this study. Far from being just rhetorical or erudite embellishments (a view of literature and literary study prevalent among too many scholars), they illustrate not only the mental states of the Italian immigrants, but also their reaction and adjustment to the new environment, their complex relationship to others – Italians and non-Italians. They also help to connect certain modes of behaviour to a more universal human condition; to show that their history – words, deeds, thoughts – is not just a local truth or history; that the material and spiritual forces in the human struggle and progress are similar in the small as well as in the large society or community ("the sum of these private stories forms a large-scale history").[30]

There seems to be, therefore, no absolute, comprehensive system or method in the pursuit of historical truth; and even the "term 'truth' is excessive," says Braudel. "There is no scientific truth without control.

That is why the hard sciences have been able to alter the 'truth' over the past two centuries, and they continue to the extent that their development forces them to confront new realities ... History also confronts certain realities."

Perhaps a good model of historical inquiry for today's needs could be derived from a balance between Braudel's "New History" – defined in the subtitle, "Musings on an 'Interscientific' Quest for Truth" – and Struever's analysis of the connection of rhetoric and history in the Western tradition. On the one hand Braudel makes it clear that "history is a serious thing. A historian cannot let his imagination run wild and write like a novelist." But on the other he warns us against the excessive trust placed in "statistics." Similarly, Struever's aim is to present "rhetoric not as a historical constant, but as a thread of possibility, a strand of choice which the Humanists self-consciously exploited in the web of assumption and motive which gives shape, density, and strength to their historical consciousness and historiographical achievement."

In other words, statistics and empirical data as well as rhetoric, in its widest sense ("rhetoric is concerned with content as well as form"), are equally valid in our continuous search for the ever-changing historical truth. The scientific, positivist method and rhetorical structures – poetic and literary inventions – go hand-in-hand. They are complementary. In brief, the intuitive approach is just as valuable as the gathering of hard evidence in seeking certain truths; each can often lead to similar conclusions.[31]

At times, true, unchecked intuition may transgress certain limits, and this study may even appear at times to be rhapsodizing, moralizing, romanticizing, or eulogizing. But I believe that, if they are really present, these elements can be justified, at least in part, by the very nature of oral history: by the immigrants' own dramatic and passionate testimonies, which, after all, form the main thread of their collective story; by the gamut of emotions that are an integral part of a study about the disrupting experience of migration, the painful separation from the *paese*, their native village, and the difficult reconstruction of a new, more familiar ambiance in a faraway land. I believe also that the writer's occasional empathic participation in relating an immigration experience, not unlike his own, can be equally justified: it is further evidence of their intense feelings. They too are part of history: "Rhetorical structure can be a source of historical insight," as Struever again clarifies. At any rate, the dramatic forms or personal feelings are not present in such an excessive or extravagant manner as to diminish the desired level of balance, proportion, or objectivity.

Besides, opposite views were often presented throughout the study. A critical attitude was applied mostly in the analysis of their ideas, behaviour, and achievements. Criticisms of the community by its younger members were amply and prominently illustrated (not easy to do and often not possible when the community itself finances or commissions the project, yet wholly accepted; see chapter 10, especially "The Young People's Confused Values"). Occasional eulogizing, mostly by the protagonists, does appear, but the work as a whole is far from being an idealization of a community or a group.

Moreover, the interpretation of the causes and the assessment of the importance of certain events or facts have been enhanced, not hindered, by the literary references. The evaluation of causes and effects has been highlighted by the presence of literary parallels. In fact, it must again be said that literature is also a "serious business," no less than history or any other form of inquiry – art or science. Of course, by literature is meant those classics of prose and poetry that best combine beauty and wisdom, enjoyment and edification: the time-tested models and widely accepted products of world literature that delved deeply into the human condition as perhaps no other art or science has yet done as fully. That is the type of literature that was used in the study: not the contrived serial romances or novels usually found on supermarket checkout shelves, but those literary creations that foster awareness, scholarship, and "real" scientific objectivity.[32]

Objectivity: there's a shibboleth of modern times! Perhaps no other notion or myth has helped to unjustly exalt or discredit human beings and their activities (scholarship included) in our contemporary quantity-oriented society, deluded daily into a false security by the "scientifically tested" products. In defending the validity of my method, I do not wish to appear to be what I am *not* – an opponent of science or the scientific method. Nevertheless, I am impelled to restate that scientific objectivity remains for the most part, if not a fallacy or a deception, an elusive goal. And this is demonstrably so in objective history. My experience and my readings in both literature and history have taught me to be very cautious, especially when the accounts make explicit claims of objectivity. Quite often, under the overwhelming accumulation of facts, figures, and statistics; beneath the very impressive, but well-selected archival and bibliographical references; and beyond the cold, impassive, erudite interpretations there lies an almost completely camouflaged self-serving thesis or an outright bias.

The questions remain: Is the scientific, positivist method more scholarly, more academic, more scientific than the intuitive, rhetorical, poetic, or lyrical method of presenting views, or extrapolating meaning from human or natural events?[33] Are the views or meanings thus reached less valid than those that creep into any interpretation?

An answer to be considered is suggested by Struever in her description of "Thucydides' relationship to Sophistical rhetoric ... Both the form and the content of the speeches in his history express his affinities with rhetorical attitudes ... Thucydides justifies his invention of speeches in much the manner of Gorgias justifying the myths of tragedy" (i.e., creative literature, fiction). "Gorgias claims that the dramatist has created a deception (*apate*) 'in which the deceiver is more honest than the non-deceiver, and the deceived is wiser than the non-deceived.'" Similarly, writes Struever, "the [Italian] Humanists are convinced that the use of rhetorically instead of logically oriented discourse leads one to reality through illusion ... The Humanists, like the Sophists," continues Struever, "embrace the distortive power of language; they accept the complexity of discourse as an attempt to reflect the complexity of phenomena," and she concludes, "artifice is all we have to express truth."[34]

A conscious use of literary artifice is more honest than an unconscious adherence to scientific objectivity or a rigid practice of the scientific method. Because I am aware of my method and process, I am also constantly conscious of the need to control language and style, and my views, feelings, or personality. But they do have a part in the work, without altering the truth of the story. They add a feature to the book: they make it more pleasant and, as a result, both entertaining and informative, as Umberto Eco clearly states: "I wanted the reader to enjoy himself ... In amusing himself, somehow, he has learned ... something either about the world or about language."[35] In particular, the study of literature and specifically the study of Italian literature especially outside of Italy, assumes a new, more concrete meaning when the works are placed in the context of the Italian experience in Canada. The parallels that clearly exist between that literature or literature in general and that experience or life in general (as Ricci's *Lives of the Saints* proves) emphasize the need to place the Italian authors within a context more familiar to our students and to all readers.

NOTE ON INTERVIEWS

In most references to interviews, in both the text and the notes, the names of the Leamington Italian families were omitted in order to respect their desire for anonymity and to direct the readers' attention from the person to the issue.

A Unique Italian Canadian Community

DISTINCTIVE CHARACTERISTICS

Near Windsor there's a smaller industrial city named Leamington. It has a large colony of Italians. The odd thing about them is that something like a third of them have come from a small hill-town in central Italy called Villa Canale. The first men came out in 1924 [i.e., 1923]. Their reports drew others. Over the years, a third of the whole village has packed up and migrated to Canada – most of them to Leamington. There they could find work in factories or food-processing plants. But most of them became prosperous by farming the rich soil, and selling fruits and vegetables [primarily to the fresh produce market and] to large canneries in the neighbourhood.[1]

The Leamington (Ontario) Italian community, in its essential form, was already clear in that mid-1960s description "by E.W. Dewlin, Radio Canada, as published by *Il Cittadino Canadese* [Montreal], December 23, 1966." A.V. Spada quoted the passage and simply listed the Leamington Roma Club members (about 180 men and women in the Leamington-Kingsville area) and added a few of his own observations. In spite of a few inaccuracies and some excessive praise, he provided a further glimpse of the community as a whole by highlighting some of its particular features: their "multi-million dollar [greenhouse and fishing] businesses" built through "hard work, long hours and perseverance," the presence of "entire family groups ... called from Italy," and having "three things in common: they are groups of relatives, they came from the same Italian village, they love the land and make it rich with their tender care and ceaseless labour." Exaggerated or not, one of his observations pointed to another central aspect of the community: "Of course not all [Leamington-area Italians] are prosperous but not one is unsuccessful. It is hard to distinguish the rich from the not so rich. Perhaps long association with the area would permit some sort of differentiation but only in the area of economics. In all other fields they consider themselves equal." Among the common aspects, that feeling of being equal was not only an effect of, but also quite an influence on, the unique growth of the community.[2]

The evidence gathered in the research carried out in the late 1970s and early 1980s clearly shows that, despite changes, the Leamington-area Italian community has retained the basic characteristics noted by others almost two decades earlier. The community is, as it has been, a rural, mainly agricultural community; it has remained relatively compact; and almost all of its 550-odd families (see appendix A) originate from the *Meridione*, the South of Italy, particularly Molise (or Abruzzo-Molise), Lazio (Latium), and Sicily.[3] Whether inherited or developed, or both, they have been the constant features that all Italians in the area shared: the distinctive characteristics that shaped the community in a relatively brief period of fifty-odd years, and quite early differentiated it from most Italian and immigrant communities in Canada.

The story itself of this relatively small Italian community, also unique to the extent that it derives mostly from the memories of the protagonists themselves, is more than a portrait of the lives and fortunes of a few individuals or of a particular group, and it illustrates certain facets of the history of two countries, Canada and Italy, of twentieth-century Italian immigration and of the larger phenomenon of mass migration.[4]

The Leamington Italian experience constitutes an exception to the general trend that Italians preferred to avoid farming in Canada.[5] Almost 60 per cent of the 430-odd families participating in the research-study are engaged in farming: either directly as field crop, vegetable and orchard growers, and/or greenhouse operators; or indirectly in agriculture-related industries such as Heinz and Omstead Foods (chapter 9). In earlier days, immediately or shortly after their arrival in the Windsor area, almost all Leamington Italians worked on farms, by chance, by choice, or out of need. The community pioneers themselves, a group of about a half-dozen men, reached Essex County via Montreal, by pure chance, as railroad gang workers (1923–24). They were in need of work, any type of work, even farming, though less profitable than factory or construction jobs. They soon sponsored other men, some of whom had to sign an agreement to work on the farms for several months and even up to two years; and a group of them became farm labourers in the tobacco fields of Essex County. Shortly after, some of them were joined by their wives and children; they all settled in the area, worked on the farms, and became the nucleus of the community (chapters 4, 5).

The extreme flatness of Essex County, the fertility of its soil ("unsurpassed, not even by the alluvial deposits of the Valley of the Nile"), and its moderate climate ("the result of its proximity to the Lower Great Lakes and of its southerly latitude, which approximates that of Rome and Northern California") made "The Sun Parlour of Canada" appear as a sort of Eden.[6] Unlike the hilly, rocky, over-exploited little farms they barely survived on in the "Old Country," the area offered new opportunities, not just to the pioneers and their immediate families but to many of their *paesani* as well. Over the years, they sponsored entire lines of relatives and friends from the same towns and surrounding areas in Italy. They eventually bought the farms, transformed many tobacco fields into orchards, and later developed a state-of-the-art, multi-million-dollar greenhouse industry. The Leamington Italian farming community, mainly the result of a spontaneous, if not haphazard, growth during five decades of chain migration, of slow, laborious settlement (1925–75), is a unique development among the several recorded attempts and failures in Italian farming ventures in Canada.[7]

The close-knit nature of the community rests upon strong family, regional, and linguistic ties. Some of the first men who started it all were already related, either belonging to the same family – the two sets of brothers (Ingratta and Moauro) – or through marriage (Pannunzio and Ingratta); and they had all been friends since childhood. Through the years this bond was strengthened by further intermarriage (Pannunzio and Cervini, Mastronardi and Moauro) and by the sponsorship chain, which often restructured in Leamington the Old World extended family and village. The inhabitants of one village in the Molise Apennines, Villa Canale, near Agnone (Isernia), have moved in bulk to the Leamington area. The Mastronardis, with more than fifty families, along with the numerous Ingratta, DiMenna, and Pannunzio families, all from Villa Canale, make up almost one-fifth of all the Italian families in Leamington. If the nearby Molisan villages of origin are also considered, the ratio almost doubles (chapters 7, 8, 10).

Hardly noticeable are the linguistic and cultural differences between the two large groups of immigrants from the two adjacent regions of (Abruzzo-) Molise and Lazio; and those that may have resulted from the later influx of immigrants, or particularly from the postwar growth of the Sicilian group, did not threaten the unity of the community. On occasion, *campanilismo*, though not in its extreme forms (blind parochialism or exaggerated attachment to one's own hometown or region), may have generated competition among them, as individuals or groups, but never such deep-rooted rivalries or unbridgeable divisions as to splinter the community into community centres or clubs along regional lines[8] (as is evident in other cities, including Windsor).[9] They all grouped around one Italian cultural and community centre, which served and spoke for the whole community, especially in matters common to all. If there were persistent parochial views of life, they were often smoothed away by interacting within the walls of their Leamington Roma Club, which most considered "their second home" (chapter 11). The name of the club itself, "Roma" (recently changed to the "Roma Club of Leamington"), by recalling Rome – both the historical reality and the myth – suggested and nourished pride in one common origin.[10] At the same time, the other part of the name expressed their loyalty to the new community and to Leamington – a feeling that was at times stronger and more cherished than the memories of the old town or country of origin.

The presence of an Italian priest, the establishment of the Roma Club (early 1960s), and the rediscovery and re-enactment of old village traditions and pageants reflected and simultaneously promoted the close-knit growth of the community. The size of the community itself, its relative geographical and cultural "isolation," affected also by the distance (about fifty kilometres) between Leamington and Windsor, have also played a role in drawing its members closer, even as a measure to counterbalance the inevitable assimilative forces, or protect their ethnic identity (chapters 12, 13).

Not even the stronger centrifugal tendencies of modern life, which often enhance generation conflicts, have profoundly disrupted the community's compactness. As expected, an increasing number of young people have been moving into the city to work or to pursue degrees in higher education, away from their parents' activities. Some parents even encouraged the new generations to embark on other careers. Still, in spite of the often harsh criticism levelled by the younger generation against aspects of the community, there were no visible indications of a breakup of the community (chapter 14). The community, in fact, even served as a source of self-discovery and renewal (chapter 15).

The bond, whether natural, traditional, or the result of environmental conditions and needs (survival, security, mutual assistance), served variously as a form of control and as a base for social and economic advancement. A sign of this bond, a measure even of the compactness, became visible in their political behaviour. The development of the community over the years, the economic advance of many of its members and its general well-being coincided mainly with the success of one political force in Canada – the Liberal Party. Firm political belief or personal gain may, of course, have been specific causes for this behaviour through the years. But in order to totally justify why an entire community remained faithful to one party for decades, other reasons were variously suggested in their own testimonials: Be it collective gratitude, a sense of security or guarantee for future progress, a feeling of commitment to the new land or simply political sheepishness, herd instinct, the Leamington Italian community, in exercising their democratic rights, has indeed proven to be compact, almost monolithic (chapter 13).

A COLONY WITH COMMON TIES TO THE FORGOTTEN "OTHER ITALY"

Almost 100 per cent of the Leamington Italian families originate from the regions of Central South Italy, South Italy, and Sicily – a factor as unique as it is important in the compact growth of the community. Though diverse, these southern regions are usually referred to together as the *Meridione* or *Mezzogiorno*. The imaginary line that divides Italy into two parts cuts across an area about one hundred kilometres south of Rome (and for investment purposes the demarcation line is real, extending even to north of Rome). The southern half of the peninsula, shaped by centuries of different political, economic, cultural, and philosophical development, has always constituted "another Italy."[11] A highly marked differentiation between the two parts persisted until recent times; and, in spite of the postwar boom, the advances in technological communication and the special 1950 South Italy Investment Fund (Cassa del Mezzogiorno), the disparities have perdured (chapter 7); the split is evident even today in the average per capita incomes, in the general standard of living, as well as in the unfortunate derogatory terms used by each part of Italy for the other, which also indicate "the mutual mistrust and misunderstanding which separate the Two Italies."[12]

A form of dualism between North and South seems to have always existed; and with it that intriguing contradiction or paradox of Italy: politically divided or splintered, but culturally and spiritually one. At any rate, even in ancient times, the "other Italy" was already a different entity composed of "peoples" or cultural groups to be conquered or subjugated. The Romans in their southward expansion devastated and depopulated the areas in order to subdue such powerful opponents as the Volscians of southern Latium, the Samnites in the area of Molise, Abruzzo, and Campania, and the Greeks of *Magna Graecia* (Great Greece) in Calabria, Sicily, and parts of Puglia and Basilicata. The

Byzantine and Lombard conquest and rule (sixth to eighth centuries) and the Islamic invasions (ninth and tenth centuries) further enhanced the social and cultural division. In the later Middle Ages the decline of the independent southern maritime cities, and for a time powerful trade centres (such as Amalfi), was due partly to the bitter rivalry of the northern maritime republics (Pisa, Genoa, Venice). While the northern cities were laying the economic, political, and legal foundations for the cultural Renaissance, in the South, the Norman occupation (eleventh and twelfth centuries), the defeat of the enlightened king of Sicily, Frederick II, and of his Hohenstaufen successors by the northern forces (Benevento, 1266), as well as the failure of the "Sicilian Vespers" rebellion against the French, marked the end of a splendid period in history and the beginning of the foreign domination of the lower part of the peninsula and of Sicily, which lasted until 1860.[13]

An event that had "incalculable consequences for the future history of Italy" was the birth of the state of the church, especially as a result of "a forged document, known as the Donation of Constantine" (CE 728), which also marked the birth of the temporal power of the popes. The resulting Papal States – the narrow strip of territory from Rome to Ravenna – were a wedge in the heart of Italy, a geographical and political corridor between North and South for more than a thousand years.[14] More than a physical obstacle in the way of Italian unification, it constituted a psychological barrier, even after unification. Though temporarily put aside by the Lateran Treaty signed with Mussolini (1929), the thorny issue of church–state relations between Italy and the Vatican has been affecting Italian political life down to the present day.[15]

Nor did Italian unification resolve the divisions and splits. The South looked upon unification as a conquest by the North, an expansion of the Piedmontese state.[16] For centuries a subjected and exploited region, after unification the South became a constant source of cheap labour for the expanding northern Italian industries or the expanding economies of the Western world. For decades it remained an impoverished, depressed, unproductive region with a vast illiterate population.

The "Southern Question," as it has come to be generally known, was thought falsely to have a solution in emigration, to have found in it *la valvola di salvezza* (the safety valve) of the *Mezzogiorno*.[17] Instead the result was depopulation, which further aggravated the South's "precarious economy" – itself the main cause of emigration, and mostly of "young men." It became a never-ending cycle that, in the course of a century, caused the exodus of over ten million people from South Italy (and Sicily and Sardinia).[18] Many of them came to Canada, first as seasonal workers and later as permanent settlers. Between 1925 and 1975 over 2,000 people from these southern regions settled in the Leamington area.

Except for Basilicata (and the island region of Sardinia), all the regions of this "other Italy" are represented in the Italian community of the Leamington area. But three main areas have been identified as the origins of the three largest groups of families that participated in the study:

1 The Molise region (Abruzzo-Molise until 1963): mainly the province of Isernia (till 1970 part of Campobasso Province), particularly the villages and towns of Villa Canale, Agnone, and Poggio Sannita; only a few from the Campobasso province (i.e., without the Isernia province).
2 The Lazio (Latium) region: particularly the province of Frosinone, called also *Ciociaria* ("*Chocharia*" – normally taken as the area dividing North and South Italy), specifically from the towns of Ceprano, Ripi, Patrica, Castelliri; with only a few from the Rome area.
3 The island of Sicily: mainly from the province of Trapani (northwest coast), specifically San Vito Lo Capo.

The relative concentration of each group was as follows: Villa Canale and only four surrounding municipalities, nearly 45 per cent of total entries, or over 96 per cent of the (Abruzzo-) Molisan contingent; Frosinone Province alone nearly 34 per cent of total entries, or over 95 per cent of the Lazio contingent; and San Vito Lo Capo alone nearly 10 per cent of total entries or over 71 per cent of the Sicilian one. The other regions (Abruzzo, Puglia, Calabria, Campania, Marche, Emilia-Romagna, and Veneto) make up less than 5 per cent of the total.

In reality, the entire Leamington-area Italian community consists of two major groupings, clearly distinct on the basis of geographical area of origin and dialectal affinity. Those from the first two areas (listed above) – southern Lazio and (Abruzzo-) Molise – constitute one group: most of their towns are located within 40 kilometres on either side of a line that runs from Frosinone (approximately 80 kilometres southeast of Rome) through Isernia to Campobasso. Therefore, approximately 80 per cent of the Leamington Italian community derive from a rectangular area of Central South Italy measuring about 120 kilometres long by 80 kilometres wide, and mostly from the mountainous districts, the scarcely populated pre-Apennine and Apennine towns and villages, within a thirty- to thirty-five-kilometre radius around Isernia. In fact, the province of Isernia, or more specifically the village of Villa Canale, emerges as the centre of this general area of emigration, both geographically and numerically. It is an area that includes parts of four present-day regions – Abruzzo, Molise, Lazio and Campania.

However, their proximity, their common physical aspects and their shared historical events have produced a linguistic and social affinity that makes the regional boundaries disappear. The general area's common characteristics constitute a unity which was eventually reflected in the growth of the community. While many from this area became farmers, those that came from Sicily tended to engage in the fishing industry. Occupation was also an indication of a measure of differentiation between the two major groups of the Leamington-area Italians (i.e., those from [Abruzzo-] Molise and Lazio together and the Sicilians).

Nevertheless, even in spite of the differences (linguistic more than cultural) between the two major groupings, a harmonious interaction prevailed. The strongest bond consisted of a common Italian origin and especially of a common experience in the new, strange, and often hostile environment. Their shared history, which had shaped their Southern Italian life and character, proved stronger and more effective than the differences in speech and customs inherited from their particular regions or towns of origin. They had all belonged to that "most derelict" Italian *Mezzogiorno*, where "emigration was the only way out"; to that "land of despair," or simply to that "other Italy" that so many for more than a century longed to forsake to seek a better life elsewhere: in Europe and the Americas.[19]

THE "RURAL" AND "URBAN" ITALIAN EXPERIENCE IN CANADA

"Emigration," remarked the Italian historian Gianfausto Rosoli, "has constituted one of the most complex social phenomena in Italian history, for its close connection with the economic situation and the policies of the country of origin as well as those of the receiving countries." This was especially true during a period he called "a century of Italian emigration: 1876–1976" (the translated title of the book he edited, *Un secolo di emigrazione italiana: 1876–1976*). The "close connection" between Italy and Canada coincides also with this period. The first "truly Italian" immigrants begin to arrive in Canada about the middle of the nineteenth century, in time for many of them also to participate in the Canadian dream to link the new country by rail from east to west, while the great wave of Italian immigration to Canada occurs after the Second World War.[20] The Leamington Italian community, like other communities, expands during the latter period. But its origin, early development, and present configuration are unlike those of most other Italian Canadian communities.

The majority of Italians in Canada in the 1980s (a rather heterogeneous group of about a million people representing about 4 per cent of the Canadian population and the fourth-largest Canadian ethnocultural collectivity)[21] resided in urban industrial centres: Toronto, Montreal, Vancouver, Edmonton, Hamilton, Sudbury, Sault Ste Marie, Thunder Bay, as well as Windsor. All have an Italian community.[22] In many cases the Italians are concentrated in a particular area of the city, traditionally referred to as "Little Italy."[23]

Only in the early years of mass migration, later part of the nineteenth and early twentieth centuries, were large groups of Italians found working in rural or isolated areas (in the mines of northern Ontario, British Columbia, Nova Scotia, or along the transcontinental railway path). But most of them were transient workers who either returned to Italy or moved into the cities. It can generally be said that, though originating from rural areas in Italy, once in Canada, the great majority preferred to settle in urban centres. To our knowledge, except for smaller groups of Italian families engaged in farming in the Okanagan Valley, British Columbia, or the Niagara Peninsula, the Italian community of the southwestern Ontario town is the only one that has developed in rural Canada. And unlike other immigrant farming communities, it is not the result of a pre-established settlement program, nor the outcome of a pre-arranged land investment or development.[24]

The history or story of any Italian immigrant community or "Little Italy" is a slice of the history of Italian emigration in modern times. To retrace their growth is to follow in part the development of both modern Italy since unification (1861) and of modern Canada since Confederation (1867) – two almost contemporaneous events.

The Leamington Italian community, though relatively small, constitutes another stone in that historical mosaic. Its characteristic features provide another perspective to the emigration-immigration phenomenon and to the connection between the two countries, at least in the latter part of the period of Italian immigration to Canada. Its Southern Italian identity brings into focus the "Southern Question," highlighting two specific areas: one continental and mountainous, the other insular and coastal. At the same time, because of its compact, rural quality, the community also serves as an alternative indicator of the degree of ethnic and cultural retention and of the level of integration or acculturation into Canadian life: its manageable size, circumscribed within a relatively small rural town and designated farming (and fishing) area (Essex South / Lake Erie), favours the analysis and assessment of its interaction with and impact on the town and area as a whole. Its unique aspects also offer an opportunity to relate the community to earlier experiences and episodes of Italian presence in Canada.

THE CENTURIES-OLD ITALY-CANADA LINK: EARLY EXPORTERS OF *ITALIANITÀ*

A Canada-Italy connection can be established also for the period before Italian mass migration and settlement. Accordingly, the five centuries of "Italian" presence in Canada can be reduced to three main cycles: the first, from the end of the fifteenth century to the end of the nineteenth century, can be defined as the cycle of decline (from navigators, explorers, entrepreneurs, and missionaries to railroad/industrial navvies, street peddlers, and hurdy-gurdy men).[25] The second cycle, the first half of the twentieth century, can be called the rise and fall of the Italians in Canada. The third cycle, which begins in the second half of the twentieth century, is marked by rapid growth, expansion, and impact on Canadian and Italian society at the economic, political, and cultural levels. The cycles or phases mirror the particular situation and the changing fortunes of both Italy and Canada throughout the modern period. The type of Italian that comes to Canada is a barometer of the political and cultural climate in each country and/or on the international scene.

The two Italians who discovered and claimed the Atlantic coast of Canada – the (Genoese-born) Venetian Giovanni Caboto for the English (1497) and the Florentine Giovanni da Verrazzano for the French (1524) – reflect the Italian paradox at the dawn of the modern age: the "greatness and decadence" of Renaissance Italy.[26] The land that Francesco Guicciardini hailed as "the richest, the most cultured ... and the most illustrious ... of Western Christendom"[27] was nevertheless deplored by both Guicciardini and Macchiavelli as the land of "calamities," the divided, weak, corrupt prey of a foul "barbarous domination."[28] Italy's "historic disaster" (1494–1530), which the two political thinkers both witnessed and analyzed, increased the number of Italian expatriates, merchant-bankers, and intellectuals in the courts and cities of Europe, where they had been active since the fourteenth century (the Bardis, the Medicis, Petrarch).[29] Military leaders, seafarers, and scholars (including Leonardo da Vinci) had to take service (sometimes refuge) with foreign sovereigns, in Europe and in the New World, which they helped discover and explore, often risking their money and life (as seems to be the case of both Caboto and Verrazzano).[30] Their voyages of discovery – including those of the Genoese Columbus for Spain and of the Florentine Vespucci for Portugal – "while opening a new world to trade and industry, [slowly] shifted the commercial center of Europe from Italy and the Mediterranean to the [strong unitary monarchical states] facing the Atlantic"; and while exposing the growing conservatism, if not short-sightedness, of the Italian cities' ruling merchant aristocracy, they ironically brought about changes that eventually led to, if not hastened, Italy's political and economic decline.[31]

Nevertheless, as adventurers-entrepreneurs they were also men of vision and learning, who, with some luck, held or gained prestigious positions.[32] Versed in letters and sciences (navigation, cartography, cosmography, and mathematical sciences), they reflected that early Italian "capitalistic" individualism and Renaissance humanistic spirit of enquiry that first emerged from their own native or adopted cities.[33] The city-state experience of Genoa, Florence, Venice, Milan, and others in the fourteenth to fifteenth centuries has been recognized as "one of the bases of the modern scientific renewal," of "a new vision of the world." But the new attitudes toward life and nature were reaching full expression at the moment of decline of those very cities and urban outlook that had nourished the new image of man and human culture. The crisis of Italian liberty, Italy's failure to emerge as a nation state, in spite of "Italian cultural hegemony" in Europe and in spite of a "strong national consciousness,"[34] excluded Italy from having a relevant, albeit dubious, military and colonial role in Canada and the New World. Yet Italy was not totally absent: it was indirectly present through men like Columbus, Vespucci, Caboto, and Verrazzano.[35]

The cosmopolitan Italian "immigrants" first carried their language, culture, expertise and symbols to Europe, and then as discoverer-explorers to North America: both Caboto and Verrazzano spoke Italian.[36] Verrazzano's "Report" of his discoveries to King Francis I was "written in Italian," a language the French king and many at his court knew well;[37] and Caboto, upon reaching Cape Breton, raised a cross and both the English and Venetian flags, that were also hoisted on his caravel the *Matthew*.[38] The toponyms on the early maps of the North American eastern seashore are also a clear indication of Verrazzano's Tuscan origin and humanistic education, as well as of his loyalty to his royal patron and some Italian financial sponsors: "Arcadia" – part of Delaware, Maryland, and Virginia, later Acadia or Acadie, Maritime Provinces, Canada – derives from the *Arcadia*, the title of a popular Italian pastoral romance by Jacopo Sannazaro; New York Bay bore such names as

Angoulême and *Ste Marguerite* in honour of both Francis I and his sister Marguerite d'Angoulême, the enlightened princess, poet, and patron of the arts; Cape Cod was Cape *Pallavicino*, for his friend Gian Ludovico, the Florentine army captain killed in the battle of Pavia (1525) in the service of Francis I; Goat Island, Rhode Island, was *Pietraviva*, for the wife of the Florentine banker in Lyons, Antonio Gondi, a backer of the expedition. Verrazzano, in fact, in claiming all the lands he discovered or explored from Georgia to Nova Scotia (or probably from Cape Fear, North Carolina, to Newfoundland), named them first *Francesca*, for Francis I, and then applied a term he himself coined, *Nouvelle France*.[39]

An early Italian connection, though more indirect, can also be established with other toponyms and with the purpose of the voyages: "Montreal" itself originates from Cardinal Ippolito de' Medici, archbishop of "Monreale," Sicily, who was instrumental in obtaining from his uncle, Pope Clement VII – a dispensation from the Treaty of Tordesillas, which cleared the way for Jacques Cartier's voyage in 1534.[40] The search itself for the dreamed-of "westward passage" to the spices, treasures, and legends of Cathay (China) and "Scipango" or "Cipango" (Japan) was not only dictated by the advance of the Ottoman Turks into the Levant (their conquest of Constantinople, 1453), but also by a challenge to "the privileged place Italy had so far held on the economic level and in the sphere of international relations" through the monopoly of the spice trade by such Italian cities as Venice and Genoa.[41] Some of the protagonists in this search, hired by the competing major rivals, were Italians from those same cities: Florentine, Venetian, and Genoese citizens or merchants, and also, as in previous centuries, "travellers [and] adventurers who did not hesitate to put themselves at the service of anyone who was ready to pay them."[42] They were, nevertheless, important links with the heritage of the Italian communal "revival," and with that Italian humanistic, "intellectual revolution" that was transforming European civilization.[43]

Italy's presence in early Canada was particularly in the form of the new spirit of enquiry, navigational expertise, and scientific knowledge. If Marco Polo's story of his travels to China was the common inspiration for all the late fifteenth-century adventurers and explorers, all vying to seek wealth and glory in the fabulous Orient, Paolo del Pozzo Toscanelli's "new representations of the world" provided the scientific base for the trail-blazing voyage of Columbus as well as for the explorations of the new world by Caboto, Verrazzano, and others. In brief, even if the Italian origin and national identity of the discoverer-explorers of the American continent are sometimes forgotten or questioned, Italy's determinant role in this historic achievement and its connection to the New

World and Canada remain solid by virtue of "the great discovery made by Humanism, that of the objective and pure nature of research [which] applies to every form of human knowledge."[44] Wealth and power were not the only motives for the great voyages of discovery. Similarly, economic conditions, while most important, are not the only reasons for migrations of people, as the Leamington experience also showed. The spirit of adventure and a degree of folly have also played a part (chapters 3, 5, 15).

"Independent in 1494, Italy forty years later had become merely an appendix to the history of the great European powers," and remained so for the next three centuries: under church and foreign domination (Spanish, French, Austrian), in a state of economic stagnation, a French colony to be exploited even during the Napoleonic era of liberation, and in the early nineteenth century still a political nonentity, or in "Metternich's unsympathetic dictum ... only a geographical expression." In spite of sporadic political and economic reforms, its limited participation in the illuminist movement (eighteenth century), some outstanding achievements in the arts and sciences (Galileo, Vico, Beccaria) and its leadership in music, "Italian society was effete and sterile," Italy continued to be on the fringe of Europe and of its industrial and political revolutions.[45] In the mid-nineteenth century Italy was still weeping over her plight and longing for unification.[46]

Just as the "poor, fragmented, impoverished" peninsula was carved up and engulfed by the great powers, so most Italians who came to Canada during the earlier centuries in the service of the colonial powers were slowly assimilated into their systems.[47] Yet some of the more noteworthy individuals and groups had significant roles in Canada's history in every century, as explorers, administrators, and defenders of New France and Canada, as well as businessmen and educators – the Tontis, Marinis, Crisafis, Burlamacchi, Malaspina, Donegani, Bruschesi, Rusconi, Forneri, and others such as the railway builders (Capreol, Veltri). One of them (Bressani), a missionary-historian, wrote one of the earliest histories of New France (1653) in Italian.[48]

But none formed a nucleus of a rural or urban Italian colony: neither the soldiers (i.e., those of the Piedmontese-Carignan Regiment, mid-1600s; those in the Seven Years War in Canada, mid-1700s; or the mercenaries who became farmers after the War of 1812), nor the merchant families and group of professionals and tradesmen who settled in Montreal (late eighteenth and early nineteenth century). Most intermarried and were also absorbed, though some descendants of the Montreal settlers who still understood Italian did act as intermediaries for the political exiles and Italian navvies who arrived later, especially during the first Italian exodus (1870s–1915).[49] By this time, after the centuries of foreign despotism (Italy's long torpor since the Renaissance), Italian "national awareness" was a vague thought, even in spite of the rebirth of nationalism in the Napoleonic era (1796–1814) and the civic passions generated by the Romantic culture of the *Risorgimento* – the struggle for Italian unity and freedom (1820–60). "We have made Italy," observed a nineteenth-century Piedmontese unifier of Italy, Massimo d'Azeglio, "now we must make Italians."[50] Most Italian immigrants of that period (late nineteenth to early twentieth centuries) identified with regional or village customs more than with Italian language and culture: "An intense provincialism [was] coupled with an exceptional lack of nationalistic feeling" (*campanilismo* more than *nazionalismo*).

With the large influx of immigrants, mostly from the peasant masses, the status of Italians in Canada and the attitudes toward them steadily declined, to reach one of the lowest points at the beginning of the twentieth century, a period one referred to as a "decade of brutality, 1902–1912."[51] Italians were usually recruited for menial chores and became regarded mostly as beasts of burden (*bestie*), gangs of knife-carrying, dangerous, and violent migrant workers – a needed but undesirable lot. More generally, they became, in Canada, a mirror of "the backwardness of Italian social and economic structures" after unification: of the tragic conditions of life in rural areas; the poverty, the illiteracy (78 per cent in the 1870s), the degradation of the peasantry; and of the unwillingness of Italian politicians to apply the remedies proposed in the many inquiries of the time into these conditions, especially into those of southern Italy (undernourishment, disease, death). They highlighted a primary failure of the new nation: the high price paid by the rural areas and southern Italy for Italian unification.

The peasants in particular became the victims of all the crises that followed it, of the "gap between the government and the governed." Many of them "seized by the resolute and desperate desire to escape from the spiral of poverty and degradation in which they were imprisoned" gave rise to the first phenomenon of Italian mass emigration that poured thousands of illiterate immigrants into Europe and the Americas.[52] The stereotype of Italians and Italy in general, often reappearing even today in various pockets of Canadian society, became rooted during that period. As victims of the land of origin and of the receiving country, as well as of the unscrupulous merchants of immigration, of the official and public attitudes (indifference, prejudice, racism) on both sides of the Atlantic, they reflected the entire system at the turn of the twentieth century.[53]

THE CHANGING FORTUNES OF THE ITALIANS
IN CANADA AND IN LEAMINGTON

Between 1910 and 1935, in spite of the dubious activities of the *padroni* (labour agents), the Italians in Canada were slowly gaining social respectability through the emergence of honest community leaders, institutions (clubs, mutual aid societies, parishes) and increasing interaction and participation in the affairs of the larger society. As allies during the First World War, Italians and Canadians experienced a new solidarity reinforced by the Italian contribution to the Canadian war effort in the form of volunteers from across Canada (*il treno degli italiani*) and funds: "Service to Italy and loyalty to Canada were possible simultaneously." The new Italian-Canadian patriotism was transformed into Italian-Canadian pride in the new Italy and in their Italian origin, especially as a result of a series of events: Fascist Italy's interest in the forgotten immigrants; the Canadian acceptance of Fascism as a political belief; the reconciliation of church and state (Lateran Treaty); and the respect and admiration won by Mussolini (the enemy of Bolshevism) among world leaders including Churchill and Mackenzie King.[54] Italian Canadians were enjoying a newly established rapport with other Canadians, a new status in the adopted land, until all was shattered again by events in the land of origin.

Between 1936 and the end of the Second World War, as a result of the Fascist invasion of Ethiopia (1936) and the declaration of war on Britain (June 1940), the "place of Italians in Canadian life was at its nadir." Though not comparable to the experience of the Japanese Canadians, many hundreds of Italian men and some women, British subjects or not, were placed in internment camps as "dangerous enemy [aliens]" (including a Leamington Italian pioneer; chapter 6). The "enemy alien" designation was rescinded between 1947 and 1951 partly because of the desire of Italians in Canada to reunite their families and particularly because of "Canada's need for unskilled manpower." With both governments encouraging emigration/immigration after the restrictions of the 1920s, 1930s, and 1940s, the chain migrations resumed, first from Friuli and parts of Veneto, then from Molise, Abruzzo, and other central-southern areas. Whole villages were slowly transferred to Canada, such as Pisticci (Basilicata) in the Toronto area, and Villa Canale in the Leamington area. About one-third of the Italians now in Canada entered during the first three decades of the second half of the twentieth century. From 1951 to 1961 alone, the number had grown from 150,000 to 450,000.[55]

Though still in the making, the postwar Italian immigrants constitute, a new Italian-Canadian community, a new era of the presence and history of Italians in Canada. A heterogeneous group, much different from the pre-war Italian settlers, they reflect the changes that have taken place in Italy and Italian society in the three post-war decades: those who came to Canada in the fifties were mainly unskilled workers, labourers, small farmers or farmhands, and some skilled tradesmen; those who arrived in the 1960s and 1970s were primarily skilled workers, technicians, industrial workers, and professionals as well as entrepreneurs and investors. On the one hand, the number and their origin expose the post-war Italian economic situation, specifically the limitations of the Italian "economic miracle" of the 1950s and 1960s, which did not benefit every part of the country. On the other, the change in the type of immigrant in this period indicates the radical transformation of Italy in one generation: from a mainly agricultural land in the 1950s to an industrialized nation in the 1970s, one of the seven most industrial democracies in the world. At the same time, the return of many Italians from Canada is also evidence of a different trend in the Canadian economy and life.[56]

The status and respect gained by the Italians in Canada and by Italy in Europe and the world, in the last decades, have also favoured the study of the long-forgotten earlier Italian "heroes" of Canadian history and the more recent Italian immigrants of more humble origins. This new interest is more specifically a reflection of the political, cultural, and attitudinal changes within Canada in the latter part of the twentieth century. It is partly the result of the large presence of Italians in Canada and their increasing socio-political awareness, and partly the outcome of the Canadian multiculturalism policy, which favours the rediscovery of one's heritage and identity.[57]

Particularly significant and timely, in light of the present Canadian linguistic dualism and constitutional impasse, and especially of Canada's multicultural reality and ideal, is the rediscovery of even a small strand of our collective past – in this case, the often neglected, earlier Italy-Canada connection.[58] Italy's sixteenth-century catastrophe, its absence as a nation-state in early modern times, and the transformation of the names of the early Italian "immigrants" to Canada or the New World (Gallicized, Anglicized, or Hispanicized according to the nation served or colony settled) have often led unaware or zealous historians to over-look, question, doubt or deny the *italianità* (Italianness), the Italian identity or origin of many of them over three centuries:[59] John Cabot may be known to have claimed Canada for the British Crown, but he is hardly recognized as "Giovanni Caboto," the Italian navigator and "Discoverer of Canada." Similarly buried is the identity of Verrazzano, the Tonti brothers, Burlamacchi, and others. The name alteration – a practice that continued down to the twentieth century, whether resulting from their own cosmopolitan outlook or the pressure of the prevailing cultural climate – has also helped to camouflage and diminish the Italian role in early Canada.[60] Jacques Cartier was indeed the first explorer of the Gulf of St Lawrence and the discoverer of the St Lawrence River, including the "area between [Stadacona] and Hochelaga" (i.e., Quebec City and Montreal), but Verrazzano was his "teacher and guide," the founder of the *Francesca*, the "land of Francis," the "true father" of "New France" more than the "godfather" as Biard wrote in 1616, "*le Parrain de ceste dénomination de Nouvelle France.*"[61]

The issue itself of *italianità*, though more extensively treated in relation to the Leamington Italians' identity (chapter 12), requires that it be immediately placed within its appropriate historical-cultural context. Thus, to apply to Italy the concept of nationality strictly based on nation-state is historically inappropriate and misleading. A national Italian awareness predates the Italian state by many centuries, as Procacci among others points out: "The Italy of the communes as a whole, in spite of its many-centredness and its particularism, acquired a certain homogeneity: that of an intensely urbanized area, the most intensely urbanized of all Europe. In the long run this was bound to favour the formation of a sort of national Italian consciousness, above and beyond the divisions of local patriotism; and this slowly took shape from the thirteenth century on."[62] Nor was this a process that involved only intellectuals, as Migliorini observes in his overview of the sixteenth century: "Although Italy did not achieve the political unity which other great European nations already enjoyed, a consciousness of belonging to a common civilization became general among her inhabitants."[63] For the Italians, Rome always represented a unifying force, "their moral and spiritual inheritance," writes Barzini,

> their soul ... their pride and their will to live as one nation ... the symbol of the national existence. Italians had not achieved unity, but had always felt themselves to be a nation nevertheless formed, not like others, by kings, soldiers and statesmen, but by *churchmen, poets, artists* and *philosophers.* This *spiritual country* which Italians loved desperately had a capital which was Rome, not the stone Rome on the banks of the Tiber, but the ghostly city to be found in books and legends. It had bewitched Dante, Cola [di Rienzo], Petrarch [and it] was to bewitch all great Italians in the future. *Rome* was the great mother, the womb from which everything Italians held dear had come.[64]

The early Italian navigator-explorers, mostly from the central-northern urbanized areas, were part of that learned group of great Italians representing that common civilization whose roots were the double heritage of Rome (the "mundane, humanistic" traditions and Christian beliefs and practices).[65] They were of course much unlike the Italian immigrants of the "great exodus" (1870s–1915), especially those from that "Other Italy," for centuries a separate entity or state, then "annexed" to North Italy, and generally neglected after unification: alienation and deracination were only bound to generate in them a loyalty to the *paese*, the village of origin rather than to the new nation.

Nevertheless, that uniquely Italian "capitalist and commercial revolution" of the thirteenth century allowed Italy to acquire "a certain homogeneity" that, according to Procacci, favoured "the formation of a sort of national Italian consciousness." In "Italy, as in the rest of Europe, agricultural and urban development were correlated and interdependent." But in Italy this process represented "a new trait in the evolution of Italian society ... in much of Italy this economic interdependence allowed a fusion of city and country also on the territorial, political and human level ... and this is one of the key points of Italian history." As a result even the *paese*, the village, however removed or isolated, absorbed some of the aspects of the Italian city-civilization that since the thirteenth century, moulded an Italian consciousness or a common *italianità*. "This Italian awareness," writes Procacci, was to appear fully formed in Petrarch [for whom] Italians were the most legitimate heirs of the Roman tradition.[66]

After Italian unification, the unpopularity and distrust of the official Italian state did not preclude the presence of a common *italianità*, even among the sometimes "campanilistic" immigrant *paesani* – an *italianità* discernible even in their mostly Latin-derived dialects; it was particularly visible in certain traditional characteristics, "cultural" traits, habits, tendencies, practices, good and bad, that Barzini called "*cose all'italiana*" (things Italian-style);[67] and that Indro Montanelli reduced to the combination: "the total lack of moral commitment [and] instinctively kind."[68] However vague or unconscious, that feeling of *italianità* was also quite evident among the Leamington Italians, especially in their choosing *Roma* as the name of their common centre or "second home": it coexisted with their good feelings toward their adopted land.

The first two Italians in Canada (Caboto, Verrazzano), for their tragic end and for the subsequent historical distortions and amnesia, can almost be made metaphors for both Italy's "historic disaster" at the beginning of the modern period and for all non-English and non-French immigrants and settlers in Canada, whose achievements and legacy continue to remain unacknowledged, by the dominant cultures, as integral and equal parts of the nation's history and makeup. Therefore, "the accounts of the antiquity of the Italian presence in America" and in Canada, far from being, as they once were, a sort of ethnic countercharge by "filio-pietist ... crusaders,"[69] serve instead to place the history or story of a particular group, or individual, within a Canadian historical context. They are a recovery of a significant reality that is essential to the building of identity, community, and nation. It is within the larger Italy-Canada connection, created by the Italian expatriates and immigrants in Europe and Canada, that the unique aspects of the Leamington area or any other Italian community can be better analyzed, be better understood, and have meaning.

The settlement and growth of the Leamington Italian community coincide with one of the three basic cycles of Italian presence in Canada: the middle two quarters of the twentieth century: 1925–75. The base of the farming community was firmly laid during the first quarter (1925–50), which may seem unusual in view of the unfavourable events of the period: the Italian Fascist regime restrictions on emigration especially toward North America, the Great Depression, the anti-Italian hysteria and "enemy alien" status and the Second World War (1930s–1940s). On the other hand, those same events, or the Italians' reaction to them, may have decisively contributed to the consolidation of that first nucleus of the community, so that by the end of the war the Leamington Italians were ready to receive on their farms the relatives and friends whom they were able to sponsor more easily because of farm ownership.

Moreover, the Italian farm owners and/or workers in rural Leamington, though closely surveilled throughout the war period, were mostly spared official harassment (dismissal from work, arrest, internment) that many Italians in the urban centres (including Windsor) had to endure (chapter 6). The Leamington community not only reflects rapid numerical expansion and economic progress in the second half of the twentieth century. In the smaller farming community, the trend and process of change emerge more apparent, especially in the increasing occupational differentiation in the two main groups: the development of the fishing industry mainly by the Sicilians, who came after the war, and the changes brought to the farming industry, mainly by the earlier settlers or descendants from (Abruzzo-) Molise and Lazio. The development of the greenhouse industry alone, during the latter period (1950–75 approximately), gives substance to a statement that even two decades ago seemed mere exaltation: "Canadian farming ... was not for Italians ... Yet some Italians did try it: and, wonder of wonders, they made it."[70]

Not only! They themselves believed and often claimed that both Canada and Italy benefited from their "hard work ... and perseverance." If, on the one hand, they helped transform the rich soil of the Leamington area into giant orchards, on the other, they had at least alleviated Italy's unemployment problem. Where would Italy have "put all the people," mused one of the pioneers, "if we hadn't gone all over the world?"[71] Alex Colasanti (1924) was, in his own way, referring to the view of emigration as Italy's "safety valve," especially in relation to the Southern Italian situation, which most Leamington Italians had experienced.[72]

In sum, the Leamington-area Italian immigrants were mostly farm workers or small farmers from rural South Italy who, in a few decades, formed a unique, relatively close-knit agricultural community in rural Southwest Ontario, the southernmost corner of Canada. The community's final configuration is as unique as its origin: it is composed of a series of interrelated family chains (see chapter 10), and it began with a small group of people who happened to go to that area in the mid-1920s.

Clandestine Emigration
and the South

THE MOLISANI: FLIGHT FROM *MISERIA* OR SEARCH FOR *FORTUNA*?

There wasn't much in my town.
If I hadn't come to Canada, I would have gone somewhere else.

The whole "Southern Question" (*la questione meridionale*) of the politicians, historians, and sociologists was thus reduced by a post–Second World War Leamington Italian immigrant to a simple and poignant statement: it underlines the continuity, the permanent character of the question and its connection to the phenomena of political corruption and of emigration throughout the period of Italian national history. For the historian Villari, the central factor of the question was Italy's "radical refusal to involve in the process of renewal of the country the ... human, economic, political, and intellectual resources of the *Mezzogiorno*." According to the meridionalist polemic, the South was "exploited, as a financial reserve and as a colonial market" to the advantage of the northern industrial apparatus. The overall effects were blocked development of a modern, productive, southern agrarian middle class; the persistence of the traditional semi-feudal immobility in the ruling classes; and extreme poverty, sporadic rebellions, and emigration among the peasants.[1] Meanwhile, "in the [northern] regions surplus of labor force expelled from rural areas tended to become absorbed in stable industrial occupations which provided an alternative to emigration, *in the [southern regions] emigration was the only way out*, nor did the return flow of money and migrants serve to modify the structural situation in any way" (italics mine).[2]

The two great waves of Italian emigration coincided with the periods of pronounced Italian industrial expansion: 1876–1915 and 1946–76.[3] In spite of lower emigration levels between the two wars (1916–42), the flow continued; thus, between 1876 and 1976 almost twenty-six million people left Italy. More than half (54 per cent) emigrated during the first "great exodus" (1876–1914/1915), and more than one-third of the 100-year contingent left in the first fifteen years of the twentieth century.[4] During the entire first period the most striking manifestation of the crisis and especially of the worsening of the southern problem, provoked by the Italian industrial revolution, was the unparalleled exodus of the rural population toward transoceanic countries. Between 1901 and 1913 over 4.7 million Italians emigrated to America; of these, close to 3.8 million emigrants came from the South.[5] Bearing in mind that 8.5 million returned to Italy over the 100-year period, the massive dislocation of Italians, especially from northwest, northeast, and southern Italy, changed the face of the country forever, influencing its domestic and foreign policies as well.[6] The effects on the South, though not as positive as many Italian leaders believed in the 1880s, were indeed "revolutionary."[7]

The southern contingent (including the islands of Sicily and Sardinia) for the 100-year period consisted of over ten million emigrants, or 40 per cent of the twenty-six million people who left Italy. The southern proportion in each of the other periods of Italian emigration ranged from about 35 per cent in the first two periods, to over 50 per cent in the most recent exodus.[8] Moreover, between 1876 and 1976 the massive internal migrations from South to North (two million people to the northwest "industrial triangle" and 1.8 million to the Rome area) brought about the "re-equilibrium of the distribution of the Italian population," contributing to the post–Second World War downturn in the southern population (from 37 to 35 per cent of the Italian population), with continued negative effects on its economy.[9]

Italy's betrayal of the solemn promises of ample social justice programs ("land to the peasants") led to widespread social unrest and struggle after the First World War and, in 1919–20, to the peasants' occupation of the landowners' estates, from which they were driven out by force.[10] The year 1920 was also the year of maximum emigration for 1916–42: the expatriates from the southern regions constituted more than half of the year's total, and the highest emigration rates occurred in Abruzzo-Molise (37 per cent) followed by Calabria (36 per cent) and Sicily (30 per cent).[11] "Over 75% of Italian immigrants to Canada," wrote Sturino in 1988, "have come from southern Italy, especially from the regions of Abruzzi-Molise and Calabria."[12]

The causes of emigration varied according to region and period. Two main reasons identified by the Italian Statistics Office for the first period (1876–1915), and differentiating southern and northern emigration, seemed increasingly interwoven in the subsequent periods in southern emigration. They were *miseria* and *miglior fortuna* – to escape *misery*, destitution, wretchedness, and to seek *better fortune*. The latter motive – the desire for a higher level of prosperity or well-being – became more prevalent at the beginning of the twentieth century when (according to Francesco Coletti) the "migratory contagion," spread by the returning emigrants and shipping line agents, "assumed even the form of collective psychosis." In some situations, it may have been what Sidney Sonnino called in 1879 *slancio industriale* – spontaneous entrepreneurial daring, spirit of adventure – that drove them out. But for the southern peasantry *miseria* was the main motive: it was "poverty," which in their area was "much more widespread and acute than in other regions."[13]

Emigration was the only alternative for the cruelly oppressed southern peasants (the *cafoni*, rubes); and initially not even that option existed, for they were denied the very freedom to emigrate. Many simply fled to escape the rapacity of the well-to-do and their allies (all the petty local tyrants, state officials, municipal bureaucrats, usurers, usurpers, and parasites). Flight or emigration offered a door to freedom from the state of feudal servitude still imposed upon them by the absentee landlords (the *signori*) and by the much loathed class of the *galantuomini*, the propertied gentry of the South, who formed an alliance with the industrialists and political leaders of the North[14] ("the pact of wickedness").[15]

During the first fifteen years of united Italy, the social ills of the *Mezzogiorno* had been completely neglected,[16] and after 1876, in spite of some social legislation, misery and discontent became more acute.[17] Southern brigandage – whether an explosion of common delinquency or, as it was also called, a social war, guerrilla warfare, or a pitiless rustic war against unification and the new order – had been ruthlessly suppressed.[18] The struggle for land and for some form of regional self-government or autonomy (the "Sicilian Question") had been lost (again militarily repressed).[19] The great agricultural crisis (1880s), the vast importations of American and Russian corn, the crash of produce prices, the rise in rental fees, and such financial pressure on the rural areas as to further aggravate the wretched conditions of Italy's cultivators of the land wiped out the meagre livelihood of farmers (*contadini*) as well as of tenant or contract farmers (*affittuari*) and day-farmhands (*braccianti*). The government's industrial protectionist tariffs (1887), the banks' swindle ("the banking carnival"), and the frenzy of a few speculators resulted in the ruin of the economy of the South, and the hope of reviving its agriculture was forever lost.[20] The prospect of further division and distribution of public lands and large estates had also vanished with the re-annexation by the landowners of the unproductive fragments of lands distributed in earlier divisions.[21] All the questions converged into an end-of-century crisis, the decade of revolts, the tragedy of 1898. A turning point for the Southern Question had been reached, and the trench, opened forty years before, split further apart national government and *Mezzogiorno*, revealing in the political significance of the existence of "two Italies" – industrial North and agricultural South.[22]

The South, moreover, began to be viewed as a ball and chain at Italy's feet; and the Southerners, according to the racist theories of positivist sociologists, an inferior race, "the cause of disorder in Italian public life."[23] Ettore Ciccotti provided an ample view of the conditions of the South and its people: "Slaves of need, slaves of ignorance ... they have no voice; and, if in part they have succeeded in having the vote ... the right to vote is usually, for [them], another sort of service they have to render to the [ruling] class."[24] Poverty, injustice, usury, heavy taxes, semi-feudal oppression, prejudices, and malaria combined into an explosive situation for which emigration provided the only "safety valve." "If it weren't for emigration," declared a peasant during an early twentieth-century parliamentary enquiry on the southern peasantry, "in order to live, we would have been at each other's throats with knives."[25]

EMIGRATION:
ITALIAN IGNORANCE AND OFFICIAL AMBIVALENCE

Emigration, an unprecedented subversion of the status quo and a panacea for the southern ills, intensified and complicated the North-South debate. The governing classes saw the exodus as another manifestation of peasant wanderlust, anarchism, ignorance, and gullibility (easy prey for false advertising); as insubordination and desertion that threatened class equilibrium, provoking reduction of the labour force, rise in salaries, and changes in the contractual system. Emigration was therefore to be discouraged, opposed, and repressed, especially the clandestine shipping of emigrants by emigration agents. Besides, it was an embarrassment in the face of Italy's quest for a world mission and colonial empire. On the other hand, exponents of colonialism in Parliament argued in favour of a policy of free emigration to establish new markets, a base for colonies and Italy's expansion. Ironically, the emigration-colonialism link provided rival factions with an inauspicious point of agreement.

Southern reformers (according to Rosario Villari) insisted on the connection between the rural exodus and the general conditions of life and work in the rural areas, presenting the social question as a fundamental Italian problem. But, while at first the reformers deplored emigration as a symptom of impending perils, they later accepted it as a necessary evil and even hailed it as a peaceful social revolution. Especially in light of the remittances pouring into Italy (by 1907, according to an American estimate, as much as US$85 million),[26] most southern socio-political writers anticipated the positive effects of emigration: total renewal of the South through autonomous development, set in motion by emigration, then pushed forward by government initiatives. Emigration was thus forecast as "the *natural* and *spontaneous* way to solve the Southern Question," a harbinger of a new rural democracy risen from work that would permit the South to become an integral and equal part of the Italian nation. Besides, emigration had also eliminated the danger of other tragic insurrections as experienced in the last decade of the century. Emigration was therefore to be favoured, directed, and controlled for the benefit of the South and of Italy; and the emigrants to be helped and protected from the hardships encountered in their journey and in their work in distant lands.

Italy generally accepted the ideas of the reformers, but not to the advantage of the Italian South: money pouring into Italy from America was absorbed partly by the banks and industries of the North; and the lack of capital was partly the cause of the failure of the dream to create a rural democracy through the division of public lands. In fact, the meridionalist views on emigration helped prepare the psychological climate for Italy's first colonial ventures (resulting in two military disasters: at Dogali in 1887 and at Adua in 1896). The debate went on: emigration was neither opposed nor protected; it became a police matter, a problem left to customs officers, or just a source of much irritation for consular offices; it was at best treated with benign neglect, or taken advantage of. "Emigration," proclaimed a landowner, "was born as a *need*, has grown as a *desire*, has become an infectious plague."[27]

Amidst much public indifference, confusion, ignorance, and official rhetoric and ambivalence, emigration flourished, with millions leaving, unassisted by Italy, and often at the mercy of exploiters and fate. By the end of the second decade of the twentieth century, the millions who had returned, or had travelled back and forth to America with increasing frequency and ease, were spreading the fever and challenge among the new generations. Their showy wealth, more modern American ideas, and sense of independence were activating the spirit of adventure among those who, though not poor, were growing dissatisfied with their state and impatient with official procrastination in adopting programs and measures leading to the permanent solution of the Southern Question.[28]

Nevertheless, emigration, war, universal suffrage, and postwar social agitation had shaken the compact agrarian block. But the semi-feudal client-patron structure continued to suffocate further democratic progress in the South. The solution for some was a "southern revolution," which was also to be an "Italian revolution."[29] Others sought reforms: Father Luigi Sturzo's Popular Party might have broken this obstacle were it not for the disastrous events of October 1922. The law on proportional representation had been approved in 1919, and the law on the expropriation and division of large estates was still being debated in Parliament in July 1922. But the Fascist conquest of Italy three months later interrupted his party's work, while his popular program produced a backlash: it strengthened ties between the agrarian class and Fascism. In spite of Mussolini's propaganda on agrarian reforms (the "Battle for Wheat," "Land Reclamation Programs"), Fascism was against the peasants. Between 1920 and 1923 the Fascists terrorized and crushed the Communist-led peasant organizations and movements. The 1922–23 laws of the Fascist government eliminated all peasant institutions and rights, and restored landowners' right to drive peasants from their lands and raise rental fees. By siding with the landowners, Fascism perpetuated and aggravated the Southern Question, partly also by opposing independent emigration.[30]

THE PLIGHT OF UPPER MOLISE

It was this general climate as well as the situation in the Molise mountain villages that made many emigrate, and that also nourished the desire and the plan of the six young men to leave Villa Canale and Agnone in 1923. The Abruzzo-Molise area, formerly the northernmost part of the Kingdom of the Two Sicilies, had been a land of emigration since the eighteenth century: entire families moved from their depressed areas to work in the neighbouring Papal States. Instead of improving the situation through reforestation and small industries, the kingdom tried to prevent emigration through laws, heavy taxes, and the threat of confiscation. In the nineteenth century, emigration to the Americas became regular, beginning in 1870, and vigorous after 1879, first the exodus from the rugged mountain areas, then the departure of the less distressed *mezzadri* (tenant farmers) from the plains. Emigration was a need, at least at first for reasons of poverty, hunger, low productivity, petty wages, sterility of deforested lands and pastures, and the boldness of the inhabitants, for centuries accustomed to internal migrations as labourers and shepherds.

In the following decades, in spite of better conditions, emigration increased, but for a set of different reasons: to maintain or improve the economic levels reached; the obsessively growing attraction to "America"; and the decreasing fear of travel. Using their instinct of self-improvement and experience as guide and norm, they became their own agents. Since its inception, they were part of the first "great exodus" and of subsequent immigrations to Europe, the Americas, and the Italian African colonies, so that by 1920 the Abruzzo-Molise region registered the highest migration rate for 1916–20.[31]

Molise alone (split from Abruzzo-Molise in 1963 to become the youngest and the second-smallest Italian region), like Abruzzo, was an area of high emigration for over a century. Between 1861 and 1981 the resident population decreased by over 3 per cent (from 335,138 to 324,741).[32] The municipality of Agnone in Upper Molise has records of emigration at least since 1870 when the first few labourers left for America. The steady, irregular flow throughout the 1870s grew from 70 in 1871 to 1,293 emigrants in 1879, to reach the peak in 1906, and by then about one-quarter of the population of Agnone had crossed the ocean. Between 1912 and 1943 many of them emigrated to the Italian colonies (Libya, Eritrea, Somalia, Ethiopia, and the Dodecanese Islands), and after the Second World War the exodus continued toward Europe and Canada, especially to the Leamington and Montreal areas.[33]

The majority of the Leamington Italians interviewed stated without hesitation that in order to achieve anything worthwhile they had to get away from the life of their hometowns or villages. For the Leamington pioneers, like for those who emigrated before the First World War, the destination was generic "America" – no distinction was made between the United States and Canada, which often caused complications, particularly if the approximate destination was a border area such as Windsor-Detroit. However, the town lore had its own simple and colourful way of distinguishing North and South America.

THE "RIGHT" AMERICA AND THE "WRONG" AMERICA

Stories about "America" circulated in the hill towns of Molise in the early twentieth century. The young people of Agnone and Villa Canale formed their first impressions of the land of plenty from the stories of those who had been there to work for a few years and had returned to Italy (see chapter 15, "The 'Migration' Parallels," and "Conclusion"). Tony DiMenna (1898–1989), at age eighty-two, still vividly recalled those times: "Around our parts, there was talk about America – *l'America 'dritta' e l'America* '*storta*.' The 'right' America was Argentina and the 'wrong' America was the United States, because *gli antichi*, the old people, the very old ones who used to come here to the United States, came only for a year – one, two, three years – made some money and went back and told the story that over here the winter was long and cold ... They had to explode mines in the earth to break the ice in the areas where they were sent. They were sent up north ... They came here, they put away seven to eight hundred dollars – a thousand dollars – but not one with the intention to stay."

In the view of the Leamington Italian pioneers, it was relatively easy to go to America before the First World War: "Italy could still travel by sea," Tony DiMenna remembered, "but after America joined the war, everything was closed." Several early immigrants who settled in Leamington had been to the United States before and after the Great War, but they all returned to their hometowns before sailing again. The stories of pre–First World War Italian migrants were told by their children and grandchildren. Henry (Enrico) Ingratta (1883–1971) – according to his son Marius Ingratta, who remembered well what his father used to tell him – spent many years in Ohio in the quarries. In 1912, he returned to Villa Canale, fought in the First World War with the Italian army, and spent two or three years in Romania as a prisoner of war. In 1925 he came back to "America," this time to Canada, first to Windsor, then Leamington, where he died in 1971.

Ralph Ingratta of Leamington (1953) related the story of his grandfather, Raffaele (Ralph) Ingratta (1923), who also had gone to the United States, where he remained for awhile, then returned to his hometown, Villa Canale.

Luigi, father of Marius Mastronardi, made his first trip to the United States at the age of seventeen. He worked there for two or three years and then returned to Italy, where he served in the army through the First World War. Marius seemed certain that his father was with Henry Ingratta: both worked in the same mine.

At the age of sixteen, in 1913, Domenico (Domenic) Pannunzio, a Leamington Italian pioneer, went to the United States "to earn some money" with his brother-in-law Giuseppe (Joseph) Mastronardi. They soon discovered that "times were just as hard in America," and Giuseppe convinced Domenico to return to Italy. Shortly after their return, the First World War broke out and Domenico and Giuseppe were sent to the front, where Giuseppe lost his life. Domenico served in the Italian army for three and a half years.[34]

Antonio (Tony) Cervini (1893–1991), from Ripi (Frosinone, Lazio), went to Detroit in 1912, then returned to Italy in 1915 "to defend Italy" in the First World War in the Italian army. After his discharge in 1920, he went back to the United States. But jobs were scarce, so once again, in 1921, he returned to Italy. Up to that time, Cervini said, he "was free" to go back and forth. But "then the United States closed immigration";[35] and in 1923, when he decided to leave Italy again, he left by the infamous clandestine route. As a result, he was prevented from entering the United States; he was held in New York for seventeen days and then sent back on 5 April 1923. The roundabout journey home to Ripi did not dampen his desire to return to America. In 1927, this time with the proper papers, he came to Canada, and in 1938 he settled in Leamington. (A fuller story of his wandering will be told in chapter 4.)

Albano Valeri, from Fara Sabina (Rieti, Lazio), northeast of Rome, "called by a friend in Detroit," went to the United States in 1912 with the intention, quite unusual for that time, just to visit: but he liked it, found a job at the Ford Motor Company, and settled in Detroit. During the First World War he worked for eighteen months for the American army in the United States. After his discharge, he lived in Italy for six months, and then returned to Detroit. During the Second World War he served in the American army in Detroit and shortly after, in 1946, moved to Windsor. On one of his frequent visits to Windsor and to the well-established Italian community, he met a woman from San Daniele (Friuli) whom he married in 1940 in one of the earliest marriage ceremonies held in the still incomplete St Angela Merici Church (corner of Louis and Erie Street East in Windsor, the heart of Windsor's "Little Italy"). In October 1978, Albano and his wife Giacomina moved to Mersea Township to be near their daughter Ines (or Enes) Brunato. He returned to Windsor in 1983.[36]

"Right" or "wrong," America was a desired destination, even by the clandestine route, if necessary, especially after Mussolini came to power (1922). Nevertheless, the few who came to the Leamington area during the Fascist regime, after the settlement of the first groups, were able to reach it through sponsorship: according to one immigrant, "Mussolini let you leave the country to work if you wanted to, but you had to have someone to call you over." After the Second World War, North America became again particularly alluring, even though at times the desire and the need to leave the devastated southern villages took them at first to other destinations in Italy, Europe, or South America.

Of the thirty men who entered Canada shortly after the Second World War, several had spent time outside their villages: in the army, on the front, or as prisoners of war in Europe and Africa. Though only one said he had been in other places in Italy after the war, two of them had jobs that probably often took them out of their town. Another worked in Africa before coming to Leamington.

Quite a few Italians who settled in Leamington during the second postwar decade worked first in various Italian cities (Rome, Florence, Turin, Reggio nell'Emilia), where "you could work in a factory or in an office or at various other jobs," and later in other European countries (Germany, Belgium, France, Switzerland, England), sometimes in more than one city and more than one country. Some had first spent time in larger Italian cities and later in South American countries (Argentina, Venezuela, Brazil). Especially in the later decades, Germany was the most popular destination: "People who could not come to Canada went to Germany," said one of those who came to Canada in 1966. "They didn't need immigration papers and it cost less."

Men who had spent time in Italy and other countries while serving in the military were usually first to leave their villages. Some of them, as well as a few women, and mainly in the later period, also left for the larger towns or cities in order to continue their studies. But apart from the relatively small group who did leave their native areas for military service or school, most of the Italians now in the Leamington area left their hometowns and Italy mainly for economic reasons – not for *miseria* (poverty) but mainly for *miglior fortuna* (better life).

The men who had travelled back and forth to Italy, before and after the First World War, were the first links in the chain migrations to come in the later decades. They nourished, often also enkindled, in the hearts of the younger generations the desire to go to North America. For Marius Mastronardi (born 1922, emigrated 1933), "the letters from relatives in Canada" (particularly from his father Luigi, who arrived in 1925) were, from a very early age, what made him dream about Canada, the "land of opportunity." Tony DiMenna himself (1923), during his first trip back to Villa Canale in 1933–34, influenced many a young man with his stories of Canada: "I was a kid in 1933," recalled Guido Pannunzio (1948), "but I picked up all he had to say about the 'great country' Canada."

But the earliest catalyst – at least in the Upper Molise area – the man who started it all in the 1920s, was Angelo Moauro. Angelo and his father Francesco had gone to America (to St Paul, Minnesota, according to Tony DiMenna) in 1915. In 1921–22 they returned to Italy, to Agnone, and spoke a great deal about America with the young men in the Agnone-Villa Canale area. Once the bee was in the bonnet, there was no turning back.

A casual conversation between Angelo and Tony DiMenna led to their decision to emigrate to North America, to Canada: "*Maledetto quel giorno che sono ritornato*" (Damn that day I came back), Angelo cursed on one occasion. And sixty years later Tony DiMenna still remembered Angelo's words that made him decide to join five other men from Agnone and Villa Canale in the first unfortunate attempt to get to Canada: the clandestine way, in August 1923.

THE ILL-FATED FIRST TRIP

On the morning of 30 October 1922, Mussolini arrived in Rome and took over the government of Italy. He did not come on horseback, as Fascist art of the time depicted.[37] He came by train and was met with little resistance. The "March on Rome" may be a myth, but what followed was a harsh reality. The Italian people would soon realize what they had lost, wrote Angelo Tasca in 1938, "when they allowed Mussolini to ride to power in a sleeping car, on the 30th of October 1922, preceding that march on Rome that 'never took place.'" Mussolini's intent was to exterminate democracy as well as socialism. The aim of Fascism was not just power, but total power.[38] And this became immediately clear to those who had plans to leave Italy.

Shortly after midnight on 26 August 1923, four men from Villa Canale and two from Agnone started out on their long journey to "America": first on foot through hills and fields as far as Pietrabbondante, then by train to Sulmona (Abruzzo), Rome, and Cuneo in northwest Italy, and by automobile to Borgo San Dalmazzo, on the Italian-French border, where the "emigrant guide" was to meet them. The guide never showed up. Instead, the French gendarmes handcuffed them and handed them over to the Italian *carabinieri,* who sent them back to their town, perhaps frightened and humiliated, but not totally discouraged.

The trip had been on their mind for several months. Ever since his return from the United States, Angelo Moauro thought of only one thing: going back to America. But when he returned to Italy he didn't have the papers prepared for the return trip. In 1921 the United States established an emigration quota, and those that did not have the return trip papers had little chance of going back. He often complained to Tony DiMenna about this, comparing his life in America and the miserable existence in their hometown: *"In America si sta bene, qui si zappa dalla mattina alla sera"* (It's a good life in America, here you break your back on the hoe from morning till night).

Angelo and Tony often talked to each other during these months. The DiMennas had a parcel of farmland next to one owned by the Moauros. There the land had more stones than earth. The five or six families who lived there, "jealous of one another," just piled up the stones and left them there, though "they could have been used for building." One day Angelo saw Tony in the fields and called him: "Damn it! We can't work here with all these stones. I'd like to talk to you about something: I was in Naples; I wanted to leave. They put me on a boat, but they caught me, but they let me go. But if I can, I'm going to leave again because in America it's a good life, but here ..." Tony DiMenna understood and agreed: "Well, Angelo, if you try, let me know ... when you try."

Everything quickly fell into place. As Tony DiMenna recalled, it seemed as if the lid on a box of secrets, sealed for decades, was being slowly lifted:

At the *contrada* of Pietrabbondante there was a *cantina* – a tavern in the countryside, where you could eat and drink wine in the middle of the woods. The son of the owner of this *cantina* – or whatever you want to call it – was a *carabiniere* (a police officer), and he had been to San Remo where he met a certain Gennaro. This Gennaro was involved in "contraband," in smuggling people abroad to one place or another.

Angelo went to talk to this guy and said, "We have to leave right away."

Angelo was from Agnone, and he came to my place in Villa Canale, but he didn't find me; he found Domenico Pannunzio ... I was out in the fields ... Anyway, they knew each other quite well, Angelo Moauro and Domenico Pannunzio, having neighbouring farms and so on ... and Angelo says, "I'm looking for Donino" (instead of calling me Antonio – dialect, softer).

"What do you want to tell him?"

"*Ho una* [I have a] *masciata*" – dialect meaning "story, a secret."[39]

But Domenico Pannunzio says, "Oh, come on, tell me ..."

And he told him.

And so Domenico says, "I'll come too."

So when we decided to leave ... we were told that four people could go, not counting Angelo Moauro and his brother. They were going too, but exactly four from our town were going ... There was myself, Domenico Pannunzio, Domenico Ingratta – who is now [1980s] in Argentina – and Tony Mastronardi, who was from Vallocchia, but always in Villa Canale, not far. Tonino Mastronardi was my cousin ... us four, and two of them ... Angelo Mauro and his brother whose name was Peppino – Giuseppe ...

So, after midnight, casually dressed, we made our way on foot from Villa Canale, crossing Vallocchia, the river [Verrino?] and the hills to Pietrabbondante in order to get the electric train ... We didn't want to go by way of Agnone, so as not to show that we were leaving because there was envy ... And from Pietrabbondante, we took an electric train and another train and then another.[40]

Tony's memory, at times, seemed to fade away. The faster they moved away and the farther they were from the familiar places, the more uncertain and confused the memories became, unless the events were of particular significance to their undertaking and destination. It seems unlikely that the train took them to Castellammare (di Stabia?) on the Gulf of Naples, in the opposite direction from where they started out. It is more likely that they followed the Pescolanciano-Sulmona-Rome route.

There may have been a mingling of previous trips and activities, especially in Tony DiMenna's case: his experiences as a soldier in the Italian army during the First World War, his active duty on the Isonzo-Carso front (Italy-Slovenia border), where he was wounded, and on the Western front (France), as well as his convalescence and work in different Italian cities, before his permanent discharge in 1919. After so many years it was indeed remarkable that he clearly remembered as much of that first trip as he did.

On the other hand the shock of uprooting could never be really forgotten. Emigration was often presented as a permanent division in one's existence: an end and a beginning, a sort of death and rebirth. In the immigrant's life, every subsequent experience found some meaning when held up to the light of that event or decision: a moment splitting life into two parts, yet joined in a never-ending comparison of one with the other, often without certainty as to which was more real. Emigrating, both the physical move and the consequent spiritual shift or separation, especially if occurring after adolescence or in extraordinary circumstances, coloured every thought, word and deed that followed (chapter 12, "Attitudes toward Italy and Canada"). The memory of that moment may have faded, some details may have been heightened or discarded, but it was never lost. Tony DiMenna gave the best illustration of all its effects (chapter 3, "The Southern Italian 'Dream of America,'" especially note 22; chapter 5, "The Hardships"; chapter 15, "Conclusion" and note 83).

On their way to Cuneo, the six men stopped in Rome and visited the Vatican. But they did not see it as tourists. That visit was secondary, a by-product of their objective, a means to pass the time while awaiting instructions.

They were even afraid to move around, afraid they would be caught and beaten by Fascist gangs: "If they suspected anyone ... they would

beat you up ... It was an ugly dictatorship." They were already foreigners in their own land, in their own capital. The much longer second portion of the journey, along half of the Italian peninsula, seemed
almost not worth mentioning: "And then from there we went to Cuneo
in Piedmont." The cities, the mountains, the seas that passed by them
didn't have much room in their memories. They did not relate to their
main objective: emigration.

But what happened in Cuneo was not easily forgotten. The car that
was to be waiting for them was not there. Since it was the middle of the
night, they had to sleep in a cornfield. In the morning the car arrived.
They were taken as far as the mountains and were left at the foot of the
Tenda mountain pass (Colle di Tenda). During the night they crossed
the mountains on foot. Their guide was "one of those people who went
for coffee to France to bring it back to Italy ... and they knew all the
mountain roads. And to this guide that brought us across the mountains that night, we gave 1,000 lire ... and then we went to Tenda"
(Tende, France).[41]

At Tenda they waited in a restaurant for a day and a half for another
"guide that was supposed to come and get us from France." But the
next day "the French *carabinieri* came – and they spoke nice Italian –
they came to this restaurant ... it appeared there was envy between one
restaurant and the other ... and told us: 'Get out boys' ... And we left
... They took us to the Italian *carabinieri*. The Italian *carabinieri* took
all our clothes; they left us with no clothes on whatever ... all six of us
... They took our clothes ... and they took our money." And they were
asked many questions.

In relating this part, Tony DiMenna again recreated the scene, casting
himself in every role and commenting at the same time:

"Which one of you has been to France?"
    No one answered ... but I was in France during the war. I said,
"I've been to France."
    "Are you the guide of these guys?"
    "No!" I said, "I was in France, but I was there during the war ...
and no one's a guide here! With this much money! See!" Altogether,
they found 43,000 lire on us ...
    So they said: "With 43,000 lire, you're looking for work?"
    "If we can't find work, we don't want to stay here. We have the
money to go back home." I was trying to build an excuse for ourselves ...
    He said, "We'll see!"

They handcuffed us ... and they brought us to [Borgo] San Dalmazzo by train. I said to the *Maresciallo* [marshal].[42] "After serving in a blessed war, this is what we deserve – chains?"

The six men remained in the Borgo San Dalmazzo prison for four days during the investigation. A telegram to the Agnone authorities sent the local *carabinieri* to Villa Canale to ask many questions: What was the son of Domenico DiMenna, along with the son of Francesco Pannunzio, doing on top of this mountain so far away? The whole town was shocked:
"*Signor* Domenico, do you have a son by the name of Tonino?"
"Yes!"
"And where is your son now?"
"Since he's come back from the army, I can't tie him down ... but has he done something, some crime?"
The mayor of Agnone, Francescopaolo Covitti,[43] was a good friend of Tony's father; besides, a cousin of Tony's mother was a priest not too far away. The *carabinieri* were convinced that they had not been involved in any crime in Villa Canale. They had just left for *"al loro destino"* (an adventure). The telegram from Agnone assured the Borgo San Dalmazzo police that they had not committed any crime. They were given back their money and belongings, and released, but on the condition that they leave town and return directly to the authorities of Agnone within four days. The penalty for not doing so would be three months in jail. There was no point in running that risk, so "with money in our pockets, we went to eat and drink, and went back home."
Three or four days later, only four of them went before the mayor of Agnone: Tony DiMenna, Angelo Moauro, Peppino (Beppe) Moauro, and Tony Mastronardi. Domenico Pannunzio and Domenico Ingratta remained in prison in Borgo San Dalmazzo, on suspicion of participation in anti-Fascist activities.
According to Tony DiMenna, sometime earlier there had been a revolt in Villa Canale. During the elections a group of Fascists, about fifteen young men, were sent to town with a letter for Deputy Mayor Cervone. The people in Villa Canale met them outside of town, first taunting them by yelling *"Fascisti, Fascisti, Fascisti,"* and then attacking them with fists, hoes, and pitchforks. The *carabinieri* beat the attackers and those who came to help them. They all ran away, but the names of many of them were kept in a special register and the Agnone authorities kept a record of the "most suspect faces." The *carabinieri* at Borgo San Dalmazzo soon discovered that Ingratta and Pannunzio had not been involved in that incident, and three or four days later they were sent home. Two weeks

after the ill-fated trip had begun, all six men were back in their home-towns, deeper in debt, but much wiser. That experience would be of great benefit to those who followed in their footsteps soon after.

THE FEAR OF FASCIST VIOLENCE AND MILITARISM

The political upheavals of the time made the men increasingly apprehensive and more eager to leave: Fascism, in DiMenna's words, was "an ugly dictatorship." Mussolini's "reign of terror" (1922–24) was annihilating recent gains by peasants and farmers and the democratic Italian state. Between 1918 and 1920, though defeated in their struggle for land, the rural inhabitants had achieved economic, political, and moral victories that allowed them to raise their standard of living and self-respect (collective contracts, suppression of feudal obligations, salary increases, agricultural cooperatives, government loans, even the right to occupy lands left uncultivated by the landowners). Above all, by 1919 all rural municipal councils were in the hands of the peasants.

But the big landowners sought vengeance, and Fascism offered them the terrible means: from a small movement in 1919, so catastrophically defeated in the elections that Mussolini himself reconsidered emigrating, in 1920 Fascism became a terrorist organization of the industrial and landed middle class. Thousands of peasant leaders, including hundreds of rural parish priests, were imprisoned or massacred; the peasant leagues were destroyed; the popularly elected municipal councils were replaced with Fascist appointments; and the 1925–27 "laws on the *podestà*" wiped out the last vestiges of democracy and popular freedom.[44]

At the national level, in order first to achieve power and then to transform his position from prime minister to dictator and consolidate his regime, the *Duce* allowed lawlessness to spread by employing every form of intimidation and brutality. The crimes perpetrated by his own *squadristi* (the personal squads that he had legalized into national militia), by hired thugs and criminals, or by the so-called *ras* (the local bullies or the Fascist extremists in the provinces), not only went unchecked and unpunished, but were often encouraged from his office and assisted by the Italian police (especially in raids against "Bolshevists"). The 1921 "elections took place in conditions of unusual violence," in an atmosphere of "officially permitted intimidation." In "some areas of Italy ... virtually under Fascist control [the] socialists could not even hold their election meetings." The result was that Mussolini, who in 1919 had received almost no votes at all and no deputies, in 1921 picked up thirty-five parliamentary seats – about 7 per cent of the total – as well as immunity from prosecution of a judicial case pending against him for "intent to overthrow the government by violence."

In southern Italy the Fascist movement had gained momentum and strength even before the March on Rome. At the Fascist mass meeting in Naples on 24 October 1922 the plan for insurrection crystallized. In his speech, Mussolini threatened that unless the Fascists were allowed to govern, they would seize power by force, and "take by the throat the miserable political class" that governed Italy. Before they left Naples, the Fascists "also devastated the offices of the opposition newspapers." What followed was the "March on Rome" (28–30 October 1922) and relentless escalation of violence, corruption, and fraud in order to silence and eliminate all opposition. "During the first twelve months of fascism," wrote Denis Mack Smith, "the newspapers reported an average of five acts of violence a day. Most of these were against leftist politicians or were acts of private vengeance." The "Reign of the Bludgeon," as Gaetano Salvemini called it, most intense during 1923 (when DiMenna and his companions decided to leave Italy), reached a peak on 10 June 1924 with the assassination in broad daylight of the Socialist leader Giacomo Matteotti, who had dared to reveal in parliament that Mussolini and his Fascists had won the spring 1924 election by fraud and violence.[45]

In the hometown itself, the political situation was always the same, before and after the war: the party of the *signori* – the rich and the powerful – against the party of the workers and the farmers. "As far as I was concerned," said Tony DiMenna, "Socialism, more or less, I agreed with, but Communism no." And it got worse with Fascists and Communists clashing in the streets.[46] Dislike for the Fascist dictatorship, reiterated by Domenico Pannunzio, was intensified by a general fear of another terrible war in 1923. Most of them had intimately experienced it. Like most downtrodden peasants who had been the bulk of the Italian army in the First World War and the unwilling mainstay of the Italian imperialist wars, they were left dissatisfied: they had had enough of it!

The painful memories of the war in Tony DiMenna's mind were as fresh as the wound on his foot (and the scar was a constant reminder). Called for military duty in January 1917, joining the 68th Infantry Regiment at Campobasso (Molise), after a brief period of training at Sansepolcro (Arezzo, Tuscany), in April he was sent to the Isonzo-Carso front in northeast Italy. On 2 October, on San Gabriele Mountain northeast of Gorizia (former Yugoslavia), he was hit by shrapnel and almost lost his foot during night-long bombing, which prevented his immediate transfer to the First Aid Post. After a few weeks at the hospital in Carrara (Tuscany), he was sent home for two months of convalescence with a wound that "didn't want to heal." But in early February 1918 he was back on duty. After a brief but pleasant stay at the hospital for the disabled in Milan, though unfit for action, he was assigned to an Auxiliary Corps, and in early February 1918, 1,500–1,600 of them were sent to the Verdun area of France. Whatever front they fought on, it was the psychic scars, more than any physical infirmity left by the Great War, that deeply affected all the men of Tony DiMenna's generation.

TONY DIMENNA'S WAR MEMORIES: HISTORICAL TRUTH AND ITALIAN PRIDE

On the French front, in addition to the hardships of digging trenches and putting up barbed wire to resist the German advance, Tony DiMenna and the other Italians had to bear the condescension and insults the French reserved for the Italians. The immigrant, gathering his deeply felt Italian sentiments, even sixty years later defended the Italians and their role in the Great War, proclaiming that "the 200,000 Italian soldiers in France … saved the war … The Italians saved France … The French were running away … The Italians [did act] with treachery in retreating from Monte Santo … but the French retreat was desertion … They were abandoning their positions."

The proud Italian soldier of long ago, along with thousands of other southern Italian peasants, had done more than his share in the so-called war to end all wars:

When I was there at … Amiens and Soissons – I went after Verdun – there was the great retreat … We had to do 150 kilometres on foot to get away … without eating for five days … and with bombardments … They took the Marne that was 50 kilometres or · miles from Paris … Germany made a cannon that would fire a long distance so that they could bomb Paris; and they fired … this cannonball went 48 kilometres or miles … It didn't make it to Paris, but it was near … And France was afraid … and when we were retreating, the French would say to the Italians: *"Italie, la France est perdue … La France est partie!"* France was lost … But everything stopped at the Marne.

Tony DiMenna himself stopped for a moment. Then, as if pointing to a scene projected in front of him, he began to describe the deployment of the troops: "Here, there were the English … in the middle the Italians, and here, on this side, the French … each holding their own zone."

Tony went on to give a rapid and vivid description of the battles and the participants:

Each maintained their own zone ... But the French ... with the powerful attack that Germany made ... to break through ... with the [asphyxiating] gas ... and bombardments ... the French abandoned the line ... and so the Italians spread out with their machine guns ... across the water ... on this side ... Then also the English abandoned the line, for they could not resist this gas, the burnings, and so on ... So the Italians spread also to the English line, and the Italians maintained the French and English zones ... They maintained the fort for three days ... And then America that had two million soldiers there in Europe ... though they weren't at the borders yet, brought reinforcements, strength. With the Americans, they began to push back the Germans ... And Germany said, "Coward Italians, go and defend your nation!" Because they stopped the Germans at the Marne ... The gas killed the people ... but then we had masks ... Germany was the one that used the gas for the first time ...

Then ... after they signed the papers ... D'Annunzio thought that Italy didn't get enough ... so, he formed a group of sharpshooters ... to conquer Fiume ... and Fiume fell, but he wanted to go further on ... to Dalmatia ... They stopped him at Fiume ...

But, thinking about it ... really, Italy was not really prepared for a war so large ... It had to get prepared ... I think they had help from England ... from America also quite a bit ... With the Americans, they began to push back the Germans ...

It was Italy that made the first peace ... the fourth of November ... But the Peace Treaty was signed on November 11 at 11 o'clock ... there are three elevens: the eleventh month, eleventh day, and 11 o'clock ...

But at 10 o'clock there was bombing ... at the camp where I was staying ... we had to run at 10 o'clock ... in November ... in France.

More than historical truth, what is significant in Tony's account is the reality of the war as seen and experienced by a simple individual who did not need more than his grade three education to understand that, to people like himself, war left only sorrow, fear, and disruption, forever. And yet surprisingly, many of Tony's recollections do coincide with history; and both the events of the period and the men's personal experiences, which filtered or enhanced the events, united all former soldiers and immigrants like DiMenna, who became in a way their spokesman.

DIMENNA'S MEMORIES AND THE HISTORY BOOKS

Italy entered the First World War on the side of the Triple Entente (Allies) by declaring war on the traditional enemy, Austria, on 24 May 1915. The Italian front stretched from the Stelvio alpine region to the Isonzo River – a corridor between the Alps and the Gulf of Venice. For the first two years the Italian armies were deployed on two main fronts: the Trentino (Adige River valley, Asiago plateau, northwest) and the Isonzo-Carso area. But the Italian offensive concentrated mainly along the Isonzo (Soča River) to the Carso (Karst/Kras) along a front of about 100 kilometres on both sides of the present Italian-Slovene (former Yugoslav) border. The Italian advance, part of a vaster Allied plan meant to support Serbia and establish contact with the Russians to the east, was also to reach Trieste, with Trento the main Italian Irredentist objective. The Isonzo theatre was for the Italians a place of "tragic valour" and often "vain heroism." Two such places were the localities remembered by Tony DiMenna – Monte Santo and Monte San Gabriele (today Sveta Gora and Sveta Gabrijel): they were two bridgeheads of Austrian defences on the Isonzo; and after the Italian victory at Gorizia they became with Ermada the main Austrian strongholds.

DiMenna was on this front during the last two Isonzo battles (12 May–18 June 1917 and 18 August–12 September 1917). The plans of the two battles were tragically almost identical: outflank the Austrian frontal defences in the Gorizia basin. In the latter, the three separate, badly coordinated offensives (Tolmino, Bainsizza, and Carso) prolonged the fighting so much that it turned into a battle of attrition. Till the end, the San Gabriele, with Tolmino and Ermada, remained the pillars of the Austrian defences on the Isonzo-Carso front, where the war of attrition went on until the Italian collapse at Caporetto (October–November 1917). As a result of his wound, DiMenna left that front before Caporetto and the Italian retreat to the Piave River, where they held the line until the final victory at Vittorio Veneto a year later (October 1918), when the Italians took both Trento and Trieste.[47]

On the Western front, reached by DiMenna in 1918, after the French-German reciprocal massacre at Verdun (February–June 1916), the French launched a costly and ineffective offensive on the Champagne front (16–20 April 1917). Consequently a climate of discouragement and distrust spread over France, expressed in strikes, political unrest, and desertions, resulting in the execution of twenty-three leading socialist and pacifist agitators (15 May 1917).[48]

Similarly, in Italy in the summer of 1917, General Cadorna complained to the Italian prime minister that lukewarm government support, internal political squabbling, and defeatist attitudes at home were destroying the discipline and morale of the army, contributing to their fatigue and discouragement; and reminded him of the mutiny in July of one of their best brigades, the Catanzaro, and the increase in desertions, in spite of the twenty-eight summary executions. A large number of Italians also deserted after the defeat at Caporetto (October–November 1917). DiMenna's references were quite correct, on both French and Italian desertions.[49]

History further corroborates DiMenna's general comments on the war, particularly those about its fourth year, 1917. This year of exhaustion, increasing aerial bombardments, submarine warfare, dwindling food production, and steady diminution of the ordinary securities and honesties of life, produced appeals from all sides for peace and armistice in order to stop the "useless slaughter." But neither side was willing to desist from the war.[50]

Even the part in DiMenna's story that sounded like a patriotic exaggeration seems to have some foundation in fact. As a result of his wound, he may have avoided the Isonzo carnage at Caporetto, but he had to live through one of the worst periods on the Western front: the "Battle of France." Though DiMenna was not a combatant himself, many other Italians distinguished themselves on the battlefields of France. Italian participation on the French front in 1918 went beyond the role of Auxiliary Corps; their involvement was neither less dangerous nor less important during the relentless German attacks and advance toward Amiens and Paris from April to July of that year.

In the first German offensive of 1918 (21 March–5 April), which "began with a bombardment of 6000 guns and a heavy gas attack ... [the] British line broke and in a few days the Germans drove in the British line to a depth of about 40 miles." In the second great German blow (south of Ypres, 9–29 April), the Germans opened up "a wide breach in the British front." Such was the crisis that the British were moving toward the Channel ports for withdrawal from France; a turning point resulted partly from a unified command of the Allied armies in France (14 April 1918). Similarly, in the Battle of the Aisne (27 May–6 June) the Germans attacked the French between Soissons and Rheims; the French were "driven back 13 miles on the first day. The Germans took Soissons (May 29) and May 30 reached the Marne River, only 37 miles from Paris." While the French retreated beyond the Marne, the

Germans threatened Paris itself with the continuous bombardment from their "big Bertha" cannon.

In the subsequent German attack toward Compiègne (9–14 June) the Germans "advanced about 6 miles, but ... the French and the Americans who joined them were able to meet it," also because by this time an American division had joined them. It was during the Allied counterattack of 18 July that the German advance was finally broken. Fifty thousand Italians, led by General Albricci, blocked the German advance at Bligny Hill (near Rheims), thus contributing to the salvation of France and to the veracity of DiMenna's recollections.[51]

DiMenna's rapid and fragmented summary of events, with no attention to chronology, served a double purpose. While providing a clear background for the group's 1923 venture, it seemed to fulfill a compelling need to have his memories quickly recorded in order to share them ("lest we forget") with posterity, his own Leamington Italian and other communities. The repetition itself of certain aspects helped to emphasize his own awareness of the Great War and its effects. "The horror it brought to individual lives," in the words of R.R. Palmer, "cannot be told by statistics, which drily report that almost ten million men had been killed, and twenty million wounded."[52] At the same time, DiMenna's ardent defence of Italy, of that same Italy that he and his companions had to leave at any cost, was also an illustration of the eternal dilemma and contradiction of all immigrants vis-à-vis their land of origin: simultaneous dislike for the government and a strong Italian sentiment or *italianità*!

DiMenna felt he had to respond to the charge of cowardice, just as Italy since the start of the war had rejected the unjustifiable accusation of treason by the former members of the Triple Alliance, especially by Austria, first for Italy's neutrality (July 1914–May 1915) and then for her denouncing the Alliance (3 May 1915). Austria's offensive against Serbia was, Italy argued, incompatible with the terms of the mainly defensive alliance; moreover, contrary to the terms, Austria had not informed Italy of its ultimatum to Serbia (23 July 1914); had not respected Article VII of the treaty regarding Italian compensations in the Balkans, nor shown itself to be favourable to yield to Italy the Italian territories of Trento and Trieste during the long negotiations before Italy signed the Secret Treaty of London with the Entente (England, France, and Russia, 26 April 1915). As a result, General Conrad, with his "unwavering obsession to teach the former ally a lesson," launched the *Strafexpedition*, the "punitive expedition" (15 May 1916). The formidable Austro-German offensive on the Asiago plateau (Trentino front) was, however, a total failure, mostly because of the heroic Italian counterattacks. Italy's success in the "hurricane," as the *Strafexpedition* was defined, changed public opinion and the course of the war for Italy: war was declared on Germany (28 August 1916) for her participation in the punitive expedition, to which the Italians, encouraged by their action in the Trentino, responded immediately with their own offensive on the Isonzo, resulting in victory at Gorizia (9 August 1916) – the Sixth Battle of the Isonzo (6–17 August 1916), where "for the first time, after fifteen centuries of history, an all-Italian army defeated in a great battle an all-foreign army."[53] DiMenna's proud defence of Italian bravery was at least partly justified.

The First World War presented a new type of warfare of such complexity that it exceeded everyone's expectations for its form, duration, total involvement of nations and resources, and for the use of the "horrible device" mentioned more than once by DiMenna. Poison gas – chlorine – was first used by the Germans in the spring of 1915, in the opening of the second great offensive upon the British (second Battle of Ypres, 22 April–25 May), against Algerian and Canadian troops. Subsequently, poison gas was used extensively by the other powers. In the Battle of Arras (9 April–4 May) the British made use of the gas projector for a heavy gas attack. Could DiMenna's simple association of poison gas and empires suggest also a parallel between the brutality of war in general and the fatal collapse of empires? In the Great War, not only the two mentioned by DiMenna collapsed – the German and the Austro-Hungarian empires – but also the Russian and Turkish or Ottoman empires![54]

DiMenna's sudden shift and projection to the postwar Fiume episode was his own reflection on the link between the war and the partial failure of Italy's imperialist goals, and on the subsequent general dissatisfaction that led to the Fascist dictatorship. On 12 September 1919 Gabriele D'Annunzio seized Fiume with a band of volunteers and proclaimed it an independent state, to serve as a base for expansion in Dalmatia; that is, to occupy those territories promised to Italy in the Treaty of London (April 1915) and denied to her in the postwar peace treaties.

On 12 November 1920 the Italians, tired of war with their neighbour, Yugoslavia, signed the Treaty of Rapallo and renounced their claims to Dalmatia (incompatible from the start with their own irredentist claims). But D'Annunzio, whose action had been disavowed in 1919, resisted and practically declared war on the Italian government. Italian troops bombarded Fiume and forced the wounded D'Annunzio to evacuate. According to Nino Valeri, the Fiume expedition was the first grave armed rebellion against the Italian state, and it offered Mussolini the pretext to initiate his struggle against the liberal state, against its old institutions and against the international order that emerged from the Treaty of Versailles.[55]

The southern Italian farmer's acute awareness of what he and many others were experiencing was manifested in his simple comparison of the immensity of the war and Italy's conditions. As the historian Procacci explained it,

> One is bound to wonder how a country which had for fifteen years followed a policy of appeasement and was completely unprepared for war could suddenly have taken the decision to enter the struggle. The question is all the more legitimate in that the country as a whole, without question, did not want war ... So Italy entered the war psychologically and militarily unprepared ... The Italian army, which had lost 600,000 men, had fought well, and the peasants flung into the trenches had done their duty with the same resigned determination that they applied to their daily tasks as civilians. If one considers that, at least in the first two years of war, the Italian army was one of the least-prepared and worst-armed that fought on the various fronts of Europe, one cannot but feel respect for the tenacity and self-abnegation of the Italian soldier.[56]

DiMenna's very use of language revealed both his own and the more general and increasing disaffection toward the Italian governing classes. The pronoun "they" alluding to the industrial-military complex, to the "official Italy" that had to get reinforcements from other nations, was in contrast to the more frequent use of "Italy" and "Italians" (or "we" in relating the "Corfu incident") when referring to the Italian people and soldiers. It reflected a state of mind that emphasized his own dissociation from "them," as well as most of the peasants' "declared opposition"[57] to "their" war that Italians alone could not support. In fact, after the Battle of Vittorio Veneto (24 October to 4 November 1918), the "Victory Bulletin" included the following section: "The gigantic battle, engaged on the 24th of October last with the participation of 51 Italian, 3 British, 2 French, one Czechoslovak Divisions and one American regiment, against 73 Austro-Hungarian Divisions, has ended."[58]

DiMenna often mentioned American involvement in the war, with some admiration; after all, Palmer wrote, "American assistance was decisive in the defeat of Germany." Even though it came late, when the others were weary, "the mere beginnings of it were enough to turn the scale." On the other hand, DiMenna also understood, perhaps with

equal admiration, the great benefits America derived from its war investments; at least according to Palmer: "Aid flowed to the Allies. To the
loans already made through private bankers were added some ten billion dollars lent by the American government itself. The Allies used the
money mainly to buy food and munitions in the United States. American
farms and factories, which had already prospered by selling to the Allies
during the period of neutrality, now broke all records for production.
Every possible means was employed to build up ocean shipping, without
which neither American supplies nor American armies could reach the
theater of war. By such means the United States made enormous stocks
available for its Allies as well as itself."[59]

On 29 October 1918, the Austrians offered to surrender uncondition-
ally to the Italians. But on 30 October the Italians advanced to Vittorio
Veneto; by this time "the Austrian armies were in a state of dissolution,
several hundred thousand being captured and the remainder stream-
ing back toward home." On 3 November at 3:15 p.m. the Italians took
Trento, less than two hours later Trieste, and at 6:00 p.m. at Villa Giusti
near Padua, there was the signing of the armistice that came into effect
on 4 November 1918. On the Western front, hostilities ceased on 11
November at 11:00 a.m., and the armistice was proclaimed in London
at about 11:00 a.m. on 11 November.[60] If war veterans in Italy remembered the end of the Great War on 4 November, Italian Canadian veterans had the benefit of two "Remembrance Days."

The war ended and peace came on the "three 11s," but DiMenna's
memory returned to the tenth hour, to the moment before the armistice,
when they were still scrambling to hide from the bombs and escape the
rage of the war.

The events that followed the Great War increased the dissatisfaction;
it was the period of incubation of the desire to emigrate. In 1919, to continue with the example of one of these men, Tony DiMenna, after a brief
stay at the Army Medical Unit in Milan, was sent to serve at an army
hospital in Varese. But as a result of a telephone conversation with a girl,
he was removed for obstructing the hospital telephone line and activities. After another assignment with a small salary in another hospital, he
was promised, in his own words, a 200-lire *complimento* (bonus) to buy
his girlfriend a gift, and sent home. The wound on his foot continued
to give him problems, mainly because of the initial improper dressing.
The *complimento*, adding insult to injury, was a poor recognition for
what one had done. What a miserly reward for the sufferings and scars
received for the sake of one's country!

THE REWARDS OF THE "UGLY WAR":
HOPELESSNESS AND OPPRESSION

The experience made Tony reflect: "Here I am in this condition, and I have to accept it, just like that. After the 200 lire they won't give anything more." Then quickly Tony added, "And they didn't give me anything more ... the 200 lire didn't come either." (In fact, Tony DiMenna, not unlike others, finally received his army pension from the Italian government in 1987 at age eighty-nine, ten years after submitting his application.) How could one possibly look forward to a good future? "There was also fear that we would return to war once again ... and then ... dictatorship ... We weren't happy there, that's all."

Tony's thoughts were the thoughts of many others; his story typified a general attitude. "Once the storm was over," wrote Procacci,

Italy realized she remained a poor country and, what was more, heavily in debt to her allies. The peasants who came back from the war found the same poverty that they had left behind, fields that were more badly worked and stables more empty; and the glittering wartime officers faced the prospect of uncertain salaries of inflated money: a far from exciting or attractive reward for men who had fought for three years in the trenches ... Few years in the history of modern Italy, and perhaps none save 1943, were years of such deep and general social and political crisis and revolutionary ferment as 1919. Labour was greatly agitated ... There were strikes [all over Italy] ... In the countrysides of Lazio and southern Italy the peasants, now war veterans, organized and ... occupied the big estates ... In June a number of cities experienced violent demonstrations against the cost of living ... and in July, a general strike ... was put into effect, as a display of solidarity with revolutionary Russia. Then in September came D'Annunzio's invasion of Fiume, achieved with the connivance of the military authorities. This was ... the first of a series of subversive acts from the right that was to culminate in Mussolini's march on Rome.[61]

Tony DiMenna's doubts and fears were shared by all his companions. They had all served in the army: Domenico Pannunzio for three and a half years, two years in the war where he had lost his brother-in-law, Giuseppe Mastronardi, with whom he had gone to the United States in 1913, killed on the Carso front, where Tony DiMenna had been wounded. The experiences and thoughts of those who left later in the 1920s were similar. Costantino (Gus) Moauro (1923) had spent four years and eleven months in the Italian army and almost three years in the *carabinieri* corps after the war; Luigi Mastronardi (1925) had fought both in the Libyan Campaign (1911–13) and in the first World War (the above-mentioned Giuseppe, married to Domenico Pannunzio's sister, was his brother). They had all been soldiers, including Henry Ingratta (1925), Alex Colasanti (1924), and Tony Cervini (1927). As a matter of fact, according to DiMenna, the documents the first six men were asked to take with them to Cuneo in order to leave from France were their army or military discharge papers, evidently to prove that they were not deserters running away from Italy (see appendix C).

In 1923, war seemed quite imminent. There was much talk about it; even those who had been discharged could be called back. According to Tony DiMenna, none of those born between 1894 and 1910 could not emigrate anywhere. In fact, "the idea to leave Italy" at this time was also, in his words, the result of "fear of this new war that could come about ... In the month of August ... the twenty-sixth of August ... in Greece ... they opened fire and killed five to six [Italian] soldiers ... Italy sent ships to Bari ... they wanted to bomb Greece ... we [had just] finished a terrible war ... what [was] happening?"[62]

What was happening was the "Corfu Incident" or "Corfu Episode" (August–September 1923), that, as DiMenna vaguely but essentially described, brought Italy close to war during those same days the six men from Molise were experiencing their misadventure. What was happening was "the first venture" of Mussolini's adventurous, bold foreign policy, his vision of national greatness, his imperialist goal to give Italy an active role in international politics. Since the beginning, the Fascist movement, reversing Mazzini's ideal of Thought-Action, advocated first of all action, and action usually meant violence. With Mussolini in power, politics and violence became one and the same thing, at the national as well as international level.

The belief that war and violence were inevitable was shared by many movements, thinkers, and poets of that time. Philosophers like Georges Sorel exalted violence as vital energy. Poets coined aphorisms in praise of virile aggression. D'Annunzio's *Memento Audere Semper* (Remember to be always daring) was based on the initials of the name of the Italian motorboats used in the First World War to sink submarines – MAS – *Motobarche Anti Sommergibili*. His dictum was similar to Mussolini's slogan, "One must act, do, be what one does." The 1909 manifesto of the Futurist movement contained a section (9) that glorified "war – sole hygiene of the world – militarism, patriotism ... and scorn of women." In fact, the early twentieth-century Italian trio, "D'Annunzio, Futurism and Fascism," according to Cantarella, "sought and extolled the animality in the Italian man" at the expense of the Italian humanistic traditions and humble people.

Mussolini's belief that war was "the most important thing in a man's life," and that peace was "just a pause between wars," as well as his policy of national expansion and not excluding "his usual anti-English spirit," led to the rigid policy of Italianization in South Tyrol or Upper Adige (July 1923), the reaffirmation of Italian power in the Mediterranean (Dodecanese), and the ignominious Corfu episode (August–September 1923). After the assassination of General Tellini and four members of his staff on Greek soil (27 August 1923), Mussolini ordered the bombardment and occupation of Corfu (31 August 1923). When Britain and other powers protested, he ordered the naval authorities "to prepare for a possible war against Britain." But a month later, he was forced to withdraw in defeat and with the reputation of a bully.

Nevertheless, in Italy, Mussolini's foreign policy was enthusiastically received, and it helped to consolidate his power and continue his violent campaign to "[bend] people to his will," to persuade Italians, by means of the wooden club (*manganello*) and castor oil, to "believe" and "obey" him, and to "fight" for the greatness of the Fascist state and Italy (*credere, obbedire, combattere*).[63]

In simple terms, to DiMenna this meant that "Fascism ... didn't want people to go out," to leave Italy. The "*signori* who were in power in Rome" were preventing him and his friends from getting a passport. "We didn't like that law [or what] they were doing ... we made up our minds to emigrate, to go somewhere." The main reason for this decision, at least for Tony DiMenna, was more political than economic; after all, his family "*stava abbastanza bene*" (was doing fairly well). Tony was quite specific: "Fear of a new war ... Fascism ... dictatorship" caused his leaving his homeland. And the only way out was flight-in-the-night emigration. The decision itself to engage in a clandestine operation, as well as their ill-fated first attempt, turned them into "outlaws," "rebels," or even "resistance fighters" against an unlawful and oppressive regime. Thus began their own revolt against social and political injustices.[64]

3

The Second Expedition: The Ordeal of the First Molisani

Noi eravamo all'oscuro: Dove si andava, non si sapeva!
We were in the dark: Where we were to go, no one knew!

THE LESSONS OF THE ILL-FATED FIRST ATTEMPT

The first attempt ended in humiliation, but not in total defeat: for some of them at least it was a test, a trial run. Nevertheless, the immediate effects were more than a failure to reach a destination. The six men, travelling mostly by night, hiding like thieves, caught like criminals, had undergone a frustrating and frightening experience, and caused turmoil in family and village life.

It had also been costly. After the initial contact with Gennaro the "smuggler," a go-between (*la ruffiana*) instructed the six men to bring with them five thousand lire each for their meals, travel costs, and the network of guides and contacts, who exploited them on each leg of the journey. Debts accumulated. Tony DiMenna was forced to borrow the money. His father, who had the money, refused to give it to him, not because he was an unkind father, but simply because, after Tony's experience in the war, he did not wish to see his son go away again. His father's reaction was the first indication of the disruption that the incurable yearning to emigrate brought to the patriarchal order.

The departure in secrecy in the middle of the night and the events that followed shook the entire village, leaving widespread envy, alarm, concern, and suspicion in its wake. They had barely left when the woman who had lent Tony the money started to complain, regretting her decision. To avoid gossip, Tony returned the money immediately. The wives and parents were afraid that tragedy had befallen them when the police came to ask questions. And their return home in defeat brought satisfaction to the envious and drew derision from the gossips.

The burning desire to emigrate drastically changed their way of life. Their first flight had already caused much sadness, tension, and a tragic split among members of the family. In one case, the parting might have been made easier by a paternal embrace. But on that first night the deep sorrow in the heart of Tony DiMenna's father exploded: "Where are you going?" asked his father.

"*Alla fortuna!*" (In search of my fortune), Tony answered.

Instead of saying "God be with you!" his father shot back, "*Vatti al diavolo!*" (Go to the devil.)

Only deep sorrow could make such a scene comprehensible: death had robbed Tony's father of his wife; now a dream of success in a distant land was robbing him of his son, who, in his eyes, had no reason to leave, for he had inherited enough property, to lead a good life at home. But by then circumstances made Tony's stay almost impossible.

Not filial piety, paternal love or anger, not patrimonial inheritance could keep Tony and the others home. Italy's turmoil was cause for deep concern and fear, and each had strong personal reasons to get away from their village life: Angelo Moauro, to escape the backbreaking work on his family farm and return to the "good life" of America at any cost; Domenico Pannunzio to go back to America for economic and political reasons. The other four–Tony DiMenna, Tonino Mastronardi, Domenico Ingratta, and Peppino or Beppe Moauro – had never been to America, but the bright vision of it was stronger than any hardships or sacrifices they could imagine in order to reach it. They were unhappy, dissatisfied with Fascist arrogance, the privileges of the rapacious *signori*, the aristocrats, and the entire Italian class structure.

On the other hand, with the benefit of hindsight, one may wonder why they even considered getting themselves to America through clandestine operations, and three of them attempting it a second time in the span of two months! What made three of them withdraw and five others rush to take their place, in view of recent experience? What other motives could there be to again venture into the unknown? Definitely not *miseria* (poverty)!

They were not the typical Southern *cafoni*, the indigent and often illiterate peasants forced to seek that American heaven-hell, amply portrayed in the type of politico-social study known as "meridionalist literature"[1] and the veristic literary works.[2] Domenico Pannunzio, who had experienced America, the army, and the war, while declaring his dislike of Fascism described Italy as being just "a *little* poor." Farming was indeed backbreaking work, and hardly efficient or profitable on their hilly, stony parcels of land scattered around the village and countryside. Nevertheless, the farms belonged to their families, to themselves. They were small proprietors, not poor peasants exasperated by that notorious and chronic southern social problem – the struggle for land (*la lotta per la terra*).

THE FRAGMENTED UNPRODUCTIVE FARMLANDS

The plague of common land, characterized by the expropriation and partition of ecclesiastical and feudal estates, had existed since long before Italian unification: for decades at the centre of the North-South contradiction and of the Southern Question, the problem of land was also a primary cause of a bitter and anachronistic class struggle. Italy was perhaps the only Western European country where the privatization of public lands and the formation of a progressive, landed middle class were never totally accepted as ultimate goals. In the eighteenth century, political economists such as Antonio Genovesi and Gaetano Filangieri had already proposed enlightened agricultural reforms to solve the question; and in the early twentieth century the leftist thinker Antonio Gramsci offered a more revolutionary solution ("political alliance between the workers of the North and the peasants of the South in order to remove the middle class from power"). There had been sporadic partitions (*quotizzazioni*) of common land for over two centuries but hardly to the benefit of the poor peasants.

During two phases in the nineteenth century (1806–60 and 1860–77) several hundred thousand hectares, generally the least productive or barren, had been divided into a few thousand parcels and distributed among poor peasants. But most of these parcels were reabsorbed by the grasping landowners or the municipalities, in spite of laws against land alienation and concentration; and those not reincorporated or reappropriated did not permit the "lucky" grantees to escape the "abject condition of *cafoni*." The lots assigned after 1806, for example, varying from eighty-three *are* (one *ara* equivalent to 100 square metres, or 119.6 square yards) to one and a half hectares (15,000 square metres, or 3.7 acres), depending on the fertility of the soil, were "too small to provide subsistence for one family." The result was a vicious circle of baronial or landlord monopolization and peasant struggle for partitions; or the "antichretic contract" – by which the creditor takes possession of the land in place of the accumulated unpaid interest on the borrowed capital); while contracting or working land on shares (*métayage*), either on a 50:50 basis (*mezzadria*) or on a one-third/two-thirds basis (*terzeria*), so favoured the landowner that the peasant and his family were no more than feudal serfs (for the sharecropper had to furnish seeds, fertilizers, and even tools, and the children could not marry without the owner's permission). Scarce production, soil exhaustion, high rental fees and taxes, lack of capital for improvements, few markets and low prices for produce perpetuated and exacerbated the ugly cycle of illegal reintegration and often violent revolts, usually followed by repression and victory of the *galantuomini* (the well-to-do class).

The 300,000 hectares of productive land still available for division at the end of the 1800s were the subject of many studies, legislative proposals, and parliamentary debates for over twenty years. But after the 1904 legislative attempt, the "sepulchral stone again fell on the much vexed, unresolved question." Luigi Sturzo's complex plan after the First World War was interrupted by Fascism, and the ordinance on public lands of 22 May 1924 was not even brought before Parliament. The effect of decades of partial, incomplete, inefficient measures was the breaking up and squandering into bits and pieces of the public demesne.[3]

The Agnone–Villa Canale situation provides a good illustration at the local level of this general Italian land question. This area of Upper Molise had been a feudal possession of the Caracciolos di Santobuono, titular princes of Agnone, since the seventeenth century. The village of Villa Canale had its origins in the early nineteenth century, when the Caracciolos realized that agricultural production would benefit more from a permanent resident population than from seasonal farmworkers. With the 1806 law on the abolition of feudalism (first promulgated by Joseph Bonaparte and then implemented by both Joachim Murat, king of Naples from 1808 to 1815, and then by the Bourbons themselves, after their restoration to the throne of Naples) the Caracciolo lands of Villa Canale became state lands, which the rulers in Naples then turned over to the municipality of Agnone to be set aside for cultivation and assigned to those who requested them.

The public lands were thus divided into small parcels and rented out to peasant families who either moved from Agnone, or were "imported" from nearby villages to what was to become Villa Canale. (In fact many of the families who formed the early nucleus of Villa Canale bore the same names of those now found in the Leamington area: DiMenna, Ingratta, Mastronardi, Pannunzio as well as Cappussi, Cacciavillani, DiCiocco, Marcovecchio, and others.) At first the results were quite positive: the demographic growth of the village was accompanied by a standard of living relatively higher than that of the earlier feudal period. But also as a consequence of the land fragmentation, the initially quite fertile soil had slowly become sterile and unproductive, and by 1845 the peasants preferred to give the lands back to the municipality in order not to pay taxes needlessly.

Villa Canale and area were thus plunged into a "dark period" of *miseria* (poverty) that dragged on until 1860, becoming worse after Italian unification as a result of the tenfold increase of taxes and other burdens imposed by the new government. Thus began for the people of Villa Canale and Agnone, as well as for those in other parts of Molise and of the entire South, that "sorrowful but necessary phenomenon of emigration to the new lands beyond the ocean," first to Argentina, then Brazil, and later Canada. At first, the few years spent abroad allowed them to return home with a little nest egg, to bring some relief to their families, and at times even to buy that small parcel of farmland that the family longed for; but the benefits were short-lived; the need to emigrate again arose; and in the twentieth century the phenomenon resumed, and this time it was often a one-way journey![4]

Nevertheless, those who owned some land in the South in the early part of the twentieth century could be considered fairly well off, however small and fragmented the family property. (And the fragmentation resulting from the haphazard distribution of public land was further enhanced by the practice of dividing the family property among the heirs, so that members of the same family, according to various Leamington Italians, owned pieces of farmland in different parts of the countryside.) The DiMennas, for example, according to Tony owned a house as well as sixty to seventy *tomoli* (approximately equivalent to as many acres) of farmland in various *contrade* (rural districts).[5] They had vineyards, olive groves, fruit trees, wheat, corn, vegetables, and lumber, which were in part sold in nearby markets. They even rented out some of their lands, or hired workers when they themselves, though a large family, couldn't do all the work. Most of the families of the America-bound first six men seemed to be in essentially the same situation.

THE SOUTHERN ITALIAN "DREAM OF AMERICA": REALITY AND FICTION

Want was definitely not what made them so determined to go after an unknown *miglior fortuna* (better fortune): they were leaving behind a small family "fortune" that would become their own, as well as father, family, friends, and way of life. Nor did they lack cash: the 43,000 lire the *carabinieri* found on the six men in Borgo San Dalmazzo was a substantial sum. (In 1917, a Turin industrial worker earning 30 lire a day, in the eyes of a Sardinian peasant who earned 1.5 lire a day, was a *signore*, a rich man;[6] compare also with the 200-lire bonus given to DiMenna when he was discharged from the army in 1919.) If emigrating, according to Francesco Coletti's 1911 study on Italian emigration, was said to "assume at times a form of revolt" not suitable for the weak-minded, the six men also were part of the multitude of brave farmers turned emigrants. But while they were not like the many *cafoni* (indigent, often illiterate peasants) who, forever victims of natural calamities and oppression, either emigrated out of despair or stayed behind with indifference or even "animal resignation," they were also unlike the farmers of the Emilia-Romagna region who, "out of pride," according to Coletti, did not leave in order to "attempt their revolt on the home front." The six Molisani's reasons for emigrating, and by extension some of the causes of the whole phenomenon of emigration, were not just to be found in the quantifiable political and economic injustices (violence, taxes), but also in what Coletti called "the stirring of the boldest desires ... the call of those who left before ... psychic contagion."[7]

The words and phrases the Leamington pioneers often used to describe their action offered clear glimpses into their deep-seated restlessness, their vague but unquenchable yearning for a better life, which also took the form of a romantic, reckless adventure: they went off *all'oscuro*, in the dark, pressed by a *slancio*, an impulse, a sense of daring, *alla fortuna*, trusting chance or toward good fortune, *alla ventura*, in search of a dream. They were words that evoked descriptions of experiences by the emigrants of the "first exodus" (1876–1915) and that also distinguished their own experience from that of most Leamington Italians who came after and often through them.

Some of their expressions of disappointment following their return home from America, or their state of mind that inspired their first attempt, coincided almost totally with those found in southern political writings and literary works. Angelo Moauro's contrast of the hardship in Italy with the good life in America and his imprecation, "Damn the day I came back," echoed the words and feelings of earlier emigrants quoted in Coletti's study: "You can't live here ... The soil is scorched ... Here you have the *bitter* mountain ... Why should I stay here?"[8] Similarly, Giovanni Pizzilli, one of the *"Americani"* in Carlo Levi's *Christ Stopped at Eboli* (*Cristo si è fermato a Eboli*), also compared, complained, and cursed: "Damn 1929 and what made me come back!"[9] Moauro's words, whether original or recalled from memories of earlier readings or conversations, while describing their situation, also reflected a more general attitude and the close link between Southern Italian reality and literature in that period.

Especially in reference to the Italian Southern Question, art explains life as often as one imitates and informs the other. Since the late nineteenth century, according to Pasquale Villari, "the writings of men of letters were united to the works of economists and sociologists in a common political battle." They all shared the same outlook and method that distinguished the liberal reformers: the direct, scientific observation of reality.[10] Thus, in many Italian literary works of the late nineteenth and early twentieth centuries, the plight of southern rural communities and the causes and effects of emigration were given highly realistic and dramatic representation. In the more "backward regions," observed a historian in the 1970s, "life does not differ radically from the village life described in the novels of [Ignazio] Silone or Carlo Levi."[11]

Silone's "*Fontamara* is the story of the struggle for survival of the exploited people of a small Abbruzzese [*sic*] village during the Fascist regime ... Silone's vivid portrayal of Fontamara offers a perceptive view of the life of the southern Italian peasant." In fact, "*Fontamara* is the story of all remote southern villages ... [where] all of man's history unfolds ... dominated by the most powerful of all forces, *miseria* ... a combination of poverty, helplessness, squalor, and suffering ... the father's only legacy to his son, the tragic heritage of the land."[12] Giose Rimanelli, himself a fugitive from Fascism and an immigrant to Canada and the United States from Molise, in his 1954 novel *Peccato originale* (Original sin), has a former immigrant couple recall and debate, as did many Leamington Molisani, the ambivalence of their experience: on the one hand, the vision of a better life in America; on the other, the hardships and sacrifices emigrants must endure.[13] Another Molisan writer, Francesco Jovine, a native of Guardialfiera (the town of origin of at least one family from Molise now residing in Leamington), dealt especially with the eternal condition of servitude of the Molise peasants.[14]

Similar themes of suffering, revenge, emigration, and revolt are present also in the works by writers from other regions, such as Corrado Alvaro (Calabria),[15] Elio Vittorini (Sicily), as well as the other Sicilians, Giovanni Verga[16] and the 1934 Nobel Prize winner Luigi Pirandello.[17] In many cases the works were based on not only the political debates and sociological studies on the South, but also on the writer's life and direct experience: in the case of the Piedmontese Carlo Levi, his *Christ Stopped at Eboli* was the result of his two-year political confinement by Fascism to a remote area of Lucania (Basilicata) where, he wrote, "men do not consider themselves 'Christians' (men), but beasts of burden and are convinced that 'Christ' (Civilization) never succeeded in reaching their barren mountain villages but stopped to the North, down on the plains around the city of Eboli."[18]

The authors' intent was as much artistic achievement as the raising of social consciousness among the ruling class, in the vain hope of translating the *miseria* and the struggle into radical social reforms and renewal. In order to move the authorities to action, a turn-of-the-century political writer emphasized the harsh reality of the Sicilian situation – the violent reaction against the oppression of the feudal families (*galantuomini*) – by resorting to fiction. After quoting a vivid scene in one of Verga's short stories ("Liberty"), Napoleone Colajanni remarked, "Art could not summarize better the hatreds generated by centuries of injustices."[19] Similarly, emigration, or the urge to emigrate in the first Molisani (i.e., the two 1923 groups), gave rise to a "reality" in life that closely paralleled "fiction," that is, the "reality" of literary creations.

The attitude and experience of the six Molisani before and after their first flight were comparable to those of two of Verga's characters. Turiddu in *Cavalleria Rusticana* (Rustic chivalry) and 'Ntoni in *I Malavoglia* (The house by the medlar tree) are two tragic literary representatives of the dissatisfaction, restlessness, and yearning that often lead the young to incalculable risks and, as in the case of the two literary heroes, to disgrace and even death. After a more cosmopolitan experience (military service in Turiddu's case), the two protagonists are consumed by longing for self-fulfillment outside the restrictive, closed, and stagnant village environment. Turiddu, senselessly undermining the sacred institution of marriage, the dignity of the family, and the religion of the home, meets a violent death at the hands of the jealous and betrayed husband. 'Ntoni, tired of toiling endlessly to pay off a crushing family debt, becomes a smuggler, is sent to prison, and dishonours the family name: his deviant behaviour helps precipitate a series of tragic events leading to the degeneration and final breakup of the patriarchal family. He later returns home and would like to stay. But he who had detested village, home, life, and work, now realizes he is a stranger, an outsider. He must leave and never return: "*qui non posso starci ... Andrò lontano, dove troverò da buscarmi il pane, e nessuno saprà chi sono*" (I can't stay here ... I shall go far away, where I shall be able to earn a living, and no one will know who I am.)[20]

Though not as tragic or dishonourable, the situation of the six men after the hapless Cuneo episode was not dissimilar. It presents some common basic elements: discontentment, debt, desperate and illegal action, imprisonment, break with the family, dishonour, return home with more wisdom but also with fear, and realization in some of them that it was no longer possible to remain in the village. Art and life seemed quite interwoven, even in the limited episode of the six Molisani "fugitives."

Tony DiMenna's sorrowful clash with his father at departure, like the rebellious acts of Verga's tragic heroes against the time-honoured, unwritten laws and patriarchal wisdom, equally exemplified the strain placed on the traditional close-knit family by the two by-products of Italian unification – the Southern Question and especially emigration. "The shock that emigration might have on the ancient unity of the family especially in the rural areas," would not be as severe as feared, wrote Coletti (rather prophetically) in 1911: the negative effects would be transitory, and after some expected disintegration in the transitional period, the family would establish a new equilibrium. Nevertheless, it would be transformed into a more modern structure, characterized, observed Coletti, by "the disappearance of the patriarchal type family, the decrease of male supremacy and the increase of the woman's role." But it would not become, as some forecasted, incompatible with the "spirit of solidarity and affection essential to any normal family."[21]

The disruption in home and village life, set in motion by the departure of the six men, was itself a symptom of a more radical and enduring social change that literary and historical writings were equally portraying. The senior DiMenna's answer to the *carabinieri* inquiring into his son's whereabouts and activities, while manifesting fatherly concern, indicated a sense of annoyed acceptance of his son's growing assertiveness, of the weakening of paternal control over him "since he's come back from the army." The choral response of the other families, of the village as a whole, with the generic phrase *"al loro destino,"* which served also to justify their children's going off "to their own destiny," revealed a sense of the almost inevitable breaking away from the family of the younger generations "in order to seek their own lot in life." In this sense also, the men were unaware participants in a wider silent revolution. Their emigration experiences, however circumscribed, inform the evolution of the basic human structure in the modern period; their actions add substance to, and simultaneously link, the insights provided by historical analysis and literary invention; and through this connection, each assumes significance within today's immigrant and general Canadian context.

Furthermore, this interrelation provides another key to further clarify and highlight the mix of powerful emotions and facts behind the men's action, and emigration in general. Besides the unsatisfactory economic conditions and the foreboding political climate, restlessness and illusions were activating in them the natural human tendency (Coletti's "stirring of bold desires") to seek greener pastures. Some of them longed (as Verga's heroes) to recapture the way of life previously known, albeit briefly, in

"America" (Moauro and Pannunzio); others yearned for the opportunity to discover it for themselves (DiMenna, Ingratta, Mastronardi, and Giuseppe Moauro) as much out of personal dissatisfaction with what they had, as for the influence of others (Coletti's "psychic contagion"). The "lure of America," the theme of many literary works, public debates, and individual dreams was already widespread, and Angelo Moauro had spread the "disease" among his companions. And yet they were all quite aware that America (as Carlo Levi's characters and some political writers warned) was as much a "hell" as it was a "heaven." Domenic Pannunzio himself, in his previous trip in 1913, had discovered that "times were just as bad in America." But what prevailed, at least at that moment, was the vision of paradise.[22]

The young Molisani reflected a general confusion. They were part of a collective hypnosis: Was the emigrants' illusion any different from the rather naive notion of many southern writers and politicians (including many Italian Socialists) that emigration would be the remedy for all southern political and cultural ills? Where was the truth? Neither the emigrant's vision, nor the politician's "idealistic" interpretation, nor the novelist's "realistic" portrayal of emigration and its effects was completely untrue. The "fiction of reality" and the "reality of fiction" seemed fused if not confused in the Italian emigration question. A picture closer to the truth rested in an integration of the "truth of history" and the "truth of poetry," in the interaction between historical insight – the "scientific" investigation of the various visible signs – and creative intuition – the "poetic" observation of the human psyche.

The combined forces of "need" and "dream" underlay the action of the six Molisani and of many others before and after them. They were essentially the same material needs and ideals that sustain and promote life, progress, and civilized society. But in the emigrant they often took the form of illusions that tend to make what humans imagine more appealing than what they actually see, or a distant place they wish to reach more beautiful than their native soil.[23] In the case of the six men, all the forces had been reduced to *slancio, fortuna, ventura* (impulse, daring, vision of fortune – mainly but not exclusively material); a desire to seek a better life beyond their native boundaries. They were urges deeply at work, cancelling the effects of defeat and humiliation of the first attempt, making at least some of them even stronger and encouraging them to boldly look forward to the next undertaking.

THE EIGHT MOLISANIS' DESTINATION: SOMEWHERE, CANADA

The ordeal of the first group had lasted less than two weeks: 26 August to 5/6 September 1923. They had started off exactly four years to the day after Tony DiMenna's permanent discharge from the service – 26 August 1919. A second group of eight men began a more successful journey a month after the first one had ended. It was 6 October 1923.

The regrouping again took place *sotto cappa* (in total secrecy). Domenico Ingratta and Tony Mastronardi, frightened by the first experience, did not participate. Domenico Pannunzio was reluctant, but encouraged by his mother, Custode Santangelo, who made a sacrifice to finance his trip, as well as by Tony DiMenna, Domenico decided to join Tony and the others: Angelo Moauro, of course, his brother Costantino, replacing the other brother, Beppe, who withdrew, frightened by those few days in prison; Geremia Capussi, Michele Capussi, Giovanni Ingratta, and Raffaele Ingratta, nicknamed "Big Fellow."

Only three of the first group of six took part in the second trip: Tony DiMenna, Angelo Moauro, and Domenico Pannunzio. Of this group of eight, six were from Villa Canale and two from Agnone, the Moauro brothers. In addition to the Moauros, there was another set of brothers, the Ingrattas, and a set of cousins, the Capussis. This group, rather than following the Cuneo route, went by Monte Carlo, using different guides, but the same agent system, involving the usual costs, and more – no longer 5,000 but 6,000 lire were required. And this time they also had a passport, of sorts.

When the six men of the first group returned home, they immediately went to the Agnone town hall to present the documents that the *carabinieri* had given them at Borgo San Dalmazzo. The mayor, "Cicillo" Covitti, mockingly questioned their behaviour: "What I'd like to know is what you people are up to. How did you put into your heads the idea of leaving the country without passports?" The men were surprised, for they did not think that passports could be requested. "Of course they can be made," proclaimed the mayor, offended in his authority.

Therefore, before leaving, the eight men in the second group first paid a visit to the town hall to have their passports made. But they were told that what was available was only the "passport for the interior," for use within the country, and only for one year. The man in charge, on recognizing the men involved in the first trip, offered friendly advice: "Wouldn't it be better if you stayed home?!" And punning in dialect on the name *Passaporto per l'interno* changed into … *per lantern* (for/by the lantern), he joked: "OK, you'll have the passport *by lantern*, but you'll return by *electric lights*." It was his way of telling them that he doubted they would make it even this time. But the men were satisfied. That passport, after all, allowed them to travel through Italy without being disturbed by the police or by Fascist agents in plain clothes who regularly requested identity papers along the way (see appendix C, "Antonio DiMenna, *Passaporto*").

In Monte Carlo they waited three days for the guide and were each given French citizenship papers; then on to Paris, where they "found the Italian consul and the Fascist captain." In their office they were shown a map of Canada, and the captain pointed out their destination: "You're going to this town here, Grenfell, in the west of Canada, way out west! ... Some place, eh!" he added with irony. Whether Grenfell or Burrows, Saskatchewan – localities recorded on the "Declaration of Passenger to Canada" of seven of them – their destination remained always unclear. In fact, they never got to Grenfell, Burrows, or the West.

They were puzzled when they were asked whether they knew anyone there. "We didn't even know where this Grenfell was." It must have been obvious. But the two men insisted: "But you *do* know someone in America." The hinting made quite evident to the eight men the type of answer the two were looking for: some sort of statement, even an invention, to satisfy requirements. And the travellers readily obliged them: "We looked at one another, and what were we to say ... that we knew *nobody* in America? We gave them the name of Colamario [Nicola Mario] Capussi, who lived in Chicago" (the grandfather of Tony Capussi, who immigrated to the Leamington area in 1949.[24]

In fact, according to the "Declaration of Passenger to Canada" for each of the eight men, the name "Capussi" or "Capussi Nicola" appears only in the "declarations" of the group of four men whose destination was "Burrows, Saska," while the names of fictitious relatives are recorded in the "declarations" of the group of three whose destination was "Grenfell, Saska." In the case of one of them, no name was recorded, and the document stated that he was "destined for Montreal for business"; he was immediately deported.

For no clear reason or consideration, at Cherbourg the eight companions were split into three groups and placed on different ships, sailing at different times. The four who were destined for Burrows, Saskatchewan, included Antonio DiMenna, Antonio Pannunzio, Geremia Capussi, and Michele Capussi. They sailed on 31 October 1923 on the SS *Empress of France* and reached Canada on 9 November 1923. Naturally, upon landing in Quebec, Capussi was not there to meet them, nor could he be located to guarantee to the Canadian immigration officials, as the system required, that they would be taken care of. Without much money left, without a job or a place to stay in Canada, unable to communicate well, even though Tony DiMenna knew some French, they were detained until they could be sent back.

It is unknown exactly what happened to Angelo Moauro! Angelo, who sailed by himself on the SS *Andania*, probably from Liverpool, in October 1923 and reached Quebec City on 4 November 1923, before the other seven. But he, who, more than the others, yearned to get back to North America, was detained immediately upon arrival, rejected, and deported to France shortly after (perhaps as a result of his dubious declaration as a businessman, which was clearly contradicted by fifty dollars in his possession). He sailed again on 12 December 1923 on the SS *Minnedosa*, and in spite of other clear discrepancies in his "declaration," was admitted to Canada at St John, New Brunswick, on 24[?] December 1923. He then joined his brother Costantino in Cowansville, Quebec, and later returned to St Paul, Minnesota, where he had been before the First World War.

Costantino Moauro, Raffaele Ingratta, and his brother Giovanni, who were destined for Grenfell, Saskatchewan, left Antwerp on the SS *Melita* (not *Miladi*, as they called it) on 25 (or 29?) October 1923 and reached Quebec City on 9 November 1923, the same day of arrival as the other four men. In spite of the fictitious relatives recorded on their "declarations," they were immediately admitted, and the next day they took the train from Quebec City to Montreal in order to reach their place of work. Although at the Italian consulate in Paris, according to Gus (Costantino) Moauro, they were provided with train tickets to travel in Canada, they didn't know exactly where they were going, except that it was "up north in the West" of Canada. But they apparently had better luck at Immigration: "A Catholic priest" (probably the same priest who helped his companions in the other group) "advised them against going there and to stop in Montreal or Quebec; and this is what we did," Gus Moauro explained, "and we found some work during the winter ... and we were lucky ... because it was the month of November when we landed, and in Quebec it was cold." It was in the town where they found work, not "Covensville" as Gus called it, but Cowansville (about eighty kilometres southwest of Montreal), that Angelo Moauro and another *paesano* joined this contingent of the original group. They worked and lived there, boarding with a "very Catholic" French couple, from November/December 1923 to the end of March 1924, when the whole group was reunited in Montreal.

The four who were detained in Quebec City for deportation – Tony DiMenna, Domenico Pannunzio, and the two Capussi cousins – had arrived on the same day as the group of three, 9 November 1923. Their experience was quite different: a difficult "rite of passage."

While they were awaiting deportation, an Italian man convinced them to try a possible way out of their predicament: "Boys, it's quite apparent that your papers are not in order. This person they're searching for in 'Grenfell' doesn't exist ... Besides, in Grenfell there's a lot of snow! What are you going to do? Do you want to starve to death? Appeal to the government, build a case in your defence, appeal! ... A boat won't be coming back to this place until next spring. You will probably have to remain here all winter. In the meantime, who knows what will happen?"

He made it sound like a good plan, a stalling tactic. But the men were concerned about the costs, perhaps thinking of the many immigration profiteers they, too, had encountered along the *via dolorosa*.[25] How could they appeal with hardly any money left! He assured them that it didn't matter: "Appeal!" he insisted.

The priest who tried to help them when they were brought before the Immigration officials – probably the translator, for though "he knew some Italian words ... he managed quite well" – thought he could do more for them by encouraging them to speak frankly. "Boys, you have to tell the truth. You lied to Immigration about who lives there [in Grenfell] ... They can't find this person who is supposed to receive you and give you work." The priest may have brought them comfort, but he could not get them out, at least not that way.

They four men chanced the petition route, drafting a letter outlining the hard years as soldiers in the World War, the difficulties at home after their discharge, the struggle to make ends meet, their wanderings to find a better life, the worrying for their wives, children, and parents faraway. Surely they were worthy of some understanding, especially in consideration of the fact that Italy and "America" had been allies during the war.

When the letter was finished, they were asked to disburse five to six dollars each (twenty to twenty-four dollars seemed a rather large sum in view of what they earned later).[26] Then the letter, translated into French by the priest, was submitted to the authorities. But even their resourcefulness in drafting the petition was not enough to bring them their freedom.

Ninety miles north, in the woods, an Italian engineer with a crew of French workers was building a dam for a paper mill. With temperatures thirty degrees below zero, many of the French workers left the site. An advertisement in a Quebec newspaper, requesting Italian or Arab workers to replace the departing workers, was noticed by the priest, who immediately informed the company about the four men: "Very good Italian workers, without work, and nowhere to go." He then approached the detainers with the advertisement and a supplication on behalf of the four men: "Let them go free! pardon these poor, unfortunate breadwinners [*questi poveri padri di famiglia*]. The company will take them." The Immigration officers agreed on condition that the company guarantee them work for two years, thereby fulfilling government regulations. The plea of the priest and the company's reputation, as verified by Immigration, finally allowed the men to hear the result: "You're free, you're free."

WHAT PRICE LIBERTY!

The four men were released to the care of the priest on 17 November 1923, and they left immediately for their place of work. They soon discovered the truth behind the tales of early transient workers and the meaning of the "Wrong America" – the Canadian winter, coupled with hostility toward immigrants (see chapter 2).

On the day they left, a man from Chicago came looking for them. During their "confinement," the men were not just waiting for things to happen. They had written for help from Nicola Mario Capussi, Geremia's father and Michele's uncle in Chicago. Apparently, they were told later, Nicola Mario ("Colamario" or "Colamariu," as they called him) went looking for them with three thousand dollars in his pocket to get them out: his intention was to find a way to obtain sponsorship for these men, even by buying land in Quebec, if necessary, in order to secure them work and freedom. When Colamario was told where they had gone, he followed them into the woods. But especially with all the money he carried, his fear grew, and he went back home to Chicago.

Meanwhile the four men reached the Donnacona Mill labour camp (about thirty miles above Quebec City) and met their unwitting benefactor, "the Italian engineer: Fracasso was his name; he was the son-in-law of a Quebec judge," a Canadian of Italian descent. The labourers at the camp resented the Italians so much that the four men, and the other two Italians at the camp, had to be lodged in a tent.

The six Italians made the best of their makeshift shelter. They had to improvise and invent! For mattresses, they spread pine branches on the ground. As heat from the stove was less than enough, to defend themselves against the cold, they laid blankets on top of each pile of branches so every two men had twelve blankets, rather than six each. Wedged between the two six-blanket layers and sleeping two to each "bed," generating and sharing more body heat, they avoided freezing to death during the cold nights. It was so cold that "in the morning you could scratch out your name on the ice formed on the inside walls of the tent." Nothing could be left exposed: to cover their heads and faces they used their jackets and trousers, which proved to be comfortable head-rests and kept their clothes warmer for the morning.

The work was difficult and dangerous: dynamite was often used to blast through rock and ice. But their co-workers' hostility made their situation much worse. The six Italians were probably experiencing first-hand the already widespread and well-documented dislike, if not hatred, toward a class of foreigners referred to as the dangerous migrant work-ers, the knife-carrying Italians, the scum of southern Europe!

By 1905 Montreal had a well-established Italian colony and a group of influential leaders (*prominenti*, *notabili*). But the Italian migrant workers or navvies, who often gathered in overcrowded dwellings in downtown slum neighbourhoods, caused concern for the authorities, especially because of sensational coverage of "incidents such as fights, knivings [*sic*] and duels [that] were recurring items in the daily news." What worried observers "was not the overcrowding itself, but the fact that, coupled with prolonged idleness among sojourners, it tended to foster criminal behaviour." A *La Presse* reporter who tried to "discover some association between the living conditions of Italian sojourners and their proclivity to criminal behaviour ... concluded [that the street where a particular] crime had occurred ... was a 'ruelle infecte ou [*sic*] vivent des centaines d'Italiens de la classe miséreuse.'" The resulting harsh judgments, that of "crime as a pathological manifestation of a cultural group ... were also reinforced by the creation of a cultural stereotype ... Italians were portrayed as being hot-tempered, uncivilized in their manners, quick to take the law into their own hands, with a proclivity for violence and the use of the knife."[27]

Whatever the reason – stereotype, xenophobia, or personal antipathy – the six Italians at the work camp suffered segregation and hardships; but the harsh treatment was surely aggravated by the men themselves, "who worked like bandits ... like horses, even on Sundays." The antag-onism of the French-Canadian co-workers was not completely unjustifi-able, and indeed quite normal. In fact, as it was related, the work at the camp, which was to last until 15 January 1924, was completed earlier than expected, and by 21 December 1923 they were all out of work, government or no government regulations.

But with the most important festivities of the year approaching, the four men were probably quite happy to get out of that harsh isolation. However unbearable, the five weeks at the work camp enabled them to put away some money: earning "five dollars a day," including meals and lodging, in spite of the long hours, "was pretty good in those days." With money for their room and board, they went back to Quebec City, where they joined the ranks of *bordanti* (boarders),[28] fortunately with an Italian family. This is where they spent their first Canadian Christmas and the first few days of 1924.

ANNO NUOVO, VITA NUOVA!

The "new year" did bring the men "new life": the beginning of their slow trek toward Southwest Ontario – Chatham, Windsor, Leamington – of course not without other jobs, layoffs, and unfortunate and fortunate encounters.

Through the help of the Italian engineer, Fracasso, and his father-in-law, they were able to find a second job in Trois Rivières. It was not as hard as the first, but it still consisted of difficult winter construction, such as breaking ice and pouring cement. But luck was again on their side. A northern Italian foreman who "liked them very much," perhaps as much as "he liked drinking," allowed them to earn more money, in a not altogether honest way. They marked, as they were told to do, more hours than they actually worked. Thus, instead of earning the "normal five or six dollars a day," they collected "seven or eight dollars a day" and sometimes as much as "eleven or twelve dollars per day." It is hard to imagine how the high daily earnings could have been justified at the pay rate they mentioned: "thirty-five cents an hour." Nevertheless, for the Italian immigrant workers this favouritism was a windfall (see chapter 9, "The Wages"). They must have been doubly sad when this job reached its completion toward the end of March.

Their next stop was Montreal, where they lived again with an Italian family according to Tony DiMenna, at 92 St Timothée Street, a downtown area with low-cost dwellings where Italian migrant workers had tended to congregate since the end of the previous century. Later St Timothée and Ste Agathe were "two streets often referred to as the 'quartier italien!'" After the establishment of the Italian Parish Church of Mount Carmel in 1905, the number of Italian families in the Montreal "Little Italy" increased from about thirty to fifty-one, mostly large families, and for the most part from the Campobasso province of Molise, or approximately the same area of origin as that of Tony DiMenna and companions.[29] In Montreal, their six- or seven-day search for work was fruitless, but the frustration was alleviated by a joyous occasion: the reunion with their four *paesani* and former travelling companions, from whom they had been separated in France almost six months earlier. The four men had, in fact, gone to Montreal because they had received word from the Capussis in Chicago, to whom they continued to write, that the other group that had also sent letters to the Capussis in Chicago, was in Montreal. Apparently they met at the home of the same Italian family where they went to board.

The eight men, together once again, and without work, decided to enquire at the railway station. They were immediately hired by the Grand Trunk Railroad, each given a train ticket and sent on to the Chatham area to work on the railroad tracks. They were only getting twenty-five cents an hour: "Instead of advancing we were getting less." But they were happy to be working again, particularly "in the open air, under the pines."

Unfortunately, this job was also of short duration: from Chatham in early April, "little, by little, by little we arrived at Windsor, and the boss of the tracks crew said to us, 'Boys, the work is finished ... you have to get yourselves another job.'" By the middle of April 1924 the eight men were again unemployed. But it was springtime, and the men were beginning to discover, if not enjoy, the much warmer weather of Canada's "Sun Parlour": the area that was to become, for most of them, their final destination.

COULD SOME RISKS HAVE BEEN AVOIDED?

It had taken them six months of wandering, anxiety, discomfort, good luck, and a great deal of determination just to find a place in Canada that they finally chose as their home. Along the way, many of their experiences that at times threatened to turn their dreams into nightmares could have easily been prevented by a little more awareness, civil responsibility, and a little less dishonesty. True, these men were not, as earlier emigrants, the victims of the greed, callousness, and fraud of the merchants of immigration; of the agents who recruited immigrants for Canadian establishments; of the vicious *negrieri* (slave traders) in the system who exploited the immigrants and migrant workers. These men did find good, kind men who helped them. Nevertheless, they too had been misled by the general ignorance about Canada: they were, at worst, victims of the insensitive and inhuman behaviour of the two Italian officials in Paris.

The two men were partly responsible for many details of the process: they arranged for their regular Italian passports "with the official signature of His Majesty the King," the exchange of their lire and francs into dollars, the passage on the ships and their train travel in Canada; but they did not provide them with guidance that might have rendered their journey, arrival, and first experiences in Canada less difficult. On the contrary, they were the coordinators in Paris of an imbroglio that sent men off into an unfamiliar land, to an uncertain destination, to their own fate. Their actions started the chain of difficulties that the men encountered along the way: separation, detainment, deportation, humiliation, fears, all often in a hostile environment. It was perhaps even hard to imagine such official irresponsibility, but the eight men quickly realized that "some people will do anything for money." Their own experience was further proof of the unchanging, contradictory nature of Italian migratory policy wavering between, on the one hand, indignation for and prevention of the "moral illness" and, on the other, a liberal or indifferent laissez-faire and exploitation of emigration, as a source of wealth for the nation or as an economic and political safety valve: a policy marked by ignorance of the true migration reality, especially after the movement became settlement.[30]

On the other hand, the two bureaucrats could be held only partly responsible for the men's later mishaps; after all, in their eagerness to embark on their "adventure," the men exposed themselves willingly to the risks they knew they had to face and were quite aware of, in light also of their chosen mode of emigration: three of them at least had had a variety of experiences (work, army, war). They were not illiterate; and the section on the "duties and faculties of the discharged soldier" in Domenico Pannunzio's "military discharge papers" might have helped them avoid many of their problems from the start. Pannunzio's papers, issued at Ancona (11 April 1920) and signed, as was required, by the mayor of the municipality of residence (Agnone, 15 April 1920), contained specific instructions about the passport for travel outside Italy: "Intending to go abroad before his twenty-eighth birthday, [the discharged soldier] must request authorization for it, through the mayor [of his municipality], from the commander of the military district that recruited him, indicating the reasons for his departure, the locality he intends to go to and possibly his new address: the purpose of that is to obtain a passport."

The men could not satisfy all the requirements, least of all indicate their exact destination, and most likely did not want to: four of them, including Tony DiMenna and Dominic Pannunzio, were under twenty-eight years of age and, the papers stated, "In the event of a call to arms [especially those in that age bracket] are under obligation to repatriate for [military] service" unless otherwise exempted. Thus, partly out of fear of arousing the suspicions of the military authorities and of the new Fascist regime (resulting in further delay if not rejection of their requests), partly to avoid the villagers' envy (and sometimes with it the curse of the evil eye), when the men went to the mayor for the "passport for the interior," they did not ask him to apply also for their overseas passports. They preferred to be smuggled out of Italy into France, and then "regularize their position": that is, obtain a regular passport as well as the "dispensation" from service (as they were allowed to do, according to the papers, by going before any Italian consul abroad).[31]

All of them, moreover, and especially the two who had been to America, could and should have been more familiar with the warnings of the Italian government against "clandestine" emigration. The Italian government, which had investigated the dangers and hardships the emigrants faced, particularly in the early phases of emigration, in Canada and elsewhere, had passed laws to protect and assist Italian emigrants (31 January 1901; 2 August 1913) and by 1901 had created the Commissariato Generale dell'Emigrazione (General Emigration Bureau) to protect and guide emigrants. By 1923, the bureau had an office even in Ottawa. Through such offices as well as other authorized emigration agencies and *Avvertenze per l'Emigrante Italiano* (Instructions or advice for the Italian emigrant), an attempt was made to help emigrants every step of the way. The first piece of practical advice in such notices dealt with work and a work contract: "The emigrant has to make sure he has a remunerative job immediately upon arriving in the country he intends to go to. It is advisable that he secure himself a work contract beforehand; only the emigrant going to the United States does not require a contract, in other cases he will run the risk of being sent back." The notices also provided addresses of emigration offices and suggestions regarding the necessary medical certificates; passports (which could be obtained free of charge just by presenting two photographs signed by the applicant and witnessed by the mayor of the town); proof of military service and discharge; sale of personal things before leaving; what to carry with them (and what not to place in suitcases – precious objects, money, food or liquids); how to identify baggage; how to behave during the journey, on the ship (be clean, use ship's library, avoid idleness), in the foreign land (avoid drinking and gambling, work, save, and remit savings to family through authorized agencies); and always be proud to be Italian. The most important warning was against the lures of improvised agents offering special insurance, information, jobs, and other good deals abroad: in brief, to seek help only at authorized Emigration Offices.

And yet, it was perhaps the recommendation regarding *"Il sentimento d'italianità,"* their retention of the feeling of being Italian, however noble the intention, that manifested Italy's lack of a real understanding of the nature of emigration. The exhortation seemed to enhance a contradiction:

on the one hand, condemnation of those who exploited emigrants; on the other, establishment of a system that took advantage from the phenomenon for national aggrandizement – not just from remittances, which were to be channelled through Italian agencies, but also from the very presence of Italians in other lands, who could be used to boost Italy. The emigrants, therefore, were strongly advised not only to retain but to transmit to their grandchildren their cultural heritage and love for their homeland faraway: "Even if they should become citizens of the lands where they live, they should never deny or forget the sublime spiritual heritage of their ancestors ... and thus remain forever unfaltering sons of a great and strong Italy in the world." What culture? What love of homeland? one might ask, in light of the level of illiteracy and of the way they were treated by the motherland! And the frequent negative reactions to Italy by many Leamington Italians were a good indication of these sentiments (chapter 12, "Attitudes toward Italy and Canada").

Some *Avvertenze* even appeared on passports. In Domenico Pannunzio's 1913 passport issued to him by the Italian "Office of Emigration" in Ottawa on 14 November 1924, the inside cover has the *"Avvertenze agli Emigranti"* (warnings to emigrants). They were thus advised to use "authorized offices" in Italy and to "refuse every offer made by emigration agencies established outside Italy, which [aimed] to draw them to foreign ports for embarkation, because, by accepting, they might incur serious inconveniences: higher expenses, often a longer journey, lack of protection on board by government Commissioners, the need to appeal to foreign courts in case of litigation, and costly stops in foreign sea towns to wait for departure day."[32] The *Avvertenze* did not, however, protect them against being taken advantage of by Italian public employees, as manifested by the consular officers in Paris and the Pietrabbondante policeman (*carabiniere*) who, according to DiMenna, first informed Angelo Moauro about the clandestine emigrant operation in San Remo.

Nevertheless, by the time the eight men reached Windsor in April 1924, the nightmare was well behind them. The six-month experience was a sort of initiation, a baptism by fire that prepared them for the difficulties they were to meet on their continued, tortuous, albeit shorter, trek from Windsor to Leamington.

4

1925–1945:
The Slow Growth of Solid Roots

Windsor was at the height of an unprecedented boom when the eight Molisani immigrants arrived in April 1924. Since the early years of the century, it had been enjoying "a period of phenomenal growth" that reached its peak during that decade: in general, a period of important industrial expansion, large-scale development at industrial plants and of new industries (including the beginnings of the Chrysler and General Motors plants), and rapid urbanization – between 1908 and 1928, the population of urban Windsor, Walkerville, East Windsor, and Sandwich increased five-fold from 20,760 to 105,200.

The 1920s were a time of unceasing construction: new commercial and office buildings, hotels, banks, medical centres, schools, new units in hospitals, and the Walker Airport. The Ambassador Bridge, a wonder for that time, was completed, as was the Windsor-Detroit Tunnel. As a vital link in the Great Lakes–St Lawrence system, Windsor offered ample employment opportunities, if not in the automotive and other industrial plants on the Canadian side of the border, in the many industries just across the river, in Detroit, one of the largest American cities. And if these could not provide work, as happened during the Depression, there were always the fertile farmlands of Essex County.[1]

Italian migrant workers passing through Windsor in 1904[2] would have found few Italians settled in the Windsor area, but the group had begun to take shape. Growth of Italian settlement had been slow and sporadic throughout the first great exodus (1876–1915): while the first recorded Italian living in the area dates back to 1861 (John B. Veste, labourer, age twenty-two, male, single) and the first "prosperous commercial merchant" to 1881 (Michael Cauzillo, from Genoa, grocer/fruit dealer),[3] by 1901 there were still only fifty-two Italians, and ninety-five in 1911.[4] Nevertheless, the earliest known reference to Italians as one of Windsor's national groups dates back to 1 June 1904, even though the Windsor newspaper drew attention to it in relation to the immigrant flow at the Detroit-Windsor border: "Immigrants at this period are passing through Windsor at the rate of seven or eight families a day, or about two hundred persons per week ... They may also be found settled all over the various portions of our city. There are, besides those of British birth, Germans, Austrians, Norwegians, Swedes, Chinamen, Syrians, Jews, Greeks, Roumanians [sic], Armenians, Russians, Poles, Swiss, Italians, Dutch, and others. No doubt the greater number, who are responsible people, make responsible and good citizens."

After an attempt to categorize the incoming settlers by their "varied facial expressions" and through current stereotypes, the reporter commented on the Italian group, showing some familiarity with their characteristics: "Then there are our old friends the Italians. Of all foreigners who land in this county the sons of sunny Italy are the most communicative and seem extremely anxious to ingratiate themselves with the community. They rapidly acquire the English language and soon become settled down in the country of their adoption."

With mass migration well under way by this time, Italian workers were being recruited and transported across Canada to work in mines, on the railways (especially since 1881, when work began on the Canadian Pacific Railway), or in the cities as ditch diggers. By the early century, many had also settled not just in the larger centres such as Montreal or Toronto, but in the greater Windsor area as well, or just across the river in Detroit where, by the turn of the twentieth century, the Italians numbered over 9,000.[5] Others were attracted to the area by a grand project: on 1 October 1906 the Michigan Central Railroad began construction of the almost two-mile-long railroad tunnel under the river, the "electrically operated ... Detroit River Tunnel," celebrated as an "engineering feat" (even in postcards) at its official opening on 1 July 1910.[6] In fact, the first substantial growth of Windsor's Italian population occurred during the second decade of the century: by 1921 the number had more than quadrupled to 429 Italians (270 of whom were Italian-born). Windsor's proximity to the United States was also a factor in this growth, as indicated by the continuous arrival of Italians from Michigan and Detroit, where the number of Italians prior to the First World War had climbed to 25,000.

The first well-known Italian to come to Windsor from the United States in the second half of the nineteenth century, and live there for some years, was Pasquale Palmieri (1826–1916). A Neapolitan patriot who had fought with Giuseppe Garibaldi in the defence of the Roman Republic (1849), in 1850 Palmieri went into exile in France and then England, where he studied engineering, and from there to Quebec to work as a supervisor in a mine. He later became a travelling companion of a Protestant preacher, Alessandro Gavazzi (1809–89), with whom he toured Canada and America preaching the gospel to the Italians and the freedom of Italy to the Americans. After leaving Gavazzi, he lived in Buffalo, where he taught languages. From there he went to Windsor and then Detroit where, in 1865, he was a photographer. Between 1868 and 1871 he resided in Windsor with his wife Mary, a music teacher, but returned to Detroit in 1872 as a fresco painter and decorator. Palmieri lived most of his life in Detroit, where he was very active in local Italian affairs: he was the founding member and first president of the Italian Benevolent Society, organized in 1873, and devoted much of his time to assisting immigrants to Detroit. But he still had close ties with Windsor: in 1910 Palmieri, now eighty-four years old, returned to Windsor to live with his daughter, Mrs George Mitchell, at 181 Windsor Street, where he died on 26 February 1916.[7] (See also Italian violinist Rocco Romanelli, appendix B.)

By the turn of the century, Detroit was not just a crossing point to Canada (in fact, "the lower lakes route ... was easier than that by way of the Ottawa River" since the early expeditions in this area). By then, Detroit itself first attracted many Italians to the area, as indicated also by interviews with various Windsor Italians. Mario Sellan (in Windsor since 1924) remembered his father first coming to Canada in 1911: "He went to Iroquois Falls, the coldest place in Canada ... He knew someone there, so he went." After several trips back and forth between Italy and Canada, "he went to live in Sudbury" where a friend told him about the opportunities in Detroit. In 1919 they both came to Windsor "for the purpose of going to Detroit, but met friends in Windsor and never got to Detroit." After the war, this route seemed to become a pattern, though Mario Sellan also remembered that Windsor by the 1920s was "a very busy city ... really booming," and "many Italians came to Windsor itself in the 1920s from other parts of Ontario ... Fort William, Sault Ste Marie ... to work in construction, factories, car plants ... Ford, Fisher Body, and others."[8]

By the time the eight Molisani arrived, the Windsor Italians formed a well-established community. Their activities since the 1880s ranged widely from menial labour (perhaps even in the nearby Anderdon Township quarry in the late 1800s) to flourishing independent businesses and professions, from artist and broker to soft drink bottling and wine manufacture, and included retail and wholesale operations (three run by women, in the 1920s), building enterprises, restaurants, and three hotels (the Hotel Milano, owned by Frank Grimaldi, as early as 1920/21), as well as a wide variety of trades and service agencies (banking and loans, insurance, and immigrant placement). By the end of the 1920s, with over 150 people of Italian origin in business and the professions, the Windsor Italians could live their entire life almost without going outside their community to satisfy their material, recreational, or spiritual needs: a Dante Alighieri Society with forty members, formed on 18 December 1920, to foster Italian culture and inspire new Canadians with a higher ideal of citizenship, met regularly in the Builders' and Contractors' hall on Ferry Street;[9] on 1 February 1925, the Giovanni Caboto Club (presently the oldest and largest Italian Club in Windsor) was founded, with over one hundred active members by the end of 1925; and in 1929 there was the official opening of the Italian Chapel (the first step toward the building in 1939 of St Angela Merici Church, the hub of Windsor's "Little Italy").[10]

By 1931, the small but dynamic collectivity had grown five times to 2,023, and though in the following decade it increased by only 430 people, after the Second World War exodus, the number climbed to over 20,000, approximately to what it was in the early 1980s (according to the 1981 census about 19,000 or a little less than 8 per cent of Windsor's total population). But the community took definite shape in the period of Windsor's first expansion (1908–28) and especially during the "Roaring Twenties," in more ways than one for Windsor, whose population had more than quintupled by the end of the decade. It was during this same period that the Leamington Italian community took root, but not before still more meandering by its pioneers.

JOB SEARCH, SEPARATION (AGAIN), AND SETTLEMENT

A combination of circumstances made conditions more favourable for the new immigrants to the Windsor area. However, it was no paradise. The Italians who came to Windsor in the 1920s had no difficulty finding work, but it was mostly seasonal. Unemployment insurance was non-existent and job security still unheard of. Therefore, the men had to move around, go where jobs were available in order to earn a living: ditch digging, factory, construction. and farm work, or anything else they could find.

It was in the search for work that the group of eight split up once again. It is sometimes impossible to follow their labyrinthine path in this search. For the remainder of 1924 most of them worked in the Windsor area: from April till September Raffaele and Giovanni Ingratta worked at an ice plant for the Michigan Central Railroad just outside Windsor. It is not clear whether Geremia Capussi and Costantino (Gus) Moauro worked there during the same period, but they were there when Domenic Pannunzio started in September of that year.

Michele Capussi, after seeing an advertisement in a newspaper requesting workers for a tannery in western Canada, went there for almost a year. Eventually, the two Capussi cousins went to the United States, illegally, were caught in Chicago, were deported in 1933, and never came back to North America.

Angelo and Costantino Moauro, who had discovered Detroit night life, "the clubs, the shows," moved to the United States. They lived in St Paul, Minnesota from the end of 1924 to 1932, until Costantino moved back to Detroit. While in the United States, Costantino worked at various jobs – slaughterhouse, drycleaner's, laundry, and Swift (& Company?)[11] – before returning to Canada in the early 1930s to join his companions and other *paesani* on the farms in the Leamington area, where he spent the rest of his life until his death in 1980.

After their arrival in Windsor, Tony DiMenna and Domenic Pannunzio worked for Chick Contractors, on the Cottam-Essex section of the highway, from April to September 1924. Then Tony worked at the Meretsky junkyard (where Angelo Moauro also worked for awhile) till the end of 1924. Then from the end of 1924 till the end of 1928/early 1929 he worked in Detroit, first at Briggs Manufacturing, a body plant, then at Murray Body Corporation. But he continued to live in Windsor with Italian families (e.g., Ettore Chiarini, Mercer Street). In fact he found his job in Detroit by getting a visa to visit friends in Detroit, but instead of visiting friends "I would visit the factory." The 1929 Depression brought his Detroit job to an end, and in 1930, after a few more months in a Detroit factory, he settled permanently in Canada. It was at this time that he moved to Eighth Concession, Mersea Township, west of Blytheswood (a village just north of Leamington on Highway 77), to work on Joe Henry's farm with other *paesani* who had arrived in 1925 (Armando Mastronardi, Luigi Mastronardi, and Joe Pannunzio), as well as with his former travelling companion, Domenic Pannunzio.

After the highway job, Domenic Pannunzio went back to Windsor, and, on the recommendation of Raffaele ("re-baptized" Ralph) Ingratta, joined the others at the ice plant in September 1924. Domenic worked there until the end of 1925 or early 1926 when he slipped, and his heel was caught in the saw that cut the ice into blocks. He spent the next two years in hospitals in Windsor and Toronto, then in 1928 he joined the small group of Molisani near Blytheswood, where they worked as sharecroppers for Joe Henry. Though Tony and Domenic were among the first pioneers to reach Essex County, they were not the first to work on its farms.

Of the group of eight men who had set off from Villa Canale and Agnone on 6 October 1923, only four settled in Essex County during the 1920s: Tony DiMenna and Domenic Pannunzio, permanently; and Raffaele (Ralph) and Giovanni (John) Ingratta until 1928. These four started the immigration chain from Molise to Leamington. The first sponsored immigrants from Molise reached Essex County by the end of 1925. With sponsorship (see chapter 7), work contracts, and other guarantees or travel arrangements, the later arrivals avoided complications that beset the earlier group: they were certain of their destination, and someone was there to welcome them, to help them during those first most difficult days in the new land.

During 1924–27, two independent groups of immigrants from two different parts of Italy also arrived and settled in the Windsor area and the farmlands of Essex County. Alex Colasanti and Tony (Amato) DeSantis arrived together in June 1924; shortly after, they began the immigration chain from the Lazio region of Italy. Vito Peralta arrived in Windsor in 1927 and settled in the Leamington area in 1943. Nevertheless, he was the first immigrant of the third-largest group of Italians to settle in that area: the Sicilians from San Vito Lo Capo (Trapani). The men who served for several decades as first links in the immigration chains from the three main Italian regions of origin – (Abruzzo-) Molise, Lazio, Sicily – to the Leamington area, all settled in southwestern Ontario in the 1920s. The nuclei of the Leamington-area Italian community appeared towards the end of that decade.

RESTRICTIONS AND IMMIGRATION
BETWEEN THE TWO WORLD WARS

The 1920s were the peak of a period of prosperity for Windsor. But the benefits of success did not always reach every level of society: for the early immigrants the advantages were few and as temporary as their many jobs. The handful of men and their families from southern Italy who laid the foundations for the Leamington-area Italian community settled there during one of the worst periods in modern times: a time of ideological conflicts, dictatorships, depression, and a devastating war. Though most of these developments occurred far away, they profoundly affected their lives. Not only were employment opportunities reduced; life was made more difficult by growing anti-immigrant attitudes, which resulted in a drastic reduction in Italian immigration to North America throughout the period.

Immediately after the First World War, Italian immigration to North America was on the upswing. Between 1916 and 1920, over half a million Italians entered the United States and Canada (United States over 512,000; Canada almost 12,500). That represented almost half the Italian immigrants who entered the United States and Canada between 1916 and 1945. If considered separately, the picture is slightly different for Canada: of the total number of Italians (about 48,000) who entered Canada between 1916 and 1945, more than one quarter came between 1916 and 1920. By comparison, from 1911 to 1915, over 70,000 Italians entered Canada, and over 65,000 during the first decade of the century.[12]

The downturn in Italian and southern European immigration to North America during the 1920s, and further reduction in the 1930s, were due to "events and currents of thought in both Italy and North America": the "xenophobia and racialism" that swept the United States and Canada after the war and the Russian Revolution; Italian legislation in 1924 and 1929 that drastically reduced the flow from Italy (from 6,000 legal entries in Canada in 1923, to below 2,000 in 1924, with the annual number never rising over a few hundred until after the Second World War, and only farmers permitted to enter Canada after 1929); the interruption of most village chains of migrations, though some fixing of passage by go-betweens continued; the Depression, which sealed the fate of open immigration; and Fascist Italy's opposition to emigration and promotion of settlement in Tripolitanian and Eritrean colonies.[13]

In spite of Benito Mussolini's restrictions, about two million Italians left Italy between 1925 and 1945, and few went to the areas preferred by Mussolini: the Italian overseas colonies.[14] The majority chose Europe and the Americas: many tried to reach North America, particularly the United States. The few who did come to Canada legally were either "government recruits," with a bond and an agreement to do farm work or other work where available, or sponsored by their relatives and friends.[15] All of them had to agree to work on a farm for at least a year. Of course there were still those who entered illegally. They came directly to Canada or entered Canada via the United States, often crossing the border at Windsor. The flow went both ways, and many were sent back from both sides.

THE FIRST MEN FROM LAZIO

The first two men from the Lazio region to settle in the Leamington area ventured out as recruits whose destination was rarely clear. For Alex (Eleuterio) Colasanti and Tony (Amato) DeSantis – the first from Ceprano, the other from Arce, two small towns six kilometres apart in Frosinone province – it was emigration at one's own risk; but they considered themselves fortunate to be able to escape the "work, work, work and no money" hometown situation: "Italy ... was poor, really poor."

In late 1923, four months after his discharge from the army (see appendix C), Alex Colasanti heard a rumour about "a ship full of emigrants to Canada." He immediately submitted his name with a travel agent and obtained the necessary documents, especially the $500 bond that was required by the Canadian government as security during the first year (the money to be returned at the end of the year), and on 1 May 1924, he boarded the *America* for "America." On 13 May, Alex Colasanti and Tony DeSantis, whom he had just met, as well as the other 450–500 immigrants carrying "all the proper documents," reached Halifax and a brutal reality.

"What did you come here for, *Italianos?*" they were asked. "There is no work here!" They were detained in Halifax for over twenty days in an empty hospital building. With very little to eat, they passed the time praying, or playing cards or bocce balls made from Gyproc; and a priest who visited them daily made them kneel on the floor and ask God for help. Alex was puzzled by their treatment; after all, they "were legal." But in spite of the bond and "proper documents," immigration authorities had to ascertain where work was available, or whether the men knew anyone in Canada: "You gotta have somebody," said Alex. "You gotta go and meet somebody to take care of you. Otherwise they're afraid you go on welfare or something ... like that." The documents of both Colasanti and DeSantis included the name and address of a friend in "Ford Can." (Domenico De Luca and Nicola Mocini, respectively). But that did not seem to help them.

But eventually they were all let go, a few at a time, probably as jobs became available, as requests for immigrant workers came in, or as the immigrants themselves understood the reasons and said they knew somebody in Canada. When Alex heard Windsor-Detroit mentioned by chance, he declared he knew know someone in the area. His brother Frank had been in the United States since 1922, and at least two people from Ceprano lived in the area at that time, "but one lived in Detroit and only worked in Windsor." Finally, Alex Colasanti, Tony DeSantis, and five or six other men were also released, the last group allowed to leave on the pretext that they knew someone in Ford City.[16] They reached Windsor in early June 1924.

Each man, according to Alex Colasanti, went his own way: some worked in Kingsville, others worked in Harrow but later left the country. Some returned to Italy, others went to the United States, as some of the earlier Molisani had done. Only Alex and Tony DeSantis remained in the area. After a year on the farm with Alex, Tony worked for about a year in a Windsor car parts factory and then moved to Kingsville, where he was joined by his family from Italy in 1926. The process to sponsor his wife Gaetana and their two children was initiated while he still lived in Windsor as evidenced in the Immigration Records (1925–35), which indicate their destination as "husband [father] DeSantis Amato 301 Wyandotte Street East or [handwritten below] 401 Mercer St Windsor Ontario."[17] Alex worked for several years on Kingsville-Leamington farms, then was employed for about twenty years at H.J. Heinz in Leamington, where he bought a house in 1955 (108 Erie Street South) and lived for the rest of his life (see chapters 8, 9). On the day after he arrived (5 June 1924, Alex went directly to farm work, first for a week (though mostly to wait for a job) on the Luigi Meconi farm (Fifth Concession) and then on the Bob Conklin farm, near Kingsville (both in Gosfield South Township). Along with Tony DeSantis, who was with Alex initially (1924–25), he may be considered the first of the Italian pioneers in the Leamington area to work on the farms.

The two years that followed were a rough period for Alex Colasanti. In Windsor there was "absolutely no chance to get work." He did not want to be smuggled to Detroit on "a little boat in the middle of the night." Too many had been caught and sent back to Italy. The only route left was to fulfill his farm work agreement and get his money back. In fact, Alex Colasanti emphasized the concern and fear of those early immigrants about losing the bond money if they did not honour what was, in their view, a binding farm work contract or agreement.

Whether they came on their own (as did Colasanti and DeSantis in 1924) or through sponsorship (as the four in 1925), they had to agree to work on farms. In the case of the four Molisani sponsored in 1925 – Armando Mastronardi, Luigi Mastronardi (no relation), Enrico (Henry) Ingratta, and Giuseppe (Joe) Pannunzio,[18] "Part of the agreement between these four men and Canada's immigration authorities was that each of them post a $200 bond, with the provision that the money be refunded if the men worked in agriculture for the first two years of their lives in Canada." Similarly, Saveria Magri, who arrived with her husband

and son in 1927 (chapter 5), referred to a $500 bond (like Colasanti's) and to a "Canadian law" related to two compulsory years on the farm: "*Quando sono venuta io qua siamo venuti come contadini ... Altre cose non potevamo fare: due anni obbligatori della legge canadese*" (When I came here we came as farmers ... We couldn't do otherwise: two compulsory years by Canadian law).

Whatever the amount posted, at that time it seemed a large amount to lose. Therefore, however difficult the work, many chose the farm work just to get their money back. The farm work requirement, widely used after the Second World War in the sponsorship of friends and relatives, also became an added incentive for the newcomers to buy their own farms.

On the same day he arrived, Alex Colasanti, who had been told before he left that his bond would be refunded after one year, went to see Meconi, who at that time "used to take care of us immigrants." In fact, the Meconi brothers (from Faleria, Viterbo, Lazio) owned and operated businesses in Windsor and area: Clemente, a grocery store; Mariano (the first president of the newly created G. Caboto Club, January–June 1925),[19] a winery; and Luigi, the eldest, the Meconi Bros & Company Steamship Agents, one of the two largest Windsor Italian agencies (the other operated by John Borio), which provided a wide gamut of services, from post office and legal counselling to "immigrant assistance and placement."[20] According to Alex Colasanti (and as attested by a deed of 23 September 1924), Luigi Meconi had also "a farm ... at Fifth Concession [Lot 11, Gosfield South Township] ... purposely for the immigrants that [came] in." He would "bring them down there and then go around and look for a farm" where they could work and live, as required, for at least a year. Of course he would get some "money – ten, fifteen, twenty dollars – just for his trouble" (for Alex, at that time equivalent to almost one month's pay). So in early June Meconi took Alex Colasanti and five to eight other men to the Meconi farm, where they waited "for somebody to come and get us." Alex and his companions may not have had to bear the cold and complications experienced by the 1923 group of men, but the first Canadian lodgings were equally miserable: "We stayed in a barn for a week, we slept in the hay." And waited until they were "picked up" and taken "some here some there."

Deplorable working and living conditions were common, even throughout the obligatory farm work period. Many of the early immigrants were often required to live and sleep in cold, damp basements or other squalid places. For Alex Colasanti and his group, it wasn't any different. From June to December 1924, while working at the Bob Conklin farm, east of the town, they slept in a garage, had very "little to eat," were paid "not enough money," and felt lonely and isolated. There were no Italians in Kingsville then: "To see Italians you went to Windsor, and those other guys came a year after" (referring especially to the four Molisani sponsored in 1925; see chapter 5). Other Italians, according to Alex, had been there working on the railroad, but had left when the work was completed. Then "if you get twenty-five dollars a month, [even] if you get fifteen dollars a month," stressed Alex, "You got to stay, otherwise they kicked you back to the old country."

Moreover, since they spoke no English, they could not properly communicate their complaints to the man in charge at the farm. They were even afraid to risk it with their "tough boss ... from North Carolina," Alex pointed out, as if to stress that no nationality had a monopoly on harsh treatment of immigrants. And during the winter months the garage became an "icebox"; so unbearable was the cold that it became impossible for them to stay through the winter and complete the term. They moved to Kingsville, where they were fortunate enough (in light also of the "five–six dollars a week" earnings) to find work in a tobacco factory (December 1924–March 1925). Only a year later, at the end of his farm work term (April–December 1925) and the uneventful winter of 1926 spent in Kingsville, did things really begin to improve for Alex Colasanti. Besides, by then he "got [his] $500 back."

The two-year endurance test over, his attention and energies were directed toward pursuit of some of his dreams. Not that sharecropping was easy work, but at least the hard work and the long hours offered some benefits to the workers as well as to the owner, barring the latter's attempts to cheat them (but Alex managed to obtain forty dollars a month, at least for awhile). In the spring of 1927, Alex began to work as a sharecropper on the Jack Noble tobacco farm in Harrow,[21] the same farm where, Saveria Magri remembered, some of the Molisani were also working shortly after her arrival, July 1927 (see chapter 5). Alex continued doing this type of work for several years, later alternating between the farm in the summer and the Kingsville tobacco factory in the winter (most likely at both Hodges and Consolidated Tobacco).

The year-round employment gave Alex the means to "call over" (sponsor) his brother Loreto (June 1927), rent a house in Harrow, where Loreto also lived for awhile (1927–29), visit his parents in Italy for three months (1930–31), and shortly after his return, set up family (1932). Loreto (Lawrence), after working with the group of Molisani on the Joe Henry farm on Seacliff Drive (1929–early 1930), joined his other brother Frank (who had just moved from Detroit to the Leamington area), and together for the next seven years (1930–7) they were sharecroppers on farms owned by Conklin.[22] Alex may have joined them upon his return from Italy in early 1931, but only for a short time. In spite of much confusion in his story, the indication is that he was alone for a year, sharecropping on a 50:50 basis for "another farmer" (probably Bob Conklin) in the Kingsville area. His being alone was also a reason for his decision to get married, as he quickly did in a civil ceremony in Detroit in March 1932, and "ran away" with his wife to Canada (see chapter 5). Afterwards, the Colasanti couple lived in Kingsville, Gosfield South Township, as also recorded in the August 1935 documents when Alex and Emma renewed their vows in a religious ceremony (St Michael's Church Records). In 1937 Loreto married his brother's (Alex) sister-in-law (Emma's sister, Mary) and moved to Detroit, where he lived for the rest of his life, while Frank, by 1941, was also back in the United States (see appendix B).

Frank Colasanti, who had been in the United States since 1922, had moved to Canada in 1930 also because (according to Marius Ingratta) in the United States, "for some reason," he could not sponsor his wife Palmina, who arrived from Italy in 1930 and joined him and Loreto on the Mersea Township Conklin farm. In 1938 Frank bought a farm east of Leamington (see chapter 8), where he and his family lived until the summer of 1941. By then personal tragedy and political events had changed his life completely: in early winter 1940, while on her way to work at the Hodges Tobacco factory in Kingsville, Palmina was killed in a collision; and since after June 1940 all Italians had to register as "enemy aliens" (see chapter 6), Frank, found to be an American citizen, was deported to the United States with his children. Then, partly also for health reasons, Frank sold his farm and moved to the warmer climate of California where he lived for the rest of his life. Therefore, Alex Colasanti (as his early experiences also indicate) was the first of his family to settle in Canada and for a time the only Colasanti to be permanently settled in the larger Leamington area (including the eastern part of Gosfield South Township adjacent to Mersea Township).

In the meantime, other Italians were arriving in the Leamington-Kingsville area. In late 1925 or early 1926, Alex met the first four Molisani sponsored by the pioneers from Villa Canale and Agnone.[23] By early July 1927, when the Magri family arrived, Alex and the four of them were sharecroppers on the Jack Noble farm in Harrow (Colchester South Township); and in the same year, with one of them, Alex bought his first American automobile – a Model T. A more permanent job, if not two jobs, the advantage of growing most of their own food and having plenty of it, and the increasing presence of *paesani* and other Italians offered a more comfortable and less lonely existence. During the

1940s Alex sponsored other relatives and helped other *paesani* from his area settle in the Kingsville-Leamington area, thus recreating the much sought-after hometown *ambiente* (milieu) that reduced the sense of isolation. In 1940, after years of much hard work and saving, Alex and his wife bought their own farm and a greenhouse, today quite popular throughout the region (see chapters 8 and 9). He had achieved one of his goals, but, as Alex stressed, not without the help, support, and equally hard work of his wife and partner for thirty years.

Tony Cervini was the second early immigrant from the Lazio region to the Windsor-Detroit area. By 1921 he had been twice to America and back: 1912–15 and 1920–01. After five years of service (1915–20) in the Italian army and in the national police corps (*carabinieri*), he was given a free passage to America and went to Detroit where he worked for a year. In 1921, since he was out of work ("it was hard for a labourer to find a job") he went back to Italy. When he tried to go back to the United States in 1923 he discovered that immigration had been closed: "I was caught in a trap ... so I tried to come by the clandestine route."

Cervini's plan was daring, and its execution now may even appear romantic. But it was an imbroglio that was bound to fail. He gave his name as Antonio "Carpentiere" (Carpenter) and convinced a travelling companion, Adolfo Piselli, to also use an assumed name: Angelo Rubero. It might have worked except for the confusion their false names caused them when they were called out by the United States immigration authorities in New York.

Not only! Cervini had also falsified his date of birth, which compounded the confusion. Eventually, all raised much suspicion. While they were being held in a "huge hall" with hundreds of other immigrants (likely first on Ellis Island and then at the Battery – two US immigrant processing stations) – the authorities tried to verify all the information, including the name and address of Cervini's brother-in-law in Detroit, that Cervini had provided in the documents.

After seventeen days they were brought before a judge. The Italian interpreter, evidently an immigrant from southern Italy, let Cervini know that even he was aware of his scheme: "So you say your name is 'Carpentiere,' and you come from Frosinone ... I'm from northern Italy and my name is '*Mangiapolenta*'" (corn porridge eater), alluding to the slightly derogatory term used by southern Italians for northern Italians).

The judge was more severe. He read off to Cervini all the correct personal information, including part of his family tree. Cervini, dumbfounded, asked the judge where he had obtained the information. It had come from his brother-in-law in Detroit, who knew nothing of Tony's ruse. Obviously he had not received the telegram Cervini had sent him shortly after he was detained. The judge reprimanded him: "You're trying to make a mockery of the laws of the United States of America. You have false documents." But he also showed some kindness by offering Cervini a way to remain in America: he had to find someone willing to guarantee for him with a bond of $1,000, or appeal his case. Cervini decided to do neither, and on 5 April 1923, he was on his way back to France on the steamship *Roussillon* or, as he jokingly called it, *Ruzzolone* – a heavy fall, a tumble – an appropriate reference to his own situation.

If not a tumble, it was indeed a zigzag journey home. Lacking the proper documents, a clandestine traveller could not go across the French-Italian border by regular routes. Within a few days smugglers laid out for him a "Mediterranean cruise": first across France by train to Marseille; then, by ship, south to Corsica, on to Sardinia with a second ship, and with another one to Sicily; then, almost retracing the route, north to Livorno, on the Italian coast. There he was detained for three days until the police had his identity verified and cleared by the authorities in his hometown. Finally, he took the train to Rome and to Frosinone.

Immigration for the undaunted Cervini became a bad habit. In August 1927, "tired of Italy," he decided to return to North America (immigration records show arrival in Halifax on 24 August). Since he had no relatives or friends in Canada, he had to find someone else willing to sponsor him. A *paesano* in the nearby town of Ceprano had a brother-in-law in Canada, a farmer who agreed to have the documents made for him.

Cervini went to Windsor, where he lived and worked as a labourer for eleven years, and in 1938 he moved to Mersea Township, where he worked on a tobacco farm. After the arrival of his family in 1939, they sharecropped Bob LaMarsh's farm (Talbot Road East, east of Erie Street, Leamington), then (1940–42) Frank Colasanti's farm (just northeast of LaMarsh), and for the next two or three years Parnell's farm on Albuna Town Line Road and Highway 18. For awhile Tony also worked in construction. In 1945, as compensation after an accident in which he fractured three ribs, he obtained a monetary settlement that he used as down payment on a house and a farm on Erie Street North (or Highway 77). Southeast of Cervini's new property was Carl Attwell's farm (later Domenic Magri's), where John Cervini, Tony's son, had also worked during this period.

Because he didn't move to the Leamington area until the end of the 1930s, Antonio Cervini, though aware perhaps of the presence of other immigrants from the Lazio region in that area, didn't share the early experiences of either that group or of the Molisani. Yet, because he had arrived in the Windsor area in 1927, he was among the first immigrants from the Lazio region to this area: the others, Alex Colasanti (from Ceprano) and Tony DeSantis (from Arce) had arrived in 1924, while Loreto Colasanti came in 1927. Cervini was most likely the first immigrant from Ripi to this area.

THE FIRST SICILIAN

Vito Peralta, the first Sicilian to settle in Leamington, followed a similar path in those early days of emigration, yet his life in Canada during this period was made more difficult by world events and his domestic situation. Instead of working on a farm, as others had done, he practised his trade in the city. Above all, he was alone in Canada, separated from his wife and children for twenty-two years, and with neither enough money nor the opportunity to return to Sicily to visit them.

Vito's decision to come to North America was reached suddenly. A letter came from his brother or cousin in the Ontario-Michigan border area, and he just decided to leave. He knew absolutely nothing about Canada and left *"all'avventura,"* trusting his luck, as many had done before him.

The route he followed was in part similar to that taken by the first eight men from the Molise area in 1923: from San Vito Lo Capo to Genoa and on to Paris; from Paris again by train to the port of departure. He sailed from Cherbourg on 13 January 1927, landed in Saint John, New Brunswick (Immigration Records, 1925–35), then travelled by train through Montreal to Windsor.

It is not clear whether Vito was fully aware of his destination. The fact that he had relatives in the United States was good reason to go to Detroit, and likely he thought he could persuade the Canadian authorities to allow him to go there. But it is doubtful that Vito was aware of the border that separated Windsor and Detroit. And even if he was, what difference did it make? "America was America": it was all *America* for Italian emigrants, even for those who came later in the 1950s and 1960s. But Vito soon discovered, the hard way, the clear distinction between Windsor, Canada, and Detroit, United States.[24]

Of course there was no one to meet him in Windsor. His brother (or cousin?) came across the border to Canada and convinced Vito to go with him: "What are you going to do here all alone? You don't know a soul; it's better if you come to Detroit." The problem was that Vito had no visa for the United States, nor could he get one. Therefore he had to be smuggled in. But he was caught, placed under the surveillance of the consulate for six months, and sent back to Canada. The next fourteen years were spent in Windsor, where he worked as a shoemaker, the trade he had learned in Sicily.[25]

He did not earn a great deal, but given the times, he was happy to be working even a few days a week. Between 1927 and 1933 he took whatever he could find: for a period he worked for Steve Paris, who owned several shoe-repairing/clothes-cleaning shops in Windsor. Then for most of the following years 1933–40 he operated his own shoe repair shop. An agreement struck with Rivard Cleaners on Wyandotte Street enabled him to set up the machinery and do repairs in an area of the same establishment. Instead of a rental fee, he paid 25 per cent of his profits. He was on his way to becoming a self-employed businessman when he, like many Italian Canadians, was almost destroyed by the repercussions of events in Europe. The resulting internment experience (1940–42; see chapter 6) determined his final settling down in Leamington, where he became the pioneer of one of the three major Italian groups in the area – the Sicilians.

TRULY PIONEERS

The Italian presence and settlement in the lower Great Lakes region have been continuous, if sporadic, throughout the centuries. Italian-Canadian pride and self-identity benefit from a general awareness that among the multiple Canadian historical roots are also included some noteworthy Italian precursors. But none of those early Italians – individuals or groups – constituted a base for an early, permanent, and distinct Italian settlement in the Leamington area before the arrival in the 1920s of the three groups from southern Italy – (Abruzzo-) Molise, Lazio, and Sicily.

Thus, except for their common land of origin and pioneering work, no other links can be established between the founders of the Leamington Italian community and the Italian explorers, adventurers, traders, soldiers, and priests who had paddled with the French voyageurs along the north shore of Lake Erie from Niagara since the mid-1600s.[26]

Nor did a different outcome seem possible in light also of the uncertain links between this area and the small number of Italians present elsewhere in Canada in the earlier centuries.[27]

Similarly, it is not known whether any contacts with this area were made by the Italian merchants, artists, and professional people who settled in Canada in the nineteenth century.[28] Nor is it certain whether the Italian *girovaghi* (itinerant artists and entertainers) in Toronto (late 1880s) reached the Windsor-Detroit area; or whether any exchange took place between the Toronto Italian community, about 4,000 strong by

1902, and southwest Ontario in general or the small Italian group settled in the Windsor area by the turn of the century.[29]

The Italian veterans of the war of 1812 who had been granted lands along the Canadian-American border from Quebec to southern Ontario were quickly absorbed by the dominant society and their names often changed, as had been the case of the two Italians Michel and Jacques Campo (gallicized into Campeau), who in the early 1700s came from Montreal to Detroit, and whose descendant Nicholas Campeau in 1748 had been granted the Huron Mission farm on the west side of the present Huron Church Line Road (Windsor).[30] While both may be considered examples of Italian involvement in Canadian farming, no association can be made between them and the small Italian agricultural community that was taking root in the Leamington area between 1925 and 1945, except perhaps that they were all pioneers. Nor again can any links be made between the first Leamington Italian immigrants and the Italian stonecutters and masons who were working in south Anderdon Township in the later 1800s or early 1900s.[31]

The earliest possible links between this general area of Canada and of the United States and the three main groups of Italians that eventually made the Leamington area their home can be sought only in some stories and events of the first two decades of the twentieth century:

a   The tales about America, and the trips to the United States by relatives, friends, and the men themselves who eventually settled in Leamington, sparked their interest and kept alive their yearning to go or return to America: Angelo Moauro and Domenic Pannunzio, participants in the two 1923 expeditions; Raffaele Ingratta, a member of the October 1923 group from Agnone, Villa Canale; as well as Henry Ingratta (1925), Luigi Mastronardi (1925), and Antonio Cervini (1927, Ripi, Lazio), had all previously been to the United States, in some cases more than once (chapters 2, 4).

b   The presence of relatives or *paesani* in the Great Lakes region of the United States encouraged many to attempt to reach them via Canada, especially after the United States instituted its immigration restrictions: Vito Peralta from San Vito Lo Capo (Sicily) unsuccessfully attempted this route in 1927. The Capussi cousins of the October 1923 group of Molisani hoped to reach Colamario Capussi (Geremia's father and Michele's uncle) in Chicago, but that didn't work out too well: both were deported. Saveria and Michele Magri (1927) had an uncle and some *paesani* in Cleveland, as well as an uncle in Essex County; while Alex Colasanti (1924) had just a vague idea about his brother, Frank, and some *paesani* in this general area of North America. (The post–Second World War immigrants, as the Leone family indicated, continued the pattern, with the usual failures, if not unfortunate results.)

c The earlier presence and/or settlement of Italians, in some cases of *paesani*, in Essex County suggest stronger immigration links between the earlier and later settlers in the Leamington area. But as their stories illustrate, the clear link was more an exception than a rule.

There were no links between those Italians present on Essex County farms before 1924/25 and the pioneers of the Leamington Italian colony. Vic Delzotti, considered by some "the first Italian to work on an area farm," was in the Leamington area in the early 1920s (and probably even before that, but how he got there no one could remember). Vic sponsored his brother Pietro (Pete), and both worked on area farms as farm labourers before any member of the community founding group. Vic went back to Italy (probably Puglia region) while Pete remained in the Leamington area and continued to work as a farm labourer and sharecropper. In 1948 Pete married Isabella A. Catauro, and in October of the same year they bought a farm on Highway 77 north of Leamington (Concession 3, Lot 6; see appendix D). But other than the fact that Pete married Isabella by proxy and sent for her in Agnone – the town and municipality of the first (and many other) Leamington Molisani – there was no connection between the Delzotti brothers and the 1923 group prior to their arrival in this area (and no Delzottis are in the area now). In some cases this link did not seem strong, even among close relatives: the presence of Vito Peralta's brother, Giovanni (John), in Detroit (and perhaps a cousin in Windsor) did not make his situation after his arrival in Windsor in 1927 any less difficult; and prior to his departure, Alex Colasanti had no link with the *paesani* he said he met in Windsor when he arrived in 1924.

The accounts of the pioneers and the early immigrant families to the Leamington area clearly indicate that they met or became acquainted with the other Italians in the area, earlier settlers or not, after their arrival. The Delzottis are hardly mentioned, except for Pete, remembered by Tony DeSantis (1924) as one of the few Italians living in the area in the late 1920s. The Pasquale Sasso family, remembered warmly by Saveria Magri (1927), may have owned a farm in the McGregor–River Canard– Amherstburg area, as Saveria variably calls it, but, without available documentation for either family or farm, it is uncertain whether they were early settlers in the area. Even if they were, they clearly did not constitute a link with the founders of the Leamington community. As for the Meconi brothers, their connections with the first Italian immigrants were purely business, especially through Luigi's all-purpose agency and Clemente's grocery store (Wyandotte Street East), as well as through their Essex County properties: Mariano's farm or vineyard in Gosfield North Township, north of Highway 3, east of Essex Town (or even through his Windsor winery, The Border Cities Wine Cellar Company, on Langlois Street) and Luigi's farm in Gosfield South Township (Fifth Concession). But even if their activities (including grocery deliveries) covered all Essex County, their main base of operation was Windsor.

The few other men or families mentioned in the interviews settled later in the area, or there is scanty or conflicting information about them: Francesco La Rosa (Puglia region) lived with his family in the town of Essex, worked every day with the Magri family when they were sharecroppers on the Mariano Meconi vineyard, but nothing is known about them before 1930; Mike Totaro (from Foggia, Puglia?) may have arrived, like his friend Costanzo Carlone (Saveria Magri's uncle), in 1924, but except for 1948/49, he lived and worked (with the Canadian National Railroad) in Windsor, and played no part in the Leamington area;[32] the DeLellis family (Joe, wife Maria, and five children, Louise, Alfonse or Al, Hazel or Isotta, Mary, and Lina) moved from Colorado, where the children were born, to Detroit before the Depression, and in 1931 moved to Leamington, where they bought a farm on Highway 18 West (known also as Seacliff Drive West or First Concession Road), where the family still lived in early 2000. Joe Matassa (Lazio region) had immigrated to Montreal in 1918, and after some years, because of the climate, moved first to Windsor,[33] and then to Leamington where for several years he worked as a farm labourer (spring and summer) and in the tobacco factories (winter) until he bought his own farm (1941) in First Concession, east Mersea, and grew vegetables. The other Matassa's arrived after the war, when Joe and his brother John (Giulio?), a Detroit doctor, sponsored Attilio (1948), his wife and six children, who in the mid-1990s still lived in both Leamington and Windsor. The Brunatos, Louis Bernachi, and Nick Cicchini went to Leamington in the late 1930s; while Albano Valeri, who lived in Detroit as early as 1912, moved to the Leamington area in the late 1970s, and stayed there only for a few years (see chapter 5).

As for Saveria Magri's uncle, Costanzo Carlone, he was in the Windsor area since 1924, perhaps even earlier. He had already been to the United States (Cleveland and Detroit) illegally, had been deported, and, unable to go back to the States (apparently his American citizenship had expired), entered Canada as a clandestine in 1924; on his way to Alberta he was rerouted to Windsor-Detroit, met Domenic Pannunzio, Tony DiMenna, Raffaele Ingratta, and Mike Totaro (in Montreal), and travelled to Windsor with them. No proof could be found, however, of his owning or living on a farm in the nearby McGregor–River Canard area (closer to Windsor than Leamington); he certainly did not become a part of the Leamington-area Italian pioneer group. According to Saveria Magri's interview, he did sponsor the Magris in 1927, and with the help of his friend John Bondy (probably related, through marriage, to a Molisan family from the same area as Carlone's) found the Sasso farm for them; but until that time he had not sponsored his wife or daughter, and no indication was given about Costanzo's brothers (Francesco and Valerio). Costanzo acted as a link with at least one pioneering family, but they were from a different area of Molise, Saveria, from Campodipietra and her husband, Michele, from San Giovanni in Galdo. Besides, by the time he sponsored his niece in 1927, the other Molisani were already in the area, and the Magris them-selves did not move to Leamington until 1940.[34]

Similarly, the Windsor Italian community, which by the mid-1920s consisted of well over one hundred families, had not established a per-manent base in the rural areas for the development of the rural commu-nity. Some Windsor families (such as the Meconis) did act as links in the settlement on Essex county farms of some of these men who had come to Windsor, often by pure chance. But those families were only interme-diary agents, not settlers of the rural areas.

In sum, the Leamington-area Italian community did not begin as an extension of the Windsor Italian community. It was not the result of the Windsor Italians moving toward the county, even though some of the Leamington community pioneers had lived and worked in the Windsor area for a few years. Windsor was just a stepping stone for some of them. A unique aspect of the Leamington and area Italian community is its spontaneous development: slow and insignificant during the two decades between the wars, then growing rapidly in number and in importance in the three decades following the Second World War (see chapters 7, 8).

5

1925–1945:
L'unione fa la forza (Strength in Unity)

FIRST LINKS OF THE SPONSORSHIP CHAIN

In the period between the two wars, Canadian and Fascist Italy's restrictions on immigration/emigration discouraged but did not prevent Italians from emigrating, even to North America. The Fascist regime, in fact, offered some assistance to the many eager America-bound emigrants, in an attempt to reduce the effects of false advertisements by competing ship-line agents.[1] On the other hand, even the tightly closed doors of the Canadian immigration policy allowed some to slip through: those who could afford bonds, who were sponsored by their relatives in Canada, and who agreed to work on the farm from one to two years.

The relaxation in the policy, however limited, was due partly to a situation not uncommon to most industrialized countries in periods of rapid growth: lack of manpower and/or unwillingness of the local population to perform menial jobs (often for low wages), even in times of high unemployment. Then, like today, many farm labourers had to be brought into Canada to harvest the crops, and especially for the most unpleasant task of "tobacco-picking" (as the immigrants called *suckering* or *priming* tobacco, according to Gino Pannunzio).[2] The first immigrants to this area from the Lazio and (Abruzzo-) Molise regions of Italy also took advantage of this situation in order to have their relatives join them here.

Domenic Pannunzio, Ralph Ingratta, and others of the 1923 Molise group did not wait long after their arrival in Windsor (April 1924) to go to the Meconi Agency to prepare sponsorship papers. They were informed that they were allowed to sponsor "only two persons, and no more than two." This regulation puzzled them: "I don't know," one of the pioneers started to say during an interview, but suddenly he became reticent and continued only after he was assured anonymity, "why they were so strict during those few years ... I don't know, I wish I knew ... I got an idea why, but I don't want to put 'em here ... You know the English people ... they all want to work in a bank, in the office, in immigration, but they don't want to work on a farm, like we work, it's hard ... You come over just as long as you work on the farm and don't take away their jobs in the city."

If they themselves found "work on the farm ... hard," why would these men encourage others to come to Canada, let alone sponsor them? The search for an answer can easily lead to shallow speculation. It was not, however, mere theorizing that led Francesco Coletti to write in 1911 that, in spite of many hardships, emigration brought "more and more tangible benefits." Earlier emigrants made quite apparent that emigration, after all, "spread *benessere* (economic well-being) and raised the morale of the people who went through the trial."[3] Others also pointed out that the myth of America lived on through the 1920s, the 1930s, the 1940s, and beyond: it may no longer have been a *un tarlo che rode, una malattia che s'attacca* (a gnawing termite, a contagious disease); and the "lure of prosperity" was less powerful than it used to be before the First World War when "many naive and destitute peasants left." But people still desired to leave! By the 1920s the Italian emigrants were more aware, more expert in the ways of the world: the Great War had matured them a little; many southern peasants had gone north and learned a few things; they had become surer of themselves, less naïve, and less afraid of the adventure they were about to undertake. "The psychological motivation was different: they left, less out of destitution, and more to seek their fortune."[4]

The same dreams and illusions that had made the first men leave Italy were influencing others; nor had these feelings suddenly disappeared in the pioneers themselves upon arrival, even though the expectations had exceeded reality. The streets of America were not paved in gold (see chapter 9); fortune did not lie around the first corner. But there were other corners ahead. In general, their visions of prosperity were often strengthened by a renewed sense of optimism, even in the face of sacrifices. And they continued to be nourished by those left behind, who firmly held on to their desires to follow in their path. Besides, if there was some little success at the end of the hard journey, it only bolstered the illusions, rather than weaken them: It was proof that they were not, after all, complete self-deceptions. At times it came to be "emigration by imitation." But in general, the psychological motivation behind the entire phenomenon was complex as all the dreams, hopes, and sense of daring required in any quest or enterprise in the human journey: those ideals that lead to action, failures or achievements; all those subtle impulses that move human events or history were as decisive as economic conditions or material needs. Or, as simply put even by a post–Second World War arrival, "We came for change, *per il progresso* [a better chance of progress]!" (see chapter 15, "The 'Migration' Parallels").

It is said, also, that misery loves company. Was it selfishness, satisfaction of a human need that made these early immigrants sponsor their relatives and, therefore, keep their illusion of "America" intact by minimizing the hardships? Was it simply a disavowal of failure for which they would be mocked and humiliated were they to surrender and return to their hometowns? It had already happened to some of them! Was it a question of honour, principle, that made them fall into an irreversible "do-or-die" with no choice other than to "stick it out" at all costs? Was it the challenge, a newly found tenacity, a new frontier spirit, a dogged belief that hard work conquered all? The weighing of all these and other factors may indeed result in a more complete answer to the complex question behind emigration of peoples and similar "revolutions."

The answers offered by the immigrants themselves, if not explicitly stated, did refer to these various factors. But what had a prominent place was their recognition of the potential of this vast, rich, relatively unpopulated new land: Canada undoubtedly offered a clearer vision of possible success, after the initial hard period; life in Canada was much better than in Italy. The work on the Essex County farmlands was just as hard, but at least they yielded good crops and greater monetary rewards than those in their hometowns.

Alex Colasanti's thoughts on the differences between the two ways of life and his consideration of the choices, while echoing those of others, touched upon some aspects of the Italian debate on the "Southern Question," the difference between North and South, and the effects of emigration:

> I had a cousin in Detroit and he used to come down here to see me … once in a while; so he wrote to his mother: "I went to Canada to see my cousin."
>
> "Oh," she answered. "Oh my son, you shouldn't go there; it's bush, it's all bush! You'll die there, bush here, bush there … it's Canada."
>
> That's what they thought! I don't know who put "bush" in their heads, who invented it … and to tell Italy that! … It may be so out West someplace, in the North, but … not here!
>
> When I came here the first year and I see they grow corn, really big, nice, long corn; everything grows good here … but down there

[in southern Italy], boy! you work all summer digging the damn ground ... never rains ... I told my mother ... "Tell my cousin that he doesn't know what he's talking about ... *I'd rather stay here dead than in Italy alive.*"

I explained after that when I look around ... boy! nothing compared to what people say ... It's a nice country, beautiful country, and you got a lot more to eat; the stuff grows a lot, more better than they grow down there, because ... around our town there's poor land ...

North Italy is good ... You don't see too many North Italians come here and work on the farm, because they got good land there ... I have been all over Italy, the North is beautiful, past Rome now it's good living ... near Cassino and Naples down there is poor, much poorer ... Italy was poor ... There you work all winter ... July comes, no rain, and the corn would be like this [as big as a finger] ... Can't make no living ... that's all! ... Our family was big ... nine people ... It's better here ... even if there wasn't much work here, still, better than there ... I took a chance ... There's gotta be something better ... something better than that.

Everybody was coming here ... to stay here ... very few go back ... At that time there was too many people in Italy. Now, hell, they make a good living because the people are all over the world ... If we hadn't gone out all over the world they would have over 150 million people over there. Where are you going to put them ... like sardines?

In the early twentieth-century Italian discussions on the advantages and disadvantages of emigration for Italy, it was often observed that the departure of masses of unemployed reduced the possibility of social unrest in Italy, and the decreasing demand for work improved the condition of the workers who remained in Italy. Above all, money sent by immigrants to their families in Italy helped the precarious economy at the turn of the twentieth century. And of course, as Alex Colasanti stated, it reduced the population. On the other hand, that also meant more land left idle; and the building of the railroads in North and South America, made possible also by the arrival of masses of immigrants, was one cause of the 1880 Italian "agrarian crisis" following the collapse of the price of cereals on the European market because of the cheaper imports from America.[5]

Also, Colasanti's contrast between destitution in Italy and a life of plenty in the Canadian cornucopia was repeatedly emphasized by all early immigrants, and at times innocently exaggerated to a level of absurdity: "The type of life the farmers and workers have here, not even the richest people in Italy have it." The sacrifices, frustrations, harsh climate, squalid conditions, and loneliness, all the negative, discouraging elements vanished in the light of one thought that reverberated throughout their accounts: "Canada was the best place in the whole wide world" (see chapter 12, "Attitudes toward Italy and Canada").

The choice was clear, if not all the reasons for it. Those who stayed immediately began the sponsorship chain, and their number slowly and gradually increased: "One drew the other, and then another" until a close network of relatives and friends was formed. The sponsorship lines often read like the biblical "begats" (Genesis 5:1–31), and are just as repetitious and confusing, particularly for the Leamington Molisan families because of the recurrence of the same surnames of people who often are not related at all (e.g., DiMenna, Mastronardi).[6]

Confusion about sponsorship was often increased by discrepancies, reticence about certain events, or simply bad memory.[7]

However, 1930 was a period of intensive sponsorship. In February, John Ingratta's son Vincenzo (Jim) and Henry Ingratta's son Domenic joined the two men on the farm bought by the three Ingrattas in Rodney (Elgin County). In October, the four Ingratta men were joined on the same farm by John's wife (Chiarina DiMenna) and their other two sons (Louis and Mike). Illness detained Henry's wife ("Merceda" or Mary Mastronardi) and two of their children (Mary and Marius) until December 1930; upon arrival in New York they were held for two or three days at Ellis Island, then arrived in Canada on Christmas Eve, and finally joined Henry and Jim and the other Ingrattas on the Rodney farm.

A group of other Molisani working as sharecroppers in the Leamington-Seacliff area sponsored their relatives at the same time,[8] and the chain extended through the 1930s. Domenic Pannunzio, who was also on the farm in the Seacliff area, sponsored his wife, Fenizia (or Finizia) Ingratta, their son, Gino, and their two daughters, Maria and Fiorina.[9] They arrived in 1931 (23 June, at Bridgeburg, Ontario; see appendix C). Luigi Mastronardi sponsored his wife Paolina (also née Mastronardi but not related), their son Marius and their two daughters, Ida (married to Frank Moauro Sr) and Filomena (Florence). They came in 1933.

In 1936, Costantino Moauro, who at Tony DiMenna's constant urging had moved from Detroit to the Leamington area (most likely before 1934, as some stated, since his certificate of Canadian citizenship is dated 1936), sponsored his wife, Paolina Sabelli, and their son, Frank. They arrived about a month and a half after the arrival (May 1936) of Tony DiMenna's second wife, Antonietta Appugliese, and his son Gino;

and joined them on Mrs Graham's tobacco farm in Harrow, where the two men were then sharecropping. In 1939, Antonio Cervini, who had just a year before moved from Windsor to Leamington, sponsored his wife (Rosa Fratarcangeli) and their three children, John, Loreta, and Sandy (now in Detroit). In 1938, Angelo Moauro, who had just moved back to Canada, visited Italy (Agnone) and returned to Canada with his son Rocco (who died in 1962); while Angelo's wife (Angelina Sabelli) and their daughter Esterina arrived from Italy in 1939. By the end of the decade, almost all the immigrants who had arrived in the 1920s had sponsored their families or some of their relatives.

There were, of course, exceptions. Tragedy prevented Tony DiMenna, one of the first group of eight men, from sponsoring his family before 1936. A few months after he arrived in Canada, in early 1924, his wife Prudenzina died while giving birth to his son Gino (January 1924). Political and financial circumstances not permitting Tony to return to Italy, Gino did not meet his father until ten years later, and the only mother he knew or called by that name was Fiorina Ingratta, a neighbour (who never came to Canada): "She nursed me," said Gino, "and her ultimate generosity saved me." (And the episode, while illustrating some of the more tragic aspects of emigration, was also an example of the *baliatico*, the practice of hiring surrogate nurses, quite widespread and lucrative at the turn of the twentieth century.)[10] Tony went back to Italy in late fall 1933 and returned to Canada alone in spring 1934. In September 1935, he married Antonietta Appugliese by proxy, and shortly afterward he had the sponsorship papers prepared for both his wife Antonietta and his twelve-year-old son Gino. They joined him and Costantino Moauro in May 1936 on Mrs Graham's tobacco farm in Harrow, where Costantino's family also joined them shortly after (at Ridge Road, eastside, Colchester South Township).

Raffaele (Ralph) Ingratta's experience was also different and quite unpleasant. At first a disagreement between him and his cousin Henry resulted in the dissolution of the partnership (1932) formed among the three Ingrattas when they bought the farm in Rodney in 1928, and the withdrawal of both Raffaele and Henry. Then, in the 1930s, since Raffaele's wife (Ernesta DiMenna) refused to move to Canada, he went back to Villa Canale a few times, and on one occasion could not leave because of the war. After several years he returned to Canada, where he died in 1951.

Alex Colasanti did not need to sponsor his wife from Italy. He found her in a unique way: he went to Detroit and found a girl who eloped with him to Canada. His visit to Italy in 1930–31, mainly to see his parents, had offered him a good occasion to look for a wife but he "wasn't ready to get married." At twenty-eight he felt he "was too young." But on his return to the farm and to his "little house" in Harrow, life was not the same; his three-month stay in Italy had again accustomed him to the advantages of family life; and the sharecropping to which he returned made him feel that it was really time to have a woman in his life. His own boss encouraged him: "You got to have a woman to take care of the house, you can't stay here alone." He was convinced, but didn't know how to solve his problem: "Who the hell am I going to find here now ... There's no women around here, no girls ... If you don't speak good English you no find no girl ... so I had to go to Detroit."

On one of his frequent visits to Detroit, and with the help of his friends, he found a wife "in four weeks ... I only saw my wife twice ... three times ... We got married ... end of March, the twenty-nine, 1932 ... I brought my wife on this side, and the first of April I took her to plant tomatoes. She never saw tomatoes in her life ... We had a greenhouse and we planted tomatoes."

She was an American of Italian parents, born in Youngstown, Ohio, and "raised in the city." Her large family was not faring well for lack of work, "even in Detroit." One night, as a result of an argument with her brother who refused to buy her a coat, and angry at her mother who didn't want her to go to Canada with Alex, she just left with him: "We ran away! We made an appointment some place. She went out of the house little by little ... She took some clothes next door to a friend. Then one morning I called up and she went next door to her girlfriend and I picked her up there. I took a couple from Detroit to make the witness to go in court ... and we went right downtown and got married ... in Detroit ... and came across this way ... After, the mother was tough ... 'I'm gonna kill him' ... For months I couldn't go there. She done a lot of work, my wife, the other wife, the first one, a lot of farm work, and she took care of everything."

But after Alex's first wife, Emma Colagiovanni, died (Leamington 1975), and Alex decided to get married for the second time, he too went back to his hometown, Ceprano, and in 1977 married Anita Marinelli, and took her to Leamington with him (to the Colasanti farms in Ruthven, Gosfield South Township).

There was, of course, the very particular situation of Vito Peralta who lived here alone for twenty-two years. He didn't sponsor his wife, their two sons, and three grandchildren until the late 1940s/early 1950s, when Canada again started to open its doors to Italian immigrants.

SAVERIA MAGRI AND THE FIRST WOMEN

Unlike most interbellum groups of Italian immigrants, that eventually became the basis for the Leamington Italian community, the Magris were, if not the first, among the first to come as a complete family. They were most assuredly the first family from the Campobasso area of Molise to settle in the Leamington area during this period. Saveria, her husband Michele (Michael), and their twenty-month-old son, Domenico, arrived in Windsor in early July 1927, after a "frightening," thirteen-day ocean voyage from Bordeaux to Halifax and an exhausting train ride to Windsor beset with fatigue, hunger, foul odour, delays, and frustration. When Saveria's uncle, Costanzo Carlone, their sponsor, was not at the Windsor train station to meet them, they took a taxi and bravely continued their journey to the McGregor-Amherstburg farm, where they lived and worked for about two years, and from where they began their thirteen-year "trek" in an irregular southeast direction through the towns and farms of Essex County toward their final destination – Leamington, in 1940 (see chapter 8).

Saveria Magri, with a great deal of pride, which, in addition to the passage of time, may have coloured her recollection, proclaimed herself *"Io sono stata la prima donna italiana tanto a Amherstburg e tanto qui a Leamington"* (the first Italian woman not only in the Amherstburg area but in Leamington as well). She did subsequently concede that the first woman was Gaetana "Matuccia" DeSantis, Tony DeSantis's wife who arrived in 1926.[11] She nonetheless defended her own claim with a final modification, "but she was in Kingsville."

It is unlikely that Saveria Magri was the first Italian immigrant woman in the Amherstburg (McGregor–River Canard) area or in other southeastern parts of Essex County along the thirty-odd-kilometre Amherstburg-Leamington corridor. However scanty the information available, it seems certain that other Italians had settled there before Saveria's arrival, but there is no clear indication of the presence of Italian women other than those few whom Saveria herself mentioned. Saveria spoke at length about her family's first two years on the Sasso farm in the Amherstburg-McGregor area (Anderdon–Colchester North Townships), owned by Pasquale Sasso, who also became the Magris's *compare* (or, as they called it, *parente*, relative, most likely through godparent-hood); and of a "thirteen-acre farm with vineyards" near the town of Essex where the Magri family spent a most difficult year (1929–30), which belonged to Mariano Meconi.[12] However, it was not possible to establish ownership and the nature of their operations with certainty: whether the owners lived and worked on these farms with their families all year long, or just kept them as investments, offering them to immigrants on a sharecropping basis, or as temporary quarters upon their arrival (as mentioned also by Alex Colasanti, who spent a week on Luigi Meconi's farm in Gosfield South Township in June 1924).[13]

It was while they were sharecropping on the Meconi "vineyard" that the Magris hired farm labourers, among whom was an Italian, Francesco LaRosa, whose daughter was baptized in 1930, in Essex Town, with Saveria acting as baptismal sponsor (thus becoming their *comare*).[14] The LaRosas, whose date of arrival in Canada is not known, continued to live in Essex after the Magris left the Meconi farm. Saveria also mentioned that she worked with two Italian women in the 1940s: Maria Matassa, most likely Joe's wife (who may have been in the Leamington area even before Saveria); and Esterina Moauro, daughter of the same Angelo who had been part of the 1923 group of immigrants from the Agnone–Villa Canale area; but Esterina arrived in 1939, a year after Angelo moved to the Leamington area. There was, of course, Saveria's own uncle, Costanzo Carlone, in this general area since 1924, but he had not sponsored his wife and daughter because of an illness. The two quarry families in the Amherstburg-Anderdon Township area (the Rosatis and DiNunzios remembered by Eugene Whelan) most likely arrived in the 1920s, if their children, in elementary school in the early 1930s, "were little kids" when the parents came from Italy. Saveria's claim may very well be valid, at least in part, and will remain so until it can be put to the test by further research and studies on the Amherstburg and Windsor Italian communities, and in particular on the early migrations and settlement of Italians in the entire area of Essex County (see chapter 4, "Truly Pioneers").

"Matuccia" DeSantis arrived in this area before Saveria. But more important, perhaps, than the chronological primacy or order of arrival of the first Italian immigrant women to this area is Saveria's account itself of the immigration experience seen for the first time through the eyes of a woman, a wife and mother. Because it is her account, she emerges as the main protagonist in her family's frustrating, painful, and costly decision to emigrate and in the entire, "extremely difficult" experience itself. But even if Michael Magri, who unfortunately passed away in 1974, had left his own account, it is doubtful that it would have drastically changed the uniqueness of the experience of the Magri family, or Saveria's role. After all, she remains the only woman throughout this period who did not come after her husband had settled in this area; and it was mostly her strength of will that prevented her family from being split by emigration (even though in 1970 Michael and Saveria did separate; see chapter 10); or, at least, that determined their coming to Canada as a family group.

The Magri-Carlone families were far from destitute. Saveria's own father as well as two of her uncles had been or were in America: by the time she arrived in Canada, her mother's brother (Francesco?) had been living in Cleveland for thirty years, where Costanzo Carlone had also spent some time as a young man before going to Canada (1924). The Magri family, though large, had property distributed among the children. When Saveria married Michele, they were given seven *tomoli* of land and a house. They were also involved in a brick factory, and Michele was a musician in the *carabinieri* band. They were not rich, but they had a good life: "Life in Italy was easier for me ... more comfortable ... We had a beautiful house, property ... vineyards, fruit trees ... We didn't suffer during the war ... We always had something to sell from our lands. My husband's family was well off too ... we lived well in Italy."

But "things changed and we had to get away." They had incurred debts in the acquisition of "barracks" near Campobasso: "When Mussolini gained power, to meet government costs he sold the barracks and the jail ... There was a court case ... *e quello ci ha rovinato noi* ... and that's what ruined us." Saveria and Michele were ready to leave for North America together in 1924 or 1925, with the sponsorship papers arranged by her uncle Costanzo. But Michele changed his mind when Saveria objected to his going alone, especially since they had been married for just a little over a year (25 January 1923).

As a *carabiniere*, Michele was increasingly aware of the Italian situation; and when a Fascist friend, Michele Marino, insisted that he join the Fascist rally where their band was playing, Michele refused to go and play for Mussolini: "If I have to find myself in a pack of trouble with these people, it's better that I get out of the country." But this time it was more difficult to obtain emigration papers, and approval for the family's second application took three years. Again Saveria objected to her husband's plan to go alone or to her going alone (as it was not uncommon for the woman who had relatives in North America to precede her husband and then sponsor him): "It cannot be ... A woman is not left alone. You have to be with me." She was quite determined, especially after losing a child, to go wherever her husband went. She even sold her house in order to raise $500 to send to Canada to be used, with the financial help from the relatives in Cleveland, to "buy a farm," as well as prevent her uncle Costanzo from being deported to Italy (for his 1924 clandestine entry? chapter 4), or to post the bond and allow them to go to Canada as farm labourers.

Thus, Saveria looked forward to her new life, packing quantities of Italian seed along with her optimism. But, however strong and ready, she never could have imagined, the hardships along the way: seasickness afflicted both her and her child, and fear completely overcame her when the old, overcrowded *Roussillon* was forced to dock in Portugal for a day for repairs, before being able to complete her last trip. The family experienced further distress and humiliation on the passage from Halifax to Windsor by "cattle train": the delay for Dominion Day, the wrong transfer to an Alberta-bound coach, the restricted quarters, the three-day journey on "a loaf of bread and a can of sardines" each, given to them in Halifax, "some bread" bought with luck in Toronto, and "a few pieces of old salami and cheese" left over from Italy. Nevertheless, upon arriving at the Windsor station, and not seeing her uncle who was quite convinced "they were no longer coming," after he had gone twice to the station, the determined Magri family got in a taxi and went directly to "their new home."

In those early days immigrant men and women needed perseverance and an indomitable spirit to overcome the physical obstacles, the material hardships, and, above all, the mental stress caused by displacement: the painful irony of the immigrant situation, the trauma of separation an isolation, were given concrete form by Saveria's simple, spontaneous, almost lyrical phrases: "We lived well in Italy ... But when I came here ... *senza mamma ... senza padre ... senza casa* ... no mother ... no father ... no house ... I was all alone."

However one-sided, Saveria's account of her experience is an ample illustration of the role of all the early Italian immigrant women. It is also a challenge to the widespread notion of the Italian woman's secondary role in the Italian family. It may have been a traditional social reality in southern Italy, but in the emigrant Italian family, as Coletti had very early observed, the immigration experience also became a great equalizer.[15] The experience was just as harsh for women who came in their husbands' wake. Many made their journey to the new land alone, often with small children. Almost immediately after their arrival, they began to work in the fields or in the factories while bearing children, raising a family, and taking care of the house. They shared with their husbands one of the most difficult periods in their lives.

By the end of the 1920s, only six women, including "Matuccia" DeSantis and Saveria Magri, had arrived or settled in this area. Four came in 1930: Lisetta Mastronardi, Armando's wife; Adorina (Audrey) Pannunzio, Joe's wife; "Merceda" (Mary), Henry Ingratta's wife; and

Chiarina, John Ingratta's wife. However, only the first two remained in Essex County; the latter two joined their husbands on their farm in Rodney, Elgin County.

By the end of the 1930s the number had doubled. Fenizia Pannunzio joined her husband Domenic in 1931. Emma (Colagiovanni) Colasanti, who married Alex in Detroit and came with him to this area in 1932, was an immigrant from a large city and quite unaccustomed to farm work. Paolina Mastronardi joined her husband Luigi in 1933, while Antonietta (Appugliese) DiMenna, Tony's wife, and Paolina (Sabelli) Moauro, Costantino's wife, came in 1936. Angelina (Sabelli) Moauro, Paolina's sister, and sister-in-law of Angelo Moauro's wife, arrived in 1939 along with their daughter Esterina. Last, also in 1939, after the long separation and a long journey from Ripi through Naples, New York, and Buffalo, Rosa (Fratarcangeli) Cervini, Antonio's wife, and their daughter and two sons arrived in Leamington. They were the last Italian group to reach the Leamington area from Italy until after the Second World War. Whether they came in the 1920s or the 1930s, with their husbands or alone, the dozen or more Italian immigrant women were a courageous, untiring lot who willingly accepted the challenge of immigration and often took the lead in the struggle for survival during those two very difficult decades. The immigration experience made the woman increasingly the centre and often the real ruler within the Italian family (see chapter 10, "The 'Special' Role of the Woman").

Unlike the men, who had more occasions to meet other Italian men in the workplace, the women's chances to socialize with other Italian-speaking women were few, unless they worked in the factories or in the fields. That rare moment in around 1930 that brought together the first two Italian immigrant women to the area – "Matuccia" DeSantis and Saveria Magri – was a revelation and a celebration: "There was a party in Kingsville, and I was speaking Italian with my husband ... that's all I could speak ... Matuccia turned to me, '*Eh, tu sei Italiana?* (Eh, are you Italian?') 'Oh yes, I'm Italian ... !' We talked ... we got to know each other ... we agreed to exchange visits."

STRENGTH IN UNITY

By the late 1920s, very few Italian immigrants working on the farms of Essex County (many of them most likely former "clients" of the Meconi Agency) knew one another or were bound to meet and strike up a friendship. Upon their arrival in 1927, the Magris had also met some of the men who had arrived in 1924 and in 1925; among the first were Alex Colasanti, Armando Mastronardi, and Henry Ingratta, "who," according to Saveria, "had a farm in Harrow."[16]

Likely the Magris also met Joe Pannunzio and Luigi Mastronardi, who, along with Armando and Henry, had also been placed on the Jack Noble farm where Alex Colasanti was already working as a sharecropper. Of course the five men became friends. Then, in 1927, Alex and Armando pooled their resources (seventy-five dollars) and bought their first car together. More than an indication of their increasing prosperity, it was a concrete sign of the cooperation and closeness that quickly developed among the immigrants from different regions of Italy – Lazio and (Abruzzo-) Molise.

By the end of the 1920s, most of the Italian immigrants who had arrived during that decade seemed to be well acquainted. Some moved closer to the Leamington or Mersea Township area (as the Magris, by 1930 in the Cottam-Kingsville area, on Sixth Concession at Division Road, see chapter 8). Others who had remained in Windsor or had gone to Detroit to work came to the area for the first time and joined their relatives or friends, as Domenic Pannunzio and Tony DiMenna did. They all regrouped on farms and lived together. Domenic and Joe Pannunzio, Armando and Luigi Mastronardi, as well as Tony DiMenna lived on Joe Henry's farms – first (1929) near Blytheswood (Eighth Concession), then (1929–34) at Seacliff Drive West, where most of them were joined by their wives and children. Those who arrived subsequently, whether sponsored relatives and friends or unrelated immigrants (e.g., Vito Peralta), were readily made to feel part of the small but growing Italian settlement. They were even encouraging others who had left the area to come back.

Many who had arrived during the 1920s did not settle in the Leamington area immediately; some left and returned, others never came back. Of the 1923 Molise group of eight, six left Windsor and Essex County, two of them shortly after their arrival and permanently: the Capussi cousins, Geremia and Michele, went to Chicago, were deported, and never returned; after working in Windsor till the end of 1924, the Moauro brothers, Costantino and Angelo, went to the United States and did not return until the 1930s; and the Ingratta brothers, John and Raffaele ("Ralph") – as well as their cousin, Henry (1925) – who in the deed of land of 29 February 1928 are recorded as "Labourers ... all of the City of Windsor in the County of Essex," by early that year were on their jointly bought farm in Rodney or, as the deed states, "in the Township of Aldborough, in the County of Elgin."

All four men who arrived in 1925 – the second group of immigrants from Villa Canale – first worked together on the Kingsville area farm of Bob Conklin (their co-sponsor), and then to Harrow, on the Jack Noble farm (except for about one year, 1926–27, when Joe Pannunzio was on a farm in Rodney, Elgin County; while Henry Ingratta was across the road from Conklin's, on the McCraken farm). They were the first from (Abruzzo-) Molise to work on the Essex County farms, but a year after Alex Colasanti (Lazio, 1924). But while Armando Mastronardi, Luigi Mastronardi, and Joe Pannunzio went on to Blytheswood in 1928, Enrico (Henry) Ingratta moved with his two cousins to Elgin County, and from there he went back to the Leamington area with his family in 1933. Of the five men who arrived in 1927, two of them – Antonio Cervini (Ripi, Lazio) and Vito Peralta (San Vito Lo Capo, Sicily) – did not become part of the Leamington-area Italian community until 1938 and 1943 respectively. Henry Ingratta's wife and children and Giovanni Ingratta's wife and children, who arrived in 1930, went directly to their farm in Elgin County.

Therefore, of the twenty-three adults who arrived from Italy in the 1920s – eighteen men and five women (excluding the ten children ranging in age from a few months to sixteen years) – only thirteen – nine men and four women – lived in the Leamington-Kingsville-Harrow area by the end of that decade: Tony DiMenna (1923); the Pannunzio brothers, Domenic (1923), Joe (1925) and his wife Adorina (1930); the Colasanti brothers, Alex (1924) and Loreto (1927); Armando Mastronardi (1925) and his wife Lisetta (1930); Luigi Mastronardi (1925); the DeSantis family, Tony (1924) and his wife Matuccia (1926); and the Magri family, Michael and Saveria (1927). According to Tony DeSantis, "twenty-three or twenty-four Italians" lived in the Leamington area a few years after he arrived (about 1930). If the DeSantis, Magri, and Mastronardi children (particularly Luigi Mastronardi's eldest son, fifteen-year-old Alfredo, 1930), as well as the Delzotti brothers, particularly Peter (Pietro) mentioned by DeSantis, and Frank Colasanti, who arrived in 1930 from the United States, were included in the total count, his estimation would seem to be close to the exact number (see appendix B, especially 1 to 18).

"Up until the war years," stated Marius Ingratta (Henry's son), "the only families that were here [in Leamington] were the two Moauros, Angelo and Gus [Costantino]; the two Pannunzio families [Domenic and Joe]; the Mastronardi families [Armando and Luigi]; one Ingratta family [Henry] and one DiMenna [Tony]." When Vito Peralta went to Leamington in 1943 to work in (John and Ines) Brunato's shoe repair shop, he noticed "nine Italian families in all." Since Vito lived in the centre of town, he may not have considered in his total some of the families living in the surrounding area. In reality, by then (since Loreto and Frank Colasanti had moved to the United States, and excluding the Brunatos, from Guelph, and the DeLellis family, from the United States), the Italian families were exactly one dozen. In addition to those mentioned by Marius Ingratta, there were four other families: the Colasanti, DeSantis, Magri, and Cervini families. Naturally, each family had several children.

The common conditions and goals in those early years, as well as the common origins, generated a tendency to help and to support one another. It was easier to survive and to succeed by banding together. Some of the families lived and even moved together in the 1930s: Tony DiMenna, Domenic and Joe Pannunzio, Armando Mastronardi and Luigi Mastronardi continued to live and work as sharecroppers on Joe Henry's farms (1928/29–34), even after the wives and children of the latter four arrived (at Seacliff Drive West). In 1934 they were also joined by Gus (Costantino) Moauro, and in 1938 by his brother Angelo. Tony DiMenna, after a year (1935) with Armando Mastronardi at Bill Setterington's farm, sharecropped in partnership with Gus Moauro on the Graham farm in Harrow with a one-year contract (1936). After a hailstorm destroyed their tobacco crops, Tony and Gus and their families, who had recently joined them, worked together as sharecroppers for one year (1937) on the Bill Setterington farm, west side of Erie Street South in Leamington (Concession 1, Lot 6). Between 1934/35 and 1940, according to Marius Ingratta, "Armando and Henry practically lived together and worked together many, many times." The acquisition in 1934 of the first greenhouse plant by the Italian immigrants was the result of a partnership among three families: Domenic and Joe Pannunzio and Luigi Mastronardi (see chapter 8). It was quite natural in such circumstances to apply the wisdom of the ages inherent in the proverb: *l'unione fa la forza* (strength in unity).

This unwritten reciprocity policy established in hard times was seldom abandoned. It became a mainstay of the community, in its numerical and economic growth, especially after the Second World War (chapters 7, 8). The eight families listed earlier by Marius Ingratta "were all growing tobacco through the 1930s on shares with local farmers ... on most of the farms you see here today." During that same decade they initiated a "process," as Marius outlined, that transformed themselves and eventually the area's agricultural and economic scene. "The Italians were to a great degree responsible" for the "creation of the greenhouse industry" and the "parallel development of the related marketing and distribution industry" (see also chapters 6, 9). Thus, Marius concluded,

The Italians moved in and bought these farms ... most of them worked on at one time before the war and even after ... There was a process over a period of years where, as others moved into this community from Italy, they worked with their relatives for a year or two and then moved to better jobs and contracted ... A lot of them moved back to the farm by way of buying their own ... and this, over the last twenty-five years, has been the gradual process of the greenhouse industry ... When these people moved into these farms, most of them didn't have any greenhouses, but were able, with their families, over a period of time, to develop a greenhouse industry, which today is basically much of this area, still owned and operated by the same people who started twenty-five, thirty years ago.

The "good neighbour" policy was not limited to just a circle of relatives and friends. It extended to all the *paesani*, regardless of region of origin. When Vito Peralta, the first Sicilian and the last Italian until after the Second World War to settle in Leamington, arrived there all alone in 1943, following his unfortunate internment period, he recalled being treated "like one of their own ... I was all alone, I didn't know anyone. First I met Costantino Moauro ... then Armando Mastronardi ... Cervini ... Tony DiMenna ... Joe Pannunzio ... I found friends in all of them ... one day I would visit one ... the next day another one ... They always respected me like a relative."

However, the Italian immigrant families were not building a protective fortress around themselves. The mutual assistance pattern, common to all immigrant communities, especially small ones, strengthened them but did not totally isolate them from their non-Italian neighbours. Their growing security, as well as needs, made them more open toward the larger community, in spite of perduring prejudices on all sides.

THE HARDSHIPS

The first years after immigration and the Depression that followed, perhaps more than the Second World War years stand out as the harshest that most early Italian immigrants to the rural areas of Essex County remember, at least from a material standpoint. The recurring theme among men, women, and children was the anguish, common to all déracinés, caused by the separation from all known places and faces, by their being torn from their native soil and catapulted into an alien world.

Nevertheless, these were not obstacles that resourcefulness, pulling together as a family or group, and hard work could not overcome; and for the pioneers in those earlier days, work, above all else, became not just a means to achieve material advancement, but also a way to forget their anguish. Work allowed them to escape that initial daily "state of suspension and scission": that "sentiment-torment" that firmly lodges in the emigrant heart; that "nostalgia, homesickness, painful longing for the native land and hearth." And in "America," as they discovered, *"quando uno non trova lavoro sono guai ... qui chi non lavora muore di fame"* (when you can't find work, you have real problems ... here if you don't work, you starve).[17] Physical work ransomed them, united them, and eventually brought them closer, physically and socially.

During the Depression, even very hard work became scarce. The immigrants were the first to lose their factory or construction jobs. In 1929, Tony DiMenna, unable to find another job in Detroit or Windsor, joined his *paesani* on Joe Henry's farm, at first temporarily, and in 1930 permanently (when the October 1929 Stock Market Crash created increasing unemployment). "Jobs were not there for us," said Saveria Magri, whose husband was allowed to work only three days at the Ambassador Bridge (completed in 1929).

During the Great Depression men were either out of work or worked very hard for very little; women had to scrape and improvise in order to feed the family, and worked just as hard if they could find a job; and children shared house and field chores, and walked several miles to school, which in the rural areas was usually "one large room" for all the eight grades, and (as Eugene Whelan himself who grew up in rural Essex County remembered) with no hydro, no inside plumbing, no central heating, only outhouses.[18]

Italian immigrants often applied *l'arte dell'arrangiarsi* (the art of making do with what one has, or manage as best one can), as did Saveria Magri, who became an entrepreneur: she made embroidered pillowcases and slipcovers and sold them door-to-door. Instead of money, she was given "flour and butter," which she gladly accepted: *"Non si poteva campare"* (We could barely survive). And to survive, she made use of all resources available: "I cooked tons of dandelion ... I kept a goat until it was very old, and with that goat I raised all my children ... they came one after the other ... I raised a family with goat's milk ... it's the best ... with the leftover, I made cheese and ricotta [Italian cottage cheese] ... I have always been a woman ready to make the best of any situation."

And she made sure that nothing was wasted: "There was no meat ... there wasn't even money to buy bread ... A wolf-dog killed some sheep ... we cut around the part that was bad ... took the good part and we put it in a barrel and we put salt to cure it ... The first time it was three sheep, the second time two of them, and we did the same thing ... we preserved all of it ... that was our fridge."

"When there was nothing else to eat," added Saveria's daughter, Ida, "we used to put lard on our bread and sprinkle sugar on it."

"Those were rough years," stressed Ida's brother, Domenic. Ingenuity had to be combined with very hard work, and most immigrants like the Magris never shied from any job: in the fields or in the factories, or even at a brickyard on Division Road, where Michael Magri might have been able to work had it not gone bankrupt. They also worked at different places at different times of the year; sporadically, in Michael Magri's case, with Gosfield South Township, as remembered by his son Domenic:

> I recall going ... to get my dad's cheque in Kingsville ... He worked for $1.60 a day for about eight years ... In the winter ... he didn't work all the time ... He worked in a tobacco factory in Kingsville called Hodges Tobacco, and I was there with him as a youngster at the age of fourteen trying to get a job ... There were as many as 300 men standing outside the gate looking for employment ... and occasionally they would pull one or two in on a given morning and they'd tell the rest to go home ... so things were tough ... in the 1930s.

Even Saveria, though burdened with family responsibilities, especially with five children, continued to work or look for a job in Kingsville or Leamington: "I took the streetcar [most likely the Windsor, Essex, and Lake Shore Electric Railway in service from 1908 to 1935/36] in front of my house on Division Road to come to Kingsville ... from Kingsville to come here to Leamington ... to look for a job ... and I got my job," probably at the Imperial Leaf Tobacco Company of Canada Limited, Oak Street East.

In the factory or on the farm, the pressure was often intolerable. The piecework system and related pittance (i.e., two to three dollars per acre of tobacco "primed"[19]) generated a race against time, stiff competition among the workers, especially among those of different nationalities, with results varying from fisticuffs and hair pulling to insults and much resentment. Saveria found herself in such a situation on a tobacco farm: "You goddamn woman," cursed one of the Polish or German workers, "you want to beat me." Naturally, Saveria counteracted the abuse by humiliating the men: "They couldn't keep up with me, I finished my acre before them ... even with a horse they couldn't keep up with me." What distressed her most, however, was the owner's attempt to cheat her out of her pay. "They took advantage of us for we couldn't speak ... For a week I walked five miles a day to collect my pay." This was the straw that broke the camel's back. The work and the stress took their toll, and her "nerves went sky high."

It was also a most difficult time for immigrant children who, like many other children, had to work as hard as their parents, around the house after school, and on other jobs when no longer of school age. "I remember," said Domenic Magri, "the potbelly stove in that school on No. 3 Highway before you get to Cottam [approximately four miles east] ... that same building [later moved to and still] situated in Oldcastle where the [Michigan Central Railway/Conrail] tracks cross Highway 3." Domenic remembered much more:

> When I came home from school I had to carry water, light the stove, go for milk half a mile or three-quarters of a mile ... I recall in the fall riding my bicycle from school to Jack Miner's to husk corn for three cents a bushel ... If I made twenty–five cents after school, often riding ten miles, I earned something ... I was thirteen or even twelve years old.
>
> There was hardship during the Depression years, and I think it sort of left a bit of a scar on me to some extent ... If there would be a disaster – hopefully we'll never get one – I think I could adjust easier than some people ... When you're without hydro, without water and inside plumbing ... if you're not used to it, if you've never lived through it, it would be very difficult to get used to it.
>
> I think people make a lot of fuss when we get a storm and they're without hydro or something like that ... But in those days it was a way of life and we never thought nothing of it ... It's much nicer today, but under those conditions, we managed ... If you don't have it and you can't afford to buy it, you do the next best thing.

"The next best thing" to toilet paper was an "Eaton's or Sears catalogue," or any other old paper. Even owning an automobile, as some immigrants discovered, seemed more of a nuisance than a comfort. It could be used only in the summer since there was no antifreeze, and it was dangerous: "broken wrists and sprained shoulders" were not uncommon if the crank had to be used to start it (perhaps indicating that the immigrants were buying older models or Model Ts with a crank, since the self-starter, first adopted in 1912, by 1920 "was standard equipment on virtually all cars").[20]

The common and basic human problems of survival – food and shelter – were all-consuming worries for the early immigrants. Equal only to finding a job, any job, was the concern to secure adequate accommodations and proper protection against the Canadian climate. In the rural areas especially, it was a constant struggle.

For the pioneers of the 1920s, shelter, or lack of it, proved to be the first inhuman Canadian experience. Some had no more than a shakedown to sleep on, and quite often on the floor of unheated tents and barns in the dead of winter; others lived for months in unhealthy, cold, damp garages and basements. The shack-like houses of the 1930s were just a little improvement – very cold in the winter and very hot in the summer, lacking all facilities: "no bathroom, no water, no hydro ... not much of a change from conditions in Italy," recalled one of them who went to Leamington in 1939. In the 1940s, 1950s, and even 1960s, whether sponsored or not (as the Leone family indicated), immigrants had to accept whatever inadequate accommodations a relative, friend, contact, or farmer offered, or whatever they themselves could find in the rural areas, if they were not placed in the House of the Immigrants (chapter 7).

But in the 1920s and the 1930s, years before they were turned into enemy aliens, the Italian immigrants had to bear a hardship that neither hard work nor ingenuity could counteract: hostility and discrimination from other Canadians (see chapter 9 and chapter 13, especially "Group Interaction and Intercultural Prejudice"). Ray A. Young (b. Wheatley 1899), GM products salesman and dealer from 1916 to 1981 (for thirty-nine years with his own dealership at 11 Mill Street East and a used car lot at 148 Talbot Road East in Leamington), offered more than just dates for the cars sold to the first Italians (a "convertible GM" in 1929 to Joe Pannunzio, Tony DiMenna, Louis Mastronardi, and Armando Mastronardi, who was "the only one who could drive ... to have a licence"; and then one to Domenic Pannunzio). He also related the warnings he received more than once about "doing business with Italians: People in town were scared of the Italians ... Al Capone was wild in Chicago ... and people here heard bad [things] about Italians, due to the newspaper top stories on criminals such as Al Capone. An old lady called the Italians '*desperados*'" and was angry with Ray for selling them cars and befriending the Leamington Italians. Once, on coming home and seeing her husband "lying on the floor" (drunk), the lady "immediately called the police saying that he had been knifed by some Italians." But Ray Young, unaffected by the events or the stereotypes of the time, "was never scared of Italians," even "when he didn't know the men." He understood their predicament: "When they arrived, they naturally stayed together; they were new in town; they minded their own business, so the others were curious and suspicious of them."

The Prohibition-related activities, the illicit sale and smuggling of liquor in the 1920s and early 1930s in Windsor and Essex County, had also negative effects on some Leamington Italian immigrants. Moreover, the gang wars and related crimes to control the very lucrative business, not only in Al Capone's Chicago but in nearby Detroit, made life difficult for many Italians then living along the shores of the Detroit River and Lake Erie, the very centre of contraband operations by the "rum-runners." According to Windsor and Detroit historians, as much as 85 per cent of all liquor sent to the United States from Canada was smuggled across the Detroit River. The traffic was so heavy that this route, especially after the completion of the Ambassador Bridge, 1929, and the Windsor-Detroit Tunnel, 1930, came to be known as "The Windsor-Detroit Funnel." At times the business amounted to 500,000 cases a month, and "the value of the liquor carried across the Windsor-Detroit border in the 1920s" was estimated at "hundreds of millions of dollars."

The illicit liquor traffic involved others in addition to local operators. Detroit's most vicious Purple Gang as well as Chicago's two rival gangs, Bugs Moran's and Al Capone's, also moved in. Both gangsters visited Windsor and vicinity several times: Capone himself was once in Belle River (a few kilometres east of Windsor on Lake St Clair) to strike a deal with Blaise Diesbourg (known as "King Canada" of bootlegging); more than once at the Windsor export docks to meet those in charge (Dave Caplan and Lou Harris); and at least once in Amherstburg to inspect the export docks, warehouses, and clearing houses that covered the waterfront along the river and lakes, including townships of Essex County where the Leamington Italian pioneers were settling in the late 1920s.

Canadians of many origins and nationalities were involved in the illicit business, condoned by the majority and hardly opposed by the often helpless police force. (Carl Farrow himself, provincial constable in Amherstburg from 1928 to 1934, met Al Capone during one of the latter's visits in the area.) Various Italians, beside Capone, also took part in the smuggling operations (from Hamilton's Rocco Perri, who resented being labelled "criminal" because of a "law which the people [did] not want," to the Detroit mobsters Sam Cantilonotti, Gaspare Scabilia, and the Pete and Yonnie Licavoli Squad, the equally vicious rivals of the Purple Gang, which had links with Capone, with the Little Jewish Navy gang and with Canadian operators in Sandwich, Windsor, and Belle River). Not their number, but the nature of some of their activities brought notoriety to Italians: above all, Al Capone! "Capone developed most of the rum-running activities in the United States," and syndicates, such as that "led by Al Capone, moved in and the smuggling of beer and whiskey from the Windsor area became a well-organized big business." Capone is said "to have accumulated up to $100 million per year from contraband beer sales alone." And the countless killings, he is also said to have engineered, as well as the 1929 St Valentine's Day Massacre in Chicago, could only increase people's fear and suspicions of Italian immigrants to this area.[21]

After their two-year stay in McGregor on the Sasso farm in the nearby River Canard area, the Magri family accepted Mariano Meconi's offer to work on a sharecropping basis on his Essex farm. The experience became very unpleasant, not only for the poor living conditions ("we slept in a cold garage") and the disadvantageous agreement ("we got no money for the fertilizer … and farm help"), but also for the aggravations caused by the "beer and whiskey smuggling activities" by some of the people they met on these farms. They thus looked forward to freeing themselves from that situation as much as from their "two-year farm-work stint," and to moving on. But they too found themselves in the grip of the October 1929 Great Depression, as was described also by Saveria Magri: "Then came the Depression here also … Where could we go … no car … no warm clothes … not able to speak … We couldn't do any-thing … I had to work outside on the tobacco farms … at the Cottam Canning factory … do backbreaking work picking sugar beets."

The suffering caused by their leaving their homes to settle in a new land was the result of their own decision, and they bore the consequences with stoicism and great hope. The Depression struck everyone more or less equally, though for them it may have been a little harder because of the initial language barrier, restricted circle of friends, and little or no familiar-ity with the system or social structures. But the unusual hard times were met as if they were part of the initiation, another blow in the immigration and settlement process, which the resilient newcomers were prepared to absorb. The Depression may have slowed their quest for a better life, but it never decreased their determination. In fact, both the immigration expe-rience and the Depression may have better prepared and tempered their will for the adverse times during the Second World War.

PRIDE AND SURVIVAL: "WE ARE NOT MAFIOSI!"

They were able to adjust, therefore they managed to survive. In need, they applied hard work and their wits, trying always to avoid the ever-present temptation to borrow, beg or steal. Their basic sense of propriety and their pride, above all, would never have allowed it, and they resented those who did it! It was as if it were a challenge not just to them but to all Italians. They had to prove that, as newcomers, as Italians, they were just as good as, if not better than, all the others, who, regardless of their ethnic origin, in their eyes, were *Inglesi*, all *English*. The contrasts and comparisons were often based on racial or national characteristics, as Saveria Magri readily pointed out:

> We Italians are accustomed differently. We are used to a hard life ... This other family ... a neighbour ... who maybe are English, they are people more *rabusciata* [run down]. They suffered, they starved ... They came to my house: 'Give me some flour, I'll give it back to you.' How could they? They never had anything! They always borrowed, never gave back: the tub to wash clothes, soap, preserves, cheese ... everything. When I wasn't home, they went in my house and took everything ... and the filth in their house! We lived in a shack and they lived in a better house, but it was dirtier than mine ... What are you going to do?"

Nevertheless, they became the "best of friends," the newcomers and the *Inglesi*, who soon began to admire the way Saveria raised her family. They soon realized "what we – " Saveria stopped to go back to the time she worked in the fields faster than anyone else:

> Now they are behind and we went ahead, like the horse, no? Before we were donkeys, now we have become horses ... and the horses have become donkeys ... Who straightened out Leamington? ... All the Italians have done something here ... That's why they like us ... Of all the nations, who made the most progress are the Germans and the Italians ... the Germans for Alberta ... and we can be proud ... We Italians have a good name ... They say we are Mafia ... We are not Mafia ... Whatever we do is Mafia ... but look here, now, this is a name that was stuck to us ... but they know what they are saying ... They also know what we are doing.

Saveria, like DiMenna during the war, proudly defended the progress and the name of all Italians, not just her own, with words often heard throughout the Italian communities in Canada: "*Mica siamo tutti mafiosi qua* [We are not all Mafiosi here]." Having said that, the conclusion was always the same: "But Canada is the most beautiful country of all the many other places." Such conclusions were not reached without reason or reflection, and they were often reached soon after their arrival in Canada, as both Alex Colasanti and Saveria Magri indicated: in Saveria's case, after the first five difficult months in McGregor, during the visit of some *paesani* from Cleveland.

The occasion was again a disagreement over Saveria's place in her husband's plans and the future of the Magri family: "If things are so tough," the friends noted, as reported by Saveria, "the best advice, Mike, would be to send your wife back to Italy ... You can come with us to Cleveland ... and find a good job ... as a musician."

"We had a fight ... 'How can you ask that?' [she told her husband] 'You came here for me, now you want me to go back ... you go if you want ... I'm staying right here ... and if you go to Cleveland I'll come too because I have my mother's brother there.' I didn't want to go back," continued Saveria, "I saw what Canada was ... A friend before coming here told me about Canada, its vegetation, its people; he told me I'd be happy here ... I never forgot those words ... He wanted me to go back to Italy! 'You can go back, not me!'" she insisted. In spite of the difficulties, Saveria had made up her mind then and there about Canada, about her choice in life, "not that I want to go against Italy ... but Canada is better ... It's much better here than there, in those mountains." And her conclusion, more balanced than Alex Colasanti's rash rejection of Italy ("I'd rather stay here dead than in Italy alive"), was also an early indication of the typical immigrants' double pride, the tendency to defend both Canada and Italy or even their readiness, when necessary, to criticize both (chapters 12, 13).

Besides, in spite of some hostility, good relations and friendships between the small Leamington group of Italians and other Canadians, *gli Inglesi*, were also developing, as evidenced not only by Saveria and her neighbour, but also by other examples. Ray Young, the Leamington car dealer, knew well what the "Italians were doing": they were becoming "good customers ... There was no credit in those days, they paid cash." But it wasn't just for that reason that they became "great friends of his," nor simply because he "was never beaten by them in his whole life." As far as he was concerned, right from the beginning, "five nicer or finer men have never come to this district," and he defended them "even before he knew them," and then admired them for their generosity, kindness, and industriousness.[22]

The partnerships, or the sharecropping agreements between the Italian newcomers and the Canadian landowners, could not have been built on just need and profit. The sharecropping "contracts" were normally written (and signed by both parties), but very rarely in the form of documents drawn up by lawyers; and such was the practice even at the beginning, shortly after the first men from Lazio and Molise (1924/25) had started working as day labourers on the Essex farms. The very first agreement was made, probably, as early as 1926 with Bob Conklin, and certainly in 1927 with Jack Noble. Such accords, especially in the early years, required trust and understanding. In general, even though rapport between the two Canadian ethnocultural groups later underwent strain as a result of international events (chapter 6), and in spite of fears and suspicions caused by the press about Capone and the Chicago Italians, or about the Mafia and Cosa Nostra, the examples cited were indications of the very early bonding that occurred not only among Italians themselves but also among new and native Canadians in the Leamington area.

6

The War Years: "Good Canadians" and "Bad Italians" or Vice Versa?

SUSPICION AND SURVEILLANCE IN LEAMINGTON

Resentment was strong during and following the war ... There was a period when we had to report when we left the town of Leamington. We couldn't go out of town without the authorities knowing where we were going. Precautionary measures used during the peak of the war ... made us feel a little uneasy. You felt as if someone was watching you all the time. Some Italians here were put in concentration camps for a while ... Funny feeling to be under observation ... You don't feel as free as you should when you know that ... What could you do to harm the country? ... What could you do really ... especially when you're so far away from the action? ... I think what started to break the ice was ... the mayor of Leamington ... wrote to some office in Ottawa and told them that "these Italian people did not need such surveillance" ... There was only a handful of us, and he felt we were good citizens, and I know we were good citizens.[1]

For the Italian immigrants, the feeling of being prisoners in their own home, aliens in the "new motherland," was more unbearable than the first years in Canada, perhaps even harsher than the "tough" Depression period or starving thirties: it was not so much the privations, the "rationing of butter, coffee, sugar, gas, rubber tires ... and everything needed for the war effort ... the many things you couldn't buy," remembered Domenic Magri. Barely fourteen and out of grade eight, Domenic was working in a burley tobacco field near Olinda (Gosfield North) "when the war broke out in September 1939, and Mr Upcott [the owner] told us of the news." What disrupted their lives was, above all, the sudden change in their status from "good citizens" to "enemy aliens."

The tragic period following that fateful 10 June 1940 is enclosed in Magri's first and last words in the opening quotation: "resentment" and "good citizens." Other key words and phrases trace the dramatic events in those "tight few years": the reporting to the police, the confinement, the denial of civil liberties and fear of internment ("concentration camps"); the general bewilderment, questioning and reaction against police "surveillance" and the suspicion of treason; the slow "breaking of the ice," the protest of some politicians, the easing of tension and the feeling that the "Italian people" deserved to regain their freedom as good Canadians. The words describe a common situation throughout the country, including Windsor.

Even though the Leamington-Italian experience had its differences, almost all who lived it stated emphatically "how rough things were for the Italians ... when Italy went against the United States, Canada and England"; that's how Saveria Magri saw it, explaining that "we belonged to England then ... They believed we were involved in acts of sabotage ... They put a watchman in the tobacco factory fearing 'some revolution from us.' Maybe there were bad people around ... but we were good." Their "resentment" was caused largely by what they considered unjustified widespread surveillance, suspicion, and investigations to which they were all subjected: "I was sixteen years old when the war started," said Gino DiMenna, who associated the beginning of the war with the period when "discrimination started ... Although we were Canadian citizens, in Ottawa they felt they couldn't trust anybody and because we were of Italian descent and Italian-born ... They figured they better keep an eye on us. We had to report every month, then every six months, then once a year, and then they never bothered us any more ... But they still looked at us as an enemy, as Italians ... 'Your country declared war' ... The [Italians] were enemies, so they looked at us in the same way ... It was stupid, but that's the way they felt."

It was a "stupid" situation: the immigrants were again innocent victims of international politics. As Italians, they were enemies by association, by birth, or by descent; and many (including in Windsor, but apparently not in Leamington) "anglicized their names and denied their ethnic background ... Lobianco became Mr White."[2] Others, especially in rural areas such as Leamington, had practically cut all ties with their land of origin or were afraid to proclaim themselves proud Italians; and yet they were no longer accepted as citizens of Canada, their adopted land. They were made to feel as social outcasts, especially the young men: even as they were called for duty, they were suspected of not being true Canadians. They were all prevented from just being what they were – proud Canadians.

What permeated the accounts of the Leamington Italians was a feeling of being Italians and Canadians, but neither one nor the other: suspended in no man's land, belonging to two countries or none, having two identities or none according to the moment. They felt squeezed between the jaws of the two identities: as Italians they were registered and fingerprinted like criminals, as Canadians they were still bound to serve their country.

At first, the Italians helplessly bore the situation with hope that it would soon pass. In the meantime, it was bewildering them, and frightening their children, who could hardly understand why they also were being picked up by the police: "We were just kids," recalled Frank Moauro Sr, "we were in school. The policeman came, called our names ... and we had to go with him: 'What did we do wrong?' we would say. We knew nothing about the war." The initial uneasy feeling, the uncertainty and disorientation that threw their loyalties and patriotism into disarray (but, as Saveria Magri said, "never discouraged" them) turned into anger and protest. The restrictions and contradictions could not foster a favourable attitude toward Canada, toward military service, and much less toward the war, even if it was to defend democracy against Fascism and Nazism. Some were convinced, by the way the Italians were treated, that it was not their fight. Consequently, they tried every means to avoid military duty; and if that was impossible, they made every attempt to avoid being sent to the front lines in Europe.

When he was reprimanded for not reporting for duty after several notices, Marius Mastronardi (Luigi's son) defended himself by questioning his status as a Canadian: "I sort of blew my top ... Look, I've had to register like a criminal ... Now you want me to fight for Canada? ... How can you trust me?" But Marius was eventually called, and although he was not sent overseas, he did perform his duty as a citizen, however unwillingly.

Frank Moauro Sr (Costantino's son) protested vehemently against the general situation and the treatment by the police; and his reaction may have been partly responsible for his not serving at all: "So when I got called in the army, I just wrote a letter back to the army and told them I was treated in a rough way ... that I didn't like it and I wasn't going to go and fight ... and I got away with it."

Nevertheless, like many others from most Italian communities across the country, several Italians from Leamington served Canada during the war, at home or overseas: Alfred Mastronardi (Luigi's eldest son), Ollie Mastronardi (Armando's son), and John Brunato (whose store was then managed by Peralta) were mostly in Newfoundland; Gino

Pannunzio, who after finishing grade thirteen had worked for a short time for his father, "was called in the army in 1941" and spent "four and a half years in England ... Holland and Belgium," as well as in Canada: "I was a Canadian citizen," pronounced Gino with pride, as if to counteract the distrust for his being "Italian-born," which precluded him from joining the navy or air force for active duty, as well as to stress the commitment he and other Italians felt even then, in spite of the enemy alien status.

As the war progressed, the surveillance and the tension eased, and the reporting to the police, as DiMenna indicated, became less and less frequent. The reasons for unlocking, if not opening the prison gates varied from the reactions of the Leamington Italians themselves to local politicians' protests against unfair treatment of Italians. Perhaps they were all echoing the attitude of some farmers who, according to Saveria Magri, "defended us" from the beginning, convinced that the Italians were not "saboteurs." Besides, Mussolini was being "soundly defeated" on all fronts between 1940 and 1943;[3] and their own status as farmers gave them certain privileges, as many of them believed.

Initially, the general distrust and suspicion directed toward the Italian-Canadian population may have helped them avoid performing their military duties; but later, as Frank Moauro suggested, likely his work as a farmer "had more to do with it than me writing a letter ... They respected farmers ... They wanted people to work on the farms." Gino DiMenna emphasized the same point:

> The Canadian government didn't take people in the army if they were working on the farm ... They wanted to keep them there to produce food. But we had to prove to them that we were on a farm: myself, Domenic Ingratta, Marius Ingratta, Frank Moauro, the two Cervinis, all had to go in the army, but just because we were on a farm they left us alone ... In the winter time they wanted us to work in some industry ... I had to go to Ford's ... for war purposes ... They kept changing the laws ... Marius Mastronardi, Gino Pannunzio, Alfred Mastronardi, Fred DeSantis, Roy DeSantis, those guys had to go ... The only fortunate thing, when they did go to the front lines, the war was over ... When things did get tight in Europe, they needed men; then they abolished farm and everything ... they called everybody ... I had to go too ... But I had an infection in my ear ... so they sent me home for six months and then I had to go back ... but then the war was over.

THE WAR BONANZA AND THE "NEW LANDOWNERS": FROM TOBACCO TO VEGETABLES

A factor more important than government respect for the farmer was government's policy toward the war: total mobilization of the country for war, but limited direct involvement; or, in accordance with Mackenzie King's plan, "[judicious] avoidance of large-scale infantry combat until the end was in sight." The government's "commitment to total effort in war-production," and its control and management of Canada's food and industrial products resulted in the "war bonanza" that also benefited the Leamington Italians. "After three or four years," said Frank Moauro, "there was quite a noticeable change ... The war changed a lot of things and there was quite an improvement ... There was more employment ... and things just improved generally, housing, transportation, automobiles." In fact, between "1939 and 1941, the GNP increased 47 per cent as the output of primary commodities doubled and levels of secondary manufacturing trebled ... Thanks to the war, an industrial worker in 1941 earned twice as much as in 1939." Also, by 1940 "employment was nearly full," unemployment insurance legislation had been passed, and the requirement that in the winter months farmers "work in some industry," as DiMenna also stated, offered the farmers additional personal and financial advantages.[4]

Paradoxically, the war that had made them enemy aliens produced such an economic recovery for Canada, a general boom, that for the Leamington Italians it meant increasing prosperity. In contrast to the Japanese, who were deprived of their property, the Leamington Italians, despite discrimination, emerged from the war with secure landholdings. By the end of the war, the Italian pioneers to the Leamington area were very well established – most of them living on their own farms, which they had bought before or during the war. Except for Luigi Mastronardi and the two Pannunzio brothers, who had jointly bought a farm as early as 1934, the others bought theirs between 1940 and 1946: Armando Mastronardi and Alex Colasanti in 1940; Costantino (Gus) Moauro, Luigi Mastronardi, and Henry Ingratta in 1942; Angelo Moauro and the Magri family in 1944; Antonio Cervini in 1945; and Tony DiMenna in 1946. The Ingratta brothers (Giovanni and Raffaele) and their cousin (Enrico or Henry) had, of course, bought their farm as early as 1928, but in Elgin County; though, by 1933, Henry had moved back to the Leamington area where, by 1942, he and his family had their own farm (see also chapters 5, 8).

The war boom was a favourable coincidence that permitted the pioneers to buy the farms. But their personal makeup and work played important roles: hard work and resilience saw them through the gruelling emigration-immigration experience; resourcefulness and more hard work helped them overcome the privations during the 1929 Depression, and tempered their spirit to bear the hostility after 1936 and especially after 1940; and determination and still more hard work led them to become owners of a few acres of land or part of those farms that they and their relatives, as Marius Ingratta pointed out, had to work on for others on contract or as shareholders. Partnership among relatives, pooling their resources and work-power (including men, women, and children) had also a great deal to do with it, especially at first. After all, at least two of the families (Ingrattas and Pannunzios) had bought them long before the war started.

The fact that almost all of them had been farmers, and/or owned farms in Italy, was another incentive, though in the case of Antonio Cervini, it was also a construction accident that permitted him to buy his farm in 1945: after falling building material broke two of his ribs and unable to receive further compensation, he sued the company, obtained about $7,000, after legal expenses, and invested the amount in a farm with practically nothing on it, except a "small greenhouse … just a frame," which he then rebuilt with the salvaged lumber. With hard work he eventually converted the farm from tobacco to vegetables. The war boom helped, but as Gino DiMenna himself stressed, "it was also hard work."

The tobacco market situation, just prior to the war, was an additional factor; but they also had to be on "top of it" and ready to respond accordingly. After 1936 and especially after 1940, explained Gino DiMenna, tobacco was no longer profitable, particularly because of increasing competition from the southern United States and especially from the Delhi, Simcoe, and Tillsonburg areas of southern Ontario, where land was cheaper and the soil much better for tobacco than in Essex County; in fact, one acre of land in those areas produced a tobacco crop double that of the Leamington area, where the terrain is "sandy … almost blow sand." Besides, tobacco-growing required at least fifty or sixty acres of land, which was a great deal more than the few acres acquired by the pioneers.

As a result of the competition and the 1938–39 depressed market situation, the eight Italian families, who according to Marius Ingratta "were all growing tobacco through the 1930s on shares with local farmers," had converted their farms by 1941–42 to vegetable growing (tomatoes, lettuce, celery, cauliflower, cabbage, and others). In a way, the Italian immigrant farm workers seemed long prepared for "the big change to vegetables … in the 1940s": though "flue-cured tobacco was the main crop [in the] 1920s/1930s, tomatoes and cantaloupes were supplementary crops ... at that time." At any rate, not only was their decision to convert timely, it also proved to be a wise one, especially when they became proprietors: as owners of relatively small farms, they could hardly compete with the larger tobacco growers, but they were able to expand as produce-growing became increasingly profitable.

According to Gino DiMenna, whose family was the last to have a tobacco crop, on only seven acres of land, a crop of tomatoes "gave a tremendous return, especially during the war when there was no competition from the southern United States, mainly because the means of transportation were mostly used for war materiel. But even after, in 1947, a case of celery sold for eighteen–nineteen dollars." The Italians, who had no contracts with Heinz of Leamington, "because we were Italians," grew their vegetable crops for markets that they themselves searched for, not just locally, but in Toronto (1950s) as well as Montreal (1960s/70s). A world conflict and local economic trends may have provided the occasion, but they themselves, besides investing money, hard work, and family cooperation, had to deploy vision and enterprise.[5]

By 1946, the Italian pioneer family groups owned twelve farms, all except one in the Leamington area (nine in Mersea, two in Gosfield South Townships), and ten of them purchased between 1940 and 1946. Out of the twelve, ten (including the one in Elgin County) belonged to the Molisan families (seven of which bought during the war) and two to the immigrants from the Lazio region.

Throughout Italian history, in times of crisis, "a massive drift to the land" was common: "difficult times ... reawakened and revived in Italian merchants and burgesses that *rentier* spirit that had always existed in them, from their beginnings ... It seemed clearer to them that property investment, whether in lands or houses or in public bonds, was the only way to protect from the blows of circumstance the wealth they had accumulated by trade or speculation," or simply by other forms of employment or activity.[6] In a similar way, the war and its consequences materialized the thought, long in the minds of the Leamington-Italian pioneers, to buy a farm, a piece of this rich, fertile land. In their view also, land was not just a good investment, but the best protection against a possibly recurring economic depression or recession, and exploitation: the landowners made sharecropping a little hard sometimes, even in Canada. (In fact, in the early Leamington-Italian accounts, the term *carogna*, literally "carrion" or "despicable person," appeared more than once in reference to both Italian and non-Italian landlords.)

Thus, during the war, the farm offered some security against widespread suspicion and possible political repression, as well as against loss of job, livelihood, and savings, as was happening to many Italians, even in nearby Windsor. It served also as a demonstration, for those who were suspicious, of their commitment to their adopted land; a guarantee of their citizenship. It was *terra firma* that helped dispel that sense of precariousness that the immigrant status always entails. It was tangible proof of their hard work and courage that had helped them through difficulties and anguish: a well-deserved reward. Above all, during those months and years after June 1940, when their status was in a limbo, the farm offered the enemy aliens a bit of refuge, a sense of belonging, an identity. And after the war, it became the base for continued sponsorship (chapter 7).

VITO PERALTA IN WINDSOR: VICTIM OF FASCISM AND CANADIAN "JUSTICE"

Vito Peralta's arrest, internment, and uncertainty, from June 1940 to the end of 1942, followed a pattern of events common throughout Canada; his experience was like that of many other Italian Canadians. But he was the only Leamington Italian pioneer to have had that experience. In fact, it was his internment that interrupted his life and work in Windsor and led him to work and live in Leamington in 1943. His experience also serves to compare and contrast the urban and rural situation before and during the war.

From the comparison emerged a distinct difference between the life and fortunes of the Italians who had settled in Canadian cities and the conditions of those who lived in the rural areas. The Italian immigrants who went to work on the farms may have lived under harsher conditions in the early period, but later were a little more secure, from the severest blows of the Great Depression and from the political repercussions of the war. In the rural areas, livelihood was not entirely dependent on factory work or the law of supply and demand of the international market. The farm work and products provided a protection against hunger and against being rounded up, arrested, and detained.

By 1940, the Leamington Italians, not more than two dozen families, were well known and well established in the small rural community, and the risk of being sent to internment camps seemed more remote than in the impersonal climate of the larger city. As both Saveria Magri and her son Domenic pointed out, the local farmers and the politicians defended the integrity of the Leamington Italians: "You can rest assured Italians are not saboteurs." They helped the Leamington Italians avoid the more drastic measures enacted by the Windsor Municipal Council (later deplored by its mayor) against that city's Italians. The Leamington

Italians were not arbitrarily and summarily removed from their jobs, homes, and families; the new way of life they had struggled so hard to slowly get used to, their years-long efforts to adjust to the new land, were not completely wiped out. Though they felt – and were – confined, often taken abruptly to the police station and registered as suspects and parolees, their lives were not totally disrupted: they were not sent off to internment camps as many in other cities had been, often for absurd reasons, even for non-existent "incriminating evidence," as in the case of Vito Peralta. In fact, after his internment, the only job Vito could find was in Leamington.

In a more general way, Vito Peralta's experience is a concrete example of the sudden reversal of Italian-Canadian fortunes throughout the country after a period of steady rise in the first two or three decades of the century (chapter 1). Whatever stability and success they had achieved was suddenly destroyed by Mussolini and Fascism. Fascist Italy's nationalistic rhetoric may have given Italian immigrants some pride and self-respect, but its empty propaganda and militaristic imperialism took much more away from them: from many Italian-Canadian women, first their jewellery, then their men, and then from all their freedom and dignity as human beings and citizens.[7]

The disruption in Vito Peralta's life can be best understood by projecting his experience against the backdrop of the world scene and events: this was the era of dictatorships of the right and of the left. The European stage was dominated by Mussolini and Franco, Hitler and Stalin. It was the period of Mussolini's mad dream to recreate the Roman Empire. The "children of Italy" in the world had been indoctrinated for years in Fascist Italy's glorious modern mission. They were the outposts, and they too in large numbers had contributed to the conquest of the first colonies.

The effects of Fascist "overt political activity" in Canada, as well as of Fascist Italy's aggressive foreign policy in the Mediterranean and Africa, on Italian Canadians also help place Peralta's personal experience in better perspective; in particular, growing hostility of Canadian public opinion toward Italy and Italians everywhere, especially after 1936; denunciation by the English-Canadian press of the conquest of Ethiopia and of local Fascist activities; and increasing confusion of Italian Canadians, torn by a "conflict between loyalty to Canada and their sympathy for the mother country." That conflict was quickly resolved for them, but violently, and replaced by a state of total bewilderment, by both Mussolini and the Canadian Justice Minister La Pointe, on 10 June 1940, when LaPointe announced in Parliament, "The very minute that news was received that Italy had declared war on Great Britain and

France, I signed an order for the internment of many hundreds of men whose names were on the list of the RCMP as suspects."

Surprise raids and mass arrests followed immediately and in total secrecy, in order not to hamper the minister's plan: "Those arrested were denied their rights of habeas corpus, and [this] denial of civil liberties extended not just to known Fascist sympathizers but to all enemy aliens and even to all those of 'Italian racial origins who [had] become naturalized British subjects since September 1, 1929.'" Vito Peralta belonged to this category, and he, like many others, too preoccupied with earning a living, was not fully aware of what was happening across the ocean and didn't understand why he was being arrested. Among those arrested, there were prominent men from every *colonia* in the country who had been active Fascists; but paranoia and anti-Italian hysteria led Canadians down an unfortunate path: first, to confuse *italianità* and Fascism (nationality, citizenship, and ideology); then to round up and intern many loyal Canadian citizens, and to perpetrate "many travesties of justice."

All across the country, Canadians of Italian descent were swiftly subjected to violent attacks and ill-treatment (not as vicious as those inflicted on the Japanese, but worse than those directed against the Germans, especially in the extensive Montreal raids). In Toronto, Italians were met with cries of "Down with the Jackals," and their store windows smashed; in Glace Bay, Nova Scotia, Italian miners were repudiated by long-time friends and fellow workers; in various cities, people with Italian surnames were "denied their right to municipal employment or welfare" – a brutal step for those families whose men were interned; and there was frequent harassment by officials and estrangement among friends and neighbours. Men like Vito Peralta with well-paying jobs, including those who "held government contracts to produce war materiel, soon found themselves shipped to Camp Petawawa, where they languished or wasted their talent building wilderness roads."

While the internees were distraught with concern for their dependants, "moving letters were written to the camp commander and to the newspapers about the plight of Italian-Canadian families who were without their breadwinners in the cruel winter of 1940–41." And according to Spada, "The anguish of the families of internees was heart-breaking. Some were destitute, but through direct and indirect help and solidarity, all desperate cases were taken care of." It was indeed a most tragic period for all Canadians, for the nation as a whole, and a moment when, as R.F. Harney almost aphoristically stated, "The place of Italians in Canadian life was at its nadir."[8]

FASCIST AND ANTI-FASCIST ACTIVITIES IN WINDSOR

In the "'hotbed' of Fascist activities," as Windsor came to be known in the 1930s, "things were very, very bad, awfully bad," when war broke out in 1940: "Thirty or forty men were sent to concentration camps in Fredericton," remembered Windsor resident Gilda Meconi (Clemente's wife).[9] Several months later the mayor of Windsor, Arthur J. Reaume, described the Windsor Italians as "having a hell on earth," declaring the council's measures, that had led to suspension of those of enemy alien birth from work, as more drastic than those in other cities; the "grave injustice" done to Canadian citizens of Italian birth by the city, said another city official, was worse than some of Hitler's actions.[10] Only a year later had attitudes begun to change a little, but by then, hundreds of Italians, including Canadian citizens, had been detained, fingerprinted, registered as "dangerous Italian elements," and, according to an RCMP sergeant, "interned without further questioning."[11]

A large number of Windsor Italian Canadians were affected, especially after the changes in the 3 September 1939 "Defense of Canada Regulations." Accordingly, the 1940 regulations required that all Italians and Germans, naturalized since 1922 and no longer since 1929, register under enemy regulations and report regularly to the police. The Order in Council, which seemed intended expressly for the Italians, was based on the view that any Italian naturalized after Mussolini came into power in 1922 was open to suspicion, because Italian consuls were known to be converting Italians in Canada to Fascist principles since that time. In fact, "whereas no arrests were made in the German raids," conducted two weeks before those on the Italian residents, "heads of every Italian home visited, were taken into custody and are still held."[12] Though it is not known how many of the "1,117 native-born Italians" living in Windsor on 12 June 1940 were affected, the August 1940 changes added "at least 200 more Italians" to the list of suspects and parolees.[13]

Moreover, in the Windsor Fascist "hotbed" not only had the police been aware of Fascist groups and activities for some time, they had themselves taken part in their public celebrations. In his October 1933 speech to the Sandwich Co-operative Commonwealth Federation (CCF), John Artico of the Workers' Educational Association warned against the spreading of Fascism in Canada, the attempts to establish "Black Shirt" and "Blue Shirt" movements in Windsor, and the support given them among local Italians.[14] At least since May 1938, the Windsor police had known of Toronto's appointment of Luigi Meconi as head of the newly formed Windsor Fascist Section. The RCMP also had the benefit of information on Italian suspects: public reaction against Fascist activities had prompted government investigations in 1938 into the promotion of Fascist doctrines by both the Toronto and Detroit Italian vice-consuls, especially by the local Italian language classes ("Fascist Textbook Scandal").[15] "Records gathered then," wrote the *Windsor Daily Star* on 12 June 1940, "are believed to be playing an important part in the current drive" to round up Italians.[16]

The Windsor Italian community, like other communities in Canada, reflected and reacted to the political events in Italy, as well as in Canada, through their cultural and political associations. During the Fascist regime, Windsor had pro-Fascist and anti-Fascist groupings or clubs. Their activities were conducted in public, and in general the public was itself not only aware of the activities by some local Italian Fascist clubs, but they often gave them tacit and open support. In May 1936, at their annual banquet attended by 150 members and their wives, the Windsor Branch of the Italian Legion publicly endorsed Mussolini's invasion of Ethiopia in the presence of a representative of the chief of the Windsor Police Department.[17] The speeches at the banquet repeated the arguments in favour of Mussolini's action that had been presented in an earlier public speech in Windsor by the visiting Italian vice-consul. On that occasion, Vice-Consul George Tiberi also reassured the Canadian public of the Italians' loyalty to the British Commonwealth, as evidenced also, his local supporters pointed out, by their attendance at the memorial service for the late King George V.[18]

Tiberi's visit was the first of two incidents in the 1930s that saw the clash of the Windsor-Italian opposing factions, resulting in headlines in the local newspaper with reverberations in provincial and national capitals. The 100-member Italian Cultural Club opposed attempts by the Italian vice-consul and local Italian Fascists to solicit financial aid and moral support for Mussolini's Ethiopian Campaign.[19] But the supporters of Il Duce won (partly because protesters were silenced by boos and heckling from the crowd, or scorned as communist sympathizers). On 26 January, at a meeting at St Alphonsus Hall ("held under the auspices of the Italian Veterans Association, the Sons of Italy and the Italian Independent Political Club," as well as the consulate of Italy in Toronto), the over 300 Italians attending cheered Vice-Consul Tiberi's specious justification of Mussolini's invasion of Ethiopia, and most of the women responded to his appeal by handing over to the Italian officials "their gold wedding rings to help *Il Duce*."[20] Tiberi's visit bolstered patriotic fervour and the prestige of some Windsor Italians; but the repercussions of the "victory" of the Windsor Fascist faction devastated the whole community. After 10 June

1940, there were no longer "Communists" in the community: the Italians, in the eyes of other Canadians, were all "Fascists."

The second episode occurred in 1938: the use of Fascist books and teaching material in the Dante Alighieri Society–sponsored Italian language classes provoked a controversy involving not only the Italian community and the school board, but city council, the Italian vice-consulate, the Department of Education, and Canadian Immigration. For five days, from 14 to 19 May, the *Windsor Daily Star*, which had exposed the scandal, gave extensive coverage to every aspect of the battle: the meetings, the declarations, the charges and countercharges, the challenges and accusations against the critics and rivals who were again discredited as advocates of Communism. The Windsor Fascist Italian school was probed in Ottawa (which also launched a full-scale investigation in similar schools in Toronto and Hamilton): the classes were discontinued, the two Italian teachers were barred from Windsor and Canada, and local officials were reprimanded. At one point, Charles Quenneville, secretary of the Windsor Separate School Board, stated that he had found nothing "abnormal" in the books, considered them preferable and healthier for children than those of the Young Communist League, upheld the Fascist teachings as an antidote to the spread of Communism, and condemned the critics as enemies of the common good.[21] In fact, the government investigation found the schools to be part of an international Fascist program of indoctrination under the supervision of the Italian Foreign Office, and the texts a glorification of Fascism and Mussolini with "exhortations to unselfish sacrifice of self for the future of Italy."[22]

Some results were positive: more awareness of the Fascist threat and increased opposition to Fascist activities by the general public. But the effects were mostly negative for the entire Italian community: further alienation, division, confusion, and fear (especially of reprisals against Italian anti-Fascists who refused to be identified when they opposed the school and its organizer in letters to the editor);[23] therefore antagonism toward all Italians, since the distinction between Fascist and non-Fascist sympathizers became more difficult, and dishonour to the whole community "for the actions of a few." Hostility against Fascist sympathizers and Fascist activities, generated especially by the "textbook scandal," became indiscriminate hostility against all Italians: the entire community paid dearly for it when the blow fell on 10 June 1940.[24]

The explosion of anti-Italian sentiment set off on that day tore apart homes, lives, and families, with some effects still felt today.[25] "Scores of Windsor Italians Arrested in Fascist Purge," read the titles of the *Windsor Daily Star* of 12 June 1940, just two days after Mussolini's declaration of war. The Windsor "four-day drive to round up and arrest the enemy aliens" was described as "the most extensive in the city's history with more than 150 policemen and citizens participating." The surprise aids and the ransacking of homes, did produce "firearms, ammunition and literature," according to the *Star*, as well as "military-style shirts with 'Blue Shirts of Canada' crests," but no evidence of sabotage, subversion, or espionage. Nevertheless, "the sudden change of events" made the "bewildered" Italians "virtual prisoners of war":[26] "Because they were Italian," said Elvira Montanari (in Windsor since 1926), "they thought they were all Fascists ... It did not make a difference if one was an Italian citizen or Canadian. They took some wrong people ... All one had to do was point a finger at you." Not even women were spared: "A girl's mother was sent to a concentration camp."[27]

In Windsor also, however justifiable in time of war, xenophobia and paranoia, particularly after June 10, had such a grip on public opinion as to suppress all moderation and compassion. The Italians lost their freedom and their jobs and found mostly injustice, scorn, and "social ostracism." City council even "banned the use of the Italian language at church services."[28] Among the twenty-two people ordered suspended or "stricken from payroll" of city departments after 12 June, most were Italians: Constable Nero (Nereo) Brombal (1897–1974) was the only Italian-born member (for twelve years) of the police force;[29] Joseph Diodati (Public Works) was a Canadian volunteer-veteran of the First World War, whose son had left a forty-dollars-a-week position to enlist with the Royal Canadian Air Force. In a letter to the mayor in 1941, Airman E.A. Diodati pointed out with indignation his father's "desperate situation ... rent is owing on [his] home and he is threatened with seizure of his furniture ... What gets me is my dad, a returned soldier, kicked around like a dog."[30] Joseph Falsetto (Liquor Control Board of Ontario), who spent more than three years at Camp Petawawa while his two sons were fighting for Canada, was released only after his eldest son, Hector, was killed in Holland and the younger Anthony, a survivor of a torpedo attack on his aircraft carrier in the Arctic Ocean, wrote to Ottawa threatening not to return to active duty. Natale Soda (Sanitation Department) was sent to Camp Petawawa for two years, in spite of his pregnant wife and six children, who were evicted from their home and forced to live in an overcrowded "barn-like area" with "other destitute families."[31]

The suspension of employment, the freezing of bank accounts, and federal control of financial properties of internees resulted in the loss of homes and businesses. The Government of Canada assumed full financial responsibility only for the families of enemy aliens interned, and

only on the basis of the relief scale allowed indigent Canadians, about
twelve dollars a month.[32] Those not interned were "unable to obtain
employment and provide for their families."[33] Joe DeSanti, in his letters to Mackenzie King, asked why his father Attilio, whose "prosperous
construction business" was totally dismantled and sold "dirt cheap" by
the government, "was being treated like a traitor while his older brother
Edward was fit to serve in the Canadian Army." The Dominato, Minello
(Mary), and Soda families also gave accounts of loss, pain, anger, anxiety, and struggle for survival, even after the return to Windsor of their
husbands and fathers, who were usually not given their jobs back: neither did the city rehire Natale Soda, nor the Ford Motor Company
Angelo Dominato, not even as a low-level labourer in spite of his foreman position prior to his arrest.[34] One cruel solution was to urge authorities to deport the interned men and their families to Germany and Italy,
the lands they were "so anxious to serve: Send Enemy Aliens Home ...
That would solve the problem of keeping them in internment camps in
Canada, and it would also allow the families to be kept together."[35]

The Windsor-area members of Parliament, who not long before had
courted the Italian voters and sung their praise and loyalty to Canada, cast
off all Windsor Italians on the same day the raids were reported:[36] "'Me
help 'em, Nuts!' said Paul Martin, MP for Essex East – or, at any rate,"
commented the journalist, "in words to that effect." Norman A. McLarty,
minister of labour and MP for Essex West, to whom the Italian Liberal
Club only a few months earlier had "expressed unanimous support,"[37]
was reported saying, "No political influence in behalf of enemy aliens ...
You can make that as strong as you like"; and Murray Clark, MP, Essex
South: "They needn't look to me to get 'em out of trouble." The first politician to come to the defence of his oppressed citizens was the mayor of
Windsor, Reaume – but not until 20 January 1941, when he made a plea
for tolerance toward the foreign born, particularly the Italians.

The *Windsor Daily Star* added insult to injury with its comments on
Italians, their former political influence, and their falling out of grace
after the politicians' about-face on 12 June 1940:

> The Italian colony ... is deriving no support today from their repre-
> sentatives even though the Italian vote had been known, more than
> once, to have swung an election ... The members of Parliament are
> today unanimous in passing up spaghetti for the roast beef of Merrie
> England ... So far as the Italian voter is concerned, the "Walk In"
> sign on the door has been covered over by "Out to Lunch" ... That
> shuffling sound today was Canada's political pachyderms backing

away from lighted firecrackers. Or, rather, from spluttering sticks of dynamite ... in ordinary times ... merely innocuous Roman candles labelled "Made in Italy" [which] shoot pretty balls of fire into the firmament and help mightily to illuminate the tricky path to the ballot box ... Today, they're high explosives and the politicos won't touch 'em even with the proverbial forty-foot pole.[38]

Canadian citizens of Italian origin were summarily tried and condemned, not just by the government and the police, but by the press and public opinion as well.

That example of journalism, teeming with innuendos, could only lead to further community alienation, recharge anti-Italian sentiments, escalate slurs, harassment, persecution, and ostracism, along with fear and grief: "We were all afraid," said Gilda Meconi, "people would be in front of the church calling us 'wops' ... We would keep quiet and go home."

"They went as far as throwing stones at me," recalled Marina Ferranti, "while [they were] yelling, 'You Mussolini's girlfriend' [and] telling us to move ... You couldn't talk Italian ... there on Marion Street ... We couldn't get together or else [they] would become suspicious: 'Oh look, they're having a meeting' ... So I would just wave to my friends from far away ... We used to cry."[39]

It was quite a fall for the Windsor Italians who only thirteen years earlier had enjoyed the esteem of high-ranking representatives of the English-speaking community. Italian and Fascist pride was perhaps at its highest point during the 1927 inaugural celebration of the new 141-member Loggia Generale Umberto Nobile, Number 1442, of the Order of Sons of Italy in Ontario: with the "Flags of Italy and Britain Entwined in Good Will at Cenotaph," "high tribute was paid to the Italian nation and the Italian people for their service in alliance with Britain during the [First World] war, for her leadership in science and art and commerce [and] the cordial spirit of good will engendered by the conduct of Italian residents in Canada."[40] The sudden disappearance of their public support and prestige was a blow for the Fascist activists within the order.

Nevertheless, in Windsor as in Leamington, the early Italian immigrants, familiar with hard times, weathered this storm also. Even at the moment of the raids, the *Windsor Daily Star*, taking notice of the general Italian mood, wrote: "No one said a word, neither did they complain. They just appeared bewildered ..." Joseph Diodati's reaction to his "desperate situation," presented by his son in his letter's closing remark, summarized an attitude expressed in other interviews in both areas: "But he is proud and weathers well." Also, while the assumed disloyalty of many Italian Canadians was being proclaimed and punished everywhere, the Italian communities responded with demonstrations of loyalty and commitment to Canada: with financial contributions and a "disproportionately high number of volunteers in the Canadian armed services" – as evidenced in Windsor by Diodati, DeSanti, and the Falsettos, as well as by the 20 March 1942 donation of $1,200 to the Red Cross by the Italian Mutual Benefit Society (with contributions even from Italians who had not worked for several months but had never forgotten the assistance received in harder times).[41]

PERALTA'S "BOARDING-SCHOOL TERM": LESSONS OF INTERNMENT

On 10 June 1940, Vito Peralta was an innocent bystander struggling to build a new future, who had little time for politics but was under suspicion, rounded up, indexed, filed, registered, and sent away for no reason at all. He was a hard-working, law-abiding citizen caught in madness and megalomania that justify "defensive" wars of conquest, self-protective prejudice, and unavoidable inhuman acts. He was simply a humble person made to bear the burden of ill-advised decisions, policies, and laws that violate human rights. Peralta and hundreds of other Italian immigrants were the victims of the long arm of Fascist Italy's "ugly dictatorship" and the temporarily unenlightened Canadian democracy.

Vito Peralta was neither pro- nor anti-Mussolini; he was not a "dangerous Italian element." He was a new Canadian citizen whose modest, hard-earned, and proud achievements were threatened by stupidity and hysteria, as he described during his interview forty years later:

I never lost a day of work ... I was making eighteen dollars a week, because I worked Saturdays and even Sundays ... There was a guy who was envious because he earned ten dollars a week, but I told him, "You get drunk on Saturday and Sunday and you don't go to work on Monday because you're still drunk: a man must do his duty, and my boss pays me what I deserve because I do mine."

But when the war came ... there was a big meeting at the Windsor Arena with all these *inglesi* who wanted information; they wanted to know if there were some "bad people" against Canada. Someone told them, "Add this guy here to the list too." So I was listed, and as soon as the war began, on June 15, I was working on Ouellette Street and the police came to ask me questions:

"What's your name?"

"Vito Peralta."

"You're under arrest."

"And what's this for?"

"Because Mussolini declared war on Canada."

"And what fault is it of mine?"

"You must come with us."

Can you understand this? They arrested me and took me to the concentration camp and with my citizenship papers ... and I was a prisoner there for two and a half years.

Vito was first sent to the internment camp at Petawawa and was then transferred to another camp in New Brunswick. He really never understood why he was arrested. As far as he was concerned, it was the work of evil, occult forces, *"il segno del malocchio italiano"* (the mark, curse, hex of the Italian evil eye) (see chapter 11, "The Pastor's Views" and notes 39–41). But later in court he was given a more specific reason, which turned out to be as ridiculous as others might have considered his own.

The three judges asked the Mounted Police to present the charges, and an envelope was shown.

Vito felt secure: "I knew I had done nothing wrong; there could be no serious charge against me."

A judge opened the envelope, looked at the contents, and said, "Very nice, fine looking boys."

Then he showed them to the second judge, who also said, "Very nice." Finally, after a brief look, the third judge repeated, "Very nice."

Then one of them turned to him: "Mister Peralta, are these your sons?"

Vito took the photo (which the Peraltas still have) and saw his young sons wearing the sailor uniform of the Fascist youth organization (to which all Italian school children had to belong at that time). His two sons appeared so handsome to Vito, with their sailor hat and on it the writing *Balilla*. He kissed the picture.

The judge again asked the officers for the charges.

The answer was as expected: "That's all!"

"What do you mean 'That's all'!" the three judges asked, glancing at one another.

Of course there were no charges! There was no substantial proof, because he was never involved in anti-Canadian activities. There were only allegations, suspicions, and lies, possibly fabricated by an envious acquaintance-turned-informer.[42] The "incriminating evidence" for his alleged association with the Fascists, for his arrest, incarceration, humiliation, loss of employment and freedom, and above all for two and a half years of incommunicado captivity and incalculable hardships for his family far away, was none other than a picture: an innocent photograph of his little boys – sent by his wife from Italy – dressed as Fascist "Boy Scouts," in a compulsory uniform for all Italian boys, from eight to fourteen years of age, who were organized by Fascism in a paramilitary formation and called *Balilla*.[43] In fact, according to Salvatore Peralta, he and his brother (Girolamo) had not been in the *Balilla* movement at all: "The *Balilla* uniform in the *marinaretto* [little sailor] picture belonged to the photo studio." In contrast, Gino DiMenna of Leamington had been a *Balilla*, but was not interned.[44]

In order to secure such *corpus delicti*, the guardians of law and order had gone to his place of residence, dumped and scattered his modest belongings on the floor, and searched everything. Whether it was fear, ignorance, or overzealous execution of one's duty, an innocent man, a Canadian citizen was pronounced guilty, judged, and sentenced: he was stripped of his human rights and dignity. Above all, the act was a cynical violation of the most honoured traditions of fairness, justice, and legal procedure. No wrong can ever be corrected by another wrong. It was not just the Italians who had reached the nadir of Canadian life at that time. It was Canadian life itself, civilized society, that had reached one of its lowest levels of degradation. If "histories make men wise," as Francis Bacon wrote, and past experiences hold valuable teachings for the individual and society, then a most endurable lesson can be drawn from the story of this simple immigrant. And Vito himself made an effort to point it out afterwards.

Vito Peralta had been gravely wronged, and the judges at the hearing realized it. Perhaps in an attempt to make amends by recognizing the injustice, they asked Vito whether he was "angry at Canada." Vito's answer was that he was indeed angry, but not at Canada, only at those who had made false accusations against him. His answer, whether the result of a noble sentiment, true love for his new land in spite of his ordeal, or desire to ingratiate himself with the authorities, carried a warning for all: the judges, the police, and the Canadian people in general, whose fears and hasty judgments had turned "good citizens" into "prisoners of war," and opportunistic informers and racists into patriots.[45]

"Those people who accused us," Vito told the judges, "wanted to harm Canada," clearly suggesting that those who abuse democratic freedoms to curtail the rights of other citizens are the real saboteurs and traitors to be closely watched, if not interned.

Vito Peralta had no time for anger or resentment. He had to rebuild his life and business. Above all, he had to think of his family who, throughout this time, had received no news from him: "no financial or moral support" (as his sons sadly stated forty-five years later). However, Vito remembered one man from that trying period. When he and the other thirty to thirty-five Italians suspected of pro-Fascist activities were rounded up for questioning, it was Luigi Meconi, who was himself arrested and sent to internment camp for four years, who defended them: "'I am the only Fascist here,' that's what he told them," Vito quickly added. "'There are no Fascists among these poor people present here. I am a Fascist.'" Of course Meconi's appeal was in vain. But Vito clearly recalled the speech, perhaps with admiration for Meconi's courage, even though Meconi could hardly deny his Fascist ties.[46]

Just as quickly, though, Vito dismissed that moment with resignation: "*e così è passata la vita!*" which may be interpreted as "And this is the way life went" or "And so life went on." This concept, part work and hope, echoed the words, attitudes, and deeds of both Windsor and Leamington Italians during that period. They inherently understood that sometimes some things cannot be changed, at least not immediately; that it is more advisable and convenient to bide one's time, to accept with resigned courage things that are or can be inevitable and sorrowful: the will of God, fate, or whatever fortune presents. During the raids and at the height of hostility, some Windsor Italians cried with fear, others responded with anger, and most were just bewildered, did not say a word or complain; they weathered the "desperate situation" well and, as indicated by Saveria Magri, they "didn't get discouraged," because life must go on.

"NO MONEY, NO APOLOGIES SUFFICE" FOR YESTERDAY'S WRONGS

In general, Italian Canadians responded generously toward Canada, not just by serving in the armed forces or by giving money, but by laying that sad period to rest. Like Vito Peralta, many "did not forget but forgave." A former Glace Bay Italian miner, who during his internment had lost everything, in a 1990 CBC interview stated that he preferred to "let bygones be bygones," or as another said in Italian, "*mettiamoci una pietra sopra*" – "let's put a stone over it" or "let's bury the past." Vito Peralta himself was satisfied with the answer he gave the judges and the message he left for posterity.

However, as evidenced by the WICCC interviews with Windsor Italians in 1985, by a series of articles in the *Windsor Star* in 1989, as well as by a brief submitted to the Canadian government by the National Congress of Italian Canadians (1990), some Italian Canadians believed, and requested, that some form of redress was due to them for the wrongs done to the 700 Italian internees and/or their families: if not a monetary compensation, as in the Japanese case, at least an official acknowledgement of this suffering for all the 100,000 Italian Canadians of that time, and of shame for the entire nation.

On 4 November 1990, at the urging also of some Italian Canadian members of Parliament, Prime Minister Mulroney "broke half a century of silence" and offered, "on behalf of the government and people of Canada, a full and unqualified apology." In recognizing, the prime minister stated, "the indignity suffered by the Italian-Canadian community between 1940 and 1943 ... the brutal injustice ... inflicted arbitrarily, not only on individuals suspected of being security risks but also on individuals whose only crime was being of Italian origin ... an act of prejudice ... organized and carried out under law ... [for] none of the 700 internees was ever charged with an offence ... I ... extend a formal apology to all the Members of the Italian Community for this unspeakable act, and to other Canadians who have suffered similar grievances."

But the "historic day," as one called it, did not promote more agreement on the whole issue among Italian Canadians or Canadians in general. Contrary to those who cheered Mulroney's "courage to reopen and correct a page of our history," some considered the government's apology unsatisfactory, belated, or opportunistic.[47] In Windsor, Tony Soda, whose family had lost the house when his father was interned, felt the reparation was "fifty years too late" and of no benefit to those who suffered most, since they were no longer here. Nevertheless, Soda himself, Antonia Dominato, still defending her "father's innocence," as well as other Windsor Italian families of internees, all still feeling the scar of "enemy aliens," proposed that the government provide some form of financial retribution, such as funding for worthy community projects and programs: community centres, homes for senior citizens, scholarships for Italian Canadian students, expansion or creation of Italian language and culture and/or multicultural education courses and programs. Such monetary redress, "symbolic, creative and imaginative," seemed the only proper one to a Canadian English-language newspaper that made similar suggestions: "Why not create education programs dealing in minority rights? Or a display in the museum of civilization to educate future generations about the sad period in Canada's history when there was rampant racism and discrimination."[48]

On the other hand, the families of some internees, such as the sons of Vito Peralta (Jerry and Salvatore), were opposed to any form of "collective economic acknowledgement." They were indignant at the suggestion that the entire community be the beneficiary of financial compensation that rightfully belonged to those who suffered the wrongs: internees and families. "To assume that the Italian community at large be at all involved in this highly and emotionally charged issue is absurd." They, in fact, wondered whether "any money or any apologies will ever suffice" to right the wrongs![49]

"Is there any honour to be brought to this man who was honest [and] honourable," asked Helen McCrory of Windsor, whose father "Giuseppe Giovanni" (Joseph) Diodati (1894–1980) felt "very humiliated at being let out of his job [at] Windsor Utilities." What suitable reparation could there be for the wrongs done to Diodati's family? "We the children," McCrory wrote, "suffered humiliation and degradation from lack of food, and none of us 5 children received an education past grade 8. One brother even changed his name so not to detect he was Italian." Is a plaque like the one erected by the Windsor Police to honour the memory of Constable Brombal sufficient?[50]

The polarization went beyond the Italian community: direct compensation of Japanese Canadians, however deserving, was seen as a dangerous precedent, an opening of a Pandora's Box, since not only Italian Canadians but also "Ukrainian- and Chinese-Canadians ... all have legitimate complaints, deserving of some kind of [economic] redress," and perhaps even "those 450 individuals rounded up without charge during the 1970 October Crisis." These protesters were, therefore, opposed to any direct compensation of Italian Canadians: "At some point it must stop. Claims cannot go on forever."[51] To others the apology was simply crass opportunism by a government that was low in the opinion polls. Others even questioned whether all Italians deserved an apology at all: in their view, there were pro-Fascist Italians in that era; thus the confusion of *italianità* and ideology, which had condemned innocent people to internment camps in the 1940s, was reappearing to cast suspicions on all Italian Canadians fifty years later!

Nevertheless, in one case at least, Frank Moauro made an attempt not only to understand but even to justify why the Italians were treated as they were in the early part of the war:

They came to pick us up ... and fingerprint us ... But, in a sense ... possibly you can't blame them ... At that time, before this war took place ... these guys here didn't quite realize what was across the ocean ... In a sense they were scared ... But once they got to know what the Italian people were and what the other foreign people were

... once they got to know the other countries and the way the other people were living ... they realized that they weren't as bad as they were supposed to be ... They got more or less the idea that we were the same, made of the same blood as they were.

Atrocities of war are never outweighed by its benefits. But, as Frank Moauro suggested, one good result was that it broadened the horizons of the Canadian people: they began to learn more about other nations and about other peoples who came to be part of Canada. Moauro's final reflection on that bewildering and tense period in Canadian life was a fitting message for today's multicultural Canada and humanity in general: fear and distrust among people of different origins and races can be overcome only by knowing more about one another. Though a very high price to pay for a lesson on the benefits of harmonious coexistence, the Second World War did provide an occasion for mutual discovery, as well as for Canada's economic recovery, and increased prosperity for the Leamington Italians. "War," said McLuhan, "is accelerated social change."[52]

The war for Peralta was a personal disaster, but his internment, in his view, was also a preparation for better things, an education, his *"anni di collegio"* (college years), as he called it. (He had even mastered his carving skill, as shown by a wooden tray made during his internment.) When he returned from internment camp on 23 December 1942, he faced other hardships: there was no work for him in Windsor. The man Vito suspected of having falsely "fingered" him to the RCMP was working in the shoe repair shop where he had worked previously. "There isn't much work now," he was told. "I have the other man now. Come spring [1943] you'll be back working here again." Vito could not afford to be without a job for three months or more. But he was not discouraged: *chi cerca trova* (if you seek you'll find).

THE PERALTAS REACH LEAMINGTON

A young Italian couple owned a shoe store in Leamington. Vito had known them since they were quite young. John Brunato had been away, serving as a soldier in the Canadian army, for longer than expected. His wife needed help to run the store, which in her husband's absence was not doing well. When she heard that Vito had come back from camp, she asked him to manage the business for her. Vito accepted the offer and never regretted moving to Leamington, in spite of the initial difficulties: particularly loneliness and isolation, since he didn't know anyone, nor was he aware of the presence there of a few Italian families. At first he lived with an English family who liked him and respected him. Once they even brought back an Italian newspaper from Detroit for him. Later he lived in a room behind the shoe store. But it was hard; he worked long hours and had to prepare his own meals. He was alone, even though he soon became a close friend of the Leamington Italian families (such as the Moauros, Mastronardis, Pannunzios, Colasantis, Cervinis). In the meantime, Vito's family was still in Italy. Ironically, it may have been partly fortunate that they were not in Canada during his internment. Now that he wished they were with him, it was more difficult to have them come over (because of the "enemy alien" law). He nevertheless went ahead with the application, especially since he was already thinking about buying the store and repair shop, and settling down in Leamington, which appeared to him "the best place in the whole of Canada."

Vito's wife (Giuseppina, Josephine, Milana, whom he married in 1924) and their elder son (Girolamo, Jerry) finally arrived in Canada (via Halifax on the Italian ship *Vulcania* – the same ship and voyage as the Leone family but unaware of each other) on 31 March 1949, after living apart for over twenty-two years. Vito and Josephine had spent the best years of their conjugal life alone, without each other's comfort and support; he had not seen his twenty-three-year-old son since he was a baby. He was so excited when he went to the Windsor train station to meet them that at first he could not find them and feared that they were lost. One can imagine the surge of emotions on seeing his wife step off the train, and the feelings of both during their embrace. What might be more difficult to imagine were the feelings of father and son during those first moments of their first encounter as adults. The wife-mother respectively of the two men made a brief and rapid introduction: "*Questo è tuo padre*" (This is your father). Only then did the two "strangers" embrace.

But the real strangers for Vito were his other son (Salvatore, Sal), who was born shortly after Vito's departure for "America" (1927), and his son's own family. Salvatore came to Canada in 1950, while his wife (Pietra Adragna) and their three small children arrived two years later (1952). It was only then that, for the first time in his life, Vito saw his younger son and his three grandchildren: "*non conoscevo nè padre ... nè figli*" (I knew neither the father nor his children) ... twenty-three years without me," Vito remembered sadly; and then, perhaps as a form of self-justification, quickly added, "But I never forgot my family."

Vito did finally buy the store (1956) at 9 Erie Street South in Leamington, where for twenty-six years he sold, cleaned. and mostly repaired shoes. Vito came to Canada as a cobbler and remained a cobbler all his life. His sons, who had lived a different life, took a different road. After working at Heinz, Salvatore went into the fishing industry and later became part owner with his son, also named Vito, of a food processing company (Etna Foods Limited). His other son, Girolamo (Jerry), who before coming to Canada had completed his training as a *carabiniere*, was not accustomed to country life and farm work. After working for some time in Leamington, he found a job in the Detroit area, where he and his wife (Agatha Zichi) settled permanently shortly after their marriage in 1953 (and where he operated his own barbershop for many years). Nonetheless, the Peraltas did finally come together as a family, all living in the same area, on the same side of the ocean.

THE PERALTAS AND EARLY SICILIAN IMMIGRATION

Vito Peralta's immigrant experience, though similar in many aspects to that of other early immigrants to the Windsor-Leamington area, is distinct: unlike the others, Vito had a trade, a skill, that remained his livelihood; his many years spent in an urban setting caused him to endure a situation from which those in the rural areas were mostly spared. Among those interviewed, he was the only one to be interned. His story offers a different view of the immigrant condition and the Canadian reality, as well as a measure for comparing urban and rural life during those early years, the advantages and disadvantages of the two environments: the opportunities and the risks of the one and the isolation and greater security of the other. The internment episode helps illustrate the Windsor reality of the time and the similar experience of many other Windsor Italian Canadians who were more hesitant to discuss it or were deceased. This particular experience also exposes some ironical aspects of immigration and of immigrant life: many often left their homeland to escape political and economic oppression only to find worse conditions in the land of their dreams, if only at first.

On a personal level, perhaps Vito postponed bringing his family to Canada because he intended to remain only for a few years and then return. Yet he became a citizen as soon as the required five-year residence period had elapsed. Nonetheless, this was not the pattern of others who immediately sought to surround themselves with family and *paesani*. Some Italian emigrants forgot the families and towns they left behind, at times with tragic consequences, as when some men set up new families in the New World and cut all ties with the old ones, which were often plunged into destitution and despair. But if, as Coletti observed, the "islanders" – the natives of Sicily – "are more attached to their native villages than those on the continent," then for the Sicilian Vito, the long absence and separation from family and town must have been especially painful, particularly during those months of internment, when he was forbidden to communicate with his family.

His experience also exemplifies Sicilian emigration to North America in the early part of the twentieth century. Sicily was not immediately affected by the great exodus from continental southern Italy. Emigration from Sicily "developed vigorously only after 1900, but it quickly became quite intense, surpassing in a relatively short time the development phases that in other places required several more years." The leaders were the areas of Messina and Palermo on the northern coast of the island, more exposed to contacts and influences. Emigration from Trapani on the northwestern seaboard, where Vito's town (San Vito Lo Capo) is located, developed later. In fact, the coastal areas held off longer than those in the hinterland, where discontent was more general and deeper because of poverty and the "prevailing feudalism." In general, the departures from areas on the seashore were frequent before the First World War, and usually the determining factors were greater familiarity with the concept of travel and easier communication, as well as the "fortunate example of others." When the steady flow started, the Sicilians preferred the United States because it offered greater opportunities America offered; and very quickly, emigrating to America came to be regarded as "a natural fact of life," a basic *need* that "young children suckled with their milk."[53]

The Sicilians also, albeit later, succumbed to the lure of America, *La Merica*, as it came to be popularly known – the mutilation of the name suggesting familiarity, awe, and scorn; that ambivalent America of wealth and loneliness, of work and nothing else (*"si lavora, si lavora e poi si muore"* – "you work and work and then you die"), as Sicilians remembered it (wrote Leonardo Sciascia) even beyond the 1920s. For the inhabitants of the ancient centre of Greek civilization, "America" assumed aspects of classical mythology: it became a new Circe, a sort of modern siren that enchanted young men to its shores while wives and mothers, cursing her as if she were a wicked woman, wept and waited, and the wait was often long, as was so poignantly described by Maria Messina in "La Merica" (published between 1910 and 1928): *"Tutti partivano ... non c'era casa che non piangesse. Pareva la guerra; e come quando c'è la guerra, le mogli restavano senza marito e le mamme senza figlioli."* (They were all leaving ... there was no home without tears. It seemed like war; and just as when there's war, wives were left without their husbands, and mothers without their children.)[54]

Vito's own odyssey – from his farewell to his young pregnant wife and a two-year-old son to his encounter a generation later with his wife, sons, and three grandchildren – assumes in a similar way almost legendary and mythological aspects: like the Homeric Odysseus who, forced by the wrath of the gods and mortals, was away from wife and son for twenty years fighting wars and roaming the seas even to the shores of Sicily, the Sicilian immigrant, under the spell of wealth and fortune or buffeted by adverse political winds, was separated from wife and family for over twenty-two years on the shores of America. Giuseppina, like Penelope the faithful wife, could only wait for his return or for news of his better fortune; and his children, like Telemachus, grew up without their father's guidance. Vito also, like Tony DiMenna before him, embarked on a "*folle volo*," a "witless flight ... to venture the uncharted distances ... to reach" America, driven, like Dante's Ulysses, by a "restless itch to rove," that neither "tenderness" for his son "nor the wedded love that should have comforted" Giuseppina "could conquer" in him. The recurring theme of the emigration experience – that disrupted lives, kept loved ones apart, and confused values – created automatically a link between Vito Peralta and Tony DiMenna, and through them a parallel between the Sicilian and Molisan experiences (as well as with the *Ciociari*, especially Tony Cervini, himself without his family for years): a common chord that helped draw all the Leamington groups closer.[55]

The humiliation and alienation, often from both country of origin and country of adoption, as in the case of Peralta, was a high price the immigrant paid for "wealth" or "fortune." The enemy alien status placed the Italian Canadians in a psychological state analogous to that experienced by the earlier migrant worker or navvy who was considered "a necessity for the economy but not a desirable immigrant." In the Leamington case, the farm was a "salvation." Therefore, poverty (*miseria*) and politics, as well as "dreams," may have forced many southern Italian peasants away from their "miserly" fields to become migrant workers, then immigrants; but economics, politics, as well as "psychology" often turned them back toward farm work and the land to eventually become successful farmers; thus contrary, at least partly, to Spada's observation of Italians in Canada not being farmers, and to Sergio Romano's statement that in the eyes of southern Italians "the land became synonymous with wretchedness and despair."[56] By 1945, thanks also to the war and in spite of it, the Leamington pioneers were already disproving such observations. They were all well placed in Leamington, including Vito Peralta. They were no longer the "bewildered Italians." Some had even achieved, at least in part, "their fortune," and as Tony DiMenna aptly put it, "They were glad they tried emigrating ... They had good fortunes. Because of their *slancio* [daring] to go abroad ... many people were able to come over and settle in Leamington."

After the war, when immigration to Canada was again possible, the farms offered the first Italian-Canadian families in Leamington the stability, guarantees, and power to initiate the second great wave of immigration from their regions of origin: (Abruzzo-) Molise, Lazio, Sicily. The farm would then become the first base for the growth of the community in the postwar period.

7

Postwar Growth

FROM AN OLD "ITALY IN PIECES" TO A "YOUNG BOOMING CANADA"

After the Second World War the widespread shortage of labour caused by a booming economy, as well as Canada's new obligations within NATO, once again made the country receptive to Italian immigration. Postwar immigrants comprise almost 70 per cent of the Italian Canadian group.[1]

THE WAR AND ITS EFFECTS ON SOUTHERN ITALY

"Italy," wrote Procacci,

> emerged ... happily on the whole from [the second postwar period] much better, certainly, than from the first postwar years. Whereas in 1919 it had been possible to speak of a "mutilated victory," in 1948 it could be said that though she had lost the war, Italy had won the peace ... The years 1948–53 were still difficult years from the economic point of view, but from 1954 onwards recovery has been rapid, and since 1956 and Italy's entry into the European Common Market, overwhelming. This was the so-called "economic miracle": production figures, the national income, consumption, all began to rise dizzily. No sector of industry was excluded from the general growth ... Finally, after years of stinting and privation, the Italians discovered a certain well-being.[2]

Then why was there, after the war, "the impetuous resumption of emigration, [especially] from southern Italy, which, after 1956, caused a veritable depopulation of many municipalities"?[3]

Postwar Canada had plenty of attractions for Italian and other immigrants. By 1945 it had attained international stature and even with a relatively small population had reached the number three position in industrial production and number four position in strength of its armed forces.

On the other hand, postwar Italy held little promise for many Italians. In the words of Attilio Matassa (1897–1980), a decorated Great War veteran and one of the first post–Second World War Italian immigrants to Leamington, "*Era un'Italia dopo la guerra un pò a pezzi*" (It was an Italy after the war a bit in shambles) – This is the reason we emigrated.

In 1943–44, Attilio, his wife, and seven children, caught between the retreating Germans and the advancing Allied Armies in the Cassino area, southeast of Rome (Casalattico), were rounded up by the Germans, and all were sent for seven months to a German concentration camp in Cesano (north of Rome), which resulted in the illness and death of their eighteen-month-old child. Once back in their destroyed, deserted town, the loss of everything they owned, followed by two years of "*miseria nera*" (utter poverty), convinced them that the only choice left was to be sponsored by Attilio's uncles Joe and Giulio, in Leamington and Detroit respectively, and go to Canada. Matassa preferred to cut short what he called "*una storia molto dolorosa ... per i guai dell'Italia*" (a story filled with much sorrow ... due to Italy's troubles), but similar stories were told again and again by those who came to Leamington immediately after the war, be they from Lazio, Molise, or Sicily.

"Italy's troubles" had begun long before the war, which for many Italians was just the culmination of twenty-one years of Fascist arrogance. Italy's unpreparedness for the Second World War was much worse than for the First; and the Second, while devastating and nationally traumatic, was again disastrous for the poor and the peasants. While their sons were sent unequipped to be massacred on all fronts, from Greece (late 1940) to Russia (early 1943) or Africa (as indicated also by several Leamington Italians who had fought on many fronts), the *figli di papà*, the pampered children of the rich, evaded conscription, just as their privileged fathers, including the Fascist *gerarchi* (bosses), resorted to the black market to evade the regulations rationing foodstuffs and essential goods. In fact others wrote, "The war meant nothing to the Italian peasants. Started by a distant tyrant in Rome, continued ... by foreigners from over the mountains and the seas, this war was no different from all the others inflicted on them over the centuries. Of this war, like all the others, the peasants knew only one thing: whoever won, whoever profited, they would suffer."[4]

The year 1943, which also began the Matassas' "very sorrowful story," was like 1919, one of those "years in the history of modern Italy of ... deep and general social and political crisis and revolutionary ferment." The second half of 1943 particularly was a period of destruction, confusion, and division, due also to the unprecedented "foolishness of the Italian ruling class." After the defeat in North Africa (May 1943) and the invasion of Sicily (10 July), the occupation of southern Italy by the Allied Armies was quick: by 22 July, half of Sicily was occupied; Trapani and Palermo fell a day or so before the coup against Mussolini (24/25 July) – "virtually a revolution" against Fascism that the euphoric Italians thought would soon end the war and the dictatorship. Mussolini was forced to resign, and Marshal Pietro Badoglio declared the Fascist Party dissolved (28 July) and opened negotiations for an armistice. But during "August 1943 ... Allied air-raids rained tons of bombs on Italy's towns every day." By 2 September, after the fall of Messina (18 August), the Allies had crossed into Calabria (southern tip of Italy), and a month later, after the Salerno landing (9 September), they had entered Naples (1 October) and were advancing slowly northward along the peninsula toward Rome. But "winter weather, the mountainous countryside, and stubborn German resistance stopped the Allied advance on a line south of Cassino."[5]

The announcement on 8 September of the Italian "unconditional surrender" to the Allies was followed by disbandment and chaos among Italians, the flight from Rome of the king and premier of Italy (9 September), the German rescue of Mussolini (12 September), and the pouring of German divisions into Italy to occupy strategic points and leading cities, including Rome. Italy, left without a government, was split in two, each area with a puppet government of an army of occupation: Allies and Badoglio in the South, the Nazi-Fascists and Mussolini in the North. It was a tense, tragic situation for Italians, especially for those around the German defence lines: the "Gustav Line" (Garigliano, Rapido, and Sangro Rivers – by way of Monte Cassino) held until the liberation of Rome (4 June 1944); and the "Gothic Line" (Leghorn, Ancona/Viareggio, and Rimini) held until "Liberation Day" (25 April 1945).

All of Italy, during this same period (1943–45), experienced "the horrors and miseries of a civil war." The Resistance fighters, in spite of Allied objections, engaged in a "war of liberation" of their own against the Germans and the Italian Fascists. The results included sabotage, demolition, and frequent acts of cruelty by all sides in reprisals, manhunts, torture, executions, deportations of Italians to Germany, and massacres of partisans and civilians.

Unlike the First, the Second World War involved the populations of the Italian South directly and fully. The Allied invasion of Italy had started from Sicily (the first foreign conquest of Rome from the south since the time of the Byzantine general Belisarius in CE 536). Cities, towns, and villages on the coast and in the mountains from Trapani and Palermo to Villa Canale, Isernia, and Cassino were subjected to bombing from both the Allies and the Germans, sometimes reducing them to piles of rubble and the countrysides to deserts of mud: the fields and farms overrun by troops and vehicles and tanks were turned into cement-like surfaces, when they were not minefields or thoroughly sown with booby traps. Especially in the general chaos and anarchy following the September 1943 Italian surrender, the Italian army ceased to exist: some soldiers joined the Resistance fighters or the Allies, others were taken prisoner, sent to concentration camps or dispersed without trace, and many were massacred by the Germans. The Italian population – "no longer an enemy, but not yet an ally" – was distrusted by the conquering Allies and hated by the retreating former allies, the Germans.

After the taking of Naples, and in spite of the costly beachhead at Anzio (22 January 1944), the Allied advance to Rome was blocked for months in the "murderous battle" fought in the rugged mountains south of Rome: first on the German line of defence along the Volturno and Biferno Rivers (Campania and Abruzzo-Molise regions), and then on the "Gustav Line" (the place of "the most painful defeat that the Americans suffered in the war in Europe") to the Sangro River on the Adriatic side (Lazio, Campania, and Abruzzo-Molise regions). The trenches and pillboxes along the lines of defence were usually built by Italian labourers hired "for food or tobacco" or "just rounded … up at the point of a gun" from the surrounding areas. Attilio Matassa had been among the 200 men taken from the concentration camp at Cesano to dig the trenches along these lines of defence near Cassino.

"The Italian campaign turned into a long and disheartening stalemate" – a battle of attrition that resulted in destruction and death along the Gustav Line, especially in the "long, fierce, bloody battle of Cassino." The "focal point of this line of defense was the hill on which stood the abbey" of Monte Cassino itself. The fourteen-centuries-old centre of monastic and artistic life, "one of the most sacred of Christian sites" that many believed would never be bombed, became the sanctuary for hundreds of people from the town of Cassino or from hamlets or farms in the neighbouring valley. But after months of deadlock, the abbey was first battered daily by German and Allied artillery for two weeks in February 1944, then for three days, 15–17 February, the Allies dropped tons and tons of bombs on it: the ancient Benedictine abbey – "falsely described as a German fortress" – was totally destroyed. It was perhaps the only way for the Allies to "strike at" what Churchill called "the great political and psychological prize of Rome."[6]

That "prize" was extremely costly for Joe Colasanti, whose "father died ten feet away from him ... when many bombs" fell everywhere, and "German soldiers were around just like leaves." It was a tragic, frightening experience for the family, forced also to abandon their town of Ceprano. In September 1948 when he arrived in Canada, Joe was only sixteen and had never before seen his uncle Alex Colasanti, his sponsor, but had already planned to stay. Anna Barraco, one of the ten Barraco brothers and sisters related to Vito Peralta who, except for one, immigrated to Canada in 1950 and after, found it difficult to speak about the suffering of her brother Pietro, a prisoner of war in Germany for seven months, but not about her state of terror before and during the Allied landing in Sicily: "bombing and fires at Palermo, on the seacoast, on the boats; fires and trouble near San Vito Lo Capo [Trapani], evacuations of cities, and people dying everywhere." Vittorio (Gino) Guerrieri (1949) from the Cassino area of Lazio (Patrica), had spent eight years in the army and the Italian wars from 1934 to 1942.

Many of the men, women, and children from the Villa Canale–Agnone area, who came to Canada in the years immediately after the war, also had direct experiences with the world conflict and its effects. Some of the men had served on many fronts: in Greece, Albania, Yugoslavia, and Germany, like Mike DiMenna (1949) – for eight years in addition to time in the hospital with a frozen foot; in Italy, Sardinia, and Tripolitania from 1935 to 1945, as in the case of Nick Mastronardi (1950); and from Ethiopia (1935–38) to Bari (1939–43) like Ercole Mastronardi, who came to Canada in 1949 "on the same boat that took him to Ethiopia in 1935."

While the men were away fighting the war or being taken prisoner, the Villa Canale women and children became helpless victims of the war. They lived with constant fear after 1943 when "airplane bombings ... destroyed some towns," remembered the then twenty-year-old Carmela (Mastronardi) DiMenna (1954); and the "Germans caused disaster," according to Bambina (Ingratta) DiMenna (1951), whose husband Pacifico (1949), "at war for fourteen–fifteen months ... walked two days and two nights to go home from Campobasso"; and when the "Germans came to Villa Canale in 1943," said the then seventeen-year-old Rachelina DiMenna (Alfino's wife, 1952/53), they were "extremely frightened ... Though they [the Germans] didn't damage the house, they took everything." "We had to hide our belongings," said Irene (DiMenna) Mastronardi (1951), whose husband Francesco (1949) also served through the war. "We were constantly running and hiding from the Germans," as well as from "the bombs and the shrapnel," recalled Joseph Mastronardi (Agnone, 1949), then nine or ten years old.[7]

The children were generally frightened and confused: Austin Pannunzio (1951), five years old in 1943–44, had only bits of memories, but quite vivid: "terrified by the Germans," the "Americans ... good to him," his "father ... always away at war." In fact, their father Henry (1948), clarified Austin's elder brother Frank, "had been drafted, sent to Greece and then prisoner in Germany for two years." Frank Pannunzio, who left Italy "by himself" in 1949 when he was sixteen, while remembering similar experiences during the war, pointed out that "right after the war ... the Christian Democrats were in power," and "the situation was not very stable [with] clothing and food rationed." And he knew then that "to better himself" he had to join "his relatives in Canada," that Canada was "much better than Italy ... Canada was a young country."

POST-FASCIST ITALY

Ercole Mastronardi, who had lost his first-born son while he was in Ethiopia, and many years of his life serving Italy, still thought that "Mussolini was a good man. But," he reflectively added, "he made a big mistake." Alluding to Mussolini's (15 September 1943) establishment of a "Republican Fascist Party" (whose total subordination to Nazi Germany initiated "the tragic and bloody epilogue of the Fascist parabola,"[8] as well as "Italy's troubles" of 1943–45), Ercole Mastronardi emphasized that "his mistake was letting the Germans into Italy." But Mastronardi referred also to other "mistakes" of Fascist Italy that lived on after Mussolini; one reason for his leaving Italy in 1949 was his anger at the "Amministrazione," the arrogant bureaucratic ruling class, the surviving Fascist system. According to Mastronardi, "Mussolini's law still ruled in Italy in 1949."

From the April 1945 "Liberation Day" to the April 1948 elections, which for Italy marked the end of the second postwar period (following the 1946 referendum abolishing the monarchy and the 1948 Constitution), the Italians aimed to quickly rebuild the "new nation." But its foundations, laid upon the ruins of the war, also became the basis of discontent, disruption, and emigration. Many Italians, preferring to leave the nightmare behind and start living again in "peace and quiet," "refused to take a straight look at the reality of Italy, with its old evils, its inadequacies and injustices." They resented and objected, for example, to Roberto Rossellini's neo-realist films (*Rome Open City, Paisà*) depicting not only the spirit of the Italian resistance but also Italy's miseries:

the spreading prostitution, unemployment (over two million people in 1948), inflation, the black market. They were mostly "unaware of the political implications of their attitude" that, in fact, opened the way to a "political movement with markedly reactionary characteristics" (*qualunquismo*). Consequently, the forces of conservatism and privilege, just like after the First World War, "managed to find consensus and mass basis that allowed them to retain their dominance."[9]

Moreover, the "increasing intensity of the Cold War" caused the campaign in the 18 April 1948 elections to degenerate into dramatic choices: freedom or communism, America or Russia; or a crusade: "Christ versus anti-Christ," "Rome versus Moscow," "exploiters versus the exploited." With American pressure, promises (the Marshall Plan), and parcels (containing not only food and clothing but also clear election messages) that almost every southern Italian family received from their Italian-American relatives, the only choice for Italians was "to vote ... for the party trusted by America" or the "choice of civilization." Following the overwhelming victory of the Christian Democratic Party and the establishment of its hegemony, the new Constitution's "plan of a republic 'based on labour,' as its first article declared, and with wide possibilities for social demands, seemed already to have been left behind by the course of events. The unity of the resistance ... had been swept away by the Cold War," and doomed with it were also the goals of the Committee of National Liberation: mainly the workers' and peasants' claims.[10]

In the South of Italy, the effects of the conflict, the fall of Fascism, the peasants' participation in the political struggle, and the decisive role played by the leftist parties (Socialist, Communist) had shaken the old political system based on privilege, favouritism, and the formula of political reversal (transformism) that had kept Italy split since unification. The debate on the "Southern Question," interrupted by the advent of Fascism, revitalized a central interest in restoration of the democratic state, in light also of the misery and devastation caused by the war, the renewed separatist movement in Sicily (and Sardinia), and the new wave of emigration, which, after 1956, was depopulating entire southern municipalities. The programs of renewal outlined between 1945 and 1950, which reflected the Resistance ideals (and partly Antonio Gramsci's ideas of the common goals of workers and peasants), slowly lost support with the removal from the national government of the two Marxist parties (May 1947). In fact, because of the Cold War, even the left-wing "Christian Democrats were eased out of positions of influence by 1949."[11] And after 1950 there was a partial return, among the pro-peasant forces, to the "traditional ultra-conservatism" (*immobilismo*).

Piecemeal implementation in the 1950s of the program in favour of southern industrialization and agrarian reforms brought only limited results: the almost 420,000 hectares expropriated and assigned to poor peasants, along with some technical assistance and credit, did not end the entrenchment of land monopoly and the antiquated, anachronistic land contracts and social relations. By the end of the decade, most of the agricultural lands were still in the hands of absentee landowners; the land was not worked by small proprietors, but prevalently by non-landowning peasants (*affittuari* – tenant farmers; *mezzadri* – sharecroppers; *coloni* – husbandmen), along with a large number of "associates" and hired workers (*compartecipanti, salariati, braccianti*). The cry and the struggle continued to be for *"la terra a chi la lavora"* (land for those who work it).

The investments and incentives, particularly through the Cassa per il Mezzogiorno (South Italy Investment Fund, 1950), failed to set in motion a "mechanism of development" for a global renewal of the South.[12] The policies were different in quantity but not in quality: in spite of visible improvement, the late 1950s statistics on per capita and global income, unemployment, and emigration (of such proportions as to threaten every hope of southern renewal) confirmed the inadequacy of the program, the failure of the development of autonomous productive forces in the South. *The Italian Economy from 1861 to 1961* included a study by Pasquale Saraceno entitled "The Failure of Italian Economic Unification One Hundred Years after Political Unification."[13]

Italy's 1950s "economic miracle" was only a "half miracle." Just like the first industrial boom in the 1880s, it coincided with an agricultural crisis and a new wave of Italian emigration, of which it was partly the cause. Just as in the first boom, it was the privileged classes, the northern industrialists, and the southern big landowners, or what Gramsci called "the agricultural-industrial bloc of the Italian dominant classes," that mostly benefited from the postwar political choices and stability, the economic policies and growth: the 1947 "credit squeeze" stemmed inflation and saved the lira, but "production ... stood still, and unemployment rose to the terrifying figure of 2 million." The peasant struggles in the South were sometimes marked by bloodshed: in 1947, when the bandit Salvatore Giuliano massacred workers gathered to celebrate May First at Portella della Ginestra (Sicily), Giuliano, the outlaw and sort of folk hero, was in the pay of the big landowners.[14] The only welcome gifts the poor had in those hard times were the American parcels of food and clothing. The only other choice was emigration.[15]

The massive "exodus ... of workers from the countryside that from 1951 to 1978 decreased the agricultural population from 8.6 million to a little over 3 million,"[16] depopulated inland villages and areas to such an extent, at times, as to make their revival practically impossible. Especially after the 1956–67 "sudden industrial expansion ... millions of peasants left the countryside to look for work in the cities of the industrial north." That large-scale internal migration may, indeed, have been "the greatest mixing of population" since Italian unification (1861); but it also "made more acute the crisis of [Italian] agriculture" and the North-South split: Italy's "double face [had] become even more marked."

In the late 1960s, at least according to Procacci, Italy manifested certain basic traits that were not unlike those presented in Antonio Labriola's 1896 description of the country: "A modern state in an almost exclusively agricultural society creates a universal sense of unease; that is, it creates a general awareness of the incongruity of the whole, and of every part." Postwar Italy may not have been the Italy of the "two worlds" that Labriola spoke of in the late nineteenth century ("on one side the Germanic-Roman cycle, on the other the Byzantine-Islamic world"). After all, by the 1960s Italy had "managed finally to break the chains of backwardness in which she was held for centuries," and join "the small number of industrially advanced countries." Nevertheless, it was still an Italy that left "many Italians perplexed and sceptical," for the simple reason that the "economic miracle [brought] no parallel social progress."[17]

In other words, the "old Italian incongruity" had "by no means disappeared, but merely been reproduced at a higher level. Italy [was] still the country ... where the rich [were] really rich and the poor really poor"; and that incongruity, even in the late 1960s, continued to generate "a universal unease, and [those] same Italians who [had] benefited from the economic miracle [did] not believe in their prosperity, but confine[d] themselves to enjoying it as noisily and unthinkingly as they [could], while it [lasted]." In the 1970s it also took the form of terrorism of the left and of the right, resulting in the kidnapping and "execution" of Aldo Moro (1978). That "universal unease" continued to influence Italians, albeit in smaller numbers, to emigrate in the 1960s and 1970s.[18]

POSTWAR MOLISE

The Italian "incongruity of the whole, and of every part" becomes more apparent in considering an area like Molise. On the whole, Abruzzo-Molise was not a fortunate beneficiary of the South Italy Investment Fund, as indicated in its ten-year balance sheet (end of the 1950s). Between 1951 and 1959, the average rate of growth of the global income of the South had not only been lower than that of the North but also less than half the figure aimed for at the start of the program. The percentage of investments in the South had also fallen from 24 in 1951 to 20.5 in 1959, and their distribution had been quite uneven: two-thirds of the investments had been absorbed by two regions – Sicily (42.4 per cent) and Campania (23.6 per cent). In fact, about 39 per cent of the total had been concentrated in two cities: Siracusa (Syracuse, Sicily, 21.3 per cent) and Naples (Campania, 17 per cent). Sardinia held third place with less than 10 per cent, and Lazio, fourth with 7.6 per cent. The remaining 16.5 per cent had been distributed among the other four regions as well as the island of Elba and the southernmost province of Le Marche (Ascoli Piceno).

Abruzzo-Molise during the period had received 6.6 per cent (or 24.6 billion lire) of the total investment: less than the amount invested in the area of southern Lazio, Latina, and Frosinone (*"Ciociaria,"* on the Molise border), which between 1947 and 1956 had been designated part of the *Mezzogiorno* to allow them to benefit from the laws favouring South Italy. Such classification, further extended to include some municipalities around Rome and part of Rome itself, worked totally against the South: its effects were viewed as "deadly" to the southern policies, since the extension favoured the concentration of industrial projects in the areas nearer to the capital.[19]

In 1966, according to statistics, Molise was still considered what it had been for centuries: a mostly underdeveloped, isolated area; and in 1983 it was still characterized as a "subsidized region."[20] Its share of the Abruzzo-Molise 1950s government funds had been limited; and later they hardly reached their destination mainly because of the "excessively intricate [and] sieve-like" distribution channels and much waste.[21] Besides, many *Abruzzesi* considered "Molise a subdivision of Abruzzi and not a separate region."[22] After 1963, when it split from Abruzzo to become the twentieth region of Italy, with Campobasso as its capital and only province, the renewal programs tended to favour Lower Molise. Upper Molise, the ten-municipality *Comunità Montana* (mountain community) with Agnone as centre, tended to be, marked by very slow progress, if not almost forgotten; and it continued even after 1970 when Isernia became its second province. Its birth, which the Agnone area supported, brought so few advantages to Upper Molise, deplored a 1987 article, "as to make one wish for reannexation to Abruzzo." Throughout the 1980s the "Upper Molise" newspaper repeatedly denounced the bureaucratic delays, indecision, and lack of vision at all levels of the administration, bitterly wondering at times whether the politicians preferred that they all desert the Agnone area.[23]

In general, Molise's isolation from the rest of Italy was due chiefly to its prevalently inland position: its territory is mainly mountainous and outside the main north-south commercial routes. Its physical features tended to encourage its neglect and "desertion" rather than investments for economic and social progress: very limited plain (two-thirds clayey mountains, one-third hills); a continental climate (rain, wind, ice, snow: on 10 March 1988, the Agnone area reported snow from over 1 to over 1.5 metres deep); frequent earthquakes and landslides; inadequate, endlessly winding roads (due to fragmentation of mountain masses), making the donkey, estimated at 20,000 head in 1966, the common means of hinterland transport; no mineral deposits and, at least in 1966, scarce hydroelectric power (the water of its main river, the Biferno, was partly diverted by a tunnel from the Adriatic to the Tyrrhenian side to supply the aqueducts of Naples); and in 1986 a population of 334,195 in an area of 4,438 square kilometres, one of the lowest density rates in Italy (seventy-five persons per square kilometre), with heavy depopulation of mountain villages and countryside.

Nevertheless, Molise also had favourable characteristics, some economic resources that could have served as a basis for improvement, renewal, and job creation: agriculture, though "diligently practised," remained poor because of lack of mechanical and technical assistance; and yet its wheat production (in 1966) surpassed that of Sardinia and equalled Calabria's; widely grown were cereals, vegetables (especially onions and tomatoes), and melons; and quite developed were also viticulture (table wines) and olive growing (olive oil), as well as sheep raising (in its ample pasturelands), to which was tied cheese production. There had been some small-scale manufacturing activity for centuries: scissors and knives (Frosolone); bobbin lace – *merletti al tombolo* (Isernia); copper utensils; and the world-famous bell foundries (Agnone); as well as gold crafts. By 1966 there were also some nascent industries (food, chemicals, textiles, cement, furniture) but located primarily in its main city, Campobasso. Tourism development had possibilities, not only at the Adriatic Sea resort at Termoli, but also in Capracotta, the highest village in the Apennines, for winter sports and summer recreation.[24] On the whole, however, its potential and the few initiatives in the 1960s offered only hopes (and partly so, even in the 1980s, in spite of talks and plans for an industrial park or "service technopolis").[25] The only highly noticeable phenomenon in the mid-sixties was the "frightening exodus": the emigration and movement to the cities, which enhanced the cycle of depopulation, with decreasing interest in renewal projects for the area and further emigration of young people.[26]

The southern investment distribution statistics for the 1950s are conversely reflected in the number and area of origin (regions and towns) of the Leamington immigrants in that decade and the entire period (1940s–70s): Molise and Villa Canale (Isernia) registered the highest number of entries of the three main regions and towns respectively. The fact that Agnone in the 1960s surpassed Villa Canale, if only by one, confirms the rule: the lower the regional investment, the higher the rate of emigration. The population of Villa Canale decreased from 1,160 in 1939–45 to 752 in 1961 and to about 300 in 1985,[27] while that of the municipality of Agnone, which includes Villa Canale, decreased from about 8,187 in 1961 to 6,170 in 1988.[28]

Villa Canale was already deemed "too small" and a "depressed area" when Floyd Cacciavillani left it for Canada in June 1948: "It couldn't support all the people who lived there ... There had to be people going out and bringing the money back or people going out and staying out ... It's been the history of the town to emigrate; God knows since when, maybe since the time of my great grandfather ... Canada, United States, France, Germany, South America ... anywhere." Quite a few Leamington Italians (particularly the DiMennas, Mastronardis, and Ingrattas) mentioned brothers, sisters, even parents who had emigrated to Argentina. Cacciavillani himself, who left Italy at the age of eighteen, "wanted to go someplace" where he could "put it together," and he knew from his uncle, and sponsor, Domenic Pannunzio (1923), as well as from school, that "Canada was large and had rich resources, many opportunities," and he "looked forward to the challenge."

REASONS FOR EMIGRATING (1948–1970S)

In general, the thirty or so men who came in the late 1940s, as well as the majority who arrived in the 1950s, gave reasons that reflected the economic, political, and socio-psychological climate of postwar Italy as a whole and of their particular area: initially the devastation and disorder during the war, then the confusion, the misery, "*povertà*," and dissatisfaction during the "reconstruction" period (from the betrayal of the 1948 elections' "*impegno d'onore*," the "commitment of honour" toward the South, to its "economic regression" after 1949; from the absence of an effective global industrialization and agricultural reform strategy in the 1950s to the increasing North-South disparity, as well as the marked class distinction and bureaucracy). In addition, there were ills caused by the "economic miracle" itself: that pervasive "universal unease," that "incongruity," those contradictions in Italian life, that living "unthinkingly" and beyond their means, along with the ills of industrialization in the late 1960s.[29] Some of the Italian ills that Procacci referred to in his

History were noticed by Cacciavillani himself during his visit to Italy at the end of the same decade: "a funny way of life in Italy today; they live too much expensively and can't afford it, and ... the bureaucracy and nonsense."

Political discontent, though not widespread, was often expressed and sometimes bitterly: Mussolini was spoken of with some admiration, even by those who were in the war, but he was generally blamed for that war: "Wartime was terrible ... Mussolini ruined Italy." With respect to postwar Italy, the harshest criticism came from Gus Mastronardi, who came in 1953 at forty-nine years of age, with no war experience but eighteen months of military service: "If Italy were good ... I would not have come to Canada ... The government in Italy was too selfish ... didn't help anyone; people dying of hunger in Italy didn't get any help from the Italian government." Even when he went back in 1978, though he found "Italy changed 100 percent," he saw "people ... still hungry ... no one wants to work ... Everyone that was good took off ... emigrated to other countries."

Although the war damages in the Isernia-Agnone areas were mentioned, what emerged as a fundamental reason for leaving Upper Molise (Villa Canale–Agnone) was the unproductivity of the land: "the poor ... split-up pieces of land, *molto lavoro e sacrificio e poco profitto*" (hard work, many sacrifices, and little profit). In 1948, when Frank Mastronardi (Domenic Pannunzio's nephew) left, "many people in Villa Canale wanted to come to Canada" mainly for that reason, and "*se potevano venire venivano tutti*" (if they could have, the whole town would have left) with him. In Villa Canale, said David Mastronardi (1953), life was like this: "You worked, walked for an hour to work; you had a donkey, some animals, a big stone house and some farmland ... not too much, so I decided to come to Canada."

Those who came later did admit that Italy was "not bad," "a little better," and they themselves "were faring quite well." But they all believed and often heard from their relatives already in "America" that they could find better fortunes, that Canada was "the land of opportunity"; and some came "expecting a paradise," a place where "one worked little and made a lot of money." In general, they felt that they had "a better chance for *progresso*" (progress) in the land that had also won the war.

The lure of America had not died. The "Italian myth of America" had become even stronger among many who had witnessed the power and wealth of the *Americani* during the war and occupation; or among those who had travelled beyond their mountain villages. Since the 1930s America had been a "gigantic stage" or a "gigantic screen" for many

Italian writers. Their "long-cherished vision of an America of the mind" (which was partly also shared by earlier emigrants) had been particularly reinforced by American films, much admired even by Mussolini's son Vittorio. In 1940 alone, sixty-three Hollywood films, or 34 per cent of the total imports, entered Italy, and their distribution increased immensely after the war (296 in 1946; 515 in 1948; 406 in 1949). By then, in spite of "heroic attempts to declare that the myth was gone forever, what had [earlier] affected a few anti-fascist intellectuals had begun to spread among a more mysterious, less articulate entity, the so-called popular culture, exposed to a large amount of no longer prohibited American books (in translation) and dubbed American films, as well as American music, food, clothes, and ways of life."

The "more than 5,000 American films ... circulating on [the Italian] screen between 1945 and 1953" greatly contributed to the Italian search for some aspects of the "American dream" in the postwar period.[30] Entire families, however poor or isolated, had had a chance to see some of them in local cinemas or in the village church halls. Many Italian school-age children in that postwar period dreamed of one day seeing in reality the "Far West," of being part of that vision of America they had become so familiar with, not only through films but also from such widely read and collected comic books as *Il piccolo sceriffo* (the young sheriff) of Prairie Town, and *Pecos Bill*. On reaching Canada in 1952, one person was rather "upset on seeing all the cities" instead of "cowboy land."[31]

CANADA: LAND OF OPPORTUNITY
FROM ATLANTIC TO PACIFIC

Canada itself, after 1950, became increasingly known as a land of opportunity in its own right. Canadian forces had also been part of the Allied Army that invaded Sicily in July 1943: they too, like the Americans, had been in a sense "liberators." The parcels that Italians received in those difficult postwar years had partly originated from Canada, manifesting its abundance, especially if accompanied by the increasingly common pictures of relatives and friends in bright kitchens, in front of electric stoves or open brimming refrigerators. Canada itself contributed to the image in the 1950s with a fully illustrated 125-page booklet, including a foldout map of Canada and charts showing its natural resources and vital statistics, written all in Italian and distributed to immigrants or prospective immigrants. The title, on a green cover showing Canada on the globe, was IL CANADA: *dall'Atlantico al Pacifico*.[32]

Any Italian, living in any village or city with the piles of rubble and ruins of the war still around years after, could not but be spellbound by such a "paradise on earth" stretching *dall'Atlantico al Pacifico* (from the Atlantic to the Pacific). The pictures alone were sufficient: from the fertile valleys of British Columbia to Newfoundland's picturesque Pouch Cove; from a neat Ottawa River valley farm to the plentiful potato crops of the New Brunswick–St John River valley; and all that just in the first five pages! And each of the following pages showed increasingly captivating scenes: from the cattle roundup in the Alberta Milk River valley and Saskatchewan wheat fields to the Welland Canal locks and the "Canadian steel capital," Hamilton; from the Arctic "steppes" and the Yukon River to the aerial view of Toronto's "sky-scrapers" and Winnipeg's "world's largest private railway station"; from the gold mines of the Northwest Territories and the orchards of Ontario to the "new buildings" of the University of Montreal and the busy port of Halifax; and children were everywhere, frequently portrayed at school or at play. Nor excluded were the commonplace images of Canada that especially appealed to Europeans in general: the mountains and the forests, the "Indians," the "Eskimos" and the cowboys, the totem poles and the Mounties; nor omitted were those that might awaken Italian pride: Garibaldi Park in British Columbia, Signal Hill in St John's, Newfoundland, where Marconi received the first transoceanic radio signal.

If one could and wished to read, the opening paragraph of the booklet began, "Il Canada è un territorio vastissimo. È il paese più grande dell'Emisfero Occidentale, il terzo, per estensione, in tutto il mondo [Canada is an extremely vast territory. It is the largest country in the Western Hemisphere, the third largest in size in the world.]" How could Canada not become the favourite destination of Italian emigration, especially from the South, in the postwar decades! Thus, Franc Sturino states in *The Canadian Encyclopedia*, "Over 75% of Italian immigrants to Canada have come from southern Italy, especially from the regions of Abruzzi-Molise and Calabria, and about three-quarters of these immigrants were small-scale farmers or peasants."

SPONSORSHIP AND FARM WORK

The pattern of growth of the Leamington Italian community, during the three decades following the Second World War, reflected the national immigration trends. In the Leamington area, almost all Italian immigrants originated from southern Italy: almost half from Abruzzo-Molise (more precisely, especially after 1963, from Molise); 35 per cent from Lazio; 13 per cent from Sicily; and the other regions (less Abruzzo, 2.07 per cent) make up a little over 2.5 per cent. Of the 434 family units interviewed that settled in the Leamington area, 417 or 96 per cent arrived during the period 1948–79. Fifty per cent of them arrived during the peak of the immigration wave in the 1950s, as indicated in settlement figures:

1 1948/49: 28 males (often representing family units), or 6.5 per cent of the total number of families;
2 1950s: 210 males, or 48.3 per cent of the total;
3 1960s: 143 males, or 32.9 per cent of the total;
4 1970s: 36 males, or 8.3 per cent of the total.

Growth of the Leamington community after the war was mainly the result of sponsored immigration, which, as illustrated by Sturino, reflected a pattern: "Men often arrived under one-year contracts to do hard physical labour similar to that of their earlier compatriots, though now the great majority came as permanent settlers, later sponsoring wives, children and other relatives. Family 'chain migration' from Italy was so extensive that in 1958 Italy surpassed Britain as a source for immigrants."[33]

The inhabitants of Upper Molise, particularly Villa Canale and Agnone, and those of the surrounding or bordering regions of Abruzzo and southern Lazio (Ceprano and other villages of hilly "*Ciociaria*"), as well as those of northwest Sicily (San Vito Lo Capo, Trapani), had additional incentives to choose Canada and southwest Ontario in particular: the well-established, pre–Second World War relatives and *paesani* who could facilitate emigration–immigration through their sponsorship, which after 1947 became a requirement: "Italians were permitted to come as next of kin or as farm hands. To come to work on the farms they had to secure a [contract] of employment from a Canadian farmer guaranteeing work for twelve months. Never was a more unrealistic Canadian immigration rule more favourably greeted by the Italians in Canada. Now they could free their relatives of the miseries of postwar life in Italy."[34]

Almost all the 1940s and 1950s entries referred to a farm work, agreement even though, according to Gino Pannunzio, "the immigrant was expected to work one year on the farm but there was no such thing as a contract." There might have been no formal written contract between the emigrant (who was still in Italy) and the sponsoring farmer, but there was, as has been documented, a duly notarized document signed by the armer in the presence of a notary public and two witnesses. A copy of such a document (sent by a Sudbury sponsoring farmer to A. Temelini, the writer's father, in 1950) bears the title "Guarantee for Expatriation." The paragraphs under it listed the sponsor's responsibilities toward the immigrant from the very moment he arrived, as explicitly outlined in one section: "The sponsor declares to be in the condition to receive the above-mentioned person, to employ him as farm worker on his farm, and he ensures that, upon his arrival in Canada, he will provide suitable work, food, lodging and all the necessary attention, protection and assistance, and he also binds himself to furnish, if the case arises, the necessary means for his return to his homeland."[35]

Moreover, the sponsoring farmer declared to have obtained, from the Canadian Department of Immigration and Citizenship, the proper documentation authorizing the entry into Canada of the person named herein, which had to be duly noted in the "Guarantee" and attached to it. In the same request, the farmer asked the Italian authorities to "issue the necessary passport and all the particular documents," so that the person mentioned could reach his destination in Canada. The document was then read and signed by all four present. A copy was sent to the nearest vice-consulate or consulate of Italy and then to Italy to the person being sponsored.

In the "Guarantee" quoted, there was no mention of the length of time the immigrant was required to spend on the farm; but it was clearly one year, as Pannunzio himself stated, and as others besides Spada and Sturino have documented. References to the one-year farm contract appeared also in at least two *Windsor Daily Star* articles in the 1950s: one relating to the Windsor Italians,[36] and another about some Italian immigrants, apparently not connected in any way to the Leamington group, working on Kent County farms (Tilbury East Township) in the fall of 1951. In featuring Antonio (Tony) Tomassetti (thirty-four years old, Chieti province, Abruzzo) and Salvatore Papia (twenty-one years old, Agrigento province, Sicily), then on the farm of Bernard and Maurice Quenneville, the reporter pointed out that "unlike some of his friends who came to Canada last April and have already left farms for the more lucrative construction fields around Sarnia and other points, Tony is going to fulfill his bond of staying with the land for a year at least"[37] (see also chapter 4, "The First Men from Lazio").

The immigrant was then well aware of the terms of the agreement, which was binding for both immigrant and farmer, even if it wasn't strictly observed. The farmer sometimes consented to the immigrant's leaving the farm even before the year was over. (In the case of the person whose "Guarantee" was cited, he came to Canada in 1950 and was released months before the end of the agreed term, but only after several requests and after securing work in his own occupation.)

The farm work immigration rule, for the twenty or so pre-war Italian men or families in the Leamington area, became a convenient means to get relatives into the country and to grow tenfold by the end of the 1950s. Farm ownership (or in the case of Peralta, his "managerial" position in a small business and his connection with the farmers) offered a solid guarantee for sponsorship, enabling them also to establish good rapport with the immigration officials. Relationship, the other requirement for sponsorship, was no problem: the endogamous practices in the area of origin and in the community itself, particularly among the Molise families but also with those of the nearby Lazio, resulted in complex ties, especially among the Pannunzio, Ingratta, Mastronardi, and DiMenna families, but also through other intermarriages with and among the Moauros, Magris, and Cervinis. Frequently, the family links were multiple and quite confusing when husband and wife (though not related or distant relatives before marrying) had similar surnames. Brothers of one family often married sisters of another family; and in one case (DiMennas), the son married the sister of his father's second wife. In the long run, such intertwining enabled them to sponsor entire clans: first, the members of the immediate families who then, independently and/or in cooperation with their sponsors, continued and expanded the sponsorship network to include even distant relatives.

The groups leading the sponsorship chain in 1948/49 had mostly the same surnames as the pioneers and represented the three main areas of origin: Pannunzio, Mastronardi, DiMenna, Magri (Abruzzo-Molise); Colasanti, Matassa (Lazio); Peralta (Sicily, 1949). Though the names Ingratta, Moauro, and Cervini did not appear among the 1948 entries, some of them were related to those pioneers also: a Pannunzio was a grandson of Henry Ingratta's (1925), a nephew of the Pannunzio pioneers, Domenic (1923) and Joe (1925), as well as related to the Cervinis (Domenic's daughter had married a son of Tony Cervini, 1927) and to the Moauros (a son of John Ingratta, 1923, Henry's cousin, had married a daughter of Angelo Moauro, 1923). Floyd Cacciavillani, among the June 1948 entries from Villa Canale, who in confirmation of the rules remembered that the "only way one could come out in those days [was] by somebody sponsoring you, and actually showing some kind of relationship," was himself sponsored by Domenic Pannunzio whose wife's niece was Floyd's mother. Floyd, with the help of the Pannunzios, immediately began his own sponsorship line and "reunited the whole family within three years" in Leamington. Such was the pattern that continued through the rest of the 1940s and in the following decades.

RELATIONSHIP AND "QUEST FOR SPONSORS"

All thirty or so 1948/49 entries (nearly fifty, including the year 1950) were sponsored by the pioneers or through them; the only exceptions were the Leone and Mastromatteo families (1949), as well as Father Ugo Rossi (1948) who did not go to Leamington until the 1960s. All the 1949 entries from Agnone and Villa Canale, always the largest contingent, were related to the pioneering families, and most had their patronymic names (DiMenna, Ingratta, Mastronardi, Pannunzio). The DiCioccos (Agnone), the only family besides the Cacciavillanis (Villa Canale) not showing the pioneers' surnames, were related to Angelo Moauro's wife (Sabelli family); similarly, the first of the Barracos (Jim) and of the Maniacis (Salvatore) to arrive from San Vito Lo Capo, Sicily, in 1950 (in addition to Salvatore Peralta, Vito's son), were sponsored by their uncle Vito (although in Salvatore Maniaci's case, his father had been in Windsor since after the Depression, but had died before Salvatore's arrival).

The pattern was similar for the Lazio area, though some variations began to appear in the 1949 group. Some of the sponsored relatives had surnames similar to those of the early Leamington Italian families (Colasanti, Cervini); others were related through the mother's side of the family, such as the first of the Corpolongos, Umberto (Pastena), who was sponsored by one of the first families in the Leamington area, but not part of the community pioneers – the DeLellis family (uncle Joe and cousin Al).[38] At times, it seemed as if the family tree were closely reviewed in the hope of finding some relative in "America": the first of the Carnevales, Luigi (Pontecorvo), had an uncle (in Detroit since before the war) whose maternal grandfather was a brother of Alfonse DeLellis's grandfather. Luigi was thus able to emigrate through the intercession of his mother's brother and through the DeLellis's distant relationship and sponsorship.

Often the Leamington pioneers offered assistance in sponsoring their friends' relatives: Alex Colasanti, as a favour to a friend in the United States and an uncle of Augusto Carducci, found a farmer in Ruthven willing to sponsor Augusto, from the same town as Alex, Ceprano, also partly destroyed by the war; in the case of Vittorio (Gino) Guerrieri (Patrica), his wife had a sister in Canada whose husband knew Antonio Cervini who found Vittorio a sponsoring farmer in Ruthven. Later these men sponsored their families and settled in the Leamington area; but unlike the relatives of the pioneers, who for the most part went into farming, they pursued other employment (Heinz, fisheries), most likely because of the first unpleasant farming experience with strangers, often non-Italian.

Some of the late 1940s entries from other Italian regions, who had relatives in Canada or in the United States but not among the Italian farm owners in the Leamington area, fell into that category characterized by abuses that had crept into the immigration rule, or what Spada called "the quest for sponsors": "The Italians in Canada set about visiting nearby farmers to ask them if they would be kind enough to sign applications to allow Italians to come to Canada to work on their farms for twelve months. Of course, the farmers signed, and applied the law of *do ut des* [I give that you may give]. Who can blame them?" It was quite profitable for the farmers, since thousands of them "came [to Canada] by virtue of a request signed by farmers who never intended to give them work. A few tried to get work from their sponsors but were turned down. The whole procedure was a burden on relatives and friends. This incongruous situation was later modified. No longer did the Italians have to ask favors from the Canadian farmers."[39]

In 1949, such was the situation of Italo Baldassare, one of the first postwar immigrants to the Leamington area from Ortona (Chieti, Abruzzo): unable to join the police force after four and a half years in the army, in an "unnecessary but inevitable" war that, by German hands, "destroyed ... totally" his Adriatic coast hometown, Italo "wanted to get out of Italy because one could not survive; so [he] wrote to his uncle" (in Windsor since 1938/9, but earlier in Montreal with another uncle of his), and he "got a farmer in Leamington to sign the papers." But when Italo arrived, the farmer didn't need him, and because he couldn't work anywhere else, he had to live with his "uncle for about one year" until, made aware through an ad in the paper that "a farmer in Tecumseh needed workers," he worked there "for a month ... for sixty dollars ... including food and sleep," consisting of insufficient "leftovers" and a "barn." Nevertheless, Baldassare, who had come with "the intention to stay," after a few better jobs (first harvesting tobacco in Delhi for 300–400 dollars for forty days, then at the Ford factory and later in St Thomas as a bricklayer) was able to sponsor "his wife and two daughters ... within a year and a half."

Two 1949 entries as family units, the Leones (San Pietro Avellana, Molise) and the Mastromatteos (Puglia/Veneto), seemed in a category of their own: not only were they among the first postwar family groups, their migrating to Canada also seemed to indicate a lack of uniformity, or a certain flexibility in the implementation of the postwar Canadian immigration rules. Prior to and after emigration, the two families shared almost common characteristics, similar or analogous circumstances: level of education and socio-economic status better than average among the period's emigrants; occupation or work experience; no urgent need to leave Italy, except to seek a better future for the children; regret and adverse reaction to their decision from other members of the family; brothers in the United States but no relative in Canada, yet no impediment to their admissibility; extreme difficulties during the first months in Canada, and regrets of their own about the drastic change in lifestyles they had brought upon themselves.

Upon their arrival (early November 1949) via New York, Nick Mastromatteo (Peschici, Puglia), his wife Maria (Veneto region), and their four children were accompanied by one of Nick's brothers living in the United States (Detroit) to the farm they had found for them in Leamington: they immediately realized they had "made a mistake in coming to Canada ... [they] were better off in Italy." Even though Nick had been a prisoner of war in Germany for two years, he "found *l'America dura*" (America hard). In Italy he was a *carabiniere*, a police officer; in Canada he "had to work hard." Maria Mastromatteo's contrasting image of Canada and Italy, and of their torn state of mind, was one of the briefest and most poignant ever presented with respect to that time: "[In Italy] we both went to school ... here we learned to work on the farm; *l'inverno qua è lungo, a Padova è corto* [winter here is long, in Padua it is short]; enjoyment was limited; learning English was hard working at home, and then became harder to learn. I didn't like Canada when we first came, *ora non-mi è niente più* [now it has no more meaning for me]. I visit Italy ... but I have to come back ... the family is here ... The children are Canadian citizens."

Although the family "knew nothing of Canada" before emigrating and had no related guarantor in Canada, they stated that it "was easy to get passports." The initial shock and the accompanying sense of nostalgia and loneliness were revealed especially by the northern Italian woman, one of very few in the Leamington area. Nevertheless, she herself had sponsored one relative: "I called over ... just my brother." Nick, on the other hand, shortly after their arrival, thought that life was better in Canada than in southern Italy; and in 1950 he and his brother in Detroit sponsored their sister, her husband, and four children, the entire Stramacchia family from Peschici (Puglia).

Gabriele Leone, his wife, and two children, who similarly had no relatives or friends in Canada, had "no problem ... at all ... in leaving

Italy ... or in entering Canada ... no need of special documents or anything." Gabriele simply obtained his "discharge papers ... and went ...
fully uniformed ... to the Canadian Consulate ... It was not at all difficult." The reasons, according to Gabriele, were not just his uniform,
rank, and "twenty-year service in the Italian navy and police force," but
also his "grade-school diploma and navy technical training," as well as
his "machinery and office work experience." In spite of their relatively
"good ... life" in postwar Italy, his wife Rosina's initial unwillingness
to emigrate, and the grief their decision caused both their families, the
Leones also felt that it was the right thing to do, "not so much for themselves as for their children." Besides, they were going to join Gabriele's
brother in Pontiac, Michigan. Since their application to emigrate to the
United States had not yet been approved and immigration laws were
such, their son Reno recalled, "You could not make a direct approach to
the United States from Italy ... [they] came to Canada first ... [for] just
sort of a pit stop ... to the States."

Like the Mastromatteos, they quickly discovered how very unexpectedly hard it was to adjust to the type of work they had to do in order to
survive: Gabriele as a caretaker of farm animals, his wife as a domestic
servant, especially for the first month or so with the "sponsoring" family on a farm in Denfield (a village about ten kilometres northwest of
London); then "more hard work" in Ruthven on Ross Bruner's farm, a
place found through a well-known agency, through a long-established
system:

> My brother met a certain Meconi who brought us to Ruthven.[40] We
> worked there all summer with Ross Bruner ... At that time all spon-
> sored immigrants had to work on a farm for a year, and then one
> could go to work in a factory. There were about fifty of us Italians on
> that farm ... We worked with vegetables, picking tomatoes, onions,
> potatoes, and also peaches and apples ... Then I went to another
> farm until November. But during the winter I could not do anything.
> When I arrived with my family ... in Ruthven ... there was what they
> called *La Casa degli Immigranti* [The house of the immigrants].

That's where they lived for a while, always hoping to go to the
States. But Canada, the "pit stop ... to the States," became their permanent home: by the time their application to the United States was
approved (ten years later), the Leones were well settled in Leamington
and part of the community. After the initial shock and the first "hard
months," they were quite pleased to have found so many good friends

and "*gente tanto gentile*" (very kind people), in the neighbourhood and in the area, especially Alex and Emma Colasanti, "their closest family," the Pannunzios, as well as "a most helpful German family" and other non-Italian immigrants. With the help from their relatives and new friends, and above all with very hard work and sacrifices by both of them, in a relatively short time the Leones were able to achieve one of the first most cherished goals of all immigrants – *la casetta in Canadà* (the little house in Canada):

> In the morning we started to work at six o'clock. It would hurt us to have to wake up the baby, for we had to take her with us. My wife had to work and look after the baby. But the boss, Ross Bruner, was good and kind to my wife and baby ... He allowed my wife to work in another area so she could look after our three-year-old. That's how we managed all summer ... until September [1949]. In those days the pay was almost nothing ... but we saved ... my wife was good at that ... We always managed to put a little away, even though it was little. We got $25 a week: $5 went for the rent for each of the two rooms [in The House of the Immigrants] so we were left with $20 per week each. With these $20 and the help of my brother in the States who visited us often, bringing all kinds of things ... by the end of September ... I think ... we had $900 saved up and ... with $1,300 from my brother we bought a small house and we came to live here in Leamington. And never moved again.

By 1950, after going to school to learn English, Gabriele had found a permanent job with Heinz, where he worked all his life and "never had a layoff"; and by 1951, the Leones had begun their own sponsoring line with Donato Puglia (Teramo, Abruzzo) who in 1962 married their daughter Colomba. Donato in turn sponsored two of his brothers: Bernardo (1953), who sponsored his wife Gina D'Antonio (1955), and Domenico (1954); as well as two brothers-in-law: the husband of Gina's sister, Ada – Adamo Clerici (1959, Ascoli Piceno, Marche) – and his sister Serafina's husband, Tito Norcini (1963) who then sponsored Umberto Norcini (1966, Tofo S. Eleuterio, Teramo). Initially, some of them lived with the Leones, thus helping them avoid the usual tribulations. Like the Mastromatteos, the Leones also "had to change a lot": although "one can never forget the nation where one was born and grew up," and "*il pensiero è lì e qui* [one's thoughts are both there and here]," the Leones "never wished to return forever." They adjusted quite well and were satisfied with their new life.

Clearly, all entries during the early postwar period had relatives in the general area, whether in Canada or the United States, and all had to agree to work on farms in order to stay in Canada. But the advantages enjoyed by those sponsored by relatives who owned farms (especially the Molisani) were quite a contrast to the many and varied difficulties encountered by those whose relatives went on a "quest for sponsors." In spite of the help and kindness offered by the pioneer families, as the many tributes to them indicated, there were instances (one mentioned by Luigi Carnevale) of people returning to Italy shortly after their arrival.[41] But in general, people came to stay, some "looked forward to the challenge," and others even made false declarations about their farming occupation in Italy, as long as they could get away to Canada.

CHAIN MIGRATION

Such a stratagem was hardly needed by the immigrants from Villa Canale and Agnone: most were farmers in Upper Molise, and, as the year 1950 alone indicated, they continued to constitute the highest number of entries (eight out of eighteen recorded). The general patronymic connection with the pioneers from all three main areas was also high (ten out of eighteen): one of each of the Peraltas, Cervinis, DiMennas, Ingrattas; two Colasantis; and four Mastronardis. By this time, a name connected to the 1923 Molisani group had also appeared, the Capussis (with the 1949 arrival from Villa Canale of Tony Capussi, son of John killed in an accident in Chicago in 1926; or grandson of Colamario, the "Capussi of Chicago," who in late 1923 had gone to Quebec in his attempt to "rescue" his other son Geremia – John's brother – and his nephew Michele who, along with Tony DiMenna and Domenic Pannunzio, had been detained for deportation; see chapter 3, "The Eight Molisanis' Destination…; chapter 9, "The Significance of 'Farming'…"). The year's entries indicated also that the sponsorship chain was increasingly reaching into the second level, to nephews, nieces, brothers-in-law, cousins, with both similar and different surnames, such as the Maniacis and Barracos through Peralta (San Vito Lo Capo, Sicily); the Marcovecchios and the Sabellis (Agnone, Molise) through the DiMenna-Appugliese and the Moauro-Sabelli families respectively; while those sponsored in the previous two years began to sponsor their own family, such as Guerrieri, his son (Patrica, Lazio).

They each then began sponsoring other related families, and the latter still others: one Sicilian line, begun by the pioneer Peralta, first involved the Maniacis, who sponsored their relatives the Aiutos and the Agostas, who in turn sponsored other Aiutos and the Coppolas, and they went on with other families; another line involved the Milanas (Vito's wife's relatives). The same pattern occurred in the other major groups, especially among the *Molisani* from Villa Canale and Agnone throughout the 1950s, 1960s, and even 1970s, in spite of changes in the rules. "Starting in 1967," Sturino pointed out, "new immigration regulations based admissibility on universal criteria such as education; this 'points system' restricted the sponsorship of relatives, so that Italian immigration dropped significantly."[42] The general decrease was also reflected in the Leamington area after the 1950s. But there was no clear indication that sponsorship played a lesser role than education in the Leamington Italian immigration chain in the latter decades.

The occupation accounts for the 1960s and 1970s entries did indeed indicate a steady increase in the number of persons with technical skills or trades (to reach two-thirds of the 1970s entries). But no less important was the fact that by the mid-sixties almost all of them had relatives in the Leamington area or other parts of Canada before their arrival, including those few known to have entered Canada independently, as skilled workers or at times as tourists or visitors. Frank Tannini (Rome area, 1966) admittedly "didn't know much about Canada" prior to his arrival, but he had a stepbrother in the Leamington area; Armando Bonfiglio (Alia, Sicily, 1967) left England for Canada, no doubt influenced by youthful wanderlust and Canadian demand for skilled people, as much as by the presence in Ottawa of his sister and brother.

A few others, who arrived in Canada in the 1950s and 1960s and later moved to the Leamington area, where prior to their arrival they had neither relatives nor sponsors, gave no indication of the presence of such links at their first Canadian destinations or places of residence: Sam Catrini (Noto, Sicily, 1965), Isidoro Spano (Vita, Sicily, 1952), and Reno (Rino) Melatti (Treglio, Abruzzo, 1956) moved to Leamington from Toronto, the first in the late 1960s, the last two in the early 1970s; Peter Lusetti (Reggio nell'Emilia, Emilia-Romagna, 1956) moved to Leamington from London (Ontario) also in the early 1970s. While Melatti was only eight years old on arrival in Canada, and Lusetti was an electrician (a trade learned in Belgium), only Spano mentioned that, besides entering as a skilled worker, he had been sponsored by a Toronto Calabrian friend of the family and contractor.

In general, for only about a dozen men among the 1960s entries interviewed (143), and for only 3 of the 36 entries in the 1970s (besides Melatti and Lusetti), it was not possible to establish with certainty the presence of a relative in Canada prior to their arrival. Moreover, for those

Italians who went to Leamington, especially in the 1960s and 1970s, from the countries of earlier immigration or of birth in certain cases (Argentina, Brazil, France, Germany, Switzerland, Tunisia, Venezuela, and the United States), most already had relatives in the Leamington area. Thus, a high percentage of the entire postwar Leamington Italian immigrants from all areas of origin were sponsored and/or had family links in the Leamington area or in other parts of Canada prior to arrival.

The "chain migration" phenomenon is made clearer in the breakdown by region, province, and especially town of origin of those who settled in this area during this period. The highest numbers of families derive from the three regions of Italy that gave Leamington its Italian pioneers: (Abruzzo-) Molise, Lazio, and Sicily, with respectively 204 (47 per cent), 153 (35.3 per cent), and 57 (13.1 per cent) of the number of families for the entire period. The other regions make up less than 5 per cent of the total, with Abruzzo 9 (2.07 per cent), Puglia 6 (1.38 per cent), and the rest (Calabria, Campania, Marche, Emilia-Romagna and Veneto) less than 0.5 per cent each. The figures change very slightly if only the postwar period is considered, for it is mostly a postwar chain migration.

Most of the immigrants originate from three main provincial areas of three regions: for Molise, Isernia province with 198 families of a total of 204 (97 per cent) of the region (bearing in mind that up to 1963 Abruzzo-Molise formed one region; and up to 1970 Isernia was part of Campobasso province; see chapter 1, especially note 2); for Lazio, Frosinone province ("Ciociaria") with 146 families out of 153 (95 per cent); and for Sicily, Trapani province with 49 out of 57 families (86 per cent).

The best indicator of the mass migration for this whole period, and in particular for the postwar decades, is the high number of immigrant families originating from the same towns of the above three regions of Italy. Villa Canale in the Isernia province of Molise is at the top of the list with 109 families, of which 102 arrived between 1948/49 and 1979. Thus, the Villa Canale group represents about 25 per cent of the 446 families interviewed, 53 per cent of the Molise region, and 55 per cent of Isernia province. Villa Canale is truly representative of those many hill towns throughout Italy that have been decimated by emigration. No other single town has given Leamington so many families. Next in line in that same region are: Agnone with 41, Poggio Sannita with 26, Belmonte with 13, and Capracotta with 6; and in the Campobasso province, Campodipietra with 4.

The most represented towns from the Frosinone province (Lazio) are Ceprano with forty-three families, Patrica with thirty-four, Castelliri and Ripi with thirteen each, Pastena with seven, Pofi and Torrice with five each, Arnara and Boville Ernica with four each, and Ceccano with three. There are also four families from the city of Rome, while all other towns range from one to two families each.

The town in the province of Trapani (Sicily) that exported the largest number of families is San Vito Lo Capo (forty-one), followed by the island municipality of Favignana with three families. All the other towns in Trapani Province are represented with one or two families, while of the other Sicilian provinces, Palermo gave four and the rest one or two families each.

Only two towns in two other regions are represented with more than one family: Scapriano (Teramo, Abruzzo) with three; Peschici (Foggia, Puglia) with five. On the basis of the interviews, three regions of central north Italy appeared with only one unit each: Le Marche, or The Marches (A. Clerici, Roccafluvione, Ascoli Piceno, 1959, but married to a woman from bordering Abruzzo); Emilia-Romagna (Peter Lusetti, whose wife was Belgian); and Veneto (Father Ugo Rossi, Vicenza, entry New York 1948, since 1967 the Leamington Italian priest). Campania and Calabria were mentioned only as the birthplaces of children of families from other regions: Bruno Matassa (San Felice a Cancello, Caserta province, Naples area), son of Attilio, Lazio; Reno Leone (Nicastro, Catanzaro province), son of Gabriele, (Abruzzo-) Molise. In Matassa's case, Bruno's mother (Rosa Capomacchio) was a teacher at San Felice at the time of his birth. In Leone's case, Gabriele and his wife Rosina had moved to Calabria, where Gabriele was a prison guard at the Lamezia (Nicastro) penitentiary.

INDIRECT ROUTE TO LEAMINGTON

Among the exceptions in the sponsorship and settlement pattern were those who, whether sponsored or not, had never planned to work on the farm or settle in the Leamington or any other rural area: they preferred to seek better or more lucrative jobs in the city, in construction or in the factory, as indicated also by those working on the Tilbury farms in the 1950s. In certain cases, however, unemployment forced them to seek the more readily available farm work. In 1954, Domenic Iarusso (Agnone), who had been sponsored by his brother Felix, went to live with him in Windsor. But after three months without work, both Domenic and Felix moved to the Leamington area. Others went to the Leamington area from the larger cities for altogether different reasons: the Sicilian Sam Catrini (Noto, Siracusa), who had arrived in Canada in 1965, went in search of open spaces: "Not satisfied with the job in Toronto ... [and]

used to the outdoors ... [I] had heard about fresh water fishing on the Great Lakes ... I then drove along the lakefront to look for the fisheries. My search took me to the Omstead Fisheries in Wheatley ... After a while, I bought, along with my dad, a fishing boat and then ... a second one ... [I] have been in the fishing business for eleven years."

In the 1960s, with the easing and then change in regulations, non-sponsored skilled workers or those with some specialization became more common. In 1966, "no one called over" Frank Tannini (Lazio), a "specialist" with "a job waiting for" him in Montreal; but rather than stopping in Montreal, he decided to go to Leamington, where his stepbrother Angelo Cervini lived. Tannini also thought that his "was a special case, just for orphans, not for everybody." Similarly, in 1967 Armando Bonfiglio (Alia, Palermo) "came on [his] own: No one made papers for me." Armando, at twenty-one already a mechanic in England for three years, came to Canada, where his father was visiting. But when he arrived, his father had already left for Italy, and he spent the first few months in Ottawa with his sister. The Ottawa climate ("too cold") and a better paying job that a friend had found for Armando, who was a skilled worker with a knowledge of English, persuaded him to try Windsor, where initially he had "no real intention to stay," especially since he lived all alone. But then he met and married (1971) a Leamington woman from one of the Paglione families (Capracotta, Molise), the first of which had settled in Leamington in 1955 (Vittorio, married to a Marcovecchio, Agnone, and related to more than one of the original families).

In the case of the three 1950s entries who settled in Leamington in the 1970s, the routes and the reasons were somewhat different: Isidoro (Sid) Spano (Vita, Trapani, Sicily, 1952), not a bricklayer as per work contract provided by his Toronto Calabrian sponsor, but a tailor, during his first five years in Toronto was employed by a Canadian clothing company, then turned entrepreneur involved in various enterprises (bakery, restaurant, pastry shop, including a wholesale operation). After selling his Toronto business (to Italfina), Spano bought the Village Inn in Leamington, which the Spano family – Sid's wife Rosa (née Mirra, from Toritto, Puglia) and their two children – and a junior partner, Joe DiFalco, have operated for several years.[43] Peter Lusetti (Emilia-Romagna, 1956) seemed to exemplify those Italians who paved the way to Canada through an earlier immigration experience: while in Belgium, besides marrying a Belgian woman, Lusetti acquired his electrical trade and most likely a little of another language, which undoubtedly helped him enter Canada (especially if he did not have a sponsor) and gain employment. In 1972, after a stay in London (Ontario), the Lusetti family moved to Leamington, where he set up his own business. Reno Melatti (Treglio, Chieti, Abruzzo), quite young when he arrived in Toronto with his family in 1956, became a teacher and moved to Leamington in 1972 when he married the Leamington-born Lena (Lina) DiMenna, herself a teacher. Generally, however, the non-sponsored, independent entries – those who had no previous contacts with the Leamington Italian community or became by chance part of it – were in the minority.

"THE HOUSE OF THE IMMIGRANTS" AND OTHER EARLY LODGINGS

In the 1940s, 1950s, and even 1960s, sometimes even when they had relatives, the immigrants had to accept whatever inadequate accommodations the relative, friend, contact, or farmer offered, or whatever they themselves could find in the rural areas. For many post–Second World War immigrants, the first temporary dwelling place in this area was *La Casa degli Immigranti*, as the house was named by the different people who lived there while serving out their farm work stint. It was then owned by Alex Colasanti, one of the Leamington Italian pioneers who, according to Gino Pannunzio, sponsored so many Italians to Canada that he always had the house full of Italian immigrants. As they settled and moved from the house, he would "call" more: "It was like a rotating 'Ellis Island'" (a U.S. immigration centre from 1892 to 1954).

The Leone family, after moving from the farm near London (Ontario) to Ruthven in 1949, lived in that house: Gabriele Leone left the only description available of a "moment" in "The House of the Immigrants":

It was a red brick house ... It's still there ... On the first floor there were five men. They gave us the second floor; there were two rooms; one we used as a bedroom and the other as a kitchen. But there was nothing ... We had to put in our own stove ... no toilet ... the toilet was outside ... and for water we had to go get it from a well ... In the summer, the well would even dry up, so we had to go to Emma Colasanti [Colasanti's farm, north of the "House"] ... After ten hours of work, tired and dirty, we had to cart water for quite a distance, wash, and then prepare our meal ... And the heat! It was so warm that the other men sleeping in the other rooms went outside to sleep. There was quite a group of friends there ... Rocco Peschisolido, Gino Guerrieri, Salvatore [Fazio] from Sicily [later in Windsor] ... Catenacci [later in Detroit? New York?] and Luigi Meconi's brother-in-law [Augusto Cocchetto, later in Windsor] ... quite a group ...

they all slept outside ... It was so warm, it was impossible to sleep at night. I couldn't join them outside, I had my wife and two small children: Colomba just three years old and Reno nine.

The temporary lodging was not used exclusively by the immigrants whom Colasanti sponsored, nor by those who had no relatives in the area (as in Leone's case). Augusto (Gus) Cocchetto was, of course, related to Luigi Meconi, whose wife Emilia was Augusto's sister, and to the other Windsor Meconi families; Gino (or Vittorio) Guerrieri, whose daughter Teresina later married Rocco Peschisolido (owner of a business in Kingsville), had a sister in Windsor and was sponsored by Cervini. Though Catenacci could not be identified and precise documentation was unavailable, it seems that through the years many others used the "House." In any case, after months of sacrifices and frugality, they moved to a better place or, as the Leone experience exemplified, they bought their own home. The Italian immigrants in that situation were eager to simultaneously free themselves from the farm work bond and the discomforts of "The House of the Immigrants." The "House" was eventually bought from Colasanti by one of its previous immigrant occupants. "It's still there," on Third Concession Road West, just west of No. 3 Highway: for some of them, "It's still there" as a reminder of all their struggles and dreams.[44]

Though many on arrival did live with relatives and sometimes comfortably, their sponsorship did not always guarantee living quarters, at least not in their homes, partly because sometimes the immigrants came in groups. The scarcity of available dwelling places and their generally poor quality throughout the 1950s – the decade of highest number of entries – aggravated the culture shock. The types of accommodations recorded during this time ranged from inadequate to squalid, frequently excessively overcrowded and lacking basic facilities. Some lived in almost primitive, frontier conditions: on top of garages or bowling alleys, and in various structures or areas designated for farm purposes: a tobacco kiln, boiler rooms, or stables, as Luigi Carnevale (1949) pointed out: "We had a barn ... split in half: horses on one side ... and we slept on the other side ... or in the room above the boiler."

The shack-like *"casette"* (little houses), as the immigrants called them, with no facilities at all, were not uncommon: "two rooms, one a kitchen, a coal stove and no water or toilet" (A. Carducci, 1949); where sometimes three or four men "lived and cooked their meals for three years" (Luca Mastronardi, 1949). It became unbearably ironic for some of them whose apartments in Italy had "a bathroom and running water," while their first "house" in Leamington in 1950 "didn't even have an indoor toilet." A 1951 entry "lived in basements ... freezing cold in winter, hot in summer," and in the hope of finding better quarters "from 1954 to 1960 moved from house to house." In 1952 a family had to share with two other families "a three-room 'house' with no doors, just curtains." It was probably the same "garage turned into house with no indoor facilities" rented to a 1957 immigrant family.

The "little house" that the immigrant was often happily welcomed to in this period had to be generally shared with many others: sometimes "from fourteen to eighteen people under the same roof." Lucy (Gabriele) Paglione recalled as many as twenty-one people living together in her first residence in 1959 (Pulford Street).

Finding an apartment or a house to rent was "a problem" even in 1959, especially if "you had children, or one small child." The Italian immigrant families were particularly appalled by the "no children" restriction. Inevitably, the alternative was adjusting to uncivilized, miserable living conditions: no electrical facilities nor hot water, no furnace nor insulation, and sometimes no furniture, no outdoor toilets, and all clothes hand-washed; apartments were sometimes infested, and the families had to put up with bugs and mice, as well as extreme heat, cold, and dampness. They had to become particularly resourceful in order to survive: "It was so damp," said a 1952 immigrant, "we burned wood to soak up the humidity," but that often caused a great deal of smoke. If they couldn't afford a fridge, like the family living in the "garage made into an apartment" on Highway 18, they "kept the food between the window and the screen during the winter ... and in the summer, bought enough food for one day at a time." Like many others, Nick Mastronardi in 1953 "kept the milk downstairs between some concrete to keep it cool ... and the meat ... in a cold storage locker in town ... rented annually for two dollars."

Not all were that unfortunate! Upon arrival, some immediately lived in "a good home" with all the comforts: one in 1957 even had the luxury of "an air-conditioned house." In many cases, both low quantity and poor quality of housing facilities were incentives for hard work and sacrifices in order to buy a little house as soon as possible, however rundown, that they could slowly improve or add to before sponsoring other members of the immediate family, as in the case of the Leones in 1950. Of course, the pioneers had homes with "all the conveniences," as recalled by Francesco Mastronardi who in 1949 went to live with his sponsor, his uncle Armando Mastronardi (1925).

By the late 1950s some of the first postwar Italian immigrants to Leamington also had a type of house celebrated in the very popular

1957 Italian song "La casetta in Canadà," the lovely "Little House in Canada" with "ponds and little fishes and many lilac flowers" so much admired by "all the girls," and no doubt the subject of "much envy," as was often the case in Leamington, of passersby as well as of neighbours. And if *la casetta*, just as in the song, should happen to burn down, it was immediately rebuilt.[45] It might have been totally coincidental, but the following year, in 1958, "Italy surpassed Britain as a source for immigrants" to Canada,[46] and by the end of that decade the number of the Leamington Italian families had grown to over half of the total for the entire sixty-year immigration period.

The Settlement Pattern

THE EARLIEST CORE AREA: SEACLIFF WEST

The newcomers' first place of residence was usually temporary. They were always on the move, in search of work wherever available. In the earlier days, they were scattered on the farms throughout Essex County. As time went on, they gradually converged toward the three townships that approximately make up the southeast quarter of the county: Mersea and Gosfield South and, to a lesser degree, Gosfield North.

The Italian settlement in the Leamington area was gradual. It is useful to remember that not all of the eight men who left Villa Canale–Agnone in 1923 reached or settled in Leamington, and those who did, didn't get there until the late 1920s or early 1930s. The eight men, reunited in Montreal, reached Windsor together in spring 1924, but they were soon scattered again (chapters 3, 4): the Capussi cousins eventually settled illegally in Chicago and were later deported to Italy for good; the Moauro brothers (Angelo and Gus) went on to Minnesota and did not reach Leamington until the 1930s; and by 1928 the Ingratta brothers, John and Ralph (i.e., Giovanni and Raffaele), along with their cousin Enrico or Henry (sponsored in 1925), were living on their jointly owned farm in Rodney (Elgin County), where John and family settled permanently, Henry and family resided until 1933, and Raffaele for about two years. After selling his shares to his brother John, Raffaele moved to the Leamington area; but since his family remained in Italy, in the subsequent twenty years (until his death in Canada in 1951), he travelled back and forth a number of times. In fact, he was in Italy during the Second World War, an active period of farm acquisition by the Leamington Italians. Thus, only Tony DiMenna and Domenic Pannunzio remained in this area since their arrival – Windsor (DiMenna on Mercer, Tuscarora,

Pelletier Streets) and/or Detroit first and then Leamington. They are, in fact, the only two members of the 1923 group of Molisani to have lived permanently in the Leamington area since the late 1920s (along with some of the relatives "called over" from 1925 onwards).

Generally, for the newcomers to this area, particularly in the 1920s, the city of Windsor or nearby areas and Essex County farms were stepping stones to Leamington. This was true for the other Molisani (e.g., the Magri family) as well as for the pioneers of the other two major groups: DeSantis and Colasanti (1924) from Lazio; and particularly Vito Peralta (1927) from Sicily. However, unlike the others, the first two men from the Lazio region went to work on county farms (Kingsville) immediately after their arrival (see chapter 4, especially "Truly Pioneers").

The reasons for this direction toward the rural areas were mainly economic: work and survival. The farm was seldom a voluntary choice: at first, for the contractual requirements or out of necessity – lack of jobs in the city, especially in the "starving thirties" – then for the stability required to sponsor the family, and during the war for all those reasons, including protection against a possible worse fate (internment as enemy aliens). Subsequently, however, the farms attracted them: the fertility of the land and the opportunity for an independent, more secure, albeit hard life convinced them to settle in the familiar rural areas and buy the farms they had worked on or managed as sharecroppers for so many years.

In the late 1920s, Joe (Joseph) Henry's Blytheswood farm (Concession VIII, Lots 2/3) became a gathering place and the last stepping stone to the Leamington outskirts for five Molisani: two of the 1923 group, Tony DiMenna and Domenic Pannunzio, together again after a four-year separation (1924–28), and three of the first group of sponsored relatives (1925) – Joe Pannunzio (Domenic's brother) and their sister's brother-in-law, Luigi Mastronardi, as well as Armando Mastronardi who, while related to his sponsor Raffaele Ingratta, was also Tony DiMenna's cousin. For some of them, it was the first occasion to be together with the others.

In the earlier period (1924–28), their search for work had often scattered the Molisani of both groups throughout the larger Windsor-Detroit area or even beyond. At times they had worked together, but only for short periods: Tony DiMenna and Domenic Pannunzio (1923 group) for the same contractors, April–September 1924 (chapter 4). The four men sponsored in 1925 had worked together for longer periods after their arrival (Bob Conklin's farm, Kingsville; Jack Noble's farm, Harrow). But they too had been separated, if only for about a year (1926–27), when Joe Pannunzio went to Rodney (Elgin County) and Henry Ingratta went to the McCracken farm, though only across the road from the other two companions, Armando and Luigi Mastronardi, at the Conklin farm (Kingsville). Besides, the four men had also been divided from their sponsors, who in some cases were also their relatives, their only family. In fact, especially during those first years, each of them, related or not to the other *paesani*, looked upon the entire group as their only family.

Thus, after a period of uncertainty, anxiety (especially for Domenic Pannunzio who, as a result of his accident, spent some time in the hospital), and hopscotching from job to job in Windsor or Detroit, or from farm to farm in Essex or even Elgin County, the Blytheswood reunion offered the first opportunity to form a more closely knit group, at least for five of them. Henry Ingratta (1925) did not join them: that same year (1928), he went with his cousins (John and Ralph, 1923) to their farm in Rodney (see chapters 4, 5).

For the next six to seven years the five men lived and worked together as sharecroppers on Joe Henry's farms: first in Eighth Concession, Blytheswood (1928–29), and in 1929 when Joe Henry sold that farm, they moved as a group to his other farm also in Mersea Township, on First Concession Road West or, as it is better known now, Seacliff Drive West (Concession 1, Lot 4). It was, in fact, in the same Seacliff area where, only six years later, three of the men bought their own farm (Concession 1, Lot 5) or "up the road" (about 1,000 feet west) from where Gino Pannunzio's son now lives, a half mile outside the town limits. The five men had thus formed the first small Italian cluster in the vicinity of Leamington, at least until the end of 1934 or early 1935. Tony DiMenna and Domenic Pannunzio even had a souvenir of their stay at Joe Henry's: a photo in front of the plane that carried mail between the mainland and Pelee Island, and that they proudly took care of (on Henry's farm itself, which, according to some, had the "second airfield in Ontario").

The Seacliff area on Highway 18 (west of Leamington), to some Italian immigrants appearing "all bush" even in the 1950s, had been a developing farm, park, and residential area for at least a century.[1] In the early 1930s it had also become the earliest core area of settlement of Italians, or at least the first permanent settlement by a small group of Italian families, who indeed found that "all bush" designation by their newly sponsored relatives quite annoying. Even in the early 1930s, it seemed inappropriate for a newcomer to say that "there wasn't much to Leamington." By then Heinz had "many buildings west of Erie [which] was the core of its manufacturing area." It was also rather offensive to the long-settled pioneer families when postwar immigrants described Leamington "just as four corners:

its roads ... narrow ... its fields ... empty ... Heinz ... small, and the rest all bush, especially on Highway 18." It was particularly irritating when, though in jesting exaggeration, they compared their new home to Siberia (*Questa è Siberia*). The contrast in perceptions, while indicative of how views are relative to experience, also revealed the level of adjustment of the older immigrants, how quickly they had "become accustomed to their new surroundings." They thus resented hearing what they themselves had at times expressed twenty-five or thirty years earlier.

On the other hand, anyone arriving in Canada, even from a rural area in Italy and even before the industrial boom that encroached on farmlands, was invariably struck by Canada's rich, abundant, lush green vegetation. Therefore, however developed the Highway 18 West area might have been in the 1950s, it still impressed on the newcomers, especially on those from the sparsely wooded hills and mostly barren farms of Upper Molise, an image of "all bush," in the sense of all green and not necessarily wild or backward. It is the perception or feeling also of anyone who comes to Canada from the overcrowded and congested towns and cities of Europe or of other parts of the world. A journalist for *La Gazzetta* arriving in Windsor from Rome some years ago asked, *"Dov'è la gente?"* (Where are the people?), simply because there were no crowds in the streets. They are all expressions of surprise and awe for the wide-open Canadian spaces, of "the immigrant's fear of the landscape": a sense of isolation that Northrop Frye (*The Bush Garden*, 1971) called "the feeling for the immense searching distance ... which is the primary geographical fact about Canada which has no counterpart elsewhere." Some scenes can evoke "the frightening loneliness of a huge and thinly settled country."[2]

The postwar Italian immigrants were awed by this land: as they travelled by train from Halifax to Montreal they were "deeply impressed by Canada's hugeness ... miles and miles without seeing a house" (B. Matassa, 1948); often after two or three days of "just trees, water, sky ... and not ... one village, [they] wondered where [they] were going" (I. Baldassare, 1949). In winter, the snow made them reflect (in a way echoing Voltaire's vision of Canada as a few *"arpents de neige"*) about their going from the "land of the sun to the land of the snow ... It seemed as if I had entered into a desert full of snow and nothing else" (Rolando Paliani, 1954). Yet almost all, after their first deadening encounter in Halifax with Canada's "cold, *mondo morte* [death-like world]" as they approached Leamington, though "small," found it "clean and warmer" (F. Pannunzio, 1949). And for a few, Canada itself was a place of "beautiful houses" and unique natural beauty: "Like a dream" or truly the "land of 100,000 lakes" as described in school geography books (A. and

B. Matassa, 1948); and Leamington "a great town"; "the best place" (Floyd Cacciavillani, 1948; Levino Mastronardi, 1958; see also chapter 12, "The View of Canada").

By 1935 the Seacliff Drive or Highway 18 West area, where Italians bought their first farms (in 1931, the DeLellis family), had become the home of at least six entire family units: the DeLellis family and the families of the five Molisani pioneers. By the end of the war, the number had decreased to two or three families, but it grew very rapidly in the decades following the war. Today the whole length of Seacliff Drive West is quilted with Italian families, some bearing the names of those first immigrants: DiMenna, Ingratta, Mastronardi, and Pannunzio.

In the 1930s and first part of the 1940s, the growing trend among the early immigrants toward Mersea Township produced other small Italian clusters in and around Leamington. A few came back to the area after several years: Henry Ingratta (1925) and his family, after selling their portion of the Rodney farm to his cousin John, moved from Elgin County to Leamington – first (1933–40) they worked on the Conover farm (Concession 1, Lot 6); then they sharecropped the Parnell farm after Armando Mastronardi left it in 1941 (later owned by Luca Mastronardi, Tony DiMenna's brother-in-law, on Seacliff Drive West and Albuna Townline, Concession 1, Lot 1); and finally, in 1942, the Ingrattas settled on their own farm on Talbot Street West.

Similarly, Gus Moauro (1923) moved from Detroit to become Tony DiMenna's sharecropping partner for a while, first (1936) on Graham's tobacco farm (Ridge Road, Harrow, Colchester South Township), then (1937) on Bill Setterington's farm in Leamington (just south of H.J. Heinz, west of Erie and south of Oak). In 1938 Gus left the Setterington farm and Tony DiMenna, to work for the Angus McCharles farm (near Ruthven, Gosfield South Township, north of today's Colasanti enterprise), where for one year (1938–39) he worked with his brother Angelo and Angelo's son Rocco. But in 1940 Gus left Ruthven for the Brown farm (Fifth Concession, Mersea Township), and two years later he and his family settled on their farm on Hodgins. In the meantime, his brother Angelo (1923) also returned from the United States to settle in the Leamington area (1938), where he was joined by his family from Italy (1938/39). After the McCharles farm in Ruthven and sharecropping first (1939–42) on Bob LaMarsh's farm (Talbot Road East or Highway 3, southside, approximately 1.5 kilometres east of Erie Street, Leamington) and then (1943–44) on the George L. Cole farm (Talbot Road West, approximately 1 kilometre west of Leamington), Angelo and family moved to Morse Lane (1945) and began working the farm they had just bought (14 December 1944). Thus, it is very unlikely that Angelo was, as some said, one of the first Italians employed at Heinz (chapter 9).

Others, after some meandering in the adjacent townships, moved closer to Leamington (in Mersea and Gosfield South Townships): Tony DiMenna (1923), after Blytheswood and the Seacliff area on Joe Henry's farms (1928/29–1934), worked for one year (1935), along with Armando Mastronardi, at Bill Setterington's farm. From 1936 to 1940 (for the first two years, 1936/37, in partnership with Gus Moauro) he sharecropped first Graham's farm (Harrow) and then again Bill Setterington's farm (Leamington). Then DiMenna spent the next six years (1940–46) on three different farms in Mersea Township until he finally settled (1946) on a farm near Leamington, but outside Mersea Township (Gosfield South Township). Armando Mastronardi (1925), after two years as a farm labourer and sharecropper in Kingsville and Harrow (1925–27) and after sharecropping with the group of five in Blytheswood and Seacliff Drive (1928–34), worked for about two years (at intervals with Tony DiMenna) at Bill Setterington's farm (1935–37), and then he share-cropped with his son Bert on Parnell's farm (1937–41) until he and his family settled on their own farm on Oak Street.

The Magri family (1927) moved to Mersea Township in 1940, after working as day labourers or sharecroppers on farms and at various other jobs throughout Essex County: McGregor-Amherstburg area (two years), Essex (one year), Cottam-Olinda area ("ten years" on the Upcott farm), and in Windsor (briefly). Their residence for about ten years (1930s) was the Cottam-Kingsville area, in the Sixth Concession at Division Road, Gosfield North Township (probably on or near the site of what was the Primo Food Plant, north of Highway 3). Their neighbour there was Joe Matassa, who also moved to the Leamington area around the same time. From 1940 to 1945 the Magris worked in factories and on farms, at times as sharecroppers: on the Bob LaMarsh farm (1940–42), almost at the same time as Angelo Moauro; on the Peter Smith farm (northeast of LaMarsh and north of Frank Colasanti's farm) as tenants; and on another farm near Olinda, belonging to (according to Gino DiMenna) a "northern Ontario Italian gold miner," or (according to the Land Registry records) owned by Natale Cuzzilla, and situated on Concession Four, Gosfield South Township. In March 1945, they took possession of the farm they had bought four months earlier in the Talbot Road East area also called North Talbot Road Concession (or NTR Concession). In the early 1950s, their daughter Ida's Italian grocery store, the first in the Leamington business section, helped to attract more Italians to the downtown area (chapter 9).

Antonio Cervini (1927) also moved from Detroit to Windsor and then to Leamington (1938), and after working in construction as well as on the farms of LaMarsh, Colasanti (Frank), and Parnell, which he share-cropped after the Ingrattas, he settled on his own farm (1945) on Erie Street North (or Highway 77, where he still lived in the 1980s). Tony DeSantis (1924) was residing in Kingsville by 1926, but from the late 1920s or early 1930s onwards he worked on different Leamington area farms, including one owned by Dr E. Cook (Concession 3, Lot 1, Mersea Township). By 1946, according to employment records, he was working at Heinz in Leamington (thus becoming most likely the first Italian to be permanently employed by that company; see chapters 4, 9). Tony finally settled in Leamington, in the house he bought in 1955 at 108 Erie Street South, where he died in 1982. Joe Matassa, a Windsor resident in the late 1920s (chapter 4) and then in the Kingsville area, had also moved to Leamington by the early 1940s, and to his own farm in Mersea Township by April 1941 (see appendix D).

Vito Peralta (1927) seems to have been the first Italian immigrant to settle in the downtown area of Leamington. Nick Cicchini and Louis Bernachi (both shoemakers) had been there before him, 1939–42, to assist John and Ines Brunato in their downtown shoe repair shop (see chapter 9). But they did not settle in the downtown area of Leamington. Their residence was Windsor, where they had been at least since 1926 (Cicchini at 1453 Tourangeau; Bernachi at 514 Erie East). In 1943, after his return from Camp Petawawa to Windsor, Vito moved to Leamington to manage Brunato's shop located on the west side of Erie, north of Mill, south of Talbot. For years he rented apartments nearby, where his relatives also lived after the war.

Only a few of them did not settle in Mersea Township: John (Giovanni) Ingratta (1923) lived in Elgin County from 1928 on, first with his brother, Raffaele, and their cousin, Henry (whose farm shares John purchased when each one moved to Leamington) and then with his family. Loreto Colasanti (1927), after working on various farms in the Leamington area (1927–37), moved to Detroit (see chapter 4). His brother Alex (1924), after Harrow (1927–30) and perhaps a brief period in Mersea Township in the early 1930s, always lived and worked in Gosfield South Township, first in Kingsville, and after 1940 on his farm in Ruthven, which is only five kilometres west of Leamington, in the same township where Tony DiMenna bought his farm in 1946.

By the time the postwar influx of immigrants started, not only were most of them well established in Leamington and area, but the majority also owned farms and greenhouse businesses. The three Ingrattas had, of course, led the way with their joint ($5,000) land purchase in 1928; but their 100-acre Elgin County farm – that John's family held onto at the end of the partnership (early 1930s), and where his sons still lived in the 1980s – was well removed (about 100 kilometres east of Leamington) from the main Italian settlement area. Joseph and Alfonse DeLellis (father and son) may very well have been the first Italians to buy a farm in the Leamington area, according to the date of purchase – 30 September 1931. But the DeLellis family, who had first moved from Colorado to Detroit, went to the Leamington area only after contacts made with the Leamington Italian pioneers and *paesani* from Lazio and Molise: Joseph and his wife Maria were born, respectively, in the Ceprano area of Lazio (Pastena?) and in Agnone (Abruzzo-) Molise. In fact, recalled Gino Pannunzio (who had just arrived from Italy), in the summer of 1931 Joseph worked with the five Molisani "on Joe Henry's farm, for board only, in order to familiarize himself with Canadian farming" before investing $12,000 in the thirty-seven-acre farm west of Henry's farm, in the same Seacliff Drive West area (Concession 1, Lot 2).

THE PIONEERS: FROM SHARECROPPERS TO OWNER-FARMERS (1934–1946)

Among the Italian pioneers themselves, the lead in farm purchase and development in the Leamington area was taken by the two Pannunzio brothers, Domenic (1923) and Joe (1925), in association with their sister's brother-in-law, Luigi Mastronardi (1925). With a deed signed on Christmas Eve 1934 (and registered the day after Christmas), the three partners became equal owners, with 33.3 per cent each (though Domenic advanced 50 per cent of the $7,000 down payment), of a twenty-eight-acre farm purchased from James and Maude Bradford for $13,500. Located, according to the deed, "in the First Concession" and "composed ... of the east quarter of Lot Number Five (5) and the west one-eighth of Lot Number Six (6)," the farm became the second one bought by Italians in the Leamington area and on Seacliff Drive West. But at the same time it became the first Italian-owned "greenhouse operation" in the area (and consisting of three greenhouses and boiler room or power house with boiler and heating system). With the purchase in 1935 of three additional acres to the west of the farm, the three Molisani families of the Pannunzio brothers and of Luigi Mastronardi showed themselves to be pacesetters among the Leamington-area Italians.

The others followed their example but did not start until almost six years later (excluding Frank Colasanti, Alex's brother, who had bought a farm on Talbot Road East, northside, i.e., North Talbot Road Concession, or Lot 240, east of Highway 77, on 15 February 1938, but had sold it in the early 1940s after moving back to the United States). Nevertheless, by 1946 almost all the early Italian immigrant families, including one of the younger generations, had purchased parcels of land, with farmhouses and sometimes greenhouses, in both Mersea and Gosfield South Townships. By 23 September 1940, Armando Mastronardi and family owned a farm on Oak Street or Second Concession Road West, southside or Concession 1, Lot 5 (where the family settled in 1941). On 2 September 1943, he also bought a house for himself and his wife on the west side of Churchill Avenue (north of Oak West), while his son Bert (Umberto), who since his marriage in July 1943 had been living with his wife in an apartment on the corner of Mill and Fox, in the fall of that year moved with his wife into the old family house on the farm both families worked (just west of the house on Churchill Street).

In 1942, three others followed: Costantino "Gus" Moauro (on the 4 February deed said to be "of the Town of Leamington") bought his own farm on the west side of "Hodgson," i.e., Hodgins Street, south of the Chesapeake & Ohio Railway, Concession 2, Lot 5. Between 25 February and 11 March, following the sale to the Pannunzio brothers of their shares of the farm held in partnership since 1934, and after sharecropping for George L. Cole (Talbot Road West), Luigi Mastronardi, his wife "Palina" (i.e., Paolina) and his two sons, Alfred and Mario (i.e., Marius), became "joint tenants" of over twelve acres of land and greenhouses on the "Ridge," at 425 Talbot Road West, south of the Chesapeake & Ohio Railway, Concession 2, Lot 2. And on 28 July of the same year, Enrico (Henry) and his wife Maria (Mary/Merceda) Ingratta bought over six acres of land also on the "Ridge," at 391 Talbot Road West, where their son Marius then lived (Concession 2, Lot 2, east of Luigi Mastronardi).

In 1944 and 1945 three other pioneers ventured on their own in Mersea Township. On 14 December 1944, Angelo Moauro invested $18,700 in seventeen acres west of Morse Lane, north of Third Concession Road or Wilkinson Drive (Concession 3, Lot 4). On 1 March 1945 the Magri family moved to the 35-acre farm they had bought on 13 October 1944, on Talbot Road East (NTR Concession, Lot 243), southside of Fourth Concession Road or County Road 18 and east of Highway 77. And on 13 March 1945, Antonio and Rosa Cervini bought their 9.6-acre farm in Concession 3, Lot 6, on the west side of Highway 77 (which is the name of Erie Street North at the northern Leamington town limits). On 20 October of the same year, Gus Moauro's son, Frank Sr, and his wife Ida (Luigi Mastronardi's daughter), also made a $4,000 purchase of a 9-acre farm on Talbot Road West, east of her father's farm and just south of his father's farm (Concession 2, Lot 5). Their action provided the earliest indication of a widespread postwar tendency that produced clusters of relatives and close friends around the areas of the pioneers' farms, especially in Mersea Township.

Only two of the pioneers bought farms in the bordering Gosfield South Township: Alex Colasanti and Tony DiMenna. On 18 October 1940, after his eight or nine years of summer sharecropping and winter factory work, Alex or Eleuterio (as per deed) and his wife Emma became joint tenants of a 19.75-acre farm, lying north of Third Concession Road and west of Highway 3, near Ruthven (Concession 3, Lot 9). But, at least until 1944, Alex continued to work both in the factory (Hodges Tobacco Company), as inspector, and on the farm, this time his own, during the evenings and other periods of "free" time.

Tony or Antonio DiMenna, after leaving Bill Setterington's farm in Leamington (1940), resumed his meandering through Mersea Township for six more years, working two years on each of the farms owned by John Tew, Concession 4, Lot 1, north side of Fourth Concession Road east of Albuna Road (1940–42); Hazel or John Stockwell, Concession 2, Lot 1, north side of Talbot Road West, east of Albuna Road (1942–44); and Harvey Hilborn (since 1953 owned by Floyd Cacciavillani) in Concession 2, Lot 3, at 263 Talbot Road West, at Fraser Road (1944–46). Then on 23 December 1946, Antonio and his wife Antonietta became joint tenants of a 7.5–acre farm in Gosfield South Township at Union on the Lake (east of Union Road or Essex County Road 45 and south of Front Road or Highway 18). Following a pattern established years earlier, in September 1957 Tony's son Gino, in partnership with Joe Marcovecchio (Gino's brother-in-law) also bought a farm "just across the road" from his father at Union. Subsequently owned solely by Gino, the 7.5-acre farm included 1.5 acres of covered greenhouse producing mainly tomatoes.

In 1931–46, according to Mersea Assessment Rolls and Deeds, at least fifteen parcels of land, varying from six to thirty-seven acres, were purchased by Italian immigrants in the larger Leamington area:[3] two of them already mentioned in Gosfield South Township (T. DiMenna and A. Colasanti); and the other thirteen in Mersea Township, if included are the three purchased by Frank Colasanti (in 1938), Giuseppe (Joe) Matassa (in 1941), and a northern Italian and former Windsor resident,

Fred Belluz or, as in deed, Fernando D.B. Belluz (in 1944).[4] But the latter three were situated east of Leamington (the first in the North Talbot Road Concession, Lot 240; the second in Concession I, Lot 13, south side of Oak Street East or Second Concession Road, about three miles east of Erie Street; and the third in Concession C, Lot 13, just north of Pelee National Park; see appendix D.)

Since the farm of the pioneer Magri family was also in the North Talbot Road Concession (Lot 243), albeit only about a half mile east of Erie Street North, nine of the thirteen Mersea Township Italian farms were situated in a relatively small area of the township west of Leamington; more precisely within the south-to-north-arranged First, Second, and Third Concessions and within the west-to-east-numbered Farm Lots 2 to 6 (the latter immediately west of Erie Street, which divides the town into East and West). Three of them were in the First Concession, also known as Concession I (between First Concession Road or Seacliff Drive and Second Concession Road or Oak Street, which west of Fraser Road becomes Talbot Road or Highway 3). Four of them were in the Second Concession or Concession II (between Oak Street/Talbot Road/Highway 3 and Third Concession Road or Wilkinson Drive). And two of them were in the Third Concession or Concession III (between Wilkinson Drive and Fourth Concession Road or County Road 18). This small portion of Mersea Township, measuring approximately three by four kilometres, became the area where the children of the pioneers tended to buy their own farms, and where most of the immediate postwar arrivals went to work and live, especially on the farms of the pioneer families from (Abruzzo-) Molise.[5]

In fact, of the fifteen farms bought in this period (1931–46), eleven (including the one purchased by Frank and Ida Moauro) were owned by the families of the 1920s immigrants from Lazio and (Abruzzo-) Molise: nine of them were in Mersea Township, and eight of the nine within the above-mentioned rectangular portion of the township, some quite near to one another and to the Leamington town boundary. Armando Mastronardi's farm, described as part of Registered Plan 440, which was a parcel of land severed from Farm Lot 5 (Concession I), was situated just northwest of the northern boundary of the Pannunzios–Luigi Mastronardi property. In 1953, after Gino Pannunzio, Domenic's son, bought his own farm in the same farm lot, west of, but not adjacent to, his father's property, Gino and Armando became almost neighbours: with only a few hundred yards between them, the western boundary of Gino's farm (north of Seacliff Drive West) was in a direct line with the eastern boundary of Armando's farm (south of Oak Street West). The

DeLellis farm, also in Concession I (Lot 2), was about 1.5 kilometres west of the Pannunzio farm (i.e., in Mersea Township, but not among the above-mentioned eleven, or nine farms).

Similarly in Concession II, the property that Henry Ingratta bought five months after Luigi Mastronardi (in 1942) was in the same west part of Lot 2 and separated from Luigi's farm by a three-acre tract of land (with the latter at 425 and the former at 391 Talbot Road West, both were roughly one kilometre north of the DeLellis property, at 435 Seacliff Drive West). Northeast of Luigi and Henry and directly north of the farms of the Pannunzios and of Armando Mastronardi (Concession I, Lot 5) were the farms of Gus Moauro and of his son Frank, the one just north of the other in Lot 5. It is the same northeastern corner of the lot where in the late forties and in the fifties other Moauro relatives invested in real estate. Rocco Moauro, Angelo's son, with a deed of 12 January 1950, took possession of a house and about two acres of land just north of his uncle Gus (Concession II, Lot 5); while in November 1952 Rocco's sister Pasqualina and her husband Enrico DiCiocco (name misspelled in deed, DiCiocca), both postwar immigrants (Molise, 1949), bought about one acre of land also in Concession II, Lot 5, just east of Rocco (and later sold it to their cousin Ralph Sabelli). Rocco himself, from 1953 to 1957, was joint owner with John Brunato – the same Leamington merchant who owned the shoe shop managed by Peralta – of a ten-acre farm in Concession III, Lot 1, or north of Third Concession Road West (where the Brunatos, who bought the farm from Rocco, then resided). Finally, Rocco became owner of a few acres severed from his father's farm (Morse Lane), where he built a house, as well as, along with his father, a greenhouse plant (sold, after Rocco's death in 1962, to Moretto Ingratta).

On 30 July 1957, Domenico Sabelli, a nephew of Gus Moauro on his wife's side, also purchased about 2.5 acres of land (in Concession II, Lot 5) north of his uncle's farm and south of the 2-acre property that, since 15 November 1952, belonged to another postwar family: Tony DiMenna's brother, Pacifico (1949), whose wife Bambina (née Ingratta) was a close friend of Domenico Sabelli's mother in Italy (and besides, the two Moauro brothers, Angelo and Gus, were married to two Sabelli sisters, Angelina and Paolina, respectively). West of the above Sabellis, Moauros, and DiMennas, in Concession II, Lot 3 (or 263 Talbot Road West) was located the 39-acre farm purchased, on 1 October 1953, by Floyd Cacciavillani (1949) and family. In the 1940s, while it still belonged to C.H. Hilborn, the farm was not only the place of work of Tony DiMenna for two years (1944–46), but also the pre-arranged destination" in March 1949, of Tony's nephew Adelchi DiMenna (as indicated in handwriting on Adelchi's Italian passport).

In Concession III, about 1.5 kilometres northwest of his brother Gus (and after 1952 even closer to his daughter Pasqualina), was the property of Angelo Moauro (in Registered Plan 615, the "severed" west quarter of Lot 4). About 2 kilometres east of Angelo was the farm of another early immigrant: Antonio Cervini (Lot 6); and north of Cervini was located the farm of one of the first Italian farm labourers in Mersea, Peter Delzotti (in deed Del Zotti), who purchased it in October 1948, three years after Cervini and probably the first after the war. (In 1963 the seventeen-acre farm was sold to Beato Mastronardi, who still lived there in the 1990s.) The farm of Michael and Saveria Magri, though east of Erie Street, was only a short distance from the farms of the Cervinis and Delzottis. A little farther away, 4–5 kilometres from their parents, were Domenic Magri, Saveria's son, and his wife Loretta, Cervini's daughter, who bought their own farm in Concession II, Lot 3, in November 1955. But by then the Leamington Italians were more than a few families.

The postwar Italians continued to buy land throughout the three Mersea Concessions, and beyond. But the highest concentration, since the early days, occurred in Concessions I and II, especially along Seacliff Drive West and Talbot Road West, as far as the boundary line between Mersea and Gosfield South Townships, and thus closer to the two pioneers' farms in Gosfield South. The two Gosfield farms themselves were already relatively close: Tony DiMenna's in Lot 10 (First Concession, Eastern Division); Alex Colasanti's in Lot 9 (Third Concession), or one east and the other west of Essex Road 45, which at Ruthven turns into Highway 3. In fact, the distance between Essex Road 45 and Erie Street in Leamington, following Highway 18, is about six kilometres, which is almost equal to the distance from Blytheswood, the village or more precisely Joe Henry's Eighth Concession farm north of it – the place of the 1928 regathering of the five Molisani pioneers – to the Leamington "Four Corners" or main intersection at Talbot Road and Erie Street.

Still, in that early period the Italians were few and somewhat scattered; and for reasons of both economic survival and companionship, they made every attempt to live and work as near as possible to one another, as well as to the town of Leamington. Some of their farms were in its immediate outskirts and have been since incorporated into the town, particularly those situated in Lots 5 and 6 in both Concessions I and II. Within the present town limits can be found, for example, the farms once owned by the Pannunzio brothers, by Gino Pannunzio (after 1984 by his son Gerald) and by Armando Mastronardi, as well as those once belonging to Gus Moauro and to Frank Moauro – Frank's property was later used for the expansion of the Leamington and District High School (today, Leamington District Secondary School). As Leamington continues to expand, others in Concession III will most likely also end up within the town's perimeter (see appendix D, especially section ii).

Only one of the 1923 Molisan pioneers and only two of the 1920s Italian immigrants, who eventually settled in the Leamington area, did not become owner-farmers. Raffaele Ingratta (1923), though among the first farm owners, worked as a sharecropper (on a rented farm east of Erie Street South, opposite Pulford Avenue) after leaving Rodney and the partnership. Vito Peralta (1927) remained a tradesman and then became a merchant. Tony ("Amatuccio") DeSantis (1924) and family were for a period tenant farmers or sharecroppers, but never owned farmland. At the same time that the other pioneer families were investing in farms and greenhouses, Tony's family was struck misfortunes: the loss of his wife and a daughter as a result of illness, as well as the induction of his two sons into the army during the Second World War, deprived Tony of the comfort, moral and physical support, and financial base necessary to achieve that goal.

By contrast, the account of Tony DeSantis may help illustrate a more general situation. If the few Leamington Italian families were able to become a major force in the farming and greenhouse industries in the area, one reason was because there was the opportunity for family members and families to work together, for sons and daughters to buy farms near their parents, at times in partnership with them or with other relatives. Another reason was the willingness of all to do hard work. That was generally a practice adhered to throughout the early period, and partly followed in the postwar decades.

THE POSTWAR SETTLERS: TOWN AND COUNTRY

After the Second World War, though "Canada's need for unskilled manpower helped to overcome residual hostility and prejudice against Italy as a land of emigration," and to rescind, "between 1947 and 1951, the 'enemy alien' designation against Italians,"[6] the farms served as necessary points of passage. For some, farm work may have been a necessary evil. Nevertheless, the farms were also the "safe" springboard to the larger community, and sometimes the focal point around which Italian neighbourhoods arose. The intensive immigration and the exponential growth of the Leamington Italian community in the postwar decades might never have occurred had not the early Italian families firmly established themselves on their own farms.

The majority of those who arrived in 1948/49 lived and/or worked on the farms of their relatives. Luigi Carnevale (whose mother was a Corpolongo) and his cousin, Umberto Corpolongo, worked with their newly found "American" relatives, Joe and Alfonse DeLellis (Seacliff Drive or Highway 18); Floyd Cacciavillani, sponsored by Domenic Pannunzio (whose wife's niece was Floyd's mother), for the first year (1948–49) worked with the Pannunzios (Seacliff Drive); Domenic Colasanti, a cousin of Alex, and Joe "Pino" Colasanti (whose father, Alex's brother, had been killed during a 1943 bombardment in Ceprano), went to Alex Colasanti's farm (Ruthven). Frank and son Joseph Mastronardi (son and grandson of Rosina Pannunzio), as well as Ercole (killed in a 1952 auto accident) and his brother Francesco Mastronardi, all stayed at uncle Luigi Mastronardi's farm (Talbot West). Michael DiMenna was at his uncle Tony DiMenna's farm (Union on the Lake), and so was Tony's brother-in-law, Luca Mastronardi. Stanley Cervini went to the farm of his uncle Antonio and cousin John Cervini (Erie North or Highway 77); Carmen DiCiocco was on the farm of his grandfather, Angelo Moauro (Morse Avenue/Lane); and Frank Pannunzio lived on uncle Domenic Pannunzio's farm (Seacliff Drive).

Domenic and Joe Pannunzio also took care of a brother each at this time. Henry and Antonio (1948) both worked on the Pannunzio farm (Seacliff Drive West), but while Henry lived in Domenic's house, Antonio lived with Joe. Guido Pannunzio, who had arrived with his father Antonio (1948), on the other hand, went to live with his grandfather Henry Ingratta and his maternal uncles Domenic and Marius and families (Talbot Road West). After the arrival of Antonio's other son Goffredo (1949) and his wife Aquilina (Henry Ingratta's eldest daughter) and the other three children (Mary, Fiorina, and Pierino "Perry," 1950), the family reunited on a farm they took on shares on Fifth Concession Road (just north of Leamington). Igino Ingratta (who was the son of the same Fiorina Ingratta who had nursed Gino DiMenna, and the husband of Fiorina Mastronardi, Armando's sister) lived on the farm of his brother-in-law, Armando, who had also sponsored him (Oak Street West).

Some also lived and worked on the farms of friends and neighbours of their relatives: Floyd Cacciavillani worked for a brief time for Cervini, and after the arrival of his father Corrado, whom he sponsored in 1949, they went to work on the farm owned by Pete Williams, Domenic Pannunzio's neighbour across the road on Seacliff Drive West (south-side). Attilio Matassa (1948) lived with his brother Joe, on the ten-acre farm that Joe had owned since 5 April 1941, on Second Concession Road East (southside, east of Noble or Bullock Road). Over 60 per cent of all postwar immigrants lived with either their relatives (57 per cent) or friends of their relatives (4 per cent), while 35 per cent rented, and 4 per cent bought their own place within two to three years. The percentage of those who lived with relatives in the immediate postwar period (late 1940s including 1950) is almost 100. Thus, the first place of residence for the great majority was on or near the farm where they worked.

Only a few were on their own: some in "The House of the Immigrants" (chapter 7) in Ruthven, such as Gabriele Leone and Vittorio Guerrieri; others lived in apartments, especially those who settled downtown, such as the Peralta families and the other Sicilians whom Vito sponsored in the 1950s. Vito himself, most likely the first Italian immigrant to settle in downtown Leamington (Brunato, Bernachi, Cicchini or Bert Mastronardi were or had been there but only briefly, 1939–43), probably stayed, at first, in a room in the back of the shop he managed (at 9 Erie Street South, west side, opposite the Bank of Montreal at number 10). But mostly, during the first six years (1943–49), he lived in "a room here ... a room there" until the arrival of his wife, Giuseppina, and their son, Girolamo (March 1949). Then the three of them lived in an apartment above the F.W. Sorrell Jewellers store (30 Erie Street South, east side, north of Mill Street, near the former site of the Greyhound Bus Station). This apartment was also the first residence of Vito's other son, Salvatore, and of two nephews, Girolamo (Jim) Barraco and Salvatore Maniaci, upon their arrival (1950), as well as of Maniaci's wife (Giuseppa Senia), a year later (1951). They all lived there together.

In 1952, when Salvatore Peralta's family arrived, each family rented separate apartments, but very close to one another. By September 1952 (according to the *Bell Telephone Directory*), Vito's residence was at 111 Talbot Road West (east of Elliott Street); and his son, Salvatore, by 1954 was residing at 16 Erie Street South, a few doors north of his cousin Maniaci, who kept the apartment at 30 Erie Street South when the others moved out (and by January 1965, perhaps earlier, the same apartment was the residence of another relative, Girolamo Agosta, who arrived in 1962). Jim Barraco (1920–68) went to live on Fraser Road, north of Seacliff Drive West, at the Don McCarty farm (later owned by Moretto and Olindo Mastronardi, father and son). Though later some moved to new subdivisions, others remained in the downtown area, Barraco himself at 41 Fox Street, while a Minaudo family related to him resided at 108 Erie Street South (between Robinson and Montgomery Streets), in the house owned by one of the pioneers from Lazio, Amato DeSantis (1924). Another Sicilian, Pietro Panzica from Caltanissetta (San Cataldo, 1950), later in Windsor, lived for twelve years at 70 Talbot

Street (i.e., Road) East, in a room in the back of the Princess Grill he owned and operated.

Another group of 1950s arrivals, mostly from Lazio (i.e., *Ciociari*), also resided in the Talbot East area: Loreto DelGreco (1952), Joe (Giuseppe) Maiuri (1953), Mike Molliconi (1954) and Tony Zompanti (1955) rented apartments above the Vogue Theatre (80 Talbot East), subsequently part of Gabriele's Furniture, Carpet & Appliance Centre (76–88 Talbot East) owned by Vittorio (Vic) Gabriele, one of several families also from Lazio (Castelliri, 1950s).

By the late 1940s, besides the Peraltas and most likely Amato DeSantis (by then a Heinz employee), the Leone family (Molise, 1949) also had their residence in the downtown area: at 80 Victoria Avenue (east of Erie, south of Montgomery) in a house they had bought in September 1949. They were, in fact, the first among post–Second World War Italian immigrants to own a house in the downtown area and so soon after their arrival. Gabriele Leone, his wife Rosina (Colaianni), and two of their three children (one was born in Canada) had travelled to Canada at the same time and on the same ship (the *Vulcania*) as Giuseppina and Girolamo Peralta, Vito's wife and son. But the two families only met in downtown Leamington, where there were very few Italians in the late 1940s; and they became friends and then *compari*, like one family (Girolamo and his wife Agatha were the godparents of Josephine, the Canadian-born daughter of the Leones; see chapter 10, "The Extended Family: The *Comparatico*").

The presence of the Peralta and Leone families in the downtown area helped attract more to the "urban" area, which many postwar Italian newcomers seemed to prefer to the rural setting, for both work and entertainment. If the Sicilians generally tended to live with or near Vito Peralta, those from other regions of Italy, particularly Abruzzo and Molise, sponsored or not by the Leones, often found a place in the house of the Leones or its vicinity. In fact, at the very beginning, before the (1952) opening of the first Italian grocery store in downtown Leamington (just west of the "Four Corners"), the house of the Leones was often the gathering place for all, especially the new Sicilian friends. "They all came to the Leones; it was the only Italian house in town then." And since 1949 the house has always been on Victoria Avenue, first at number 80, then at number 70 and finally at number 68.

In general, the Sicilian immigrants did not have relatives with farms. Mainly concentrated in downtown Leamington, after fulfilling their farm work requirement, in the early 1950s they constituted the first nucleus of another small Italian neighbourhood. Some of them may not have worked on the farm at all, since at times, after 1950, the immigration regulations regarding farm work were not followed, nor apparently enforced until the Immigration Department was informed. Some went to work in construction or the factories, including Heinz (e.g., Salvatore Peralta, who had arrived in early June 1950, by 14 August of the same year was already employed at Heinz).[7]

Besides the Seacliff area in the 1930s and afterwards, another early small concentration of Italian families began to form in the 1940s and 1950s around the main intersection of Talbot and Erie Streets. In the northeast it included Nelson, Clark, and Ivan Streets; in the southeast, the south side of Talbot, east side of Erie, and Victoria Streets; in the southwest, Fox and Mill; and in the northwest, Elliott, Clark, and John Streets.

Another area settled early by a small group was on the west side of the town, south of Talbot, north and south of Oak, along Churchill and LaMarsh Streets: the area where Armando Mastronardi bought his farm in 1940 (south of Oak) and his house in 1943 (Churchill Street, north of Oak). In many cases, therefore, the farms bought by the early immigrants clearly served also as centres of subsequent settlements (some temporary, others permanent). Gus Moauro's farm on Hodgins Street and Antonio Cervini's farm on Erie Street North also attracted some families to settle there in the 1950s (on both sides of the Chesapeake & Ohio Railway, east and west of Elliott Street and at Erie Street). A few others were sprinkled around the town on Georgia, James and Pulford streets and at the corner of Erie and Seacliff Drive.

By the early 1950s, except for the Seacliff Drive West area, then outside the town limits, the main concentration of Italian families was within the town limits, all north of Oak Street: along the north and south side of Talbot from Churchill and Fuller Streets on the west, past the Erie intersection to Victoria Avenue on the east, and along the Chesapeake & Ohio Railway, from Hodgins to Erie Street North. The heaviest concentration was around the main intersection where Italians soon established their own little enterprises – the first grocery store (Ida Magri's Italian Grocery) in 1952 at 54 Talbot Street West, not far from the first Italian shoe repair shop, which Vito Peralta managed since 1943 and purchased in 1956 (Leamington Shoe Repairing, at Erie Street South); and by the mid-1960s, other small Italian businesses and shops (tailor, barber), including at least one other grocery business (chapter 9).

However, as the new (post–Second World War) immigrants became increasingly successful, they moved to new and more elegant dwellings and neighbourhoods, often in houses built in new subdivisions that Italians themselves developed (an example of which is suggested by Paglione Drive, off Seacliff Drive West, formerly the property of Vic Paglione). It is this area, Seacliff Drive West or Highway 18 West (hardly "all bush" even in the 1950s) developed into one of the most elegant areas in Leamington. Also called "Seacliff Village," with spacious, wooded lots near the water, it has become one of the most prominent Italian neighbourhoods, where as much as 75 per cent of the property is owned by Italian Canadians. But, whether in town or in the rural areas, the early Italian settlements were few and sparse, not more than a handful of families in each cluster. The recurring complaint concerned the hardship in communicating with those they met, since there were so few Italians around. The others with whom they came in contact, on the farms or in town, were not only the "English" people, but immigrants of several other nationalities. For many Italians, this first and sudden encounter and imposed interaction with people of diverse backgrounds was confusing and challenging. Saveria Magri was one of the first to recall the rivalry that developed between her – a woman and an Italian – and the Polish or German worker in the tobacco fields in the 1930s (see chapter 5, "The Hardships").

THE ITALIANS AND LEAMINGTON'S ETHNOCULTURAL DIVERSITY

The Italians were apparently the real latecomers to this area, not, as was pointed out, the Belgians or some other groups. Several Belgian families had settled in the Leamington area during the First World War, and about thirty families of Russian Mennonites from western Canada, in 1925. They were followed by a second influx before and after the Second World War.[8] Even in 1950, an Italian arriving in Leamington, who did not know "how to speak English," said he often "communicated with hand signals" because there were "not too many Italians around." Though the 1951 Census of Canada did not provide statistics by ethnic group for the Leamington area population, the 1941 figures show the Italians to be fewer than those making up other groups in the area (e.g., Dutch, German, Polish, Russian); and even with the new arrivals at the end of the 1940s, the Italian group was still relatively smaller.

The Italian community and settlements grew within a multilingual, multinational, heterogeneous environment. Since the beginning of the century, Leamington and Mersea have been developing into a multicultural society, to become today almost a microcosm of Canada. Among the thirty different ethnocultural groups, the Italians represented in the mid-1980s over 7 per cent of the population, and the third-largest group.

The Italian community and the Leamington area, in fact, present a parallel growth, demographically and commercially. The population of

Leamington Town grew from 4,351 in 1925 to 7,525 in 1950, and that of Mersea Township from 4,172 to 6,106.[9] In that period, the number of Italian families had more than doubled. By 1971, according to the Census of Canada, the Leamington population was 10,435 and the Italians were 1,045 or 10 percent of the total population, and the third-ranking ethnocultural group after the Anglo-Celtic and German groups. Similarly, in Mersea Township, according to the 1971 Census, the total population was 9,075, while the Italians numbered 650 or 7 per cent of the total, and also constituted the third-largest group.[10] This pattern was maintained in the 1981 Census: the population of Leamington and Mersea Township was 20,870; the Italians were 1,505 or just over 7 per cent of the total, and the third-largest group.[11] The census totals do not include the Italian families that, though residing in the Ruthven and Kingsville areas (Gosfield South Township), i.e., outside Mersea Township, in this study are considered part of the larger Leamington area. The Italians grew from a dozen or so families in the late 1920s/30s to well over 500 families (late 1970s) in this general southeast area of Essex County (see appendices A, B).

The expansion of Leamington occurred mainly during the same decades and especially from the 1950s to the 1970s: incorporated in 1890 amidst much boasting about its "city-like appearance" and mud-free streets year-round (though its main intersection at Talbot and Erie was not paved until 1914–15), from 1901 to 1975 Leamington's population increased by 351 per cent, and by 52 per cent between 1950 and 1975. Leamington's uninterrupted construction period began about the time the pioneers settled in southeast Essex, with work projects in every decade from 1929 to the present, for both new buildings and additions to existing ones: schools, hospitals, libraries, post offices, homes for senior citizens, and churches. The new town hall was completed in 1966.

Many Leamington residents considered 1975 (the year after Leamington's centennial) "the first year of unprecedented growth." A *Star* journalist, reporting on the town's rapid growth in the previous seventy-five years – its increase in population, construction activities, development plans, and especially its progress in the agricultural industry – commented, "History has shown [Leamington] to be the 'Sun Parlour of Canada' ... Historically, the first 100 years have proven steady and economically sound for the community." Highlighted in the historical overview was "the major or key industry in Leamington ... the giant H.J. Heinz Co. Ltd complex [whose] growth can be reflected in the growth of the community."[12]

In 1908 the town of Leamington invested $10,000 to purchase a tobacco factory – the old Ward Tobacco building (southwest corner of Erie South and Oak Streets) "reputed to be the tallest wooden structure (six stories and 116 feet high) on the North American continent" – and had turned it over to the H.J. Heinz Company, which "promised to manufacture food products in Leamington for a period of at least five years starting in the 1909 season. It agreed to manufacture the products of at least 400 acres of garden produce during the first year of the factory's operation, and at least 1,600 acres over the succeeding four years ... During the summer of 1909 district farmers brought cucumbers, beans, cabbages and cauliflower to the plant for pickle production. About 60 men were hired and a giant in Canada's food processing industry was in the making."

One of the town's two newspapers, the *Post*, in its editorial of 22 October 1908 urging the taxpayers to vote in favour of the investment, justly argued and anticipated that to Leamington it meant returns of "hundreds of thousands of dollars" (and in the 1980s with over 1,200 employees – millions of dollars). But as much as the city's monetary investment (which included a twenty-year exemption from most municipal taxes), what helped Leamington secure the industry was what the editorial included among the area's advantages: its "general climate ... geographical position and ... excellent fruit land ... presumed the best in Canada for an industry of this kind." They were basically the same advantages that also attracted first the Italian pioneers (as Alex Colasanti pointed out; chapter 5), and eventually hundreds of Italians, to settle and/or become farmers throughout the Leamington area.[13]

What the 1975 *Windsor Star* article failed to mention in its brief survey of Leamington's twentieth-century growth was its people: the influence of its ethnocultural communities, or at least the connection between this "great manufacturing company" and Leamington's ethnocultural diversity, increasing and changing through the decades, as indicated also by the census figures.

The Leamington area demographic transformation (1901–81) can be best illustrated by considering the population designated by the census as groups of British origin (English, Irish, Scottish, Welsh, and Manx): in 1901, they consisted of 5,556 out of a population (Leamington Town and Mersea Township combined) of 6,615, or 84 per cent; in 1941, of 8,225 out of 11,412, or 72 per cent; and in 1981 (according also to the "Leamington Census Agglomeration: Distribution and Percent of Ethnic Origin Groups") 8,520 out of 20,870,[14] or just over 40 per cent. From a relatively homogeneous society at the beginning of the century (and still so forty years later), by 1981 Leamington Town and Mersea Township had become an ethnoculturally diverse or multicultural area, though not totally a Canada in miniature in this case: the French, with 4.8 per cent of the total population, did not constitute the second-largest but the sixth-largest group; the German group was second with 16 per cent; the Italian, third with 7.2 per cent; the Arabic, fourth with 6.2 per cent; and the Portuguese, fifth with 5.7 per cent. Also, with respect to "Mother Tongue Groups," the 1981 census recorded the official languages combined at 66.9 per cent (English 64.6 per cent; French 2.3 per cent) and the total non-English, non-French, and non-American languages at 33.1 per cent, of which 23.6 per cent was made up by German (12.5 per cent), Portuguese (5.8 per cent), and Italian (5.3 per cent) combined.[15]

GROWING TOGETHER: THE ITALIANS AND LEAMINGTON

The Italian community itself, though Italians were relative latecomers, by 1975 had shared in and contributed to the demographic and socio-economic growth of town and rural areas: in the earlier days in a small way with their work as sharecroppers or as labourers on area improvement projects. (At least two of the 1923 pioneers, Domenic Pannunzio and Tony DiMenna, both employed with Chick Contractors, April–September 1924, worked on the Cottam-Essex section of Highway 3 between Leamington and Windsor, which was not completely paved until 1926.)[16] The rapid postwar increase in their numbers, accompanied by progressive changes in their needs and interests, influenced the establishment of small business enterprises in the downtown area also (barber/tailor shops, grocery stores).

The 1952 opening of the first Italian grocery store (54 Talbot Street West), besides making their shopping easier, the food on shelves more familiar, and their reliance on "pictures on cans" less necessary, also helped the Leamington economy. They no longer needed to go to Meconi's Grocery in Windsor, or to have the goods delivered to Leamington. By 1953 they were able to "shop Saturday nights and congregate in front of the Italian Grocery in Leamington." Though in 1956 one still said that "everything was difficult," he also observed that "every place you went you could find other Italian people" that a new arrival could spend some time with, especially downtown.

Whether settled in rural or urban neighbourhoods, most postwar arrivals recognized that the "earlier immigrants already had the road built for them," and together they continued to be part of the general expansion. By 1964 they had completed their own gathering place – the Roma Club and Community Centre – which in 1967 became the base for full participation in the Canadian Centennial (see chapter 11). Growth in number and activities through the decades had influenced their own general well-being, as well as the quality of life of the entire community: through their increasing involvement in the farming and greenhouse industries, business and construction, fishing and general service enterprises, as well as in Leamington's key industry, where hundreds of Italian men and women had worked or have been working occasionally, seasonally or full time.

By the mid-1960s, Leamington and area appeared quite different to the new Italian immigrants. In the eyes of Bernice Ingratta, seventy-five years old when she arrived from Villa Canale in 1966, the new place was, as reported in the *Canadian*, "at least a branch office of the Promised Land ... just like she imagined Heaven would be." Perhaps in an attempt to clarify her statement, the interpreter Gino DiMenna (president of the Leamington Roma Club) quickly added, "And if you have seen Villa Canale, you'll understand how she feels." However, whether or not a wilful exaggeration from a kind newcomer, the praise reflected the sentiments of many at that time, both immigrants and old settlers; and it anticipated the opinion of many Leamington residents who in 1975 declared that it was the place where they "most like to live."[17]

Unlike the 1975 *Windsor Star* article, the 1966 story in the *Canadian* about "the big move" or the immigration en masse of Molisani from Villa Canale to Leamington, dealt also with the endeavours of the Leamington Italian community, with emphasis on their multi-million-dollar greenhouse businesses, as well as their "$207,000-headquarters building [and] its modern 700-seat banquet hall ... proudly" shown to the Ontario Citizenship Minister John Yaremko at its official inauguration in October 1964. The article implicitly suggested that the growth and prosperity of a town and community were not due to just a key industry, but also to the work and entrepreneurship of its people, to the role also played by a particular group in the community through the years.[18] By 1974, the "prosperous" Leamington Italians, more securely integral parts of the town and area that they "helped build," expressed their Italian-Canadian pride and praise by commissioning a fountain in the downtown area (northwest corner of Erie and John Streets), opposite the Leamington-Mersea Municipal Building, not far from where the first Italian neighbourhood had emerged in the 1950s.[19]

9

Employment

I came to make money ... I heard I could make good money here.

A Leamington Italian

THE QUEST FOR THE "STEADY JOB"

The myth of a distant land of peace or plenty is ever-present in the human heart: Utopia or Shangri-La, Arcadia or El Dorado. In more recent times, "America" has served as the fabled place where streets were paved with gold.[1] Immigrants arriving early in the twentieth century probably wondered in a lighter moment whether they had arrived too late or landed in the wrong place. The harsh reality must have made the self-deception even more bitter. But as they learned to do in time with other disappointments, this also was turned into bantering self-ridicule. One story in the immigrant community dealt with this vision of their future employment: "Apparently, upon disembarking, one of these early immigrants was automatically convinced he had reached the land of opportunity; lying at his feet, on the pavement, was a ten-dollar bill. About to pick it up, he quickly resumed his erect position, kicked it aside, and walked away, saying with an air of sufficiency: 'I've just arrived, I can't start working right away.'" Especially among the pioneers, who in order to earn even half that amount had to do many days' work, if they could find it at all, the story always produced roars of laughter.

Chronicles of early life of Italian pioneers in the Leamington area often read like beautiful inventions. Their spontaneous, vivid, unpolished narrations about finding a job, the work and the drudgery, the subhuman conditions and slave wages, vicissitudes of fortune seem like folktales and romances. Indeed, in order to capture the grim reality of those days, in order to present a composite picture of that experience some writers have resorted to literary images and epic metaphors.[2] Their own quest for employment thus became a sort of "Herculean labour," an "Odyssean journey" in the still strange and unfamiliar environment of Essex County or beyond the Detroit River, constantly at the mercy of adverse natural forces – the seasons, the weather, the crops – often "ship-wrecking" against the reefs of employers' attitudes and bias, or buffeted by the ill will of human demigods wreaking economic and political havoc on the earth, then freed by lucky encounters, benevolent spirits, good Samaritans and, above all, by their own "superhuman" strength of body and mind – wit, cleverness, and even ruses – until they reached safer waters, the more secure ports of a permanent job or self-employment. "There was absolutely no chance to get work … Jobs were not there for us … so you moved around to get anything you could find … ditch digging, highway construction, railroad, canning or tobacco factory, ice plant, junkyard, brickyard, slaughterhouse, meatpacking, drycleaner's, even peddling … anything: factory, farm … fields … picking whatever was in season … tobacco, sugar beets, fruits, vegetables … When there's little to eat, if you're offered $15 per month, you had to stay … or they kicked you back to the old country."

The search for work scattered the first group all over the county and the country. Some suffered injuries (Domenic Pannunzio), others deportation (the Capussi cousins). Though one, by "tricking" the authorities, succeeded in working in Detroit while living in Windsor, others, for fear of being caught, never tried it and lived precariously. They "lined up at factory gates," sometimes with 300 hungry men and little hope "to be pulled in even for a day or two," until "they'd tell us to go home." Some travelled many times by streetcar halfway across Essex County looking for a job, and often "walked miles to collect [their meagre] pay." Invariably the seasons or events limited opportunities, giving rise to harsh competition aggravated by exploitation and intimidation: "They took advantage of us … afraid to risk complaining." Resentment toward immigrants in general was common: "Work and don't take away their jobs in the city"; and discrimination often directed toward a specific group: "Whatever we did was Mafia … Italians enemies … equal Al Capone. If you weren't removed from the job because they needed you on the farm, you were closely watched."

As work became more available, all had to adapt. Many alternated between two jobs – at first equally temporary – the factory during the day and the farm in the evening, even rushing home at noon to put in an hour's hard work on the farm the family sharecropped. The whole family, including children, laboured at tasks around the house, husking corn or "picking tobacco" (i.e., "suckering" or "priming" tobacco). Then things began to change: from piecework to sharecropping, and eventually to farm ownership, which often brought equally severe and continuous trials, but also a progressive liberation from servility, an end to the client situation: "You came here with only a suitcase ... you automatically know that you have to work under someone." In time, their hard work and resourcefulness gained the pioneers a degree of independence, acceptance, and respect; and in spite of all the troubles, they hardly ever regretted their move or condition, as some of them indicated quite unambiguously: "I'd rather stay here dead than in Italy alive"; "Italy never gave me anything"; "I forgot Italy the day I arrived."

THE POSTWAR FARM LABOURERS

While the pioneers, who by the end of the Second World War had survived their twenty-odd-year struggle, were extolling their relatively better life in Canada, a new group began a similar process, even though it was easier for those who came to look for work and better conditions in "America" after the war. By 1948, the Italian pioneers to the Leamington area were all well established – the majority with their own farms. Most postwar immigrants arriving in the Leamington area were thus in a relatively better position: they had a job waiting for them, either with their relatives or with other farmer friends. Nevertheless, even for the sponsored immigrants (though such links and home environment often eased the shock), the farm contract and work presented unexpected hardships, at least for the first few months: a long workday, low wages, and an "unusual" type of work. For the most part, they worked the standard ten hours a day, but often as many as thirteen or fourteen hours or, as one claimed, "from 7:00 a.m. to 1:00 a.m. with one half-hour break." They were mostly unaccustomed to the farming methods requiring "crawling on hands and knees"; many were "disappointed to find that farming was more difficult in Canada than in Italy: in Italy you used a hoe, but in Canada you used hands ... Fruits and vegetables were planted and [at times] cultivated by hand."

A few immigrants, especially those without relatives or friends to welcome them, found themselves in oppressive situations, even reduced to lowly farmhands or domestic servants, performing menial tasks that they regarded as a self-inflicted fall from their previous station, an almost unbearable humiliation. Some, in fact, would have left, had they had the money for the return trip.

The early 1950s were generally described as particularly bad times for employment. It is not even necessary to look back to the days of the pioneers to get a glimpse of the clash between the persistent myth of

"America," with Canada also quickly gaining distinction as "the land of wealth and opportunity," and the often shocking reality: "I heard that I could make good money here. But when I came, it wasn't easy. Jobs weren't easy to find. I cried every day. I came in February and started to work in May. It wasn't even steady ... I went door to door looking for work ... I was so tired at night" (1952). The words and images used to describe the employment situation, even by those who arrived later in the 1950s, sound like rhetorical exaggerations: "[I] heard some things about Canada but didn't find a shovel full of money" (1956); "For the first few years, it was not 'America,' it was *fame, hunger*!" (1958); "In Canada you even have to buy the sun that comes up in the morning" (1958).[3]

The central preoccupation was the need for steady employment. The primary motive for emigration had been financial, and the main attraction of the new country was its potential for economic gain. Unless one could earn good wages, and quickly, the purpose of emigration was defeated. Surviving the long winter months of unemployment, when farm work stopped and other jobs were scarce, added frustration to loss. Some men, after working and saving all summer in order to pay off their debts or to bring over their family, saw all their savings used up for their own meagre sustenance. Rather than being reduced, their financial burden was aggravated.

As sponsored newcomers, they were ineligible for unemployment benefits under the Unemployment Compensation legislation, in effect in Canada since 1940, partly because the sponsoring farmer and/or relatives were responsible for them.[4] But if sponsorship was offered only as a favour to the relative of the immigrant, and the farmer had no need of the newcomer, he found himself in a situation similar to that of Italo Baldassare (1949): he had no job and could "not find work because [he] didn't have an unemployment book." Without work or money, they were often forced to borrow, live off their relatives as long as they could, or suffer with strangers who needed cheap labour, and who often fulfilled their food and lodging obligations with a haystack and "leftover chicken bones." Whenever they could, they just settled for anything, and the postwar, southern Italian immigrants were often well equipped to do so.

In southern Italy, up until the 1950s or just at the beginning of the second great wave of Italian emigration, it was not uncommon for a large class of people to grow up with knowledge of two or more trades or skills, one of which was farming. "To speak of farmers in the strict sense," wrote Saverio Strati, "is not altogether exact," because not all those who worked the land during the Fascist era were *zappatori* (hoers, tillers of the soil), and not all those who asked landowners to rent them a piece of land were *giornalieri* (farm day labourers). To describe this class of people, Strati used a term that was well known in Calabria and southern Italy but hardly familiar to those who dealt with the "Southern Question": *mastro massaro* (literally a tradesman/artisan-farmer or "master farmer"). Bricklayers, carpenters, blacksmiths, cobblers, and even tailors, barbers, and the most sophisticated craftsmen, those least suited physically for farm work, rented small pieces of land from the rich landowners. All these men were called *mastri massari* (and the woman, such as a seamstress who also worked on the rented piece of land, *maestra massara*). The children of such families had to learn, at a very early age, "how to cultivate the land and [with a bricklayer father] how to erect a wall" (and the practice seems well reflected in the many southern Italian family names beginning with *Mastro*, as evidenced also among the Leamington Italians: *Mastr*angelo, *Mastro*mattei, *Mastro*matteo, and the frequent *Mastro*nardi; i.e., "Master-Angelo," "Master-Matthew" and "Master-[Leo]nard"). Since the Italian state had not yet begun its long-range, public works projects (housing, roads) and apprenticeship was almost impossible, the young people inherited their parents' skills and instruments: besides the "hoe," it was usually the "trowel."[5]

Massive emigration changed all that: in the long run, it created problems that remain largely unsolved in both lands (depopulation and socio-cultural deracination); and it slowly brought an end to both the *scambiaservizi* (services-exchange system, replaced by monetary transactions) and the traditional transmission of skills from one generation to the next. Nevertheless, such long-practised customs proved to be advantages to pre– and post–Second World War Italian immigrants. Thus, Baldassare, who, like many others in Italy, had been a farmer, fisherman, and bricklayer, to name a few, in a span of a few years was able to move from one job to another: for a month or so on a Tecumseh farm; forty days at Delhi harvesting tobacco; one and a half years until layoff at Ford; for a year bricklaying in St Thomas; and finally with Ray Allen for thirteen years doing "all kinds of jobs all over Windsor."

Sixteen years later, the skills were different but not the process: by the time eighteen-year-old Sam Catrini reached Canada (1965), besides his "first class seaman" registration and fishing experience, he had obtained a technical high school diploma; at first, that helped him secure employment in Toronto as a hairdresser; then, having "discovered" the Leamington–Lake Erie area, he returned to his preferred outdoor occupation – fishing. In general, given the situation, they had to take advantage of every available opportunity: work at different jobs day and night, "on the farm during the day ... at Heinz during the night"; and that was often the case not just in the 1940s but also in the 1950s and 1960s: "I worked for two months, and six months later I still couldn't find a job ... I had to borrow money for food ... Sometimes I had one job, sometimes two, sometimes none. When there was work, I took two jobs if possible because some months there wasn't any work" (1959).

Work – too little or too much of it – was the main concern. By the 1960s the opinions about Canada had become more balanced. The portrait became more realistic, and sometimes the scale tipped a little toward the negative: "I heard good and bad things about Canada: Some say they never see the sun in Canada because they're too busy working nights" (1965).

From preoccupation, it often became total occupation: Italians, they said, worked so hard and so much that they had lost "the meaning of Sundays, Holy Days and Patron Saints' Days." Work became the sun around which life rotated: "People in Italy would ask when they met you on the street, '*Come stai?*' [How are you?] In Canada it is, '*Eh lavori?*' [Hey, are you working?]" (1965).

Work, a job, employment were metaphors for greetings and salutations, synonymous with good wishes, health, success, identity; and the lack of it, the opposite. Were the Italian immigrants so obsessed with work because of the earlier experiences? Was it a way to escape poverty, to give meaning to immigration, or were they becoming workaholics, slowly assimilating the North American work ethic? Perhaps a combination of all of them! However, there was no evidence among Italians of a sense of personal failure, of total identity crisis, resulting from job loss or unemployment, as was more apparent in the Anglo-Saxon Protestant environment. Italians tended toward blaming the system more often than themselves, and often found ways to beat the system.

The farm, farm work, and farming were the first three essentials in the immigrant reality: the farm (or farmer) provided the guarantee for their immigration papers; farm work was the bridge most had to cross upon arrival; farming remained an important occupation for many of them. In fact, they helped transform the farming industry, not only in the conversion of crops – from tobacco to vegetables – but also in market development and in adoption of fully automated production. Yet, in spite of this ever-present importance in their life, not all Italians became engaged in farming.

Many of those arriving in the mid-1950s, and especially afterwards, preferred to remove themselves as far as possible from farm work once the term was completed. At times, they did not even serve out their full year on the farm, as was required and often expected. They sought factory jobs in the fishing and food industries (particularly at the H.J. Heinz

Company and Omstead Foods Limited) and in construction; but especially in the factories, mainly because of the shorter hours and a secure paycheque. These were reasons most often given even by those who held two jobs, since the shorter day offered them a chance to work on their own land, and the extra earnings helped them to pay off their farm, or complement the income from it: "I liked the work in the factory better ... It was lighter work and I made more money."

THE FACTORY: H.J. HEINZ
AND OMSTEAD FISHERIES/FOODS

The two major industries in the Leamington area that many Italians aspired to be part of through the decades are food processing companies. Inextricably related to the main activities and resources of the area, farming and fishing are good Canadian examples of commercial synergism. The H.J. Heinz Company Limited in downtown Leamington, considered the largest company in this activity in Canada, "the major or key industry" in Leamington since 1908–09, by 1980 had more than 1,200 year-round employees, and hundreds more during the summer harvest time (see chapter 8).

Omstead Foods Limited, established in 1911 in Wheatley (Ontario, approximately ten kilometres east of Leamington),[6] was first involved exclusively in fish production, marketed day-to-day, then in processing "over a quarter million pounds [of fish] ... in a day" (to make them leaders in the industry and "Wheatley the freshwater fish capital of the world"). Omstead later turned to agriculture, to freezing, packaging, and canning vegetables, and reached a processing capacity of up to 200 tons per day. In 1975 it boasted three processing plants involved in fishing, agriculture, cold storage, and transportation; and the status as "Ontario's and Lake Erie's largest freshwater fish processor."[7] Annual output of both companies ranged in the several millions of dollars, several of them put into the local economy. At Heinz "the wages and benefits are about the best paid in the agricultural industry today."[8]

Employment in a factory offered many advantages. But at the beginning, it was neither easy to obtain nor to hold on to, and for many Italians the factory environment was far from ideal: "There was a time when you could not get a job at Heinz because you were Italian ... the result of the war I think ... I was mistreated at Heinz by fellow employees." It was, of course, a more general situation, not just particular to Heinz. During the whole war period, as well as before and after, Italians would not be hired by factories, including the Ford plant in Windsor.[9]

The H.J. Heinz Company

By following the Heinz example, it is possible to obtain a general view of the predicaments and progress in factory work through the decades. It is most unlikely that any Italians worked at Heinz before the Second World War – as confirmed by the memory of the immigrants themselves and of Bill LaMarsh, a retired personnel officer, as well as on some post-1950s company records – except for very few seasonal workers in the late 1930s (such as Gino Pannunzio and Alfred Mastronardi, fall 1938). There are no prewar employment records to substantiate LaMarsh's statement that "the first Italians that worked at Heinz starting in 1934–35 were Tony [Amato] DeSantis, some of the Cervinis, one or two Mastronardis and old Mr Moauro (thought of as old *patrone*)." But it is clear from the interviews that most of them at the time worked on farms; in fact, two of them (Tony Cervini and Angelo Moauro) settled in Leamington in 1938, and their families in 1939 (see chapters 5, 8).

However, the 12 August 1954 Heinz Plant-Wide Master Seniority List (which shows chronologically each male employee hired since July 1921, with respective clock number, department, and hiring date) has the following entry at the 159th place: "Amato DeSantis – Clock No. 3343 – Can Filling Department – Hiring Date: 8-20-46." DeSantis, whose name appears also among the retired members in the 1981 Heinz Veteran Employees Association, was clearly, if not the first, among the first Italians hired permanently by Heinz. Tony himself, during his interview, stated, "I worked at Heinz ... twenty years" (see chapters 4, 8). The first Cervinis appearing in the 1954 Seniority List were Pasquali [*sic*] Cervini (Can Filling Department, 6-23-53, "Re-ins[stated]" 5-27-55 in the Material Handling Department); and John Cervini, Tony's nephew (Storage Department, 6-24-53, "Re-ins[stated]" 5-27-55 in Material Handling Department). The first Mastronardis listed were Luigi Mastronardi (6-12-52, Cereal Department) – not the Luigi (1925) who had bought the farm in 1942, but one who, after retiring from Heinz, went back to Italy; and Gim [*sic*] Mastronardi (6-11-53, "Re-ins[stated]" 5-9-55). But none of the Moauros ever appears in the lists consulted (the 1954, 1955, 1983, and 1990 Seniority Lists and the Veteran Employees Association lists from 1981 to 1990).

Whenever LaMarsh needed an interpreter in an injury and Workmen's Compensation case, he may indeed have turned to the elder of the two pioneer Moauro brothers, Angelo.[10] Bill and Angelo were neighbours when the latter was sharecropping on the farm of Bill's cousin, Bob LaMarsh (1939–42). Angelo was also known to aspire to and often assume a *patrone* or leadership role in the small community, just as he had done years before in the first clandestine emigration venture. But the recognized mediator, the man who first had the complete trust of the people at Heinz and of the Italian newcomers, was Gino DiMenna (Tony's son): It was through Gino, and after, not before, the war that some Italians became full-time employees at Heinz. Particularly in an "emergency ... when workers were badly needed, even temporarily," according to Gino DiMenna, LaMarsh was thus able to find "the best" Italians and convince the management to hire them: "In 1951 Heinz needed help badly, but Heinz was afraid to hire Italians. Bill LaMarsh wanted to hire them, but ... the head of personnel put a stop to it ... Bill LaMarsh talked to someone higher and convinced him that these new Canadians were fine people ... and they agreed to hire the six people who wanted the job, on the condition that Gino [DiMenna] went with them and acted as an interpreter ... The six immigrants were Nick Appugliese, Mike Appugliese, Pacifico DiMenna, Allen DiMenna, Mike DiMenna, and Luca Mastronardi."

Among them was Gino himself, who had been working on his father's farm and had "no plan to work in a factory." In fact, according to the 1954 Seniority List, some of them were hired or rehired permanently: Pacifico DiMenna (4-26-51); Mickele [*sic*] DiMenna (3-6-52); Allen DiMenna (5-27-53, "Re-ins. 5-9-55"), and "Geno" (i.e., Gino) DiMenna (8-16-54, "Re-ins. 6-15-55, Bldg Service Department"). For about ten years, even after buying his own farm in 1957, Gino functioned as the in-house guarantor, interpreter, troubleshooter, and link with the Italians, with those already employed and those who aspired to become Heinz employees; and there were many others that he, in cooperation with LaMarsh, "brought in" during that period and after. A "lot of Italians were farmers, but," pointed out LaMarsh, "a lot knew about machinery and factory work too, which was good." Whatever form of antagonism, resentment, or even discrimination there was in the company against Italians at first, it soon disappeared, as a result also of Gino's intermediary role. At least Bill LaMarsh had "absolute confidence in them and in their judgment," and except "maybe [for] three or four Italians [he] wouldn't rehire," he thought Italians were generally "extremely good workers."

They were hired mainly because they were needed. By 1950, according to Gabriele Leone, who applied and was hired that year (9-13-50, according to the list), it was a "busy time" at Heinz. Nevertheless, even Leone, whose education and technical training might have favoured him to be "one of the first postwar Italians hired at Heinz," did not discount the help of the pioneers in "opening the company's doors," for him and others employed after him, such as Salvatore Peralta, 9-14-50, and his cousin Salvatore Maniaci, 3-8-51 (all three in the Vegetable Department, according to the list). Naturally, those who came "later found it even easier because they had friends or relatives who had been there for a while." Along with the pioneers, they all served as character references, as sort of "sponsors" for factory employment as they had been for immigration and farm work.

Most of the hiring, according to the records consulted by Jack Parsons in the personnel office at Heinz, was done in the 1950s: a few each year up to the 1955 recession and many in 1956, or generally at the height of the Italian influx. The Seniority Lists confirm these trends, even though retired employees are not accounted for in the subsequent lists. Thus, according to the 1954 list, the numbers of Italian males hired yearly were two in 1950; three in 1951; nine in 1952; fifteen in 1953; eight in 1954; and only one in 1955 (but, indicatively, out of the twenty-three men hired in 1953 and 1954, nineteen were reinstated in May and June of 1955).

Similarly, according to the 12 August 1954 Plant Wide Master Seniority List of female employees (dating back to March 1923), nine Italian women were hired between 1952 and 1954. Among the first five were Letizia Matassa (2-14-52); Rosina Leone, Angela Colasanti, and Mary Marcovecchio (6-11-52, all three); and "Sovi" (Saveria) Magri (7-18-52), who was clearly not the first woman to be hired as LaMarsh stated while recalling that "[he] got a kick out of trying to understand her English, because she talked so fast." In fact, of all nine, Letizia Matassa was the only Italian woman who reappeared on the 1 January 1955 Seniority List (six were crossed off and later reinstated, and two designated as having lost seniority).

Nevertheless, by 1955 Heinz had hired forty-seven Italians (including those reinstated and those who left). In 1956, according to the 1983 List (dating back to November 1942), twenty-six Italian men were hired; and in spite of subsequent fluctuations in yearly hirings (four in 1957, five in 1958 to reach again a peak in the mid-1960s, twenty-four in 1964, and twenty-five in 1965), the overall number grew steadily, so that at one point about 15 per cent of the whole factory payroll went to Italian workers. By the early 1980s, according to John Ingratta (grandson of the pioneer John Ingratta, 1923) who quoted payroll records, there were over 200 Italian workers at Heinz, or about 20 per cent of the total workforce. The Seniority Lists of 1983 and 15 November 1990 indicate almost the same percentages: out of 986 and 932 employees, respectively, 201 (almost 22 per cent) and 207 (almost 21 per cent) were of Italian origin.

The issue of discrimination against Italians, a recurring theme in the interviews, revealed a split into opposing factions, at least among some former Italian Heinz employees. Some claimed they had experienced hostility, but in some cases identifying as reasons the "arguments ... about speaking Italian amongst themselves," which "Canadian" co-workers did not like. But even as late as 1957, with relatively fewer Italian workers some felt that the "trouble at Heinz" was that they were "looked down upon: people did not want ... anything to do with Italians." On the other hand, while some maintained that after they learned the language, the situation became generally better, and Italians established themselves quickly in the company, others insisted that the problems were hardly over after the non-hiring hurdle had been overcome. The Italians were generally still "not welcome at Heinz; they were always the first to be laid off from work." But "layoffs," objected others, "were common anyway. Italians only suffered because they were the most recently employed."

For a small group, the deep resentment against Italians came from a different source: not so much from management, or any company structure, as from the fact that "many 'English' employees [were] jealous of the success of Italians ... who earned the same wage but had more to show of it." Nevertheless, most were satisfied, glad, and even thankful that they had a job and "made money," especially when it was quite difficult to find any work: "I liked my job at Heinz ... a good job for a labourer, especially for immigrants without a trade or without a Canadian education ... I made the best of my job."

Bill LaMarsh tried to present a balanced view of Italian workers and their position within the company. He admitted that there might have been at play "a natural bigotry perhaps we all have [but] without any nastiness that is without animosity; and it never really came from the top management but from the average guy: 'What are you hiring so many of them for?'" As proof, he indicated the positions of responsibility some Italians had achieved: "Albert Magri was made head of the union or [the] factory ... Italians [were placed] in quality control." On the other hand, he recognized that in viewing the situation "from the other side of the fence, the Italians might have felt some discrimination." But in his opinion, it was what "any group of people [feels] for two years or so until they can understand English." Many agreed with him: Gabriele Leone (1949), while appreciative that the "foreman watched after them until they understood what they were supposed to do," stated that he himself had no problem either with the "English," who were in the majority when he started at Heinz, or later with "all other immigrants – Portuguese, Lebanese or Italians ... They all liked me." Perhaps one of the reasons for the Italians' advance was what LaMarsh pointed out in an interesting comparison between Italian and Northern European workers. Regarding the latter, he had learned that "they either ran you or you ran them with your foot down. They'd always say, 'Boy if I were in [my old country] I'd do it this way.'" It was a situation he never ran into "with the Italians ... [They] never felt inferior or superior to you; it was important for their personality."

But Bill LaMarsh did not refrain from referring to a certain Italian modus operandi which was, or may still be, neither unusual nor totally reproachable – the wine offerings and the letters from Italian doctors. The "only trouble I had with them was over wine; I never drink, and many Italians would come over to bring me wine; but I had to refuse the wine; I never wanted anyone to say they bought their job." With the other issue LaMarsh was more delicate. But it was not hard to detect that he was aware, that he understood: "maybe three or four times they'd get letters from Italy, from doctors, on how sick they were, so they wouldn't lose their seniority ... letters always came in Italian, and Mrs Garwood [the nurse, wife of Dr Gordon] would translate them ... basically they were obeying the law."

Anyone unfamiliar with the more tragic aspects of immigration might quickly judge and condemn such acts. But during his thirty years in personnel, Bill LaMarsh had come to know well the immigrants and some aspects of their plight. Sometimes he wondered "how Canadians would do in such predicaments in foreign lands." He understood, perhaps because he always tried to follow the advice given to him when he started his job: "If you don't love people ... get out of this job." And he "loved his job and ... he liked people." There "are wonderful things to say about all new Canadians, but [LaMarsh] had a great affinity for Italians]." He admired them for their "thriftiness [and their] strong sense of family." As a result, Bill LaMarsh interpreted and recognized such acts as expressions of resourcefulness on the part of a people, a group, that had been for too long accustomed to struggle and sacrifices, that was striving to build a better life by every acceptable means. He tended to overlook whatever tinge of chicanery that might have leaked through, or "basically they were obeying the law." Yet, his words did suggest that, besides the initial language-related tensions, these practices might have also been partly the cause of some of the problems and antagonism toward Italians in their workplace.

As for himself, he always had a "wonderful relationship with Italians." He never doubted their integrity. He even learned a few words in Italian and he hired them, as many as he could find: "ninety per cent ... within the year of their arrival." He hired them even when he was told that "[they'd] like to work for five or six years and then start a farm." Some of his words of praise stand out like an epigraph: "We could learn a lot from these new Canadians ... the company and the country benefited from the Italian immigration ... the Italians have done marvellous things [for themselves, their family] for their own people."

Omstead Foods and the Fishing Industry

There is no record of any Italian immigrant working in the fish production or fishing industry before 1950. In fact Omstead's "move into agriculture in the early 1950s" coincided favourably with the large wave of Italian immigrants, many of whom, after the more or less compulsory year on the farm, were hired by this company. According to Jake Omstead (interviewed by the student-researchers in 1982), "the Gabriele family [Castelliri, Lazio, 1951] was one of the first Italian families to work at Omstead's" (namely, Guido and his daughter Clara, hired in 1952, and Guido's wife, Maria, in 1953).

The employment situation at Omstead's was well described by Jake Omstead himself:

> At this time the business was very labour intensive. The work was money. They worked hard, and when they were not working at Omstead's, they worked picking tomatoes. Since it was seasonal, people were only called when the weather was fishing weather. However, the working environment or atmosphere was always a happy one, even though the conditions were not good ... because they were getting established, and at the same time they were helping Omstead's get established ... Without the immigrants, Omstead's would never have had [that growth ... they really needed a job ... they helped provide the manpower and Omstead's] made the working rules flexible, and at times women would bring in their children if there was no one to babysit them ... The advantage of working at Omstead's was the piecework: they offered any hard worker the opportunity to make money ... the people welcomed the long working hours because they needed the money.

Many Italians, according to Omstead, "heard of the job through word of mouth," and many of them were hired because "it is obvious that Italians are hard workers." In fact, "at the peak, there were at least 50 per cent Italian employees," while "today [early 1980s] there are only approximately 20 to 25 per cent." (According to a 1990 list, by the late 1960s the Italian employees at Omstead's numbered about 200.) Omstead's, which owned five to six boats, also engaged independent boat owners. At one time, all of the Italian boat owners, "the majority from southern Italy [and] Sicily ... worked for them." But at that moment, Jake Omstead pointed out, they did not have "any Italian fishermen working directly" for them. Omstead's statement was a direct reference to the transformation that had also occurred, in a way similar to the one in the farming industry, in an activity in which many Leamington Italians were involved: the fishing industry.

Management and labour views, more often than not tending to differ, were on this occasion quite concordant. The immigrants' accounts of their employment at Omstead's basically coincided with Jake Omstead's interview. On discrimination, Omstead did not feel it was ever a problem, since their employees came from "all kinds of ethnic backgrounds," and there was "mutual support between them and the company." At Omstead's, said an Italian immigrant, there were "many nationalities working – Lebanese, German, French, Polish, Portuguese, and Italians ... The employer was very fair ... gave work to anyone ... no discrimination against nationalities ... Even when there was no work, he found work for them ... Working conditions used to be pretty bad before ... Water [was often] above their feet ... Union came in about 1969 ... drug and dental plan with the union ... Working conditions are better now at Omstead's."

The only difficulties reported by Italians working at Omstead's were not related to company attitudes and conditions or to tensions with non-Italian workers. They were problems, to some not at all surprising, among the Italians themselves, above all "a lot of jealousy" and sometimes meanness: "The first year ... Italian women would scare me and say if I didn't work the boss would send me home." Yet some preferred to go to work in that "Italian atmosphere" at Omstead's, rather than bear the humiliating mockery "at Pyramid's ... with not too many Italians" in 1959.[11] And there were also other advantages at Omstead's in the 1950s: a fish cutter, paid by the pounds of fish cut, had a chance to make twice as much as on the farm.

Conditions being equal – long hours, pressure, quotas – factory employment was generally preferred to farm work. The mostly language-related "discrimination" initially felt in the factories was an obstacle eventually overcome, at least in part, but often sufficiently to enable some of them to get away from farm work. Even "work on the railroads was better than on the farm," in spite of the wages and "boxcar" living arrangements that some did not mind and even liked: "They fed me ... gave me a place to sleep ... and paid me sixty-five cents per hour."[12]

FARM AND FACTORY EMPLOYMENT

Even so, more than a farm/factory polarity, there seemed to have been a farm/factory employment integration all along, as was particularly evident in the 1950s, so much so that a general pattern of employment can be established. Most immigrants first found work on the farm, remaining there for a few months or a few years. They would then attempt to secure a factory job, working on the farm and in the factory simultaneously, and return to full-time farm work (if possible) when laid off from the factory. (The rapidly growing greenhouse industry ensured that some farm work was also available in the winter.) Thus, they either waited until they obtained seniority and secure, steady employment at the factory, or purchased their own farm and eventually quit their factory job.

The transitional period was feverish and worrisome. On the one hand, there was the strain of commuting between two jobs, often pirouetting between Heinz and their farm work during their lunch break; and of working fifteen to sixteen hours a day (a ten-hour night shift at the factory and four to six hours on the farm); as well as the risk of illness and its long-term consequences. On the other hand, they subjected themselves to a stressful daily existence because they remembered their earlier jobless days; and they lived in constant fear of being left without a job, since farm and factory work were mostly seasonal. In order to secure year-round employment and a future, they had to make provisions, use foresight, and exercize all the stamina they could muster. The solution for a while was just as dangerous – a balancing act between two uncertainties. But they skilfully interrelated and took advantage of the two realities – the farm and the factory.

However wise their building toward more than one option, at a certain point a choice had to be made. Many chose the farm: postwar newcomers to the Leamington area, as well as the children of the Italian pioneers, followed in their forerunners' footsteps and went into farming. Others chose the factory: as times changed, as "Italians built a good reputation for themselves," they were able to rise through the ranks and reach positions of leadership and responsibility as foremen and supervisors. Both outcomes were already taking place in the mid-1950s. But there were also those who chose neither: as years passed, particularly the children of Italian farmers often went into other forms of employment, which was not necessarily a disappointment to the parents. During periods when farming had to face severe crises and "growing financial problems" due to natural disasters, market conditions, or government policies, the families were especially happy that their children had chosen different professions: "I'm glad my sons are not farmers ... One is a factory worker; the other is an industrial engineer ... less worries."[13]

THE WOMAN'S "DUAL RESPONSIBILITY" AND CHILDREN'S CHORES

Immigration, by necessity, transformed as many members of the family as possible into workers. Most women worked, and if Saveria Magri's experience was an indication, they often worked very hard: in and around the house, on farms, in factories, and wherever they could find a job. It was probably not very different for Maria Matassa and Esterina Moauro, who in the 1940s worked with Saveria Magri at the Imperial Leaf Tobacco factory in Leamington. Sometimes they had to bring their infants with them on the job: on the farm, as in the case of Rosina Leone, and in the factory, as in the case of others working at Omstead's. It was also their hard work that enabled the family to move quickly out of its difficult times and save for a house and a piece of land of their own.

For some of the women, however, it was often difficult to adjust to this new reality. Unlike the women from Villa Canale (Molise) who had been familiar with farming life, some of the women from the province of Frosinone (Lazio), and most of those from Sicily were accustomed to a different situation: "My life here was harder because I always had to work ... In San Vito [Sicily], the women didn't have to work; but then we had to think twice before we bought something ... When I first came, there was little work and there was little money ... I had to work here if we wanted to get ahead ... It was more necessary for the woman to work here, because there were more expenses than there were in Italy."

Here, the women frequently stated, they had a dual responsibility: a job and raising the family. They had to rise early, send the children off to school or to the sitter, then go to work themselves. In the evening they made supper, cleaned the house, and tended to the children when they returned from school or from a day's work. This daily routine went on for many years, down to the present day. Many Leamington Italian women today work at the factory or on the farm, while maintaining the household. Although, for the most part, it is no longer a financial necessity to work outside the home, many prefer to keep their jobs: "I don't have to work, but I like the money."

As in the larger community, work and money have enabled the Italian woman to gain greater independence. While customs and traditional attitudes persist, especially in a small, isolated community, the status of Italian women has been progressively changing. The new environment sometimes required that they take charge of the situation: they often became head of the family. Since the earlier days, they proved to be and were often recognized by men as equals in their work, and by their husbands as partners in their investments and in their business. Alex Colasanti remembered his first wife Emma not only as a hard worker, but one "who took care of everything," as an equal partner. Saveria Magri did not allow any male worker to humiliate her and did not refrain from humiliating them by showing she was better than they were, even in hard tasks.

After 1952, when the first Italian women started to work at both Heinz and Omstead's, many others were hired, including, in each of the following decades, the daughters and granddaughters of the women pioneers. According to both companies' 1990 lists of employees (from the 1950s to the 1980s), out of the 207 Italian employees at Heinz, thirty-seven (about 18 per cent) were women, while at Omstead's out of about 250, 170 (68 per cent) were women (and in the 1950s alone they numbered fifteen out of the twenty Italians hired by Omstead's). The women showed the same energy and ability as the men in farm and factory work, as well as in managing a business, including the Roma Club (chapter 11): Ivana (Colasanti) Ercole (Ceprano, 1952), as manager (1983–94); Margaret (Ricci) Ingratta (Poggio Sannita, 1954), as president (1993–94; 1999–2000). The younger generation of women pursued positions in other fields, particularly in education (see also chapter 10, "The 'Special' Role of the Woman").

The children worked just as hard, before as well as after the Second World War, as Domenic Magri well remembered (chapter 5): "If I made twenty-five cents after school … I earned something." In the earlier days, even twelve- and thirteen-year-olds had to find ways to help the family in household chores or on the farm. Domenic Magri, at thirteen, was husking corn after school for three cents a bushel, and at barely fourteen, working on a tobacco farm near Olinda. After the pioneers bought the farms, the children carried out as many duties as the parents, especially if during the day the parents were working in the factories. For some children, life was quite hard, even later: "My brothers had it more difficult than I did … They had to work every night after school and on weekends … My parents always pushed work … and my brothers had to give their money to my father … I didn't have to go to work after school because by that time they were pretty settled ... I was able to keep the money I earned."

The difficulties varied according to age and sex. The economic burden of the family was more greatly felt by the older children, and more by the boys, who had to work, than by the girls, who were often confined to the home. The daughters' main problem was, of course, that confinement: the lack of freedom to go out in the evening, which the boys almost never experienced. In fact, both the imposition on the son to work and give up his salary, and the restrictions placed on the daughter were often the cause of many family arguments and distress. In some cases, it may also have been the main motive behind the children's efforts to pursue a degree in higher education, a well-camouflaged and justifiable pretext to leave home (i.e., a better program in a college or university farther from home). But that experience often produced an opposite effect: a desire to go back home as soon as possible and cherish even more the warm family environment. Besides, by then they had a diploma, a degree, or a profession that afforded them greater freedom (see chapter 10, "The Challenging Balance"; chapter 14, "The 'Uncertain' Legacy" and "Bases for Balance").

THE WAGES

The pay was as irregular and varied as their jobs and the hours they worked. But wage levels and oscillations depended also on the location, the seasons, the economic and political events and climate, as well as on other factors not easily quantifiable, such as attitudes and luck. It was almost impossible to establish with precision any pay standards for the different decades or periods (Depression, war years, or time of arrival) or different jobs (i.e., farming, factory, construction, or other trades). There were just indications that the wages were generally low, and lower in some jobs than in others.

In the 1920s, Gus Moauro stated, he worked for as little as seventy-five cents a day, for ten hours. But he was probably referring to the United States, where he was already working at the end of 1924. (Nevertheless, in such cases, the fifteen to twenty dollars the agent charged for finding them work on the farm was approximately equivalent to a month's wages; see chapter 4, "Job Search," and "The First Men from Lazio.") Some of the men earned one or two dollars for a day's work on the farm. This often included the dubious benefits of food and lodging. For at least four of the pioneers, this was far less than the five dollars per day each earned shortly after their arrival in Quebec, December 1923. But it was winter, in the middle of the bush, and very hard work in a primitive labour camp. In fact, the same four men earned even more, subsequently, on a construction job in Trois-Rivières in the winter of 1924. Although the pay rate was thirty-five cents per hour, through good luck and a very friendly Italian boss, they were able to work more hours and even collect more than the hours worked.

A similar windfall would not be experienced again for a long time. In their next job, with the Grand Trunk Railway, which in early 1924 took them to Windsor, they earned only twenty-five cents an hour; that regressive step anticipated the situation on the Essex County farms where the wages were as low as fifteen dollars per month, or about less than half of what some others earned toward the end of 1924. Between 1924/25 and 1926, Alex Colasanti seemed quite satisfied with some of his earnings, ranging from about five or six dollars a week in a tobacco factory to forty dollars a month on the farm, both in the Kingsville area. Ten or more years earlier at Ford in Detroit, "$2.75 a day or less was standard pay for unskilled or semi-skilled labour," and after "January 12, 1914 ... each production worker [was] paid five dollars for an eight-hour shift." Improvements for some, at least up to the Depression, may be illustrated by the fact that in 1927 two of the more recent arrivals were able to buy an automobile for seventy-five dollars, even if they had to pool their resources.

However, besides wiping out jobs, the Depression decimated wages and fixed them at the same or lower levels for quite some time.[14] In the 1930s Michele Magri worked for eight years as a labourer with Gosfield South Township at $1.60 a day. In the same period, according to Saveria Magri, piecework in the tobacco fields earned her $2–3 per acre, but she did not specify how long that required. At Heinz, although it was not clear when, Tony DeSantis earned twenty-five cents an hour. By comparison, an independent trade or self-employment could generate quite a larger income: Vito Peralta's shoe repair business in Windsor in the late 1930s earned him as much as $18 per week, but he had to work on Saturdays and even Sundays. By the time the RCMP closed him down (1940), he was making almost twice the $10–11 weekly average.

The war-related production re-established and surpassed employment levels of the pre-Depression era: "There was full employment." After all, by the early 1940s few were counted in the unemployment statistics since not only Japanese and Germans but Italians as well were in internment camps or stuck on farms, as were the Italians in the Leamington area. "Thanks to the war, an industrial worker in 1941 earned twice as much as in 1939, and he or she was twice as likely to be a member of a union."[15] But even in the late 1940s, the wages paid to some immigrants were quite low, as indicated by the earnings of Gabriele Leone and his wife from their farm work in Ruthven: twenty-five dollars a week each, less five dollars a week for each of the two rooms rented from the farmer. The monthly rate for the sponsored immigrant on the farm of relative or friend for the first year averaged fifty to eighty dollars plus room and board. The factory workers, according to Gino DiMenna who worked at John Wyeth's in Windsor, were already earning fifty cents an hour years earlier.

The farm rates reached fifty to sixty cents an hour in the early 1950s, and about seventy-five cents an hour by 1959. Some felt they were still lower than in other jobs and left the farm in hope of earning a little more. In the early 1950s in some railroad jobs, workers received sixty-five cents an hour with food and lodging. The Canadian Pacific Railway paid seventy-five cents an hour, perhaps less, as one pointed out, than what Canadian-born workers were paid, but definitely more than one earned on the farm; and again with food and lodging, even if it was in a boxcar. From the mid-1950s on, when the factories began to hire immigrants, many found that the wages were better than on the farm. In the late 1950s a fast worker at Omstead's earned seven dollars in half a day, the same amount, at least according to an interview, earned in a whole day on the farm. In the 1960s and thereafter, particularly in the factories, the working hours and wages became progressively standardized. In some cases the introduction of a workers' union began to regulate job security, plant conditions, and pay rates; and, as Jake Omstead pointed out, the needs of the workers changed: as people became "settled, they did not need the long hours."

Omstead's observation may very well indicate that the wage disparity between farm and factory was just an impression: the larger earnings seemed the result more of long hours, type of work, and speed, than of differences in rates of pay. (On the Delhi tobacco farms in the mid-1950s, one could average over ten dollars a day.) The difference in wages was not substantial, so marked as to make a difference between poverty and quick riches. But the factory work, even if temporary or seasonal at first, besides the immediate advantage of the salary, offered additional security; if not real, it was an important sensation or state of mind: another door unlocked and opened on their future.

Nevertheless, those who remained on the farm outnumbered those who left it, except in the more recent years; and besides, many of them had found a way of combining farm and factory employment. They were sufficiently satisfied that they had a job; holding two jobs seemed like good fortune. By the 1960s they were well on their way: either on their farms, even by then already a multi-million-dollar investment; in the factory, where they eventually obtained seniority, security, and some lower management positions; or in other industries such as fishing and construction, as well as trades. In general, there were more complaints about the long hours, hard work, and conditions than about low wages.

EMPLOYMENT AND TRADITION: FARMING AND THE MOLISANI

Another pattern emerged from the interviews and documentation: the Italian immigrants to Leamington tended to choose occupations that were related to those they had before, in Italy, the countries where they had gone to work, or places to which they had immigrated, before reaching Canada (particularly if admitted to Canada as skilled workers; see Lusetti or Bonfiglio, chapter 7). Naturally, the new immigrants aspired to belong to the "self-employed" category, as implied by a postwar immigrant who became a greenhouse owner-operator: "There are two categories of Italian workers: self-employed and factory workers ... Many liked to be their own bosses."

In the "self-employed" category can be included the trades or the fishing industry. But in Leamington, after the Second World War, "self-employed" frequently meant aspiring to become farm and greenhouse owners, like most of the pioneers who had sponsored them; and this tendency was particularly strong among the Molisani, specifically among those from the Agnone–Villa Canale area. After all, of the twelve (out of the fifteen) farms bought between 1931 and 1946 by the Leamington Italians, nine belonged to Molisani, eight of whom were from Agnone and Villa Canale (chapter 8). The postwar immigrants, almost all farming people like their pre-war predecessors from that area, tended naturally toward farming. But just as decisive for the postwar Molisani was that they too were immediately impressed and attracted by the arability of the rich, flat, fertile land of southeast Essex, in contrast to the meagre, hilly, stony plots they had been used to in Upper Molise. Quite a few worked toward owning, as soon as possible after their arrival, a part of that land as well as a greenhouse business.

Statistics illustrate the trend for each decade and for the overall period. Among the 1948/49 arrivals from Italy, 16 of the 28 men listed farming as their main employment, and 13 (81 per cent) were Molisani (compared to 2 Laziali and no Sicilians). Of the 1950s arrivals, 203 (out of 210) gave their occupation: out of the 66 who listed farming (only), 59 (89 per cent) were Molisani; if included are those in part-time farming 65 out of 79 (82 per cent), (compared to 6 Laziali and no Sicilians)

Among the 1960s arrivals, 130 (out of 143) listed their occupation: of the 27 who listed farming, 22 (81.5 per cent) were Molisani (compared to 5 Laziali and no Sicilians). And of the 1970s arrivals, 35 listed their occupation: of the 4 in farming (only), 2 were Molisani and 2 Laziali (no Sicilians).

For the overall period of immigration and settlement, 1948–79, of the 396 (out of 417) males who indicated their occupation at arrival and their later permanent area of employment, 113 listed farming as their only occupation, and 96 (almost 85 per cent) were Molisani. If in the total are included those who listed part-time farming, it would be 104 out of 128 (81 per cent). By the early 1980s, the farmers from the Agnone–Villa Canale area of the (Abruzzo-) Molise Region of Italy represented a sizable portion of the extensive greenhouse-growing industry in the Leamington area. According to the 1980 Leamington-area membership list of the Ontario Greenhouse Growers Marketing Board, 40–45 per cent of the 170 farmers were Italian families. In other words, over seventy-five farms – varying from approximately seven to thirty-five acres (only one with over sixty acres) and including covered greenhouses ranging from about 55,000 to 100,000 square feet – were owned by Italians. Over sixty-five of them belonged to Molisani, fifty of which to four family groups with roots in the Agnone–Villa Canale area (Villa Canale alone forty-eight) and with the same names as those of four of the first (i.e., 1923–25) immigrants: four Pannunzios, six Ingrattas, eight DiMennas, and thirty-two Mastronardis.

Clearly, the Molisani were also well represented in three other categories: out of a total of 159, 50 (31 per cent) gave "factory" as their place of employment, 24 of 49 (almost 49 per cent) "construction," and 12 of 42 (28 per cent) declared they were involved in "other" occupations. However, none of the Molisani listed "fishing."

THE "COLASANTI FARMS LIMITED" AND OTHER *LAZIALI* ENTERPRISES

The most notable exception in the farm-greenhouse business is Colasanti's complex in Ruthven, established not by a member of the Molisani group but by a pioneer from the province of Frosinone, Lazio region of Italy: Alex Colasanti, who, along with Tony DeSantis, was the first among the Leamington Italian pioneers to go to work on an Essex County farm, in 1924 (chapter 4). Nevertheless, the majority of immigrants from this area south of Rome (*Ciociaria*), opted for factory jobs, particularly at Heinz or Omstead's. Indicatively, the first full-time Italian employee at Heinz was Alex's travelling companion, also from Lazio and a former *carabiniere*, Tony DeSantis (hired in 1946).

For the postwar *Laziali* immigrants, farming had often been only a sideline in Italy – their five to six acres (or even less) of "low productivity" land used mainly to grow food for the table. Steady employment was sought in industry, the trades, or services in the Frosinone-Rome area or in other parts of Europe. Besides, unlike the Upper Molise towns and Isernia province, which were isolated geographically and politically (Molise was attached to Abruzzo until 1963, and Isernia was part of Campobasso until 1970; see chapter 2), Lazio's Frosinone province, more favoured by location as well as by the 1950 "South Italy Investment Fund" (chapter 7), is and has been much more industrialized.[16]

Statistics indicate the trends for the *Laziali* from 1948 to 1979: "factory," 83 out of 159 (52 per cent); "construction," 14 out of 49 (28.5 per cent); "farming," 15 out of 113 (13 per cent). But the *Laziali* were high in the "other" category, specifically the trades: 20 out of 42 (47.6 per cent). One, Gino Perciballi (Boville Ernica, 1967, age thirteen) was apparently the only non-Sicilian to list his new occupation as fisherman; but Gino had married a Sicilian woman of the Causarano family, owners and operators of a fishing business.

THE SICILIANS' TRADES AND BUSINESSES

Farming, in Sicily, had not been considered profitable by most postwar Sicilian immigrants in Leamington. Many had turned to manual labour in construction, marble work, and fishing; those who had to earn their living in the marble quarries considered excavation very dangerous. Others had engaged in basic trades – barber (or hairdresser), tailor, bricklayer, and shoemaker (like their pre–Second World War pioneer Vito Peralta). Those Sicilians especially who had spent some time in other countries (England, France, Germany, and Tunisia) had learned other skills (mechanical, electrical, welding), and several who came from sea villages had become fishermen.

Only a very few had been involved in farming, in spite of the efforts, between 1950 and 1955, to revive Sicilian agriculture with the "land reform" and large investments in the sector by the *Cassa per i Mezzogiorno* (82.5 per cent of the expenditures of the "Southern Fund" in Sicily in that period went to agriculture; only 9 per cent to industrialization). But the division and distribution of 87,311 hectares of land to the people, an average of less than 3.7 hectares per grantee, did not prevent the decrease of the labour force employed in agriculture. The island, the celebrated "granary of Rome" of antiquity, in the late 1960s was in fifth place among the Italian regions in wheat production (and had to employ twice the area cultivated in the northern Po River valley).

While Sicily is rich in citrus fruit production (in the late 1960s two-thirds of Italian oranges and tangerines, almost all lemons) and in other products (wine, oil, nuts, cotton), as well as having industries (food, textile, mechanical, and chemical, including some oil refineries), its most important asset is the fishing industry (about one-fifth of the national production), including specialty fishing (tuna and swordfish). But for decades and more the island has had an abundance of vexing problems: aridity, an average income about half that of the North, mismanagement, and a series of contradictions that parallel Italy as a whole (the traditional regional East-West or Catania-Palermo dualism, economic disparities between coastal and urban areas, the depopulated hinterland and, some would say, the influence of certain "organizations"), have made Sicily, since the 1901–10 exodus, the largest Italian exporter of its labour force (1975 calculations indicate that, of the six million Italian immigrants abroad, as much as 40 per cent may be Sicilian).[17]

The area of origin of the majority of the Leamington Sicilians, Trapani province and particularly San Vito Lo Capo (in recent years fast changing into a tourist "golden beach," thanks also to the Detroit-Windsor and Leamington *Sanvitesi*), had been a "poor area for decades."[18] When they arrived in the Leamington area, the postwar Sicilian immigrants, for the most part, tended to go into construction, factory work, and fishing. Of the eighteen people who listed "fishing" as their main occupation for 1948–79, all except one (and he had become part of a Sicilian family) were Sicilians (94.4 per cent). The first time this category appeared in the 1950s, the only five to list "fishing" were all Sicilians. In other categories we can observe the following for 1948–79: "factory," 20 Sicilians (which is a higher number than that given for fishing, 17, but much lower in percentage); out of 159 listing "factory" work, 20 (12.5 per cent) came from Sicily; "construction" has 8 out of 49 (16 per cent); while "farming" has none, with only one Sicilian in "part-time farming/part-time factory/construction"; the "other" category lists only 2 for the entire period.

The Sicilians have become owners of a variety of businesses (construction companies, a hotel-restaurant establishment, as well as fish processing facilities/outlets, i.e., Etna Foods and Lake Erie Foods). But it is perhaps in the fishing industry that expansion has been visibly continuous. For years, as Jake Omstead indicated, their boats were engaged by Omstead's, but later most became independent Great Lakes fishermen and entrepreneurs: the Figliomenis, Catrinis, Rubinos, Causaranos, and

Peraltas. One of them, Vito Peralta, is the grandson of the first Sicilian in the Leamington area, Vito, the shoemaker from San Vito Lo Capo.

The career of the younger Vito is an example of the employment pattern of the later generations and more recent immigrants. Born in Italy in 1948, he arrived in Leamington in 1952, with his mother Pietra Adragna, his sister Giuseppa, and brother Nick (joining his father Salvatore, 1950, as well as his grandparents and the rest of the Peraltas). From age eight he worked as a shoeshine boy at the family shoe repair shop, as a fish-cutter at Omstead's, then as a foreman and engineering technologist. In 1975, Vito started his own company, Etna Foods Limited, and by the mid-1980s, he had sold the Mediterraneo Fish Market (located in Windsor) to another Sicilian, Frank Aiuto, and he owned five fishing boats. In the early 1980s, a many-year-long legal battle, engaged against the Ministry of Natural Resources over fish quotas, again forced a Vito Peralta, thirty-five to forty years after the pioneering grandfather, to appear before a Canadian court to defend his rights as a citizen of Canada.

As if to illustrate, on a small scale, Giambattista Vico's course and recourse theory, history was repeating itself.[19] In a more general way, what was also repeated in the Leamington Italian community was the southern Italian tradition of securing economic safety by engaging in more than one occupation. Considering all areas of employment, according also to Joe Colasanti (Lazio, 1948), "Ninety per cent of the Italians have their own business ... Even if they have a job, they have something extra going because they like being self-employed."

ITALIAN AND NON-ITALIAN
EMPLOYEES AND EMPLOYERS

Intergroup relations in the workplace did not always emerge in a clearly defined pattern. The positive and negative views and attitudes toward other workers of different nationalities were quite balanced. Some had no problems with "the others"; others preferred to work where there were "more Italians." The reason most often given for this preference was communication rather than inherent national hostilities or outright discrimination: "People made fun of me because I couldn't speak English." However lighthearted, that sort of "making fun," for the recipient, could be quite cruel; but perhaps more cruel, as well as ironical, was getting this kind of treatment, and sometimes worse, from the other Italians in the workplace. More than once, reference was made to such problems as jealousy (envy), petty quarrelling, and scare tactics, or what today would be called "harassment in the workplace" ("Italian women would scare me"). It is not clear whether the cause was invidious competition or simply garrulity. There was, in fact, a situation when too much talking in Italian at work jeopardized their jobs.

Somewhat different and a little more complex was the Italians' relation to the "Canadians," also referred to as *Inglesi* (English). These terms were often used to identify two amorphous groups: sometimes all those who did not speak Italian, or with whom they could not communicate in Italian and, most often, all those born in Canada, particularly the Anglo-Celtic group, the "English." Often, the Italians could not understand "why the Canadians felt some resentment for them." Was it because they looked different or simply because they were foreigners?

Gino DiMenna was uncertain whether the prejudice he experienced in the schools was "on purpose" or "perhaps the teachers were afraid of losing their jobs." He also wondered, along with others, whether the discrimination against Italians was the result of the Second World War or "perhaps jealousy" over their "success." Some thought that the "Canadians" saw the Italians as threats to their jobs: "Why hire so many of them?" This perception of the immigrants as scapegoats for unemployment or some economic ills has been invariably applied to different groups at other times: Irish, Jews, Blacks, Japanese, Asians, and others. During and after the Second World War it was particularly the turn of the Italians, especially in the 1950s when they constituted the largest group of immigrants to Canada (see chapter 13, "Prejudice").

Generally, all newcomers were (and are) made to feel inferior, "looked down on" or "eyed with suspicion." ("*I Canadesi mi guardavano brutto*," DeSantis, 1924). The immigrant reaction to this "Canadian" attitude varied according to individual and also to group, and it took various forms of rebellion or withdrawal. Two different examples of immigrant self-defence in the workplace appeared in Bill LaMarsh's interview. Though barely touched upon, they were clear in his final comparison of Italian and other workers: open criticism or resistance on the one hand, silent endurance on the other.

An attitude of superiority appeared through their direct challenge of the skill, knowledge, and authority of the "Canadian" co-worker and foreman, of the efficiency of the "Canadian" system: "They'd always say, 'Boy, if I were in Germany, I'd do it this way.'" It was not uncommon and not very different from the often-heard English or British declaration, "At home, we'd do it better." Whatever the source, it wasn't kindly received. In some cases, such conduct could also be perceived as "insubordination," or at least as disrespect for the person in charge; and that required resuming control quickly and running "them with your foot down" before they started running you. In most cases, however, it was less an expression of aggressiveness or arrogance than a form of protection of one's identity, so closely linked among immigrants with the group and/or land of origin ("their cultural roots").[20]

It was also a natural response to what LaMarsh described as "a natural bigotry perhaps we all have ... a habit [Canadians subconsciously have]." However unintentional, this attitude had deeper implications that the immigrants felt compelled to counteract. However inadvertent, it suggested to the newcomers that they were automatically inferior – at least a few degrees below the status of the "more fortunate" Canadian-born worker, the established Canadian – simply because they had been forced for whatever reason, economic or political, to leave their native country and seek refuge and a *better* life in Canada. The newcomers knew they were expected to be grateful for this generous Canadian act, but they weren't at all ready to be obsequiously so. Therefore, their subconscious "offensive" reaction was a way of re-establishing a balance: an overcompensatory declaration of their equality.

The other reaction, defined as silent endurance, was of a different mode, but the goal was the same, as revealed by LaMarsh's observation of Italian workers, and also by the workers themselves. This should not, however, suggest that the Italians did not at times consider themselves superior to the "Canadians," and their own ways better! On the contrary, the feeling was (still is) quite widespread. It can even be detected in many of their jokes, which tend to demythologize Canada, or in the "desecrating" parody of the Canadian national anthem.[21] Oblique and direct comments were often made on "Canadian" casualness in dress and behaviour, in their eyes unsophistication and sloppiness; on their gullibility, particularly in political matters; and their poor eating habits: "a matter of cookies and potato chips" (DeSantis). An early example was Saveria Magri's compassion mingled with disdain toward her "Canadian-English" neighbours, who, though better off than she, kept their house "dirtier," and not having anything to eat, "borrowed" things from her, a recent immigrant.

The general feeling was that Italians were better because they knew how to endure and overcome the harshest situations; and Saveria again summed up the reaction and the outcome with the "donkeys" and "horses" analogy (chapter 5, "Pride and Survival"). On the other hand, "Canadians" were sometimes regarded as a "naive, narrow-minded, and complacent" people; or they were referred to – both mockingly and affectionately, since at times the term was used for the Italians' own Canadian-born children – as *"mangiachecc"* (a typical Italian-Canadian erm composed of the Italian verb *mangia*, eat, and the Italianized English word *cake*: therefore, "cake eaters," that is, "over nourished" but "underdeveloped" beings).

At times, the Italian immigrants did not hold back their anger toward the "Canadians," particularly during the war years, for the suspicion, distrust, fingerprinting, surveillance, and general rough treatment: "I sort of blew up" (Marius Mastronardi); for the false accusations, arrest, and especially for depriving him of his livelihood (Vito Peralta); and after the war for being generally derided and mocked. After Bruno Matassa arrived in 1948, he "was called DP [displaced person] several times ... got used to it, but at one point I had to answer back," and he reacted to the offensive term with a general challenge: "Well, I'm better off than you. I was at least chosen to come here; you just happened to be born here, and maybe you would not have been chosen to come here like me because of your attitude."

They didn't lack reasons to feel and express anger. But unlike their northern European colleagues, most of the Italians preferred to keep under control whatever sentiments of superiority or anger they harboured. They had to keep them well hidden in order not to further aggravate their already difficult situation, particularly in employment opportunities. This was apparently equally true for those who came before and after the Second World War: Gino DiMenna, who was twelve years old when he arrived (May 1936), observed that the "children born in Canada have different ideas," and went on to clarify that "the people brought up in Italy are all good people, but reserved ... The older people are more careful, [while] the people who came after the war are afraid ... to be frank."

Whether "reserved" or "more careful," both groups were generally less outspoken: almost afraid to openly proclaim to their "Canadian-English" co-workers or foremen their true feelings, their real worth! Their challenge had to take a different form. The reasons were many, and they knew them! First of all, they had to break through the powerful barriers of some deep-rooted prejudices, stereotypes, and residual distrust of the war period: the short, handwaving, boisterous "Eye-alians, with dark complexion, from 'Mussolini-land'"; the "jackals"; the "enemy aliens" of a few years before; or the Mafiosi compatriots of Al Capone. Laws and regulations changed, but attitudes, perceptions, and old fears lingered.

It was already quite difficult to find work in the 1950s: the ingrained bias made it even more difficult for Italians. To react against the slurs openly could have meant being barred completely from many jobs. To be without a job meant not just poverty, but total failure. "To be unemployed," a Canadian journalist even in 1986 noted, "is to be a leper." One must have work "to be respected by a society that values work so much."[22] In order to find and keep a good job, the Italians had to prove, first of all, that they were not what they were perceived to be.

They could not, therefore, say what they were able to do. They had to try to prove it to the Canadians with positive deeds: bide their time, take advantage of every opportunity that would make the Canadians take notice, and convince them of the Italians' good qualities. Thus, just to get a foot in the door of a factory, they had to accept even "two hours of work" at "half an hour's" notice. They, of course, tried different strategies to obtain that important job, even offerings of "bottles of wine"; buy it if necessary! That was less a concern than not having a job at all. Besides, wasn't it, after all, normal here? Didn't the other immigrants have to pay the farm agents in the earlier days? (chapter 4, "The First Men from Lazio").

They felt they had to use various means to win over the Canadian employer or boss: his favour, his sympathy, his trust, even his admiration, first in order to obtain the job and hold on to it; and then in order to reach seniority and security, even through medical certificates from Italian doctors. But above all, they worked very hard in order to impress the employer, to prove that they were what Bill LaMarsh eventually recognized them to be: diligent, dependable, reliable, honest, extremely good workers, even accommodating. They had to stoop to conquer: act humbly and submissively without losing dignity; show superior ability and cleverness without offending or challenging; be what LaMarsh observed about them: "never inferior or superior to you."

In the long run, how did they prove that they were equal to and even better, in certain ways, than the Canadians? How did they ingratiate themselves with the employer, win his respect, while defending and protecting their integrity and dignity? Through what they knew best: "work, very hard work!" The same words echoed through the years and the interviews: Saveria Magri's "hard life" – forged Italians (1930s), Bruno Matassa's "very productive and proud" Italian workers (1940s), Gus Mastronardi's "sturdy race" of hard workers and thrifty Italians (1950s), and Guido Mastronardi's 1970s view that "Italians work hard and take on a lot of responsibilities."

The Italians, in short, channelled all their anger and other feelings which they could not express otherwise, into work, work, and work. Each one became engaged in a sort of competition, or challenge, not first of all against others, but against oneself. In the long run and on the whole, it was a challenge as a group against all "Canadians." Not only did they have to prove that they were "extremely good workers," but also that they had the courage and the strength to hold two jobs; and that they were thus as good as, if not better than, the "Canadians" at their own game of making money quickly. The goal was not simply to keep up with them, but to surpass them: buy a house, even two, and remodel them with style; buy a farm or a business, make them profitable, become independent, and then perhaps even hire "Canadians" themselves. In other words, they tried to achieve as quickly as possible, through hard work, all those things by which Canadians measured success, reputation, and worth, and dispensed respect.

Once the break had been made and their reputation established, jobs were much easier to find, especially for those arriving in the later decades; by then, non-Italian employers knew that "what they could get from the diligent, hard-working and dependable Italians, they couldn't get from anyone else." "Bosses liked me," said one of them, "they treated me well because I treated them well. I did my work." Even during the 1950s, the newcomers would often start with a non-Italian employer; the only reason that made them seek out an Italian employer, especially upon arrival, was their need to communicate: "Here, the first day, I worked for an 'English' foreman ... I was dead tired ... no one to talk to; no one to relax with." But they soon found that Italian employers were generally more demanding ("harder to work for"). They expected more of their employees, and because of the bond of nationality, the latter sometimes felt more obligated to "put out." Non-Italian employers, on the other hand, would often tell their Italian employees to "take it easy" – a phrase the Italians often translated literally, without realizing its fullest implication.[23] Nevertheless, at least one comparison did not lack some insight: "1956 ... 1958 ... little work ... farmers made them work like animals ... Think: better to work with 'English' [non-Italian employers]. They do not push as hard as the Italians ... Italians work a lot harder because when they first came it was hard to find a job, so they worked harder and faster to keep their jobs ... Italians were born to work hard, so Italian bosses were tougher ... made you work hard."

It was not simply a blind or cynical profit motive, hard-and-fast deadlines, or production quotas that made Italian employers drive their Italian employees so hard. There were deeper historical, social, and psychological reasons. For the most part, the Italian employers were pre–Second World War Italian pioneers and families who had known only hardships and work, who had had to prove their worth through hard work. They viewed work as a national characteristic, an inherent, almost predestined quality of the Italian people ("used to a hard life"; "born to work hard"). For them work was the very essence of life, existence and identity: *Work* was what distinguished them from Canadians, what made them progress or advance from "donkeys to horses." Work was seen almost as a direct link to their former village life and even to the new Italy, to "Italianness."[24] The postwar Italian immigrants also knew that hard work was the only way out, but they preferred not to be driven by employers, and they were not as driven from within. They also held somewhat different views about life and work: one had to work for life, not live for work. The basic principle was the same; the emphasis had changed.

But, whether they worked for Italian or non-Italian employers, they were all in agreement about the beneficial effects of their work on the whole Leamington community. Echoing Saveria's words of many years before, time and again the Italians claimed due recognition of their efforts and contribution. Above all, they wished for an end to the Canadians' attempt to belittle or deny their success through their insinuations about the usual Italian association or "connection": "Who straightened out Leamington? ... All the Italians have done something here. We can be proud ... We Italians have a good name. They say we're Mafia ... a name stuck to us. But they know what they are saying. They also know what we are doing" (see chapter 5, "Pride and Survival").

GENERAL EMPLOYMENT TRENDS
AND THE PLACE OF FARMING

Substantial changes can also be observed by comparing the occupations with the first place of employment (i.e., upon arrival) and the current place of employment: a decrease in farming (from 44 to 28 per cent) and construction (from 10 to 6 per cent); and an increase by almost five times at Heinz (from 5 to 23 per cent). As expected, there was also quite a shift in the miscellaneous categories (from 25 to 36 per cent), which includes the trades, businesses, and professions, produce workers and housewives. The appearance of the "housewives" category is an indication of the decrease in the number of women seeking jobs outside the home. On the other hand, there is an indication of either a modest increase or no change at all in the percentage of women in the various categories: from 10 to 13 per cent in "farming"; from 10 to 12 per cent in "other"; and in both periods, 0 per cent in "construction," and 10 per cent in the food processing industry, i.e., the total of the female percentages at Omstead's and at Heinz (the only change was in the place of employment, from Omstead's to Heinz). In the latter period, the percentage of women (13 per cent) and the percentage of men (15 per cent) in "farming" were almost equal.

However, in spite of continuous postwar occupational and commercial differentiation, partly fostered by the newcomers in each decade from the late 1940s to the late 1970s, farming remained a central activity among the majority of Leamington Italians. As already noted, all the pioneer families (except two, Peralta, DeSantis) had become owner-farmers (and Raffaele Ingratta, a tenant farmer) by the end of the Second World War; and after the war several of their children (and later some of the grandchildren) also bought farms.

After the war, several trends emerged. About 60 per cent of the 1948/49 male immigrants, or 17 (with one in part-time farming) of the 28 newcomers, started out and remained in farming (well over 90 per cent if included are those who were initially in farming and later left it for other activities). In the 1950s, the peak decade of Italian immigration to Canada and Leamington, four times the number of the 1940s newcomers chose farming, but only about half the percentage of that of the earlier decade (66 out of 210 entries or 31 per cent). Each successive decade registered a decrease in both figures: in the 1960s, 27 out of 143 entries (18.9 per cent); 1970s, 4 out of 36 entries (about 11 per cent).

For the entire postwar period (1948/49–1970s): out of the 417 male entries, 113 (27.1 per cent) listed "farming only," while 15 (3.6 per cent) were in "part-time farming" for a total of 128 (30.7 per cent); and 268 (64.3 per cent) were in non-farming activities. But during that period, 120 (28.8 per cent) had been initially engaged in farming and then left it (that is, about 45 per cent). Thus, out of the 396 males, 248 (over 62 per cent) were or had been involved in farming in the Leamington area in the postwar period. In other words, 148 individuals (35.5 per cent) were never engaged in farming in that same area and period. In spite of variations, this seems to corroborate the general trends presented by the student-researchers in what they themselves labelled their "not ... most reliable" employment charts.[25] Even though the higher 1940s–50s farming occupation figures may reflect the immediate postwar farm-work requirement, on the whole they reconfirm the central role of the agricultural industry among the Leamington-area Italians.

Generally, the decrease in the number of those giving farming as their main occupation corresponds closely to the increase in the number of those entering the non-farming activities. Thus, the "factory" category increases from 25 per cent (1948/49) to 44 per cent of total entries (1960s), and though in the 1970s it drops back to the same figure shown for the 1950s (about 36 per cent), it continues to be in first place (except in 1948/49, held by farming with about 57 per cent). Overall, factory employment absorbed the largest number of newcomers entering the workforce or switching occupation, to give it the largest percentage of all categories (38–40 per cent). Factory employment, temporary and limited before the Second World War, and a goal for many Italians, was mainly a post-mid-fifties development.

The other three areas of Italian employment – "construction" (about 12 per cent); "fishing" (about 4 per cent); "Other" (miscellaneous trades and professions, over 10 per cent) – make up a combined percentage of about 26 per cent (and a combined number of 109 out of 417 interviewed, or 27.5 per cent of 396 occupational listings). Generally lower than both "farming" and "factory" figures, they were on the increase from the 1950s to the 1970s, though not steadily or uniformly. For example, the 1970s "construction" percentage – 30.6 per cent of decade entries – was double that of the 1960s (15.4 per cent), while the respective number of those choosing that occupation was exactly one half the other one (i.e., 1970s, 11; 1960s, 22); and while the "fishing" percentage more than quadrupled from 2.4 per cent in the 1950s to 11.1 per cent in the 1970s, and the number of respondents in this occupation went from 0 to 5 to 9 in the first three periods, in the 1970s it dropped to 4 units, even though it represented over 11 per cent of that decade's total.

While the establishment of the first construction companies and the earliest involvement in the fishing industry date back to the earlier part of this period (1950s), the independent businesses grew in the latter part of the period, in spite of the 1960s–70s decreases in the "other" category, with the professions on the rise with the emergence of the third generation (late 1970s–80s). In general, the figures indicate similar overall trends: an increase in factory employment at the expense of farming (with Heinz's percentage almost four times that of Omstead's); and a decrease of those involved in construction toward the end of the period (from 22 to 11 units, from 10 to 6 per cent).

Considered globally, the "non-farming" activities make up the highest percentage (64.4 to 67.6 per cent); but, if viewed separately, with the exception of the factory (38–40 per cent), farming remains the major single activity, with over 30 per cent – if part-time involvement is included. Moreover, factory work in Leamington (the Windsor automotive industries and other factories absorbed only a small minority) is closely related to the farming and fishing industries, or food processing industries (Heinz, Omstead's). Furthermore, in growth of independent commercial enterprises, farming or farming-related industry has clearly been in the lead among the Leamington Italian Canadians throughout the period.

Therefore, in spite of the numerical decrease, the farming, agricultural, and greenhouse industries have been expanding in importance, production, and dollar value. In great measure, this expansion has been the result of the work and vision of the approximately one hundred Italian families engaged in this industry in the Leamington area, in both greenhouse and field-grown produce (fruits and vegetables). During the last forty or fifty years, those same people whom Marius Ingratta described (chapter 5) as laying the foundation of the farming community, also led the transformation of the agricultural industry: the process had actually begun in the 1930s and 1940s when they bought the first tobacco farms, which they slowly converted into giant vegetable gardens, and eventually into model farms of the future. In the 1970s and 1980s, they developed highly sophisticated businesses with state-of-the-art automation (computerized systems in the greenhouses to control feeding and watering) in order to have maximum yield. Thus, the Leamington Italians see themselves no less than major protagonists in the "revolutionizing" of the industry, especially "in the last five to six years" (late 1970s, early 1980s) when, in the words of Gino Pannunzio, "the level of automation has been truly amazing."

Just as determinant has been their role in creating marketing channels for their ever-increasing production: the Sun Parlour Greenhouse Growers Co-operative (late 1950s, with largest presence of Italians who also served in various administrative offices including that of president)[26] and the Ontario Greenhouse Growers Marketing Board.[27] In both groups, Italian owner-farmers constitute an important component numerically and in production volume. "The biggest growers in the Co-op are Italians," according to Gino Pannunzio, who served first as director (1959–62) and then as president of the Sun Parlour Co-op (1962–67). Pannunzio described briefly their unique achievements: "Italians made the greenhouse industry viable ... because they are good growers, good farmers, and, regardless of what some people may say, good businessmen ... It's amazing what some of them have done without [higher] education. The Leamington farming industry is perhaps the most advanced scientific farming industry in the world today." The Italian farmers and greenhouse growers clearly played an important part, albeit not as large as "the giant H.J. Heinz," in making the Leamington area more than the "tomato capital" of Canada, a truly agricultural wonderland of Canada.[28]

SELF-EMPLOYMENT: COMMERCIAL INSTITUTIONS

Farming was certainly not the only area where "many [Italians] liked to be their own boss." Out of the approximately 65 per cent of those postwar immigrant males in "non-farming" activities, about 40 per cent became factory employees, while of the other 25 per cent, many followed independent routes. They formed construction, fishing, and food processing companies; became involved in trades and small businesses (from music stores to insurance and real estate); and later their children began to enter the self-employed professional field or with firms or institutions in and out of Leamington (engineering, teaching, law, medicine). Besides the farming business and John Brunato's (later Vito Peralta's) shoe repair shop, the first small commercial enterprise established by an Italian was the Grocery Store.

The First Italian Grocery Store

Italians of any social status do not need dieticians to advise them on the importance of a balanced diet and health: "Not everyone in Italy may know how to cook, but nearly everyone knows how to eat. Eating in Italy is one more manifestation of the Italian's age-old gift of making art out of life.

"The Italian art of eating is sustained by a life measured in nature's rhythms, a life that falls in with the slow wheelings of the seasons, a life in which, until very recently, produce and fish reached the table not many hours after having been taken from the soil or the sea."[29]

Marcella Hazan simply echoed what has been part of the Italian tradition for centuries, perhaps millennia. There are numerous proverbs and sayings (some going back to the eighth-century Salerno School of Medicine) that establish the relation of good eating habits, good nourishment, and good health: *"Prima digestio fit in ore"* (Digestion must first occur in one's mouth). *"Molto cibo e mal digesto non fa il corpo sano e lesto"* (A lot of food badly digested makes the body unhealthy and congested). *"Piglia il cibo con misura dai due regni di natura"* (Take food with measure from both realms of nature).[30]

It is no surprise that the Italians in Leamington pursued farming and fishing, and that the first businesses were food stores. There were many complaints among early arrivals about the insipid and unbalanced quality of Canadian meals. Meat and potatoes and gravy followed by pie was not considered a hearty meal for people who had to work hard. They missed the pasta, the fresh vegetables, fruit and cheese, and the glass of "blood-giving" red wine. They couldn't find these goods in the Leamington stores, so at first they had to provide for themselves by making their own spaghetti, bread, and wine (see chapter 11, "The Italian Art of Eating").

Many of the first men lived together so they could share their own homemade meals, for which they had to change attitudes and become especially resourceful in order to have the best results. "In Canada I had to get used to cooking. [I would] sometimes eat at the Ruthven General Store ... [But I] preferred to buy Italian goods from Meconi in Windsor [who] used to come around and sell us food" (Neil Salvati, Lazio, 1951). For Luigi Carnevale (Lazio, 1949) and his friends, it was not always that easy: "[We'd] buy flour, eggs, and make our own spaghetti and eat ... That's all we knew [then, besides] work and sleep." After the wives arrived, they would rush home from the factory not just "to put in an hour's work" but to eat the homemade meal, for there was no lunchbox elaborate enough to provide the nourishment they needed.

The grocery store was a natural outcome of this need. Nor was it seen as just a business; it was an essential Italian institution, basic not only to survival but also to the enjoyment of living, through the rediscovery and practice of the art of eating. By 1952 the Leamington Italians were finally able to obtain Italian groceries right in Leamington: at the "Italian Grocery" at 54 Talbot Street West (late 1960s at 34 Mill Street West).

Ida Magri, the Canadian-born daughter of Saveria, no stranger to the hardships of immigrants, embarked on her venture with the same pioneering spirit her mother had shown through the Depression and war years. To set up the store required $3,000, and she had only $110; she had no knowledge at all of the grocery business, and though she understood Italian, she did not speak it. But with her family's financial help (even though her father "was not happy"), she followed the suggestion of a Windsor friend, Tony Montello.[31] He not only thought it timely to open an Italian grocery store in Leamington, but told her of a friend who was selling a store in Windsor from whom she was able to buy all the necessary basic equipment (such as a freezer and a meat slicer) at a good price and good terms with a three-year credit. She also solved her linguistic problem: with all the Italians flocking to her store, she soon learned how to speak Italian.

"During the first year, business was good." The other merchants showed no resentment: "they welcomed the opening." She also carried both an Italian and a Canadian line of goods, which she was able to sell at competitive prices because she bought some supplies (olives, peanuts, and others) in bulk. Most of the goods were ordered monthly from Primo and Lancia Foods in Toronto. When she first opened, spaghetti was sold at nineteen cents a pound, and most people bought three or four cases at a time. Because of the variety and prices, the store attracted a general clientele, including many from the growing Portuguese community whom Ida especially "liked because they paid the price [she] said," unlike the Italians who "always tried to barter with [her] for groceries," and often frustrated Ida the Italian businesswoman.

But Ida, the daughter of Italian immigrants, did more than provide an the full gamut of Italian goods for her Italian customers and friends. Her Italian store, more than a commercial enterprise, became a comprehensive institution in those pre–Roma Club days: a gathering place ("Italians would come to the store to visit with other Italians"); a "bank" ("They would always come to her to cash their cheques because they didn't have time to go to the bank"); a real estate agency, an income tax office, and a general information centre ("finding apartments, making appointments, reading letters, filling out forms"). Raised and educated in Canada, Ida was more familiar with Canadian ways and thus became the link between the Italian immigrants and Canadian society. She helped out many of them every day, running errands for them, sometimes even five or six times a day. Besides being good, neighbourly deeds, they also constituted a good business policy. When competition became more intense, her customers continued to appreciate her and remained loyal to her store.

Competition came soon. Within a year, another Italian grocery business opened, and within three years there were four in operation, including Ida's store: Domenic Capogna (Patrica, Lazio, 1951) had a little one, Corky's (corner of Fox and Askew streets); Rolando Paliani (Patrica, 1954) ran another one; and Luigi Carnevale, beginning in 1953, went from house to house selling his goods with his "store on wheels." But they didn't last long. The real competition came from the chain stores that began to carry Italian goods in her last two years in business (1957–59). Italians continued to frequent her store, but by the end of the 1950s it was becoming too difficult.

Though she enjoyed the independence and the people, the store demanded total commitment of her time and energies: "I was tied down six days a week, sometimes even on Sundays when people came even from Windsor, and for many hours each day, since I would close up at night at no specific time but only when the customers stopped coming. I did have some help from my sisters and a couple of young Italian boys (Frank Gabriele and Tony Cianfarani) but not enough to allow me to take holidays: I would take about three days off every year and a half." Moreover, because good help was hard to find, she was needed on her father's farm. Therefore, she spread the word that she was selling the store.

Two people became interested: Angelo Iacobelli (Casalvieri, Lazio, 1954) and Ivana (Colasanti) Ercole. In October 1959 she sold it to Ivana. Even though Ida's father had sold the farm, Ida never regretted selling the store. She was happy to leave behind the preoccupations and aggravations – especially from customers asking for credit, which caused her a loss of $1,000. Free from this commitment, she was able to do what she couldn't do for many years: go away. In fact, she moved to Chicago. But years later she returned to Leamington and made it her residence.

Ida Magri, like her mother, Saveria, was a pioneer: Saveria was one of the first Italian women to work on the farms and in the factories in the Leamington area; Ida was the first woman to start an Italian business in downtown Leamington. Ida was also known as a fighter: as a member of the Leamington Chamber of Commerce, she even joined a group of merchants who had proposed that the town change the by-law to allow late store hours for Fridays rather than Saturdays. The town finally approved it; and more pleased than the store owners and their employees were the customers who, mostly workers, preferred to shop on Fridays and have Saturdays free for other activities. She was indeed missed by many for her store, her services, and community involvement.

By the early 1960s Leamington had two well-established Italian grocery stores located for a while a few doors away from each other on Mill Street West: the other was Roma Grocery, first owned by John Mastromatteo and after 1965 by Luigi Sperduti (Patrica, Lazio, 1955), who in 1967 transferred it from 48 Mill Street West to 54 Talbot Street West (on the former premises of the Italian grocery that Ivana Ercole had moved to 34 Mill Street West). If both stores were enjoying a healthy clientele, it was due partly to Ida Magri's 1950s initiative and her legacy of continued good service for six long years; and she was deservedly remembered, especially by those Italians who were spared the same experiences others had prior to the existence of Ida's Italian grocery: "When I would go shopping, I would calculate in my head how much the bill would come to and then hand the cashier more than that amount. I did not know the language. Actually the cashier could have cheated me, and I would have never known."

With Magri, the Italians were able enjoy haggling over prices and to obtain credit, which they would not even think of asking for in non-Italian-owned stores. And the reasons were not just language difficulties, but pride or even fear of giving the "English" proprietors the wrong impression of Italians, whose goal was always to project a reputation of being "cash-on-the-barrelhead" customers, a successful group. Ida Magri provided a hometown, village atmosphere for Italians even in this respect, while safeguarding their reputation.

The Leamington Shoe Shine and Repair Shop

When Ida Magri opened her grocery store in 1952, the only other Italian business in downtown Leamington she remembered was Vito Peralta's Shoe Repair Shop. The store was not yet owned by Vito, though he had been managing it since 1943, but by John Brunato, a Canadian-born Italian unconnected to the new group of Italian immigrants who were settling in the Leamington area in the 1920s and 1930s. Nevertheless, this store, purchased in 1939/40, may be considered the first Italian small business in downtown Leamington (at 9 Erie Street South).

John Brunato (born in Guelph in 1918) moved to Windsor in 1936 to help Louis Bernachi (Bernacchi), who was married to his aunt. Bernachi (according to Nick Cicchini's interview) was part owner of Humphries Shoe Repair on Erie Street East, in Windsor (where Cicchini also worked when laid off by General Motors or Ford, 1933–37, and in 1939 before he moved to Leamington). When Louis and John expanded their business by buying the shoe repair shop in Leamington from a Greek family, they moved there and left Cicchini to run the Windsor shop alone for six months. But Bernachi, unable to bear the stress of travelling back and forth between Windsor and Leamington in order to help Cicchini, eventually moved back to Windsor. John Brunato took full possession of the Leamington shop and hired Nick Cicchini to help him. In 1940 John was drafted into the Canadian army and Nick Cicchini managed the shop alone until 1942, when he himself was drafted. John's wife, Ines, hired someone else to look after the shop, but he proved to be unsatisfactory. Then Cicchini suggested to Ines Brunato that he approach Vito Peralta, whom she knew well and who had just been released from the internment camp at Petawawa.

Vito Peralta's only desire after his return was to rebuild his shoe repair business in Windsor where, since his arrival in 1927, he had been doing quite well, at least until an acquaintance, "jealous of his success," falsely accused him to the RCMP as a Fascist sympathizer. But, unable to find a job in Windsor, he accepted Brunato's offer, moved to Leamington, and in 1943 started anew as a shoe repairman and manager of Brunato's shop. Vito's initial hesitation was justifiable: he knew no one in Leamington and probably wondered about his position upon the return of the other men: John Brunato and Nick Cicchini. In fact, after the war, John and Nick came back to the shop. But since there wasn't enough work to accommodate all three, Nick Cicchini volunteered to search for another job (in Windsor, where, according to the *City Directories*, he eventually operated for years Humphries Shoe Repair), and Vito was able to stay on at Brunato's shop.

Vito continued to operate the store for the Brunatos until the mid-1950s. By then the business was identified more with Vito than with the owners (as Ida Magri herself pointed out). Besides, during this time, John Brunato had gone into the greenhouse business in partnership with Rocco Moauro (Angelo's son). After four good years together (1953–57), Rocco sold the farm to John, bought land near his father (Morse Lane), and developed a greenhouse business with him (see chapter 8), while John continued farming (on the same farm the Brunatos still owned in the 1980s), and in 1956 sold the shoe repair shop to Vito Peralta.

Peralta had come to operate and then own the first Italian shoe repair business in downtown Leamington by pure chance and as a result of his misfortunes. But through hard work he made a success of it. There were two other shoe repair shops in Leamington, but most people went to him. He "felt no discrimination" against him, and if there had been, he was sure he could overcome it by pleasing his customers, whether they wanted shoes made, repaired or cleaned. He was a master cobbler who had started in his trade as an apprentice at the age of eight, and by the time he was sixteen years old he was able to make an excellent pair of handmade shoes. He was a fine businessman who got to know his customers well and, from experience, knew his suppliers and salesmen in Windsor, where he obtained most of his material. Soon after he sold the store in 1968, when he retired, his successor had to resell the store because he was losing most of the customers who had been accustomed to Vito's promptness and workmanship.

Vito Peralta's shoe repair shop was not his own creation, but creation is not always starting something from nothing. In this sense, Vito was the first Italian small business operator outside the farming industry, in downtown Leamington. Since both Ida Magri and John Brunato were Canadian-born, he was the first Italian immigrant to operate and own such a business as a permanent settler in Leamington. After the arrival of his family – wife, children, and grandchildren (late 1940s to early 1950s) – it became a family business. They were all involved in it for a while, as they looked for other jobs or before embarking on other ventures, such as fishing, as in the case of his grandson Vito. The business was also a stepping stone into Canada for numerous Sicilians, who never forgot

Vito the pioneer. The yearly celebration in his honour and memory (organized by the San Vito Lo Capo Club and often held at the Windsor Sicilia Club) is a simple but fitting recognition of the man and his work: a public expression of gratitude to the first immigrant from San Vito Lo Capo to settle in the Leamington area, a tribute to the "founder" of the Leamington and even larger area Sicilian community.

Construction and Other Small Enterprises

From the 1950s to the 1980s, several other businesses were started or purchased by the Leamington Italians. Among them were a tailor shop by Milvo Costanza (Patrica, Lazio, 1954), a real estate business by Pat Cervini (Ceprano, Lazio, 1954), a beauty salon by Salvatore Ligotino (Partinico, Sicily, 1971), a hotel-restaurant by Isidoro Spano (Vita, Sicily, 1952), and barbershops, bakeries, pizza parlours, restaurants, and produce and fruit stands, as well as food processing enterprises. Two of them – Onorio Iacobelli (Casalvieri, Lazio, 1954) and Gino Saccucci (Isola Liri, Lazio, 1967) – became owners of Sun-Brite Canning. Vito Peralta (a grandson of Vito the pioneer) in 1975 started Etna Foods of Leamington, which grew in less than ten years from three employees (all relatives) to ninety-five seasonal employees and "a monthly payroll that often exceeds $60,000."[32]

On average, the post–Second World War newcomers had a higher level of education and often knew a trade. Many had worked as skilled workers in Italy or in other countries, which was also a reason for the increasing number of people involved in non-farming activities. After the adjustment period, many of them resumed their original trade, often as independent operators: general mechanical contractors or owners of auto body and automotive repairs, boiler repairs, welding, and general maintenance. A business that also attracted many Italians, perhaps because it offered a personal challenge and some independence, was selling insurance. In Leamington, Fred DeSantis, who arrived in the 1920s when he was three years old, started and operated his own insurance company for years. For some, the real estate business offered a similar attraction.

Specialized stores or boutiques also appeared. Besides offering entertainment, music had been a livelihood for many Italian immigrants for decades, by teaching, playing in a band, or organ grinding in earlier days. One immigrant, who arrived with his family at the age of nine in the late 1940s, became the owner of Leone's Music Store, located for many years on Talbot Street East in Leamington, but later moved to Windsor, where it attracted a larger clientele. More recently, the adoption of traditional and completely Italian names, such as La casa del corredo for a trousseau shop (41 Erie South); La Piccola Capri Fine Imported Shoes (6 Erie South, owned by a pre–Second World War immigrant, Gino DiMenna, son of Tony the pioneer); and La Molisana for an agriculture-related business, is perhaps an indication of the increasing popularity and acceptance of the language and of the group in the Leamington area.

The widespread stereotyping of Italians as construction workers, and the often unkind if not coarse jokes surrounding this occupation, are all too well known.[33] From the very early days, construction (road, railroad, drain, sewer, or building) frequently offered Italian immigrants the only livelihood available in North America. Of those who arrived in Leamington after the war, at least forty-nine went into construction. Before the 1950s, there may have been some Italians in the construction-related business, but it was not until the 1950s and later that many of them started their own companies. Bruno Matassa's company, among the first and then among the biggest in the area, was mostly the result of the 1950s demographic growth and lack of housing.

Bruno had no experience in the building trade. When he arrived with his father Attilio in 1948, at seventeen years of age, he followed the usual work pattern: two years on farms (his uncle Joe's, George Cole's, Angelo Moauro's), then three and a half years at Ford, and two more at Chrysler, until he was laid off. While living with his parents in Leamington (in the Queens Avenue house, which they kept for the married children to settle in until they built their own), Bruno saw their new home being built (on Nancy Avenue): "That's when I decided that *that* was the business I liked to go into." Bruno referred to other factors, besides the favourable market situation, that influenced him and other Italians to become builders and/or contractors: Canada's "opportunity to build things for yourself and your family," the contrast in modes of building, or in Bruno's words, "In Italy, everything was made of stone, here homes looked like they had paper walls," a situation that Italians everywhere in Canada have demonstrably tried to balance especially in their homes; and the availability of an experienced workforce, particularly of "very good ... excellent ... conscientious ... Italian workers," many of whom Bruno sponsored, especially when "only skilled people were allowed to immigrate."

In the mid-1980s, more than a dozen construction companies and several related contractors and independent tradesmen were providing services, from excavating to roofing (bricklaying, carpentry and woodwork; electrical, plumbing, heating and air conditioning; building supplies, trucking, painting and decorating). Their evolution followed the expansion of residential areas of Leamington: much of the land between Talbot and Oak, east of Whitman Avenue and east of Lutsch Avenue, was developed after 1964 and 1970 respectively, as was most of the area east of Danforth between Oak and Seacliff Drive. In 1977 Vittorio Paglione (Capracotta, Molise, 1955), whose brother Italo (1957) had a construction company since the early 1960s, began to develop an eight-acre farm that he had owned since 1963 off Seacliff Village: two of the several Paglione families who settled in Leamington (1950s/60s) in the 1980s resided on the street bearing the family name – Paglione Drive. In Bruno Matassa's view, "Perhaps Italians aren't great financiers but they are great builders; they have been nation builders for many years, and without a doubt, they have contributed to Leamington and to Canada."

THE FISHING INDUSTRY AND THE SICILIANS

In his interview, Jake Omstead (Omstead Foods Limited) stated that in the earlier days all of the Italian boat owners, "the majority from southern Italy [and] Sicily," worked directly for Omstead's. It is not known whether there were any Italians working as fishermen or for Omstead's before 1950, but of the 210 male immigrants in the 1950s, 5 listed this category as their area of employment: they were all Sicilians. One of them, Diego Barraco (San Vito Lo Capo, Sicily, 1953), who had been sponsored by Vito Peralta, was likely the first person employed in this area: he started out in Kingsville in 1953. His son Nino, who arrived in 1954 when he was one year old, later started a fishing business.

In the 1960s, apparently only 9 (8 of whom were Sicilians) out of the 143 entries chose fishing as their occupation. But shortly after their arrival, some of them bought their own boats and became independent fishermen: A. Figliomeni (1967), Nicola (Nick) Rubino (1968), and Salvatore Rubino (1968), all three from Favignana (an island off the western coast of Sicily, part of the Egadi Islands, Trapani Province). Sam Catrini (Noto, Siracusa, 1965) left his factory job in Toronto and later set up Catrini Fisheries with his father (chapter 7). Only four (all Sicilians) of the 1970s immigrants chose the fishing industry; but during this decade, several earlier Italian immigrants ventured into the industry on their own – from the Peraltas, whose roots in this area go back to the 1940s and 1950s, to the Causaranos who arrived in the early 1970s. When John Causarano was interviewed in July 1980, seven Italian fishing boats were operating in the area. But the number was most likely higher in the 1980s, since in November 1984 alone, Vito Peralta's company counted as many as five boats. Generally, the boats operate out of Wheatley Harbour, though the companies' head offices may be in Leamington or Windsor.

The independent boat owners, explained John Causarano, run their "business like a free enterprise." They have no contract with Omstead's, though "most of the selling is made to Omstead's." But they "can just as easily sell elsewhere." In fact, some of the Italian boat owners established their own food companies and/or fish marketing outlets, such as Etna Foods and Mediterraneo Fish Market by Vito Peralta (who later sold the fish market to another Sicilian, Frank Aiuto who, as a bricklayer on his arrival in the 1950s, was involved in construction jobs, but later decided to be in the fishing business like his father, already a fisherman in Italy); or Lake Erie Food Incorporated (Captain Nick Rubino, president). "Only three Italians," according to Causarano, "sell strictly through contracts to Omstead's; the rest [like him] are independent." The Sicilians, like the Molisani in farming, have been quite prosperous in the fishing industry. John Causarano's own fishing business has been successful since its establishment in 1973.

After his arrival in Canada in 1972, John Causarano first moved to the United States, and six months later to Leamington (March 1973). In the same month, after he and his father had sold their fishing business in Ragusa, they bought their first boat (the 45-foot *Adria*) which they sold in 1974 to buy the 70-foot *John D'Eau* (one of the largest fishing vessels in the area if the standard size is taken to be 60–65 feet long).[34] Therefore John Causarano's experience presents a different and more recent example of involvement and development in the fishing industry.

With his Italian experience, Causarano's comparison of fishing in the Mediterranean and in the Great Lakes offers a general view of saltwater and freshwater fishing, and similarities and contrasts in the nature of the industry. Size of vessel was more or less the same. In Italy the fishing season was year-round, two weeks at a time, night fishing included, but idle "when the sea gets rough, you cannot go out on certain days"; while in Ontario it runs from the first or second week of March to the first or second week of December, every day, 4:30 a.m. to 4:00–6:00 p.m., returning to port each day. Sea catch was not as ample, but prices were higher, especially for lobsters, whereas lake catch was abundant and varied – perch, pickerel, white bass, especially smelt. In both places, profit margins were subject to quantity and quality of fish, market demand, and labour costs: there was good profit in Lake Erie bulk fish, but little money in the variety fished year-round, such as smelt, and there was higher Italian demand for most Mediterranean catch. Labour costs were about the same.

In general, sea fishing is more dangerous, but also more exciting because of possible unique catch (large tuna or shark). One major difference in the Great Lakes is that Italian boat owners with Portuguese crew often learn each other's language. Overall, "Financially it is better in Canada, but as a type of life, perhaps it is better there: more adventurous."

Causarano's interview also presented other aspects of Great Lakes fishing: basic on-board equipment – types of nets (gill netting, nets with weights and a heavy "door" attached to a 450-foot cable that drags behind the boat for smelt fishing); radar, navigator, compass, and radio (useful to establish vicinity of the American border, or to find where gill nets were placed the day before); fish finder (to find fish and measure water depth). He described the tasks of the crew (usually six) on the fishing vessel, particularly sorting out fish from netting, which is not difficult but exhausting (using a special hook, they pick the fish out of the netting and simultaneously poke their eyes out); and the attitudes or virtues needed in the business: stamina, but also trust that no one takes anyone else's nets, and secrecy as a necessary preventive measure. The good fishing spots are sometimes disclosed only to close friends in strict confidence. Perhaps these are the qualities that allowed Causarano to never have any problems, and always have a good catch, "the best [consisting of] approximately 6,000 pounds of fish."

John Causarano and Vito Peralta present two different Italian-Canadian experiences in the Great Lakes fishing industry. Though both Sicilian, their earlier development was different. Also, while Causarano stated that he never had any problems, Vito Peralta was at the centre of a complex legal battle that involved the Ontario Ministry of Natural Resources, the Ontario Supreme Court (1984–85), and the Supreme Court of Canada, as well as a supporting group of "about 35 fishing licence holders ... from as far away as Lake of the Woods and Lake Superior" to the western basin of Lake Erie. The protracted court fight over unfairly allocated and (according to an October 1984 ruling) unconstitutional fishing quotas had Canada-wide ramifications and attention: it was not just an issue of fish quotas and conservation in the Great Lakes, but a dispute with "wide-ranging implications ... not only on fishing but other natural resources." It was such a complex problem that it was felt that "the Supreme Court of Canada [was] the proper place to settle the issue because of the case's ramifications for Nova Scotia and British Columbia and its central relationship to the Canadian Constitution" (i.e., to a clearer definition of federal and provincial jurisdiction, control or power).[35]

The legal dispute appeared also as a classic struggle between the "little guy" and "dictator"-like public officials; or as a challenge of private, dynamic, free enterprise against big government and bureaucratic interference. In fact, a relatively small and new Canadian entrepreneur was again being unfairly treated by the older, more powerful establishment: "government officials" were not just "hassling" boat owners or even workers "unable to speak English," but were also "enforcing" a system "without lawful authority" or engaging in unlawful seizure and confiscation of goods and property and disrupting businesses and livelihood.[36] It was thus a citizen's battle against a minister's "outrageous display of political indifference."

It was also a question about not just the strength of the industry, freedom of action within the law, but also equality and harmony within a racially and ethnoculturally diverse Canadian society. "The gulf separating 'have' from 'have-not' can also be drawn along racial lines," observed a *Windsor Star* reporter:[37] "Although there are exceptions, many of the fishermen with low quotas are Italians and Portuguese. Peralta says comments made by Steve Getty, president of the Ontario Council of Commercial Fishermen, as quoted in the *London Free Press*, have not helped ease tension between the Italians and Portuguese and the established fishermen. 'They just jump off the boat and they're supposed to have as much quota as someone who has been working here for generations,' Getty was quoted as saying."

The struggle of newcomers or established minorities against overt and subtle prejudices and discrimination is perhaps the same in every age. And every age provides its own means to fight against injustice. In response to Getty's comments, Peralta pointed to the Charter of Rights and said, "A third-generation Canadian shouldn't have any more benefits than a first-generation Canadian." The 1980s Vito Peralta (grandson), like the 1940s Vito Peralta (grandfather), showed faith in the Canadian democratic system: "I feel good about our judicial system. It's the watchdog that makes sure government abides by the laws of the land." The controversy made him more aware of it, and he began to use that system to defend his rights and those of other Canadians: "Before his legal battle with the Ministry of Natural Resources over fish quotas, Vito Peralta was a typical 'Oh well' Canadian. If the government said, 'Jump,' the burly Peralta said, 'How high?' But after spending a year wrangling with the ministry over fish quotas, the normally placid Peralta was forced to break out of the traditional mould cast for Canadians. He stopped being apathetic and started complaining ... loudly. And when that didn't work, he and a group of Great Lakes commercial fishermen took recourse in the Canadian court system."[38]

Vito Peralta, Sicilian immigrant, Leamington Italian Canadian, and successful businessman fully benefited from Canada's vast opportunities and resources without losing, at least at that time, his sense of fairness ("Treat your employees, partners, and buyers fairly and you will succeed"). In 1984, at thirty-six, he could have easily remained smug. "But," he said, "there comes a time when you have to put your foot down and say 'No!'" Peralta even apologized to his colleagues, but he didn't give up his Canadian right to fight: "I'm sorry if I created problems for other fishermen. I only did what any Canadian has a right to do: Protest if I feel I'm not being treated fairly." Regardless of the outcome of the court fight and the personal advantages (or disadvantages) for himself, Vito Peralta's stand, his decision to protest, especially his greater awareness of the power of the law, may serve as an example for all Canadians, particularly for ethnocultural, racial, or other minorities who feel that their rights have been in any way or at any time infringed.

Ethnicities in contact (almost inevitable in Canada's diversity), especially in the workplace (as evidenced by the Italians in the Leamington factories), may produce opposite effects: at times, advantages (as Causarano noted regarding Italian boat owners and Portuguese workers learning each other's language); at others, tensions (as also reported in the *Windsor Star* during the fishing quota dispute). Conflicts can also arise also among new Canadian groups themselves. Ethnic relations can become particularly tense during management-labour disputes, as Vito Peralta himself experienced later with his Portuguese workers. Perhaps temporarily forgetting his own fairness credo, Vito's vain attempt to oppose his workers' rights to form a union helped generate an unpleasant situation for all, and was most likely costly for Vito, both financially and in reputation.

Vito Peralta indeed looked after himself – in both disputes! But at least in the fishing quota battle Vito's own interests coincided with those of many others; his standing up for himself was also identified with a fight for a more general or greater cause; he became a defender of his profession, a champion of the rights of a group of citizens, even of a principle. Therefore, again, regardless or in spite of that later labour dispute with his workers, the example he set by "[breaking] out of the traditional [Canadian] mould [to protest]" deserves praise. His own protesting workers (though ironically for him) may themselves have been influenced by his earlier stand, and the labour dispute and its outcome may have, reminded Vito of his own battle for his own rights, and that very principle of civilized living – fairness.[39]

THE PROFESSIONS

Farming and factory, construction and fishing, the trades and professions were the major areas of employment and business involvement throughout the six decades of Italian immigration and settlement in the Leamington area. Except for farming, which was the main occupation and business activity before the Second World War and through the 1940s, all the other areas gained prominence and expanded in the following decades. But whereas the middle categories (factory, construction, fishing, and the trades) were associated mostly with the period of numerical growth of the Leamington Italian community, with its adult immigrant generation; and farming can be linked to the pioneer group and their families; the professions, ever on the rise, were tied more closely to the second and future generations, the 1980s and beyond.

Since the 1950s, the entrepreneurial ability of the Leamington Italian Canadians has been successfully tested in a variety of commercial ventures (barbering and building, catering and construction, fishing and furniture, food and coffee shops, gift shops and grocery stores, garden centres and hotel, real estate and insurance, restaurant and repair shop, painting and decorating, music and others). But while the numbers abound in these fields for such a relatively small community, the professions, which require advanced education and training and involve intellectual skills, are not largely represented.

Nevertheless, the community has produced a few barristers, such as Frank Ricci, son of Virginio (Poggio Sannita, Molise, 1954), and Mario Carnevale, son of Luigi (Lazio, 1949), with offices respectively in Leamington and Windsor. The legal profession, along with the medical one, has always been regarded among Italians as prestigious. But more than prestige for family and community, the presence of lawyers and doctors in the immigrant communities usually meant having essential services in their own language. Besides, medicine and law provided safeguards for their physical and commercial well-being.

In the Leamington Italian community, Marius Ingratta (son of Henry, 1925), who arrived in Canada from Villa Canale in 1930 at age seven, tried to fulfil part of their legal needs since the early 1950s. In 1952, after his BA in economics (Michigan State College of Agriculture & Applied Science, 1949), Marius obtained a JD at Wayne State University in Detroit. But the American degree in law did not allow him to practise law in Canada; and though he had long been a Canadian citizen, he was denied a visa to set up his practice in the United States, simply because he "was Italian-born." Thus, Marius turned to farming and the greenhouse business in the Leamington area; and, although he was prevented from acting as the first Italian lawyer in his community, Marius offered them valuable legal advice throughout the years, even after the arrival of the younger-generation Italian-Canadian lawyers.

Other professions included a consulting engineer (N.J. Peralta, Vito's grandson); an electronic specialist, media centre, county school boards (Anthony Cianfarani, Castelliri, Lazio, 1956); administrators in factories such as Heinz (John Ingratta); and many teachers, including at the community college level (Ron DiMenna). At least two – Nick DiMenna (Villa Canale, 1951) and Franco Incitti (Arnara, Lazio, 1958) – were employed at the Harrow Research Station (in 1975 one of the twenty-six agricultural research stations across Canada run by the federal department of agriculture; see chapter 6, note 5). In the early 1980s only one person was known to hold a PhD (Frank Ingratta, Louis's son and John's grandson, in mushroom physiology), while a few were involved in artistic and literary pursuits. Though small, the number is rising.

The first novel of his Italian immigration trilogy was already a clear indication that the Leamington Italian community also produced a novelist of renown in Nino Ricci (the Canadian-born son of Virginio, and Frank's brother). While teaching English at Concordia University in Quebec, Ricci wrote his first novel, *Lives of the Saints*, which was immediately acclaimed in both Canada and the United States as a work "of remarkable beauty and unforgettable power," "a beautifully paced and measured first novel,"[40] and awarded the 1991 Governor General's Award for literature, as well as others (the W.H. Smith/Books in Canada First Novel Award, and the F.G. Bressani Prize for Fiction). The 1980 "Report" written mainly by Ricci, as part of the Leamington group of student interviewers, pointed to a likely successful career in creative writing. Both his research into the Leamington Italian community for the "Roma Club Project" and his 1980 report, *Radici* were clearly part of Nino Ricci's experience, the raw material that the Leamington Italian-Canadian novelist forged into a "[lucid and dazzling] gem of a novel."[41] (*Radici* and first novel are discussed in chapter 15.)

THE SIGNIFICANCE OF "FARMING" AND THE "SEARCH FOR EDEN"

Cultivation of letters (culture, the arts and sciences) and of the soil (agriculture and agribusiness), associated in Italian tradition since the first document of the Italian language (eighth century CE), require the same degree of patience, awareness, and care.[42] The conscious cultivation of the arts and letters, of the spirit, by the next generation of Leamington Italians (as Ricci's novels indicate), may just be a natural extension of the most pervasive and fundamental occupation and vocation of the earlier settlers – the cultivation of the earth, farming. All traditional areas of employment will inevitably grow and change; other commercial ventures will most likely be attempted and established; and cultural activities will probably bring some wealth and glory to other Leamington Italian Canadians, as well as honour and lustre to the community.

It can also be said that the Leamington Italian community has already had a taste of all such experiences, including the enjoyment of some fame, through and for its farming activities. In the late 1960s, in a decade when most new immigrants were choosing other areas of employment, the Leamington Italian colony was receiving the highest praise in *The Italians in Canada* for its achievements in the fishing industry, and above all, in farming. The author, A.V. Spada, who stated that the "Italian is not a farmer," praised the Molisani from Villa Canale and the *Laziali* (namely the Mastronardis, DiMennas, Ingrattas, and Colasantis), pointing to their love for the land and to the "tender care and ceaseless labour" with which they made the land rich and themselves prosperous, by building "multi-million dollar businesses," especially in the greenhouse industry.[43] Even as it shrank in quantity, as the result of natural social evolution, farming provided new challenges and new opportunities for quality development and changes. The creative application of the most advanced technological systems and scientific know-how have gained the community not only prosperity but respect and renown in the agricultural community, both in the capitalist and communist worlds (as evidenced by Mikhail Gorbachev's visit to these model farms and greenhouses when he was Soviet minister of agriculture).[44]

Farming has been a pivotal and centripetal force all along, a connective fibre for the Italian community, economically, socially, historically, and even culturally; it has been a constant throughout most of the six decades of community settlement and growth: through depression and war, hostile climate and politics, periodical market fluctuations, demographic changes, and occupational shifts. The farm meant livelihood, security, unity, strength, and stability in periods of uncertainty; satisfaction, self-fulfilment, recognition, and the base for further growth in more prosperous times. In the latter decades, in the midst of occupational diversification, determined efforts in commercial pursuits, and further exploration of other occupations and professions, farming remained a guarantee for all their endeavours, a protective cushion to fall back on if the new venture floundered: a base of identity for the new community.

Farming has provided most of them with an unbroken, vital link with their past: their town and area of origin, their heritage and traditions, especially for the founders of the community and particularly for those from the Villa Canale–Agnone area. The latter not only make up the largest number (over 60 per cent) of the Leamington-area Italian owner-farmers, but almost as large a percentage of these farming families (and about 25 per cent of the 417 postwar entries interviewed) also bear the names of the first eight men from that area of Molise. In fact, a recent farm-ownership list includes also the name Jerry Capussi, of one branch of the family of the 1923 Capussi cousins, whose relatives finally settled in the Leamington area after the war (starting in 1949 with Jerry's father, Tony, who was a grandson of Colamario, the "Capussi of Chicago," as well as related to the DiMennas and the Mastronardis; see chapter 3, "The Eight Molisani's Destination"; chapter 7, "Chain Migration"). If marriage and the extended family were considered, over half of the entire community would be found connected to a farm in some way (as well as to each other).

Farming has also been a springboard for the community's new generations, in their search for other types of "cultivation," for both material and spiritual fulfillment. Besides livelihood and a gamut of opportunities for commercial experiences, farming has offered pleasure, enjoyment, or "non-financial amenities," as they were called in a 1973 survey of Lake Erie fishermen. And what has been said about fishing can be easily extended to farming: "Aside from direct income and other forms of financial benefits," the study reported, "fishing provided certain non-financial amenities to those selecting it as a way of life. Almost all fishermen (95.1%) agreed that they fished because they '... like fishing.' Most [enjoyed] the fresh air and water ... the association with fellow fishermen [and] the opportunity to be their 'own boss.'"[45] Similar thoughts were expressed or implied by the Leamington Italian farmers (as well as by the Sicilian fisherman Causarano). But perhaps even more than fishing, farming can gratify deeper human needs and longings, as well as stimulate the imagination, and thus achieve pleasurable knowledge (i.e., *culture*).

In addition, land cultivation holds the potential to enter a close communion with one's inner being, nature, the micro/macrocosmic secrets of creation itself, and the basic substances of the universe (earth, air, water and fire). Country work and life also evoke legends and myths, which can often provide a link to history, science, literature, and religion.

From mythological figures, from gods of agriculture and of earth's golden age (Saturn) and from goddesses of prosperous humanity and fruitful mother earth (Ceres, Gea), all kept alive through time by poetic writings, also derive today's idea of the earth "in harmony with the Greek conception of the Earth as a living [goddess], as a living whole, as Gaia." This image, instinctively familiar to the responsive tiller of the soil, recently inspired a forward-looking "new scientific synthesis" viewing "the Earth as a coherent system of life, self-regulating and self-changing, a sort of immense living organism."[46] Agriculture, the first moulder of civilized society in myth and history, has always been associated with orderly living in an organized community or, in modern terms, in the "global village," in our common geo-ecological unit. Farming, the care of the earth, is an essential link to human life – past, present, and future: to the survival and continuation of humanity; to a type of human inventiveness that has to ensure increasing and safe food production for the ever-expanding world population, and simultaneously respect the human environment.

Could the Leamington Italians have intuitively grasped the full significance of their activity as they were working and developing their farms and greenhouse industries? Some did, in fact, see the advantages and the potential of the natural setting and of the greenhouse concept for a commercial as well as "artistic" enterprise, and thus for simultaneous material and spiritual gratification. Sometimes they achieved a balance in spite of changing and opposing views on agrarian life and work.

Farming has long been regarded as a wholesome occupation, and yet perhaps no other human activity has generated more simultaneously opposite attitudes: on the one hand, scorn for the earthbound, unlearned serfs, as well as admiration for the pioneering tiller of the soil; on the other, awe and reverence for the rich landowners, as well as derision of their conservatism, but at the same time imitation of their ways. In spite of the lure of the city and the increasing precariousness of farming, the simpler rural life and values have been a continuous attraction. At the same time, modern ideas of progress and excessive industrialization and domination of the natural world threaten the balance and harmony of nature, even though nature has long been associated with the human creative force, or at least has been considered a model, at times a stepping stone in the journey to artistic beauty, truth, and goodness. Like the Greek philosopher Socrates, others later exalted city life and scorned rural existence. Yet the praise of country living over city or palace life has been a constant literary topic since the (Sicilian) Greek bucolic poet Theocritus. Today, country folk in one part of the earth are destroying their own habitat, in another they still protect their "[rural] shrines ... [with] loving care and attention."[47]

"Earthly paradise" was the expression often used by both French and English explorers and settlers when they first saw the Detroit River–Lake Erie region of the Great Lakes.[48] And two centuries later the phrase has been at times applied to the southernmost tip of Canada, the eastern part of the "Garden of Canada" (i.e., Essex County), particularly to the rural setting of south Mersea Township with its mild climate, rich farmlands and orchards, its variety of fruits and vegetables, its waterways and fishing, and the unique flora and fauna of Point Pelee National Park, as well as the nearby (Kingsville) Jack Miner Bird Sanctuary, defined as "a thing of beauty and usefulness." In dealing with Point Pelee Park (est. 1918), at least one writer offered an "earthly paradise"–type description:

> Rarely is such natural beauty concentrated in such a small space [containing] some of the most beautiful woodland and lake scenery ... the peace and dignity of a great cathedral among the towering, moss-covered ancients of the forest; hanging lianas are reminders of the tropics; breezes carry the invigorating fragrance of red cedar; along the water's edge, fine beaches of white sand lure the holiday-seeker into the surf ... Even more important ... are the many outstanding characteristics of the trees, plants, birds and other animals ... Plants such as Summer Grape, Rose Mallow, Green Brier and Prickly Pear Cactus are common ... Great trees of southern species exist in the woodland. The visitor can make the acquaintance of Chestnut Oak, Hackberry, Sycamore, and Tulip-trees ... [The] most engaging natural attraction of Point Pelee is the overwhelming panorama of bird life ... such as Cardinal, Carolina Wren, Orchard Oriole ... enormous numbers of birds concentrate on Point Pelee during the migratory journeys ... [The] variety of terrain, including open beach, fields, marsh, bushland and woodland ... is attractive to all kinds of birds, from eagles to humming birds. Almost two hundred and fifty species have been recorded there ... in mid-May ... the entire park is filled with bird song and birds are to be seen everywhere ... Again, in the autumn, this parade of birds takes place ... one is struck by the wonder of migration – the mystery of the urge which drives winged creatures to make great return journeys to the south every year ... Point Pelee ... is an unusual spot, possessing valuable scientific attributes, as well as great attractiveness for recreational purposes.[49]

A rural "paradise" near the most modern urban conveniences! No wonder it has been hailed as one of the best retirement spots in Canada (if not in the world, according to a retiree from Great Britain).[50] For more than one person, retirees and writers, the Leamington area has become, as Bernice Ingratta saw it, "at least a branch office of the Promised Land."[51] In fact one area has been artistically and scientifically transformed, if not into an "earthly" paradise, quite definitely into a "tropical paradise" that one can really visit, just down the road from Windsor.

Colasanti's Cactus and Tropical Gardens, as it is now called, highlighted in a brochure advertising Windsor and Essex County attractions, has been described as a "tropical paradise ... located in Ruthven and open all year round. Stroll through 15 interconnected greenhouses presenting a display of colorful blooms amidst a wide variety of cactus and greenery ... Talk to exotic parrots, feed the animals and then relax over a hot cider under fruit-bearing tropical trees." Beyond the economic aspect and the dollar value of the enterprise for the community, it is the beauty of it and the thrill of a visit that are enhanced in the tourist brochure; and the words and photos playing on the collective fantasy transform the "tropical garden" into an island paradise. In this sense, the "farm" comes to represent a balance of needs and dreams: of financial-economic pursuits and of pleasurable and educational aspirations; of both the utilitarian and the aesthetic components of every human being. It seems to be at least one Leamington Italian-Canadian answer to the Horatian formula of the universal artistic fusion of the useful and the beautiful (*utile dulci*).[52]

In brief, farming and the greenhouse industry, which was the outcome of farming, more than any other occupation in the Leamington area, has provided the Italian-Canadian community with the satisfaction of many human desires (first of all, genuine nourishment) and the fulfillment of personal and community expectations. One of them was to be constantly linked to tradition, but at the same time be free, forward-looking, adventurous, and creative enough to experiment with new ideas and more recent technology, in a quest for more plentiful products and a higher quality of life. Some of their achievements did not go unnoticed, either to the illustrious visitor from Russia to the Pannunzio farm, or to the jury that awarded the Colasanti farms. In 1986 Colasanti Farms Limited, along with such companies as 3-M Canada and E.D. Smith and Sons, was the recipient of an Ontario Chamber of Commerce award of merit. The Colasanti enterprise/complex was one of thirty-eight businesses nominated, and one of five businesses to receive it. "The awards recognize achievement in sales and export growth, employment creation, introduction of new technologies and entrepreneurship."[53]

Perhaps, in Colasanti's case, it could have added "achievement in harmonizing science and art," a concept also quite appropriate for other Leamington area Italian farm complexes. The 1986 award to the Colasantis, occurring about a half century after the purchase of the first farm by Italian pioneers in the area – the Pannunzio brothers and Luigi Mastronardi – marked also the anniversary of the birth of the Leamington farming community and, in view of its sponsorship role, of the foundations of the Italian community as a whole.

10

Marriage and the Family

The most significant social institution among Italian Canadians has been the extended family.

Sturino, Italians

AN ITALIAN SPOUSE ...
PREFERABLY FROM THE SAME HOMETOWN

A close-knit family, while providing protection and strength for its members, guarantees the survival and transmission of traditional values and customs, which in turn reinforce ethnic identity. The married men who came to Leamington alone, between the two world wars, had their wives and children join them as soon as finances and regulations permitted. The single men preferred to live with or near Italian families who better satisfied their "Italian" needs: a warmer environment, companionship, as well as robust meals. But as soon as it was possible, they also looked for an Italian bride with whom to build a family and home, who would make venturing into the "cold" environment easier. Several other immigrants in that era came as family groups. Only one, in fact, among the first settlers lived in Canada for over two decades without his family. By the end of the Second World War, the twenty-odd families formed a relatively close-knit and distinct Italian group – "one big family" – the basis of the community, the keeper and defender of a certain degree of *italianità* (see chapters 1, 12).

In order to alleviate the anxiety of disruption and separateness, all immigrants try to recreate a familiar milieu, first by adhering to customary practices, to prescribed forms of daily and occasional rituals. Among Italians, this was especially evident in the almost inviolable mores around marriage.

Therefore, in choosing a lifetime companion, tradition offered clear though unwritten guidelines in a proverb: *Moglie e buoi dei paesi tuoi*

(Wife and oxen from your hometown). The closest English equivalent "Birds of a feather flock together," does not have the same implications. The Italian maxim is a caution. Things familiar are safer than unfamiliar ones, and different backgrounds in a marriage may be the source of problems. In other words, "Stick to your own people (when choosing a mate)."[1] Endogamy, in fact, was and still is preferred and quite high among Italian Canadians.

About half (48.5 per cent) of the Leamington Italians interviewed were already married upon arrival in Canada (the majority in Italy, three of them in Argentina, and two in Brazil). Of the other half (50 per cent), all single persons on arrival, 19 per cent went back to Italy "to visit and get married," as one of them confided. Once they felt settled, many of the men returned to Italy to marry their childhood sweetheart or any other available young woman: "[in 1950 there were] not many Italian girls in Leamington. [I] wanted to marry an Italian, so I went back to marry."

The practice was common in all Italian immigrant communities throughout the world; it even inspired Italian songs that became especially popular in these communities in the 1950s and 1960s. In a 195. hit, "La mogliera" (The wife), the immigrant-singer makes unequivocally clear his intentions and the type of woman he is going to look for in his *paese*: "*Io voglio ritornare al mio paese e mi voglio trovare una bella sposa, una sposa molto semplice e cortese*" (I intend to go back to my town and find myself a beautiful bride, a bride of very simple and polite ways). But in view of the not so simple task, before he sets out on his search, he consults his "close associate," his *compare* (a typical presence in the southern Italian immigrant community) who accordingly advises him to choose very carefully; to avoid women with extremely good or bad qualities that may make his life miserable: "If she is too beautiful you will need a sentinel; and if she is too ugly, you will be dry and dull."

In another song, "Io sono Americano" (I am an American), 1957/58 the Brooklyn-born southern Italian complains that "surely the story has made a mistake," and in both English and Italian he informs his American "fiancée" that he is going to Italy to marry what he colourfully calls a "*uagliona.*" The southern Italian dialect term for *girl* is used, in fact, not only for colour, but also to reflect the language spoken or at least understood even among the immigrants' offspring, as well as to more easily identify the area of Italy where he will choose his bride: "My baby goodbye! *Io me ne vo, e na uagliona sposerò* – I am leaving and I'll marry an Italian girl." The reality and the myth reflected in such themes were more than likely encouraged and reinforced thereafter by the popular success itself of the songs. In the late 1960s at least one occurrence of this Italian immigrant custom appeared in a newspaper title as "Canadian Women 'Frivolous': He Writes for Nice Italian Girl" *Toronto Daily Star*, 2 September 1969).

In the early years after the Second World War, it was not unusual for the single immigrant to send a photo of himself to his hometown (preferably one that revealed his new good fortune) so that his relatives, friends, or even the priest could show it around to any girl who might be interested in marrying an *Americano* from the same village. The man, as a Leamington Italian indicated, need not even go back and look for one himself; the bride was found through go-betweens and matchmakers, followed by an exchange of correspondence and photos: "I wrote to my brother [in Italy] and asked him to find a good woman for me ... My first wife died ... I felt I had to remarry because I cooked for myself, and washed my own clothes ... They were dirty after I washed them." Whether the motivation was respect for tradition or downright convenience and selfish needs, or a persisting *campanilismo* (parochial outlook), many young men in the 1950s, and even later, preferred hometown girls as wives. And convenience and needs were not just one-sided: there was no lack of young women back in the village quite anxious to make their way to "America."

However, the practice of writing to Italy for a wife or a husband often entailed some arrangements. One common procedure was the man or the woman, depending on who had a sponsoring relative, first came to Canada and, in due time, "called over" the other, and they got married in Canada. In other cases, the relative in Canada served as matchmaker and immigration link: "She found a girl for me ... I came over and got married three months later." In certain periods (not uncommon even today among more recent non-Italian immigrant groups), these arrangements, however old-fashioned, were the only way to get to Canada. However legitimate the practice, abuses were not lacking.

Among the Italians, the parents' continuing preference or tendency (if not pressure) to see their Canadian-born children choose spouses from the same hometown group may perhaps be indicated by a still widely told anecdote. It deals with a more "modern" Italian immigrant father who does not seem to be much concerned about the ethnic or racial origin of the child's future spouse, unless it happens to be an Italian, in which case he immediately inquires: "What part of Italy is she/he from?"[2]

THE PROXY MARRIAGE

The proxy system was another method used to get an Italian wife or husband from the hometown. About 7 per cent of the single men who came to Leamington followed this method, whether from Molise, Lazio or Sicily. Generally, proxy marriages were arranged between men and women who had known each other in Italy. But it was not always between acquaintances; some hardly knew each other; others not at all "I met my husband by picture at the fishery."

Proxy marriages were usually arranged because the man could not afford the time and the expense to return to Italy, and the government did not allow the woman to enter the country without the legitimate sponsorship of a relative or a spouse: "She couldn't come to Canada unless she was married, because she didn't have any relatives here ... We got married by proxy ... My brother stood in for me." There seem to have been another important reason: parents were not eager to send their daughter alone to a distant land without the assurance that she had a husband waiting for her.

However convenient it may have been for a few, marriage by proxy was described by some of those involved as a very unpleasant experience, particularly for the wives. Those women who "wanted to come to Canada," admitting they would have done "anything to get away from Italy," were of course quite satisfied with the arrangement. Besides, they generally knew their future husband. Other proxy brides, however, remembered it as a very sad and sometimes frightening episode in their life: "I married by proxy ... I had no idea of Canada ... I was unhappy to leave my relatives ... I knew no one in Canada ... I didn't know my husband before I got married; I only knew what he looked like ... I had never talked to him ... I came alone ... I cried ... I was lonely ... scared ... I had never been anywhere ... I arrived in Windsor at 7:30 and had to wait until 2:30 for my husband ... I was scared ... I took a taxi to Leamington ... I didn't understand the taxi driver." However limited and short-lived, this immigrant practice left indelible marks on some of the protagonists as evidenced by the memory of even the smallest details.

ITALIAN AND NON-ITALIAN SPOUSES

The majority of Leamington Italians who arrived in Canada as single persons chose their wives or husbands from the local communities in Canada or the United States. The rapidly growing Italian population not only in Leamington but in Windsor as well as Detroit, offered wider choices. Moreover, other considerations encouraged the immigrant to opt for a local wife; and, in some cases, the betrothed young woman in the hometown was simply left behind: "I was engaged in Italy, but I didn't want her to come here because I wanted to go back to Italy ..

After five or six years ... I felt settled [and] wanted to marry someone here, so I could better adjust." Already early in the twentieth century, an Italian immigrant writing to a friend who had second thoughts about joining him in "America" and leaving his girl reassured him by pointing out certain other benefits the new land offered: "Don't worry; even here there are beautiful ones and richer than there"; and he was most likely referring not just to women of Italian origin.[3]

The need or desire to adjust or integrate more easily into the Canadian way of life may indeed have been an additional good reason for choosing a Canadian-born wife. What may have also come into play was a belief that marrying into an "English" family increased one's opportunities or even resulted in general improvement. It was not possible to establish how widespread this notion was in the Leamington Italian community. But at least one statement by the Canadian-born wife of a 1950s immigrant was an indication that it did exist. The woman felt that since their marriage, her husband had not only "changed a lot" but had also started "to be more civilized, outgoing, not just Italian and that's it."

Whatever the reason, a conspicuous number of Italian single men in the Leamington area chose non-Italian brides. Most men in this group had come to Canada when they were young; but quite a few of them, who were in their late twenties at arrival, also married non-Italian women. Nevertheless, the exogamous category represented only 21 per cent of the total single population. The preference among the "older" immigrants was to follow tradition and marry within one's "own kind," and they generally expressed the desire that their children also marry into Italian families.

That preference was again as much the result of respect for tradition as one of more practical consideration. A number of parents felt that they would have difficulty communicating with a son-in-law or daughter-in-law who was not Italian: "It is important for me that my children marry an Italian because we will speak the same language, eat the same food, have the same religion ... [Also] if there are ever any problems with money or anything else, there is no problem for them to move to Italy to try and make a living ... They are free." But evidently, it also involved more than a question of language barrier: it was an all-embracing concern about the survival and welfare of the family. These parents believed that their children would get along better with an Italian spouse because of the shared background.

However untenable some of the arguments may appear, endogamy was strongly advised and sometimes imposed in both subtle and direct ways. Not uncommon were the doubts whether a non-Italian bride would be able to meet the "culinary demands of an Italian husband." Subjective comparisons seemed unfairly in favour of Italian over non-Italian women: "I would really like my sons to marry Italians, but now young men want the 'English' and I don't know why ... I think there would be more respect from Italian women, especially from those born in Italy.' But group maintenance was also a consideration: "When I was younger most people stuck to their own group ... Italians would marry Italians ... Today, children are becoming more Canadianized ... Cultures are being mixed [in] marriages between nationalities."

As a result of these views, most of the Italian men's non-Italian brides who were interviewed stated that the initial period was very difficult. The language barrier was much less a problem than the resentment, usually from the husband's mother. Generally, these difficulties were sorted out with time. But it was especially hard if the husband insisted that they live with his parents. Nevertheless, in the few instances where this situation occurred, the arrangement was quite short-lived, since the new couple took up a separate residence. And in the long run, contrary to some views, many non-Italian wives not only accepted the husband's family traditions, but they also learned his dialect and even became supporters of those traditions.

Time and experience changed even the strongest convictions, at least in part. Some parents, of course, didn't think it mattered if their children married Italians or not "just as long as they get along." One, however still had some reservations about interracial marriages.

OLD AND NEW MARRIAGE PRACTICES

Generally, the wedding customs practised in the hometown for generations were carried over to the new land with few variations. In fact their willingness in the earlier years to accept the proxy arrangement may be better understood in the light of certain customs in villages of Molise. The most "peculiar" seemed to be those described by immigrants from Villa Canale, where a two-tier matrimonial ritual was followed. Tony DiMenna, a widower since 1924, who himself provided the first example of proxy marriage in the community when he remarried in 1935 (see chapter 5, especially note 6), gave a brief explanation of what many referred to as the "Villa Canale marriage custom": In the old days the couple first went through a civil marriage at city hall; but it was the subsequent religious ceremony that legitimized the marriage that is, to be fully recognized by the parents and townspeople as husband and wife, the sacrament of matrimony had to be administered by the church. Usually, however, two, three, and even four years elapsed, most often at the request of the girl's parents, before this celebration took place. In the intervening period, the couple was considered formally engaged, but not formally married, since "*la chiesa era quella che contava*" (the church was what counted). Therefore, they continued to live separately, each in their respective parents' home, and they could see each other only with chaperones.

One of the women interviewed related her own experience:

Before we got married, we just knew each other ... We didn't go out with each other as young people do today ... We were married in 1944. We had a Mass, no white dress ... But we were married ... though it was more like an engagement ... Then after four and a half years we had another wedding, but this time I wore a white gown and more people came and we had a big party ... After this wedding, we started to live together ... After the first wedding we couldn't go out alone ... like on a date ... My husband visited me and my family after we were married the first time [but] he couldn't touch my hand ... He couldn't even sit by me ... Only small towns like Villa Canale ... had such extreme customs.

The proxy wedding in the Italian immigrant community seems an extension of this custom. Separation of husband and wife in the proxy arrangement could not have appeared unusual to those who were accustomed to the old village ways. Old habits die hard: according to one woman, who was married in 1956 in Villa Canale, this custom was still popular there at that time.

Nevertheless, some customs, however respected, did not survive in the clash with more modern exigencies, especially if they were deemed harsh in the first place, at least in Tony DiMenna's judgment: "I think this old, outdated custom was very bad for the young people ... That's the way the thinking went. [But now] I think in Italy they must do what we do here: When they are married they are truly married."

A custom that did not totally disappear, even to this present day in the Italian Canadian community, was the one of the extended family. In small towns, the newly married couple lived with the parents, in-laws, or grandparents; perhaps more frequently with the groom's parents than with the bride's family. This arrangement required a great deal of adjustment, but there were also advantages: "After we were married, we lived with my grandmother ... She helped with raising the children." Some explained that this was only natural, since many girls from the small town married at a very young age, "anywhere from fourteen to nineteen ... A girl at fourteen is not ready to marry, but then you always live with the family and are guided." Invariably, in situations involving young girls, the marriages were arranged by the parents – the majority of them among those who came from Sicily. One man described his marriage as "a marriage of convenience ... My family was very poor ... My wife had much property."

According to those interviewed, most marriage traditions were still carried on in Leamington. But the reaction to the more antiquated forms became stronger, especially if they had been exposed to present-day life in the old villages and were able to compare: "In Italy, I think the teens have more to do, and Italy is not as strict now ... The Italians here bring the old style and traditions with them and don't change ... My family is very old-fashioned: no dating ... very strict ... have to have chaperones everywhere you go ... I'm against this ... I believe in moderation."

The survival of some "antiquated" norms, with the resulting clash between two lifestyles, often aggravated the natural generation gap. While rejecting the old ways, quite a few daughters of those strict parents vowed never to put their daughters through the same hardships: "I got married when I was sixteen years old ... I was so young! I really didn't know what was going on ... When I was young, I was not allowed even to talk to a boy ... I don't think I will be quite as strict with my daughter because I don't want her to marry someone she doesn't really know." The survival of some of the customs was inevitably having adverse effects on the family and community: they further removed the children from their origins and tended to fragment the group.

Some aspects of the old village marriage customs were fast disappearing, but not completely, as indicated by a few: "In Leamington it is expected that sons live with their parents when they get married." Some parents planned years ahead for this event, as evidenced in the way the house was built. But this also was increasingly becoming a cause of tension and quarrels among son, father, and future bride, who most often refused the arrangement.

On the other hand, there were customs that all young and old seemed to accept, and they weren't Italian at all, or at least they had not originated in Italy. The "Italian wedding," at which the entire community seemed to be present, was a spontaneous growth of the Italian-Canadian community. Such a custom did not fail to surprise a bride arriving from Italy in 1955: "I got married fourteen days after I arrived ... We got married in Windsor because there was an Italian priest there ... We had a party afterwards which was all planned by my in-laws ... My wedding was different than the weddings in Italy ... invited [are only] close family for weddings there ... [It's] a small feast ... Here they invite friends as well as relatives to the weddings."

There were, of course, definite reasons for this development, all related to the immigrant experience, group maintenance, and community identity. In the early 1950s and before, weddings served the additional purpose of a community social function: "a good excuse for getting together." Thus, most, if not all, Italians in the area, whether Sicilians, *Ciociari*, or Molisani, relatives or not, were invited to the reception. In this way, explained the Italians in Leamington, the tradition of large weddings developed among members of their community. As the Italian population grew, and as the list of relatives increased, invitations became more selective. But because of the early tradition of inviting all the Italians, many felt an obligation to invite all those who had been kind enough to invite them to the wedding of their son or daughter. It became an expanding cycle. Insofar as it brought the Italians together and kept the community spirit alive in those early days, it was a positive custom.

But an attitude, often related to the nouveau riche, came into play in its development and proliferation. Large weddings began to be used and regarded as manifestations of personal success, a measure of the family financial strength. They often simply became extravagant public displays of wealth, reaching levels of exaggeration and poor taste: "Big parties are one way of showing off money and wealth ... a type of competition ... Here, at your wedding, you may have people you don't even know." This growing materialistic mentality, while distorting the spirit of that community custom from a civic to a more selfish act, was most probably threatening many other traditions. Often the rapid growth and resulting demise of some traditions were regarded as signs of progress; but they were also indications of community fragmentation, or at least of increasing detachment from the common cultural moorings and a decrease in the sense of security they had offered in the earlier days.

But marriage among the Leamington Italians rarely ended in divorce. Though records are incomplete (mostly due to reticence, a sense of "shame" in reporting on this matter), fewer than thirty divorces and/or separations (one involving a pioneer family) have been counted in the community for the entire fifty-sixty-year period (about 5 per cent of the approximately 550 families). Their opposition to divorce, while coinciding with Catholic doctrine, was more than a manifestation of religious rules or beliefs; not simply a continuation of the "social defect" or characteristic that Indro Montanelli ascribed to the Italians in Italy: "lack of social sense" and consequently excessive concern for "the family."

Their strong disapproval of the dissolution of marriage, and consequent splintering of the family, rested also on other considerations, some quite practical: their recent immigration experience (the need, often felt also by the younger generation, to stay and work together in a "strange" environment); a sense of pride and fear of domestic shame (especially in a small, rural, mainly agricultural and quite interconnected community); as well as respect for tradition, customary practice (one of the soundest bases of ethnocultural identity in a multicultural society). Overall, their "great opposition to divorce" was a further indication of the rural southern Italian belief in the unity and strength of the family and of the immigrant community's need for and commitment to such a family (see Ricci, *Radici*, 33; and chapter 15, "The Mores in the 'Village' and in the Community"; "Almost Parallel Communities" and notes 16, 18, 19).

LA FAMIGLIA (THE FAMILY)

When old customs and values anchoring a society were seen to be disappearing, what could be put in their place as a stabilizing force? The Italians saw to it that it remained *la famiglia* (the family)! Or in Luigi Barzini's words,

> The first source of power is the family. The Italian family is a stronghold in a hostile land: within its walls and among its members, the individual finds consolation, help, advice, provisions, loans, weapons, allies and accomplices to aid him in his pursuits. No Italian who has a family is ever alone. He finds in it a refuge in which to lick his wounds after a defeat, or an arsenal and a staff for his victorious drives. Scholars have always recognized the Italian family as the only fundamental institution in the country, a spontaneous creation of the national genius, adapted through the centuries to changing conditions, the real foundation of whichever social order prevails.[4]

The emigration-immigration phenomenon reshaped and redefined the Italian family in the land of origin and in the adopted land. Even by the early twentieth century, Coletti observed, emigration had shaken the very foundations of the southern Italian family structure, initiating development toward a more modern concept.[5] Immigration and settlement in a new land, as illustrated by the pioneer experiences of both the Molisan group and the Sicilian Peralta, had torn apart the centuries-old village family life (see chapter 3, "The Southern Italian 'Dream of America'"; chapter 6, "The Peraltas and Early Sicilian Immigration")

Post–Second World War immigrants also frequently referred to the disruptive effects on the family by the departure of one of its members: Floyd Cacciavillani (1948), whose "mother thought [he] was too young to go on his own," reflected both a general feeling about emigrating, "difficult … it disrupts the way of life," and their subsequent dominant desire "to reunite the whole family again." And quite often reunification occurred within the first few years.

But "recomposition" of the family structure according to traditional views, customs, and values was slow and often beset by confusion, conflicts, and compromises. The attempts to recreate the southern, patriarchal, close-knit family gave far from uniform results: the vision they had imported was not always or completely reflected in reality; sometimes it even seemed they had failed. In the long run, partly as a result of external and internal pressures and partly because of the clash and/or interaction of local conditions and "old" characteristics, what emerged most often manifested changes in the once clearly defined roles of each constituent member: basically a development of different rapports between husband and wife, between parents and children, and particularly a weakening of the male-oriented family concept.

Generally, the basic concept of the family, as described by Barzini, found some reflection in almost all the interviews with the Leamington Italians. Among the many divergent views regarding the methods of preserving or achieving the "Italian family," and in spite of contradictory claims within the same family about the results of their efforts, there were no disagreements on the type of family they wished to perpetuate, particularly some of its fundamental aspects: "Most Italian families are close … more affectionate … Italians think more about the family … Children are more attached to their parents … even after they marry … The bond stems from the whole family working together … The older children take care of the younger children."

Their vision of the southern, patriarchal, close-knit family as a well-coordinated unit was substantially similar to the image of it presented by Giovanni Verga's patriarchal "Malavoglia" figure: the family functioned like the human hand; each finger, like each member of the family, needed to work jointly together for the benefit of the whole structure. The need to rebuild "the power of the family" – "a stronghold in a hostile land" – was more greatly felt by the immigrants than by Italians in Italy or by some Canadians. Consequently, most Leamington Italians, particularly the first newcomers, defended the traditional role of the family: the strength of the family was life itself; the welfare of the family unit became the highest good. Inevitably their goal was not without many challenges and obstacles, both from within and outside the family unit and the community.

The first difficulty was the attempt itself to implant an "old" concept into a new and different reality: the southern family was often associated with the centrality of the male, particularly with a concept reminiscent of the ancient Roman *patria potestas* or "the power of the father" over family goods and members; the emphasis was on the male's "sense of honour," not just the pride arising from the traditional view of "maleness" or the male's privileged status, but the dignity and responsibility associated with his traditional role of paterfamilias, "head of the household," chief breadwinner.[6] Any attempt, therefore, to diminish his stature and role was often seen as an erosion of family strength, honour, and success in society. On the other hand, at times the family's achievements themselves became obstacles: work, money, education, as well as Canadian ethnic diversity and social changes in Italy were variously judged as disjunctive influences on different family members and the unit as a whole.

Conflicts were inevitable. In certain households, the men either attempted to impose an unchanged, traditional family structure, or adopted as the base of the new family certain aspects of the old one, but with little or no account for the different Canadian circumstances. In fact, in each situation the result reflected only a partial view, a misinterpretation of the conditions necessary for the existence or the growth of a "Barzini-type" Italian family. In each case there was a serious misunderstanding about the complex interdependence of the family members: the intricate and reciprocal bonds – emotional, spiritual, social, and economic – were often reduced to a simple *financial* dependence of children on their parents.

The power of the family thus came to be misinterpreted as control and submissiveness, and often on this basis alone the Italian family was claimed to be stronger than most. The illusion and self-delusion lasted as long as there were no challenges to that family standard, often set by only one of its members and fixed to a different time and place. In earlier southern Italy, at least according to those who questioned it, "family members depended on each other more so than is necessary in Canada. A son couldn't afford to argue with his father because if he was disowned or thrown out of the house, he would be lost ... When children married, they often lived with their parents because they could not afford a place of their own ... Since a son relied on the inheritance ... from his father as his future means of livelihood, he would take care to ensure that he didn't forfeit that inheritance through hot-headedness These practical considerations became translated over the years into a morality surrounding the idea of fidelity to the family and respect for one's parents."[7]

Such a limited view of the family network and structure led to other misinterpretations and misunderstandings. In comparing "Italian" and "Canadian" families, many Italians felt that family ties were generally stronger among Italians than among Canadians: in their view, within the latter there was "more independence" and therefore "lack of respect for elders"; or Canadian parents, who were more willing to let their children roam free at their own pleasure, lost respect for their children. Canadians, in brief, "kick their children out of the house as soon as they are old enough to support themselves." Italian parents, on the other hand, "work and sacrifice for their children," give them "the opportunities [they] did not have [like] going to school," and plan for their future.

That the ties among Italian family members were or are stronger may even be true. But that the consequence of more independence of Canadian children was "lack of respect" was open to strong objections from Canadians and Italians alike. A few of those interviewed had a more realistic outlook. They felt that such generalizations were unfounded: "There are bad Italian parents as well as good Canadian parents." That also applied to their children who grew up in conditions better than their parents had known: "It's easier to raise children here. The kids here are better educated … They have an easier life … There is more money here … They have more opportunity to work and earn money."

It can generally be said that the only pattern that emerged from the accounts on reshaping the Italian family was variation and lack of uniformity in ideas and results. The variants and confusion were most often directly related to the reactions, by each family group or member, to tradition and Canadian social and economic conditions. A concern of many Italian parents was to spare their children some of the hard times they had experienced; they thus encouraged them "to go to school and be something." Often repeated was "I will help them … but they have to help themselves as well," and that was to be done, of course, by following "their parents' example…and work hard." Some even went against advising their offspring to go into farming, preferring that they obtain "an education … and work that was satisfying and profitable." Others, however, held on to views that led to misunderstandings, resentment, and clashes within the new family: "Children should follow the path of their parents … Children aren't willing to help out in the greenhouse industry."

On the other hand, many parents, realizing that their children's increasing financial independence inevitably led to a loosening of the family unit, took precautionary measures, made some adjustments to their views, and compromised. They tried not to interpret their children's refusal to participate in the family business, or a son's choice of another profession, as a rejection of family traditions and lack of respect for the parents. By accepting, though reluctantly at first, some practices of the adopted land, and by respecting and supporting some of the children's wishes, they were able to repair and remould family relationships, and continue to dedicate themselves completely to it: "My whole heart is with the family," said one of them, still reflecting the feelings of the majority.

EXTERNAL THREATS TO THE FAMILY

Often the "builders" of the Leamington Italian family found themselves in a double irony: on the one hand, they were aiming for a family that worked together in order to be strong and financially secure; on the other, work and financial security offered other members the means to be more independent. Similarly, the same external pressures, against which they tried to protect the family by turning it into a sort of fortress or "stronghold," as Barzini called it, were progressively assailing and weakening the structure: "In Canada, children can afford to be much more independent ... They do not have to rely on their parents for survival ... They know that if they are thrown out of the house they can get a job and make a fairly good living." The concern or fear was that the Italian family increasingly showed the same trends that, in their view, had made the Canadian family a weaker structure: "When people have more money, they get spoiled and the family ties weaken ... I see [our] children becoming more Canadianized, and that the kids treat the parents like second-class citizens ... Before, the family depended on each other."

The recurring complaint was that the "strength of *la famiglia* is weakening ... Italian families are not as close-knit as they used to be ... The children are influenced by others and by the schools." They "do not listen to their parents." The schools that their children were encouraged to attend in order to secure a better future, seemed to receive a large share of the blame for their children's disregard for the family unit, for their ingratitude for what they had or received, and for their undisciplined behaviour: "In schools [they] teach them to be individuals, not united ... The school system is responsible for the lack of respect ... Children don't think about helping others." The "others," who were supposedly also transforming their "Italian-reared" children, included youngsters from Canada's ethnocultural diversity: "children are mixed with too many nationalities."

But neither their nostalgia for the earlier days, nor their attempts to find scapegoats could forestall the quite normal integration. The authority of tradition could not be enforced forever with the usual, simple reminder: "Well, back home we did this"; that was frequently counteracted with a reference to a more immediate, and their own, reality: "Never mind about back home, we're in Canada!" The reaction was both quicker and stronger when changes "back home" supported their arguments.

However sadly, some parents began to slowly accept that reality: "Children have different ideas … I can't raise my children as I was raised because we're in a different country." But it was still "a shock … to realize that the children are growing differently than we did." Nevertheless, at times the "shock" had positive effects: it made parents more aware that it was "a bit difficult to raise children in a different culture." It helped them to gradually relax their standards: "Children don't grow up totally Italian, because they were born and raised here… I brought up my daughter with moderation in mind … that is, not too strict and not too lenient … Parents must change with the times … Living is easier today … They get more in life … Life is more comfortable … [Therefore] children's ideas change from their parents." The recognition and acceptance of the differences in environment, ideas, cultures, and times helped to avoid or eliminate some basic causes of possible family conflicts.

In many cases the very existence of the conflicts was denied. Many parents were willing to admit that their children's way of thinking followed the "Canadian way," but only a few would accept that the differences of opinions, between parent and child, were the source of any deep tensions, let alone of family breakdown. But the accounts of the younger members of the family were often quite an eye-opener. According to many Italians who had entered the country at a young age, "a terrible strain was put on children: being raised in an Italian household had a big effect on us children … We were raised here and they were raised there … They had lived a certain type of life [and] we were expected to grow up in their way … [This] created a gap … no way can [I] get along with [my] parents … My parents' way of thinking is different … I lost the Italian language … I could hardly communicate with my parents … All my brothers, except the oldest, left home in early teens … I dropped out of school … hit the streets … got into trouble … then I met my wife [and] settled down … [I] never mixed with Italians."

THE GENERATION GAP AND THE FAMILY

"The youth of today think of eating, dressing, and having fun … [Our] generation thinks of working hard and saving money for the future … for the family." The external influences on the children increasingly fuelled what were at first latent contrasts within the family: the two pressures combined often represented formidable threats to the family structure. The different view of "work" and "money" was the first indication of a growing divide between the young and the old. With respect to money in particular, the parents' implication was that it had a tendency to spoil the young people; but its accumulation by the older generation was a more respectable pursuit because it was done "for the family ... for the future." Such contradictions, though inspired by intent to keep the family intact, were not always acceptable to the younger generation. They were seen as unfair judgments: distortions of reality that further enhanced the generation gap to the detriment of the family.

The "struggle of ancients and moderns" is a common theme of the human condition. But ethnicity confers particular features to it. In general, parents who vied to recapture the "good old times" (most likely because they were younger then[8]) were, ironically, either critical of recent developments or blamed the young for what they themselves once did or didn't do. After all, many of them had abandoned parents, family, and old ways to seek a new life for themselves. The forward-looking young, on the other hand, often rejected the old ways as well as their parents' judgment of them.

The older generation, part of a relatively small ethnocultural community, especially one in a rural area that had built its strength and pride upon traditional values, interpreted the challenge from the young as a total breakdown, not just of the family, but of the very base of their identity. The generation conflict, dangerous as it is in ordinary circumstances, was compounded by ethnicity into a bitter laceration of two familial entities. To the new generation, the traditional family concept appeared increasingly old-fashioned, anachronistic, and unsuitable to an upwardly mobile community; the old premises were less and less valid, no longer completely justifying even the need for such a family.

Sometimes *la famiglia* assumed a meaning larger than that of "good mothering and fathering." The protection of its good name often became more important than the parental care or understanding that children may have needed and rarely obtained. Personal problems and family conflicts were generally taken seriously, but they had to remain solely the concern of the family. Very seldom would an Italian "speak openly about family problems." Their exposure might lead to public humiliation and disadvantages for the family. The family must never appear to go wrong, for it would be a bad reflection on the parents, a personal defeat. "Thus if a child behaves in an untraditional or unconventional manner, they are most often reprimanded with the usual 'What will people say?'" The protection of the family from negative public perception always had to take precedence over individual needs and aspirations: strong opposition to divorce may have partly derived from this concern; but it was usually the feelings and values of the children that were sacrificed to the "strength" of *la famiglia*.

The origin of such a view is undoubtedly the heightened Italian sense of posturing, especially in the male: his self-esteem makes him self-assured, but at the same time self-conscious, oversensitive, touchy, resentful of criticism and consequently concerned and careful in *fare bella figura* (making a good impression, keeping up appearances, saving face). Public disgrace or dishonour to himself and to the family was particularly dreaded when related to doubts raised about the public behaviour or morals of the female members of the household. In order to avoid such gossip, the children were jealously guarded, especially the daughters: "Canadian girls can go out ... Italians like to keep their children in ... They do not want to make a 'bad face' [i.e., *fare 'brutta figura'*]." (see chapter 3, note 2).

Consequently, the close attachment that parents claimed to have for the children was often questioned, held up as selfishness and distrust. The cementing force of the family was also scrutinized: was it the result of inherent bonds and values, or simply a reaction to external conditioning? At times the woman-wife herself refrained from manifesting, or was kept from enjoying, her hard-earned equality within the family because it seemed to challenge her companion's self-perception of masculinity. But the major danger to the traditional family came from the clashes with the emerging second generation.

Numerous accounts of the sons and daughters of the immigrants revealed an early life full of stress and strain that still affected them existence and influenced their own family life. The confessions formed a litany of hardships and frustrations, of anxiety and resentment, as well as recurring themes of disapproval, criticism, and even condemnation of parental, particularly paternal, authoritarianism, intransigence, inaccessibility, and harshness. All in all, they exposed deep-rooted conflicts between two lifestyles and sets of values that many parents preferred not to recognize or refused to accept: "I have had problems with my parents being strict ... My parents thought I didn't respect them ... They were just old-fashioned ... too different ... [and] still haven't changed"; "I never used the *'tu'* form with my parents ... always *'signore' 'signora'*[9]... My parents had to reassert their authority ... because [we] were being influenced by other children ... Family ties were breaking down"; "I resented my parents because of the work they made me do ... I was expected to go home [from school] to help them on the farm ... Other children stayed at school to play."

Parental control of their children's lives sometimes extended well beyond their age of maturity and into their more personal affairs. While hampering the independent growth with responsibility of the children, it jeopardized the development of sound and lasting relationships. In order to break free, children were often forced into rebellious or at least self-assertive stands: "I finally told my dad that I had a life of my own to live ... I would give my parents my pay cheque up to age twenty-four when I got married."

Parents' non-involvement in the children's school activities, and their lack of understanding of pressures in the school milieu, drew many complaints. Even though justifiable reasons reduced the blame, sadness was common: "Italian parents didn't go out of their way to participate with their children at school ... They never went to PTA meetings ... I felt bad but I knew they couldn't speak the language ... They didn't know the way of life in Canada ... They didn't have time ... It was a question of time rather than interest."

Most children, especially the daughters (largely of Sicilian parents), expressed strong resentment for their parents' strictness: "I resent my parents for the way they treated me ... Because of them ... I missed out on a lot of things ... Now I can't return to what I missed out in my youth ... I regret missing the life that other children had ... I remember that my sister and I spent the night in the car a couple of times because we found the door locked ... [It was] not a happy teenage life since I was always arguing with my parents." Distrust deprived children of their parents' guiding support and forced them to become sly: "I was expected to stay at home and be a second wife ... I went to school and took part in sports without my parents' consent ... I snuck out a lot"; "Sicilians gave rough times to their daughters ... I wanted trust from my parents ... I resented the fact that they were so strict with me. I began to go out when I got married."

The reaction against authority became even stronger when its traditional underpinnings were themselves discovered to be less valid than they used to be:[10] "In Italy, even in Sicily, girls have much more freedom ... Italy has changed but the Italians here keep their old ideas and mentality." Where children could use examples from the land of origin to question the basis of the Italian customs, there was often a general disorientation. The parents themselves, unaffected by the changes in their land of origin or by the customs of the adopted land, and seeing the erosion of the formerly secure grounds for their convictions and structures, felt frustrated and lost. The tightening of control on the family, which was often the consequence, further exacerbated the parent-child differences.

A common practice in the male-dominated family, that more than others generated frequent and often deep resentment, alienation, and even hatred, was that of the double standard: "I was brought up strictly Italian and I *hated* it ... I had to stay home while my brothers could go out ... My parents gave me everything material-wise, but I didn't like the customs ... My friends didn't like the way I was brought up and couldn't understand it ... I was even afraid to look at my father."

Many of the daughters experienced fear, anger, and loneliness more frequently than love, affection, and understanding. In fact, love or a synonymous term was hardly ever mentioned in referring to the family bonds. *Strong* and *close-knit* were more common in describing the family, but not without implying that those qualities were the result of imposed rules and regulations. The words *communicate* and *communication* sometimes did appear, but only to signify a breakdown or the absence of it. *Argue* and *quarrel* were also used quite frequently. In brief, there seemed to be very little open discussion and dialogue.

Family dynamics such as these were not unique to the Leamington Italians. By increasingly absorbing the values of the host society, all immigrant families slowly experienced integration, if not assimilation, into the North American way of life. Their conscious or unconscious resistance to the external influences, while not favouring a smoother interaction of the two different ethics, gave rise to family contrasts and to inner conflicts, particularly in the younger family members, usually at a more advanced stage in integration and assimilation (see also chapter 12, "Ethnicity").

THE YOUNG PEOPLE'S CONFUSED VALUES

The effects of the attempt to straddle two ways of life became clearer in a sample interview carried out by the student-researchers with fourteen Leamington Italian young people: nine females and five males, from sixteen to twenty-five years of age, single, living at home, and most attending school (high school, college, or university). They responded to questions on a variety of topics:

1 Identity: land of origin, customs, language, Canadian ways, friends
2 Parents, children: views, double standard
3 Marriage/sexual behaviour: dating, birth control, common-law living
4 Other practices: smoking, drinking, drugs

They generally revealed that the family and the community had passed on to them quite a "mixed bag of goods."

Sense of Identity

All but two of them (both women) considered themselves Italian Canadians: one felt she was "Canadian," the other "Italian," but neither defined the term. Five neither spoke Italian (one just a little) nor had visited Italy; eight associated only with Canadians (i.e., non-Italians); three had only Italian friends; the other three, mixed friends. Except for two who had mixed feelings, all were proud of their Italian heritage. But over half (eight) did not feel different from "Canadian kids," except for the fact that Canadian young people had more freedom to do what they pleased (six). On the other hand, all but one pointed out that differences between Italians and Canadians were often the cause of misunderstandings, confusion, and clashes; and at the same time, all found some aspects acceptable in both ways of life.

Parents, Children, and the Double Standard

The variety of views and reactions was most marked in their relationship with their parents, particularly in the observance of Italian or Canadian customs or values. Generally, they felt that the older generations' attitudes toward marriage, dating, and sex were outmoded; and their outlook on financial status, lifestyles, and adherence to tradition, quite different from the Canadians' view: Italians were more hard-working, more concerned with self-improvement and saving money for a home and family needs; Canadians, on the other hand, were more carefree. Italians, according to one of them, were always trying to "prove themselves," while for another, they were "defensive because deep down they felt they're foreigners." Over all they thought the Italian family was "closer and more caring"; Italian parents did more for their children but were more watchful, overprotective, and strict with them; however, mothers were more sensitive than fathers. The children were also kept closer to home, and too much was expected of them. For one girl, the characteristic difference was the Italian parents' lack of trust in daughters, and the curfew applied to them. But only half of them had regrets or bad experiences as a result of it.

The majority of female respondents objected strongly to the different roles and treatment of boys and girls in the family and community; and all the young women, except one in the sixteen-to-eighteen-year bracket, believed the double standard was common: "Italian boys have more freedom ... [They] can go out with girls, smoke, etc. ... where girls are kept at home to raise the family ... Girls have to stay home with their parents; guys are more loose, do whatever they want ... Girls are brought up stricter, much stricter." They rejected some pretexts that parents use to support the differences: "Boys can't get into trouble"; "it's the way we were brought up"; and the tradition-imposed image of women as simply "homemakers." Two of the women made sound arguments against justification of such practice; one accusingly vindicated equality and human rights – "It is a form of sexual discrimination." The other appealed to common sense: "The differences are not justified in the fact that girls remain naive about the real world."

The message from the five men was altogether different: the men not only accepted the double standard, they did so with the usual references to tradition. All but one, in the twenty-two-to-twenty-five-year range, were aware of the situation: "Everyone knows the problems of being an Italian girl. They are slaves at home ... They never go out." One man in the sixteen-to-eighteen-year range naively justified the practice of allowing boys to go out more often and longer on the grounds that, by staying home, "girls remain pure and become good wives." An older one (nineteen-to-twenty-one bracket) seemed to repeat the words of the parents: "The way I was brought up [was that] girls are to be ladies and are not allowed out with boys until a certain age, or permission from their father." The eldest of the five (twenty-two-to-twenty-five bracket) did not justify the differences but provided a further reason for them: "Italian boys have freedom and are very aggressive in public, whereas Italian girls have to stay home and be good so that they won't be known as tramps in their parents' eyes." For one woman in the nineteen-to-twenty-one-year range, the main reason for her different behaviour was to keep up appearances more than safeguard her morals, although in many families they often meant the same thing: "I feel that I must be careful in all I do, in order not to be the centre of gossip in the Italian circle."

Marriage and Premarital Behaviour

To what extent had the younger generation been influenced by their parents' values, or to what degree had the older generation changed? What were the similarities and differences in their parents' and their own views regarding marriage, dating, premarital sex, common-law living, smoking, drugs, birth control, child rearing? In general, the older community practised endogamy. But of the fourteen young people, only two males preferred Italian women as wives: for one of them, in the sixteen-to-eighteen-year range, a self-defined Italian Canadian, it was because "Italians are good cooks and easy to get along with." Four preferred non-Italians and eight were indifferent; but a few leaned more toward non-Italians, with only one open to one or the other, and stressing "as long as we are happy."

With respect to dating and sex, the parents were generally old-fashioned, but with an increasingly flexible attitude, more open-mindedness, at least on dating. Their own views were mostly closer to today's changing views than to their parents' old views. Only one, a male, stated that his outlook was closer to that of his parents; and three, that their views were a "little of each."

Most did not consider premarital sex "as wrong as [they were] taught to believe." Only three, one male and two females, considered it completely wrong; eight, three males and five females, said it was not wrong; and the rest, one male and three females, were either wavering between yes and no, or made it depend on life's "circumstances" or "situations." But half of them were completely against common-law cohabitation, three were uncertain (depending on the situation), one didn't "think so"; only three responded positively but with qualifications: two were men, but one interjected that his parents would object; and one woman, in the twenty-two-to-twenty-five-year range, responded, "Yes, but in another town, city, or country." What seemed to be the guidelines for most were not so much traditional values or fixed moral principles as some other considerations: a flexible outlook, an open mind to life's circumstances, or the usual fear of being seen and becoming the talk of the town. The "fear of being seen" and the resulting gossip assumed a role similar to that of customs in a rural society: a code of behaviour.

Other Practices: Private Vices and Public Virtues

Morality or religiosity seemed to play a lesser role than other factors. While most parents and the community imposed certain rules of behaviour in order to avoid gossip, they did not force any of the children interviewed to attend church, since church attendance did not determine their reputation in the community (although one said that he went on his own).

With respect to smoking, for example, although only six said they did, none of them did it automatically in front of their parents: one said his parents gave him that privilege; another, a woman, did it only in front of her mother, not her father; three others smoked when not in their parents' presence, for various reasons: "They think it's disgusting … so

I'm showing respect"; "my parents don't smoke, but they know I do"; "they asked me not to." It was especially difficult for parents who had grown up in the 1950s or earlier, in rural Italy, to become accustomed to seeing a woman smoke, let alone their own daughter. That woman was still unconsciously associated with particular morals or a particular profession; therefore, some preferred not to see it, and children obliged by hiding it.

Hypocritically or not, in order to maintain appearances, the children were forced to hide more than smoking from their parents. The girls in particular were "forced" to lie or were "forced" into a self-protective deception; and yet they were most frank in answering the question of whether young people hid anything from their parents (drinking, drugs, and birth control). Seven out of nine responded positively without specifying what it was. But after her "yes" one added, "but none of the above," likely alluding to premarital sex, if the previous answers were an indication.

The different attitudes toward women in the community were again illustrated by the males' all negative answers. The family and community double standard was exercising undue pressure on young women, often placing them in an awkward and painful situation, if not harmful to themselves and the community, since they also were the future mothers in the community. In fact, on child rearing, only four of the young women stated that they would strictly follow the way in which they had been brought up; two only partly or in some ways, and three responded negatively; while only one male responded negatively, two were positive, and two in some ways. These responses did not completely coincide with their general feeling of pride for their Italian heritage.

PURSUIT OF WEALTH AND ELUSIVE FAMILY UNITY

The children, growing up in overlapping worlds, more than their parents, felt squeezed or torn by the two separate, often opposing forces. But in their endeavour to react or adjust to the dual influence, they were provided with a vantage point. What emerged as the base of many clashes and the weakening of the family, related as much to the Italian-Canadian family mentality as to the Canadian milieu: the primary concern for material comforts. Of course, material pursuits can be closely associated with "ethnicity": economic betterment was a main goal of the immigrant. What puzzled and made things harder for the children was a family that was partly anchored to seemingly outdated concepts, and partly deeply influenced by the materialistic values that more widely permeate North American society.

In their view, Italian parents, like all good parents, dedicated their life and work to the family, to the children, particularly in order to help them avoid "hard times" and "be something." Their parents' goal was to "provide them with a great many things," which were specified as a good job, money, financial security, good living, and self-satisfaction. Yet the children were often reproached for showing more interest in the things that were easily made available ("eating, dressing, having fun") than in plans for a future patterned on their parents' lives or views ("working and saving for the family"; "helping others"). Clearly the parents were providing a "house," not a "home": work, money – things – made their life more comfortable, but not necessarily happier within the family. In the long run, material *things* without companion warmth and sensitivity did not always mean self-fulfillment, nor did these *things* win respect for the parents or their ways: "My parents gave me everything material-wise, but I didn't like the customs."

Since "in Canada children can afford to be more independent," they no longer had to rely on their parents' *things*: "If they are thrown out of the house they can get a job and make a fairly good living." In turn, the parents, perceiving the children's rejection of their *things* as a rejection of their *ways*, frequently deemed their "work and sacrifices" – often considered the shoring of their self-identity – as all very sadly futile: "No son wants to do the same thing his father did ... so there's no sense in sacrificing so much for your children."

The parents may not have been completely fair in judging their children as disrespectful, irresponsible, and selfish. On the other hand, many children themselves appeared to be more materialistic and less sensitive to their parents' sacrifices. Their relation to the parents or the family was summarized in statements that seemed to place their personal interests or special wishes, relatively petty at times, above the general good: "[I] never went camping or anything like that"; "I had to be in by twelve midnight ... I never received an allowance"; "We were not treated equally"; "I couldn't go out"; "I worked and had money, therefore I had more freedom than others." Sometimes what other children did or said seemed more important than the wishes of the parents or helping the family: "I was expected to go ... help on the farm ... [while] other children stayed to play ... My friends didn't like the way I was brought up and couldn't understand it."

Things, personal comforts, satisfaction of one's own desires – going out, money, play, freedom, independence – seemed to take precedence over cooperation, responsibility, understanding, and overall peace in the family. Though seemingly united by similar interests and aspirations, sometimes parents and children appeared to be living in two separate universes with no possibility of meaningful contact. *Things*, appearing as the essence of life, pursued as mirages of freedom and independence, occupied too much of their attention. As a result, they stood in the way of true feelings and hampered communication, the real bonds of the family (or humanity).

Does all of this, then, indicate that the strong, close-knit Italian family is only a myth? Not at all! The confusion and conflicts simply illustrate the struggle between the old and the new, one outcome of the conflict, one phase in the evolution of a concept of the family. Though many pressures caused the traditional family to change, often radically, or its ties to weaken, other centripetal forces protected and strengthened it. Also, from those same conflicts that often seemed to threaten its existence sometimes came renewed strength: clashes brought reflection and awareness, new values and new balances.

Some daughters who resented their parents' strictness, and "couldn't go out and had to lie," later showed understanding of their parents' ways: "That is the way [they] were brought up"; at times, appreciation: "I realized that what my parents did was for my own good," even though, they added, they wouldn't raise their daughters "in the same way." Though they did not totally accept the Italians' preoccupation with "pride and honour," they felt they were good qualities to have in moderation. Thus, part of the legacy of the Italian family was conserved in a general guiding principle.

THE CHALLENGING BALANCE: SECOND-GENERATION FAMILIES

A variation of the traditional family, or a different phase in its development, was presented in other interviews with both immigrant and second-generation families. Expectedly, it was not a uniform picture, as emphasis on both tradition and more modern practices varied. But it was always the result of a mixture, if not yet a fusion, of the ingredients. Frequently, modifications and combinations of old and new were made through conscious effort. Both parents and children displayed more tolerant attitudes and approaches, thereby avoiding excessive rigidity or extreme positions. The family presented by this group were better able to span the gap between generations, cultures, and eras. It was still beset by confusion and uncertainty, but there was at least a desire for a modus operandi based on moderation.

Some sensitivity on both sides improved parent-child rapport: some older children noticed that their parents' attitude changed as years went by. They became "less strict ... and gave more freedom to their younger brothers and sisters." The family situation was even better when the older ones did not resent this different treatment.

In dealing with money and freedom, some parents' middle-of-the-road approach helped to reduce and even eliminate possibilities for confrontation. They still maintained that children shouldn't date early or have allowances, but neither should they be made to pay room and board, if they continued to live in their parents' home after they had found work. They continued to firmly believe that "parents should provide for them all that is possible and give the children what they want, naturally what they deserve as well ... [but] children should have their freedom too, and of course if they work, they should be allowed to have their own money." Some were even more liberal and philosophized that it was better for younger people "to have a good time when they are single, because when one is married it is hard to leave the family and go out."

What was important was the fact that they were constantly considering their options; and such reflecting led to changes – at times, to relaxation of rigid beliefs; at others, to acceptance of the new ways, often aiming at an equilibrium between authority and freedom: "I think that children have to be a certain age to go out ... it doesn't matter if they are a girl or a boy ... They need responsibility before they can go out ... If they have too much freedom, then they won't enjoy family gatherings anymore ... If I had a daughter, I would not let her go out alone in the evening ... My son can go out, but I don't like it when he comes home late."

Though the distinction in rules for son and daughter remained, the attitude was a little less strict. Of course equal treatment was much more common in the second-generation family. But even in such cases, particular precautions were reserved for the daughter: "I wouldn't want my children to go through the same thing I did ... I'll allow my daughter to date, but I would insist on seeing who she's going out with first ... I don't want her to sneak around ... My son will be raised the same way ... He'll be expected home at a certain time."

In some immigrant families there was enough flexibility to foster independence and maturity in the children without rejecting family origins: "I came at two years old ... [it was] a bit difficult for me until I was sixteen ... At sixteen I was considered mature ... I worked and had money, therefore I had more freedom than others ... I am proud to be Italian ... [unlike] some Italians who would be ashamed to admit their nationality."

But in the second-generation family, different circumstances sometimes made a particular choice necessary: "I won't keep too many Italian customs in my family ... I won't be as strict ... I wouldn't speak Italian to my children, because I speak English to my wife at home ... My wife isn't Italian." And yet some among the young "liked the way [their] parents brought [them] up," and vowed to follow the same way with their children: "I will raise my children the way I was raised ... the proper way ... the Italian way ... more strict." One daughter followed the customs even more strictly than her parents: "Even though my sister was born here, she has yet to be Canadianized ... She disapproves more of what I do than my parents."

For every view or position, there were opposite ones: some parents insisted that the young people "feel more Canadian than Italian," that "going through the school system" made it almost impossible for them to "keep their Italian heritage." Besides, few wanted "to buckle down to family tradition," nor did they show "too much interest in Italy." Others explained that their Canadian-born children didn't care to know much about their past, and when they did, they refused to believe the sufferings of their parents and grandparents, sometimes with unkind remarks: "That's your tough luck!" The parents also liked Canada, but they often complained that their children "didn't want to hear anything about Italy." Ironically, the parents themselves, with their tales of poverty and suffering in their hometown and with limited knowledge of Italy, left the children with such a negative view of the land of origin that to many of them even the thought of a visit evoked images of hardship. Consequently, they avoided Italy, preferring California and Florida as their holiday destinations, and often Italian traditions: "not ... too many Italian customs at home." In the long run, such views and practices often led to only one solution: "full assimilation."

But some families aimed at a more modern, more enlightened solution: a complete balance of Italian traditions and Canadian reality. Their endeavour "to pass on [their] values and traditions to [their] children" seemed inspired by a more forward-looking human and cultural view: "As a family we're Canadian with European heritage and customs ... Our children are strictly Canadian but proud of their Italian heritage ... We taught them about their background ... We would like our children to know about Italy as well as other European countries." The global outlook, with which the situation was resolved, places this type of Italian-Canadian family at the most advanced point of its evolution. Such a family and outlook, if permitted, will most likely play an increasingly central role in the development of the new Canadian ethnocultural family, and perhaps of a more harmonious multicultural society.

But whatever the solution or level of achievement, the attempt to find a suitable modus vivendi between two identities demanded continuous soul-searching. It presented a constant challenge: no other task seemed more rewarding or more frustrating than the attempt to transmit the two ways of life to the younger generations: "I raised my children as best I could ... Try and raise them with both Italian and Canadian customs." The brief statement synthesized the feelings of many parents: while expressing a certain sense of satisfaction, it implied doubt about the success of the effort, as well as humility before this difficult role of the Italian-Canadian parent.

THE "SPECIAL" ROLE OF THE WOMAN

Other family practices, though not as intensely demanding as the raising of children in a different culture, were also a source of mixed reactions and concerns relating to the unity and strength of the extended family: working mothers and the care of aging parents and/or grandparents. The former presented a greater dilemma because of the "special" place of the woman-mother within the Italian family.

"The family system," according to an Italian-American writer, "is, perhaps, the clearest sample of difference between the Northern and Southern Europeans and their American descendants." Quoting Alfred Stuart Queen, Ciongoli states that "the general pattern and many specific traits" of the American family "are largely English products." One basic difference relates to the role of woman: "British and American feminists ... have stressed individual fulfilment in lieu of family success. Conversely, the Mediterranean woman puts family above her personal gratification ... There is an extraordinary difference between the women of the British-American and Italian cultures. This does not express itself in terms of power but rather importance within the family."[11]

Above all, what characterizes the Italian family is the role of the mother, more than that of the father. Richard Gambino described "the Italian father as titular head of the family, and the mother as the center ... the death of the Italian father is a far less significant event to the Italian family than the death of its mother. She is the irreplaceable source of sustenance, the nurturer; he is a mere breadwinner." But even "her position of power within the family is widely misperceived by non-mediterraneans," argues Ciongoli: "As early as the third century BC, the Roman Cato has been quoted on the subject, 'We Romans rule over all men, and our wives rule over us.'" And "Luigi Barzini in *The Italians* describes ... the position of women in modern Italy as one of 'great power' and paraphrases Cato, 'Men run the country, but women run the men.'"[12]

Similarly, the "differences between the way Anglo-Saxons and Italians regard their children also has its roots in history. For centuries, English children have been encouraged to independence at the earliest possible age. In contrast, Italian children are taught lifelong family duties and responsibilities." Thus, the Italian immigrant woman's decision to work outside the home, whether resulting from need, ambition, or trend, presented more than a dilemma, a value conflict.[13]

In general, after arriving in Leamington, the Italian woman found a regular job. But she also appeared to make the difficult attempt to balance traditional and Canadian ways: on the one hand, as a sensitive, self-respecting (only seemingly submissive) companion; an understanding but firm guide for her children (especially teenage daughters); and homemaker, general dispenser, and versatile cook (to satisfy demand, taste, and quality); on the other, as a hard worker, co-provider, and powerful defender of her rights and equality, even to the point of challenging customs and practices that tended to diminish her position. In brief, she stood out as a practical and feminine human being, proud of her multiple role as wife and mother, responsible manager of the household, and worthy partner in industriousness in all spheres: home, factory, field, greenhouse, or family business.

When their thoughts turned to the children, of course both parents often regretted if their children had "suffered" because they "had to work so hard"; but the mother felt deeply sad that she "couldn't spend much time with them." Consequently, most agreed that it was "better for the woman to stay home to raise the children … That way they [grew] according to your own system," thus reducing also the possibility of their estrangement: "I want my children to know their parents … [therefore] my wife stays at home … I don't want my children to go to babysitters; they come to a point … when they don't know their parents … Italian children going to babysitters grow up like Canadian children."

The task of nurturing the traditions and transmitting them to the children seemed to fall first on the mother, the attentive guardian of customs and morals. Yet many felt that both parents should share the responsibilities of raising the children. Only a few husbands left to their wives the decisions regarding the daughter's going out, but not without reserving to themselves the last word: "If my daughter does anything wrong, she's out of the house." Some women preferred to leave the decision to their husband, "accepting" the unwritten rule that in all situations "the man must be head of the house."

But since many of the women worked, even this time-honoured tradition began to change: "I became the backbone of the family here in

Canada ... I got a job at the Sun Parlour Co-op, and so money was coming in for us, making things much easier ... I did the shopping and everything." Such a situation was not always agreeable to the husband, who may have also perceived it as a threat to his position as chief bread-winner, or even to his masculinity: "Wives can work to help their husbands out, but once established, their wives shouldn't have to work."

The Canadian custom of wives-mothers holding a regular job was generally alien to immigrants from a rural environment, even though in the land of origin, women always worked just as hard as the men, in the home and in the fields. Quite indicative was the reaction of one arriving as late as 1966: "I was shocked when I saw women wearing pants and going to work." It was probably the wearing of the pants that was more shocking; after all, the women who stayed home also worked "very, very hard ... Things had to be done even when we [the women] didn't feel well."

Situations in which both parents held jobs did not always have a totally negative effect on the children. Nevertheless, while they offered relief from some difficulties or helped them mature more quickly, they also moved the children away from the Italian family system, and toward the North American type: "My parents were a little strict, but I had quite a bit of freedom, since both of my parents worked ... no one around to tell me what to do ... I had to help myself out when my mother wasn't around to cook."

CARE OF THE AGING GENERATION

Traditionally, especially in rural Italy, placing parents or grandparents in a home for the aged was frowned on. In the Leamington Italian community, most parents repeated that just as "children shouldn't live with their parents when they're married," so parents, when they got older, did not expect to live with their children. But neither did they wish to live in a home for senior citizens: "If I cannot live alone, I will go back to Italy."

But they also knew that that was an almost impossible solution! The two customs – the one they held on to, and the other that they respected for the sake of the children – seemed to create an impasse, a heart-rending dilemma. What they said simply contradicted what they felt and expected; they clearly wanted the children to take care of them at home: "If you have children for whom you have sacrificed, it is a terrible thing for your children to put you in a home"; "I don't think old people should be sent to an old folks home ... Italian old people wouldn't be able to speak to anyone."

In general, even when there was no linguistic obstacle, the children, respecting the feelings and views of their aging parents, took care of them, sometimes by sharing the responsibility among them: "My parents rotate two weeks at a time between my house and my brother's." Though at times considered a burden, parents living with their children's family also offered advantages, especially to working or career-oriented mothers. Moreover, the extended family created a favourable method to transmit customs to the younger generations: The grandparents filled essential roles as live-in family "historians," raconteurs, and mentors to the grandchildren.

THE EXTENDED FAMILY: THE *COMPARATICO* OR *COMPARE-COMARE* "NETWORK"

Gli emigranti si fanno compari (Emigrants build friendship networks)

Proverb

A rural and particularly southern Italian tradition that gradually expanded and reinforced the Italian immigrant family (and thereby the community) was (and continues to be) the *comparatico*: the complex bond or relationship that joins the godfather (*compare* or *padrino*) and the godmother (*comare* or *madrina*) to their godchild(ren), and the nuptial witnesses (*compari di nozze*) to the newlyweds; or the group itself of godparents and intimate friends (*compari, comari*) of a particular family; or even the ceremonies – baptism, confirmation, matrimony – that produce such lifelong relationships among individuals and their respective families. Among the Leamington Italians, the tradition related to "calling people *comare* and *compare*" was quite widespread.

In general, the bonds thus established were as strong as blood ties and often even more sacred. The sponsors at baptism and confirmation, and the best man and maid of honour at weddings, became integral parts of the extended family: active participants in the fortunes of the family groups; significant components of "the religion of the family." Above all, the already strong godparent-godchild relation became even stronger among the Italian immigrants, especially in the early days of immigration: it itself developed into a "godfather-godchild religion" (as illustrated, for example, in the movie *The Godfather* when the lawyer, in order to emphasize the bond between Johnny Fontane and Don Corleone, states that for Italians that's "a religious, sacred, close relation"). In any case, the relationship entailed both rights and responsibilities.

The *compari* and *comari* implicitly understood their mutual obligations. The godparents, in particular, knew they had moral and material duties to their godchildren, not unlike those of parents toward their children (especially if, by some tragedy, the children were deprived of their parents). Thus, the godparents were supplementary guardians, surrogate parents, or even co-parents (as suggested also by the etymology of *compare* and *comare* < *compater* and *commater*; and by the literal sense of *padrino* and *madrina* – "little father" and "little mother" respectively). Besides respect, the *compari* also enjoyed other inherent privileges, such as that of being always welcome visitors or guests. Of course, the rights and responsibilities were not so much the result of calling people *comare* and *compare* as the outcome of long acquaintance and/or association, of a gradual development of deep and reciprocal friendship and trust, that were eventually solemnized through the usual ceremonies or sacraments.

The *comparatico* reflects more than just three major moments in life: the terms *compare*, *comare* in popular tradition have been applied to a variety of persons, practices, and events that range from birth to death. *Compare* can signify close friend, associate, confidant, or advisor (as in the song "La mogliera" – The wife); neighbour and compatriot, almost synonymous with *paesano*, or the more colloquial *paesá*, with reference not only to a person from the same hometown (*paese*) or region but also to an Italian in general, and especially to an Italian immigrant (as in the 1950s popular song by the Italian-American Julius LaRosa, "Eh compare"); in a rural, peasant setting it is often used as an affectionate, familiar, and even mocking title, and sometimes as a derogatory term (i.e., referring to a partner or accomplice in shady activities). *Comare*, on the other hand, can also mean "midwife," "gossip" (the English term itself etymologically linked to "godparent") and "death."[14] On the whole, the terms seen to cover the gamut of family and human life: some of the most cherished and most dreaded human situations.

In the Leamington Italian community, though aspects of the tradition were indirectly recalled, the meanings that related to family and community life prevailed. The *comparatico* custom or tradition dates back to the very beginnings of the community, and such relationships were established not only among immigrants from the same area of origin in Italy, but also with Italians from other regions whom the pioneers met after settling in Essex County and the Leamington area (and at times with non-Italians, especially when in the marriage contract or ceremony one of the partners was of non-Italian origin): Gus (Costantino) Moauro (Molise, 1923) and Vito Peralta (Sicily, 1927) became *compari* after Vito moved to Leamington in 1943 (chapter 4); in the late 1920s and early 1930s, the Magri family (Molise, 1927) formed similar bonds with Pasquale Sasso (region/date of entry unknown) in the Amherstburg area and with the LaRosa family (Puglia, entry?) in the Essex Town area (chapter 5). The custom was continued by postwar immigrants, as exemplified by two 1949 arrivals: the Gabriele Leone family (Molise) and the Girolamo Peralta family (Sicily), in 1958. However, not all marriage witnesses became *compari* or *comari*, as in the case of "Frances Major" appearing as witness in the 1936 marriage certificate of Tony DiMenna and Antonietta Appugliese; but the reason may also have been that they had already contracted both civil and religious marriage (albeit by proxy) in 1935.

Naturally the *compare-comare* network became more extended and more solid with the postwar growth of the community and the resulting increase in wedding, baptism, and confirmation ceremonies. Overall, the *comparatico* seemed to have played an additional role in the Leamington Italian community, or even to have had a particular effect on it: that of extending the family unit and interconnecting family groups to such a point as to make the community appear, as they often said, "one big family." The *compare-comare* bonds favoured closer identification of the family group with the community as a whole (and that, in turn, favoured the vision and the building of one common community centre – The Roma Club – their "second home"). In other words, this particularly rural and southern Italian tradition and quasi-institution seemed to have helped the Leamington Italians overcome the Italian dichotomy between family and society – a characteristic that Indro Montanelli in an early 1970s interview presented with his own question and answer: "Really, what is society for the Italian? The family, and that is all."[15] In their attempts to preserve and strengthen the integrity of the family unit, the Leamington Italians were also extending the family while forming links with other families, a bridge, as it were, or a union with their community – their own "society" (see chapter 11, especially "A 'Parish' for All Leamington Italians: The Roma Club"; chapter 13, "Interaction within the Community").

In brief, the Leamington Italian family may be defined as a *traditional, generally patriarchal, extended, close-knit unit, manifesting an interplay of fixed roles and attitudes: care and severity, power and devotion of parents; respect and submissiveness, security and dissatisfaction of children; a closely guarded haven or stronghold, centre of activities and intimacy, but not without challenges to the structure and with increasing tendencies toward the nuclear family.*

Social Life: Homemade Fun, Food, and Festivals – the Family, the Roma Club, and the Church

Ma non si gira, senza una lira (But you don't dance, without a pence)
"L'amore sotto la luna"

RECREATION AND PASTIMES IN THE EARLY DAYS

The verse from a 1948 Italian song captures the sad refrain in the memories of the early immigrants: "No one had money to go around" or "money was scarce … never went anywhere." The hardships and loneliness allowed very little time and rare occasions for socializing. At the beginning, the only form of entertainment was brief moments of respite from the long hours of work. The custom of *dolce far niente* (sweet doing nothing) was no longer possible in Canada, if ever it was for them. Nevertheless, the Italian fun-loving spirit was not altogether spent. They improvised even in this area: *Dove manca natura, arte procura* (where nature fails, talent prevails). They provided their own entertainment by getting together in the houses or barns, in the fields or in parks. It was often spontaneous homemade fun, involving the entire family, friends, and neighbours.

Among the many difficulties in the late 1920s and early 1930s, nature and natural phenomena sometimes provided moments of happiness. The "all-French … River Canard" area with the "so beautiful St Joseph's Church" was "a very nice place" that offered Saveria Magri some peace and tranquility: "Oh … I liked it there …" A unique spectacle that still evoked joyful memories occurred, according to Saveria, "the year they removed the tracks, 1934 or 1935 … The guy … making bricks took a piece of glass, made it black with cigarette smoke, and looked at the eclipse … when the sun and the moon meet" (probably the 14 February 1934 eclipse). As if to emphasize how fortunate they were in witnessing such a rare occurrence, Saveria added (apparently with some accuracy, in view of the anticipated eclipse on 9 March 1997): "After 1997 it will come back again ... I read it in the Italian paper" – the last statement indicating also that reading was, at times, a pastime for some of them. Rural living also offered manufactured occasions for enjoyment. Saveria recalled "a picnic in the woods" on Sasso's farm in the same River Canard–McGregor area: the large gathering, including "many people from Windsor ... talked and drank," and probably sang and danced while "Pasquale Sasso played his accordion."

Domenic Magri remembered those simpler days of spontaneous fun-making: "We made our own entertainment, basically ... They would take turns going to their neighbours' houses, maybe once a week ... There would be perhaps nine, ten couples and they'd all take a turn entertaining their particular week ... and people had a good time ... much more than today ... They did enjoy themselves ... They made their own fun ... There were more picnics ... The parks were fuller ... than they are today ... I remember going to Kingsville Park on Sunday ... That was a Sunday outing for everybody, it seemed ... Now the parks [are] deserted ... for instance at Seacliff Park in Leamington you hardly find a soul [today], but during the Depression it seemed that everybody went out on Sunday."

Seacliff Park was quite an attraction when Marius Ingratta (Henry's son) was a young man:

> I grew up [on the Conover farm] right across from Seacliff Park, which back before the war was quite a thriving entertainment spot ... Open-air dancing attracted many of the Leamington residents ... Hundreds of Michigan tourists would come to Leamington to spend weekends on the beach and in the park. I used to join in with the bathers and the dancers ... I spent a lot of time working at the pavilion on Sundays and Saturday nights taking tickets at the open-air dances ... This is how I made my spending money, because I didn't get it at home.

In those early days the occasional party outside the home, in church or other public halls, also offered much-needed distraction and relief. Sometimes meeting other Italians was a much anticipated and profound pleasure, a rare experience and the beginning of lifelong friendships. A party in Kingsville around 1930 was unforgettable and deeply satisfying for Saveria Magri and Matuccia DeSantis (chapter 5). It was the two Italian immigrant women's first encounter. The surprise and happiness were still vivid sixty years later in recollection of that moment.

Such recreation, only seemingly simple, was more than relaxation or refreshment after hard work. It often meant total delight, a gratification of the spirit. It was an experience common to many early immigrants: unexpectedly hearing someone speaking one's own language, especially the same dialect, in an ocean of quasi-incomprehensible babble, was a fleeting moment that poets call epiphany. What occurred instantly was total communication, with words, gestures, and silences: "I understood what was being said" was the recurring recollection. But above all, as recorded also by more recent lore and songs, they understood what *they themselves* were saying. The encounter of two or more Italians was like "going home":[1] an exquisite moment, a celebration of life always remembered and cherished, and regularly renewed whenever the families visited each other and at community gatherings (e.g., the banquet in honour of the pioneer families in 1977; see note 16).

But even in the earlier days, picnics and parties were not the only diversions: some played cards or bocce; some went for drives in the county, even to Point Pelee (and most likely to the Jack Miner Bird Sanctuary); others went bowling or to the show. Gus Moauro remembered a detail that he hoped would surprise others as much as it seemed to surprise him on recalling it: "On Saturday nights we went to the cinema, *che quella volta neanche parlava, il cinema*, which at that time didn't even speak, the cinema that is ..." In the winter, some went hunting, others went to Windsor to the Caboto Club, while a few of them (apparently not long after their arrival) were attracted by the Detroit nightlife: "We went dancing in Detroit, always three or four of us together" (see chapter 5). The younger ones went tobogganing (most likely on the Hugh MacDonald hill, Highway 3 and Albuna Townline Road, rather than "down Sherk Street," as others stated). Sometimes, "while the children went to the show ... the parents visited with other families." Family get-togethers became frequent. The "holidays were spent with the relatives ... and much visiting with the relatives" was done then. The majority, in fact, engaged in such homespun recreation: "Since we were so few here in Leamington ... two or three times a week we would visit: *una volta a casa vostra ... una volta a casa mia ... Si faceva qualche partita a carte, specie con un bicchiere di vino* (once at your house ... once at my house ... We played some cards, especially with a glass of wine; Gus Moauro, 1923).

THE HOME VISIT: STORIES, JOKES, AND GOSSIP

The visit or exchange of visits among families became a sort of institution with its own simple ritual. It was practised at all levels, not just among relatives and neighbours, but among friends and new acquaintances. It was regulated by widely accepted unstated norms: the invited family was expected to return the invitation within a certain period of time. A cycle of visits was soon established; as the number of families increased, the visits formed several interwoven series, then slowly expanded to include other groups of families closely linked amongst themselves, not just through marriage, but often through the even more binding system of *compari* and *comari* (or *comparatico*).[2] The result was that most free time during weekends and holidays was spent in this activity: "In those days ... nobody had a car, so you visited back and forth ... You had a gathering of the clan, so to speak, on Sunday afternoons: the kids running around playing hide-and-seek ... the old men telling stories, and the women doing the cooking ... It was family" (Marius Ingratta, 1930).

The Italian family did not take quickly to the North American practice of engaging babysitters, unless a very close relative was available. Therefore, it was understood that the invitation included children and infants. Before the era of television, the children played with whatever toys they had, found games in their school books, or invented their own, often by imitating the grown-ups. They were often a nuisance, but the parents wouldn't want it any other way: the children had to be close to them, except when the stories told became spicy; then they were put to bed or relegated to the basement or another room. Many friendships and first loves were born among the new generations during these visits.

Normally the visit was not a dinner invitation. However, if it occurred during a Sunday afternoon or holiday, the invited family was often asked to remain for supper. Generally, Saturday evening was the best time for visiting, at times Friday, if the working members of the families were free the next day. The arrival was usually early in the evening. The practice among immigrant families was to have their evening meals relatively early, between five and six o'clock, especially in winter. Nevertheless, the visit was spent not just chatting, but eating. The host family brought out the specialties of the town or area, either made for the occasion or conserved for months: jars of marinated olives, green peppers, slices of eggplant, lupini beans, chickpeas, and even fava beans, homemade salami or dried sausages, and fresh homemade bread.

Each delicacy was presented at intervals as the evening progressed. The element of surprise was an important component, regenerating interest and conversation. The hosts derived pleasure and a sense of pride from the offering and from the guests' enjoyment and compliments. They were exquisite appetizers and instant sobering countermeasures for the robust homemade wine, with which, according to practice, the glasses had always to be filled. The pièce de résistance was usually the variety of special pastries, also usually homemade, presented at the end of the evening. Even if liqueurs were available, coffee and whiskey became customary. For the sake of enjoyment, even such Anglo-Saxon practices were acceptable.

The leave-taking ritual sustained the jovial mood to the last moments. The guests renewed the invitation to the hosts, reminding them that it was now their turn to pay them a visit. But this was usually done by an exchange of a series of ironical statements. They would pretend that these pleasant activities were hardships, or difficult tasks, by using such popular expressions or sayings as "After all, a promise is a standing obligation." Also, by using other rhetorical devices such as preterition, widespread in their speech, the guests would state that they would not do what they were actually doing: "We will not thank you, for by doing so, we may suggest that we do not have an obligation toward you." It was a sort of last performance, on the one hand, to extend an open invitation to all the family, and on the other, to express that the invitation was welcome; it was a finale to the light and pleasant atmosphere that pervaded the whole visit. And it was not the result of drinking, but mainly of their spontaneous conversation and lively storytelling.

Reminiscing was inevitable, especially if the two families had been acquainted in the Old Country: they reviewed aspects of their youth, growing up, their families and common acquaintances. Sometimes they even discovered that they were somehow related to the same person, thereby strengthening their own relationship. And if they were not previously acquainted, by the end of the visit they knew almost everything about each other's lives: love, marriage, children, and respective families and relatives.

An inexhaustible topic of conversation was their immigration experience: the fateful decision, separation, journey, arrival, and new reality. Almost all immigrant stories have the potential of a five-act drama, but in such settings they were told mainly for laughter and enjoyment. However humiliating the predicaments, what mattered was their humorous aspect. Many such situations were produced by the "strange" customs and their inability to communicate in the new languages, particularly by their early unsuccessful attempts to pronounce certain English (or French) words, with unintentional results, ranging from the facetious to the vulgar.

The Leamington pioneers left some good examples of such stories: two of them told by Gus Moauro related to the first experiences of the 1923 Molise group in Montreal, just as they set off on their slow trek to their final destination. One can be titled the "bread episode": just after they arrived, they went to Windsor Station to obtain information, but none of them knew French. Every time they asked someone in Italian where they might find some Italian people, they were repeatedly told *"comprends pas,"* which to them sounded like *"compran pa(n)"* (buy bread), at a moment when they were particularly hungry: they "had not eaten for over twenty-four hours."

The second episode occurred in the boarding house in Cowansville (southwest of Montreal) where some of them were lucky to find work just after they arrived (November 1923; see chapter 3). Some of the "very Catholic" landlady's rules were that all go to church on Sunday, and no meat on Friday. But early one Friday morning, Gus's brother Angelo caught the "most devout" woman preparing a breakfast of bacon and eggs. Unable to communicate (she spoke only French, and Angelo only a few words of English learned during his previous trip to America), Angelo began to laugh. The landlady, offended, called her husband, who demanded an explanation, which Angelo tried to provide, since her husband spoke English: "Catholics don't eat pork on Fridays!" Apparently his wife, the landlady, wasn't aware that bacon was "meat." She was just following her "mother's ways." Well, her husband reassured her, they should know, "they are Catholic, and they come from Rome." Gus Moauro reported that the delicate situation ended *in una gran risata* (general laughter).

Tony DiMenna and Alex Colasanti related similar episodes about their first year in Canada, when there were "a lot of things you don't understand." Once Alex couldn't comprehend why his boss "pretty near killed" him. Alex wanted to praise his way with words by comparing him to a lawyer. But instead of "lawyer," Alex called him a "liar." "He grabbed me … What the hell did I say? … Because you don't understand English you tell something wrong all the time." And there was the time Alex didn't want to say or do anything wrong: he had to buy underwear, but he didn't know what it was called. It was quite embarrassing, but he had to slowly "open his shirt" and show it to the salesclerk. One day when Tony DiMenna was working at the Meretsky junkyard, rather puzzled, he started getting ready to go home much earlier than usual, until someone explained that the boss was asking him to go for the *chain* and not for the *cena* (supper). One of the most popular among immigrants was the anecdote about an immigrant finding money on the ground the moment he stepped off the boat, convincing him even more, but only briefly, that America's streets were truly paved in … gold (chapter 9). Tony Cervini alone could have provided entertainment for more than one evening just with his own picaresque-like immigration story (chapter 4).

Not all the stories were related to their own experience, but they provided the same effect. Famous was the anecdote of the Italian who answered an interested Canadian that he had come to Canada on a "sheep," by giving an Italian sound to the *i* in *ship*. Another did not understand why the saleswoman was offended when he thought he simply asked for a "shirt," not realizing that he had made the *r* disappear. Variants were just as funny: one concerned an Italian lady who asked a salesclerk for big "sheets," but this time the English *ee* was given an Italian sound. In some retellings the embarrassed clerk showed them the way to the washroom. But when the mistake was realized, there was general laughter. It happened often with English words containing the vowels *ee* or *ea* as in *beech* or *beach*. Embarrassingly funny was a reading of the word *focus*: a far too open sound to the *o* and the final *us* uttered like the first-person plural object pronoun. Such words as *fork, folk, folks*, and others gave rise to a whole series of suggestive jokes and as many variants, with varying degrees of spiciness as they were told and retold. Sometimes the complex misunderstandings the words created reminded one of comedy-of-errors repartee in many Renaissance plays.[3]

Some anecdotes related to misunderstandings produced by Italian words and expressions. The immigrants soon learned, sometimes the hard way, to avoid saying them within hearing distance of English speakers. Though quite proper in one language the terms for *fire, roof, enough, porter, it's warm*, and *you sing* sounded like many vulgarities to the anglophone ear.[4] At times it was the other way around: some English words to the Italian ear sounded vulgar, such as *cool*; others funny and contradictory such as *boy, bye-bye, street, talk, I'll see you*; still others sounded odd and irreverent, such as *church*, or appeared so in writing such as *Christmas*. The Italians were, of course, quite aware that the meaning of the words was not at all related to what the Italian sound suggested. In fact, the enjoyment came from relating the real meaning with the image the sound evoked. The overall effect was spontaneous, good laughter at their own expense, and often at the expense of Canada (e.g., the parody of the Canadian anthem).[5]

The laughter sweetened the bitterness of the humiliations, as a sort of personal retributive justice. However rewarding the opportunities, to a newcomer a new country appears totally strange, exaggerated, even distorted. He often feels assailed by the new ways that he must quickly adopt. He finds himself defending his identity by unconsciously exposing the exaggerations, distortions, and contradictions, real or apparent, of the new land. At first it is mockery, then laughter. The Italian immigrant found this escape in the juxtaposition of the meaning of some English words and the

Italian meaning suggested by their sound. Accordingly, what kind of land can this be, he mused, that calls a good boy *"boia"* (executioner); that to say "goodbye" barks like a dog – "bye, bye"; that calls wide streets, *"stret"* (in many dialects suggesting "narrow"); that calls the house of God a "church," sounding like the Southern Italian word for "jackass"; and calls the day on which Christ was born "Christ-kill day"![6] It cannot but be an upside-down society, a topsy-turvy world. It is not difficult to imagine the sort of liberating laughter and pleasures such inventions produced.

Whether they poked fun at themselves or at the "strange" aspects of Canadian life and behaviour, or whether they laughed over earthy stories or spicy jokes, the evening repertory seemed endless. The amusement, however simple, was general and continuous. The visit provided complete satisfaction at many levels: individual, social, and spiritual. The custom went through a period of decline with the construction of the community club and with the increasing involvement in other activities: sports, vacations, trips, or other more sophisticated pastimes. But it never lost its popularity. It remained a solid tradition simply because it offered a wholesome recreation for the entire family.

Gossiping has always been a favourite pastime: one of the best forms of entertainment and control. In the Italian communities, especially in the rural areas, before and after the coming of television, gossip fulfilled both roles, as well as others: it served as private entertainment and public control of the individual and the group. But it was gossip's influence in the public sphere that was more frequently and explicitly cited, especially by the young people in relation to their sexual behaviour. It seemed to help safeguard and strengthen group mores and morals, and it often determined their voting patterns and political allegiances. Generally, gossip's function as a village newspaper, as a sort of community information and communication system, also suggested its widespread private use, providing a great deal of enjoyment at family gatherings. But, especially with respect to this role, the information in their interviews was limited because of the hesitation in dealing frankly with the subject in general. Further studies in gossip's role as entertainment and control in such communities might prove revealing and rewarding to social scientists and the community at large (see chapter 10, especially "Marriage and Premarital Behaviour").

"*ALL'APERTO*" GATHERINGS AND OTHER PASTIMES

The women always played a central role in family recreation. Often, they also led in entertainment within the community. Emma Colasanti was often remembered as one of the first organizers of community socials, gatherings, and dances: "She enjoyed bringing all the Italian families together and having parties in a barn"; and on New Year's Eve she would rent a place and a band for the whole community. Acting as a sort of "social convener," Emma filled some of the entertainment needs of the still small community of the 1940s.

In the following decade, especially after 1952, Ida Magri's Italian grocery store in downtown Leamington offered, among many conveniences, another form of diversion: on Saturday nights Italians did not go to "their" store just to shop, but also to partake in an ancient, favourite custom: to congregate in front of it, converse, discuss, argue, and laugh. The store seemed to fill the socio-recreational needs once satisfied by establishments in the village or town of origin: the old *osteria* or wine shop, the forerunner of the Italian bar; the *Spaccio di Sali e Tabacchi* (literally "salt and tobacco outlet" (so named because salt and tobacco, being state monopolies, were sold and partly still are in government-licensed stores) or simply *Spaccio* which, in small towns or villages, also served as post office, public telephone, and as a wine shop all-in-one and often with a card-playing area like in the *osteria*. Especially for early postwar immigrants, Ida's store may have been a kind of *Dopolavoro* (literally "afterwork"), originally a Fascist government organization dedicated to popular leisure-time activities and assistance, which survived after the war as a workers' recreation centre, meeting place, for card and bocce games and sometimes as a pre-Lent dance club;[7] and the store recreated, above all, the marketplace, the village square, or the more modern café. The grocery store became a sort of multipurpose "community centre," a general gathering place.

In time, other downtown shops (tailor, barber, shoemaker, and others) also offered some relief to the gregarious Italian spirit. At times, it was not just the inclement winter that forced them to take refuge inside "friendly" stores, or that prevented them from enjoying an old Italian custom. In the 1950s and later (even today in some places), the practice of small groups gathered in "pleasant conversation on city sidewalks," in front of stores or at street corners (as earlier in the village square, church grounds, or streets) caused many unaware Italian immigrants a great deal of concern, as well as much misunderstanding or "trouble" with the local police.

The officers on patrol, not familiar with that Italian tradition (as ancient as the gatherings in the Roman Forum), "urged" the Italians to break up the group, to "move on." The Italians, who always heard Canadians boast about Canada being a "free country," often resented and reacted to such treatment, and considered the "no loitering" laws or any similar measures backward and uncivilized. The "Town of Leamington By-Law ... to prohibit loitering on any public sidewalk or street or highway or in any public place ... passed and enacted [on the] Third day of September, 1969" most likely reflected attitudes long existing in the town.[8] Even for this reason, the Italians preferred and cultivated the usual recreational activities: visit with their friends, play cards and bocce, take drives or go hunting, and participate at as many weddings as possible. Eventually they began to explore other forms of entertainment as well, both in and out of town, especially toward the end of the 1950s.

THE DISCOVERY OF ENTERTAINMENT
BEYOND THE FAMILY CIRCLE

With the 1960s a new pattern emerged. Material progress, combined with evolving interests of the older community and increasing numbers of a different type of Italian immigrants within the community, resulted in two distinct modes of social entertainment. Visiting remained a widespread and popular recreation; but it was the older group that was more inclined toward this tradition. The more recent immigrants, as well as the younger generation, developed broader views and interests and were involved in a greater variety of activities. "Things changed," said Marius Ingratta. "Other ... responsibilities came along ... kids grew up." They sought other *divertimenti*, and they increasingly found them outside the family circle or community setting.

The interviews indicated that they enjoyed masquerade parties, dances, listening to music, going to the beach at the lake or to the movies; and the places they frequented varied from hotels and clubs to public halls: the Hi-Y (149 Oak Street West, east of Fraser Road, Mersea Township, where Tony's Grocery or Variety Store was in the 1980s); the Arc Hall (Princess and Mill Streets, replaced by office buildings presently owned by Tony and son Carlo Grossi); the Auto Stop Hotel (Erie South, now the Village Inn owned by Isidoro Spano and family in partnership with Joseph DiFalco); the Seacliff Hotel (corner of Erie South and Robson, until 1978 owned by Mark Giannetta and from 1978 to 1986 by Frank and Joe Ciotoli) – all in Leamington; Surf-Side 3 (Kingsville), "where bands played every weekend"; the Caboto Club or Teutonia Club (Windsor) and other places in both Windsor and Detroit. They acted more independently and went further afield in search of a more personal form of enjoyment.

The pre–Second World War and early postwar immigrants often commented that in Italy there was little or no entertainment: "just friends, family, and a few festivals at the church or at a friend's house." They represented that group of Italian immigrants who were mostly unaffected by the profound changes in postwar Italian society. On the other hand, even if the "economic miracle" of the 1950s had not equally benefited North and South Italy, its influence had reached the small towns and villages: the more recent immigrants, especially the younger group, had more than just the hometown church hall for their entertainment. They had been exposed to different milieus, to a more varied life, through more education, trade, career, or work in other Italian cities or other countries, as well as through tourism in their own towns (especially in the case of San Vito Lo Capo) and through compulsory military service.

As immigrants, they were grateful to the earlier settlers and recognized their role, but they could neither be totally dependent on them or the community, nor be group-oriented as their forerunners were. However, trips were quite limited for everyone until more recent decades, when more time and money were available; then they could even afford to visit their hometown in Italy. Many of the young people interviewed visited Italy with their parents, especially during the 1970s.

A direct result of the growing entertainment needs and activities of the community was the Leamington Roma Club. "All came to the conclusion that the Italian community needed a place to meet, especially for weddings." The foremost reason may have been a practical one, but there were also idealistic forces behind the project. Even though at first such forces may not have found clear articulation, they were, nevertheless, at work. How else could one explain the long sacrifices, the energy, the dedication, and the self-abnegation of many promoters of this project?

Perhaps the best answer was given by a former president: "You shouldn't look for glory and praise in this type of involvement in any kind of organization; if anything, look for criticism." Some social consciousness, a feeling for the needs of the group also spurred many of them to become involved in the project, and then to continue to serve the community through the club. In their own as in other human achievements, vision and commitment appeared just as important motivators as practical benefits. Perhaps pride, a sense of altruism or idealism might help render their struggle more comprehensible, since any form of personal gain seemed out of the question; on the contrary, they often "neglected their own businesses."

The community was progressing and expanding. Material well-being increased leisure time, and with it the desire to enjoy life a little more. Not just weddings, but celebrations and other occasions for entertainment were becoming more frequent. Why rent other halls? An Italian community centre or club was timely. It could serve these purposes and others.

However scanty the documentation, it is evident that in the vision of some of the older group of immigrants, the club was also to fulfill other loftier goals. It was not to be just a place where they met periodically or held sporadic events. It was to be a general gathering place, almost a "second home" for everyone. Perhaps aware quite early that a larger community, with new immigrants and new generations, was more subject to the tendency toward fragmentation and division, they thought that a club would provide a cohesive common goal, a unifying force for the entire community, for old and new alike. Nevertheless, in their view, the first major project of the community had to serve immediate, practical, social, and recreational needs, and then aim at long-range, idealistic goals, and especially making a family out of the whole community around a common home – the Leamington Roma Club.

FROM IDEAL TO REALITY: THE LEAMINGTON ROMA CLUB – THE "SECOND HOME"

Possiamo dire che abbiamo una seconda casa … dimostra che gli Italiani di Leamington sono uniti (We can say that we have a second home … it shows that the Leamington Italians are united).

The gestation was long and arduous. The first spark may have occurred in the 1940s when Emma Colasanti was organizing parties in barns and rented halls. In the 1950s, the need for a club became clearer. At the first meeting in Mastronardi's warehouse in 1954 or 1955, "Five dollars was put in by each person" and entrusted to Emma. But fears soon damped the initial enthusiasm, and "nothing was done for a while. The money just sat there." Emma and Alex Colasanti were constantly encouraged, but "they were just scared to start something." One problem was that "no one was really a leader." It may have also been clear that it was a costly enterprise and a substantial responsibility.

The slow pace and temporary setbacks may have helped them obtain a greater awareness of the problems and to plan a little more carefully. In 1958 Gino DiMenna and Bert Mastronardi "started rumours about building a club … and had a meeting about such an organization," but again "the idea died for two years." The plan was reactivated with a better outcome in February 1960, at an Italian Carnival party at the Auto Stop Hotel (later the Italian-owned Village Inn). Gino DiMenna and Milvo

Costanza again discussed their idea and the benefits it would bring to the whole Italian community. Tony Mastronardi agreed, and "Gino was pushed on the stage to announce the idea of starting this club." Many welcomed the proposal, and a definite step was taken toward the goal. A telephone committee was formed, and with "the help from Ben Giglio, a Windsor man, to spread the news," invited the whole community to a meeting at the arena.[9] The sixty people in attendance were asked to contribute money to start the club and "everyone put down ten dollars." The funds were entrusted to a steering committee, which included Gino DiMenna (chairman), Milvo Costanza (secretary), Ollie Mastronardi (treasurer) and Lamberto Santaniello (supervisor). It was 1 May 1960 – the officially recognized date for the establishment of the club.[10]

The old fears became allayed through this union of forces (of pre– and post–Second World War immigrants), through structure and collective leadership: They "teamed up and rented a house to sell their ideas." But other obstacles, besides the task of collecting funds, had to be overcome. Planning and building of the Leamington Roma Club were not exempt from differences of opinion and conflicts inherent to any human interaction. From the very start, some community members disagreed with certain decisions, argued against them, walked away from the planning, and even refused to support the project. But, with the goodwill of the majority and the commitment of even a few believers, a good project can rarely be held back. Besides, criticism from within may have steered the organizers away from other problems and toward more solid foundations and objectives.

An obstacle from outside the community seemed to threaten their plans. Although the proper procedures had been followed, they met opposition in obtaining approval for a charter. In spite of legal counselling and help from prominent people, the provincial government rejected their application. In 1961 an appeal was made to a representative of the Conservative party, who after some time was able to explain the reason for their being turned down. He also recommended that they reapply and "leave two names out." Of the seven people listed in the first application, one was not a Canadian citizen, and the other had "a police record ... just for bringing some goods from Detroit." To avoid other possible negative reactions, this time the committee submitted the application with only three names: Aldo Ercole, Gus Moauro, and Fred DeSantis. The obstacle, whether justifiable or simply the result of well-known attitudes toward Italians even at that time, was finally removed, clearing the way for approval of the by-laws to be approved and for the election in March 1961 of a nine-member board of directors, with Gino

DiMenna, president, Gus Moauro, vice-president, and Milvo Costanza, secretary. "Everyone was enthused."

The main task of the board and officers was to secure funds for the land and building. With the mayor's help, the Site Search Committee found a piece of land on the north side of Seacliff Drive East (about one kilometre from the first Italian farm): three and a half acres at a cost of $16,000; a very suitable site within the town limits – "since the townships were dry, no liquor licence." The purchase was approved and all 100 members agreed to loan $150 each. They "were ready to build," but dances, parties, festivals, and other fundraising activities generated only limited amounts. Annual membership dues of $24 covered only a small portion of the financial requirements. A bank loan was not favoured. ("Went to the bank to get a loan, but interest was too high.") The only route left was to appeal to members for another loan of $500 each, which, besides eliminating the burden of a bank mortgage, ensured members' commitment to the club, especially during the initial difficult stages.

Begun in 1963, construction was completed in 1964, ten years after the first meeting in Mastronardi's warehouse. In October, "their $207,000-headquarters building with its modern 700-seat banquet hall" was proudly shown to the entire community.[11]

The grand opening, honoured by the presence not only of the Ontario citizenship minister but of many dignitaries, clergymen of all major denominations, journalists, and a large public, was more than a "big celebration" of a community achievement (see chapter 8, "Growing Together: The Italians and Leamington"). For the pioneers it was a historic moment: the ceremony took place exactly forty-one years after the start of the adventurous journey of the first eight men from Molise to the New World, which led to the establishment of the Leamington Italian community. It was also the inauguration of a monument to their simple heroism, a commemoration of a small triumph of the human spirit. The building of the Roma Club was the Italian community's first collective "creation."

A milestone marks a beginning as well as an end of an era. The euphoric moment quickly faded in the face of new and complex problems. The most persistently oppressive was the financial burden. During the very difficult first few years, the operational losses and growing deficit brought embitterment. As a commercial enterprise, their new creation, more than pride and enthusiasm, required refined management and organizational skills. Their inexperience in this field suddenly became evident: "lost money for two years since they didn't know how to run the business." Doubts were raised about the Italian community's ability "to support the club alone." The initial encouragement turned into criticism; support into accusations and "name calling." Collapse always seemed imminent. The overwhelming fear of failure was turning the dream into a general nightmare.

Nevertheless, disappointment, however rampant, never turned into an all-consuming despair. Pioneers do not easily succumb to what others may consider insurmountable odds. They tried every measure to contain the centrifugal forces. In 1967, "a new Board came in to try and come out of this loss … This was successfully done … Outside business came into the Roma Club." When some strategies failed, others were adopted in order to find the right direction. They hired a professional manager from the Elmwood Casino, who proved ineffective. They turned to a chef-manager, but the positive effects, as a "drawing force" in his first capacity was cancelled by his lack of practical skills in his second role. The appeal to the membership for a second loan of $500 received a good response, but it did not help them avoid the dreaded step of a bank loan and mortgage. The series of steps, not excluding trial and error, involving re-evaluation, may have turned the tide in their favour.

The final success may have also depended on more intangible factors; not least among them, their humility in confronting the task. They accepted their administrative inadequacies and recognized the need to seek the advice of experts, from the mayor and city administrators to bank managers and hotel owners. Hard-earned pragmatism enabled them to balance the "big heart" approach and adopt more unpleasant but necessary business practices, such as higher prices and financial restructuring. Above all, what they lacked in efficiency and business shrewdness was counteracted and integrated with stubborn determination, dedication, and cooperation: in brief, long hours of hard work to the point of "neglecting their own business." The pride of the whole community was inextricably tied to the survival and success of their "common gathering place," their "second home."

Consolidation and growth steadily followed during the next two decades. Amid the inevitable controversies and criticism, each successive administration made constant efforts to strengthen the organization, to implement its short- and long-range plans, to fulfill both its practical and more idealistic objectives: "to unite morally and materially [all Italians] in a bond of friendship and respect."[12] "Little changes come naturally year after year," and each administration could look back with varying degrees of satisfaction for some specific accomplishment: from "cutting down expenses" to making "the club prosper," or presiding over "the most profitable year for the club"; from having "a kitchen built" to getting "the parking lot project under way"; from seeing "the completion of a bocce field" to "setting up a soccer team" and promoting other sports,

ich as baseball and hockey; from supporting community projects, such
s the Fountain for the Leamington Centennial (1975), to initiating and
ponsoring a cultural project, such as the research into the history of the
alian community; or simply for providing a strong leadership and good
rganization to promote better cooperation and greater harmony, and
hereby achieve "a better image of the Italians in the community." Most
f the "material" goals of the club were fulfilled: the club increasingly
ecame the focus for many recreational, social, and sport activities, as
vell as for political events. By the mid-1980s, 90 per cent of the mem-
ers used the club facilities for weddings, baptisms, communions, and
ther celebrations, and the sports sponsored by the club varied from
aseball and bocce to hockey and soccer. As one president generously
onceded, they "all deserve credit." And most agreed.

In the twenty-year history, however, the frustrations were as frequent
s the little triumphs. Some of the loftier aims of the club remained out
f reach. The longed-for ideals of greater cooperation and harmony, of
ocial, political, and cultural advancements were only partly achieved.
Most presidents spoke with equal frankness about what was not accom-
lished. Their aspirations varied, from further expansion of the facilities
nd providing more recreation for the members to greater involvement
1 public charities and assistance activities (e.g., immigrant adjustment
nd settlement).

Their appeals and recommendations for quicker changes within the
lub, particularly in attitudes toward the young and women in order to
oster their full participation, were often unheeded. And yet, by 1983
woman, Ivana Ercole, was manager, and by 1992 another, Margaret
ngratta, was president of the club. One of the presidents would have
'wanted to enhance the reputation of all Italians" in order to obtain
'more recognition" and "political clout." Although some stated that
hey "wouldn't have done anything differently," many regretted not hav-
ng been able to do more for youth and culture. However limited, some
ocial and political advantages were reaped by the community through
he club activities. But the general feeling was that they had fallen short
n "realizing the full potential of the club," perhaps because they had
ost sight of, or did "not follow or respect the Preamble of their own
3y-laws." They were probably referring especially to the "Introduction"
of their 1978 booklet: "(1) To unite morally and materially [all Italians]
n a bond of friendship and respect. (2) To create and provide activities
vhich are recreational, sportive, cultural, social, and beneficial." The cul-
ural goal, though sandwiched among other goals, is mentioned, but no
eference is made to youth interests or development.

The thwarted and unfulfilled expectations, as well as the reasons fo them, were often exposed with remarkable candour by the president themselves. Most of them, while recognizing the high level of coopera tion, saw many of their efforts made futile, most often by a small, oppos ing group, whose inconsistent behaviour ranged from apathy to activ resistance: "If only there was a little more support ... just 10 per cen more cooperation ... the things we could have done!" On the one hand the obstacle may have been the leaders' inexperience, indecision, an irresolution ("They were dragging their feet") or just lack of a com prehensive plan; on the other hand, the criticism itself often blocke progress. Some spoke of resentment, jealousy, envy ("the worst Italia defect"), and other faults that tended to create uncertainty and confu sion: "Not all goals were fulfilled due to lack of sincerity, honesty, unity. Also blamed for the lack of "good cooperation" was an incomprehen sible spirit of contradiction that led one president to speculate on th nature of "the arguing quality of Italians" – the kind of stuff stereotype are firmly built on. He wasn't sure what the reason was: "Either they'r too smart or too stupid, I don't know."[13]

A sort of counterproductive stalemate may have also resulted from poorly defined positions or views on the role of the club: a profit-makin business versus a recreational centre; stress on facilities expansion versu community activities; status quo advocates versus proponents of new directions, progressive thrusts toward the future. There might also have been an underlying form of the old *campanilismo*, a tension derived from original regional differences: "A certain friction exists ... maybe becaus they're from different towns." Further progress, according to more than one, might have been hampered by "the animosity that existed betwee those who came before the war and those that came after the war." The Roma Club may have at times reflected the traditional Italian rivalries o community contrasts (interregional or older versus newer immigrants) a pattern of community development generally similar to other Italia communities; but in general both club and community revealed a funda mental deviation from the usual Italian Canadian trends (i.e., conflict or fragmentation derived from *campanilismo*).[14]

The very outcome of the dialectic process into only one club, one com munity centre for all (the "umbrella organization" other communitie only spoke of), made the Leamington Italian community unique. In gen eral, strong antagonism between the two "alignments" was infrequent On the one hand, the pre–Second World War settlers participated fully i the creation of the centre and served the organization in various capac ities, including as presidents for more than one term.[15] On the other, fo

he most part the postwar immigrants cooperated with the pioneers, pub-
icly recognized and honoured them as first promoters and co-founders
f the club and as benefactors and "founders of the community."[16] In
pite of much opposition, the sporadic, factious conduct by some small
groups was not – nor can it be interpreted as – a power struggle that
rippled or splintered the institution. The vision was the common community home; and, after all, some progress was always made!

Some very controversial issues and occasions for intense contrasts and
heated exchanges did arise, as illustrated by two events in the 1970s: the
"irregularities" employed "by a small group" in bringing about "unnecessary" and "dubious" changes to the Constitution and by-laws; and the
lub's boycotting of the visit of Prime Minister Pierre Trudeau. Neither
threatened the unity of the club, though there were, as in the first case,
a strong reaction and the charge that "it was done in an arbitrary way
vithout consultation." The result in the second case was more resentment against the *Windsor Star*'s representation of the club's action than
in internal conflict (see chapter 13). Some disruption, at other times,
vas caused by a strong rivalry between two good candidates, or by the
hallenge from a dissatisfied member and highly motivated contender
against an inexperienced or inept administration: "Sometimes there are
people involved who really don't understand what should be done."
The gap between "what should have been done" and "what was done"
always remained a source of some frustration and concern for every
administration. But only on one occasion did the members' reactions
esult in the resignation of the president.

Uncertainty and confusion over what course to follow seemed often to
be closely related to a recurring theme in the presidents' interviews. "No
one was really a leader." In the first place, many of the presidents stated
hey did not wish to fill the post. They were simply happy to work, even
or no remuneration, in all facets of the club – kitchen, bar, hall. Yet, once
elected or invited to hold that responsibility, they were ready to serve,
ome even for a second term. They felt "they had an obligation to fulfill"
and carried out the mandate to the best of their ability. Often they did not
"realize how difficult it was until they did it." On the other hand, however
eluctant at first, once in the president's chair, they all saw the potential of
heir organization. But their attempts to reach the potential of their organization were often made vain by opposition, thus their bitter reactions.
Moreover, when a resolute candidate with a clear vision emerged to offer
his strong and efficient leadership, he seemed to be met with uneasiness,
good-natured mockery, and resistance. Was it then a problem of "no one
being really a leader" or "no one being really a follower"?[17]

Was there really a lack of leadership or non-acceptance of strong lead ership that held back the club from other accomplishments? It ofte appeared that reluctant, trained-on-the-job presidents were preferre over clearly committed or more zealous candidates for the post. Thi may help explain some of the ensuing misunderstandings, disagree ments, and contrasts. But the leadership issue also offered an insigh into the group as a whole: it exposed both the weakness and the strengt of the club and the community. The disapproval, criticism, and opposi tion did produce frustrations, but they served also as checks and bal ances against ambition and grandiosity. They retained collective contro over the organization and their investment. After all, they were all awar of the level of experience of the administrators. The objections repre sented a healthy distrust of power, an informal official opposition, an a democratic spirit. If it slowed the pursuit of loftier goals, it proba bly helped the club avoid wider splits or disaffection. Their attention t more attainable, practical goals, especially the emphasis on the financia burden, may have guaranteed the very survival of the club. That alway is, after all, the major obstacle for all future plans.

Even with all its limitations, the club has been a positive force i the life of the Italian collectivity and the community at large. It is fitting conclusion to remember some of the accomplishments. By th early 1970s, they had met most of their financial obligations, especiall toward the members: in 1970 the interest was paid on the first $50 loan, and through a bank loan, the principal was also repaid; in 1974 th second $500 loan was repaid. It was no small feat for people accustome otherwise to accept a widespread Canadian institution: the mortgage The expansion and remodelling of the physical facilities were further vis ible signs of collective success. The club was gaining a good reputation and consequently the community earned more acceptance and respec from everyone, particularly the politicians. The club became recognize as an organization that "represented all Italians," and that unity als meant strength. "For example," one stated, "if you ask the mayor for favour as an organization, you have more power." As with every institu tion, the club assumed a life of its own, above and beyond the feelings o individual members or the quality of the administration.

THE UNIFYING AND MAINSTREAMING
ROLE OF THE ITALIAN CENTRE

The growing importance of the Leamington Roma Club had far-reachin effects: more than a focal point for Italians, it strengthened their identit as Italians, especially as other ethnocultural communities were expanding and building their own centres. It brought them closer together without producing, a new form of ghettoization. On the contrary, it served as a springboard, a launch pad toward the mainstream of Canadian life. By necessity the Leamington Italian leaders of the club and community had to quickly learn more about Canadian financial and organizational practices, institutions, agencies, and laws. The club accelerated their integration, especially through the multiculturalism policy and movement. It was a place where "Italians and non-Italians could mix," a home base for general interaction, inter-ethnic or cross-cultural exchanges. By participating as a club in community events and by hosting events of other ethnocultural groups, the club offered Italian Canadians the opportunity to share their traditions with others, and at the same time to be exposed to other traditions.

In the Calendar of Centennial Events for Canada's Centennial Celebration in 1967, the Roma Club is listed three times, not only for Italian activities ("September 9 – Italian Community Day ... Italian foods, music, handicrafts, costumes"), but also for other events: "January 5 – Ukrainian Christmas Eve Observance ... October 9 – Balmoral IODE Fall Fashion Show."[18] Through such activities also, however slowly, attitudes are changed, prejudices shaken, awareness expanded, and citizens built. The club was thereby involved in and fostered a more general integrative process among Canadian groups.

The broader purpose and vision were present even in the name of the club. Much thought went into the choice of the name: "They had a meeting at Joe Marcovecchio's home. They came up with the name *Roma* because there were Italians from all parts of Italy, and Rome was the capital of Italy and represented all Italians. But it would not be just the Roma Club,' since there is another Roma Club in St Catharines. They decided, therefore, on the 'Leamington Roma Club.'" Sensitive to the regional differences and sensible in avoiding further fragmentation and disunity, they chose a name that was not to be connected to a town, area, or region. The name "Roma," more than recalling the capital city of the land of origin, evoked in them other memories of leadership, greatness, order, citizenship, and civilization. "Roma" was a reminder of their common origins, a glorious past, of which they also felt partly heirs; a unifying force and a good omen;[19] and preceded by "Leamington," the name also indicated the new home, the present and the future. The emblem itself – the she-wolf inside a large maple leaf – conveyed its full significance, which most recognized and readily explained. For one early president (Donato Puglia 1967–69), the club represented "something historical: its purpose was not just to remember, but to help Italians in the future ... an organization to represent the Italians."

In sum, the organization was to reflect what the name suggested: unite, guide, represent all Leamington Italians; serve as an integrative force, a dynamic link between tradition and progress in the new land. Even if, as is often stated, culture is not always a concomitant of financial success and wealth, many attempts were made by various administrations to fill that lacuna. A major undertaking toward fulfilling that goal may very well be this present study, a project initiated by a Committee of the Leamington Roma Club. But beyond some specific noteworthy activities, that many other Italian-Canadian organizations can most likely also claim, the point must be underscored that the Leamington Italians came together into one association. By working and enjoying themselves together they were able to overcome most of the obstacles and tension and remain relatively united "under one roof."

"THE ITALIAN ART OF EATING": NUTRITION, PLEASURE, AND CONVIVIALITY

Talisman of Happiness, a seemingly pretentious title of an Italian cook book, clearly points to the status and significance of cooking and eating within the Italian tradition.[20] The term *talisman* alone elevates these activities into the realm of magic and religious rites. (In fact, "rite" was the original meaning of the word.) But even in its present, more common definitions – a good luck charm, "an instrument of success in all human situations" – it suggests power and therefore respect. When coupled with "happiness" and related to cuisine, it makes even clearer the sort of veneration reserved for any activity related to eating. A good cookbook is therefore a sort of holy book, a book of rites for human happiness. Cooking, more than an art, is a religion in which eating is the most joyous and solemn ceremony.

If in the Italian tradition the family is "the ... most ... fundamental institution," then the family dinner is its most central and sacred moment. No other Italian family tradition has held more respect among the Leamington Italians than those related to food preparation. Perhaps no other has been more genuinely preserved, and provided the family with more moments of joy and tranquility, or even a sense of unity and companionship: "One thing which perhaps helped the Italians feel a little less uncomfortable in an unfamiliar environment was the successful importation of the Italian cuisine ... they were always able to secure Italian staples." The students, from whose report this quotation was aken, had a direct experience in this activity.[21] But it had not always been as they pointed out in the final statement.

In the earlier days the main concerns of the first immigrants were not just language, climate, job, or shelter, but also eating and food, more specifically the absence of Italian food. They missed Italian cooking. They searched for flour to make their own pasta; even if it didn't taste the same, it felt like being home. Later, they travelled miles to shop in an Italian grocery, or had Italian groceries delivered to them from Windsor and even from Toronto (for example, in the 1930s, the Pannunzios and Luigi Mastronardi used a cartage company not only to ship their hot house cucumbers from their – and first Italian-operated, steam-heated – greenhouses to Toronto, but also to have Italian food supplies delivered to them: whenever they needed the goods, they prepared a list for Pasquale Brothers in Toronto, and Rowley Express Cartage would transport them to Leamington). When an Italian grocery finally appeared in Leamington, it must have seemed as if a miracle had happened. If man does not live by bread alone, Italians did not want to live by nutriment alone. Food was considered a pleasure as well as a need; and meals not merely sustenance but entertainment – an excuse to socialize: "We never eat 'English' foods ... I cook Italian style ... Never eaten Canadian food and never will."

Only Italian food and only the Italian meal could fully provide both nourishment and enjoyment. In fact, most of the Leamington Italians interviewed considered "Italian cuisine the best in the world." Many said they could never have adjusted to "Canadian cuisine." Although they never defined "Canadian cuisine," what they knew of it convinced them it could never satisfy their needs or taste: "What it's all about," remarked a pioneer "is 'hot dog ... cookie and potato chips.'" Almost everyone objected to that pale white Canadian bread which they found "too sweet, doughy and rubbery." As far as they were concerned, "Canadians are happy subsisting on canned soups and TV dinners," while "Italians take more care and pride in their cooking."

More than Italian products, the "care and pride" in their preparation distinguished the tradition and the Italian family. Without at all denying such qualities to others, the comparison served to emphasize certain uniquely Italian aspects of a common human activity. It may only be a question of degree of sensitivity, not always subject to measurement. Nevertheless, a fuller view of the implications of their statement may be possible through a better understanding of the general Italian outlook in this matter. Some experts have made this task much easier for us. In *The Classic Italian Cook Book* Marcella Hazan wrote,

Nothing significant exists under Italy's sun that is not touched by art. Its food is twice blessed because it is the product of two arts, the art of cooking and the art of eating. While each nourishes the other, they are in no way identical accomplishments. The art of cooking produces the dishes, but it is the art of eating that transforms them into a meal ... Through the art of eating, an Italian meal becomes a precisely orchestrated event, where the products of the season, the traditions of place, the intuitions of the cook, and the knowledgeable joy of the participants are combined into one of the most satisfying experiences of which our senses are capable.[22]

Tangible proof of Italians' respect for these two arts may also be pro vided by a recent protest by Italian citizens, common and prominent against an American fast-food outlet opened in Rome. It was not the more common, politically motivated demonstration against American policies, or a sudden surge of a uncommon Italian patriotism. It was a spontaneous reaction against tastelessness in every sense of the word or against, as one of the many banners and signs read, an "invasion of a subculture" that defaced and polluted a historical and monumen tal area of Rome, as well as an Italian artistic tradition. The protest which naturally closed with an open-air banquet *all'italiana* at the foot of the Spanish Steps, was meant to show and proclaim to the world the unique merits of Italian cuisine, its social, cultural, and historical significance.[23]

Not only is Italian cuisine hailed by some experts as the "mother cuisine," but apparently also as a "good mother."[24] The Italian diet has been increasingly recognized as one of the most naturally balanced diets appropriate for people of all ages and for any type of activity, includ ing and especially for athletes: people who want to ward off heart dis ease but can't stand the tedium of very low-fat diets might consider a researcher's suggestion: "Eat Italian," as was recently recommended also by a report on the research by Dr Scott M. Grundy, published in the *New England Journal of Medicine*.[25]

In this light, the Roman protest against fast foods, as well as the crit icism by the Leamington Italians of those aspects of "Canadian" or "English" (i.e., non-Italian) cooking that seemed so to them, take on a different meaning. They were not simply superficial reactions moti vated by snobbery or closed-mindedness, and even as such, they were not totally unjustified. But the rejection in both cases came from a much deeper source: it stemmed from experience, personal and collective, from good common sense, as well as from an artistic or aesthetic sensitivity. In some cases it derived from an understanding, often intuitive, of the total human being, its physical, spiritual, social, and cultural makeup.

Physical health was the individual's first concern. The ancient Roman saying *"mens sana in corpore sano"* (a healthy mind in a healthy body) has found resonance in many Italian popular expressions regarding health: *"la salute è tutto"* (health is everything); almost a "deity" to be always invoked and honoured for its continued favour: *"alla salute"* (to health). Care of one's health is, of course, closely related to the care in cooking and eating. Therefore, the first objection to those foods was also for health reasons: for their dubious nutritional value and for their possible harmful effects on physical and mental health (or even worse, "Fast Food, Early Death").[26]

According to recent studies, chronic health problems, both physical and mental and even among the very young, seem to be related to lack of physical exercise as well as to bad nutrition. Some experts even say that "juvenile delinquency" is tied to what they eat, and propose "nutritional crime prevention."[27] In 1978 Canadian Health Minister Monique Begin, at the opening session of the "Canada Food Strategy Conference," reported that the "nutritional conditions of Canadians [had] reached a state of emergency despite an abundance of food … Millions [suffered] because of poor diets." What were lacking were agricultural and fishing products, with adverse results to those industries as well.[28] Italians seem to have always known or intuited what some researchers, countries, and civilizations are just discovering: the concept that "people [truly are] what they eat," as the surreal compositions by the sixteenth-century Italian artist Giuseppe Arcimboldi aptly depict.[29]

The opposition was motivated by the possible threat to the family.[30] The harm done to one member has an effect on the well-being and serenity of the unit. Not only does eating on the run, sometimes alone, tend to destroy the participatory and celebratory enjoyment of the family meal; but it also deprives the family of those important, fewer, and shorter moments for conversation, laughter, and warmth that nourish and replenish the "spirit" (i.e., ensure a sound psychological state). The invasion of "Canadian" eating habits posed a serious threat to the Italian immigrant family; and the split was already made evident in the interviews. Some parents stated that while they strictly followed the Italian way of cooking and eating, the children liked "English foods like hamburger and hot dogs." Though what the children ate may not have always been harmful to their health (at least not immediately), having food different from what their parents were eating automatically removed a natural bond; it deprived them of a shared experience, and in the long run also impaired the integrity of the family.

Above all, the children either never developed or gradually lost their enjoyment and their appreciation of the finer aspects of Italian cuisine or the taste for certain wholesome delicacies in their own tradition, as evidenced by some negative reaction to some Italian dishes (including fish or certain vegetables). They were slowly cutting an important link with their heritage. Parents' rejection of "those foods," therefore, was also a refusal of the way of life they represented. It was also a "culturally" motivated rejection that often entailed a struggle and sometimes defeat (as well as irony, since their stand was eventually vindicated by the nutritional argument).

Nevertheless, they always hoped that the children would see that the fast-foods lifestyle did not have the fullness their tradition offered. It was, in fact, quite opposite the type of life that Marcella Hazan correlated with "The Italian Art of Eating ... In Italy," as she states, or generally in the Italian tradition: "[Eating] is one more manifestation of the Italian's age-old gift of making art out of life." The Italian art of eating is sustained by a life measured in nature's rhythms, a life that falls in with the slow wheelings of the seasons, a life in which "produce and fish" are still preferred freshly "taken from the soil or the sea. It is an art also [favoured] by the custom of [setting aside] sufficient time for the whole family to celebrate, not just the most important meal but more likely also the most important event of the day." In fact, concludes Hazan, "There probably has been no influence, not even religion, so effective in creating a rich family life, in maintaining a civilized link between the generations, as this daily sharing of a common joy. Eating in Italy is essentially a family art, practiced for and by the family. The finest accomplishments of the home cook are not reserved like the good silver and china for special occasions or for impressing guests, but are offered daily for the pleasure and happiness of the family group."[31]

Art, life, and outlook were implied in the Leamington Italian's simple statement about Italians taking "more care and pride in their cooking." The words encapsulated a tradition and a practice that the Leamington Italians had brought with them, that they wished to revive and preserve and above all transmit to their descendants. One major concern, therefore, was to counterbalance the erosion of that family foundation brought on by the more modern mechanized modes of cooking, eating, and living. This was partly achieved by their search for, and availability of, home grown goods, made easier by their main activities in farming and fishing, and in general by growing vegetable gardens or small orchards. The goal, among most of them, was to secure all goods as genuine and natural as possible; thus the do-it-yourself practices and home food processing raising animals or buying them live for slaughter, curing meats, canning, marinating, baking, and wine making – all done with the discernment and expertise of artists whose work was not always completely satisfactory. Some still found that there was "something" in the food here as compared to Italy – "a certain richness and heaviness" – which they often attributed to the fact that "the difference in the air and climate make Canadian meat [and produce] of inferior quality."[32] But the achievements were always a source of pride, as well as a saving for the family.

At times, strict adherence to their culinary traditions, pursuit of fresh ingredients and the best taste, coupled with a certain distrust for mass-produced foods, took on such extreme forms that they were not always positive for the family. Children (who along with their Canadian friends were often referred to as *"mangiachecc"* [cake eaters]; see chapter 9) reacted when too much time and dedication to these efforts deprived the family of important moments for interaction. Generally, however, the customs, sensibly followed, were maintained as "sacred" objects, as a "talisman of happiness" in their daily life. They often represented the strongest family bonds, part of the essence of their tradition and identity. Meals or banquets, at home or at their club, provided many long hours of enjoyment, often turning an already festive occasion into a celebration of life (see chapter 12, especially "Language, Culture ... and Ethnicity"; and chapter 13).

RELIGION: BELIEFS AND PRACTICES

"The influence of Roman Catholicism has been overwhelming throughout the centuries of Italian history, yet today, perhaps no more than a third of adult Italians can be said to identify with the institutional Church ... The Italian Catholic is autonomous in his conscience."[33]

The Leamington Italian community, in keeping with tradition, identified itself mainly with Roman Catholicism.[34] But in the practice of religion, the relations with the church, and general religious feelings it seemed to reflect more closely the trends of contemporary Italy than the more common patterns developed in other Italian-Canadian communities. Unlike the Windsor Italian community, for example, the Leamington community, though smaller but rural and more scattered, did not grow from a nucleus around an Italian church (often resulting also in the development of a "Little Italy," like the one on Erie Street East in Windsor around St Angela Merici Italian church).

While it grew more independently of church influence, it was also deprived of the advantages that an Italian priest and/or parish often offered. The Italian church in Windsor, completed in 1939, was about sixty kilometres away; and the services of an Italian-speaking priest did not become available to the Leamington Italians until the late 1960s, in a very limited way. Without a community church, a natural gravitational point, or an institution they could immediately identify with, the Leamington Italians had to find other institutions as meeting or gathering places (such as the Italian grocery and then the Roma Club); or partly because they belonged to various (English-speaking) parishes, a collective community attachment to the church, or to one church in particular, was less likely to become strong. The presence later of the Italian-speaking priest did offer an indication of the many possible roles an Italian church might also have had in the Leamington community. But he arrived too late (1967) to have a different impact on the religious and social life of the community.

Their church attendance, observance of the precepts of the church, attitude toward religion and the institution, as well as their general beliefs and behaviour substantially influenced the retention and manifestation of their religious traditions and practices. For the prewar and early postwar immigrants (late 1940s–50s), religion held an important place in their daily living, as it always had in the life of their towns. In Villa Canale, for example, the church served their religious and social needs. It was a place for social gatherings and entertainment. It had also some part, therefore, in keeping the family together. But some recognized that, "while in Villa Canale that was all they had ... in Canada there are other social activities other than the church." The outcome, in such cases, was that the church began to play a less important role; or at least many of those who used to go to church in Italy did not do so in Canada, or "stopped going after the war: Here I don't go to church as much ... I send my children to church."

Canadian practices, however, influenced some of them to go to church more frequently in Canada than they had done in Italy: "There is a higher emphasis placed on religion here in Canada ... There is a fairly good attendance at church." Sometimes it was simply convenience (indicating also how isolated some of them were in Italy): "I go to church more in Canada because it is closer ... Churches are further away in Italy."

The general opinion of those who came in the early 1960s was that religion was important "everywhere." But they preferred Italy, where "people not only go to church more, but [religion] is more strict and more ceremonious" (most likely referring to the practices in the villages or more isolated areas; again indicating the rural origin of many Leamington Italians). Among those who came in the 1960s and 1970s church attendance varied. Some attended mass regularly ("I go once a month here"), but most did so irregularly, in accordance more with circumstances than with church commandment or deep devotion: "Now I rarely go because I have no time ... I go on holidays."

The variation in religious views and practices in Italy and Canada apparently depended on time of immigration (before or after the Second World War); place of origin in Italy (especially degree of isolation) and diversity of local customs (i.e., role of patron saint festival); as well as the general change in attitude toward religion in postwar Italy; and more specifically their different needs and interests after immigration (church attendance was not the only way to, and at times did not, satisfy their desires for social interaction). Moreover, religion was often simply viewed as a personal matter unrelated to place or time: "Religion is important for whomever [sic] wants it to be important ... It depends on the individual, not on the country."

THE PASTOR'S VIEWS ON ITALIAN "RELIGIOSITY" AND THE LEAMINGTON COMMUNITY

Father Ugo Rossi, the Italian priest at St Michael's Parish in Leamington, readily disclosed his considerations on the state of religion in the Italian communities in general, and on the relation and interaction between the church and the Leamington Italian community in particular. The situation, as far as his purview permitted, left him with apprehension but deep understanding and hope as well. After all, Father Rossi had long been familiar with Italian communities both in the United States and Canada.

Born in Vicenza and educated at the Scalabrini Institute in Bassano del Grappa (thus one of the very few Italians from northern Italy in the Leamington area), he first spent twelve years in one of the largest Italian parishes in New York (Our Lady of Pompeii Church, 1948–60), then five years at St Angela Merici Parish in Windsor (1960–65), followed by a short stay at another Windsor parish (Christ the King, 1965–67) until he was sent to Leamington, at St Michael's Parish in 1967. Father Rossi was immediately well received among the Leamington Italians, and through the years he continued to hold their respect and appreciation. He was even made honorary member of the Roma Club. He felt honoured and happy among them, but also quite concerned for them.

Father Rossi always hoped and, above all, wished he "could do more for the community." As an immigrant himself in a way, arriving in New York without knowing English – since he was originally scheduled to work in Argentina – he gladly provided assistance as translator or

interpreter, for passports or other application forms; as adviser, confidant, friend, or just someone to talk to. But as a priest, he wanted to
draw them closer to their religion, to their church. He felt he needed to
"do more" than recite blessings and prayers, officiate at religious festivals, or minister sacraments and rites (baptisms, weddings, burials).

Rossi remembered that while in Windsor, by arranging for the arrival
of four nuns to start an Italian kindergarten and teach Italian classes,
by organizing pilgrimages to the Ohio Shrine, and especially by starting
a choir, he and the other priest drew more Italian parishioners to the
Italian church and increased regular church attendance. The first time
the choir sang the solemn mass for four voices – the *Prima Pontificalis*
by Perosi – the Windsor Italians packed the church.[35] But in Leamington,
his energy and efforts were immensely curtailed in the church and community. His attempt to start celebrating an Italian mass regularly was
at first thwarted by a reminder from the pastor (Rt Rev. L.J. Phelan,
1951–70) that he was the priest for all the parishioners, not just for the
Italian community. A year later, most likely because the other priests
(Phelan as well as the associate pastors Father C.S. Quinlan and Father
J.D. Mercer) thought that the Italians might start their own parish, an
Italian mass was allowed to be celebrated, but only once a month!

While delighted, Father Rossi did not conceal some sense of disappointment. After all, he felt that the Italians' lax observance was due primarily to reasons other than religious feelings or belief: "Many Italians
gave up mass at one time because they could not understand ... Now
they come more often because of an Italian priest ... Even today Italians
go to Italian rather than Canadian mass because they understand better.
If we could have mass in Italian every week [rather than every month]
more and more would come ... and if we had a chance to be a separate
parish, we'd probably do more."

He also believed that "the church meant a lot for most Italians": not
just for the ritual and ceremony at weddings or funerals (and even if they
were only form or spectacle of religion, they nevertheless provided some
solace or a sense of completeness to the human event); but also for the
spiritual uplift offered by individual or communal prayer, such as the
saying of the rosary: "Unconsciously, the church had an impact on them
even though they say they don't go ... [and] Italians have put an impact
on the church."

Father Rossi was proud of the Italians' favourable response in both
words and deeds to his appeal for support of the parish. When he introduced to the community the Canadian practice of envelopes for collection purposes, the other priests did not think the idea would work. But

contrary to their expectations, "within no time the donations rose at incredible speed." Italian support was expressed in other tangible ways. When the church building (probably both St Michael's and St Joseph's, the second church of the parish) required renovations, many Italians offered their help and cooperation.[36]

Italian support for the church or the parish that offered them services in Italian didn't seem to be lacking. Yet, except for Father Rossi's auspicious hypothesis about an Italian church in Leamington, no other reference was made to it. No evidence favouring or opposing the building of an Italian church was made available. No statement was made. The Italian community continued to remain part of larger congregations of various ethnocultural backgrounds: St Michael's Parish itself – which the bishop of London, G. Emmett Carter, did not wish partitioned when St Joseph's Church was built (on Sherk Street) in 1969 – included "as many as ten nationalities." Father Phelan, probably quite delighted with the multicultural composition of his parish, upon retirement stated that they were "learning to live together despite their differences." The opportunity for interaction of various groups in a parish atmosphere probably did favour more understanding and integration into Canadian life. On the other hand, in Father Rossi's view, the Italian community might have avoided some difficulties, social and religious, and become even more "united and stronger" had he been able to "do more with the Italians." Though implied, it was quite clear that he was referring to the role and benefits of an Italian church in the community.

In his interview, Father Rossi, whose experience with communities was long and varied, pointed to problems and tensions among most Italian immigrants (as documented also in the Leamington Italians' interviews). Among their difficulties, he highlighted some discrimination; their determination and hard work to escape the bad economic conditions, including "poverty"; their progress and success, but not without paying the "price of jealousy"; the envy and resentment toward them from other groups and from other Italians; the generation gap, always "getting bigger because the pace of life is ... faster"; difficulty "in transmitting certain Italian traditions to the young"; restriction on dating; marriage arrangements; general strictness on children's behaviour to avoid criticism; general tendency to gossip; and strong spirit of competition sometimes at the sacrifice of a more "human spirit."

On one occasion, however, Father Rossi seemed to give a version not completely borne out by fact. Regional tensions among the Leamington Italians seemed almost insurmountable to him; perhaps he was basing his observation not solely on the Leamington Italian community but mainly on attitudes that existed in Italy when he left it: "After the war," according to him, "Northern Italy mixed with 'coloured people' better than with the South of Italy." In his view, jealousy toward Italians were disappearing faster among the other groups than among the Italians themselves; the inter-Italian envy remained strong, again as a result of the imported interregional, North-versus-South antagonism. While admitting that it was not as evident as in other Italian communities ("for example, Windsor, the many clubs"), he felt certain that "it exists in Leamington too."

Father Rossi may not have been altogether wrong, especially with regard to Italy, as some events in 1989–90 in northern Italian cities seem to indicate.[37] However, while other interviews referred to such division in Leamington, scanty evidence did not support a deep split in the community along those lines (at least it is not as visible as in other Italian communities).[38] As far as Gino DiMenna was concerned, such divisions never existed and never surfaced; for him "Italians were Italians: not Sicilians, *Abruzzesi* [i.e., from both Abruzzo and Molise, until 1963 only one region, Abruzzo-Molise] or *Ciociari*; they were all Italians to be helped and to turn to for help." Besides, the Roma Club, to follow Father Rossi's example, was ample proof that, if tensions of that nature existed, the Leamington Italians overcame them. Nevertheless, as far as Father Rossi was concerned, social and psychological problems were preventing the community from reaching greater unity, harmony, and happiness; and he genuinely felt that such goals may have been made more attainable through greater social and spiritual interaction within an Italian church.

The Italian pastor showed particular care for the problems more strictly related to their faith and religious practices. The Leamington Italian community seemed more exposed to perplexities, to "false prophets," and even to the risks of losing their traditional beliefs. Many superstitions carried from Italy, especially from the south of Rome, were still quite popular. Though generally harmless and picturesque, some were misleading, others insidiously dangerous. Still variously practised were the *malocchio* or evil eye; the *fattura* (curse) or witchcraft and other various forms of magic or divination (palmistry, cartomancy, horoscopy) Consequently, the related popular exorcisms to remove or ward off the curses or sinister spells were also sought (a garlic wreath or necklace was thought to be effective against the evil eye; another "special ceremony" involved drops of oil in a dish of water held above the victim's head and gently moved around in small circles).[39]

Unscrupulous fortune tellers and general healers preyed upon the gullibility, phobias, misfortunes, or general anxiety of many good people

It was quite a money-making business and "there were immigrants in Leamington who turned to them." They continued to seek their services, even though Father Rossi advised them against it: "It was not right," not only because it was a fraudulent business, but above all because it made them dependent on false hopes, false powers, supernatural or unnatural, on the modern "quick fixes." It kept them from seeking both professional help, medical or psychological, and divine help in prayer and in the sacraments. However limited, and there was no clear indication of the extent of the phenomenon, Father Rossi seemed convinced that it was also the result of the infrequency of the interaction or contacts with their own place of worship, a church to which they could instantly relate, with an Italian-speaking priest only for them.[40]

They were not the only threats to their already weakening Catholic faith, which in most Italian Catholics was "habit based," according to Father Rossi. (Indro Montanelli said Italians have a "Catholic mentality [but not] a Catholic conscience."[41]) The Leamington Italians were also exposed to the public or door-to-door proselytizing by evangelical groups or sects, particularly by the Jehovah's Witnesses, who already had a rather large Italian congregation in Toronto, as well as numerous Italian converts in other areas, including Windsor (and Leamington, where apparently even one of the Italian pioneers had been converted). Their persistence and relentlessness with Catholics, particularly Italian Catholics, worried Father Rossi: "It is significant if the church loses one family." On the other hand, given the circumstances, if there were Italians being converted, Father Rossi could only show acceptance and a great deal of understanding: "But as long as the family is doing good works, and [they] remain good people, there's only so much you can do but accept them."

Father Rossi's resignation, however gracious and enlightened, was reached with regret. He was troubled over what more might have been done in the community under different circumstances. In considering the community of which he had become part, he felt like a caring parent for the family: delighted by its achievements and material success, but saddened by the many problems and the spiritual dissatisfaction and discomfort that still remained. It caused him sorrow to see some of them misguided and lured by the peddlers of rapid cures and remedies, the merchants of deceptive bliss, the worst kind of materialism. As a caring person and priest, he seemed convinced that had there been an Italian church, had he or any other Italian priest been able to play a greater role in the community, perhaps there might have been "more spiritual guidance, more relief for the stress and anxiety and more understanding and unity among them, a stronger identity with their faith." And the interviewers added, "Definitely he feels and so do the others feel that an Italian priest is a must [in the community]."

The presence of an Italian church might have made some outcomes less inevitable: he was, of course, thinking of a living, dynamic role of the church – not simply of a church guardian of dogma, teacher of divine truths or preacher of the gospel, but of a church that interacted with the community at all levels, that was always present with its priests to counsel, advise, and even offer examples in their daily struggles and moments of joy and celebration, in their daily practice of religion. That always seemed to be Father Rossi's message and wish, implied or explicit, repeatedly recorded in the interview down to the closing statement: "I [I] could do more with Italians."

But Father Rossi, in the midst of many pressures, changes, and problems affecting the Leamington Italian community, above all recognized the strong personal beliefs that had always been the guide and strength in the family and in the community as a whole: "Italians believe that as long as you live your life the way you were taught [religious practices] it is just as good as going to church ... I feel Italians want to make a better life outside the church, and [in their view] the church isn't the most important part of their religious life, although I would like to see more attendance."

He accepted the reality. Their laxity toward the church or in their observance of the Catholic faith seemed even justifiable, because of the redeeming aspects of their personal beliefs. But as a priest, though very understanding of their ways, he continued to wish them closer to the church. Only through regular attendance could they continuously nourish, renew, and strengthen the beliefs they were taught as children, and therefore their ties with their origin and identity.

However admirable Father Rossi's speculation, expectation, or wish regarding better Italian church attendance or an Italian church, their fulfilment seemed out of reach. His presence and services were needed and were good for the community. Perhaps he had come upon the scene too late, or at a point in the evolution of the community that rendered the desired changes impossible. By the late 1960s the community had built its own institution and was well-established. It had become accustomed to the lack of certain advantages and had learned to depend on its own strengths and beliefs. The Leamington Italian community was a different reality from those he had known in New York or Windsor. His satisfaction was to be found in what he had done or could still do within that reality; above all, by accepting his role, however limited, in the community and by recognizing their "development," even in religion,

With the usual resignation, he did recognize the value and strength of their own personalized form of Catholicism. In spite of their loose ties with the church, their traditional beliefs and religious customs had remained strong and had come to be essential parts of their family and community bases and ties. In comparing Canadian and Italian attitudes toward church attendance, Father Rossi stated, "Canadian people feel that the most important thing is going to church every Sunday," while Italians did not. Yet, he concluded, "Italians follow their morality much more than others." In support of this statement he proudly referred to a newspaper article reporting the results of a survey on pregnancies among unmarried girls. The fact that Italian girls were lowest on the list suggested to him that this was the result of moral values instilled in the children by their parents, as well as of a sense of dignity and family pride. He also felt that their views toward religion and morality were changing very slowly, not as fast as Canadians or Italians in Italy, because of the steadfastness of their personal beliefs and values. As a result, they accepted less readily the practices of the more "modern" and more permissive society, such as sexual promiscuity and divorce (but there were also other motives that Rossi did not seem to take into account; see chapter 10, esp. "Marriage and Premarital Behaviour"). Father Rossi recognized that, though frequent church attendance was not a characteristic of the Leamington Italians, their personal religious customs and beliefs were certainly part of the foundations of their identity.

That aspect may not have been unique to the Leamington Italians, but at least one pattern in multicultural Canada was not visible in the Leamington community. An individual or a group, whose practice of religion in the homeland had become lax, after immigration to a multidenominational milieu or society, tends to rediscover religion; if not the spirit, at least the forms and the institution which often strengthened the identity of both the individual and group. That tendency or change did not seem to have occurred among the Leamington Italians.

THE PATRON SAINT FESTIVAL

It was the religion within themselves that they rediscovered, not the institution. "The southern peasant," Antonio Gramsci observed, "is not a *clericale*, a clericalist" (i.e., pro-clergy or supporter of ecclesiastical power, nor anti-clerical), but "he is often superstitious in the pagan sense."[42] The Leamington southern Italian immigrants had brought with them not so much the body of beliefs of the organized church as the religious practices of their rural areas, their simple but profound devotion to the traditional

patron saint of their *paese*, for them more "valuable" than any other saint
In the various areas of Italian immigration, especially in the early part of
the century, this type of "religious sentiment" was "an important tissue
of [their] scattered communities."[43] It was based mainly on the recreation
of the social, public, and popular aspects of the Catholic rite. What they
observed, often quite strictly, was the liturgy of the calendar saints, special
feast days, and especially the patron saint's day.

Since the Middle Ages, initially with the support of the church, the
life of Christ and the saints had offered subjects not only for literary
miracle plays and sacred representations, but also for "dramatized interpretations of the Catholic liturgy," inside the church walls and outside
in the square.[44] Almost every town in Italy until recent times had, and
some still have, re-enactments of Christ's passion and death. The public
religious festival held the imagination, involved the deepest emotions,
evoked and often incorporated surviving ancient rituals and superstitions, and brought total participation of the townspeople. The festival
aimed at a total celebration. When the Leamington Italians organized
the St Michael's Festival, they aimed for nothing less.

In late August 1969, at a wedding celebration at the Roma Club, surrounded by his *paesani* from Poggio Sannita (Molise), Virginio Ricci's
mind momentarily wandered to his hometown in Italy, where at about
that time they were celebrating the Festival of the Patron Saint, San
Prospero, St "Prosperous" (whose feast day in the 1960s fell on the last
Sunday in August). "It would be really nice," he thought, "to have a
festival the same as the one in Italy." He made "a little speech" about
organizing a committee to start the festival. But they soon realized that
they had only four or five weeks to prepare for it. They called a meeting
for the following Friday at the Roma Club (of which Ricci was president
at that time) and about twenty people showed up.

During the discussion, however, it became evident that a festival in
honour of St Prospero could not be held. But the idea of a festival was
a very good one. In order to avoid hurting the sensitivity of the *paesani* from other towns or areas, and possible tensions, they decided
not to restrict it to the people from their own town. They recognized
that the majority of Italians in Leamington at that time were from Villa
Canale, where, "officially," the "Patron Saint is San Giocondino," but
traditionally the "most characteristic feast [has been] that of St Michael
celebrated yearly [with a village festival] on 29 September," and by the
Leamington *Villacanalesi*, with a banquet, at least since 1965–66. Besides
in Leamington they also had St Michael's Church (used by the Italians
according to parish records, since the early 1930s). Virginio, therefore

"convinced" the people on the committee (who were all from Poggio Sannita) to hold a St Michael's Festival, in honour of the Leamington (Elliott Street) church and not just in deference to the group from Villa Canale. It was a perfect coincidence that pleased everyone.[45]

The response was generally favourable, and participation was better than expected, at least for the first few years. They wanted the festival to be "just like in Italy." There was little time and a great deal of work to do to be ready for 29 September (the original date for the festival – later changed to late August). They needed and obtained many volunteers to collect money, buy fireworks, hire an Italian band from Toronto, build a platform for it, rent chairs for outside, and arrange to close the streets for the procession from St Michael's Church to the Roma Club. Though they had to charge ten dollars to meet expenses, the festival was a success: "For the first year, in 1969, there was a fantastic turnout."

The St Michael's Festival was the first of its type in Leamington. But "they really didn't have any problems; they were just asked a lot of questions, because it was all so new to the town." By this time the Leamington Italian community "had a lot of pull in the town, so they got what they wanted" (e.g., police patrol to stop traffic during the procession). In the following years the festival grew: from a one-day event, after the date change, it became a two-day festival with dancing and other entertainment, and then it became a three-day celebration. For the first five years, when Virginio Ricci was involved, the festival attracted large crowds: "They will never have the success they had in those first few years." Yet he hoped that the festival would not die. It was part of them, of their tradition, of their identity. It was a community event, a religious and social celebration originated by them for their enjoyment and elevation as well as for the whole town. In fact, Father Rossi, they pointed out, "helped out a lot," but "wasn't on the committee."

But signs of the evolving relations with the Italian priest or the church, and therefore with the larger community, could also be seen in "their" particular devotion to St Michael: one was the purchase (in Italy) of a new, wooden statue of St Michael, which was donated (August 1992) to the Leamington church in the name of all Leamington Italians; another was their serious consideration of Father Rossi's suggestion that the annual festival be no longer an exclusively Italian event but one that would include participation of the entire Leamington "Canadian" community. The developments seemed to indicate, on the one hand, the increasing acceptance of the status of Italian traditions in the area, on the other, the continuing evolution, interaction, and integration of the Italian community in Canadian society.

FROM SOCIAL LIFE TO COMMUNITY SPIRIT

Respect for the church and for the priest remained strong. It was part of the tradition: respect for an important institution in the socio-political fabric of society or for a person who held an important office. It was the same respect they would show for any educated person or someone in high office. It was not, however, obsequiousness or dependence They seemed to reflect again the "secular outlook" common among Italians in Italy and a particular "attitude" of the southern Italian peasants "summed up," Gramsci observed "in the popular saying: 'The priest is a priest at the altar; outside he is a man like all the others.'"[46]

In general, their religion, beliefs, or practices were not based on the biblical fear of God (more common among North European Protestants) but on a more human concept and approach (a balance of the divine and the human). It seemed partly reminiscent of the Franciscan idea of "a natural, spontaneous religion, to be lived more than believed or meditated." The "new form of religious feeling ... less intimidating and more familiar," which St Francis initiated, was "suited to an industrious, extrovert society: a popular religion" that reflected his "religious realism,' which contained "something that reached down to an ancient pagan substratum in the minds of the Italian people; a traditional, instinctive rustic idea of God as the daily companion of man's life, of his joy, his sorrow and his work." It is perhaps since the time of St Francis of Assisi (1182–1226) that Italians have generally perceived divinity or the supernatural being not as the All-Powerful One, as Almighty God, but as the All-Good One, as *Gesù Bambino*, the Infant Jesus.[47] If the ways people use to take the name of the Lord in vain are any indication, the Italians seem to completely lack the fear of God (see chapter 15).

The Leamington Italians seemed also to have felt the influence of Canadian religious practices less than other Italian communities. Their church attendance or observance in general was not felt to be a strict rule. Their approach was less dogmatic, less legalistic, more flexible. In fact, sometimes it became secondary to practical concerns and activities. In certain instances there was no time for the salvation of the soul It was important, but it couldn't always interfere with the "salvation of the body." The immediate satisfaction of the here-and-now was often placed before the long-range preparation for the other world, for the supernatural life. Whether it was a pretext for not attending or a genuine feeling of unworthiness, some Italians, almost in admiration of Canadian assiduousness, felt that "you have to be really good to go to mass every Sunday."

The Italians may have placed less importance on participation in the Mass; however "sublime" the Eucharistic banquet, the significance of the doctrine or concept is hardly within anyone's reach.[48] Nevertheless, their religious feelings or practices, whether originating from tradition, custom, or superstition, were genuine and deep-rooted (in fact, quite close to the etymological sense or connotation of "religion" – *religare*, bend back or again; *religio*, tie up, tie fast, bind together, collect). Their common feelings and some of their practices (such as the Festival of the Patron Saint) tended to bind the community together in communal prayer and public devotion, as well as in convivial, social celebration. What was more important to them was the "religious sentiment" that pervaded life, that was part of life's texture, an integral part of oneself, and not just the "sublime act" performed at a specific place or time. What counted was the personal, everyday practice of the feelings and of the time-honoured religious customs, not necessarily the one followed (sometimes hypocritically) just on Sunday and then abandoned for the rest of the week. The Leamington Italians can be said to be "non-practising" profound Christians and Catholics. In this sense religion, if not a powerful force, exercised a daily influence on the mores and ethics of the individual, family, and community.

A "PARISH" FOR ALL THE LEAMINGTON ITALIANS: THE ROMA CLUB

It was, therefore, not the institution of the church, but the institution that they themselves created that played a major role in their social life: in establishing, strengthening, or rediscovering their personal or community identity. Most believed that the "Roma Club is the place where you can spend time in the Italian way ... You can speak Italian, play cards or bocce ... do more Italian things."

For at least one member who had come to Leamington at a young age, participation in the club meant a more harmonious self-image and life, indicating, in part, a realization of the founders' intentions and the club's objectives: "I really started to understand Italian customs then [when he became involved in the Roma Club] ... Up until then I was always torn between two worlds – going to school and living among Canadian kids and then going back home to an Italian lifestyle."

By rallying around one common community centre since the 1960s, the Leamington Italians have made the Roma Club into more than a recreational and social centre or commercial enterprise. The Roma Club, as the only Italian community institution (with about 1,000 members) has also served as a sort of "spiritual home" for all Italians, regardless of region of origin or period of arrival (or gender, apparently, since men and women have, unlike some other clubs, equal status as members); and it was mostly so especially at the beginning, during those most crucial years of settlement and integration into the new life of the postwar Italian immigrants (a process for which the Canadian government sought cooperation of the various communities; see chapter 13, "Interaction within the Community").

For the postwar immigrants especially, the tangible "presence of the Motherland" was a great need (as Arturo Scotti pointedly remarked in one of his frequent exhortations to create not *Dopolavoro* or "Afterwork Centres" but workers' recreation centres in the late 1950s): a need equal to that of the church for the "good believer," particularly because the Italian immigrant in Canada at that time was, in Scotti's words, "fighting the most extenuating spiritual battle of his life." The Leamington Italians may not have been able (nor was it their main goal) to achieve what Scotti optimistically thought a pan-Italian organization might do in other parts of Ontario: "revive the spirit of [Italian] brotherhood, without falling into blind nationalism." But they did strive to ."better understand the ways of the new land without denying their origins."[45] Above all (contrary to Father Rossi's views), they reduced, even removed the divisive forces of regionalism (*campanilismo*) and the "old versus new" immigrant tensions (which, as Scotti also pointed out, were fragmenting other communities).

Through the continuous interaction of pre– and post–Second World War immigrants (as evidenced also in the 1960 steering committee, the list of presidents, as well as the 1977 banquet for the founders of the community), they were able to overcome even some of the inherent Italian "defects," or at least to become more cognizant of them and of one aspect of "Italian-ness" (envy, argumentative nature, mistrust of power). Above all, partly their needs as immigrants and partly the new Canadian environment helped reduce in them an Italian fault that other Italians considered a basic, historical characteristic of all Italians: the "lack of social sense," the limited public sentiment or commitment.[50] On the contrary, both Italian and civic pride was especially manifested by the Leamington Italians in the Leamington Centennial Italian Fountain Project (see chapter 8, especially note 19). Thus, in their search for an establishment that would satisfy their entertainment and social needs, the Leamington Italians also forged an extended family-like or community spirit (see chapter 10).

Ethnic Identity: Italian Canadians or Canadianized Italians?

"We ... in a strange country ... will never be Canadian."
"I became a Canadianized Italian."
"I consider myself more Canadian than Italian."

ETHNICITY: A CANADIAN AND GLOBAL ISSUE

Like three acts in a play, the three separate statements by three different Leamington Italians incisively present the uncertainty, confusion, and conflict within the individual and the group in their search for a new identity. The dramatic action, in this case, does not reach a conclusion. The declarations only represent three steps in integration into the new society, from a state of alienation toward a sort of mixture of the basic identity components. The personal conflicts revealed in the simple utterances also reflect different levels of the dilemma inherent in all pluralistic societies.

Their quest for a dynamic balance between Italian tradition and Canadian experience is, on a smaller scale, the complex Canadian drama: not just the historical conflict between two languages and two cultures, but the clash between two or more ways of life within each citizen, and the contrasts or interaction among many races and ethnocultural groups within society as a whole. Their struggle, as illustrated also by Athanase Tallard in Hugh MacLennan's *Two Solitudes*, seems a universal one: "It would be possible to find sensitive souls in any country who have struggled to reconcile ancestral claims and modern urgencies."[1]

The search for a common Canadian identity has been made even more difficult in recent decades by increasing social diversity. The survival of different languages, cultures, and traditions, as well as the attachment to the land of origin or to different sets of values, has made the goal almost elusive: "With nations, as with individuals, there are deep instinctive urges that cannot be forced into a common mould."[2]

Ethnic identity or ethnicity, as the interviews with the Leamington Italians have clearly indicated, can be such an "urge," whose effects are long-lasting. Their *italianità*, "Italian-ness," or sense of being Italian, whether neglected, forgotten, cast aside, or opposed, is ever present: consciously or subtly moulding their way of life and thinking; at times re-emerging as a guide, even among the more removed second and third generations, and in some instances causing deep conflicts and difficult choices in the immigrant child attempting to straddle two lifestyles. The Leamington young man who said he had been "raised here" had "lost the Italian language ... could hardly communicate or get along" with his parents, and "never mixed with Italians," was rejecting part of his tradition, of his essence (see chapters 10, 15). Athanase Tallard, in MacLennan's novel, is similarly "caught between two mighty opposed forces ... His tragedy is that he is driven into a position where he feels that he must renounce one of the two; he decides to cut himself off from his people and his religion. The desperate sacrifice brings no release; he becomes an outcast among his own people, and earns only the cold contempt of those whose way of life he has embraced."[3] Though the Leamington youth was not an "outcast" in the community, he had become a stranger in it, as well as in a part of his own being. In both cases, however, the outcome was just as devastating as the initial "tragedy." The dénouement in Tallard's drama – his "return on his death-bed to his ancestral faith," suggesting a lifelong search for one's origins, a need to reintegrate one's being – applies also to the Leamington man's situation.

Ethnicity, however defined, can be a straitjacket or a propelling force toward a higher awareness of the self and one's role in society. As a gilded prison, ethnicity may provide some security, but in the long run restrict vision and flexibility, encourage group re-ghettoization, involution, or a sort of "wallowing in one's roots." Static ethnicity tends toward a closed society of ethnocentric groups. On the other hand, a clear and dynamic ethnic identity can serve as a secure base for survival, development, and full and equal participation of the individual and the group in the community and in society. In other words, a Canadian identity based on ethnic hyphenation, more than just a sum of two uncertainties, can be a fruitful combination of two experiences benefiting individual and national goals: "Canada can be understood, not in terms of trade indices, nor in terms of political skills although these are important but in terms of the human values that are present in our daily life. Above all ... it is futile to try to isolate one dominant Canadian ideal. For in this country we are the heirs of many traditions that are only gradually being fused together."[4]

Within the Leamington Italian community, instances of the "gradual fusion" were visible, or at least attempts were made to resolve the conflict through reflection, through a continuous rebalancing and rearrangement of the two or more aspects of their double or multiple identity: "One must be proud to be an Italian before one can be proud to be a Canadian ... One must know his true homeland before he can know his adopted homeland." This rare but significant observation by a Leamington Italian, while indicating a way to avoid the more tragic outcomes at the personal or community levels, suggested another possible final act in the Canadian national drama: a solution attainable through a greater awareness of the two realities; which naturally entails a knowledge of the history and languages of the two countries (host and of origin), an appreciation of the cultures, traditions, and experiences of each Canadian group, and a familiarity with the institutions of the adopted land. In brief one needs to have insight into all forces that nourish the "instinctive urges" that reshape the individual in the new environment. To know oneself is also to better understand the role or impact of ethnic identity within the individual and community in Canada.[5] Perhaps then, as MacLennan seemed to suggest, "through sympathy and understanding, we [Canadians] can finally beat out a national harmony."[6]

The Leamington Italians spontaneously expressed what some Canadian writers intuitively recognized and artistically presented. Earl Birney's poetic portrayal of Canada as a gangly adolescent, almost schizophrenic, cuddled by and torn between unmarried parents, coincides with Hugh MacLennan's general outlook about contemporary Canadian life: both suggest that Canada is neither sufficiently mature nor flexible to bring about a synthesis of the many traditions and achieve a real Canadian identity.[7] Quite similar views were often found also in the confused reactions and contradicting attitudes toward the land of origin and Canadian identity among the Leamington Italians interviewed.

If, on the one hand, Canadian identity is made elusive by Canada's increasing ethnocultural diversity, vast geography, and little history, on the other, defining Italian identity is rendered just as difficult by Italy's many diversities, perhaps by too much civilization, and not enough "history of her own."[8] The Italian immigrants throughout the twentieth century knew they were Italians, and felt strongly Italian wherever they settled. But Italian self-identity or *italianità* was generally a concept as complex to them as it had been to most people who lived in Italy, as well as to those from the peninsula who roamed Europe and the world in the centuries before Italy became a nation.

If there was no Italy, could there be an Italian sentiment? If one was physically removed from the native land, what was *italianità* based on? What did it mean to be Italian? A brief overview of the Italian historical "contradictions" may better determine the quality of Italian sentiment (i.e., ethnicity) of the Leamington Italians, as well as of "some early Canadian heroes," whom Harney called "just gallicized citizens of the world," while cautioning against falsifying "the degree of their *italianità*" by acknowledging their Italian origins.[9]

ITALIANITÀ: "THE FEELING OF BEING ITALIAN" WITHOUT OR OUTSIDE ITALY

The term, according to some dictionaries, means or refers to "Italian spirit" or "Italian feelings";[10] a state of being that is in accordance with Italian temperament, customs, art, thought, or sentiment; a feeling purely and proudly Italian;[11] participation or sharing in the cultural heritage and civilization attributed to the Italian nation.[12] If strictly based on a unitary nation-state (same or similar social, political, economic institutions), *italianità* could hardly exist before the birth of the "Italian nation" in the mid-nineteenth century. But if related to "Italian spirit," temperament, customs, art, and thought, it may have existed since Roman times, and certainly since "the years around 1000."

Italy, as a political entity, had not existed since the Fall of Rome (CE 476); and even before that time, the valued status was that of Roman citizen, which also implied "citizen of the world." Even though the concept of *gens* (family, clan, tribe) remained important, its socio-political role disappeared with the noble Roman families (*gentes*). The sense of nation-spirit (*Völksgeist*), national soul, manifest in the early great northern migrations (*migratio gentium*), or in the "wanderings of the nations" of the Teutonic peoples (*Völkerwanderung*) that also animated their epics or sagas, had no parallel in the medieval Italian experience. While in northern Europe the noble families became the pillars of the hierarchical feudal system, in Italy they were attracted to the cities (became, quite early, town dwellers for at least part of each year), thus contributing to the "victory of local centres in Italian life," especially in the absence of a central and centralizing monarchy after the death of the last king of the ineffective Italian medieval kingdom (early eleventh century). Italy has been for centuries a plurality, a diversity, "a country of regions." Its history, for the nineteenth-century poet "prophet of Italy" (and 1906 Nobel prize recipient) Giosuè Carducci, was the history of its cities; and for that reason also it is still described as "distinctly different, both geographically and culturally, from her close European and Mediterranean neighbours."

Yet, in this "land of paradoxes," a sense of unity seemed to exist throughout its tortuous history: the name itself, *Italia*, Italy, dates back to Roman times, and Italian identity was always felt to be rooted in Roman civilization, which guaranteed it through its common cultural foundation. In spite of almost fourteen centuries of fragmentation, differentiation, and diversification, "Italy ... did hold," wrote Max Salvadori. "However paradoxical, regions were a factor in keeping Italy together ... Italy was the common denominator for all Italians." A "spiritual" over a "geographic" Italy began to appear at the time of the *comuni*: the struggle of the freedom-loving cities (eleventh to thirteenth centuries) against the universalistic medieval institutions – empire and papacy – was seen as the birth of the Italian people, of an Italian awareness.[13]

More than the cities' military, political, and economic exploits, what moulded pan-Italian consciousness was the elaboration of a common Italian language by the intellectuals who were simultaneously loyal to their particular city and part of a common spiritual homeland. It was, above all, the poet-philosopher Dante Alighieri (1265–1321) who, in the words of Bruno Migliorini, "performed the miracle." He "[revealed to Italy] the consciousness of its substantial cultural unity ... and thus Italy was born." In his literary masterpiece, the *Divine Comedy*, "Italians recognized their own language recast in a sublime mould."[14] Petrarch (1304–1374), "the father of humanism," "the first modern man," "the first modern historian," and himself an "immigrant" of sorts, saw Italy as a "noble country cherished by God"; and he proclaimed "the Italians ... the most legitimate heirs of the Roman tradition: *sumus non graeci, non barbari, sed itali et latini*" (we are not Greeks, nor Germans, but Italians and Latins).[15]

Fifteenth-century Italy, the land of separate states, was commonly referred to as a unit joined by "the Italian language." Paradoxically, while Italian political liberty was being crushed (sixteenth century), "a consciousness of belonging to a common civilization [linguistic, literary, artistic] became general among her inhabitants," especially as a result of the Renaissance humanists' rediscovery of the classical forms and ideas and the transference of them into Italian literature, art, and thought ("vernacular humanism"). "The very controversies on the nature of the language [Italy] should adopt showed that those taking part thought of such a language as the *vehicle for a single national culture*."

True, by the end of the sixteenth century, "the unity, fusion and harmoniousness of Renaissance culture were shattered," and what followed was "a century of stagnation" characterized by a "withdrawal into provincialism and dialect," revival of "city-patriotism," and "development of separate local cultures." But the "heritage of the Renaissance was too abundant and too recent for it not to go on exerting a strong attraction and influence." Galileo himself, "the father of modern science," after his *Sidereus nuncius* (1610) appeared in Latin, chose to write "all his major works in Italian, in spite of protests from foreign scholars," including Kepler who "accused him of *crimen laesae humanitatis*" (the crime of treason against humanity or scholarship).[16]

In the eighteenth century, "the necessity of bridging the gap ... between literary and spoken Italian," as well as public demand for "a modern, up-to-date and versatile culture, and a healing of the traditional gap between humanistic and scientific studies," made many Italian "writers ... aware of their responsibility towards their public" (especially evident in the "considerable number of works devoted to ... the 'new science' par excellence ... economics"). Thus, the "Italian intellectuals were united by the Enlightenment; once more, as in the past, they formed a spiritual community. Together with this unity, they rediscovered their social role and sense of collective responsibility for society ... Insofar as they succeeded in being Europeans, they remembered that they were also Italians." As Italians, they felt "they [belonged] to a country in which two homelands coexisted since the end of the Roman Empire: the municipal or regional homeland and the universal one of the Church ... [Since] the Church [as Machiavelli stated] was too weak to unify Italy and too strong to let others do it ... some eighteenth-century Italian intellectuals may have felt as a personal drama the absence of a national state." But as European intellectuals, "in many aspects, the intellectuals of Europe," they were also torn "between two homelands which had become the complementary components of their moral and intellectual makeup," and they were also well aware of the inevitability of foreign intervention to achieve Italian national unity.[17]

Many of them, whether enjoying "a privileged position in all the courts of Europe" or living abroad for political or other reasons, fervently defended their homeland, or publicly proclaimed their Italian pride; as did Giuseppe Baretti in England against Samuel Sharp, or as Vittorio Alfieri did in France in 1792: "Alfieri is my name, Italian and not French." "There was, therefore," commented Sergio Romano, "there had always been a feeling of identity and of belonging, so much the stronger and the more steadfast because it was expressed abroad, and often in a language different from the native one."[18]

This feeling of "double identity" is not uncommon even in today's Italy: Italians cherish their ways and proudly differentiate themselves from other Europeans, but are the least nationalistic and, according to voting patterns, the strongest supporters of a united Europe. In the 1980s the modern "Italy's daredevil entrepreneurs," such as the "global deal maker" and financier Carlo De Benedetti, or the agro-industrialist Raul Gardini, with their Italian-made fortunes contributed to Italy's rise as a world industrial power, yet they doubted Italy's "ability to modernize itself" and considered themselves the "connective tissue, the nervous system of a new Europe."[19] The controversial playwright Dario Fo's "writing ... very much in the spirit of the place of birth," has been universally adaptable.[20] Italians are a very politicized people but have a healthy "distrust of government" (more so than "contempt for the law"). For most of the post–Second World War period, the Italian party configuration itself, with its National Right and more International and sizable Left, seemed to reflect the two homelands concept.[21] Modern Italy's "unity in diversity" was succinctly described by Thomas G. Bergin: "'Italy,' as the heroes of the Risorgimento made clear, is more than a geographical expression ... much more than a political definition. It is a realm in the heart of mankind; transcending time and place, it has an image of sempiternal and universal dimensions. Many divers and precious elements have gone into the composition of the image. It bears within it the double legacy of old Rome, with its Republican virtues of patriotism, sobriety and political shrewdness, and its imperial aura of splendour and the vision of all men united under justice and law."[22]

Even from a brief historical perspective there emerges a concept of *italianità* based not so much on territory or power as on culture and ethos; an *italianità* simultaneously composed of a legacy of the "many Italies" and of an overall image, a fusion of "many divers elements"; that is, an *italianità* that incorporates both diversity and unity. Humanistic education has been recognized among "the more persistent Italian traditions": on the one hand, the humanistic endeavour to harmonize various, often rivalling human concerns (such as the practical and the rational; the mundane and the mystical); and on the other, the cultural products themselves – the literary, artistic, and intellectual syntheses – whose aim is to edify both the individual and the group. All of them, separately and together, have constituted Italy's most significant and basic cultural heritage: the characteristic and distinctive features of Italian civilization, of the "Italian spirit" or general outlook on life throughout the centuries.[23] This form of *italianità* is, of course, more difficult to achieve, more elusive, simply because it is more complete, loftier, or more abstract; it is, in other words, less municipal, less regional (i.e., parochial) and more global (i.e., cosmopolitan); it presupposes familiarity with the cultural products of Italy (language, literature, history), or with the geographic as well as the spiritual Italy.

The early North American or "Canadian heroes" of Italian origin (Columbus, the Cabots, Verrazzano, Bressani, Burlamacchi, or the Tonti brothers and others) were not, and could not be, Italian "nationals." They did not represent their native land: Italy, though "a rich, highly developed country" was excluded from the partition of the New World.[24] Nevertheless, both forms of *italianità* were present through them: the language(s), culture(s), temperament, and sometimes flags of their native cities or regions, as well as the "spirit of Italy" as a whole. Alfonso Tonti, for example, was known as "the Neapolitan" and called so, albeit in contempt, by his commanding officer himself, Cadillac.[25] Their cultural makeup allowed them to adjust to the European situation and be at the same time Genoese, Florentines, or Venetians. Those who "served the French Canadian regime," Harney himself pointed out, "were, and felt themselves to be, cosmopolitans."[26] Many Italian cultural heroes of the same period, and especially of the eighteenth century, honoured in the courts of Europe as "more cosmopolitan than their French, English or German counterparts," were said to be "demonstrating the intellectual superiority of their native land," even while expressing "with nostalgia and sadness a sentiment for a lost homeland" (e.g., Goldoni and Casanova).[27] "Degree of *italianità*" cannot be established by superimposing a North European concept of national sentiment strictly tied to nation-state.

Similarly, nineteenth-century *italianità* can neither be completely represented by the Italian patriot and cosmopolitan Giacomo Forneri, nor totally denied by the anglicized Philip DeGrassi (according to Harney, "the first two important Italians in the Toronto area"). In the 1850s when Forneri and other "immigrants began to arrive from Italy, who were," in Harney's words, "truly Italian in language and sentiment," many other Italians were not only indifferent to but opposed to the Risorgimento.[28] Even after the creation of a united Italy, the lament was that Italians were still to be made. Random examples considered separately, without an awareness of the underlying contradictions in the Italian framework, cannot be used as precise indicators of the level of *italianità* or ethnicity (see chapter 1, especially "The Changing Fortunes of Italians in Canada").

In the case of the Leamington Italians, their *italianità* was firm and genuine, even though it was based mainly on the "municipal" or "regional" homeland; and even though the characteristic, distinctive *italianità* founded on the knowledge of the language, culture, and history of the land of origin as a whole, remained, in spite of some attempts, a more elusive goal. Beyond the attachment to birthplace, hometown or village mores, or dialect, what generally appeared were vague, uncertain, mixed, or even contrary feelings towards Italy and Italians; and yet a "feeling proudly Italian" was rather common, even if it appeared more as an emotional attitude toward their particular group (at times bordering on ethnocentrism) rather than as a sense of identity with the Italian nation or people. Sometimes it appeared as narrow, nationalistic patriotism, resulting from a memory of Fascist Italy and/or Mussolini: be it for the respect he won from world leaders and pride for Italians, for maintaining "order in Italy" or, according to the common saying, for "making the trains run on time" (see chapters 1, 6). At times, Italian pride derived from vague notions about the greatness of ancient Rome, Renaissance artistic splendour, Italian historical figures (Garibaldi, Verdi, Marconi), or, rarely, on a more "cosmopolitan" awareness.[29]

Their ethnicity was marked mainly by tensions and oscillations in views between the persistence of old customs and the increasing influence of the Canadian way of life; the use of the native language and the necessity of English; involvement and participation in the larger arena of Canadian affairs and the urge to "stick close" together; ethnocentrism and integration (or assimilation). In general, though satisfied with Canadian material advantages, they found Canada lacking in other ways, and difficult to become fully part of it. Nevertheless, in a way following known patterns, they found within themselves their own sense of Italian sentiment, their ethnicity, their Italian-Canadian state of being: a simultaneous and paradoxical feeling of being part of two "nations," two traditions, yet belonging completely to neither. The dilemma, however, between tradition and experience seemed to be weakening in proportion to the discovery or rediscovery of the best qualities of both "homelands." That process made their self-identity more balanced and more secure.

ATTITUDES TOWARD ITALY AND CANADA

"The heritage should be passed on ... If one loses his heredity, he loses his identity."

Leamington Italian Canadian

Maintenance of traditional values, and therefore ethnicity, was greatly affected by the level of awareness of the "Old Country." Often, immigrants' concept of Italy was limited to only what they knew or heard about their town or region. Their determination to retain their customs was hardly matched by their attempts to know more about Italy. Even the initial strong desire to return to Italy soon faded into a romantic nostalgia for the hometown. In time, loneliness and the difficulties of language, employment, and debts were overcome by the glare of the land of opportunity and the arrival of their families. The desire to move back sometimes persisted, but it was rarely fulfilled, except by temporary visits: "I didn't like it at first ... felt lost ... took about ten years before I stopped thinking of moving back to Italy ... I haven't returned to Italy yet, but I would go for a visit." For almost all prewar settlers, in spite of the many hardships in building a new life, Italy soon became a fond but distant memory. The more frequently used "Old Country," rather than Italy, seems to suggest a detached fondness. At times, in the midst of many sweet memories of the *paese* and pride in their heritage, various negative reactions to the Old Country were expressed, in a way reminiscent of Angelo Moauro's curse the first time he went back to Italy (chapter 2). Alex Colasanti made it even clearer: "I'd rather stay here dead than in Italy alive" (chapter 5), while others simply stated "Italy never gave me anything"; "I forgot Italy the day I arrived."[30]

Among those who came in the late 1940s, mixed feelings prevailed. Some were quite critical of Italy: *"L'Italia è più brutta di prima"* (Italy is uglier than before). For many, it was a land where people lived beyond their means, earning too little and spending too much for things they couldn't afford; a land of unbridgeable social and economic inequalities: "too much of a class distinction." Others wavered between indifference, "don't curse or embrace Italy," and longing for it, "Italy ... beautiful ... ruins, climate, food ... less but better ... Life didn't offer much, but I was content ... Italy not bad ... *si stava bene* (one got along well)." Sometimes this unabated homesickness was the cause of much restlessness and anxiety, which kept many of them suspended between two worlds, in the margin of Canadian life.

The opinions on Italy among those who came in the 1950s and 1960s were as varied as the small towns from which they originated. The sources of their information were equally varied: hearsay, in large part; the English-language media with their sporadic and often superficial reporting about Italy; the Italian-language periodicals and programs, local and imported, and with their limitations; and their trips to Italy – rarely to other areas of the country, generally to their region of origin or hometown. As a result, parochial, if not distorted, views of Italy persisted.

Those few who "read Italian newspapers to keep up-to-date" generally obtained negative impressions about the rapidly changing social and political conditions of postwar Italy: "A big confusion ... The people don't know who they want in power ... The situation ... is disgusting ... everyone creates their own laws ... no government ... people do what they want ... they rob, they steal ... they kill." Some, however, admitted to reading Italian newspapers only "once in a while" or "only ... when something exciting is happening in Italy." This occasional and selective information, as well as some of the overly self-critical Italian journalism, encouraged more misconceptions than understanding about the Old Country.

The events described in the newspaper articles they read were not lived. They were disconnected from the daily flow of Italian life and reality; they were read and considered out of context. Their complexity escaped them also because it was not possible to discuss them as some used to do in their town, as Bruno Matassa (1948) remembered: "The paper would arrive in the neighbouring town and one man would go and get the paper ... Then the men would go to the café and each talk about the news for hours; but ... maybe their interest in ... the news came from the fact that there was nothing to do, so this in itself was a form of entertainment."

To the many more who seemed to follow Canadian-produced Italian radio and television programs, Italy appeared in no better light, even "worse." The usual clichés were cited: "No government ... People do what they want ... They kill, they steal ... They think and are doing very extravagant things ... build everything on credit"; and the usual comparisons made: "Italy was all right when I was there [in 1962]." Other listeners or viewers of these programs simply stated that they didn't "know much about the situation in Italy" or were "not interested in [it]." A more balanced view was held by only one among those who read Italian magazines: "The situation in Italy is not as bad as they picture it here." Of course, those who "never read the Italian newspaper" did not "care about what [was] happening there now ... *Paese che vai usanza che trovi* [When in Rome do as the Romans do]." The proverb was probably quick justification for disinterest in Italy more than acceptance of its literal meaning – "Follow the customs of the country one lives in" – for they usually followed their own particular customs more often than those found in Canada.

The possible benefit of reading and listening to anything Italian – retention of the language – was cancelled, it seemed, by the message they received about Italy. Regardless of their source of information, many Leamington Italians had a mostly negative impression of Italy; and those who read Italian often projected this impression even on those who didn't. Especially with respect to the political situation, Italy was summarily defined as *"in rovina"* (in ruins), in trouble, and getting worse: "There is too much terrorism ... Italy's political structure is weak ... too many parties and the votes are all split." In brief, "politics in Italy *è sporca* [is dirty]." "The Italian government is dishonest ... it robs people." But strangely they felt "the people have too much freedom ... everyone robs the government." Since they saw there was "no order," they concluded, as nostalgically as some did in Italy, that the country needed a "dictatorship," "another Mussolini" (in fact, one said, "five Mussolinis, one for each province; he was good for Italy"), or at least "a stricter government." For some it was still a good country, but it was being destroyed by a politically irresponsible and greedy people who deserved to be punished somehow: "Italy should have a Communist government [i.e., led by the Italian Communist Party or PCI] because they deserve it ... not because Communists are good, but they should be taught a lesson ... Italy has it good and it is trying to spoil what it has ... nobody can have two cars or homes ... you have what you need."

Economically, the Old Country was just as bad, in their opinion: low standards of living at very high cost. While one condemned the Italians for wanting or having too much, another criticized the country for providing too little: "It's harder for the people to get what they want ... They don't live as well as we do." And some were puzzled: "But they are doing well ... cars, fridge ... I don't know how they survive ... They make less money than us, pay more for food, and they go on vacations." But they quickly found themselves an answer: "Italians live on credit." Others had some odd notions about employment. It wasn't just a question of "a scarcity of jobs," but of Italians reduced to a race of parasites: "The people don't work ... they have lost [self-] respect ... everyone lives on the back of the government." In fact, some went as far as to say, "The people in Italy are lazy ... everyone lives on pensions" and especially on lies: "There is more *falsità*"; duplicity, deception seemed to them a normal way of life in Italy simply because "Italians [have] to respect the higher-class people more ... the class structure is stiffer."

They were generally as misinformed of the post–Second World War changes in the social, economic, and political life of Italy as they were unaware of its commercial, industrial, and technological progress that helped bring about what has been called a radical transformation ("the Italian miracle ... perhaps unique in the world").[31] As far as one was concerned, "Probably Italy is the same today ... People say Italy has changed, but I feel that it couldn't be much better from the situation I left behind [in 1952]."

Some were quite convinced that Italy was still a backward country, still lacking, for example, "many comforts: although it has progressed, Italy is still twenty years behind"; perhaps only "for clothing styles, Italy is ahead." Ironically, to support this point, one person chose an example from an area in which Italy has been in the forefront in the world: communications.[32] "I doubt if I would have made the same progress because of my type of business ... It is controlled by the government and this type of work is not allowed in Italy ... It is too far behind." Admittedly, even hearsay was used selectively. They often refused to believe what they heard and followed only what they thought.

Those few who completely ignored Italy neither knew nor cared whether it was better or worse off: "*Non penso per niente all'Italia* [I don't think at all about Italy]. I like Italy because I was born there, but I have no use for it now."

Nor did the widely held concept of the Old Country seem to change with first-hand contacts with Italy. The return trips to Italy made by most Leamington Italians over the years generally reinforced the views gathered in Canada. In some cases, the visit not only quenched the burning desire to see the familiar places, but made their option for Canada clearer, especially among those whose constant thought was to move back: "We returned to Italy but came back ... [We] realized that life would be better for the children here ... satisfied with the progress we've made here ... This progress wouldn't have been possible in Italy." The visit often proved to be a sad experience, overwhelmed as they were by a feeling of no longer belonging there, by a sense of separation: "Originally we wanted to return to Italy, but when we returned to visit, we found we preferred life here ... We were changing and didn't realize it ... We had adjusted to life here ... All my relatives and friends are gone ... It was as strange as when I first came to Canada."

The trip to Italy, for whatever reason – marriage, aging parents, or just vacations – often turned out to be exhilarating, but hardly ever an occasion to obtain a more objective view of their land of origin. It generally enhanced opposite emotions: a simultaneous love and hate, attraction and repulsion. Very rarely were serious attempts made to seek ample explanation or understanding of what they saw or experienced. The resulting state of anxiety and tension was often detectable in their contradictory and confused statements. Sometimes it even surfaced with full awareness: "I don't want to go back to Italy because then I'd want to stay." The conscious suppression of the attraction may have been one way of solving the dilemma: avoid the risk of a difficult, perhaps impossible decision, and accept life as it was.

In most cases the solution was found in rejection, made easier by finding or enlarging Italian defects, real or imaginary: "I could not live the life of Italy ... Too much leisure time is boring ... I love Italy for its natural beauty ... I'm sure that some people can make a go of it in Italy ... [I] would not mind living there if the government was stable." Some fearsome aspects of Italy were probably a real cause for avoiding it, but they were either blown out of proportion or simply misunderstood: "I won't visit Italy anymore ... In Italy there's too much terrorism ... Bad people are in Italy now ... Communists ... I really never thought of returning to Italy ... I decided quickly to stay here ... I liked the flat land in Canada, the comforts of modern living here and the police system." In one case, total detachment from anything Italian did not preclude choosing Italy as a final resting place: "I don't think of Italy ... It's as if I wasn't born there ... I'm happy here ... We've progressed ... Maybe when I die I'll return to Italy, but as long as I live, I'll remain here."

"OUTSIDERS," "PRISONERS," OR SIMPLY LIVING BETWEEN TWO WORLDS?

This tension was more intensely felt and clearly revealed by the older generation. For them, readjustment was practically impossible. After having spent half their life in Italy, it was difficult to adapt to a new environment. They were outsiders and remained so, even after many years. They barely learned the language and they never felt comfortable in an unfamiliar situation that could never be part of them. They often felt prisoners of irreversible circumstances. They longed to return to their homeland, but realized that such a return was unlikely. Their hearts were in Italy, but their children and grandchildren were here: "not too happy here ... much money here, but also more pain ... Life here has more sacrifices ... I would like to live in Italy now." Torn between two loves – homeland and family – though they felt they would never be totally part of Canada, they also knew they would not ever again be able to go "home" and be totally part of Italy: "We wouldn't go back to live ... now we're old ... For our children, Italy not so nice, because Canada is their home ... We will go back to visit though ... We still feel at home in Italy." This duality was especially clear among the women. The good life in the new land did not diminish the attraction of Italy: "I live well here, but the homeland always pulls you back ... my wife wants to return as soon as our son is settled ... Hopefully, when we get old we will return to Italy ... When your family is in Canada, it's hard"; "I was comfortable here after five years ... Now, I don't think of returning to Italy to live ...

My husband likes Canada ... I like Canada too, but if my husband said, 'Let's go back to live in Italy,' I would go right away tomorrow."

But concern for the children's future and later the thoughts of separation from them made it remain only a hope: "I went back to Italy in 1970 ... It was difficult to raise my children there, but now things have changed ... I wish I could have stayed ... The children stop us from moving right now ... We're too scared to take our children away from school." Sometimes there was a change of heart, but not enough to make a decision, at least not until retirement: "I've never wanted to go back to Italy until now ... I think that I might go there to retire." Often, there appeared to be no obstacles, and the social and mental state favoured a return: "Italy is a country of happiness; Canada is a country of work. In Canada there is quantity; in Italy there is quality." The more recent the visit, the greater was the surprise at Italian progress, and appreciation: "When I returned [in 1979] I found that things were much better there than here ... My nieces and nephews who are teachers, have beautiful homes ... When I returned I finally saw Italy ... Before, when I was young, I really didn't even know my hometown [Boville Ernica] ... I found that Italy was beautiful, and I would return to live there if my children would go with me."

Frequent visits also brought a little more understanding of it: "I've returned to Italy five times since I've been in Canada. Each time I returned, Italy got better and better ... There were more jobs, better jobs ... The country is nicer ... There are more villas." But some continued to disagree: "Now I would never return to Italy to live ... I went twice ... People [are] worse off now than they used to be. There, you only thought about getting by and having enough to live ... I wouldn't go back to live over that life again." And others continued to criticize Italy with a clear choice in their mind: "I would never go back to live in Italy ... I don't see much improvement since I left and when I went in 1969 ... I don't consider myself as really Italian ... Life's too hard in Italy."

Few of those interviewed would seriously consider a return to their homeland. (Of all Italian immigrants to Canada in 1946–76, only 10 per cent went back.[33]) Those who returned and decided to stay were largely outnumbered by those who came back to Canada, even after a long stay in Italy. Their return to Canada was often enough to dissuade others, including those harbouring positive feelings for Italy, from following suit. At times, their criticism of Italy, even to strengthen their justification for returning to Canada, helped to project a distorted view of Italy. In time, it became such a stereotype that it was automatically repeated, even by those who had never been there or visited Italy: "I have no idea of what Italy is like ... I would never want to live there ... I love Canada; it is nice, has conveniences ... difference in lifestyles ... Canada is freer than Italy ... Italy is much stricter [and] there is nothing to do."

But contradictions were common, even among those who at first were quite certain about their choice: afterthoughts surfaced spontaneously, sometimes exposing a deep-seated, unclear "nostalgia," an uncertain state of mind or "that 'mid-wall'[34] condition," that characterizes all immigrants, and from which escape seems almost impossible (see chapter 3, especially note 22; chapter 5, "The Hardships"; chapter 15, "Conclusion").

HOMETOWN CHANGES AND THEIR EFFECTS

Reactions to Italy depended largely on not only when the visit took place but also the area visited. The towns and regions of origin of the Leamington Italians had undergone less development and progress. In the postwar boom years, many picturesque but isolated hilltop towns were abandoned. Many who visited Villa Canale found it worse off than when they had left it. They complained that the land was no longer cultivated. The young people had deserted the area and fled to the cities. Only the old people were left, and they were all "on pension."

It was a valid observation, particularly in Molise, which even in 1983 was a highly "subsidized" region of Italy.[35] But the situation was unfortunately belittled by the final jest about retired or injured people living on government subsidies. Even worse, it was turned into a vast generalization – "Everyone has a pension, and nobody works" – later applied not just to the town or region, but even to the whole of Italy. It was, of course, impossible for them to even consider going back. After enjoying the comforts of life in Canada, they couldn't even imagine how they had ever lived in the Villa Canale area or Upper Molise. And yet, even in that area, those who returned later witnessed a noticeable improvement: "There are more cars, the homes have better facilities, and people are able to enjoy more luxuries." But, in spite of the more recent experiences, it was the notion of those who had been or gone there earlier that often prevailed. From a distance, especially if no other area had been visited, the impression left by the hometown became a metaphor for the condition of the entire country.

Those returning to visit the province of Frosinone (Lazio), the area of origin of about 35 per cent of Leamington Italians, generally had better impressions. In spite of the devastation of the war (as exemplified by the levelling of the Abbey of Monte Cassino; chapter 7), it had progressed much faster than the Villa Canale area. The visitors found much more industry, factories, and activities. They too complained about the desertion of farms for more profitable factory work, and shrinking farmlands in favour of industrial centres. But they also observed that industry brought wealth to those who owned land, as well as to the workers, as evidenced by the many villas throughout the area. But for the returning immigrant, the changed landscape evoked not just admiration for material progress, but also regret for loss of the bucolic scenes of earlier, simpler days. Duplicating a feeling expressed in an Italian song – "There, where there was grass, now a city stands"[36] – one remembered sadly, "No one works the land ... The beautiful fields of Patrica have been used for building factories ... they were ruined." Though many criticized their town for remaining the same, immigrants frequently criticized them also for having changed too much, for making them similar to North America: industrialized.

Of the three areas from which most Leamington Italian immigrants came, the San Vito Lo Capo area in Sicily underwent the most striking change in recent years. Many visitors to their hometown found it transformed into a modern seaside resort by a dynamic tourist industry. The development had increased land and property value immensely, and upon returning many of them regretted having sold property that now might have "fetched a good dollar." Quite a few confessed that, if they had kept their property, they might have gone back to capitalize on the tourist trade by opening a hotel or restaurant, and built one of those expensive villas they saw everywhere. This sort of progress sometimes excited envy (and perhaps even anger at themselves and at the whole country for "forcing" them to emigrate), but pride and fascination seemed more common. The renewed hometown exerted a strong pull upon the returning immigrant. They fell in love with it again.

Many seriously entertained notions of returning to San Vito. A few still had property there and saw the possibility of financial gain and prosperity. They were also attracted again by the beauty and climate of Sicily. Some were already making plans to move back to their native town. The attraction and desire to return were further bolstered by the Italian regional policy of *rientro*: a program devised to give assistance to immigrants in their re-entry, resettlement, and investing in the *paese* of origin. Recent trips to Canada and to Essex County by mayors of the towns of the Gulf of Castellammare may have partly served to implement this policy. But they also provided an opportunity to re-establish a bridge, better communications, a base for further exchanges between Sicily and the immigrant group: the visits not only introduced the new

Sicily to the *paesani* abroad, but also encouraged the Sicilian-Canadian group to rediscover more solid cultural bases for their ethnic identity within the Canadian mosaic.[37]

It was not just the particular area visited, or how frequently and how recently, that influenced their reactions to Italy. The exploration of other parts of Italy beyond their hometowns also contributed to their level of awareness of the Old Country: "My family and I went to Italy in 1980. I feel younger each time I go there ... I begin a life that I remember when I was young ... We travelled around in Italy ... We were only in our hometown for ten days."

Comparisons and contrasts between these two conditioning realities, while causing mild forms of personality split in the individual, gave occasion for many arguments between the detractors and the defenders of the Old Country. It was not necessarily a debate between those who chose to stay in Canada and those who intended to return. In many cases the latter felt as much part of Canada as the former, and they resented being told to "love it or leave it." They were simply opposed to the more negative views about the "homeland." Their stand was that Italy was doing fine and steadily progressing, and no longer did "people from Italy ... need to emigrate ... They have everything there." Their arguments were based on personal experiences: "When I first went back, they looked up to me because I was Canadian ... Now they don't care if I'm Canadian or not ... They're happy to live in Italy ... Today even people from my own hometown don't want to come here ... Even if they don't have a lot of money, they don't care ... [and] some have more than I have here."

The statements alluded to an earlier phenomenon when immigrants returned to the still impoverished towns and flaunted their newfound wealth. In those days the return of a "rich *americano*" was an occasion to celebrate at his expense at the local café or *osteria* (wine shop). As years passed, the reverse became more common: the townspeople not only bought the drinks but sometimes ridiculed the "rich" relative or friend from "America," especially if they knew that he was not so rich after all, or they had more money than the visitor. Some Leamington Italians had an altogether different interpretation: "The people in Italy are jealous of the Italians here." Perhaps true, at times; but, rather than envious, the townspeople were often mockingly amazed by the "unrefined" manners and speech of the returning immigrants.

A small number of those interviewed offered as explanation, for the negative attitude toward Italy, the general lack of awareness of the many changes that had occurred in Italy in the intervening years: "Italians

who came here before me [1965] think Italy is bad because that's the
way they left it ... They don't realize that Italy has changed the same as
Leamington has."

THE VIEW OF CANADA

In the parallel debate on Canada, the views were just as varied, contradictory, and inconsistent: Canada was simultaneously *terra disabitata* (a
wasteland) and *paradiso* (heaven) (see chapter 8, "The Earliest Core Area:
Seacliff West"). Comparison between the style of life they were used to in
Italy and the experience in Canada was also quite natural. It began upon
setting foot in the new land (see chapter 2, "The Ill-Fated First Trip").
There was hardly ever a notion of the difficulty in comparing such diverse
countries as Canada and Italy. Since the early days it had always been
a subjective process: what touched them most personally became the
parameter for the worth of the country and for the comparison: "You
come here with a suitcase in your hand ... and then you can buy a car ...
then a bigger one ... You can have a full fridge, but people are never satisfied and want more ... People here don't take care of their looks as much
... Here, people become attached to money ... You have more opportunity
here, but you're not content with what you have." For many Italians in the
Leamington area, Canada was "a country of the future ... a new country
[with] many opportunities ... resourceful ... a safe country ... a land of
opportunity ... nowhere to go but up."

Some considered Canada the "best country in the world" for its "conveniences and comforts ... Everyone had a television here," and with
this, they sortied into vaster generalizations: "Canada is freer than Italy
... You can immigrate very easily ... find jobs easily ... Here, we are
all equal ... no difference between people in different social classes ...
People in Italy are more segregated ... lawyers and farmers can be distinguished ... In Canada, after everyone has washed and is dressed, there is
no distinction between different professions ... Although the intelligence
is different, people in Canada are treated equally ... [We] dislike this
attitude in Italy ... [where] lawyers don't associate with farmers."

In some descriptions, Canada emerged as a modern Eden (often echoing
views quite common among other Italian immigrants and Italians in Italy
in the 1950s):[38] "There is more rapid means of communication in Canada
... a little bit faster to get things done ... You don't have to bribe anyone
to get papers ... There is more order in Canada: it is free ... no violence
... no static ... I like the fairness, organization in Canada ... the calmness
and cleanliness of the country ... The government is more organized here."

But for the majority, the best reason by far for being in Canada was "money ... a better life for the worker ... better opportunity for material growth": "I enjoy living in this country since a person can save and make something of himself ... accomplish more, even if you come empty-handed ... You couldn't go to Italy and accumulate such wealth." The general praise sometimes extended not only to life in Canada but to the whole continent: "In Italy you eat, drink good ... but here you travel a lot. [You can] go to Montreal, Toronto, USA ... You see richness all over ... This you can't find in Italy ... Not even a millionaire in Italy eats like an average person here." The last statement was hardly reconcilable with their praise and pursuit of the Italian way of cooking and eating, or their criticism of Canadian "cuisine." But harder to dispute was their belief that Canada, more than Italy, had provided to many the opportunity to satisfy their basic needs: "Here, we're happy ... We have our home, work, family ... everything is here for us ... and to top it all off, this is the country where we have progressed."

However, just as many were less enthusiastic about Canada. Sometimes the negative side of the argument reached similar levels of misconception and fantasy that made Canada just as unrecognizable. For one thing, in their opinion, children have "less respect for parents ... in Canada," because "school changes [the children]," for lack of "rules and discipline ... and the presence of drugs in school. In these high schools, too much liberty ... sends the kids on a bad road" (see chapter 10, "The Family"). In Canada, they also felt, there were "too many ethnic groups ... so there's not as much equality and fraternity as in Italy" (and there seemed to be little awareness of the irony in both statements).

For some women, life in Canada was truly difficult: "*La vita è più dura qua per la donna*" (Life is harder here for the woman). In Italy, said a 1960s arrival, "the woman is a *signora*" (i.e., lives like a rich lady), "has more fun"; and another, who arrived in the 1950s from Sicily, felt that she had more occasions for entertainment there: "*mare ... amici ... piazza ... chiesa*" (sea ... friends ... square ... church). Some of them contradicted or even interrupted their husbands' praise of life in Canada: "Women here run to work ... They run back and run to cook ... Children are raised by the babysitter ... Husband and wife work ... different shifts ... have to work in Canada to get ahead ... more sacrifices made here ... not enough time for a *passeggiata* – a stroll ... always work, work, work." In one woman's case, and her husband agreed, even her general well-being was adversely affected by the new life in Canada: "She did not like Canada ... cannot get used to it. She does not feel healthy here ... Doctors were [puzzled] ... sent her to Italy ... there she felt good" (see chapter 14, "The Never-Ending 'Passage'" and note 2).

Il dio dollaro (the god of money, the almighty dollar) that so many worshipped and praised, and for which most came and stayed in Canada, was sometimes blasphemed. One disabled person observed painfully, "Here you can only make it in life if you are able to work," and questioned the quality of life: "*La vita canadese è troppo abbreviata, fredda e piena di preoccupazioni*" (Canadian life is too brief, cold, and full of worries); Canada ... always on the go ... busy, busy, busy ... [there is] no real entertainment here ... only drinking."

Another group saw Canada as "tough and pleasant ... There is a drive to do more ... We end up having more in Canada, but at the same time we spend less time enjoying it." They regretted that money and things had become more important than other needs, qualities, or values: there were perhaps "better wages as compared to Italy [but] Canada lacked *amicizia* [friendship]." Some observations were quite realistic: "I came in 1970 ... [Now] I see the very things that drove me from Italy ... lack of jobs, bad economy, strong unions ... beginning to take hold here in Canada, but I still believe that things get better before they get worse."[39]

So many diverse views might suggest only divisions, community fragmentation, the lack of unity. But variety and tensions did not prevent them from sharing their common origins and goals. There were also internal and external forces present that helped them retain a powerful sense of collectivity. As a result of the constant Italy-Canada juxtaposition itself, many were able to develop more balanced outlooks: "Canada and Italy ... you have to work in both places ... When I first came, not everyone had a refrigerator and stove ... In twenty-seven years, things changed here, just as they have in Italy ... I would like to work here and make money, then live in Italy."

The closing statement suggested a good solution, if it could ever be implemented. What emerged was at least a better understanding of the two realities, and the dilemma was sometimes resolved in acceptance: "We like Italy for vacations ... My family, life, business are here in Canada now ... It would be hard for me to go back to Italy ... I would have to start all over again ... There I would have no house, no job, and no friends ... no I won't return ... My life in Canada has been a good one."

In the younger generation, the choice presented no mental struggle between "here" and "there," and the reasons for it often no longer existed: "I have no hope of returning there to live ... My parents have passed away ... I'm already established here"; "We both came here when we were young ... There's no reason for us to go back." The views represented different solutions to the dilemma. This healthy combination or reconciliation of the two realities was a great benefit to the individual, family, and community. The balance offered the strongest bases for a dynamic ethnic identity.

LANGUAGE AWARENESS, EDUCATION, AND IDENTITY

Opera naturale è ch'uom favella (Nature so fashioned man that he should speak)

Paradiso, XXVI, 130[40]

The Logos can express itself only in words

E.R. Curtius[41]

Language is not only the man but also the world.

Octavio Paz[42]

Language, "mankind's most important invention" and its noblest attribute, is said to be the vehicle of culture, thought, and our whole being. It is closely related to the development of one's personality and inextricably tied to one's perception of life and reality. It is our link with tradition and society, an instrument of solidarity with others and of self-fulfilment. Yet it can also be a double-edged sword that, if misused, can cause havoc.[43] Where the language spoken by a particular group is not part of the larger milieu, it can be a blunt instrument of confusion and division. In time, it may even disappear with disastrous effects on the family, especially on that mutually enriching relationship between grandparents and grandchildren, as a Leamington grandfather lamented: "Our grandchildren speak very little Italian ... I'm quite hurt because we can't communicate that well with them."

For all immigrants, language represents the first emotionally disruptive encounter. For the majority of Leamington Italians, overcoming the "linguistic shock" and then learning the new language remained a constant struggle in their attempt to adjust to the new environment. The language barrier was almost insurmountable, especially for the pioneers; the choice between preserving Italian and acquiring English was made most difficult by circumstances and their own educational background and opportunities. Initially, not only distance from their mother country, but isolation and Canadian public opinion, especially in the pre–Second World War period, favoured and encouraged integration or outright assimilation. Few Italians were sufficiently versed in English to act as interpreters. In the workplace, their inability to understand or communicate with workers or employers was often the cause of unpleasant situations. Often they preferred a workplace where communication was more difficult rather than an environment where they could speak Italian (which often led to suspicion and resentment against them), or where there were English-speaking Italians less willing to help than some Canadians (see chapter 9). In other words, some chose to be where they could more quickly turn the disadvantage into an advantage: "I was glad that I was given the opportunity to work with Canadians ... I learned the language this way."

The inability to understand or communicate was a frequent embarrassment. When help was provided to later immigrants by relatives or friends, it encouraged dependency on others, sometimes permanently. Many, especially women, depended (as some still do) on their children for translation in their activities, such as shopping or visiting the doctor: "I depended on my daughter, so I never learned English." Such situations encouraged isolation of some members of the family, and an inferiority complex in the group as a whole.

Many, however, realized that "to get further ahead and feel comfortable" in their adopted land, they would have to learn the language quickly. But they no sooner enrolled in night language courses at the high school than they dropped out. The mixture of nationalities in the class and lack of genuine interest among many students made learning difficult, and the classes not very productive. The students' tendency to ridicule anyone who made a mistake discouraged them, and they had little time for education, since the main focus of their lives was to bring home a good wage and make ends meet. They were unwilling to tolerate the frustrations in these classes, and after a few sessions many stopped attending. Ironically, practical, basic needs were obstacles to formal training in the skills that might have made those needs easier to satisfy. For many, English remained a language to be "picked up" by frequenting Canadians and avoiding Italians; and this also had an adverse effect on their retention of Italian: "I pushed myself to learn the [English] language ... School would have helped me, but I did not have time ... My wife began to learn English when she worked away from Italians."

Many later immigrants who worked primarily with Italians never felt the urgent need to learn English. They spoke only broken English until years later, when at least some of them started to "pick it up" from their children: "I was very eager to learn the English language ... I would read with my younger daughter."

However, some of them did not wait to "pick up" the language. They adopted other methods to master the language: "I taught myself, using a dictionary, to read books ... I learned with others and watching television." For a few, prior knowledge of English or another language besides Italian provided better employment opportunities. One Italian who had worked in Germany for several years easily found a job in Windsor with a German-speaking employer. Another who "knew how to speak a little English before [he] came" had fewer problems adjusting. Because he had intended "to go to England, [he had] studied English in school in Switzerland [where] the union had made schools" for such purpose. Those who understood the importance of knowing the language from the beginning, and acted accordingly, usually also developed quite a different outlook.

Generally, anyone who had come to Canada before the age of thirty had little problem learning English. The younger, unmarried men had other advantages: they "learned English by dating Canadian girls." But for the older immigrants, it remained an almost impossible task: only a few learned more than the basics. Most regretted not having been able to learn it better; and without the language they never felt totally comfortable in the Canadian environment: "My wife ... always home ... no speak English at all ... never go out ... I do all shopping ... we in strange country ... will never be Canadian."

It was primarily their inability to speak English that kept nourishing their desire to move back to Italy. A few confessed that if they could speak English well, they would never consider returning to Italy to live. But since it was so hard for them to communicate well in this country, there was always a yearning to return to a place they could converse with their neighbours and feel part of it. Ironically, they also knew that even in Italy they could no longer feel totally at ease. The immigrants' predicament was that they belonged neither here nor there, in a confused state of being due mainly to language.

Many who visited their hometowns experienced that not-so-kind attitude Italians reserved for returning immigrants, particularly for their antiquated dialect or odd blend of Italian and English, conspicuously in contrast not only to the more "modernized" local speech, but also to the more widely used standard Italian, which, even in rural areas, was increasingly becoming a sign of education or sophistication. The immigrant, embarrassed by the teasing, even in his country and town of origin, often had, if not told, to "keep your mouth shut."[44] Sometimes their predicament was revealed with a mixture of sadness and mirth: "I never learned English and I forgot Italian."

The Canadian-educated immigrant children were generally able to escape their parents' linguistic limbo but often faced other problems, particularly in the earlier period. In an age of modest ethnocultural sensitivity – light years away from multicultural equality, Heritage Language and Cultural Enrichment Programs, remedial English, or English as a Second Language training – all immigrants were pressured into "Canadianizing" themselves, and fast. Teachers and schools, besides instructing the children in the three "Rs," were to serve as well this particular purpose in earlier days.[45]

After his first day in school, Domenic Magri (1927), who spoke mostly Italian, reported his teacher's advice: "You must learn English. This is your country now. No more Italian." The "just advice," usually heeded by the parents who, like Saveria Magri, learned English themselves by helping their children, became often an urgent need to overcome the problem in order to benefit the whole family. Learning to speak like Canadian children often meant avoiding the name-calling, derision, and practical jokes to which the "foreign" children were often subjected at the hands of their Canadian schoolmates (see chapter 13).

On the other hand, among early immigrant children, the urgency to hide one's language and culture, particularly in the late 1930s and 1940s when to be Italian also meant being an enemy as well as undesirable, sometimes caused harmful psychological effects: repressed anger and withdrawal, or outright scorn and anger, which did not favour a balanced ethnicity. The resulting suppression of the knowledge of their first language also signified the loss of an essential resource at the personal and national levels. The situation of many children in pre- and postwar periods was not unlike Domenic Magri's: first he "knew Italian and little English," while today he "only understands Italian, but answers in English."

LEVEL OF EDUCATION:
THE IMPORTANCE OF KNOWING ENGLISH

The language anomaly, partly the result of the limited and unequal success of the efforts of the family and the club to retain the original language, was further enhanced by the difference in the educational levels among the generations: the trend in the younger group was to complete high school and sometimes college and university. On the other hand, though the majority of the older immigrants claimed to have had three to five years of school in Italy, a large group had only one to three years, and very few had special training beyond the fifth year (e.g., in the armed forces).

Similarly, their Canadian education experience was relatively limited. Of those interviewed in the early 1980s, 19 per cent (12 per cent of the men, 7 per cent of the women) attended elementary school; 10 per cent (6 per cent of the men, 4 per cent of the women) reached the secondary level; 5 per cent (3 per cent of the men, 2 per cent of the women) pursued a post-secondary education; and 17 per cent (14 per cent of the men and 3 per cent of the women) attended night school in Canada. In sum, 49 per cent of all immigrant Italians to the Leamington area never attended school in Canada, day or night classes. Since night classes were irregularly attended and often abandoned after a few weeks, the total of Leamington Italians without Canadian educational training reached 66 per cent.

The level of education of the Leamington Italians, assuming that 15 per cent in the secondary and post-secondary levels obtained their diplomas or degrees, was well below the 1981 percentage of all Italians in Canada with certificates, diplomas, or degrees (48 per cent). It was still well below that level with the inclusion of the 17 per cent who attended night school, assuming they had an Italian certificate, diploma, or degree. The statistics seemed to lend further support to community emphasis on material self-advancement rather than on educational or cultural pursuits, which were made difficult or impossible at times by the unfavourable social climate, as Marius Ingratta's case indicated (see chapter 9, "The Professions").

Nevertheless, as was observed by young people themselves who were usually critical of the lifestyles of the older generations, their outlook was not defined only by "their homes, cars, property – all material things." They were not educated in the strictly formal sense, but they were not unknowing; or as someone observed, generally immigrants may have been unschooled but not unwise: especially among earlier immigrants, life was their school, experience their education, trials their teachers.[46] Nor were they contrary to education; even though in their frequent condemnation of the Italian social class structure, there was a rejection of that higher or formal education, that did not equate with fairness or justice in human beings or in society. And "culture" – often associated with "power" or those who governed and were partly the cause of their problems – appeared to them as superficial, meaningless window dressing and almost devoid of social consciousness or compassion.[47] And yet some of them, guided by hindsight, wished they had gone to school to learn English or had "stuck it out" when they had the chance. They always felt the "gap" that their lack of education had made in their lives; and education in their mind was often associated with language and the ability to speak: "I still have difficulty speaking English ... never went to school ... difficult to speak to other workers ... Should force immigrants to learn English."

The last recommendation, both a revelation and a legacy, further illustrated the irony and paradox of their condition. Experience and pain had also brought to some of them an awareness that is supported by facts: Legislation, it has been sufficiently stated, cannot completely substitute education in solving social ills; compulsory education is not as effective as voluntary education or self-discipline in building an individual citizen or a society. Nevertheless, though not advisable perhaps as a mandatory statement, as a strong suggestion it is most appropriate and timely for the whole Canadian society, and in particular for the entire Italian Canadian group in the land. In Canada there are still four to five million illiterates. According to Statistics Canada (1981 Census), with respect to schooling in Canada, the Italian ethnocultural group was well below the national average and below all other groups except the Native Peoples.

However alarming or ominous the statistics, the awareness gained by at least some of the Leamington Italians was quite enlightening: their painful realization of the gap in their education and consequently in their life, as well as their recognition of the importance of language training, while applicable to society at large, constituted also a significant bequest to their younger generations, a guide in the development of a more meaningful Italian Canadian identity.

ITALIAN LANGUAGE AND *ITALIANITÀ*

And this Italian language of ours is dear to us because in it we recognize ourselves as of one and the same homeland and of one and the same tradition ... that is of a civilization which perpetuates itself through the centuries and which seems inexhaustible.

S. Battaglia and V. Pernicone,
Grammatica italiana[48]

The question of the language of origin was partly a "mirror image" of the Leamington Italians' relationship with the new language; but, by its very nature, it was also more complex. Most of the older generation of Leamington Italians often recognized the equal value of knowing the ancestral language and the language of the new land. Italian was generally regarded as an important component of their identity, of their Canadian ethnicity, at least not less than their other traditions. On the other hand, they hardly knew it; they mostly spoke regional dialects; out of necessity they often neglected it or abandoned it, and very rarely rediscovered and nourished it. Their position regarding the standard Italian language was marked by a paradox – not unlike that of Italians in Italy through the ages.

"The formation of an Italian, if not national awareness ... originated at the literary level."[49] Divided Italy had been united by one language from the Alps to Sicily more than five centuries before its political unification. For centuries, to be or feel Italian meant basically to know the language and its literature, which was very early placed on the same level of the classical – Greek and Latin – literatures, especially outside Italy. Since the sixteenth century, the language that had been produced by a fragmented land gave that same land recognition, prestige and "power." Italian language and "culture enjoyed enormous influence all over Europe. War and commerce were far from being the only reasons for the circulation of knowledge." Italy and its civilization became widely known also through some of those men and women whose *italianitá* Harney doubted, as clearly pointed out by the language historian Migliorini:

> Italians left their native land to offer their services to foreign rulers (Columbus, Vespucci, Caboto, Leonardo, Cellini). Italian princesses married and went abroad (Caterina de' Medici to France, Bona Sforza to Poland). Ecclesiastics and laymen who had renounced Roman Catholicism went into exile (Ochino, Vergerio, Morata, the Socini, the Burlamacchi, Alberico Gentile, Citolini, Michelangelo Florio, Pietro Martire Vermigli) ... Petrarchism spread. So did Italian metrical forms (the sonnet, *terza rima*). Contemporary Italian authors (Castiglione, Bandello, Machiavelli) were translated and read abroad. To know Italian became an accomplishment prized in the highest circles (Charles V, Francis I, Elizabeth I). In these circumstances the first grammars of Italian written in other European languages found a ready market.[50]

Moreover, foreign students, scholars, and individuals in Italian universities or travelling in Italy for study or pleasure, as well as Italian books, in translation or in the original, and particularly opera librettos, all contributed to its spread in France, Austria, Germany, and England, especially in the "musical century" (eighteenth), in spite of the hegemony of French language and civilization in Europe. "Nor was Italian known only in European countries. It enjoyed prestige also in non-European countries on the shores of the Mediterranean and the Levant." By the beginning of the nineteenth century, Italian had established a sphere of influence, "a peaceful linguistic domination" in a part of the same area the ancient Romans called *Mare Nostrum* (Our Sea): it was understood, spoken, and used from Corsica and North Africa to Asia Minor.

Yet, when Italy became a united country, a Mediterranean "power," her linguistic dominion disappeared. The paradox became particularly clear "at the dawn ... of unification": the Italy that had a "language greater than the state" (*Una lingua più grande dello Stato*), appeared as a "nation without a language" (*Una nazione senza lingua*). The very same language that had given Italians their first sense of unity, identity, and history, as well as artistic and intellectual leadership, was at the same time the cause of their divisions. The so-called *questione della lingua*, the Italian common language debate, dating back to Dante's time and a full-scale controversy in the sixteenth century, had been an issue limited to a relatively few intellectuals; and it had left such a linguistic chasm that one of the first tasks of the new state was a dramatic search for "unity of language ... as an important symbol of national unity." There were deep divisions between the language of culture and the language of the people, between the written and the spoken language(s); many spoke only dialects and some, including writers, preferred French. Clearly, the identity of Italy with language was more common outside than inside Italy.[51]

Italians abroad, often out of need, took the lead in bridging the gap between Italian language/culture and Italian identity, between writer and public. Since the eighteenth century, Italian writers had been confronted with the problem of choosing a language to express themselves in and be understood. Each found a unique solution and audience, at times by opting to use another language or quite often Italian: Baretti's work for the London "Italianate" middle class was in Italian; Lorenzo Da Ponte, Mozart's librettist, keeping in mind his American students of Italian, published his *Memorie* (Memoirs) in New York in Italian (1807–1830). Though "it may seem paradoxical, but it is not," commented Romano, for the Italians outside Italy "it was easier to find the solution." It seemed "as if one needed to go outside Italy to feel finally Italian."[52]

While the newly formed Italy debated and searched for a "proper" Italian language to unite all Italians, the Italians abroad often found in their ancestral language of culture a sound foundation for their identity – a foundation that, at times, seemed undermined by the language discussions taking place in Italy. Among the linguists, sociologists, or other "oracles" of modern living present at a 1978 debate in Italy, one with little concern for Italian literary traditions and cultural values went as far as declaring himself "all for abolishing the language of Dante, Boccaccio, and Moravia." The idea didn't fail, as usual, to appear in North American English-language newspapers, and sometimes as a headline: "Italy Ponders Switching to Use of English."[53] The contrary view, understandably, was presented by an Italian who had lived and worked abroad for some years: "The only thing I like about Italy," he said, "is the language."

However preposterous both idea and headline, they must have pleased budget-conscious school administrators or governments financing ancestral language classes. But they surely exasperated teachers and community leaders who for decades have been promoting Italian in North American schools and society, not only as a useful vehicle of communication and of one of the world's richest cultures, but also as a language long recognized among the moulders of Western life. To many, the suggestion appeared irresponsible and insidious: almost another betrayal, in a long list of them, of Italian communities outside Italy, an injury to their work and to their "Italianness."

The report, relating to a similar debate held in 1984 – that in the last decades the Italian language had "transformed" into a "multi-language" or into "as many and diverse languages as the number of Italian regions"[54] (if not more) – was not a revelation to many Italians outside Italy: a similar phenomenon of language change, "fragmentation" or differentiation according to local situations had long been taking place in the Italian communities abroad. In some cases the transformation has been much more distinct than in Italy, as exemplified also by the development of *Italese*, or *Italiese*, formed by crossing English, Italian, and/or regional dialects, or by attaching Italian endings to English words (e.g., job *jobba*; chapter 3, "What Price Liberty").

For a long time the Italian immigrants had felt or lived through what the Italian scholars in Italy were just discovering. The Italians outside Italy, as in the case of the Leamington Italians, disconnected from the everyday, living, and changing language and/or dialect of birth, and interacting within both an Italian and Canadian diversity, had been experiencing: the influence and interference of other dialects and languages, the changes in their speech, the struggle, confusion, and dilemmas related to their ancestral language retention, its loss or rediscovery.

The stands of the Leamington Italians on the ancestral language resembled solutions reached by Italian writers of the past: some abandoned Italian completely for English (like Casanova who chose to publish his *Memoirs* in French); others learned English and maintained Italian (like Baretti who used both English and Italian according to the situation);

still others alternated English, Italian, and regional dialect (like Goldoni, with French, Italian, and Venetian). The few who, wishing to "polish" their Italian after years of speaking only dialect, began to learn the standard Italian "language of culture," especially after a trip to Italy.

Naturally, unlike the very learned and generally wealthy Italian writers in Europe, the Leamington Italian immigrants seldom had the opportunities or means to renew the link, physically or spiritually, with the land and/or the language of origin. The obstacles to their language and culture retention and development were difficult to overcome: on the one hand, practical needs and material goals, then the pressure to become Canadians and appear less Italian, as well as the need to learn English; and on the other, uncertainty about the role of language in human affairs and their lack of an adequate educational base. Their low level of formal education rendered their task – of recovering and imparting that knowledge – much greater than the efforts required to transmit the daily customs. But all the other factors contributed also to the diminishing use of Italian in the family and the community, as well as to much of their confusion and basic dilemma.

THE LANGUAGE RETENTION/DEVELOPMENT DILEMMA

> *Un populu diventa poviru e servu quannu ci arrobanu a lingua*
> *addutata di patri*: è persu pi sempri
> A people becomes poor, a slave when it is robbed of the language
> of its ancestors: it is lost forever.
>
> Ignazio Buttitta

The use of "Italian," of the regional languages or dialects (mainly Molisan, *Ciociaro*, i.e., southern Lazio, and Sicilian) was widespread among the older Leamington Italians, within the family and the community. Parents stated that they wished their children to speak Italian at home so that they would retain the language. Thus, they spoke to them in Italian. But often the younger people, while understanding Italian, had difficulty speaking it, and answered in English. Even within the family then, the language of origin did not always create a bond. Sometimes it was a source of problems, ranging from total breakdown in communication ("I lost the Italian language ... I could hardly communicate with my parents"), to impositions on the choice of spouse ("It is important to me that my children marry an Italian because we will speak the same language").

Since the early days, the question for everyone has been whether or not the Italian language should be maintained. The answer, far from uniform, was further complicated by the contrast between regional dialect, normally spoken in the home, and the standard Italian learned in the schools. The level of knowledge or use of the Italian dialects, as teachers and students of standard Italian know by experience, can hinder the acquisition of standard Italian. But the dialect can also become a stepping stone in the learning/teaching process. The more frequent use of dialect than of standard Italian in the Leamington Italian families, presented a major obstacle to retention of any form of the ancestral language. It often led to the renunciation of the dialect and its replacement by English as a more convenient language of communication, a sort of lingua franca that helped eliminate possible confusion: "My children don't speak Italian very well ... If I can avoid speaking Italian, I do ... English is easier for me because of the different dialects ... It's too confusing with all the dialects involved ... My husband has one dialect ... I have another."

In the few cases where the distinction was made between dialect and standard Italian, there was also an awareness the importance of learning the standard language: "My children don't speak Italian ... They know our dialect ... I speak dialect to my children, and I think this is bad because they don't learn the standard Italian ... I would like my children to speak the standard Italian." Some parents, however, took steps toward finding a remedy by sending their children to Italian classes: "My oldest takes Italian classes on Saturdays ... my children understand our Italian dialect." They were anxious that their children learn the "proper" Italian to complement the dialect spoken at home: "My children went to Italian classes when they were conducted on Saturday mornings ... They understand a lot of Italian ... [but] can only speak a few words."

But, unsatisfactory results often led to frustration among the children and disinterest among the parents. Besides, it was not always the children who did not wish to learn Italian. At times parents felt that learning Italian was not important; and such a view served, in turn, to both justify the younger people's inability to speak the language and their unwillingness to learn it, as well as to render easier the older people's acceptance of a sad but inevitable reality: "My grandchildren don't speak too much Italian ... I think that English is more important to them anyway." Where both languages were used, it was difficult to ascertain whether the family was enriched or further split by such practice: "I speak Italian to my husband and English to my children."

The Leamington Italians, like other Italian-Canadian communities, also developed their own brand of *Italiese* – a mixture of "bastardized"

Italian, bits of dialect, and "badly chewed" parts of English – to which some were opposed: "I don't like Italian spoken with English thrown in ... [*Si fa*] *brutta figura* – it presents a poor picture of ourselves ... [But] everyone has learned to understand Italian mispronunciation."

The linguistic mix, a source of popular jokes and humour (see chapter 11), has been the subject of frequent academic study and codification. But less attention has been given to the possible related psychological effects of such linguistic overlapping and interferences on the individual, and to the consequent confusion and tensions in the group – such as causing its users to appear socially inferior, if not illiterate or by the mockery of visitors to Italy. On the other hand, public criticism and disgrace became themselves incentives to learn Italian, or to encourage their children and grandchildren to take Italian at school so that, as one pointed out, "our relatives won't think anymore that in our family we're stupid."

The diverse reactions to the language of origin, usually varying according to first, second, or third generation, seemed to reflect, some widely held notions and/or scholarly research. Some views seemed to confirm the findings of sociologists on the fortunes of the native language among the immigrant families and communities: the first generation retains it as the main means of communication, the second abandons it or rejects it, and the third tends to rediscover it (see chapter 15, "Vittorio: The Young Generation's Search for Meaning," "The Rediscovery of Italian Heritage").

The views of at least one group of Italian families seemed to offer further proof to a question about multiculturalism: the relationship of language, culture, and ethnicity. Jean Burnet, a professor of sociology who, as research associate of the Royal Commission on Bilingualism and Biculturalism, took part in the preparation of *Book IV* of the Commission's Report, more recently wrote, "The assertion that members of a cultural group are united by a common tongue also gives rise to problems. Are all of the speakers of French or German or English or Chinese united by a common tongue and therefore sharers of a culture? ... What about people who share an ethnic identity but speak mutually incomprehensible temporal or regional dialects or even languages, such as, for example, *those from different parts of Italy*, or for that matter, those who have retained and those who have lost their ancestral tongue?"[55]

And while using the dialect within the family, some understood its limitations and encouraged their children to learn standard Italian. They recognized the importance of knowing Italian, as well as other languages, not just to re-establish a more meaningful connection with their origins, but to strengthen the family and the group and to enrich the individual. This view, though expressed by a minority, seemed also to coincide with the answer that professor Burnet herself offered for her question about the more general Canadian situation: "Knowing more than one language means having more than one perspective, more than one intellectual tradition upon which to draw: a valuable asset for everyone, an indispensable one for a scholar."[56]

In the variety of their declarations of intention and of practices, two opposing positions were delineated: on the one hand, many of them believed that their "children [did not] need to learn Italian [to] live here." Quite naturally the children of that group of immigrants went a step further and considered "not important that kids know about Italian heritage ... I don't try to instill Italian customs in my children ... I want them to be Canadians ... I didn't feel really Italian and I'm not patriotic either."

In their view, becoming a Canadian seemed exclusive: there could be no place in it for any aspect of their parents' heritage. But in rejecting the language, they were deprived of the main link with tradition, the main vehicle for its transmission. Among them, the tendency seemed to be assimilation rather than integration. On the other hand, there was a movement within the community to reversing that tendency: Numerous families indicated by their example that a balanced ethnicity was possible to achieve by becoming more familiar with both the native and adopted "homelands."

But a third position was suggested by Domenic Magri (just a child at arrival), when he stated that he had lost the use of the Italian language, but not the "Italian feeling." This "Italian feeling" that is not predicated on knowledge of the ancestral language offers another glimpse into the Italian reality, that there have long been powerful bonds among Italians, in spite of the absence (in earlier times) of a national state; the distance from Italy (in more recent times); the centuries of Italian division and diversification; and, therefore, in spite of what Burnet hastily defined as "mutually incomprehensible ... regional dialects." Although the Leamington Italians themselves indicated that their regional dialects at times caused difficulty in communication or confusion, they seldom doubted their fundamental affinity based both on language and "Italian feeling." The fact that they often chose English to communicate seems quite normal; and it was not simply to reduce or overcome their "linguistic" difficulties but also because English is the language of the place they chose to live in.

On the nature of the "mutually incomprehensible ... regional dialects" there's also more to be said: the observation about Italy is not entirely correct (as the Italian film director Lina Wertmüller has also illustrated in some of her movies, which introduce protagonists who speak Italian dialects even as far removed and different as those of Piedmont, Bologna, Naples, and Sicily, and who, after a brief initial contrast, seem to reach almost total communication).[57] What the movies show, among other things, is that the matrix of all Italian languages or dialects is basically Latin, and that in spite of much differentiation and different influences (French on Piedmontese, Arabic on Sicilian) Italians can still communicate amongst themselves without the use of the standard language of culture (which, after all, can be said to be none other than the "dialect" of Tuscany that simply had better fortune than the others).

The centrality of language in Italian sentiment, in *italianità*, in the psyche of the Italian, and the same paradox of the standard language that seems to both unite and divide Italy and the Italians, may be just as difficult for a North European or North American to understand as is difficult for Italians to understand fully the depth of attachment, say, the English have to the their monarch. The Italians' concept of "unity in diversity," of affinity and division, seems foreign to the North American mentality, which is inclined more to the "rule by majority" than to the "rule by the consent" of all minorities, or by compromise (especially evident in the twentieth century in the political arena, e.g., a one-party majority government – Canada – does not seem to offer more stability than a five-party coalition government resulting from negotiation and compromise – Italy). In brief, in spite of confusion created by dialects, the closeness was not fundamentally affected, also because of the affinity of the dialects of the two major community groups – Molisani and *Ciociari* or about 85 per cent of total (see chapter 1, "A Colony with Common Ties").

Nevertheless, beyond the two clearly opposing stands, the issue of ancestral language and culture seemed characterized by tension, polarization, and conflict, and particularly by the "battle" between English and Italian, in which the native language increasingly lost ground, in spite of many indications of a return to it; the more they fulfilled the desire to become more fluent in English, the more they encroached on the emotional urgency to safeguard Italian and/or dialect. Their ethnic pride, evident in their treatment of food and eating, appeared to be inconsistent with their confusion about the retention of language, which was the root of many difficulties within the family and the community, in their search for an Italian or ethnic identity.

LANGUAGE, CULTURE (I.E., CUSTOMS), AND ETHNICITY

Each mother tongue teaches its users a way of seeing and feeling the world, and of acting in the world, that is quite unique.

M. McLuhan[58]

A common knowledge of the standard language is a necessity ... a precondition for democracy in today's Italy. No educational efforts should be spared to insure that every Italian acquires a firm command of the national language. Yet, the great variety of Italian dialects forms a cultural wealth one does not like to see disappear altogether. Some of the dialects ... even have developed literatures of their own, which ... should not be neglected or forgotten.

G.P. Clivio, 1979[59]

In the absence of an Italian church, and apart from the limited role of the grocery store and similar establishments, the two main vehicles for transmitting their "culture" to their descendants remained the family and, after 1964, the Roma Club. The two institutions had a positive impact on the younger generations. The family imparted to the children some aspects of their customs, especially those related more intimately to their daily life: culinary and marriage practices, values pertaining to public behaviour, and ethical standards (drinking, drugs, sex, work; see chapter 10).

The period of arrival and their age did not always determine how well culture or customs were retained in the family or community. There seemed to be just as many from the first generation as from the second or third generation who did not value the continuation of many customs, and vice versa. According to them, some of the Italian customs "should have been left in Italy." "I think my children are more Canadian ... My kids won't wear black for a long time, like my mother was wearing black for the death of her sister ... Italian customs are more strict than Canadian ones [with respect to] funerals, wearing black, baptisms." Some old folkways became insignificant when shedding them removed an obstacle to better understanding between generations and more harmony with the Canadian way of life.

Nevertheless, the majority of the Leamington Italians who arrived in the late 1940s "tried to instill Italian values" in their children, especially those related to the family: "Marriage is important; kids are important [and to] love one another." They also believed that their "children should learn the culture and language of Italy ... The heritage should be passed on ... If one loses his heredity, he loses his identity."

Among those who came in the 1950s and 1960s as well as among the children of the 1940s arrivals, there were mixed feelings and uncertainty. With them, many "Italian customs have been modified." "I hope to teach my children the traditions ... [but] with my children's generations, big weddings, the huge parties for baptism will disappear."

A few who arrived in the late 1950s were selective in the customs to be transmitted. Among the "Italian customs" excluded were the "strictness within the family," particularly the practice that "women stay at home, while men work ... I want my children to know about my heritage ... It is important for everyone to know about their backgrounds ... I don't want to be as strict as my parents ... I don't like all the Italian customs ... don't care for the big Italian weddings, etc."

Frequently the "heritage" that children remembered being passed on to them were customs associated with weddings, baptisms, or other occasions for huge parties, but particularly those connected with food – making sausage, bread, pizza, wine, and prosciutto (Italian ham cured by drying). Even though the former were deemed less inconsequential than the latter, they were all retained: "as for food, we're strictly Italian, and as for family ties [and] wedding customs, we're typically Italian as well."

It was, in fact, this close linking of their Italian self-identity to a few customs that tended to confuse, make tenuous, even threaten the family ties, and more generally their *italianità* or ethnicity. Their seeing themselves as "strictly Italian" mainly for their food seemed to be contradicted by their outlook toward language in general (i.e., English) and their language of origin in particular – standard or dialect. Their experience with language was complex. Particularly as a result of their limited formal education, they were uncertain about the role of language in the formation of the individual and the perpetuation of culture and traditions. Their argument was that if one could get by, even make good, with a few words or gestures, it was all one needed; after all, the notorious catch phrase, "Do you want good grammar or good taste?" is a reflection of a widespread misconception. Today's society, overwhelmed by the rhetoric of computer literacy and lulled in the technological panacea, has been steadily moving away from language training long emphasized by enlightened educators as the essential element of a well-rounded human being and as the foundation of a true humanity: "Language and personality development are closely related in children, as are language and mental development."[60] Language is at the very heart of one's total identity:

Language is the tool and product of all human society ... the indispensable vehicle of all human knowledge ... the basic foundation of all human cooperation, without which no civilization is possible ... All human records ... the accumulated experience of the race ... transmitted from one individual, one generation, one era, one racial group to another appear in some linguistic form ... Even those records which are nonlinguistic in the ordinary sense of the word ... must be translated into terms of language to be fully understood ... language is the transmitter of thought ... the conveyor, interpreter, and shaper of man's social doings. It is all-pervasive.[61]

The fundamental element of all Leamington Italian immigrants was language. Yet, among most of them, the ancestral tongue was not as tenaciously pursued as Italian family cooking traditions. Thus, a change in the rapport with the ancestral language directly determined other traditions, inevitably affected one's relationship with them. If language is the first shaper of experience, "speech as the expression of personality, and ordinary language as exploration of reality,"[62] then the loss of their dialects further removed or completely separated the younger generation from a sense of intimacy with the family and traditions. The children could not fully appreciate the effort expended in keeping those customs alive, the obsession with Italian home cooking.

In order to illustrate the primacy of language in human affairs, a linguist used food and eating as an appropriate example. He proposed an experiment for all to attempt: if language is not important, he challenged, try preparing a meal or eating without first saying exactly in your mind what you are going to prepare or eat. Saying it means being able to do it, and, above all, knowing it. The Leamington Italians considered cooking basic to preservation of the family and of identity but paid less attention to the other very important part of the human equation – language.

Knowledge of a language or a dialect is not necessarily a prerequisite for the enjoyment of a particular cuisine. But it can make an ordinary occasion more pleasant, turn it into a cultural or aesthetic experience. Conversely, even a small amount of curiosity to know the name and origin of the dish leads to an encounter with that language, country, and people. The point is made to emphasize the close relationship of the two human functions in general, and the importance of the awareness of this relationship in particular situations. In all the ethnocultural communities, the neglect or disappearance of languages or dialects that once held them together, besides being a great loss in itself, has adverse effects on the family and the entire community.

In the particular case of the Leamington Italian community where food and eating held a central place in the family tradition, the preservation of the dialect seemed essential: not just because the dialect is in its own right a language, but primarily because of its close connection with the Italian home-cooking traditions; and so much more because, as Hazan pointed out, "Italian cooking ... actually doesn't exist ... The cooking of Italy is really the cooking of its regions." It was, therefore, the local dialect or the regional language that first shaped it and gave it concrete form, the name of its dishes and ingredients; it was also through the regional language that it was transferred to the standard Italian to become part of the common heritage of all Italians.

Losing either language simply meant being severed from the fertile tradition, the "living organism," that produced the dishes; becoming less familiar with their intrinsic meaning or cultural value (e.g., why lamb at Easter or pork at Christmas time!): it meant being disconnected, even though one could, indeed, still enjoy the dishes when prepared by others. Without the original language, the tendency became stronger among the children to seek foods that were easier to say or imagine, or that a more familiar language made available or subconsciously suggested; and nothing today seems to be made more appealing, by the popular and uniform language of advertising, than fast foods. Neglect of the ancestral dialect may have deprived the family of readily available means, at least at first, to strengthen that important family tradition of conviviality; it may also have deprived some of its members of a great deal more in the long run.

The Italians' preference for Italian cooking stemmed from a most natural desire for familiar tastes, and simultaneously from a firm belief in its beneficial effects. Even the simplest Italian meal combines pleasure and goodness, not just for its variety but for its careful balance of the most natural ingredients. The first course itself satisfies the most diverse tastes, diets, and needs, if prepared and served properly (*al dente*, at the right consistency, neither hard nor mushy; above all, not cut, crushed, or smothered; nor eaten, as many improperly do, with bread). The pasta dish is what especially distinguishes a cook and an Italian meal.

The second course, as the ancient saying suggested, can be taken "with measure from either realm of nature," land or water – meat or fish: a vast assortment of both (not just chicken, but various types of fowl, from turkey to pigeon; not just beef and pork, but rabbit, lamb, boar, even sheep; not just "ordinary" fish, but squid and eel); similarly, prepared in a quantity of ways, but always with simple spices, wine, or herbs, and never smothered especially by garlic, which should be present to titillate and not "violate" the palate. Accompanying the meat or fish are appropriate and seasonal vegetables, not just the familiar ones, but even those some consider "exotic" (artichokes, eggplants, dandelions); and not just lettuce but mixed salad, prepared simply with the right proportions of oil and vinegar, and preferably served not before but toward the end of the meal (to help digestion).

It is the second course that is usually eaten with bread, often homemade or freshly baked; and the entire meal is graced with a glass or two of the appropriate wine, according to the meal (or the company) and/or water (preferably mineral). Rather than with cake, though not excluded, the meal ends with a variety of fruit and nuts, sometimes with cheese, followed by coffee, usually espresso (with or without sugar but no milk or cream), and also a "digestive" drink, such as amaretto, grappa, or even a *caffè corretto* – coffee with a drop of liqueur – or just another sip of wine.

If "eating in Italy," as Hazan wrote, or eating the "Italian way," as the Leamington Italians preferred, represents an "age-old gift of making art out of life,"[63] and if Italian cuisine can help "ward off heart disease" and generally protect one's health, then the loss of the Italian language, and thereby the closely connected Italian cooking and eating, meant also depriving oneself of an all-embracing art and of health itself. Moreover, the endless variety of Italian cooking and corresponding pleasures of eating involves choice; and choice entails trying, comparing, and contrasting with a discerning and open mind – a process that refines taste. Italian cuisine can, of course, be enjoyed without knowing the language, but it would be like reading a literary masterpiece in translation (see chapter 9, "The First 'Italian Grocery' Store"; chapter 11, "'The Italian Art of Eating': Nutrition, Pleasure and Conviviality").

Regardless of the many views the Leamington Italians presented on the dialects, they constituted the first essential links with tradition, with the reality of those small towns and regions of origin. They represented the firmest identity, the basic roots, almost impossible to completely shed even when consciously rejected. They were the natural links of the family, as well as of the individual, to their sister language, the standard Italian language, the language that forged a culture, a nation, a tradition out of many languages, traditions, and cultures, often blended into splendid works of art. The language that united all Italians, with which all Italians identified, was not, however, generally recognized as a possible vehicle for further nourishment and strength for the family or community. At the same time, the dialect, the particular language of the family or group, was not allowed to be enriched, and its limitations to be reduced or overcome, through conscious discovery or rediscovery of the living language of the origins, of the culture, of the entire nation.

The result was that the dialect was often abandoned, and worse, as one pointedly remarked, many "never learned English ... and forgot Italian."

Variations in the use of the two "poorly mastered" languages (Italian, English), or their combinations, suggested a confusion of tongues rather than harmony-producing communication, a fragmented rather than a close-knit family or community: numerous families alternated use of the two languages, according to family members, or certain members who were addressed in one language answered in the other; others used only English to overcome the "confusion" of dialects; and some employed neither, at the expense of any meaningful exchange between young and old.

A natural choice of a lingua franca, to overcome both the "Tower-of-Babel-like" alternation of languages and the dialectal boundaries, seemed to be standard Italian, and for numerous families it was. By cultivating their Italian (by listening to radio and television programs, and especially by reading) they helped stem the tendency to forget it. At the same time, since mastery of one's own language is a basic step in acquiring a foreign one, a stronger Italian base helped them learn English. Also, despite many differences, most Italian dialects have a close affinity with standard Italian: the former was often a stepping stone to the latter, which in turn helped them recognize and bridge the dialectal differences. In sum, standard Italian linked them closer to Italy and, as a vehicle of Italian culture, permitted them to establish a more secure base for their *italianità*.

All point to one reality: language is the most fundamental aspect of true identity. Retention of the ancestral language is at the centre of ethnicity,[64] for Italians as well as other ethnocultural groups in Canada. It may indeed be the major issue in all communities including English, French, and Native Peoples. The question is simply whether pride in one's origins can be sustained without at least some knowledge of the ancestral language. The French Canadians have given Canada their answer for over two hundred years in their continuous struggle to preserve their language. The Native peoples have also realized that their identity depends on language: "I am a Dene! Without a Dene language would I still be considered a Dene? The survival of our culture depends on the survival of our language."[65]

One regret expressed by some directors of the Leamington Roma Club was their inability to enact or pursue an Italian language and culture program more vigorously: "Not enough had been done," one lamented, "to enhance the education of the children in the areas of Italian culture and heritage." The lacuna was poignantly revealed by some presidents, whose efforts often ended in disappointments, in reference to the government-sponsored Heritage Language and Cultural Enrichment

Programs: "The Italian classes are not successful because of no club involvement." They also frequently pondered the club's ineffectiveness in promoting activities to increase participation of the "more educated and aggressive young people" with new ideas, indispensable for the further evolution of the club and the community in new directions.

Among so much individual soul-searching and community groping for answers, a small but significant group of Leamington Italian families and club leaders displayed common concerns: while aware of the problems and issues facing their descendants and the entire community, they made constant efforts to retain Italian and encourage the children to learn standard Italian as well as other languages. They pursued a sort of identity that, rather than restraining the individual within the ethnic strait-jacket, freed and developed the human being and the group, and fostered openness to other cultures and cultural groups, interaction, and general open-mindedness.[66] They made an attempt to forge a more dynamic sense of ethnicity that would permit them to preserve their Italian identity, to share their heritage, yet be fully part of Canadian society – to be, in sum, equal participants in the further development of Canada's ethno-cultural diversity into a truly multiculturally literate society.[67]

13

Ethnic Identity and the Community: Individualism and Solidarity, Parochialism and Interaction

Italians stuck together more.
The Italian community is each man to himself.

INTERACTION WITHIN THE COMMUNITY

The characteristic contradiction reappeared. But in this case it was not totally irreconcilable. Each statement separately presented a true reality, but not the total reality. It was a question of perspective. The truth was represented by both statements considered together: "Italians stuck together more, even though each man was for himself." Also, the verb tenses suggest another dimension: the evolvement of the community over the last five or six decades. The small group of Italian families in the Leamington area before and immediately after the Second World War formed a much more close-knit community. With the large wave of immigrants in the 1950s and thereafter, the community expanded and diversified radically in number and expectations. Even though it continued to evolve as a relatively compact community, to those who had arrived earlier it naturally appeared less cohesive, if not altogether splintered: "Back then [in 1948] we used to help each other without pay ... More in need then ... Now everyone wants to be better than anyone else ... The earlier immigrants were happy with what they got ... There was no need to improve ... The Italians that came later were more forceful; they expected more."

More than numerical expansion, it was money or economic growth that, while providing more comforts and more security, many saw as a prime cause for the erosion of the former interdependence, or of the communal wholeness of older days: "Many Italians ... too preoccupied with money ... haven't got time to think about friends ... too much envy for them to help each other."

Progress in general, within and outside the community, which often led to wider horizons and better opportunities in education and the professions, especially for their children, was often considered a cause of wider gaps in the community, especially between parents and children. Though partially true, even among the younger generation there reappeared, though not continuously or uniformly, a renewed and renewable interest in the emotional and social benefits of the attachment and association with the "mother" community.

Still, many complained that the community was coming apart, that the sense of community was disappearing among the Leamington Italians for other reasons: differences, divisions, and clashes were seen everywhere; they all formed a refrain in every discussion about their personal, family, or community life. The interviews made specific references, often candidly and persistently, to the flaws within the group: personal jealousies and envy among families, exaggerated vying for social and economic superiority and general one-upmanship in material display, conflicts of generations and rivalries among club members, inter-regional tensions, and misunderstanding between earlier and later immigrants.

Many emphasized the conflict between the earlier and later immigrants as an underlying cause for the widening split in the community. In their eyes, the split had been at work since the mid-1950s, with the arrival of Italian immigrants who had different attitudes and views: "My father felt that Italians who had been here longer tried to overrule them." Some felt that the established Italians, unlike the "English," were generally unkind to them: "During the first few months, the Italians who were here first treated me as a poor fellow ... The Italians especially used to take advantage of you if you couldn't speak the language ... They made fun of you ... 'English' were helpful." Children underwent similar treatment at school: "I got into fights more with Italians at St Louis, who tried to be smarter than you because they knew the language ... never with any Canadians ... nothing really serious though." Analogous situations also arose at work, even among the women: "Those three women really got me in a lot of trouble because I did not know how to speak the language or how to handle the situation ... Work was tight then, so I could not do anything that would jeopardize my job."

Whatever pain or hardship the incidents caused in the moment, they hardly had profound or lasting consequence for an entire community. In the first case, the situation was temporary and there were no wider repercussions. In the second, as indicated by the afterthought, there was "nothing really serious"; and in the third example, "It was really an awful joke." However malicious the intent, or bitter the resentment, a mischievous prank among co-workers, adolescent scuffles, or even the insensitivity of a few people could hardly constitute causes for the breakup of a whole community. They could hardly uproot the strong feelings and bonds that held most of the community together.

The factor that at times caused a sharp division between earlier and later immigrants (especially those of the late 1960s and 1970s) was the different view of Italy and consequently of Italian and Canadian ways: "I see some bad feelings between Italians here, primarily because the Italians who have been here for a while have no real understanding or knowledge of what Italy is like today ... They are too old-fashioned and they believe that Italy has made no progress at all ... The Italians who have been here for quite a while have money, but they make sure everyone knows ... They act like big shots." "Bad feelings" ran deep, reached levels of antipathy, and influenced a small group of them not to have anything to do with the community. The clash did not involve opinions alone, but also lifestyles, values, and general outlook. As such, the antagonism affected the community as a whole whenever it related to common community issues, such as the teaching of Italian language and culture, or the importance of the rediscovery of Italy as bases of their children's education, of community development, or of an ethnic identity within a multicultural Canada.

In the "prank episode" the identification of the perpetrators by their area of origin was an allusion to what some considered another cause of community "Balkanization" – inter-regional animosity. The account of the event began with a generalization implicating disparagement of a particular group of Italians: "The *'Ciociaros'* gave me trouble." It was not, in other words, a condemnation of the behaviour of three Italian women, but a criticism of a well-known community group that was singled out. Members of the three largest Italian groups in the Leamington area (including the *Ciociaros* or *Ciociari* from Lazio or more specifically from Frosinone province, and those from Molise and Sicily) often tended to band together because of the many common bonds – background, dialect, family, or marriage. For some, this represented a growing tendency toward more segregation.

It seemed to reflect a common trend within Italian Canadian communities and a common view that Italians in Canada were a patchwork of disconnected groups as a result of *campanilismo*, the old Italian regional or parochial patriotism. Apparently adherence to such beliefs played a greater role in dividing the communities than the more recent economic development, social conditions, or political affiliations. But unlike in larger centres, the Leamington community did not follow the route of regional or subregional associations or clubs, partly because it was relatively small, and partly because it was rural (chapter 1).

Although affinity tended to keep each regional group to itself and often apart from the others, and in spite of enmity, the community as a whole remained more important, their main concern. The connections became stronger than geography and dialect. They survived the tests of internal dissociative tendency and the external pressures on the associative ties. The concern for greater family and group unity was the result of and a reaction against the forces that generated disunity. However ineffective they might sometimes have been, their efforts to preserve their traditions and ethnic identity at least provided some resistance to fragmentation.

If the tendency to "stick together" remained alive, and the "glue" continued to hold the community together down to the present day, it was mainly due to the strong community foundations laid by the earlier immigrants: the pattern of cooperation, mutual support, and solidarity remained firm in the community. Those Italians who arrived in Canada in the late 1940s and early 1950s generally recognized that "the early Italians established a good reputation for the others who came over later" and "helped the new immigrants out a lot."

The early immigrants whom they generally acknowledged as community leaders and could turn to for help, included most pioneers who had brought many Italians from their hometowns to the Leamington-Kingsville area; all the men and women who provided newcomers with temporary residences, found them work, and served them in intermediary and advocacy roles: Tony DiMenna, Domenic and Joe Pannunzio, Gus and Angelo Moauro, and Armando Mastronardi (Molise – Villa Canale and Agnone); Alex Colasanti and Antonio Cervini (Lazio – Ceprano and Ripi respectively); Vito Peralta (Sicily – San Vito Lo Capo), as well as Joe DeLellis and Ida Magri, especially when she had her grocery store in downtown Leamington. Emma Colasanti, whose services as translator/interpreter proved crucial when someone was ill and needed a doctor, was especially remembered: "She helped ensure that later immigrants did not have the same language problem as Alex had had." Her lead in bringing together "all the Italian families" resulted in an early strong community spirit, which materialized in the Leamington Roma Club – the focal and gravitational point of the entire Italian community.

Among them are the Italian-born children of the pioneers, the second generation that arrived mainly in the 1930s; for example, Domenico Pannunzio's son Gino (1931), who provided the later arrivals with countless services (counselling, interpreter, clerical), especially during the "horrible ... month of April" when newcomers "found out that they had to pay income tax and file their returns" by the end of that month. Equally unfamiliar with bookkeeping and unwilling to pay an accountant (at least until the incorporation of their farms required more complex tax forms), they turned to Gino, who, "throughout the years ... did hundreds of them ... sometimes ... working till two or three in the morning" (in spite of his own "work the next day") and "never charged them." They responded with appreciation and gratitude, and "many of them" in kind, by giving Gino "a day's work on [his] farm." Similarly, Antonio DiMenna's son, also named Gino (1936), who helped many Italians find work at Heinz and other places since the early 1950s, was a community leader, respected by Italians and non-Italians alike, "who went to him for advice," also because of his role as a community "political link" (see "Political Views and Behaviour").

For all the pioneer families, sponsoring and assisting immigrants in settlement and integration had become a tradition dating back to the prewar years; and they were all gratefully remembered by the postwar newcomers: "There were the earlier immigrants who helped out when I came over ... to find work [and] to teach some words of English."

It was, after all, their socio-economic position and their cohesion, apparently sounder than in other Italian communities (at least as Scotti repeatedly described some of them in his 1957 editorials), that also enabled the Leamington Italians to perform a service that by the late 1950s neither the government agencies nor the social assistance agencies were in a position to assume full responsibility for. In fact, in 1957 the Welfare Council of Toronto and the International Institute had to urge the government of Canada to increase their personnel and invite community organizations to give their "full cooperation" in the settlement during that year of the estimated 400,000 newcomers (of whom 25,000 were Italians). In the ten years following the end of the war, "75 per cent of the Italian immigrants to Canada ... had been granted their visa ... because a relative had formally guaranteed for them." In Leamington it was almost 100 per cent: their assistance was given equally to those in the program to reunite families and those eager to come to Canada with a work contract.[1] Their involvement may have also been a source of pride; and later, attitudes, needs, and policies may have changed, but not their practice of benevolence and fellowship. Giving assistance became a community custom: "Earlier immigrants helped later ones," said a Leamington Italian. "It was a chain."

It was a chain that held together individuals and families in each successive group of immigrants without interruption. It was a form of dependence and interdependence based on favours, and at times, not with expectations of gratitude or imposition of community ways on the newcomers ("overrule them"). The initial link of giving and receiving often became intensely reciprocal, developing into a stronger bond based on mutual respect and deep friendship, reinforced by the frequent exchange of visits, marriage, baptism, and confirmation, which also established the *compare* and *comare* relationships that were often as sacred and as strong as blood ties (see chapter 10, "The Extended Family").[2] The chain and the links became a web running through and across most of the community. Besides, by the mid-1960s the Roma Club, as well as the presence of an Italian priest (1967), tended to reinforce their identity (chapter 11).

But interconnected as it may have been, it was also a complex community. However firm or far-reaching the network, it neither hampered independent growth nor stifled differences in words or deeds. All newcomers, regardless of time of arrival, had a common experience: they all felt equally different from those they found in the new land. "People in Italy have fun like the 'English' here; it is the immigrant who is different. He has to come and has to establish himself." However equal that feeling might have rendered them at the start, it was the way they dealt with it that differentiated them, made them feel more or less "Italian" or part of the Italian community.

In attitudes toward their own and other groups, and their relations with them, there were three categories of Italians (as they themselves pointed out): "One group preferred to associate mainly with Italians; they kept within their own group ... Everyone mixed with their own kind ... All the different nationalities stuck together [therefore] Italians stuck together." A second group opted to frequent only non-Italians; almost all of them, and especially those who were younger, "didn't hang around much with Italians. [They] thought [they] could learn more from others. [They] wanted to adjust to the Canadian way of life." A third category was identified by a preference for isolation; they had "no contact with anyone ... Italians don't get along and neither do other ethnic groups." The different positions reflected the tensions and divisions within an ethnically pluralistic community. But the first group represented the views of the majority of the Leamington Italians.

Similarly, although the Leamington Italians resented criticism, they dispensed it freely amongst themselves, and they were most consistent and versatile in their inventiveness. They expressed it as malicious gossip, pleasant mockery, or innocuous tittle-tattle. Criticism seemed as much a characteristic of the Leamington Italian community as it has long been national pastime in Italy. It too became part of their heritage.

To hear only some of them speak, one could easily be led to believe the community was breaking apart.

But in the Leamington Italian community, for every opinion there was an equal and opposite opinion. Paradoxically, criticism played a double role: while it dismantled, it built. It served as a restraint on behaviour, an unwritten standard of propriety, a balance in club deliberations, a guideline in all personal and community relations, and a guardian of customs. Oscillation between opposing views and tendencies was a constant. As a result, the centrifugal forces were often counterbalanced by the centripetal counterforces, keeping the community on an even keel, however troubled the waters. But contradictions and conflicts notwithstanding, the community still emerged cohesive.

GROUP INTERACTION AND INTERCULTURAL PREJUDICE

> Se porti il bene, trovi il bene. Se porti il male, trovi il male.
> If you bring good, you'll find good. If you bring evil, you'll find evil.
> Leamington Italian pioneer

> True misanthropes are not found in solitude, but in the world: because the direct practice of life ... is what makes people hate other people.
> G. Leopardi[3]

The degree of social interaction with other nationalities, as well as the attitudes towards other ethnic groups, depended on experiences and situations ranging from period of entry, age on arrival, and treatment by the host society to generation difference, level of success, and above all, language. Rapport was often determined by subjective evaluations of all non-Italians – those long-established, identified as "Canadians" or "English," as well as those belonging to other ethnic groups. Though intergroup encounters were more common and inevitable at the personal level, and, mainly out of necessity, intense in the workplace and in school, the interaction of the Italians as a group with the community was practically non-existent until more recent times. Education, better linguistic skills, increasing involvement in community projects, especially after the building of the club (1964), and their increasingly decisive electoral weight fostered a higher frequency of interaction, individually and collectively, but with effects on their Italian or ethnic identity.

Prejudice in particular played a role in the Italian community: it strengthened and weakened the community. Whether directed toward them in anti-Italian feelings or general xenophobia, or manifested by the Italians themselves in dislike, suspicion, or hostility, prejudice encouraged Italians to "stick with themselves" and blocked them from more spontaneous interaction and integration.

THE ANTI-ITALIAN SENTIMENTS OF "CANADIANS"

The Leamington Italians reflected and were deeply affected by prejudice in the community, workplace, and school, before and after the war: "In those days, the Italians were pushed around more than others ... At work they treated us as second-class people ... [There] was a great deal of discrimination then ... Italians were picked on ... Downtown, people would want to fight us in the streets."

In the 1930s there was general hostility "against Italians as well as some of the other ethnic groups ... The word that they used back then was *foreigner.*" Verbal slurs forced Italians into isolation: "I was very quiet around the 'English' Canadians ... Troublemakers looked at Italians as 'wops' ... I stuck with Italians mostly, since I was Italian and we understood each other a great deal more." Inherent ill-will often impeded good relations and disrupted family and community life. "When we moved into the neighbourhood, some of the neighbours threatened to move out because we were Italian."

In the early days, prejudice was often cause for Italians' difficulties in finding employment, especially in the factories and when they were designated as "enemy aliens." In the workplace itself, bias was at the base of much antagonism. Though it was frequently ascribed to English language inadequacy that made Italians appear "stupid" to fellow co-workers, many stated that they and Italians in general were discriminated against, even in the 1950s, and not just through frequent use of derogatory terms: "I was called DP [displaced person] several times" (see chapters 6, 9).

In school, anti-Italian feelings often assumed the cruellest forms, in words and deeds. "The bullies and smart alecks" were often relentless in name calling, ridiculing, and even physical attacks against Italian schoolmates. Domenic Magri frequently came home from school almost frozen after being pushed into a creek or ditch, once causing him "to be quite ill with pneumonia"; another time, after "an English boy" put a snake inside his coat, the whole family, unaware it was harmless, became extremely frightened. The pre–Second World War newcomers and especially those who arrived in the 1950s were constantly subjected to severe verbal abuse with the usual terms, *wop,* DP, or *stupid dago.* They were often "centred out" for their clothes and eating habits: "There were not many Italians in school, mostly Canadians ... I was the only Italian when I went to Mill Street School ... I felt different in the way I dressed, the food I ate ... Some kids always made fun of you ... took advantage of you ... I got into many fights defending myself."

At times, it appeared that they were "picked on" because of a form of "Italian" behaviour (which was, in fact, not at all just particular to the Italian heritage), but in reality it was for simply being Italian: "In high school bad ethnic feeling ... was more pronounced ... Italians were criticized for being clannish ... near brawl between Italians and non-Italians." The Italian children did not always understand their school-mates' hostility, and their rejection often interfered with their school life, educational advancement, and self-image:[4] "Most children didn't admit they were Italian, because they were ashamed ... I wouldn't communicate with the teachers at first ... I skipped school a few times, because I hated it ... Most children called us 'wops' and didn't want anything to do with me ... I was treated as if I had some sort of disease ... I felt very much discriminated when I went to school ... Their thinking was different."

The anti-Italian sentiment seemed to have had opposite effects on the community: it encouraged the older generation to seek protection in their own group, while it often influenced the younger ones to cam-ouflage their origin and dissociate themselves from it and the group. Though the lines of demarcation were often blurry, the divergence was apparent within the family and the objectives and programs of the com-munity club (see "Roma Club," chapter 11). The level of discrimination experienced and the corresponding reactions, or the way each genera-tion coped with it, influenced their attitudes toward Italy and Canada, their Italian heritage, and their ethnic identity.

However, the most harmful and long-lasting negative effect on Italians and on their rapport with other Canadians was the deeply rooted, wide-spread Italian Mafioso stereotype. It had existed since the early years, when Saveria Magri vehemently objected to it and rebuked those who used it (chapter 5). When it became slander, it most hurt, angered, and frustrated Italians. It tended to discourage them from interacting more closely with other groups, or participating more fully in Canadian life: "When one of my brothers got into town council, four Canadians said to me, 'Ah, Mafia's behind this.'"

Postwar Leamington Italian immigrants were experiencing the effects of a more widespread Canadian phenomenon: in his editorials, Arturo Scotti decried discrimination and "racial slurs" that Canadians (employ-ers, journalists, police officers, unions, politicians, and private citizens) directed against most newcomers, particularly Italians. He presented the hidden aspects of such practices, especially in employment;[5] preference for "English" or "Anglo-Saxon" employees, even when the "other" immigrants were skilled and knew the language;[6] the dubious justifications for denying the "others" work (e.g., poor language skills equalled low production – which made Scotti urge Italians to learn English as quickly as possible), or union cards (which the unions often refused); also, the immigrants' ineligibility for any substantial benefits; exploitation (lower wages paid to, and out of need accepted by, certain groups; poor protection from the Fair Employment Act); and hostility from Canadian-born workers.[7]

A number of Scotti's weekly commentaries on Canadian life dealt with biased views, false notions, or derogatory remarks about: Italian women;[8] Italy in general (by the *Toronto Daily Star*);[9] the Italian-Canadian community (by the Loyal Orange Lodge) for the Roman column donated to the City of Toronto;[10] the Italian Clubs, for their alleged pro-Fascist activities;[11] Hungarian refugees, called "second-class citizens" (by "a Halifax judge, honorary secretary of the Executive Council of the Anglican Church of Canada ... in the presence of over one hundred bishops";[12] and all newcomers, accused (by the *Toronto Daily Star*) of being "undisciplined."[13]

In one of his responses Scotti exhorted politicians to avoid the "distinction between 'immigrants from Great Britain and [those] from other countries'";[14] and he counteracted a *Globe and Mail* article containing "a series of insults directed at newcomers in general and Italians in particular."[15]

Regarding the stereotype of Italians as Mafiosi or criminals, Scotti did not deny the existence of such Italians, but he strongly objected to the generalization linking criminal activities to one nationality, to Italy or to Sicily.[16]

Scotti condemned discrimination of all types and from all sources, at times by ridiculing the perpetrators, but never attacking them personally, and usually with well-documented and balanced answers (making his editorials almost models for any journalist). His constant search for answers to the problem, at times, led him to insights that even today deserve serious consideration by all Canadians. Scotti saw "the nationalities making up the Canadian population [forming] a perfect mosaic on which [can] be built the most beautiful edifice in the world ... that new Canada ... where children of all national, racial, and religious origins are united into one world."[17] That view of the "mosaic" as the foundation for a better Canada, or "unity in diversity," anticipated by more than twenty years the underlying concept of the Canadian multiculturalism policy (1972), which envisaged a new Canada and provided a process for its renewal.[18]

THE ANTI-"CANADIAN" SENTIMENTS OF ITALIANS

But prejudice was far from being one-sided. The Leamington Italians distributed it quite freely among other groups as well as amongst themselves. Groups of Italians shunned other Italians or had "no contact" with their own or other groups. Next to other Italians, the Italians in Leamington first came in contact with "Canadians" or the "English," as they called them, usually their employers and/or co-workers. The antipathy of some Italians toward them depended partly on the way they were treated and partly on their own preconception of *gli Inglesi*.

As they often claimed, not always unjustifiably, there was "resentment from Canadians against Italians because Canada was theirs," and "Canadians gave them hard times ... even fights." The references to "fights," especially in order to "defend oneself," seem to coincide on a small scale with "some of the more pressing problems of the contemporary world" for which Marshall McLuhan "offered an explanation" in his *War and Peace in the Global Village*: "The book presented broad approaches to the themes of violence and identity. Chief among these was the notion, as McLuhan observed, "When our identity is in danger, we feel certain that we have a mandate for war. The old image must be recovered at any cost."[19]

The Leamington Italians' own "war," mainly of self-defence (as evidenced especially in their earlier work-related experiences; chapter 9), consisted of "silent endurance" and "open criticism" of "Canadians," who were variously called or considered "donkeys," beer-lovers or habitual drinkers, sloppy dressers or unrefined in manners and in eating, gullible (especially in politics) or simply "naive, narrow-minded and complacent." The insults ranged from the rather harsh, albeit rare, remark *"Canadesi ... razza bastarda"* (Canadians ... a bastard race) to the more mild or mockingly endearing *Italiese* epithet *"mangiachecc"* (cake eaters).

But at times their antagonism toward the "English" was so intensely felt as to produce in the Italians a judgment that was unjustifiably severe: "'English' are jealous ... [because] Italians work harder ... The 'English' do not care about building a house ... Most progress [is made] by immigrants ... Italians are ambitious ... There are some 'English' who get money without working." The "jealousy" or "envy" theme was so pervasive that it suggested frustration, insecurity, and an inferiority complex: "Canadians are still jealous of Italian progress because [we] have better homes ... eat better"; "'English' are always jealous of Italians because they never refuse overtime." What the Italians seemed to expect from the "others" was praise, not envy, for their hard work and advancement. In fact, the "English" might not have been manifesting "jealousy" so much as pride and condescension.[20] After all, the Italians themselves admitted that "Italian immigrants know they had to work hard and that's why they are progressing more than the people who have been here for many years." The recurring closing remark – "others are jealous of the Italians" – seemed to be a sort of self-reinforcement.

Other characteristics they perceived in the "English" were less unpleasant, but they were nevertheless obstacles that made interaction between the two groups just as difficult, if not impossible: "Canadians are easy-going ... don't take responsibilities"; "[They] don't know how to handle money: Italians save and Canadians blow their cheque"; "'English' people don't make friends with you unless they can use you." The two groups, though living side by side, remained essentially separate, if not unknown entities: if, on the one hand, the Canadians or "English" were all simply defined as more carefree, irresponsible, wasteful, unfriendly, aloof, haughty, and "jealous" of Italians; on the other, the Italians were deemed foreigners, strange (in their behaviour), inferior (at least linguistically), if not unscrupulously opportunistic, as well as ethnocentric. One seemed the antithesis of the other; and yet, if the "Canadians" appeared unsocial or disinterested in social relations with the Italians, the Italians were unwilling and unable (also because of language and their hard work) to mingle with the other. Each group seemed little inclined to become better acquainted with the other; they rarely had, or deprived themselves of, the occasion for a meaningful exchange.

THE ENDURING ITALIAN/"ENGLISH" STEREOTYPES

Intergroup marriages offered opportunities for interaction at the personal and family levels. But often the relations were strained because of family opposition from both sides. The Italians preferred that their children marry within their group. Canadians' objections and their misgivings about Italians did not work for better understanding or harmony between them. Some Canadians who married into Italian families offered other insights into the tension between Italians and Canadians in the community and into the difficult situation produced by exogamous marriages: "We're French Canadians ... my parents didn't want me marrying a foreigner at first ... My parents thought that he would make me work hard, because foreigners are just interested in getting ahead."

But the Italian attitudes toward the non-Italian wife, and Canadian women in general, at times turned into cruelty: "I don't think I was accepted right away by my husband's relatives. They tended to ignore me and talked Italian in front of me." Even though it might have been only her impression, the Italian relatives' inability and/or unwillingness to communicate with her strained their relations. In time, the situation may have gradually improved as the Canadian wives became more aware of the Italian ways and goals: "working ... saving ... Italian people believe in hard work." But the stereotypes remained.

The Canadian wives' closer view of the Italians and their qualities indicated that stereotypes were close to reality. Their portrait of Italians, the community, and even of Italy, though more positive, was largely similar to the one presented by other Canadians or Italians themselves. Though mostly based on personal and general observations, it was a repetition of stereotypes and a reflection of what Italians themselves thought, said, and did: "I understand more about my husband by seeing his hometown in Italy ... I think Italy is old, chaotic ... unorganized and undependable ... But there is a relaxed attitude ... I didn't understand the language ... My husband did all the talking ... But I think that the ambitious Italians immigrated to Canada ... Italians stick together ... They stick to the same ways ... They are afraid of being criticized."

The last reference to the Italians' "fear of criticism" was one of the Canadian wives' most significant observations of the Leamington Italians' makeup: it related closely to the Italians' own perception of the "jealousy" the "English" purportedly felt for them and their material success; it further exposed the Italians' insecurity, precarious self-importance, and uncertain self-identity; it pinpointed an obstacle to a freer, more open exchange, a less restricted participation in Canadian society. The observation could also be extended to all ethnic groups or minorities anywhere, still seeking "official" or general acceptance and recognition.

Partly as the result of such insights, the exogamous marriage tended to slowly reduce ethnic self-centredness, open wider channels between groups, and enhance similarities and mutual understanding: "My husband has some Italian in him ... This is because of his Italian upbringing ... [But he] has become more Canadianized being married to me ... My [French-Canadian] family ties are strong too ... I would take in my parents and in-laws if they wanted to live with us." Nevertheless, in many cases prejudice prevailed. Views on both sides, however superficial, exaggerated or unintentionally unkind, produced contrary effects: humiliation, anger, distrust and ongoing separation of the groups.

ITALIAN VIEWS OF THE OTHER GROUPS

For a few Italians, it was not the "Canadians" or the "English" with whom they had difficult relations, but with other nationalities: "I think there is jealousy between the different nationalities ... not on part of 'English' however ... The 'English' have a great deal of patience with Italians ... Canadians help Italians more than other Europeans." But as the Canadians or the "English" were being redeemed, other groups were being discredited. Lebanese stereotypes were even more disparaging than Italian ones: "no good ... they are zero ... too lazy ... on unemployment ... don't look for jobs ... Lebanese are lazy and dirty." However, they had some redeeming qualities: "Lebanese women are better than Lebanese men." The Portuguese fared better, simply because they "work hard ... like Italians." And yet, for others, "the Portuguese are *antipatici* [unpleasant] ... Lebanese okay."

To many Leamington Italians, so accustomed to a homogenous small village environment that even an encounter with Italians from other regions was a novelty, it "seemed a bit strange living with so many different nationalities." They often found it difficult to understand or accept "the ethnic pockets in Leamington" or the ethnocultural groups they represented. To them, some of their negative comments and attitudes did not seem unjustifiable or ironical. In fact, when thinking of Italy, one resident suggested there was less "equality and fraternity" in Canada because there were "too many ethnic groups."

Those who held such views were discriminating against those same Canadians or English whom they resented for discriminating against them. They were also exemplifying a pattern common to new, heterogeneous, immigrant societies: in the process of becoming established, it is not unusual that a group that has been the victim of discrimination tends to imitate and assume the attitudes and prejudices of the established group against the most recent immigrants. The inherent contradiction could engender an atmosphere that was unfavourable to greater awareness and understanding, and to better intra- and inter-group relations. It was not surprising that a group of Italians preferred isolation.

One comment about interracial marriage referred to Blacks as the least accepted as children's spouses. Since only a few remarks were documented, it was not possible to establish whether there was a more general racist attitude. This particular interview seemed to reveal a concern for preservation of a tradition rather than an racist conviction. In fact, almost all negative attitudes about Canadians, the English, or other groups were more the result of a "fear of the unknown," or even of imitative behaviour, than of a bias. (At least in the 1970s, Montanelli said that the Italians are such a "mixed race" that they are one of the "least racist" of peoples, simply because diverse peoples and races – German, Spanish, Arabic – have contributed to the makeup of the Italian people.[21]) Even if there were genuine racist feelings among the Leamington Italians, likely they were restricted to a very small minority. What helped to remove further speculation was documentation in support of the former argument, and perhaps the most revealing are Domenic Magri's words (especially when related to Father Rossi's statements):

> We ourselves did not mix too much with other Italian families because we were the only Italians in the community ... We were in contact with our neighbours, of course, and I know there was one family that we were always close to ... it was a Black family by the name of Smith ... They were a big family, they had twelve children, and they were a very happy family, and I envy the talent that those children had ... They could sing, tap dance ... Mr Smith worked with my father for twenty cents an hour and he raised a big family with that [and] ... I think ... some assistance.

MORE INTER-ETHNIC COOPERATION THAN CONFLICT

The general attitude of the Italians toward other groups was positive. In fact, the majority of the Leamington-area Italians clearly stated that they "were treated well by other members of the community." Many felt that they were generously assisted in their transition by other ethnic groups: "A German family that came earlier than we did helped us a lot if we needed something"; "I picked up English through a friend of Polish descent ... This man guided me around and helped me at Ford's."

Most had enriching experiences in their association or interaction with all nationalities and races: "I liked the idea that many nationalities lived in Canada ... [I] worked with Blacks, Mexicans, Chinese, and Mennonites ... treated me better than my brothers and sisters ... I don't think others are jealous of Italians ... Non-Italians went out of their way to help me understand"; "We found more honesty in Canada than in Italy ... Even if we could not speak English, we were not cheated by the others ... treated well by others ... [in the early 1950s] many Germans and Canadians ... no trouble between the different nationalities ... very friendly people here ... I found people honest and patient with the immigrants."

Also, as Italians became more acquainted with Canadians and their ways, their views and attitudes changed. Most agreed that the Canadians were very honest and that they "are more relaxed about life ... enjoy themselves more than Italians ... Italians save their money and sacrifice more ... Canadians are less self-sacrificing ... They're smarter ... They realize that when they die they can't take anything with them so they don't kill themselves working." In fact, for some, the Canadians "treated the Italians better than the Italians ... Italians are pushy." The same feelings were expressed toward the group they called English: "I don't think that English people are jealous of the Italians ... Maybe there is jealousy among different nationalities ... especially among Italians ... At first Italians visited with each other ... but with progress, friendship is lost."

Most agreed that it was necessary to get along as well as possible. All Canadian ethnocultural groups were considered an enrichment for Canada: "Canada needs all its ethnic peoples, because they have made Canada what it is today ... and besides, at one time, we were all people in a strange land." As time progressed, with increasing prosperity and self-assurance, the interaction of Italians and the various groups in the workplace or in the community became more frequent and more positive. It was a sign also that they felt gradually more secure about their own ethnic identity, which was reinforced by the building of the club, which in turn helped them "to get to know the other groups better."

POLITICAL VIEWS AND BEHAVIOUR

Liberals have helped everyone ... Always been a Liberal ... will vote Liberal no matter what.

In the exercise of their Canadian political rights, even more than in their practice of their traditional religion, the Leamington Italian community revealed a high degree of compactness, if not uniformity. In party connections, whether by omission or commission, it was a monolith.

Eugene Whelan, Liberal MP for Essex-Windsor (1962–84) and minister of agriculture (1972–84), offered a plausible explanation for the development of a one-party community: "Italians are mainly Liberal because most came when the Liberal government was in power ... Italians realize that the Liberal government was nice to them and grants their requests, and knows what their needs are."

However partisan, the view reflected the feelings of the majority. Perhaps Whelan himself, more than the party, had a role in this outcome. As a farmer in Essex County, he had known Italians long before he entered the political arena: Tony DiMenna was the first Italian he met, and through him the association with them grew, especially since he started out in politics in Leamington in 1959. Though his first bid for a provincial seat was unsuccessful, he established a lasting friendship with the Italians, and throughout his long career in the national arena he maintained a close relationship with the Leamington Italian community. He continued to receive delegations from them even when he was no longer their representative, and Gino DiMenna continued to serve as a "liaison with the Italian people"; he "got in contact at least once a month."

Whelan, more than politician and friend, came to be regarded as a benefactor, especially for "sitting in on a lot of the meetings when the Roma Club was being proposed." He was proud of this association with the Leamington Italians, and when he organized the visit to Essex County of the then Soviet minister of agriculture, Mikhail Gorbachev, it was at the Roma Club that the banquet was held in his honour.[22] If he felt that the "Italians influenced his decisions as much as any of the other people," the Italians were also deeply influenced by his attention and friendship, and they responded with loyalty and affection: "They all call me Gino." It was this rapport much more than political considerations that determined his and his party's success in the community. In fact, the party's fortunes changed only after the familiar Liberal candidate withdrew from the scene.

Particularly in the earlier days and during the period of adjustment, the Italian immigrants had too many other problems to have time for politics. As they became citizens and voters after the minimum and mandatory waiting period, they found it more convenient to follow the trends and the advice of those who preceded them, especially if language skills were insufficient. Party platforms and policy changes, often interpreted by a minority, gained their attention only if directly affecting their immediate concerns, regardless of their impact on the nation as a whole. They often reacted quite quickly and in a block.

THE "CRUELTY" OF THE CONSERVATIVES AND THE "GOOD TIMES" WITH THE LIBERALS

In the late 1950s, the decade of the largest wave of Italian immigration into Canada, many Italians developed a profound dislike for both Diefenbaker and the Conservatives for their policy and attitudes towards immigration. They also felt that in the late 1950s and early 1960s, when the Conservatives were in power, not only was immigration restricted, but it became quite difficult for Italians to obtain their citizenship. The elaborate "examinations," prior to being granted citizenship, contained questions that many could not even understand, let alone know the responses to them. The period remained a bad memory in the community: "Diefenbaker was cruel ... did not like Italians ... wanted to see immigration closed ... It was hard to get citizenship with Conservatives in power ... They asked difficult questions ... There was no work then and bad times ... When Pearson took over, things got better."

The Liberals, in their view, made things much easier, for immigration and for citizenship. Therefore, the Conservatives became a bugaboo, even for those who had not experienced the Diefenbaker years. They were identified with a "time of great unemployment," of hardships for Italians, completely opposite the period under the Liberals (particularly with Trudeau), when Italians "have been fruitful." It was "hard times with Diefenbaker and good times with Trudeau" (in spite of some contrary feelings: "happy Trudeau is out; *non ha fatto niente per l'Ontario, solo a Montreal e Quebec*" [he didn't do anything for Ontario, only in Montreal and Quebec]).

Their position remained firm, even in the midst of discontent with Liberal policies. In the late 1970s, many Italians felt that the Liberal government had been too liberal with welfare and unemployment benefits: "The government takes too much money from people who work, and gives it to those on welfare ... The Canadian government makes people lazy by giving out so much [welfare and unemployment benefits]." It was neither a sudden embrace of reactionary ideology nor a lack of social consciousness that made them oppose these hard-earned social benefits. It was simply a reaction based on their own standards and their own needs. For a group who strongly believed that work was the only way to earn one's living and reach success, welfare was shameful and bad for business, especially their own. On the basis of personal experience, they complained that many people receiving unemployment benefits refused to work. Sometimes they included all unemployed: "I have a lot of trouble now getting people to work on the farm ... No one wants to work ... People want to get paid for nothing."

The greenhouse farmers who were part of the backbone of Liberal support became the most upset. They not only had difficulty finding workers, but when they did, they knew that many of them just worked long enough to be able to collect unemployment benefits. Their situation was further aggravated when, during high unemployment, they were prevented from hiring seasonal but reliable workers from Mexico and Jamaica. Therefore, they reacted to policies restricting immigration for family and business reasons. Sometimes it was the same and only reason, since sponsored immigrants, relatives, or friends also filled their need for farm workers.

The Italians were embittered by government policies, but they were most resentful toward the unemployed. As far as they were concerned, there were plenty of jobs! People refused them because what they received for not working was often more than they would earn as farm labourers. The problem was also that high fuel costs and a low profit margin prevented greenhouse farmers from paying high wages. Besides, many workers, they saw, found greenhouse work too trying, and preferred to wait and find an easier job. To the hard-working Italian greenhouse farmer, such workers were irresponsible, parasitical citizens who would "rather not do anything at all but sit in the hotel downing draft [beer]." This attitude was shared by many other Italians who worked in the factories. They too resented the fact that their labour was supporting those "who were too lazy to work." However prevalent that behaviour among the unemployed, or even the abuse of the system, it could hardly justify generalizations that made the workers the sole scapegoats for their problems. Yet, despite their forceful concern or anger at government policies, they all remained faithful supporters of both the government and the party.

An incident in the late 1970s may have weakened the Liberal stronghold in the Italian community, but only slightly. In 1978, the local Liberal MP, Bob Daudlin, scheduled a visit by Pierre Trudeau to the Leamington area. Some Italians were incensed that the reception was to take place at the Lebanese Club rather than at the Roma Club, and accused the MP of blatant electioneering to draw the Lebanese vote away from the NDP. These Italians felt that, regardless of party strategies, Daudlin should have honoured the continued support of the Italians rather than turn to a segment of the population where he had little support. The issue stirred controversy, mainly in response to misquotes in the *Windsor Star*. The event ended rather humorously, as Trudeau cancelled his appearance because of bad weather. Some may have perceived the incident as a party letdown of the Italian community, a slap in their collective face.[23] But, in general, it did not diminish their support for the party or their candidates. They were all re-elected in the 1979 election, even though Trudeau and the Liberals were ousted from power.[24]

"ITALIAN POLITICAL CLOUT"

Interest in politics and participation in political activities among the Leamington Italians ran the gamut from commitment to apathy. Many appeared to be most interested in politics at the provincial and federal levels, at least in elections and in giving their support. Some were energetic organizers, and one enthusiastically stated that he had "strong feelings about Canadian politics ... I got people together ... got votes ... for Whelan, Daudlin, and Mancini."

Don Paterson, Liberal MPP for the riding of Essex South (1963–75), remembered having received Italian support throughout his career: "During election time they had an Italian speaker come down and present the party's views so that the Italians could feel better informed about the riding ... A few memorable things stick out in my mind ... I remember in 1963 for my first election, Ralph Mastronardi was in charge of the poll with the biggest win ... Perhaps above all was the fact that during election times I always knew I had their support."

The Italian-born Remo Mancini, Liberal MPP in Essex South (1975–93) and the first Italian Canadian from Essex County in the provincial legislature (as well as minister without portfolio responsible for disabled persons, 1987–89, and minister of revenue, 1989–90), stated that the "overwhelming support of the Italians ... made his success more assured." Though a resident, like Whelan, of the Amherstburg area, he also had been long acquainted with the Italians of the entire area, socially (most of his school friends were Italian), commercially (he had run a restaurant with his father since 1971), and politically (first elected to the Anderdon Township Council in 1972 and again as deputy reeve in 1974). In 1975, as Don Paterson's successor in Essex South, Mancini inherited a riding that stretched from Amherstburg to Wheatley, as well as the strong Italian support base in the whole area, including Leamington (where his riding office was located until his retirement in 1993).

Mancini, moreover, was not only of Italian birth, but also from the Abruzzo region (Abbateggio, Pescara), an origin or background with which many area Italians identified, and a dialect that most understood. In his case, his background assured him the support of the majority, at least originally; but he ascribed it to three specific "facts": he was Italian, he represented the Liberal party, and he did a good job. Although he considered the last one "the most important," he did not minimize the importance of the Italians' exclusive support for the Liberals: "They believe their best interests have been traditionally fulfilled by the Liberals. They feel comfortable with the party and with its diverse membership."

In Mancini's view, "the so-called spokesmen of ethnic communities" didn't "have enough political clout, and so when good candidates from their background present themselves for political representation, they should be supported. Thus, when good Italian candidates involve themselves in the political field, they should be supported by a group of Italians."[25] There was no doubt in his mind, as in the minds of many Italians, that being Italian and Liberal was a good, if not the best, combination for success. The Leamington Italian voters did, in fact, transfer their support from Paterson to Mancini, from a person they knew well and was a Liberal, to another person with a common background and who was a Liberal. Italian support for the Liberal party was just as firm at the provincial as at the federal level, even though there had not been a Liberal government in Ontario for forty years.

There appeared to be a discrepancy between the immense support for the Liberals and the widespread indifference to politics. A significant number of Italian Canadians interviewed (both men and women) were almost totally unmoved by politics: "I have few feelings about Canadian politics ... I still have to go to work in the morning, regardless of who is in power." Others, sometimes quite blatantly, declared that they just were not interested in politics: "I don't care one bit about politics in Canada." In certain cases, they not only admitted their political apathy but sadly recognized the state to which it reduced them: "no interest in politics, not here nor in Italy ... We're like sheep; we just follow the leaders and other people in this country ... But we're happy to see Italians such as Mancini in government." Many of them were quite aware of the reasons for their attitudes. Sometimes, it was not so much lack of interest as lack of understanding of political affairs: "We follow [politics] a bit ... we're interested in what's happening ... we always vote ... It's just that, well ... who can understand politics? [Sometimes] it's better not to know things in the world."

Some said it was lack of education that prevented them from becoming more interested or more involved: "I would like to, but how can you with four years of school!" This political marginalization often led to dependence on others, especially at election times: "I don't interest myself in politics ... If I have any questions, I ask my sons." Lack of interest or limited information hampered self-confidence in these matters. One woman apologized: "I can't say anything about the government because I would make a mistake ... my husband [maybe] ... He made it his business to know at least what the next guy knew."

Of course a large number had opinions on the Canadian government and the Canadian political scene, and they often talked about them but rarely got involved, mainly because of "fear ... Italians like politics but are scared." It was primarily the sort of fear caused by insecurity that results from lack of "a complete control of the English language." Therefore, many did not bother with it: "I don't understand the political system in Canada and I don't really care."

At least half of those interviewed seemed to fall into the latter categories. Thus, the indication was that wide Italian loyalty to the Liberal party was based mainly on traditional attachment to this party, and the personal involvement of the candidate in the community. Don Paterson received "their full support" because he knew the Italians, and they knew him from his various activities. Through his job at Erie Produce when he was young, "he got to know the Italian farmers." He also went to high school with some Italians (such as Marius Ingratta and Gino Pannunzio), and since he had a fabric store, he knew "many of the Italian women." Above all, as president of the Chamber of Commerce when the Roma Club first started, he offered organizers a great deal of help and guidance. Provincially or federally, the Italians automatically threw their total support behind the man they knew well, and to whom they knew they could eventually turn for help. The fact that they were Liberal made it so much the better!

Some Italians claimed that "because of the large Italian population, they exercise a strong influence on the political scene in the Leamington area." Although a poll analysis was not possible to substantiate or disprove the claim, it may be said that without the Italian community's massive backing of the Liberal party, many candidates would have had greater difficulties in getting elected, or might not have made it at all.[26] But electoral strength did not always translate into real political influence. The politicians' statements seemed more like kind gestures toward the Italian voters than recognition of their real influence. The Italians did not appear to them as forceful lobbyists. Their demands were few and limited. Eugene Whelan himself, while praising them for having become less shy in politics and in business, wondered why, although they had known him for a long time, "Italians still felt strange going to him with a problem."

Don Paterson stated that "as for the problems the Italians had during his early years of politics, they generally dealt with immigration." Though a federal concern, he tried to help them "to get more people here." Since he was more accessible than the federal member of Parliament, he handled many of the problems or referred people to others. But he went on to explain that, "as a community, the Italians did not make many demands: there were just personal demands here and there, such as citizenship papers." He recognized their economic success and their contribution to his own political success: "The large majority ... have been very successful economically ... As for the Italians contributing to my success, yes, and tremendously; there is no question about it."

But their influence on him was quite limited: "As for Italians influencing decisions of mine ... basically I was aware of their presence and of their economic activity, and naturally this influenced my actions subconsciously, but I cannot think of any specific example." What he remembered, and this surely pleased the Italians, was that "he never had any Italian welfare cases." The Italians had long been accustomed to looking after their own problems as much as possible before running for government help. Nevertheless, there were areas, according to Paterson, where Italians might have been guided by a higher degree of motivation: "As for cooperation in the community, I don't feel that the Italians participate enough in the Chamber of Commerce … Somehow they concern themselves with the immediate and leave the work for the others to do … I don't feel they are motivated to get involved in community things but … that day will soon come." And Remo Mancini's answer to the question regarding the Italians' influence on his decisions was simply: "No! Not as of yet!"

At the municipal level, an evaluation of the political interest or involvement of the Italian community as a group was rendered impossible by the little evidence available. The brief interviews with two Leamington mayors (Ralph Nicol, 1968–75; Sterling Welch, 1975–82) made no reference to Italian support in their election campaign. But they did recognize the Italian community as a civically conscious group: "The Italians in Leamington are very cooperative in community happenings." For both mayors, the "most memorable contribution of the Italians to Leamington was the fountain they donated to the town," though mentioned were also the Italian community events (St Michael's and Grape Festivals), their participation in the centennial project, and their involvement in the many festivals and the Centennial parade.

The Leamington Italians were, above all, praised by the two mayors for their contribution to the Leamington economy: for their help in shaping Leamington, "especially with their greenhouses and their expertise in construction," and generally, besides their hard work "behind the scenes … it's their thriftiness, industriousness, and aggressiveness that has helped build the town." Yet their presence was not always behind the scenes.

At least a few Italian Canadians did hold political positions in the larger Leamington area: two served on the Leamington Town Council (Frank Moauro, "elected with the highest number of votes," 1976–78; and Victor Gabriele, 1976–81: two terms as councillor; one as deputy reeve and, by virtue of that position, as Leamington's representative on the county council; as well as three terms on the Leamington Police Commission). Two others were on the Gosfield South Township Council (Ron Colasanti, councillor, 1966–72; and Ron DiMenna, councillor, 1979–85; deputy Reeve, 1986–88; reeve, 1989–91). Others held office in Kingsville: one (Salmoni) for a time councillor and deputy reeve; another as councillor (Bonnie Wilson, daughter of Fred DeSantis,

1986–91; and in 1992 appointed to the District Memorial Hospital Board); and the Italian-born Fred DeSantis, who served for twelve years on the Kingsville Council (as well as on the Utilities Commission and Committee of Adjustment) and from 1966 to 1974 as mayor.[27]

"POLITICAL SHEEP" BY NECESSITY OR BY CHOICE?

For its relative numerical strength in the Leamington area and for its compactness in voting, the Italian community may have been an electoral force, at least at the provincial and federal levels. But it did not seem to wield an equivalent political influence. The politicians did, of course, respond to their rather limited political demands, but there were occasions when the Italians' support even seemed to be mostly taken for granted. Their role had been limited mostly to poll work. There was no indication of any positions of importance held within the riding associations; and this, combined with a marked political unawareness, prevented them from having a greater voice in shaping the candidates' direction or even party policy. Their almost total attachment to the Liberal party appeared to be their strength and their weakness.

The Italians had indeed prospered under the Liberals. The Liberal policies most often coincided with their needs. The Liberal candidates and members of Parliament had generally shown support for their private businesses and community projects. Gratitude to the government, even the suggestiveness of the term *liberal*, may have indeed been a determining influence on their political inclinations. But other factors were just as important in the development and consolidation of the almost total identification of the Italian community with the Liberals. It was as much the result of a conscious choice or clear political views as, if not less than, a reaction to circumstances and events, or disenchantment (i.e., with the Conservatives). Unawareness, disinterest, and general apathy played as great a role as rhetoric, conditioning, gentle persuasion, or even subtle coercion ("We're like sheep: we just follow the leaders").

In a community where many insisted that there was a deep split between earlier and later immigrants, there seemed to be little deviation from the pattern of political behaviour established by the earlier Italians. The set of views on politics, or party to vote for, usually spread by word of mouth, became almost totally and unquestionably acceptable. It became a part of the community identity and strength, or at least an insurance.

At the same time, however, the community's unflinching loyalty to the party and to its representatives was perhaps also the cause of contradictions. Their inflexible political coherence, as evidenced at least in the interviews, ironically made them sometimes appear incoherent. For a community that often took pride in distinguishing itself from other groups in warmth or kindliness, it appeared at least in one circumstance rather insensitive to the plight of Canadian workers. Even if that insensitivity was a reflection of a more general attitude toward the unemployed, their judgment appeared rather harsh, or at least not at all "liberal," in the strict as well as political sense. However, justified by their own difficulties or personal losses and resulting anger, placing the blame on only one group was one-sided. Their unquestioning trust of the government and the party may have prevented them from being more objective in their evaluation of the government policies, as well as of their effects on the Canadian public. It may have hampered them in the search for an alternative course of action or solution. It reduced their political choices, which required a more comprehensive view of the political spectrum and political maturity.

At the end of the 1970s, many Canadians sought a solution to their disaffection with Liberal policies, and in the federal elections of 22 May 1979 they ousted Trudeau and the Liberals from power. In some communities there was a tendency toward political polarization. But in the Leamington area and in the Leamington Italian community, there was little change. Contrary to the national trend, Leamington remained a Liberal stronghold. In the Italian community, just the thought of opposing or breaking away from the Liberals was often considered a betrayal of the men who had helped them for so many years, and of the party they believed had "traditionally fulfilled ... their best interests."

It was definitely not ideology that united the Italian community around the Liberal party. Nor was it ideology that made them reject the NDP outright, but mainly the rivals' scare tactics often depicting it as socialism or communism. It was the politics of personal contacts and friendship that made Italians continue to "vote Liberal no matter what." Perhaps some evidence may be found in the February 1984 federal elections. Only after the withdrawal from politics of two familiar Liberal politicians were the seats won by candidates of the other two major parties. Particularly indicative was the fact that the riding held for over twenty years by Eugene Whelan and the Liberals went to the New Democratic Party (NDP).[28]

The victories exposed other realities and possibilities: either the Italian community showed less compactness and more political polarization, with the departure of their friends and former benefactors, or an electoral swing in other voters rendered ineffective the electoral strength they claimed they had; or perhaps both; or even during the last election the disinterested half of the community did not bother to vote. One thing became clear: in the Leamington area the Liberal stronghold had been occupied by others, at least for the moment.

It was too early to evaluate the effect on the Italian community as a whole. But there were already indications that they were slowly adjusting to the new situation. And in this also they seemed to illustrate some long-known Italian characteristics: flexibility, adaptability, or outright opportunism.[29] Whatever the case, in the absence of the familiar politicians from the local scene and from power along with the party that "united" them for so many years, the Italian community now appeared increasingly exposed to other influences, and perhaps to further growth in their political life, as in other facets of the community. If marked changes had not yet occurred in their political behaviour or outlook, it seems almost certain that, as Don Paterson anticipated in viewing the progress of the Italian community in all fields, "this day will soon come." The 1984 elections were a political watershed for the community (even though, in the 1993 Liberal sweep, the New Democrat Steven Langdon lost the Essex-Windsor seat to the Liberal Susan Whelan – Eugene Whelan's daughter).

In the span of twenty years (1964–84), three events nudged the Leamington Italians toward further change and greater interaction with themselves and the community at large: the building of the Roma Club, especially in the 1960s; the Canadian multicultural policy and "climate," especially toward the end of the 1970s; and the "radical" political changes in the mid-1980s. At least "since the [1975] Leamington Centennial," said Tony Paliani (1953) – perhaps recalling the rallying of the community behind the Italian Fountain Project (chapter 8, note 19) – "multiculturalism ... stimulated the Italians" toward "progressive" ideas about themselves as "Italians and as Canadians"; and toward, it seems, a more generous view of the "other Canadians": after all, said a woman who arrived in 1965, *"Siamo tutti figli di Dio"* (We are all children of God). Inherent beliefs, social needs, and political changes all seemed to converge toward a good effect: that of reducing contradictions within the Italian community and inter-group tensions, thereby reinforcing ethnic identity and the feeling of being more and more part of Canada.

14

Community Self-Identity:
What Is an Italian Canadian?

Sono italiano, ma sono canadese (I am Italian, but I am Canadian).
Canada number one country; Italy, second country.

THE NEVER-ENDING "PASSAGE"

The sixty-odd-year-long and arduous journey of the community toward a better economic destination was a simultaneous, though less conscious, quest for an often elusive new identity, a new self-concept. The journey of deliverance from material hardships was also a slow passage toward a greater problem: the identity question or identity crisis. The seed of the problem was sown at the moment their dissatisfaction with their lot gave birth to their desire to escape it and become emigrants. The solution became the problem; and as much as they were aware and brave protagonists in carrying out their difficult decision, they were also unaware causes and victims of the outcome. The hardships of the journey, the tension, struggles, and prejudice encountered along the economic climb, dimmed before the conflict, dilemma, and the anxiety underlying the metamorphosis of their being, their state, and their status.

Most reached their goals, and if not they themselves, their children and grandchildren. But in the process, they lost certainty of who they were, or what they had become. Prior to the transition, they were firmly Italian or at least Molisani (or *Abruzzesi*), *Laziali* (or *Ciociari*), and *Siciliani*. However dissatisfied, they were integral parts of a recognizable system; they were in harmony with their natural habitat. The urge to leave and the departure from homeland shattered the natural link with the ever-nurturing environment, severed the umbilical cord with the "mother" country forever.

They began a new life, a self-transformation: from Italians into Italian emigrants or immigrants into adventurers and wanderers, seekers, mental migrants, "exiles," and "aliens" – not simply aliens in an alien environment or politically, but aliens in themselves, alienated from their spiritual soil (the "Great Mother").[1] Having cast themselves out of their Eden, they strove to return to it by "sweat and blood"; they struggled to redefine their identity, which was distorted, denied, or rejected. They made efforts to recover that part of their being that had been lost, taken for granted, or forgotten, in order to mould and remould a newer balance; they saw themselves as Italian Canadians, Canadians of Italian descent, or Canadians and Italians, sometimes more one than the other, sometimes both, sometimes neither.

The search became a never-ending need, and the result was often more confusing. Sometimes it was the past, relived and reshaped, that helped them regain part of their identity. They often found in their common origins, traditions, customs – in their views on marriage, family, children, food and religion – some elements that distinguished them from other groups. Sometimes the new self-image was shaped more by experience and environment, by adaptation or reaction to the prevailing ways or patterns: language, values, politics, opportunities, work, wealth, success, or even the struggles themselves to overcome the tensions and the prejudices. At times, because of confusion of goals and means, the struggle and the hard work themselves became their new identity. Or the means to overcome their economic distress – the original obstacle to their greater happiness – became the barriers to a more complete identity.

In this passage from dissatisfied Italian to Canadian ethnic Italian, the Italian Canadian had lost the fixed orientation point, the core of the identity. The new identity was based on tenuous hyphenation, on relative elements, on comparisons, on degrees, on adversative statements: "I am Italian, but I am Canadian"; "Canada number one; Italy second country." It was an identity based on an ever-changing emphasis that revealed precarious social status, if not an uncertain psychological state (which, at times, affected one's physical well-being, as exemplified by the Leamington woman whose ailment disappeared whenever she returned to Italy).[2]

Was the financial or material success worth the sacrifices? Was the new self-awareness worth the loss of a secure identity? In describing the Italian-Canadian community in general, Harney wrote, "Most of the community stayed suspended between full assimilation and cherished Italian origins."[3] How does the Leamington Italian community differ? How is it unique?

FORMED BY TWO LANDS, LINKED
BY ONE COMMON EXPERIENCE

The Leamington-Italian community is relatively young: except for the twenty-odd families that arrived before the Second World War, the large majority immigrated to Canada between 1950 and 1960. However limited their knowledge of Italy, their emotional attachment to the land of birth deeply influenced their self-perception as individuals and as a community. But often they also quickly became Canadian citizens and adopted the new land as their new home. They therefore saw themselves as Italian Canadians, with varying degrees of stress on one component or the other. Only a few of them, generally those who came at a very young age, who had few relatives left in Italy or had never visited it, stressed the Canadian side of the hyphenated self-image: "I consider myself more Canadian than Italian ... I get upset when I receive stuff in the mail that is only in Italian ... I don't like to be labelled a certain nationality."

In this case, their sense of "Canadianism" was as restrictive and restricting as the reasons for objecting to being labelled "Italian" were tenuous. They simply leaned more toward Canada than Italy, because they owed much more to Canada, where, as they often stated, they "made their fortune." This position didn't seem to present any problem, until they were reminded of their origin, which remained transparent in their name, the "vowel-strewn" Italian last name.

But the majority, while grateful to Canada for their success, felt that Italy was always their *"patria lontana"* (faraway homeland). In some cases it was not just the Italy of the town of birth, but the historical and spiritual Italy:

Il nostro destino ha voluto di emigrare in Canada per il progresso dei nostri figli, ma mi sento sempre distinto e fiero di essere un Italiano ... osservando la storia di un Colombo, un Marconi, un Galileo Galilei, un Garibaldi, un Totò per il teatro, un Verdi per la musica e un Enrico Toti per il patriottismo ecc. ecc., e per di più la nostra lingua ... Viva il progresso per una vita migliore, e grazie a chi ci ospita." (Our destiny was to immigrate to Canada for the progress of our children, but I always feel distinguished and proud to be an Italian ... in observing the history of a Columbus, a Marconi, a Galileo Galilei, a Garibaldi, a Totò for theatre, a Verdi for music, and an Enrico Toti for patriotism, etc., etc., and moreover our language ... Long live progress, and our thanks to those who give us hospitality).[4]

The image of oneself as the product of two realities – of the progress that Canada signified, and the richness of history that was Italy – was indeed more balanced and more complete. Nevertheless, even in this case, as the quoted words reveal, the view of oneself as a grateful guest, even after many years in the new home, implied that the Italian Canadians felt as if they were foreigners, still living on the margin of Canadian life, far from being integrated into mainstream Canada.

That position was always a source of anxiety: like guests who, however kind the hosts, are never integral parts of the family, they were not totally part of Canada and no longer part of Italy. Their status and state were just as unclear and uncertain. Because they equated Canada only with material progress, and Italy often only with past glory, their present life appeared disconnected, suspended between past and future, between the memory of distant greatness and a future of great hopes. As immigrants, they had also known Canada as a land of hardships and suffering, even in time that image changed a little, and the adopted land became redeemed in their eyes for its promise of a better life and advancement. Simultaneously, Italy was also equated mainly with bad economic conditions and hardships, partly the reason for their becoming immigrants. Italy's recent past, its evolution since their departure, was mainly unknown to them. Nevertheless, Italy too was often redeemed, especially by the rediscovery of its past glory. But in general, Italy remained a puzzle, a confusion, a series of notions.

In fact, in their accounts, Italy emerged as several mythical lands. First, it was the land of culture and history – the most positive view, but limited. Second, it was the land that changed too quickly, and for the worse (i.e., the country of lazy people, of pensioners and liars; where students refuse to work; children don't respect their parents; the government is unstable; the Red Brigades or Communists are taking over; and everyone is always talking about politics instead of working); a view that was widespread and influential, but balanced a little by another view of a more advanced Italy with "more cars, more roads, more luxuries, better homes, more money." And last, it was the land of their sweetest memories – the romantic, picturesque, pre-evolution Italy of the 1950s. This last one was mainly their Italy: this was generally the image they had brought with them and were able to keep alive because of their isolation and the large concentration of Italians from the same region or proximate areas. In a way, the Leamington Italian community, made up mostly of this "lost" or suspended generation, became a sort of time capsule: "Italians here have brought and kept with them the Italy that they left ... We've been transplanted, then isolated and stopped right there ... until the second generation."

It was this particular image of Italy that was a determining factor in their identity. Not only had they not been part of the recent Italian transformation, they also resisted outside influence; on the contrary, the outside influence was often transformed in accordance with their life-style and standards, as was made evident by the language or dialect used in the community. The dialect, which most had brought with them and widely used, had been left untouched by the influence of standard Italian or by mass media and education. It was a "purer," older form of the one in Italy: it remained fixed to the dialect they spoke when they left, twenty, thirty, or more years earlier. The community thus became also a linguistic island, a community with its own particular language, which even incoming immigrants often had to adopt in order to be part of the group: "I think that I have changed for the worst ... When I first came here, I spoke the best Italian, but I had to start changing and speaking dialect to bring myself down to the level that other Italians were at here."

Such condescension based on language was objectionable, turning some members of the community into unlikely supporters of linguistic scholarship. Robert A. Hall Jr once defined such speech as a "relic from earlier, antidemocratic times."[5] However, a dialect is a limited language, capable only of dealing with a circumscribed reality. To any Italian who had been accustomed, especially in postwar Italy, to equate the knowledge of standard Italian with upward mobility, having to abandon it for a dialect appeared as an opposite process.[6] The statement was a clear reference to the status of the community: it was not only close-knit, but closed, almost misoneistic. It pointed to a tendency in the community to resist linguistic variety, diversity, or outside influences in general and, therefore, changes. It revealed a general community pressure toward uniform behaviour, conformity and toward a form of "equality."[7]

The conditioning effect of the dialect on the standard Italian spoken by those entering the community had also a direct effect on their sense of *italianità*: their image of Italy remained as static as the dialect they spoke; therefore, the Italian component of their identity was also static, as well as outdated, parochial, and often confusing.[8] They themselves became the image of an Italy that had almost disappeared, or had been forgotten. Their claim to being Italians was not based on the more recently evolved Italy or on historical Italy, but mainly on the Italy of their memories. The result was also a contradiction between their criticism of modern Italy and their pride of being Italian.

Some of them did, of course, realize that true pride and identity consisted in the knowledge of the land of origin and above all of its language, as the person who had abandoned Italian for the dialect later regretfully recognized: "One must be proud to be an Italian before one can be proud to be a Canadian ... One must know his true homeland before he can know his adopted homeland."

But, in general, the results were quite different. On the one hand, their attachment to a distorted or antiquated image of Italy prevented them from rediscovering the "true homeland," and thereby reinforcing their self-image. On the other, while that attachment prevented their being assimilated, it also kept them from being more fully integrated into Canadian life: from becoming more familiar with its language(s), laws, customs and traditions, and thereby able to exercise more fully their rights as Canadian citizens, or participate more directly, in the political arena; as implied also in the statements by local politicians (Whelan, Patterson, the mayors; chapter 13).[9] For a few of them, in fact, the only way to overcome the resulting duality was a totally opposite reaction: "The reason why the Italians have not learned much more is because they don't want to abandon their language and their country ... Italians should learn the traditions of the new nation." The shedding of one part of one's makeup might have been a solution, had they been able to receive a clearer picture of those traditions, or a clearer answer to a fundamental question that more than one posed: "Who are the Canadians?"

The Italian-Canadian status became progressively puzzling. Because they had partially kept the values, ideas, and mentality that they had when they left Italy and entered Canada, to an Italian from Italy the Leamington Italians appeared to be "Canadians." On the other hand, because of the traits that prevented them from adopting the Canadian way of life more completely or from being absorbed into the Canadian environment, to the Canadian they appeared to be "Italians." But to themselves they were neither and both: "I became a Canadianized Italian" or "I am Italian, but I am Canadian."

They could not claim to be Italians, nor could they claim to be Canadians, however defined. Therefore, in a certain way, the Leamington Italian Canadians were unique, insofar as their common experience had moulded a life, a history that was shared only by other members of the Leamington Italian community (even though many traits were perhaps common to other Italian or non-Italian immigrant communities).

TOWARD A SELF-DEFINITION: THE REVERSAL OF ENDS AND MEANS

In their view, there were specific Italian characteristics that distinguished them from Canadians. They were Italian traits of their own – imported, but modified and joined with other aspects developed in their new environment. They were distinctive characteristics in behaviour – mannerisms and attitudes toward work, home, food, children, and success; and with those in mind one made an attempt to sum up their self-image: "The difference in the Canadian way of life and the Italian way is that Italians express themselves with their hands; food; stay closer to home; don't go out as much ... In general Italians are better or harder workers; they have pride in their work; they set high goals for themselves ... Not only do they want to keep up with the Joneses, they want to surpass them ... They not only want to do the best for themselves but for their kids as well ... This is unique among Italians as compared to, say, a lot of Canadians."

From the confusion, at least one definition emerged. Their self-identity often rested on the same qualities that the Canadian environment or opportunities allowed them to develop; qualities that others had already noticed and praised them for (and that alone was often quite satisfactory): industriousness, competitiveness, aggressiveness, and ambition. The "uniqueness" of their Italian-Canadian mentality was based on work, dedication, self-sacrifice, thrift, frugality, and self-advancement. What once was considered a means to solve a problem now became the goal, the main support, at times the essence of their identity. It seemed inevitable in the uncertainty surrounding what an Italian or a Canadian was.

Their personal past, part of which was also a certain unawareness of the Italian collective past, was what mainly "forged their future." Most Leamington Italians had spent their formative years in Italy. While there, largely in small villages or towns, they "were faced with a day-to-day existence, with little chance to plan for the future, and with little hope that life tomorrow would be any better than life today." As a result, they had to take life as it came, "enjoying the simple pleasures of food and wine, of local gatherings, of feast days and holidays. Everyone shared a common lot, and communities were close-knit, since people found their enjoyment in the company of others." In spite of the limitations, "they were," as most of them stated and Nino Ricci also reported (in *Radici*), "fairly content with their lot" in their own environment.

Their "tranquility" was disturbed, broken by "longing for something better" or "that desire," in Ricci's words, "for the Edenic paradise which the New World seemed to offer": at least, "an existence" that offered more hope for the future, or a place "where one's children would not have to [continue] to struggle ... to put bread on the table. Emigration held out that hope." They too became part of the great twentieth-century phenomenon of the "emigration fever," and they emigrated with one thought in mind – to forge a better life, which meant mainly a life free from material privation. They came to a country that offered some chance to succeed, to get ahead, to save, to put children through school, to have comfort and to have security. They were willing to work harder than they had worked in Italy, because "here at least you had a chance to get ahead." But in so doing, their lifestyle changed: given the opportunities, they became more willing to make sacrifices, to forego present pleasures for future gain, to hold two jobs at once, if necessary, so that the mortgage would be paid off in two years instead of ten or more. In a country that offered so many opportunities, they were anxious to get and keep more and more of what they never had in the Old Country: "Italian families didn't have much when they arrived and so they want to hold on to everything they have now; they won't spend too much money ... We fixed up the basement and lived downstairs. This was to keep furniture upstairs new."

They became frugal to the point of self-deprivation; they seldom knew how to enjoy the things they had come for in the first place. They mostly forgot the main purpose of what they came to get. What prevailed was the memory of only one aspect of their past – the hopeless economic condition; and that became the main spur to obtain more and more things, to be rich, successful, to have power, and then perhaps even respect from those who had been in the country for generations, who "were dominant" in the land when they arrived.[10] Their self-advancement drive, their search for material stability thus became an end in itself, often at the price of social and spiritual anesthesia. Their hard work became their life and existence, their identity, the basis of their self-esteem: "Italians are hard workers ... Some 'English' people are jealous of Italian people ... The 'English' shouldn't tease them ... If they want what the Italians have, they have to work." They were naturally oversensitive to the criticism directed at their work and material success. They felt that not jealousy but admiration was due them, in fact, emulation: "Teasing" them about their success was an attack on their self-image.

A QUEST FOR CHANGE REDUCED TO A FORMULA

In the long voyage, more psychological than geographical, the Italians were radically transformed. They became the opposite of what they were: from a people living for the present to a community preoccupied with the future, or as a woman sententiously expressed it, *"dalla sofferenza hanno preso il lavoro"* (from suffering they took work). Work redeemed their suffering, but it also became another form of suffering

or anxiety. They were quite aware that they were not unique: "The attitude of working for tomorrow is not peculiar to Italians ... but rather
to immigrants," who mostly for this reason, they said, "surpassed the
achievements of those who had long been in the country." They nevertheless felt that they, the Italians, were quite particular, even within
this group: the Italians saved their money, "did not go to the bars every
weekend," did not make frivolous expenditures they could not afford;
and they did so in order to quickly reach a position where they were
"quite financially secure."

But were they secure? "Some questioned whether the sacrifices made
en route were worth it." They complained that the Italian community
was no longer as close as it used to be; they had become too preoccupied
with their own self-interests to think about other people: "When people
came here they changed. [They] forgot friends ... [got too] involved in
making money." They repeatedly cited examples of the growing jealousy
among Italians, their anxiety to outdo the "other guy ... If so-and-so
buys a Lincoln, I have to buy a Lincoln." They all recognized that Italians
had become too "money-hungry," too anxious to get ahead, and consequently that they spent too much of their time working: "Italians are
hard-working, ambitious and foolish also, because they don't spend any
of it for their own pleasure, but save it and spend it all at once on one
thing at a time, like a big house or car ... Here Italians only think of
money and work."

They generally described, and their own lives often portrayed, a pattern of change reducible to a simple formula: *suffering* led to *work*, which
led to *financial security*. In their perception, life was a simple equation:
material wealth equals total happiness, or at least no problems. It could
not be otherwise! Had they not learned from their earlier experience in
Italy and Canada that poor economic conditions were the main cause of
their anxiety, unhappiness, and suffering?

Suffering relates mostly to the past, in Italy and in the early days
in Canada; *work* to their more recent experience or to the present in
Leamington; and *financial security* to future happiness for them and
their children, wherever they may want to be. But formulas or equations
applied to life often present a limited and distorted view of life. They
often fail to take into account aspects of human existence that are so
basic and so inherent that people are often unaware of them and of their
essential role throughout life: For most immigrants and even for the
children of the immigrants, or for anyone living in any form of exile, it is
the native soil, the land, and language of origin and/or of tradition. The
memory of them, the nostalgia for them (as many of them often said),

or the desire at times to regain them and to reproduce them in the new land, were and are ever-present; the act itself of denying them reveals their presence, however deep in the psyche. Yet, paradoxically, they are the same aspects that the formula dangerously excluded.

They are, in fact, the very aspects that the emigrants, as they anxiously set out on their new adventure, took for granted, and unintentionally least considered. The earlier emigrants-immigrants, in particular, were neither culturally equipped nor practically prepared to anticipate and deal with the socio-psychological effects of their breaking away from home, family, and familiar places. They were generally unaware that their hometown environment, which they said caused them so much material dissatisfaction, was also providing them with some contentment – that sort of tranquility, peace of mind, even spiritual balance that one no longer feels to inherently possess after being forever uprooted from the native soil ("Life did not offer much, but I was content").

They were mostly unaware of their paradoxical situation: what they had to leave behind in order to seek a better life became the object of their search, and thus the source of new insecurity. What the formula presented as a result was itself, in fact, a cause: the *financial security* or wealth they had *worked* so hard for did not, and of course could not, erase the *uncertainty* and *anxiety* deriving from living in an environment that remained not totally familiar and somewhat alien to them: And everything seemed to indicate that the principal reason was the ongoing erosion of their "cultural-linguistic" moorings – the anxiety from lost land and language.

The slow evolution of the Italian community seems to have brought with it a confusion of views, roles, and values. The vision that emerged from their description of the different periods of their lives, as implied also in the formula, appeared a little distorted: that association of their past mostly with suffering, their present with work and sacrifices, and their future with material success presented a static view of life, implied a state of suspension, or of being "transplanted ... isolated ... and stopped there." In the transition they slowly substituted living a more complete and more pleasant present life with future financial security and perhaps illusory happiness. This almost exclusive living-for-tomorrow caused a complete reversal of the role of work from means to end, to total goal. Work and money became the polarities of their total existence, of their total identity: working, getting ahead, saving money, possessions – their accumulation and protection – increasingly defined their "Italian Canadian-ness" as much as, if not more than, their traditions, customs, dialect, or sense of family.

Material gratification became the highest reward, provided the strongest sense of satisfaction and pride. Many pointed to their homes, their farms, and the comfortable life they had built for themselves as their highest achievements. The hardships they met and overcame were themselves a source of self-sufficiency and self-satisfaction: "one must make sacrifices to get ahead"; or in order to simply do what the other Canadians were doing all along: "relax a bit, and take the occasional trip back to Italy or down to Florida." They were, nevertheless, delighted and proud that their children were in school and most likely would never have to go through the hardships that they and the prewar pioneers had experienced.

Inevitably most of them grew more and more contented with their new homeland, and they continued to regard Canada as a young country with a good future – with plenty of opportunities for those willing to work. As they looked back to their first years in Canada, when they often "were more badly off than they had been in Italy," they became even more "satisfied with how far they had come." They were justifiably proud, as well, that they had helped transform the Leamington scene, giving life to industry and agriculture, and revitalizing the landscape with beautiful homes: "Italians have created jobs … have brought development … Perhaps Italians aren't great financiers but they are great builders … They have been nation builders for years … Without a doubt, they have contributed to Leamington and Canada." In their own eyes, and that was what counted most for them, they had indeed been "most successful," and that success was the essence of their identity as Italian Canadians.

THE UNCERTAIN LEGACY:
"ONE DOES NOT LIVE BY BREAD ALONE"

At the end of their research into the life and struggles of their grandparents and parents, the student-researchers posed a question: "How far are you from that Eden that, years ago, as you stood on a rocky mountainside, you thought of as only a dream?"[11] The children of that generation of Italians who felt "transplanted … isolated and stopped … until the second generation" almost poetically sensed that the journey of the community was not yet over. They, of course, knew what was meant by their parents' wish "until the next generation." They were the generation that was to continue the journey to a loftier destination, to build on their parents' success and embody the traditions, values, and identity of the community. But they were not always certain about the essential characteristics of the community that they were expected to protect and transmit.

However, all the young people interviewed (see chapter 10) were in total agreement about the image they were given of the Italian community as a whole. Either light-heartedly or in earnest, they revealed deep concern over what they saw in the community, pointing specifically to ambition, competitiveness, and materialism – the main causes of "jealousies" among Italians:

"Money, houses, properties, the way you dress; everyone wants more and more."
"Yes! They exist, for Italians are good for gossip, especially in this town."
"There are jealousies (hidden), e.g., businessmen who take large financial steps."
"Definitely! Italian men don't like their women to flirt with anyone but them."
"They always think they own you."
"Homes, jobs, cars, property, all material things."
"Most definitely; for example: someone building a house or buying a new car."
"Have you ever driven down Highway 18 and noticed the homes?"
"Look at all the Trans-Ams and the Z28s we have in this town."
"Everyone tries to compete with each other and try to be better."
"Girls that have no freedom [are jealous] of girls that have their freedom."
"Look at their houses; one tries to outdo the other."

"Tomorrow" had arrived! The young generation, for which the "sacrifices" were made and financial security sought, did not despise their parents' success or wealth, but neither did they consider it the ultimate goal or essence of an individual or a community. They had fewer illusions about their parents' drive to own more, and their vying "to outdo the other." They tended to demythologize the Eden of "material things" sought by the previous generation(s) often at the expense of the social, psychological, and spiritual side of the "human animal" and the community. They questioned old inflexible attitudes and traditions that sometimes made women feel like chattel ("They think they own you"), with little space or freedom for self-fulfilment. They challenged the double standard. They rejected the widespread gossip that often shackled, demoralized and even intimidated the community. They sometimes objected to their parents' use of children as pretexts for their search for financial security, while exposing more probable reasons: "I think

Italians feel that they must save their money in order to build a better home, etc., in order to prove themselves"; "Italians are defensive because deep down they feel they're foreigners."

The young generation doubted the whole system of values. Though they often acknowledged attitude changes and more rapid adaptation to the Canadian way of life, they observed that material progress had engendered more material progress: "Everyone wants more and more." Financial security had often become the only substitute for emotional security or true identity: Italians still felt they were "foreigners" in Canada, or at least "guests," as some plainly admitted. Financial success became a defence for their increased vulnerability against the attacks of Italian jealousy or Canadian and English "teasing." It was an obstacle to being more Canadian, as it had been the primary cause for their severance from Italy. While it offered physical satisfaction, it had not clearly revealed the path to greater harmony in the family or community, to the tranquility of a more attainable spiritual haven. The young generation, the generation of their hope, was receiving too many double messages, too many confusing and contradicting guidelines to balance the two traditions or lifestyles.

The young people revealed, with admirable frankness, a dilemma or conflict, rather than a synthesis of the components of their Italian-Canadian identity. Most considered themselves Italian Canadians and were proud of their heritage. But because of that heritage women were not considered equal to men. They respected their parents' views, but followed others diametrically opposed, often unwillingly pretending to be what they were not. They were born or grew up in Canada, but were often considered Italians; most of their friends were Italians; and yet they hardly spoke Italian or knew little about Italy, its life, history, and civilization. They considered the Italian family in many ways better than the Canadian family, but they did not intend to marry within the Italian tradition or raise their children in the traditional way. They were all benefiting from Canadian higher education, but they were still holding on to some old-fashioned views. They praised their parents' changing attitudes, they were grateful for their sacrifices and enjoyed the privileges of their success, but questioned their way of life and material values. They were uncertain about their status and what to transmit to their own children. They were even more uncertain than their parents had been; at least, their parents' role and goal, however limited, had been clear for some years and had offered them some satisfaction.

BETWEEN THEIR HERITAGE AND NEW LIFESTYLES

Remo Mancini, though not of the same age group as that of the young
people interviewed – yet quite representative of the younger generation,
since he was only five years old when he arrived in Canada in 1956 –
offered a clear portrayal of the Italian-Canadian experience and condition; and though not from Leamington, as a politician and as an immigrant, Mancini had first-hand knowledge of the difficulties and anxieties
of the Italian immigrants in the general Leamington area. He grew up
and was first educated in Amherstburg, a small town not far from Windsor and Leamington, which already had its own tiny Italian community.
His family lived in a neighbourhood with numerous Italian families, and
the school he attended had "a lot of Italians" who "shared many common traits," so "most of his friends were Italians." Though he briefly left
the town to attend university, he returned to the area, where he became
successful in business and politics. His varied experience, as well as his
marriage to a Canadian-born woman with a French father and an Italian
mother, offered him an ample view of the immigrant struggles, the Italian-
Canadian journey toward integration, and the identity dilemma. There
was no doubt in his mind about the first difficulties the Italians encountered upon arrival: "Culture shock! Especially for those immigrants who
arrived [in the 1950s]. There was also the lack of mass communication,
many Italians had no idea of what Canada was like. Today at least they
can watch the world news on television and grasp some ideas here and
there. Then there is a major dilemma Italians and other immigrants face:
the fact that they truly want to become a part of the mainstream, but at
the same time they want to hold on to their tradition. There is the conflict
of losing part of your heritage while gaining new lifestyles."

Whether it was the first generation's self-definition – "I am Italian, but
I am Canadian"; "I became a Canadianized Italian" – or the child of the
immigrant claiming, "I consider myself more Canadian than Italian";
"Canada number one … Italy second," the juxtaposition of the two realities was ever-present in both groups. The two realities had a life of their
own, more often in opposition than in harmony. They always implied a
relative condition, a double consciousness, a two-fold state of mind and
consequently ambiguity, uncertainty, perplexity, and precariousness.

Such a dual identity or vacillating self-image could hardly be resolved
by rejecting or erasing one of the two realities, as expressed in the simplis-
tic recommendation that "Italians … abandon their language and their
country … [and] learn the traditions of the new nation." Assimilation was
an illusory solution. Besides, the suggestion seemed even "un-Canadian,"

for it tended to undermine one of Canada's fundamental policies favouring retention and integration. It ironically revealed unawareness of a Canadian historical reality and of multiculturalism, whose goal is also to promote a world view in every citizen.[12]

Empirical data and general wisdom make evident that an individual or group without a past is an entity without a future, a "nonentity." Assimilation seems even more difficult to attain than the desired balance of the two parts. As a Canadian writer has shown, one who accepts the challenge to abandon the past or one's group must be prepared for nothing less than a heroic struggle: "Noah Adler in Mordecai Richler's *Son of a Smaller Hero* also rejects 'proper appearances' [his roots] – his grandfather, family and community" – in order to search for his true identity, his true self; but at what cost and sacrifices! In fact, the Canadian critic "Northrop Frye speaks of 'the real terror (that) comes when the individual feels himself becoming an individual, pulling away from the group, losing the sense of driving power that the group gives him, aware of a conflict within himself far subtler than the struggle of morality against evil."[13]

BASES FOR BALANCE BETWEEN THE OLD AND THE NEW

The majority of Leamington Italians did not believe in leaving the past or the group, suggesting that for most of them the best solution was not in rejection of one or the other reality, but in balancing them; and this could be made even easier, according to some, by rediscovery of their past, especially through a collective community effort, through their club. The entire community, the older, the younger, and the in-between, had common experiences and achievements. They were all products of a common past; they shared a common journey and a common identity dilemma, or search.

The younger generation's frank assessment of their community also indicated their close relationship with it. Their awareness of community flaws was in itself an achievement. Recognizing and admitting one's own imperfections were also signs of maturity, of spiritual development. They did not act as aloof critics, as severe judges. They made themselves part of that criticism or that success, of that commonality. In a way, as they were dissecting the community, they were reinforcing its sense of oneness.

Above all, the younger generation's honest evaluation of their parents' pursuits underscored the need to retain and recover the linguistic-cultural components of their common past, in order to re-establish a balance in the family and community; especially in order to prepare the younger generation to interact more meaningfully within a pluralistic society. It is becoming more and more apparent that even a better education without some knowledge of the Italian language and culture is not a guarantee for development and preservation of a meaningful and creative Italian-Canadian identity, or simply for being an Italian Canadian – distinct yet fully part of the Canadian mosaic.

The arguments presented by A. Kenneth Ciongoli can also be applied to the Italian-Canadian situation: "The cultural ascent which has led to Ivy League graduation for Italian Americans is strewn with assimilation to Anglo-Saxon attitudes. James Crispino, in his 'Assimilation of an Ethnic Group,' has documented that Italian American assimilation to the mainstream American ideals is directly proportional to their degree of education. Crispino sadly informs us that the baccalaureate Italian American frequently has only the vestiges of a cuisine left from his or her old world culture."[14]

But knowledge of language without its cultural context can also result in a dangerous imbalance, according to Gian Luigi Beccaria. Language without some cultural base is speech by formulas, a string of disconnected repetitions, clichés, slogans, without any individual creative involvement. In accordance, therefore, with traditional wisdom and recent scholarship, in order to be a better human being and citizen, a good education would have to include a good knowledge of at least one language. For Italian Canadians a good education would mean the ability to speak and write well at least one official Canadian language as well as the Italian language, because "to speak and to write correctly and creatively means ensuring oneself freedom of action and of judgement."[15]

Those goals were still far from being achieved. Nevertheless, in the midst of so many perplexities, trends, tendencies, and contradictions, the community as a whole was able to strike some form of balance between tradition and experience. With respect to their traditions and customs, particularly those related to family, children, food, and religion, they were generally conservative, conforming, inflexible, even ethnocentric ("Italian cuisine the best in the world"). They were proud and sometimes scornful of Canadian ways, but not aloof, unsociable, or unneighbourly. In hardships they were strong and patient, and though embittered by prejudice and criticism, they often disarmed it with a sense of humour, without harbouring malice or grudges. They manifested flexibility in their quick adjustment to the new agricultural and lakeside area, in some cases not very unlike the one they had been accustomed to. They learned the "ways of the land" or at least to draw wealth from the soil; and, undeterred by obstacles, they slowly transformed themselves from foreigners and subservient workers to masters of their trades as well as of the farmlands. Though often self-absorbed and closed within their group, they progressed and learned to live with other groups in the Leamington multicultural diversity.

They were generally respectful of the traditional simple values and virtues they knew best, which also seemed most suitable to rural life. They were family and child oriented, and as parents they were often strict, overprotective, and possessive, but also very caring, solicitous, and generous. They were self-sufficient, economical, frugal, even to the point of self-denial, and extremely provident to the point of sacrificing present needs. They were determined, tenacious, obstinate, and stubborn in pursuit of their goals, but not ruthless: sometimes uncouth but not unkind. They were self-defensive and self-protective but not broody or inhospitable; self-satisfied and self-assured but generally not complacent, smug or condescending. They were loyal and affectionate in friendship, and in spite of increasing jealousy they continued to follow the long-established practice of mutual help. What education did not offer, they obtained from conventional wisdom, innate common sense, and perseverance. They were, above all, indefatigable workers. Their conscientiousness and conscience continually provided them with a stabilizing force in all their pursuits.

A basic moral sense, more than school and religion, seemed to be their main guide in the struggle for economic security and in the collective search for group maintenance, of which the Roma Club is a concrete expression. It accompanied the pioneers through their most difficult journey and first years of hardships. It continued to permeate all their feelings and actions. In their quest for material self-betterment and in their attachment to material possession, it gave them room to practise greed and miserliness, but at the same time maintain civilized community life. In an alien environment, in a rustic, relatively isolated area, often with limited communication skills, far removed from the land of origin and often out of touch with its language and culture, it helped to direct the community away from degradation. It kept alive and enforced those basic human qualities that allowed them to strive for the North American dream of financial success and security and cherish many of their traditions and values; as well as to cope with the paradoxes, contradictions, and confusion of immigration; at times to overcome the puzzle of their self-image, their Italian Canadian duality; and to see through their self-deception and be honest with themselves and with others.

Nowhere were these basic qualities more evident than in the interviews for their own history, the material for their self-portrait. Perhaps their greatest achievement was their remarkable self-revelation: the honesty, sincerity, and frankness with which they described themselves, their successes and failures, their virtues and shortcomings. Their conscientious self-confession, manifestly resulting from a thorough self-examination, was almost a sacramental a form of liberation; it was simultaneously a sign of a greater self-awareness and consciousness, of a presence in the community of a more advanced form of self-identity.

Materialistic needs and pursuits had not, after all, completely extinguished their hope and quest for some form of balance, for a marriage between their diminishing traditional values and the frequently overwhelming new tendencies or reality. Their very struggle (regardless of outcome) to join or separate, or even alternate, the two components of their new identity (including the attempt itself to reject one of the components, i.e., their traditions) was itself an indication of a particular self-awareness: of a need to come to terms with, adjust, and readjust the two halves of their being. At times, they even succeeded in reaching a suitable accommodation of the two parts of their hyphenated identity: "Italian-Canadian."

At least three types of outcome of their conflict-search are perceivable in their statements: one form based on cultural retention and/or rediscovery (as evidenced by the familiarity with, or recollection of, aspects of Italian civilization or historical figures, whether as renowned as Galileo or less known as Enrico Toti); another deriving from a thoughtful and wise realization that one cannot "love" or know well one's adopted mother(land) without first loving or knowing one's "true" mother(land) – as manifested in the revision of a view regarding the role of the standard Italian language besides the dialect; and a third type based on the recognition and acceptance of inherent Italian flaws or defects (especially envy and jealousy), and particularly of the more "typical" Italian Canadian characteristics by which they defined themselves: "hard-working, ambitious" and penny-pinching, "but foolish." It was, above all, this recognition of their "foolishness," of their community's own version of human folly, that while underscoring their objective self-evaluation, made their story different, if not unique.

That type of self-critical approach or outlook, however limited, tended to reduce the split within themselves as well as the generation gap in the family and the community, and simultaneously open the way toward more self-knowledge, maturity, and wisdom: the realization that material things were not an end in themselves, but a basis for further human development. This was perhaps the most valuable and enduring part of their legacy: a legacy that seemed to have already come to fruition in the search and work by the younger generation of Leamington Italians; and particularly in the accomplishment by one of the representatives of that group – Nino Ricci.

His novel, *Lives of the Saints*, may also be considered an elaborate and enjoyable exploration of the deep-rooted nature of ethnicity; of the enduring presence of ethnic identity, even in the often unaware Canadian-born younger generation of Italians. It illustrates a simple statement by a Leamington Italian concerning their puzzled state of mind or search for a self-identity – a condition more or less common to all Italians in Canada (and perhaps outside Italy): *"Siamo italiani ma non lo sappiamo"* (We are Italians but we don't know it). In fact, in order to "know it" or become more aware of one's *italianità* and real self, one needs to embark on a journey similar to that undertaken by Ricci.

The Universal Values of Ethnicity: Nino Ricci's *Lives of the Saints* and the Leamington Italian Community

THE THREE-GENERATION PARALLELS

The formation of the Leamington Italian community, almost paralleling human life, spans three generations, with each generation representing an essential step in its development. The adventurous pre–Second World War migrants – the small, close-knit group of pioneers, deeply rooted in tradition and concerned mainly with survival and security (work, farm ownership) – constitute the first generation. They represent the laying of solid physical foundations, the infancy and formative years of the community; more generally, the material or economic moment or stage of development.

The second generation – comprising the children of the pioneers and the large number of mostly sponsored post–Second World War relatives and friends – constitute the middle generation: still in pursuit of material security, respecting and imitating established community values and practices (family, community solidarity) but simultaneously modifying them, assuming a more independent outlook and lifestyle in conformity with the new environment and the pressures of the newer generation. They are the generation that, on the one hand, mark the physical growth (number, strength) and the socio-economic consolidation of the collective entity (commercial, professional diversification), and, on the other, attempt to establish a vital link between material well-being and socio-cultural fulfillment (Roma Club, community-oriented projects) and, above all, between past and future generations. In particular, they promote the rediscovery of their community's past, their total migration experience, and at the same time ensure its transmittance to the younger generation by directly involving their own Canadian-born children (i.e., the third generation or the grandchildren). They are the generation that represent the middle age, adulthood, the "socialization" moment, the self- and social awareness and adjustment stage, as well as the more reflective moment typical of the mature age.

The grandchildren of the pioneers, along with the children of the post–Second World War immigrants, constitute the third generation: a diversified group of heirs of family and community traditions and achievements, most of whom – however involved in different and independent endeavours (business, professions) and even when appearing unwilling or critical beneficiaries of that inherited, sometimes stifling socio-economic structure – continue to share in the preservation of the traditional family and community values, however transformed to suit the new environment. They are the generation that, stood on the shoulders of their parents and grandparents, have been offered a vantage point from which to see and seek material and spiritual enrichment beyond the community, without turning their backs on the community that shaped them. On the contrary, they have often made their tradition part of their further development, of their new vision – an integral part of their new self-identity (see chapter 10, especially "The Challenging Balance").

In this sense, Nino Ricci can be viewed as the best representative, so far, of that third generation, and the ongoing transition of the entire community. As a child of second-generation Leamington Italian immigrants, born and raised in the Leamington community; as a researcher and close observer of the Leamington Italian migration experience; as the compiler-writer of *Radici: A Study of the Italian Immigrants in Leamington*); and above all as a cultivator of those roots into an artistic-literary fruit – *Lives of the Saints* – Ricci represents the repository, transformer, and transmitter of fact and feeling of the three generations of Leamington Italians.

Already as a research-project leader, he guided the student-researchers toward the reconstruction of the personal life history of each immigrant, including personal opinions, feelings, moralities, and philosophies, the nature of the Italian immigrant, and the effect of the immigrant experience as a whole. His thoughtful investigation of the meaning of those particular facts and feelings is first evidenced in the string of questions he posed: "How did an immigrant's past affect his present?" What was the impact of Italian immigration on the Leamington ethnocultural diversity, "and, on a grander scale ... the effect of immigration on the nation as a whole?" What "similarities ... and differences" existed between the Italian community and "other Canadian communities"?[1] While connecting him directly to the previous generations, his inquiry clearly reveals and confirms the influence or force of ethnicity, even on the third generation.

Radici itself, more than a report on the summer 1979 student research, is also Ricci's own (and thus the community's) search for an answer to the immigrant self-identity, for a balance of his own ethnocultural Italian inheritance and the Canadian milieu. In fact, his *Radici* served two almost similar purposes: as a guideline for the present historical narration of the development of the Leamington Italian community, and as the underlying world for the fictional story about a similar close-knit rural community, where the members of three generations are also deeply affected by a clash of old values and new experiences, and the village as a whole by migration – Nino Ricci's first novel, *Lives of the Saints*.

THE SEEDS OF THE NOVEL

Lives of the Saints was not written in Leamington, but the story was conceived and gestated in the Leamington environment. The seminal idea most likely took shape during the summer 1979 interviews with the Leamington Italian immigrants, when Nino, still a student, served as project manager, then as writer of the forty-two-page report (March 1980). The framework of the novel came into being as he was shaping the material collected by the student-researchers.

Ricci took his "goods" from wherever he found them. The Leamington Roma Club project provided him with a unique opportunity to recover part of his past, to expand his knowledge of his heritage and of his community by making the community's memories his own.

In a moment of pensive anticipation of his departure and journey toward Canada, Vittorio, the young narrator in Ricci's novel, seems to have already mapped in his mind an image of his native village, "Valle del Sole, which somehow could not help but remain always visible on the receding shore" (chapter 11). Vittorio's reflection, while representing the state of mind of all those who had to leave their native soil and the memory they retain of it, is the reconstruction of the state of mind, and of the image of the hometowns, that most Leamington Italian immigrants transferred into their life stories, and that filtered into Ricci's two "stories" – *Radici* and *Lives of the Saints*. In fact, the events and memories recorded in the former "remain always visible" in the background of the latter – setting, story, characters, mores, and even language.

Radici is a chronicle of the community's birth and growth and of Nino Ricci's roots, both biographical and artistic. As a narrative of real events, as a compilation of data outlining the community's development, the report-study concludes with a clear view of the Italian immigrants' socio-economic progress and its effect on the Leamington area; it is, thus, an answer to Ricci's earlier questions: "In many ways, they have transformed the community, giving life to industry and agriculture, and revitalizing the landscape with beautiful homes." But as a search for "roots," as implied in the Italian title *Radici*, as a quest for self-identity, which involves a conscious investigation, a clear overview, if not an ample definition, of the entire migration experience, the report provides only a final unanswered question: "How far are they from that Eden which, years ago, as they stood on a rocky mountainside, they thought of as only a dream?"[2]

Ricci's question is the distant point of departure for *Lives of the Saints*, and the work itself provides part of the answer to his final question in *Radici*. First, by the very fact that, in *Lives of the Saints*, the small world of the Leamington Italian immigrants has been sublimated and universalized into art. Second, by the young Vittorio's (i.e., Ricci's) observations of the effects of migration on his village, his family, and himself – his groping for meaning or truth in the changes around him, particularly in his confused state of mind caused by separation from the certainty of his home and village and by a simultaneous need to escape into a freer but unknown distant land and vague future. Third, Vittorio's apparent intent, as a migrant himself, to always keep his village within his sight: that is, in his childlike vision of his life in Canada, he almost foresees the need to leave room for a memory of his past life in his land of origin. Thus Vittorio anticipates the elusive solution to the immigrants' dilemma regarding self-identity. Vittorio's continual "brooding" offers an insight into Ricci's artistic process and, at the same time, into Ricci's own search for a solution to the identity question: the creative use of the past in order to better understand oneself in the present, as well as the future – it is perhaps the only process to achieve a new balanced identity, however elusive.

Radici, moreover, seems to present a "process" partly parallel to that described by Umberto Eco in the "Postille" ("Postscript") to his novel *The Name of the Rose* (1980): "Writing a novel," Eco wrote in 1983, "is a cosmological affair." While as a semiotician and theorist of language and human communication Eco was quite aware of the issue, as "a storyteller [he] was a beginner"; and as he set out to write he "discovered that a novel, at its very onset, has nothing to do with words ... One must first of all build himself a world, furnished as much as possible down to the last details ... In fiction the restrictions" needed "in order to be able to invent freely [are] given by the underlying world"; it is this "world" that will also determine how the "story must then develop," as well as provide a "certain coherence" or appropriateness to all its constituent elements (characters, language, style, type of narrator as well as rhythm, mood, "pace" or "breath"). They all must reflect the "laws of the world" thus created ("The author himself is a prisoner of his own premises"; and the text takes on a life of its own, independent of the creator).

Eco, of course, chose the world he knew well as a scholar – the Middle Ages. Nevertheless, "the first year of work on [his] novel was dedicated to the construction of its world" – work that involved gathering minute documentation on every aspect of medieval life and culture – so that the story appeared to emerge naturally from it.[3] It was, in fact, *The Name of the Rose*, Eco's literary invention, more than his scholarly studies on the Middle Ages that, has been described as one of the "few, if any, works of fiction [that] have brought the cultural and intellectual world of this period, or of any other period, so successfully to life."[4]

In a certain sense, Ricci's *Radici* is to *Lives of the Saints* as Eco's "Postscript" or "Afterword" is to *The Name of the Rose*. Neither provides an interpretation of the respective literary work (which novelists "should not" do anyway, Eco says, since "a novel ... is a machine for generating interpretations," but it "may tell why and how [it has been] written"[5]). In Ricci's case, that objective was practically impossible, since *Radici* was written long before the novel; but when related to his novel, the report can be viewed as Ricci's own gathering of empirical data, a closer examination of a world he already knew quite well – the Leamington Italian community – on which he built his intuited world, which is an equally credible and "real" world.

Radici thus represents a motherlode of ideas, "the book of [his] memory"[6] and, in retrospect, a sort of "poetics": it offers an insight into the creative act itself, or at least makes clearer the process of transformation of the raw material into a successful literary work, into a "[haunting] rich and wonderful tapestry."[7] The transformation itself from *Radici* to *Lives of the Saints* also suggests an evolution that needs to occur as well in the immigrant community in order to become more fully part (like Ricci's novel) of the larger community.

THE STORY'S UNDERLYING WORLD: SOUTHERN ITALY AND THE SUN PARLOUR

Leamington itself and its Italian community are not the main setting of the story, but they are present throughout the novel. They form an extension of the world of the novel, which is quite clearly Upper Molise (XII, XXVI), the area of origin of the largest Leamington Italian group. Leamington itself appears a few times as the Sun Parlour (a popular name for the Leamington area; see chapter 8). The Sun Parlour is also presented as "part of some vast village," which includes Canada, and together forming that vague land of "contradictions ... across the sea," which the villagers in the novel (and most Italians in Italy) referred to as "America" (XXI).

Both Leamington and the Italian community are also quite transparent in references to "two men from our region [who] had smuggled themselves across the ocean and settled there" (a clear echo of the experiences of the Leamington Italian pioneers, chapter 2); the quite common departures of villagers for America and the Sun Parlour (XX, XXI), and the immigrants returning to the village of origin to marry or, as in the case of "Alfreddo" [sic] Pannunzio (XII), "to sell [his] land" and bring his "family back to Canada" (i.e., the Sun Parlour); as well as the remittances (IV), the uncertainty of factory work in the new land, the purchase of a farm before sponsoring the family, or even the primitive living quarters of some immigrants (III, XII) – they all derive from the Leamington Italians' accounts summarized by Ricci in *Radici*.

In fact, several names in the novel are the actual names of Leamington Italian immigrants, and in some cases immigrants even in the novel: Mancini, Longo, Mastroangelo (XXI), including a few of the pioneer families – Pannunzio, DiMenna, already in the Sun Parlour (XII); and the Mastronardis, still in the "village" (XVII, XIX); others, such as Amicone is the name of the village teacher (XXIII); while the last name of "a local saint [San Camillo de Lellis]" (V) corresponds to a Leamington Italian family and to the real "St Camillus of Lellis," whose feast day (in 1959–60) fell on 18 July in both the liturgy and the novel.

It is also the Sun Parlour, or at least Canada (Halifax), for which the novel's two main protagonists (Vittorio and his mother Cristina) set out toward the end of the story. Like many postwar Leamington Italian immigrants, including Ricci's parents, they too sail from Naples on the *Saturnia* (XXVI–XXVII). Many of their experiences en route are also similar: at departure (Cristina's father's anger and curse [XXV]); during the journey they have mixed feelings for both the country they left behind and the land of destination (XXVII); and on arrival, Vittorio reunites in Halifax with his father, until then almost a "phantom" (IV), since he "had emigrated to America almost four years before" (I); and their ride "together on a coal-dust-filled train ... across a desolate landscape, bleak and snow-covered for as far as the eye could see" (XXXII) – they are all clear reminiscences of the separation of the father from the family among Leamington Italians (sometimes for many years, as in the case of Vito Peralta or Tony DiMenna from his son Gino). They also recall some descriptions of their

Halifax-Windsor train journey, and some first impressions of Canada (some of the words describing the train and landscape are almost exactly those used in *Radici*, 15; see also chapters 3, 5, 6, 7, 8). Although in the novel Vittorio does not reach the Sun Parlour, his vision of the "vast village ... across the sea" relates closely to the Leamington area "with forests and green fields and great lakes" (XXI).

The area of origin of those villagers who already live in the Sun Parlour or "regularly" depart for the same destination, is the setting of *Lives of the Saints*, which is its isolated, backward, and generally poor mountain villages: the "forgotten and unsung" Valle del Sole (I), still without "electrical service" (XII); "nearby Castilucci, Valle del Sole's age-old rival" (I); "Rocca Secca ... once ... a great centre" but in decline for years because of political indifference and emigration, its "people ... moving away, to Argentina mainly" (VII); "Belmonte ... destroyed by the Germans in the second war" and never rebuilt out of fear of its sorceress (*la strega di Belmonte*), and as its residents preferred to emigrate (VI); as well as "Capracotta" (IV) and the quite far "Campobasso" (XII).

In the description of the physical setting, which as Eco states is part of the "underlying world" of the novel, not only are the actual names of the towns of origin of the Leamington Italians remembered, but also many of the reasons for emigration from the Italian South, such as the economic and political conditions – poverty, high taxes, unjust laws, the war – as well as the psychological motivations, e.g., the lure of the myth of America (XXI), and even superstition (VI).

THE PRINCIPAL SETTING OF THE STORY

Valle del Sole or Valley of the Sun, where the story mainly unfolds, is a composite village clearly based on the villages of origin of the Leamington Italians, including those of Nino Ricci's parents (in Leamington since 1954: father from Poggio Sannita; mother, née Ingratta, from Villa Canale, two Molisan villages about five kilometres apart). The name itself, *Valle del Sole*, is modelled on *Villa Canale*. And they resemble one another in other respects: in the analogous situation relating to St Michael as the patron saint (in the fictional village, the "original patron" but arbitrarily changed by the dissatisfied villagers, IX; in the real village, not the traditional patron, but "the most characteristic feast"); in the similar feast-day activities in both real and fictional villages – the procession, strolling, wine-drinking in the open air, music in the square, and fireworks (IX–XII). For the construction of Valle del Sole's *Festa della Madonna* (Festival of the Virgin), Ricci had readily available material: not only the recorded memories of the older Leamington immigrants, but also a model – the Leamington St Michael's Festival, whose promoters in 1969 included Ricci's father, who also provided a "brief history" of it.[8]

The resemblances between the fictional world and the real world are numerous and sometimes identical: the name of a street – "via San Giuseppe" (I) – is the same in both villages; some topographical features of Valle del Sole are similar to Villa Canale's – "the hollow of stony mountains that cradled it" (XXI); while the altitude of the fictional village ("not in a valley at all, but perched ... about three thousand feet above the valley floor" [II]) reflects more generally the Upper Molise highland villages – Villa Canale and Poggio Sannita, about 2,300 feet above sea level; Agnone and Belmonte, about 2800 feet, Capracotta, about 4,600 feet. Quite similar is the nature of the farms (low-yielding "plots of land scattered piecemeal across the countryside," VI), as well as some typical Christmas pastries (XVIII). More specifically, Villa Canale appeared with the name "Valle del Sole" in a 1988 publication in honour also of the *Villacanalesi* in the Leamington area: *Le due "valli del sole": Villacanale – Leamington* (The two "valleys of the sun": Villa Canale – Leamington).

THE NOVEL'S OTHER VILLAGES

"Rocca Secca," the name of an actual town, Roccasecca in Lazio, which gave Leamington several families (including one bearing the name Ricci), is based mostly on the Molisan town of Agnone (also the town of origin of many Leamington Italians, and about six kilometres from Villa Canale). Agnone is quite transparent in "Rocca Secca['s claim] to be the site of ancient Aquilonia, a Samnitic fortress town from before the time of Christ" (Agnone's claim is questioned by some historians);[9] it is also recognized in the references to the town's former grandeur, "a great centre, renowned for its goldsmiths and bronzeworks, its schools, its convents, and the seat of the region's aristocracy [and] of the most powerful family ... who owned half the land from Rocca Secca to Capracotta" (VII).

Agnone, like the fictional Rocca Secca, has also been long affected by emigration and bureaucratic neglect at the regional and national levels, and again, like Rocca Secca, which compared "to other towns in the area ... was filled with life" (VII), Agnone is still the administrative and commercial centre of the ten-municipality "Mountain Community"[10] and still enjoys some world fame for its prize-winning Fonderia Pontificia Marinelli (Marinelli papal foundry), a centuries-old casting house of church bells.[11] Agnone is also easily identifiable in the novel's historically accurate rendition of "the *tomolo* in the centre of the square, a hollowed out stone of three compartments used to measure grain for rent and taxes," particularly in the reference to "a long tradition" of publicly declaring bankruptcy (VII) or humiliating defaulting farmers who were "forced to sit naked on the [stone], with ankles shackled, for one or more days according to the seriousness of the punishment."[12]

"Belmonte" and "Capracotta" are also the actual names of Upper Molise towns and the towns of origin of several Leamington Italian families, while "Castilucci" may be based on Castelluccio, the name of over a dozen Italian towns and villages including one in Molise, near Fossalto (Campobasso province). It also recalls the former names of Castelliri (Lazio) and of two Molisan towns – Castelmauro, until 1883, Castelluccio Acqua Borrana (Campobasso province) and Castelverrino, until 1891 Castelluccio in Verrino. The latter may be the most likely source of the name, given its location – nine kilometres from Agnone, between Villa Canale and Pietrabbondante, or just south of Poggio Sannita. But it may also be a result of the union of the first part of *Casti*glione, a town near Agnone in Molise (and in numerous parts of Italy) and of *Lucci*, the name of a street in Agnone (and part of the name of a character in the novel, "Di Lucci").

Moreover, certain fictional-autobiographical parallels suggest an identification of "Castilucci" with Poggio Sannita: first, in the novel, the narrator's mother is a native of Valle del Sole (i.e., Villa Canale), while his father is from Castilucci (I); similarly, the novelist's mother was born in Villa Canale, and his father in Poggio Sannita. Second, the narrator's family lived for some time in Castilucci (IV); and again similarly, the novelist's mother lived in Poggio Sannita for four years before going to Canada. The fact that Castilucci is said to be "nearby" Valle del Sole (I) further supports that identification since, in reality, Villa Canale (i.e., Valle del Sole) is located "at almost the same distance from Agnone (i.e., Rocca Secca) and from Poggio Sannita" (i.e., Castilucci).[13]

THE NOVEL'S GEOGRAPHY AND THE LEAMINGTON ITALIANS

The link between the novel's geographical area and Upper Molise can be further established by considering the towns of origin of Leamington Italians whose family names are used for some of the fictional characters. Villa Canale is the village of origin of the Leamington (pre–Second World War) Pannunzios, DiMennas, and many of the Mastronardis (some of the last are from either Agnone or Poggio Sannita). In the novel, Alfreddo [*sic*] Pannunzio, though not from Valle del Sole but from the nearby Castilucci, is present at Valle del Sole's festival the day after his return from Canada or the Sun Parlour (i.e., Leamington); Umberto DiMenna (XII), whose new residence is also the Sun Parlour, emigrated from Valle del Sole, where the Mastronardis still reside (XVII). Also "one of the Mastroangelos" (XXI) left Valle del Sole for the Sun Parlour "around Christmas" (1960) just as the Leamington A. Mastroangelo had emigrated from Villa Canale (1952). The novel's "Amicone" – the schoolteacher of Valle del Sole and resident of Rocca Secca (i.e., Agnone) – compares to the Leamington Amicones: Lino, Lucio, and Pat are native of Poggio Sannita, while their wives are from Villa Canale (Lino's and Pat's) and from Agnone (Lucio's).

Other fictional names, though not exactly the same, also reflect reality: the "Dagnellos" of Valle del Sole (I, XX, XXI) echo the Leamington (Enrico) D'Agnillo (Agnone, 1952); and "Mr D'Amico ... who was going to America to visit his son" (XXVIII) brings to mind at least two Leamington immigrants: the Molisan Antonio Dimicco (Campodipietra, 1956) and the Sicilian Armando Bonfiglio (Alia, 1969), whose father had also gone to Canada to visit a daughter.

In general, the names of villages in the novel recall or repeat the names of villages and towns in Molise and one in Lazio. In fact, in constructing the setting of the novel, the towns of origin of the Leamington families bearing the name Ricci would seem to nearly suffice: five originate from Poggio Sannita, two from Pietrabbondante (indirectly recalled as the site of an ancient "temple or shrine" and "amphitheatre" [VII]);[14] one from Belmonte (the place of the witch, "destroyed by the Germans in the second war" [I, VI]), and one each from Ceprano (Lazio) and Roccasecca (Lazio). But it is mainly Molise – the towns and areas of the Leamington Molisani – that is recreated in the novel: its mountain geography, part of its history (even the region's pre-Roman, Samnite origins [VII]), and its distinctive dialects (including "the recognizable twang of Castilucci's dialect" [XII]; or the regional speech used by Cristina with her son, which allows Darcangelo – the *Saturnia*'s third mate – also a Molisan from the sea town of Termoli, to recognize Cristina's origin: "*Molisana* ... I thought so" [XXVI]). But it is a "Molise" that is also a metaphor of the general southern Italian situation: its centuries-long isolation, exploitation, and backwardness, its deep-rooted rural mentality, its shared identity and experience, especially through migration.[15]

The novel's world incorporates aspects of all three main groups of Leamington Italians and respective regions of origin – Molise, Lazio,

Sicily: Valle del Sole's women, for example, are clearly modelled on the southern Italian peasant women in general (I, V, VI, VII, XVIII), as well as on most Leamington Italian immigrant women. But in one particular feature, which is essential to the development of the story – the women's confinement to the home (I) – they recall a specific Sicilian tradition (which Ricci also noted in *Radici*, 4; see also chapter 10, "The Generation Gap and the Family"). Also, the reference to the pre–Second World War clandestine immigrants "from our region" who settled in the Sun Parlour (XXI) relates to the pioneer experience of all three groups of Leamington Italian immigrants, even though the fictional names and villages of origin refer to Molise: "Salvatore Mancini of Valle del Sole and Umberto Longo of Castilucci" have the same family names as those of some Leamington Italians, i.e., Domenic Mancini (Poggio Sannita, 1976); Bambino Longo (Agnone, 1967); as well as recalling Umberto Corpolongo (Pastena, Lazio, 1949).

In this case, however, at least with regard to the respective towns of origin, the fictional-real parallel does not coincide with the identification of Valle del Sole with Villa Canale, and of Castilucci with Poggio Sannita. The pattern seems almost reversed. But, after all, in reality nor had the Leamington Mancini and Longo "smuggled themselves" into Canada, nor were they, or others with such names, pioneers of the Leamington Italian community. Such and other examples, while illustrating Ricci's transformation of facts into fiction, his weaving of life and art into a unique creation, are also evidence of the omnipresence of the Leamington Italian community in the entire socio-economic and ethical world of the novel.

THE MORES IN THE NOVEL'S VILLAGE AND IN THE COMMUNITY

The fictional village reproduces the Leamington Italian community, particularly in the concept and the structure of the family ("the religion of the family"), including the generational interaction or conflict, the status of women, and related ethical standards or general moral outlook (including one basic vice – "*Invidia*, envy" or "jealousy" – the major cause, also in the novel, of family and village "troubles," VI). Again, evidence for these links can also be found in Ricci's *Radici* (32–4).

The rural, patriarchal family, exemplified in the novel by the Innocente family, is based almost totally on Ricci's analysis of the Leamington Italian family: "The morality and mythology surrounding the Italian attitude towards the family had its origin in practical considerations ... The ritual of marriage," as pointed out (according to Ricci) by Karl Marx, "first developed among primitive tribes for practical rather than moral reasons. Marriage and fidelity within marriage allowed a man to be certain of his offspring and avoided ambiguity when it came time to bequeath one's land and goods. Through the years, however, the idea of fidelity within marriage began to take on moral implications beyond the practical considerations that first led to its instigation ... A similar pattern," Ricci states with reference to the interviews with the Leamington Italian families, "may be seen with respect to the Italian attitude towards the family."[16]

According to the documentation gathered, Ricci also singles out a variety of features characteristic of the Leamington Italian family (*Radici*, 33–4): the idea of *"la famiglia"* as having "greater meaning than simply that of good mothering and fathering"; the emphasis on material possessions; the material interdependence of family members, and inheritance as an instrument of control of the offspring; "a great opposition to divorce"; the need and duty of all its members to maintain secrecy about family rifts"; the imperative to protect the family honour at all times, meaning the parents' and particularly the father's or male's standing in the community, often at the expense of open discussions or understanding of children's and women's particular needs. And above all, the fear of making public or of the public seeing the "family problems" or wrongs, especially of women's infidelity: the great fear and the major moulder of rural morality and behaviour – "What will people say?"[17] (chapter 10, especially *"La Famiglia"*).

All these features find reflection in the novel, particularly in the disastrous conflict between the defiant Cristina, married but carrying her lover's child, and her sixty-six-year-old, crippled, and autocratic father, head of the family and village mayor. Even before they "retreated" into isolation (VI), each becoming an "alien presence" to the other (XVI), there is a clear indication that material things preoccupy the father more than fatherly feelings or family solidarity or harmony. During a Sunday family dinner, Cristina, who has just "burnt herself on the cooking pot ... spilling some of the sauce onto the flagstones," is "sharply" reproached by her father, *"Stupida* ... can't you be more careful?" (V). Afterwards, a tense "shadowy silence" (IX) that had descended into their home was only, or mostly, broken by increasing reprimands, if not sarcastic comments, commands, complaints, arguments, and curses (XIV, XVII, XVIII, XX). In fact, "after months of silence [her father's] curses seemed almost comforting" (XX).

The father's curses and injunctions serve mainly as reminders of his total control over things, that his things are not to be misused, wasted, or accidentally spoiled, even for minimal comfort, such as "firewood to keep [his daughter's] feet warm" (XII); or "the chicken [she] had slaughtered" for some mysterious reason "would have to be accounted for," since he "still kept very close count of his livestock, as if every winter brought with it the prospect of famine" (XIV). They are means to enforce his rules and his will on Cristina "while [she's] living in [his] house ... while [she wants] to remain [his] daughter" (XII). When her behaving "like a common whore" brings "disgrace on [his] name," she is severely judged and condemned: "You killed your mother when you were born and now you've killed me ... I wish to God ... you'd died and rotted in the womb" (XVIII). She is threatened with the loss of her inheritance – "You'll not see a cent of my money" (XX) – and with a final harsh curse she is disowned and thrown out of the house (XXV). The father-daughter conflict also highlights the general village principles, the conventional values of the entire area (see chapter 10, especially "Marriage and Premarital Behaviour," "Pursuit of Wealth").

Concerns over material possessions, over social role or acceptability, are not only generally deep-rooted in the novel's village but are also said to be the cause of envy, enmity, and violence among neighbours and family members (VI). And the clashes and hostility are well illustrated, even for their tragicomic aspects, by the man and the boy in the hospital: A man "had a fight with his neighbour about a chicken. His neighbour came over with a shotgun, they started shouting and screaming, and, pom! the next thing you know his hand is gone, shot right off. Because of a chicken! And the boy beside him, with the patch on his eye – some of his schoolmates ... [teased] him because one eye was green and one eye was brown [saying] he had a devil in him. So ... [he took] a stick and plahck! that's the end of it. His own eye!" (III).

The two incidents encapsulate the basic outlook and behaviour of an economically and culturally deprived rural society: the fear of poverty or loss of livelihood; the fear of ostracism and of the abnormal or the strange in nature; as well as resentment and awe for the different, for the new in their midst. This attitude is well portrayed also in the "mixture of condescension and respect" reserved for the physically handicapped or "club-footed ... Marta ... as if she were both simple and yet possessed of mystical powers, a witch ... a fate" or other supernatural manifestation (II, V, XVIII). They are manifestations of the overall village religion and morality based mainly on public appearance, fears, superstitions, and a sense of guilt, and they are the causes of the downfall of Cristina and her family.

The "religion of the family" defined the fears, beliefs, and practices of the novel's villagers, and to a certain degree (as presented in *Radici*) those of the Leamington Italians: the villagers' fear of the supernatural (the devil, witches, evil eye and its agents, the snakes, I); their fear of curses and resulting economic disasters or other misfortunes (VI); particularly the fear of each other – the fear of the "villagers' instinct [for] scandal" (II) – and, thus, fears of women's infidelity (XVIII), an act that usually resulted in dishonour and social "death"; and in men's rejection of illegitimate children (XX). From the fear of women's infidelity derived the men's rules relating to the family structure: the dominance of the male; the subservient role of women and children – considered a workforce, to be closely watched as part of the male's belongings (V, IX, XVIII), their rules extended to the rearing and education of their children (stressing sense of guilt, especially in relation to nudity and sexuality [V]).

The "religion" of the family was also closely linked to beliefs in the intermediary role of saints and the Virgin Mary (IX), in miracles, confession (V), and especially in superstitions, myths, proverbs, rituals, charms, or "signs" (VI, XIV). The villagers had their own system of morals – an apparatus consisting of both pagan and Christian traditions and practices, typical of a rural area – a system that helped protect the family, avert evil spells, and preserve village traditions, institutions, and order against changes, outside influences, scandals, emigration (abandonment of fields and old people), or the reactions of the newer generations (i.e., Cristina). The fictional village was again reflecting some aspects of the Leamington Italian community where people wear around their necks both the Christian and pagan charms – the cross and the horn – for their protection, material and spiritual welfare.

ALMOST PARALLEL COMMUNITIES

Both the fictional and the real communities are rural and close-knit (in fact "half the village," almost like the Leamington Italian community, is said to be "distantly related ... by blood" [V]). In both, the highest good is the family, its public image taking precedence over private misery, or the sufferings, aims, or aspirations of individual members; and public posturing is almost an institution, a necessary attitude for the economic survival of the family. The similarity that Ricci (in *Radici*, 33) draws between the prevalent "Italian attitude towards the family" – among the Leamington Italians – and "the example of marriage" – cited from Karl Marx – may well suggest an incorporation of a memory of earlier readings (what Eco calls "the echo of intertextuality").[18]

Yet the Leamington Italian community remains the main source for the novel's family. Its structure and concept reflect a particular southern

Italian condition that Carlomagno also described, mainly in reference to Upper Molise but more widely applicable: "The economy in our mountain areas rests in large measure on the family business, in both agriculture and the trades. The family is at the centre of the economic activity, which, because of an old tradition as well as for contemporary sociological reasons, identifies itself with the local institution. It is an identity found in one's own municipal structure – the mayor and administrators – which in a mountain area is more concrete, more real."[19]

A family severed for any reason from its structure suffers economically as well as socially. The family–community relationship has been quite evident, *mutatis mutandis*, in the economic growth of the Leamington Italian community, especially in the interdependence or mutual assistance "policy" in the more difficult earlier stages of its development. And this is also the concept that Ricci transported into the novel (see chapter 5, "Strength in Unity"; chapter 7, "The Sponsorship"; chapter 13, "Interaction within the Community").

The parallels extend even to the threats against the close-knit nature or vision of the family or community posed by life itself – change, development, or what they themselves desire and call "progress"; by the increasing financial security – envy, greed (see chapter 10, especially "The Pursuit of Wealth," and chapter 11, "The Roma Club"); by better education and a variety of different views – introduced by the newer immigrants and/or generations (chapters 12, 13, 14); by the growing and inevitable interaction with other groups (chapters 8, 13); as well as by more general phenomena (war, emigration), or the natural tendency to change (chapters 2, 3, 5, 6, 7). They are all elements that affect the novel's Innocente family, especially Cristina – better off, better educated, and a "communist" involved in an affair with a "foreigner," a former enemy – a German. Cristina's situation and social status are the results mainly of emigration – earlier, by her grandfather, whose large remittances from America allowed her father "to build the house" in which they lived (XXI), and by her husband's departure for Canada and his long absence, which precipitate the novel's events, particularly Cristina's infidelity and rebellion (I, II).

Radici is again the source for some of the ideas: the effects of the Second World War and the presence of the Germans in Upper Molise and other areas of emigration; the "tremendous gamble" of emigration and a general cause of it ("the spirit of progress and betterment that has moved man forward since the dawn of civilization"); the difficult "immigration ... process" and its effects, particularly the "physical and mental uprooting"; as well as the views, behaviour, or reactions of the younger generations.[20]

Other aspects found also in Carlomagno's books are present in the novel with almost the same words (XI, XII, XXI), such as the effects of emigration on the economy of the mountain area, e.g., depopulation ("left are women and old people, the few young people, by using mechanical means, make up for the lack of human hands"). Quite alike are also the references to superstitions such as the "evil eye" and similar phenomena, including "the snake charmer": the "*ciarallo* [a being] endowed with powers to disinfect the fields from snakes" is recalled in the novel by the "powder made of ground snake skins" or the "potion bought from *la strega* [the sorceress] *di Belmonte* [to spread ... over their fields]" (I, VI). And yet, even for such beliefs, particularly for the evil eye, the most likely source is the Leamington community, especially since the term used in the novel, *Lu malocchiu* (XI), reflects the southern Italian dialect. Besides, the evil eye is mentioned more than once in Vito Peralta's interview as the cause of his misfortunes (chapter 6, "Peralta's ... Internment"); and Father Ugo Rossi, in his interview, speaks of various forms of superstitions practised in the Leamington Italian community (chapter 11, "The Pastor's Views on Italian Religiosity").[21]

Echoes of Ricci's experience in and with the community are present in details throughout the novel, perhaps even in the description of the "primal paradise" with "tropical trees" and "strange tropical birds" (VII), which seems not much unlike Colasanti's Farms and Tropical Gardens (chapter 9). The grandfather's memory of his military bravery, of "the bomb ... that ... left [him] a cripple" and of the "small pension" he received for his service and wounds (XXIV) is a clear reminiscence of Tony DiMenna's own war experiences (chapter 2). Other aspects that can be traced directly to Leamington Italians' accounts include: the presence of German soldiers in the villages and specifically in their homes (IV, VI, XVII); the effort to have the "magic" of electric power, *la luce*, brought to the Upper Molise area; the hearsay or reports about the lodgings of the early immigrants to Canada in a chicken coop or barn (XII), or about the tasteless bread eaten in "America" (XXI); as well as such Italian words or expressions as *la terza media* (Cristina's grade-eight level of education), *Don* (the common title for a priest), *contadini* (farmers, peasants), and numerous others (V, VI).

Many interviews are echoed not just in the physical setting of the novel's village and in the villagers' occupations, activities, and general outlook (I), but also in the attitudes, views, or reactions of the novel's rural dwellers: the peasants' distrust and mockery of the better-educated and often scornful local leaders (II, XII, XXII), as well as of the postwar Italian government, bureaucracy, laws, and the Italian people in general, reflected also in their firm belief that Mussolini's failure was due mainly to the Italians' treachery and cowardice (VII, XII, XX, XXIV, XXIX). Other interviews are recalled in the description of the sea voyage of Vittorio and Cristina to Canada, particularly during a storm, while Cristina is in a state of advanced pregnancy: Cristina continues to boldly manifest women's "new" attitude toward their husbands (and men in general) in dealing with the males on the ship (XXVIII, XXIX, XXX). Her attitude recalls that of a postwar Leamington immigrant woman who asked, *"Devo andare dietro di lui, io?"* (Do I have to follow him – in what he says or does), or "I have the right to my own views, don't I?"

But it is, above all, the principal "law" of the village and especially of the family – their central code of behaviour and the key to the story and its main conflicts – that derives from Ricci's examination of the Leamington Italian family and the interrelationship of its members. "Thus, if a child behaves in an untraditional or unconventional manner, they are most often greeted by the reprimand 'What will people say?'"[22] The reprimand is the harshest when the unconventional behaviour is seen to compromise the daughters' reputation or the principle of fidelity within marriage and consequently the honour of the head of the family or of the entire family (see chapter 10, "The Generation Gap and the Family").

It was mainly this ever-present fear of "What will people say?" – of gossip and ridicule, more than any religious convictions or Catholic morality, that generated in the Leamington Italian family the double standard: freedom for the sons, restrictions or confinement to the home for the daughters. As evidenced in their interviews, the Leamington daughters sometimes voiced their reaction against this unfair treatment, but more frequently resorted to hypocritical behaviour – doing "certain" things behind their parents' back, without them or the community knowing: that, after all, in the community (as in the fictional village) was preferable to any public scandal.

The only way to avoid public shame and shunning, while preserving personal integrity and family prestige, was to simply follow the Italian and community rule: *Fare una bella figura* (appear good, keep up appearances) (see chapter 3, note 2). In the novel, strife ensues, the family structure deteriorates and collapses, even the village order is shaken when Cristina violates that rule. And it is the male authority – father and village mayor – who reminds her of her irreparable wrong: "No. That's where you're wrong, Cristina. You carry your shame in the streets, you force people to point a finger at you … that's not the way to be with people" (XX). Finally, the dishonoured, humiliated, and "betrayed" (XXIV) head of the family and community leader curses her and banishes her from his house: "I'll pray ... that you rot in hell ... get out! Get out of this house!" (XXV). The sentiments, if not the words, closely parallel those of many Leamington Italians.

THE CHARACTERS AS ARCHETYPES OF THE COMMUNITY'S THREE GENERATIONS

The characters in the novel, particularly the three members of the protagonist family (the grandfather, Cristina, Vittorio), are patterned on the three generations of the Leamington Italians and their respective values. The father and grandfather respectively of Cristina and Vittorio represent the older generation: the traditional and authoritarian *paterfamilias*; the proud provider and defender of honoured family and village customs; and at the same time the old-fashioned, paternalistic, hypocritical community leader – "unchallenged [mayor] since the time of the Fascists"; regular churchgoer and blasphemer; or the reactionary old guard in general – small landlord, government pensioner, admirer of Mussolini; a sort of southern Italian *galantuomo* (I, V, XII, XVIII, XX, XXIV).

The fact that he has no name (the only one in the novel), and "in the village he was known simply as *lu podestà*," the outdated Fascist title for mayor (1960–61 is the time of the story), serves to emphasizes his symbolic role as the epitome of the village social, economic, political, and cultural backwardness and stagnation. Vittorio's grandfather may indeed recall Nino Ricci's maternal grandfather, Erminio Ingratta, who (as stated in *Le due valli del sole*, 23) was the "*Podestà* [of Villacanale]" during the Fascist era. But the novel's *podestà* is also the embodiment of the Leamington Italian men, fathers, and heads of the patriarchal families, as well as of their most traditional qualities, outlook, and ideas of power, sense of honour, and material concerns: the beliefs and customs that the children, especially the daughters, and at times the more progressive wives were reacting against – in the novel represented by Cristina.

CRISTINA AND THE BREAKDOWN OF THE OLD PATRIARCHAL INSTITUTIONS

Cristina – the rebellious daughter-wife and sensitive mother, the unrepentant adulteress and defender of women's rights, the victim of hypocrisy and of her own defiance, the outcast, the emigrant, and the tragic heroine of change – recalls the second or "middle" generation – those Italian immigrant women who through their own hard work and sacrifices were gaining or claiming more independence, equality. She also exemplifies those younger women who, influenced by the Canadian way of life, were challenging not only the double standard and their subordinate status, but also the very concept of the traditional southern Italian patriarchal family; so much so that for some of them also (as indicated in their interviews) extramarital sexual relations were not wrong – provided, of course, they could be kept concealed (see chapter 10, especially "Marriage and Pre-marital Behaviour"). What differentiates Cristina from them (as well as from the village women) is that she makes her wrong public: her sin is to allow her village community to discover her sin.

It is clearly not the adulterous act itself or resulting pregnancy that turns the villagers against her, and especially the women who avoid her "with a cold-eyed rectitude" (XVIII); after all, love affairs, pregnancy, and abortion included, were not uncommon in the village area (III, V, VI). Her crime in the eyes of her women friends is her air of superiority, her proud, princess-like indifference to the village laws, particularly to the women's code of conduct in such circumstances. Such behaviour could only bring disaster on all of them, as well as on Cristina and her family, as it does eventually – social suicide, flight from native soil, and death for Cristina; physical and mental distress for her son Vittorio; dishonour and personal and political downfall for her father-mayor; and disgrace, isolation, dismemberment, and uprooting for the family as a whole.

As a social outcast, Cristina can also be related to the small group of immigrant children whose attempt to free themselves from their parents' economic and social control inevitably led or forced them to reject the old ways and, thus, the family and the community, though not with the same tragic effects (see chapter 10, "The External Threats to the Family"; and chapter 12, "Ethnicity: A Canadian and Global Issue"). If her rebellion links her to the younger generation, her flight from the village connects her also to the pioneers whose clandestine emigration completely disrupted family and village life forever. More generally, she illustrates the inescapable fate of many of those who initiate changes in a closed, uniform society: mountain village, immigrant community, or any other (chapter 3).

Above all, Cristina represents the more progressive individuals or groups of people who are more open to change, larger events, or policies (war, emigration, education), who are more willing to influence or be influenced by those events that will transform every community, how-ever isolated. Not just her "sinful" act, but her aloofness and other basic qualities set her apart from the villagers, particularly the women, and gain her their envy: "her indifference to pain" (II) or strength of will in general; her higher level of education (*terza media*) and ability to communicate "in an Italian more rounded and precise than *la maestra*'s" (the teacher, V); her awareness and common sense ("priests?" – echoing the words of Antonio Gramsci on the southern Italian peasants' view of the clergy – "no better than the rest of us" [V]);[23] the women's superstitious practices and religious hypocrisy – "*stupidaggini*" – irrational nonsense (VI); her freedom from economic pressures, allowing her more time to spend and "play" with her son (IV, VI); and her adherence to the "communist" ideology (the same as that held by her German "communist" boyfriend, a foreigner no less," and opposite her father's, i.e., the ruling ideology) aimed primarily at bringing about changes in the village's antiquated system of values, and at gaining equality for women by openly opposing the double standard (XX).

Her presence alone is a challenge to village values and the institutions, taboos, and practices that support it: the school, education, and religious instruction – mainly dogmatic, anecdotal, unedifying, and tending to form "bored," guilt-ridden, and naive children (I, V); the economic structure and commercial practices that tend to promote greed, exploitation, and dishonesty (I, III, IV, VII, XII); the one-party political system and autocratic civic government, long based on reverence for one man, acclamation, and immobility (I, XX); and superstitions based on fear of snakes and the power of the evil eye (I, VI). Everything about Cristina is a threat to the status quo, to a system that tends to keep the peasant population "enslaved" in poverty and ignorance, and women secluded and subservient (I, III, V). Her adulterous act is the ultimate form of defiance, the highest expression or declaration of independence and freedom against an oppressed and oppressive society.

CRISTINA AND THE VILLAGE WOMEN: CHALLENGE AND CONTINUITY

Cristina is thus also the embodiment of the emerging new woman who dares to be different, at her own risk, in a rural environment where women are as closely guarded by the men as their "chickens," lest they stray "in someone else's nest" (XVIII). Not only is she not intimidated by her father or other men (II, IV, XII, XVIII, XXV, XXVI); but she also rebukes them publicly, for being tyrants with their wives, for leaving them at home while they go off to enjoy themselves or even to work (XII). She voices her resentment against her having been unwittingly involved in a ruse to mislead the wife of the *Saturnia* captain about his mistress (XXVII); and as a guest at the captain's dinner, she relentlessly questions the captain's behaviour and insensitivity to his wife's own needs, especially during his long absences – "Even a woman has an itch she needs to scratch once in a while" (XXIX).

But her deepest resentment and anger are reserved for her own husband, Mario: for his verbal and physical violence (IV, XII), for his unnecessary absence, and primarily for his attitude, which, as indicated by her father's support of him, is representative of all the villagers' attitudes. By rejecting Mario and his values (as suggested by her "tearing" up the fifty-dollar bill he had sent her [XII]), Cristina rejects them all: "He's probably slept with every whore in America by now, but for me it's a disgrace. Women have had their faces up their asses for too long, they let their men run around like goats and then they're happy if they don't come home and beat them!" (XX). Her frequent arguments against men's treatment of women, while echoing some of the reactions of the younger Leamington women, seem at times more effective on men than on the women (at least with respect to the village women).

The women themselves seem to present the greatest obstacles to her freedom (and therefore to their own). Cristina's main challenge – her rejection of the village laws governing her situation – is directed at the women; even though in the long run it constitutes a threat to the entire village system: the sacred church rites, particularly "confession," the sacrament of penance, which involves admission of guilt (V); the patriarchal tenets, enforced by the male social and political authority (i.e., her father-mayor), relating to women's morals and "bastard" children (XII, XVIII, XX, XXV); and above all, the underlying beliefs and practices that reflect the other village traditions that seem to be particularly "enforced" by the women themselves, "who watched hawkeyed from their stoops for the slow process of her disease, as if they had taken it upon themselves to keep the disease from spreading" (XVIII).

The women move quickly to advocate and defend their code. They offer advice and services to Cristina; they suggest modes to share and conceal the "disease" among the women; they urge her to end the pregnancy, to cleanse it or mystify it with the "supernatural" (with a "sign" from one or the other village religion – "make a gesture ... make a confession ... at least make a cure"). They ask her to safeguard motherhood, the village "class [of mothers]," that is, the principle or the illusion of fidelity within marriage, and thereby allay men's fears and protect social order (II, III, V, VI, XVIII). Cristina's refusal thus poses a particular threat to the women as custodians of the apparatus of superstitions and rituals, of the village parallel "religion [of the] evil eye" (I, VI). And as such they are linked to the Leamington Italian women, also the main keepers and practitioners of superstitions, and specifically the most likely source of the novel's "evil eye," *Lu malocchiu* (XI).

Cristina's "cold defiance" threatens to expose the very "crafts" the women need to survive in such an environment: mainly the facade by which they can conceal "some sin or crime for which they themselves had gone unpunished"; hence "their straight-backed rectitude"; the reason for having "been harshest towards" Cristina (XVIII). In spite of her temporary "sign" of appeasement, Cristina continues to oppose the village women, not just for accepting what men do but for hiding what they themselves wish to do or sometimes do. Concealing the truth may relieve them from the drudgery of their peasant life as wives and mothers (by gossiping about, or even secretly engaging in, love affairs); their resourcefulness in finding the appropriate remedies ("make a cure" or "some kind of a sign ... of the repentance and guilt which the villagers" always wait for [VI, XVIII]) may offer them also some control over their lives and the village situation. But in the long run, they are no remedies at all: the facade is their enemy as well as Cristina's. The same structures that they defend, and think they are protected by, keep them ignorant, poor, and subjected all their lives, first to father and then to husband (V); in fact, to the entire village which is an extended family (since "half the village [is] related" [V]).

Cristina's struggle against them and the village laws and customs seems almost doomed to end in failure and defeat. And yet, as a result of her rebellion, some radical changes are already visible in the village: the resignation of the fascist mayor (X), the fielding of a rival communist candidate "for the election of a new mayor" and the end of a twenty-year "reign," the growing "courage to raise an angry voice," and the denunciation of the scandalous immobility of the previous civic administration and of the central government (XX). By precipitating her father's retirement, Cristina opens the way for a political reawakening that may have long-term repercussions. What her story suggests is that the struggle for equal rights has risks: a message well illustrated in the migration story of the Leamington Italians as a whole (see chapter 2; chapter 3, especially "Could Some of the Risks Have Been Avoided?"; chapter 14, especially "The Never-Ending Passage").

For Cristina, also, the only way out is emigration, or even worse, self-banishment (comparable, at the literary level, to Verga's 'Ntoni, see chapter 3): a complete break with the traditional family in the hope of forming a better one in the new land. But this, too, seems to be only a path to tragedy: her death and burial at sea; and her two children – Vittorio, ill and delirious, the newborn "bastard" child in an incubator

– abandoned to an uncertain destination and destiny. And yet again, her acts and tragedy bring other positive results: her husband's fatherly attention and care for both Vittorio and Cristina's child reveal a more progressive male attitude (XXXII), at least different from the one in the village, or the one her father anticipated ("He won't have that child in his house" [XX]). Above all, they set the young Vittorio on the path toward maturity ("I brooded over the meaning of these changes being forced on me" [IV]), engaging him in a relentless, slow, and painful search for some "form of a truth" about his mother's "disease" or their "sin or crime" and about emigration (VIII, XV, XVIII, XXI).

In fact, through Cristina and Vittorio, emigration, in its concrete and metaphorical sense, becomes a central theme, almost a companion protagonist in the story. And the loaded symbolism of the snake or snakebite at the beginning of the novel confers universal meaning to the story: humanity's primordial "migration," its banishment from the ignorant bliss of Eden (the mountain village), and its journey to awareness, knowledge, love – back to an earthly paradise or forward to a similar human paradise – America (XXI).

VITTORIO: THE YOUNG GENERATION'S SEARCH FOR MEANING

Vittorio, a great-grandson and son of migrants and himself a migrant (in its various senses), like the Leamington third or younger generation (and Nino Ricci himself), is the culmination of a tri-generational family and community development, of the collective immigrant experience (in accordance, partly, with the mentioned pattern: the first generation conserves, the second rejects or reacts, the third rediscovers and redefines traditions; see chapter 12, especially "the Language Retention/Development Dilemma"). He is, thus, simultaneously beneficiary and victim of the achievements and clashes of the two preceding generations – and in his family the generational, conjugal, and gender conflict is partly the result of emigration. He enjoys the material and emotional security that comes from what some call today the "coping network"; that is, a relatively well-off rural family (IV) and small peasant community (his grandfather's "government pension," rental income, and unchallenged position as mayor; his father's remittances; his mother's open-mindedness and companionship; as well as church, school, customs, and friends).

But at the same time, Vittorio is increasingly confused and tormented by the restrictions imposed by the same village people and institutions – authoritarian and violent heads of families; "disciplinarian" priest and teacher; unscrupulous, petty entrepreneurs (III, IV, V). In fact, his discomfort is caused partly by the very practices that guarantee the benefits – such as the older generations' pursuit and/or protection of their traditional or achieved socio-economic advantages (V, XII, XIV), including the related causes and chain of effects – his father's extended absence (I, III, IV); his mother's violation of village rules (V, VI, VII, VIII, XIII, XVIII); the villagers' cruelty (VI, IX, X, XIII, XIV, XV, XVIII); the clash of reactionary and progressive attitudes or ideologies (X, XI, XX); and especially the final outcome – the collapse of the home and family, and flight (XXV). In fact, the solutions perpetuate his torment, since emigration, uprooting, "being ripped untimely from our womb, without gestation" (XXI) produces a split in the human psyche. And within a span of a few months, the seven-year-old Vittorio experiences a series of untimely separations and states of confused anxiety. His state of mind and feelings are not unlike those related by the Leamington Italian immigrants (see chapters 2, 3, 12). Vittorio, however, ponders the effects of migration (XXI) in an attempt to find his own solution to the migrant's oscillation between tradition and new experience – as seen, especially, among the Leamington younger generation (chapter 10, "The Challenging Balance"; chapter 14, "Bases for Balance").

The sensitive and inquisitive child-migrant Vittorio (like Ricci, himself, first in *Radici* and then in *Lives of the Saints*) continually "broods" over the events. He seeks explanations for the sudden disruption in his life, starting with the "snake" and the "snakebite" and their portents – which, in fact, shake him out of his semiconscious "state of indolence" (I–IV) – and then for each subsequent displacement: from his mother's bedroom (IV), from his memories-"infested" home (XXI) and native village (XXV), and finally from his motherland (XXVII) and from his mother herself (XXXI). His uninterrupted search for the truth about his mother's "sin or crime" (VIII, XV, XVIII) slowly converges into a vain effort to "bring ... into ... focus" the "visible form of a truth [that] leaving [the village] took on in [his] mind" (XXI); and toward the end his search appears as a compelling single need to "piece ... together [all the disparate facts] into a final magical solution" (XXXII).

The still unsophisticated mind of the child may not yet be able to "[work] out complicated schemes and theories," to find a rational explanation for all that is happening. But Vittorio's active imagination (in his conscious or dream-like state) allows him to intuitively figure out the hidden meaning behind the migration problem (XXI) and his mother's sin. At least one component appears to be "fitting into place like the final sum of one of *la maestra*'s arithmetic questions" (XXXII). His final and simultaneous grasp of the once puzzling "markings: 1 + 1 = 2" and equally mysterious presence of man and snake (at the beginning of the story, I) is a clear indication of Vittorio's "intellectual" growth, even though much uncertainty persists and the "final magical solution" remains elusive. Migration is hardship, but also discovery, development.

Vittorio's gradual self-transformation begins the moment he is "awakened" from his "world ... wrapped in a warm, yellow dream" by a man's muffled shout (at the appearance of the snake while the man is making love to his mother in the stable [I]). His "migration," as it were, to a higher level of awareness occurs through his coming to terms with his village traditions, or, as in the case of immigrants, through the rediscovery of their own cultural heritage. Vittorio slowly realizes that the village superstitions – the rituals, incantations, and sacrifice of chickens in moonlit nights – do not "calm the spirits" (XIV); they do not restore his earlier serenity or security. His daily singing of rhyming charms and his amulets – "the chicken head under [his] mattress" (XIV) or the lucky coin in his pocket – seem neither to be effective against the "evil eye" nor protect him against the insults and violence of the village children (XV). He thus rejects the useless magic (flings the chicken's head into the ravine). He breaks down in tears (a form of cleansing), and he becomes aware that out of fear he "had betrayed [his friend] Fabrizio" and "had sunk so low in shame that no magic or miracle could ever reclaim [him]" (XV).

However, those are the very reactions that start him out on the road of change. Vittorio, in fact, "was to be reformed" not just by "studying [his] mathematics" (I), or by learning his catechism (V), but through another "ritual," another form of "magic" that is equally part of his village traditions and educational practice – storytelling, reading the stories of the saints (V, XVI). He may have feared or disliked the "disciplinarian" village priest and teacher, but he liked Father Nick's stories, and "the teacher's tales of the saints worked on [him] like a potion" (V). He was fascinated by the miraculous "deeds of the saints," read to him by the teacher, and more so by the storytelling itself: he was "caught up by the sound of her voice" (XVI). And when he read the stories by himself, he did not leave out, as the teacher usually did, the "long words whose meanings" he discovered in his grandfather's vocabulary (XVI). Vittorio was being transported and transformed by the mysterious power of the spoken and written word. Unlike the borrowed magical formulas and rituals that prove to be quite ineffective (XIV, XV), the stories – language and literature – offered him both relief and a means of self-discovery and self-transformation.

The stories, Vittorio's reaction to storytelling represents his own, independent way of seeking for the meaning of the confusion and alienation in his life. The stories are first a relief from his painful complicity in the untruth his mother has cajoled him into (I): the tormenting conflict between the widespread gossiping about his mother's affair and his loyalty to her (V, VI, VII, VIII, XIII). They are then a temporary refuge from the "thickening gloom of [his] grandfather's house" (XVI). It is "hearing these stories" of the saints – not the "skeptical" attitude of his mother and grandfather – that starts him thinking "about religion." The shame of sinners turned saints makes him weigh his own "vices," makes him more aware of his inner conflict – his own "battle with [the devil]" – and of his having to make "a hard choice between the lesser of two evils." The "choice" is also his own way of justifying his "truancy" – the only way to avoid the "excitement and the horror [of] another vision of *la maestra*'s [his teacher's] awful nakedness" (V).

Since Vittorio's mother considered him "silly" for believing "those stories," he "guarded them from [her] like secrets" (V). In his increasing isolation – especially after the retreat into the "grim" and "shadowy silence" of his grandfather and mother and the "estrangement" of Vittorio and his mother (IX) – the stories became his only source of consolation. Shunned also by all the village children, as the truth of his mother's infidelity was progressively made evident by her pregnancy, Vittorio increasingly took pleasure in listening to his teacher read to him the stories during "what became almost a daily ritual" (XVI); and finally he reads the stories on his own, in the privacy of his room, from the "book ...' *Lives of the Saints*,'" which his teacher lent to him, that he "smuggled ... home ... under [his] books" to prevent his classmates and his mother from seeing it (XVI). The stories of the saints replaced his mother and grandfather as his role models for his search: they became his guides for his own self-discovery and transformation at a crucial moment in his life. And their role in Vittorio's life does not seem to end with his reconciliation with his mother: the teacher's parting gift to Vittorio is the book *Lives of the Saints*.

As a result of listening to the stories at school and reading them at home, Vittorio becomes a different person: no longer the "lazy ... godless boy with a devil in [him]" as his teacher mistakenly first thought of him (I, IV), or the "troublemaker" he was wrongly reputed to be among his classmates, but the "teacher's favourite" (XV), "a model student [who] took [his] books home every night and studied them diligently [and] got every question right" (XVI). He may still be "filled ... with revulsion and self-hatred" for feeling "grateful for the teacher's kindness" (XV) and "unabated ... attentions" (XVI), yet he is also totally entranced by her storytelling, by the sound of her voice (XVI). And his conversion is under way.

Vittorio's transformation is not unlike the one described in the myth of Orpheus, whose sweet music charmed wild beasts and soothed savage hearts.[24] In the novel, the reader's "voice, disembodied and pure," turns Vittorio's initial "grudging resistance" into "the vague longing [for the] teacher's afternoon readings, when [he] seemed to drift briefly out of the world as into a dream," and his "hate slowly drained away from [him]" (XVI). The teacher's "digressions to pick out saints ... special to [him]" (i.e., his "name" and "birthday" saints), and particularly his independent reading at home about his mother's name saint ("Santa Cristina ... virgin and martyr"), sharpened his self-awareness and understanding (as evidenced also by his search for the "meanings" of the "long words"). Both his and his mother's misfortunes and suffering are identified with the saints' "persecutions" and "martyrdom." The saints' virtues, their "fortitude," their "wonders ... worked through the power of Christ" are offered as guides for their own strength to overcome the village curse of the evil eye (XI, XV, XVI) or escape somehow the petty, cruel world that helped produce their unbearable situation.

Vittorio's search, self-analysis, and metamorphosis illustrate a process that is at times visible in the immigrant experience, individually and as a group. The suggestion is quite clear: in the development of both child and immigrant, knowledge of language and linguistic skills are essential. Language is paid particular attention by Vittorio throughout his story (i.e., his search); especially fluently, beautifully spoken language. He carefully singles out each speaker who uses a "burnished," "precise," "polished ... stripped clean of dialect," "florid," or "meticulous" standard Italian (the doctor, the village priest, the visiting monsignor, the ship's officers, as well as the better-educated villagers, including his mother [III, V, X, XII, XX, XXVII]). On the other hand, the village women, who "spoke the most flattened form of the local dialect ... were far from any edifying influence" (V). A better knowledge or appreciation of the standard Italian language gives young Vittorio a better understanding of himself and the world. As some Leamington Italians also realized, language is at the root of one's heritage and identity (see chapter 12, especially "Language, Culture ... and Ethnicity"). At the very end of the novel, it is again his native language – a village song buried in his memory – that spontaneously surfaces in the mind and on the lips of Vittorio the immigrant (XII, XXXIII).

VITTORIO AS "CHILD-MIGRANT"

What especially eludes and confounds Vittorio is the other puzzle brought on by his mother's rebellion – their migration – which for Vittorio, deprived by the death of his mother (XXXI), his most solid link with his life and past, comes to signify almost complete separation, physically and psychologically. Travelling on a ship "on the open sea" (XXVII), barely surviving a violent storm (XXX), and witnessing a premature birth and death (XXXI), Vittorio is all alone, in the grip of pneumonia, "in a delirium," that granted him only "a few … moments of clarity – time enough to witness [his] mother's funeral [on] the morning after her death" (XXXII). Even shortly before her death, Vittorio is generally unmoored from reality, simultaneously conscious and unconscious of "real" time and place: "I thought at first that I was in my mother's room in Valle del Sole, then remembered the ship, then thought that I was somehow on the ship and in Valle del Sole at the same time; but the effort of piecing out the truth seemed too great" (XXXI).

During "the rest of the voyage" toward Halifax "and sometime after it" his mind floats from strange dreams to delirium to semi-consciousness (XXXII). Not unlike other immigrants, Vittorio is suspended between two worlds, between two uncertainties; and like them he spontaneously seeks comfort and meaning in whatever is left to help him reconnect himself to his life. He explores his thoughts, his memories, and new or renewed relationships in his journey to reconstruct his identity (see chapter 3, especially "The … 'Dream of America' …" and note 22; chapter 5, especially "The Hardships").

Vittorio's dreamy half-consciousness is, of course, mostly the result of his physical condition, of his "high fever" (XXXII), but it is also partly due to his psychological state of separateness – the affliction of all immigrants. But Vittorio reacts. Even in his state of suspension he tries hard to make sense of events, both the blurred and pleasant ones and the clearer but tragic ones, particularly those of his mother's death and funeral at sea. During the burial service, his "few final moments of clarity" are invaded by daydreams. He rejects death as "a mistake"; he imagines "dead people … not dead" but able to "come back to life again, like that, the way the wheat around Valle del Sole, snow-covered in winter, could suddenly be green again in the spring." And he "was sure [his] mother's head would pop out of her [canvas] sack" and speak to him in her usual banter and make "everyone … laugh." Just as suddenly he is snatched back from his reveries by the final moving words of the eulogy and by "a song on a bugle." But again "before [he] could hear [his mother's body] strike the sea's surface ... [his] mind went black" (XXXII). In the sea of loneliness, the child, like the immigrant, hovers between soothing wishful thinking and the threatening new realities of life.

At the end of the story, and of Vittorio's sea voyage, another journey begins. Vittorio's thoughts, his memories of the past, seem to fuse at one point with later "future" experiences: the "two visitors [in a hospital ward]" in Halifax, the reunion with his father, and their train ride together toward the Sun Parlour are past events in relation to the older Vittorio – the storyteller – but forward projection in relation to the young Vittorio – the traveller (XXXII, also *In a Glass House* [I]). As for the first visitor, he wasn't even sure afterwards whether he had actually been there, "or whether [he] had merely imagined him [since] all these later events happened in a mist" (XXXII). Vittorio's sense of dislocation reaches into every part of his life.

The "dizzying game of flashbacks and flashforwards," as Umberto Eco calls them, may well be some storywriters' clever devices to confound their readers.[25] But in this story they also to illustrate the psychological state of Vittorio – the migrant – and the effects of migration in general. Migration simultaneously heightens and dims memory, breaks down the borders of chronology and compresses past, present and future: "all that ambiguous interplay between life and dream, past and present," writes Eco, "is ... similar to the uncertainty that prevails in our everyday life."[26] That "uncertainty" is especially felt by immigrants, by migrants in general. The same effects – time conflation, ambiguity, uncertainty – can be found in the stories of the Leamington Italian immigrants, particularly in Tony DiMenna's recounting of his early experiences (see chapter 2, especially "The Ill-Fated First Trip" and "War Memories").

It is with people that Vittorio, like all "displaced persons," needs to recreate meaningful ties. He seems to renew his relationship with his vaguely remembered father, thus re-establishing a link with part of his family and his tradition. But that reunion will occur later, and it is enveloped in uncertainty ("in a mist"). Besides, for Vittorio his father is mostly "a stranger" (XXXII) and continues to be so years later (*In a Glass House* [I, XXVII]). More significant is his attempt to form a new bond with the only living being with whom he can immediately identify: his premature half-sister, who was also, as Vittorio from his home at departure, "ripped untimely from [her mother's] womb" (XXI). She is also unconscious and unaware of what awaits them. She is his true companion; she represents the new future: its fears and hopes (XXXIII). In fact, in Nino Ricci's second novel, Vittorio, now in his mid-twenties, describes his half-sister as his "constant inner companion ... every event in my life seemed always to lead back to her as its final referent" (*In a Glass House* [XXX]).

But it is, above all, through one's native language that true identity and security are found (see chapter 12). In the very last pages of *Lives of the Saints*, when Vittorio is still in the grip of high fever, the "words of a song" – the "familiar local song ... remembering" happier days heard earlier at the village festival (XII) – are unexpectedly "floating into [his] head, surfacing like sunken relics from a place that was no longer visible on the horizon, that had been swallowed into the sea." The words, which he sings "out loud" without realizing it, while forming a contrast with another language he had just heard on the ship and "couldn't understand" (XXXIII), are a clear indication that the need to re-establish the self after migration is spontaneous, and whatever Vittorio does, indicates that the search for identity or self-discovery is and will be (as Ricci's next two novels well illustrate[27]) a never-ending task for Vittorio, just as it is for every migrant (see chapter 14, "The Never-Ending 'Passage'").

Vittorio plays a multiple role in the story. As a child-migrant he links the two human events. He suggests a parallel development or a sort of migrant-as-child correlation: both the child and the migrant experience a tearing down of their respective physical and psychological world and the concomitant traumatic moments of separation or states of separateness. Or at least both face a period of transition that requires a guide and reflection in order to maintain some sort of continuity between the old and new stage in life, and regain a sense of balance. In Vittorio's case, his constant pondering and worrying over events – "I brooded over the meaning of these changes" (IV) – constitute a journey from childlike unawareness to fuller consciousness of himself and of others (and consciousness of others is an expression of freedom).[28]

That potentially liberating effect of brooding is what seems to differentiate Vittorio from his immigrant father or the other immigrants or migrants. For them, as "for the older [Leamington Italian] immigrants, readjustment was practically an impossible task ... the older people could never complete ... integration." They appear caught between what Ricci called the reality and the fantasy of "America." They remain "outsiders."[29] They are, in a way, prisoners of both their ethnicity and their longing to be part of the American dream. They live in the new land but at the same time in the extension of the original village, between memory and myth (XXI). As in the case of other Leamington Italians, they are victims of their own rejection of the old customs and traditions (see chapters 12, 14). More than the sum or culmination of the achievements and failures of the preceding generations, Vittorio represents – as both the novel's grandfather suggests (XXIX) and the Leamington Italians wished for their descendants (chapter 14) – their future hope: Vittorio represents a further step in the fulfillment of their aspirations, a continuation of their migration journey toward a higher level of well-being, both material and cultural (i.e., spiritual).

Vittorio thus represents those of the younger generation of the Leamington Italian community (and by extension of all communities) who are reaching out beyond the physical and cultural boundaries of their worlds in order to have a broader understanding of the world they inherited and of themselves. He represents at the same time the "reader" or reading public at large for whom Ricci wrote *Lives of the Saints* – a reader who Ricci (as every writer) hopes will be entertained, moved, and enlightened as Vittorio is by his teacher's book *Lives of the Saints*.

Since Vittorio receives the book as a parting present, the hope of his teacher is that he will continue to read it and draw benefits from it in the new land (XXIII). In fact, while growing up in Canada, on more than one occasion, Vittorio fondly remembers the teacher's book and the priest's stories: shortly after his arrival in Canada, in "Mersea" (*In a Glass House* [IV]) and many years later while living in Toronto and while visiting his native village (*Where She Has Gone* [XI, XXXI]). In other words, the teacher's *Lives of the Saints* is and most likely will be for Vittorio, the immigrant, what Ricci's *Lives of the Saints* is and most likely will be for the Leamington Italian community – a meaningful and long-lasting bond with their past, with their traditions and language, with their best aspects of ethnicity, as well as with their experience as immigrants or migrants. Finally, Vittorio is Ricci himself, the writer or storyteller sharing the memories of the events relating to the early stages of his own spiritual "migration" – his journey, or as he called it, his "struggle to find a way to be good."[30]

LIVES OF THE SAINTS AS A STORY OF EMIGRATION-MIGRATION

The term *emigration* never appears in *Lives of the Saints*, except as a verb form at the beginning of the story in reference to Vittorio's father (who "had emigrated to America" [I]) or in the form *migrants* (IX, XXI). And yet the theme of emigration-migration marks a meandering course through the story. Migration is itself a character, as important as the three main ones (the grandfather, Cristina, Vittorio) – not simply a catalyst but an integral part of the story, a primary cause, a generating force behind the principal and secondary actions, and at the same time an ingredient, a side dish, as it were, in the various events and episodes. Its pervasive presence is comparable to the vision Vittorio has of his immigrant father (Mario) and of his mysterious power over his life:

> I decided finally it had been my father now who'd made me move out of my mother's bed, as if in some strange way he was able to control my life and see into it from whatever world he lived in across the sea, the way God could see into my thoughts. It did not surprise me that he had that power, because in my mind my father was like a phantom, some dim ghost or presence who could sometimes harden into the mute solid substance of a human form and then suddenly disperse again, spread out magically until he was invisible and omnipresent. (IV)

Emigration, and especially "America" – the destination most aspired to – conjure up similar phantom-like qualities and often equally contradictory forms and myths in the minds of the villagers. The process and the destination exercise a similar power on those who left and those who stayed behind (XXI). Emigration disrupts the Innocente family – both sides of the family, since Mario's father (Vittorio's paternal grandfather) dies as a result of an argument over his being in "America" while "he leaves his wife to run around like a whore!" (III). It is Mario's absence that causes Vittorio's first dislocation that in turn sets off his mental activity, his "[brooding] over the meaning of these changes being forced upon [him]" (IV).

EMIGRATION AND THE DISRUPTION OF THE FAMILY

It can almost be said that the story of the Mario Innocente family develops from an act of emigration; in fact, from an event outside or anteceding the novel's time frame. Its real "beginning" is not, as indicated, July 1960, but 1956, shortly after Vittorio's third birthday (24 August, VIII) and just before the peak year of Italian immigration to Canada, including Leamington – when Mario himself immigrates to Canada (I). "In Valle del Sole," after all, "the men had long been migrants" (XXI) for a variety of reasons – poverty, drought, dreams of wealth, even "superstition" (VI), i.e., psychological motives (see chapter 3). And in work it was normal for the village men, as it once had been for the Molisan immigrants,[31] to be away all day long in the fields, or even for months and years abroad, in spite of their "fears" of being dishonoured by their wives' infidelities during their often-long absence (XVIII).

Mario's own departure, while not prompted by want and opposed by his families, especially by his wife Cristina (IV, XII), contradicted the very proverbs, the guidelines or rules, that the village men themselves "had given birth to" in an attempt to control their women (XVIII). At least those who remained in the village, sharing the same "fears," returned home from the fields for the night, even if "after nightfall. But in our house," Vittorio interposes immediately (in the very first page), as if to regretfully underline the fundamental difference of their situation, "there were no men to go out and work in the fields" (I). The "snake bite" (IV) may very well be "a moment at which a single gesture broke the surface of events like a stone thrown into the sea, the ripples cresting away endlessly" (I); but that moment is in fact the result of Mario's unnecessary long absence – after all, for Cristina the "snake was a stupid accident" (VII). It is Mario's departure that first disrupts the normal course of his family's life, which then leads to the almost inevitable chain reaction of turbulent changes affecting all family members.

By emigrating, Mario not only deprives his family of his paternal and conjugal comfort and support, but also produces a favourable situation for the equally proud, intelligent, and free-minded Cristina to seek comfort and love with another man. Above all she's given the opportunity to seek her own mode of liberation from all oppression, and primarily from her husband, who's "probably slept with every whore in America by now," she protests, "but for [her] it's a disgrace" (XX). And Mario should know, just by heeding the village men's own proverbs, that – as Cristina herself claims – "even a woman has an itch she needs to scratch once in a while" (XXIX). Their story makes clear that migration enhances the clash between economic necessity and social or moral values. In other words, emigration makes quite difficult the reconciliation of the need to escape poverty or fulfill one's dreams and the need and desire to protect the integrity of the traditional family (as evident in the proverbs as well as in the accounts of the Leamington Italians; e.g., chapter 3, "The Lessons of the First Ill-Fated Attempt"; chapter 5, "Saveria Magri and the First Women").

THE MIGRATION FEVER/OPTION
AND ITS ENDLESS REPERCUSSIONS

The theme of emigration-migration is at the very base of not just the beginning of the novel, but also of the development and conclusion of the story. And in the last pages it gives rise to a new beginning, to a new story with the two children, both without parents, in a semiconscious or unconscious state, on a ship in the middle of the ocean taking them to a strange land, or "a new part of America called Canada, which some said was a vast cold place with great expanses of bush and snow … others a land of flat green fields … and of lakes as wide as the sea" (XXI). The act of emigration in progress anticipates its counterpart – immigration and its related difficult and, as the young Ricci mentions in *Radici*, "never" or "seldom complete process" of readjustment and integration in the new land (prominent themes in Ricci's second and third novels dealing with the Innocente family).

Whether described, mentioned, or implied, the various forms of migration and its opposite effects on the village and its people occur in almost every chapter: the "remittances" (IV), the "money from America" (XII) sent or brought back by earlier migrants, provided some material comforts, the means to build new houses and to live "in relative ease" (XXI). The substantial contributions by wealthy immigrants allowed the villagers to organize more elaborate village patron saint festivals (IX) and enjoy even a few moments of "rich modernity" with lights in the village square (XII).

But more money or new houses did not necessarily mean a better quality of life or more enjoyment, due to both *normal* misfortunes and especially fear of envy (I, II, III, IV, V, VI, XXI). At times the fathers' hard-earned "American money" was squandered by their irresponsible children; or the "fortune" itself seemed to be the cause of their offspring's degeneration (XII). By "pouring their … wealth into the festivals" the rich *"paesani"* overseas were also fuelling "village rivalries" – the battle of the festivals (IX) – i.e., localism or *campanilismo* (see chapter 1). The yearly *festa della Madonna* may have provided an occasion for the return to the village of former residents, including a few *"Americani,"* who were especially welcome since they usually brought back news and money from relatives overseas, and offered opportunities for gossip or mockery – as in the case of one whose "suit [made him] look like someone from the camorra" (IX, XII). But they also served to send back to America some poisonous village gossip (XX). They all seem to suggest that emigration, while producing "richer" individuals, also created a class of people with uncertain roots or no roots at all.

The increasing postwar departures from the village brought results that both historians and the Leamington Italians have also recorded – depopulation, physical degradation, and general economic decline of the mountain village areas, especially with the decrease of the young labour force, and thus loneliness and misery for the aging population: "whole sections of the town stood abandoned, houses boarded up and crumbling" (VII,

XI); "Just old men ... that's all there'll be left in Valle del Sole. And no one to take care of us in our old age" (XII). These effects of emigration have also been noted by Carlomagno whose work on Agnone's "traditions" includes even a photo of a house with windows boarded up.[32]

Emigration or "America" is an integral part of the villagers' existence, as much as their daily bread: its presence is taken for granted; it need not be always mentioned. They are constantly linked to it through their many relatives and friends already overseas, through their returns and departures and, as in Vittorio's case, through his father's monthly, and then more frequent, letters (I, IV, XX) – a situation quite similar to that described by the Leamington Italians (see chapter 2, "The 'Right' America and the 'Wrong' America").

The villagers always saw migration as an option, especially when the drought "would ruin the year's crops." And "when a young man returned from overseas to choose a bride, the young women of the village" would suddenly be "caught up in a dream of freedom" in what they called "Ah-merr-ica"; but just as quickly they would feel "sorry for the one who had had to leave behind the familiar comfort of family and village for an uncertain destiny across the sea" (XXI; see chapter 10, especially "The Proxy Brides"). America represents something for everyone: it is part of the children's world, of their jokes and games (XV, XXI, XXII); at times it is a source of personal prestige – Fabrizio's "most prized possession was a jackknife his uncle had brought him back from America" (IX, XXII). America is the land of all the biggest and strangest things for both children and grown-ups: "In America ... the bread sticks in your mouth like glue ... The houses [have] telephones in every room ... [people live] in houses of glass ... You can see all the women in their underwear. People look at each other all the time, over there, because nobody believes in God" (XXI). Almost all villagers seem to have at least one relative in "America," including Cristina's friends: Giuseppina Dagnello, a cousin of her husband's (XXV), and Maria Maiale, a brother (XXI).

But America is also a collective bad memory, a source of despair for many families: Vittorio's own great-grandfather had "vanished ... there"; and "others, too, had been swallowed up by America, never to be heard of again, a few like [his] great-grandfather leaving behind wives and children" (XXI). There are feelings, contradictions, events that the Leamington Italians also referred to in their stories.[33] For example, Vittorio's great-grandfather's episode recalls Alex Colasanti's words about his brother-in-law who had gone to Venezuela: "Nobody could find him ... nobody knew where the hell he's at" (see also chapter 11, "The Italian Art of 'Eating'"; chapter 12, "The View of Canada").

Migration, though frightening, is also seen as a form of escape, a way to freedom – as in the case of some of the Molisan pioneers; and "America is a big place" where one can easily hide and even start a new life – as in the case of Cristina and Vittorio (VII, XXV, XXVII). In fact, Cristina herself, despite her declarations to the contrary (XII, XX, XXI) and her silence about America with Vittorio (XX, XXI), has had emigration on her mind since the early part of the story. Fearing she may be pregnant (VII), her plan (as she relates to her friend Luciano) to "run off to America together" with her lover (VII) is already in action by Vittorio's seventh birthday (i.e., August 1960, about a month after the beginning of the story [IV, VII]). On that day she and Vittorio go to "a cold dim office [to fill out] a form" and then "into a photographer's studio" to have their picture taken (VIII), which later appears on their passport (XXI). Her intention had to be kept "secret" not just from Vittorio (XXI) but especially from the others who, in fact, realize she's not going to join her husband only on the day of their departure from the village (XXV). But their escape is a violent break: on leaving "no one raised a hand to wave goodbye to [them]," and Cristina, referring to the village as "this hell," prays to God to "wipe it off the face of the earth" with "all its stupidities" (XXV). Migration thus becomes an act of violence involving both the participants and the entire community, as illustrated especially by the departure of the first men from Villa Canale (chapters 2, 3).

THE DEPARTURE: AS IF GOING "TO THE VERY BOWELS OF HELL"

Through the two "new" village protagonists, Cristina and Vittorio, this "old" Italian phenomenon is finally brought more fully into view, along with its many contradictions. At the port of Naples, the two migrants, full of dreams and expectations, become increasingly aware of the more common and more unpleasant aspects of emigration. Both the sorrowful and humorous sides of the departure for "America" unfold, almost cinematically, before their eyes:

Amidst the porters and workers and vendors moved a floating mass that seemed cut adrift, lost and directionless, men … women … children … rope-tied suitcases and overstuffed handbags and lumpy burlap sacks strewn all over the pier like the ruins of war. Here and there whole families were bedded down on the dirty pavement with bundled undershirts for pillows and their coats for blankets; and from all along the mile-long pier came the great collective wailing of a thousand agonized goodbyes, women and men alike crying and clutching their sea-bound relatives as if seeing them off to the very bowels of hell. (XXVI)

And among them is a comic-tragic episode – which is also a memory of the Leamington Italians[34] – involving a "[frightened] old man" hugging "obstinately to his breast" a "hamper" that was finally torn from his arms sending "its contents ... flying across the deck – grain, clothes, a loaf of bread, a *provolone* [cheese], and the scrawny-headed chicken" (XXVI): they are, of course, all the precious little possessions that migrants commonly attempt to smuggle to America; or not unlike the "little packets of food ... sometimes dropped into graves to be carried to the spirits on the other side" (XXI). The incident, which appears quite humorous to Cristina but leaves Vittorio in a "serious" pensive mood, may serve also to indicate different attitudes toward migration, in general, and its disturbing effect on a child's sensitivity, in particular (XXVI).

At the moment of departure the succession of scenes takes on a more rapid pace: the ship-to-shore "final goodbyes" at times cast "to the wind. *'Addio Italia! Salve America!'*" (Farewell Italy! Hello America!) "On the pier people were shouting last-minute instructions," sometimes in jest, but all quite revealing: a more precise familiarity with America ("Say hello to President Eisenhower! And send me back an American woman!"); or that emigration is also a way to evade the draft ("Tell Giovanni the army is looking for him!"); or again that it is the cause of split-up families, of concern and anger in wives and mothers left behind ("Tell your father that when I get my hands on him, I'll break his balls!"). The departure heightens a particular effect of emigration: the separation from one's dearest friends, whose resemblance the new migrant begins to imagine he is seeing in every crowd; and the deception or trick of one's imagination can at times be, as in Vittorio's case, quite embarrassing and cruel (XXVII).

The ambivalence of emigration seems to intensify at the very moment the ship casts off from its mooring place (for the passengers their cultural moorings also): "As the gap between the rails and the dock widened ... and as the ship slipped away" from the people on the pier, Vittorio "felt a tremendous unexpected relief, as if all that could ever cause pain or harm was being left behind on the receding shore, and my mother and I would melt now into an endless freedom as broad and as blue as the sea." But at the same time, as they looked back toward the disappearing port, one (Cristina) "cried silently" beside the other; while Vittorio was pressed between two thoughts, two questions: one looking back to his grandfather – will he "die while we're away?"; the other forward to his father – wondering whether they "have to live with [him] when [they] get to America." But his queries, like many queries regarding migration, are left unanswered, suspended in vagueness and uncertainty, at least by his mother (XXVII).

THE UPROOTING: TRAPPED OR SEARCHING BETWEEN REALITY AND FANTASY

Vittorio, of course, has been trying to come up with answers, especially since he was told of the decision to leave (XX). Whether consciously or semiconsciously, and at times hovering between those two states, he makes constant efforts to discover the secrets hidden in the various occurrences, in his frequent dreams, in his conflicting thoughts and memories, even in objects; and right to the very end of the novel: he wonders whether the faint glitter of the "lucky" coin that has just "slipped through [his] fingers ... fatally ... tumbling out to sea" was sending him "some final secret message, some magic consolation" (XXXIII). And in some of his earlier attempts, he sometimes seemed more successful: at the hospital in Halifax, in the recognition of the truth about his mother's lover, and about his father, "not the black-haired ogre [he] had imagined but a tired-eyed man" who was, at least toward his son, compassionate and caring (XXXII); and during his illness, in his remembering Valle del Sole, associating it not with pain or death but with pleasant Sunday or spring scenes and renewal of life (XXXII).

But the two final acts that especially reveal the migrant's state of mind are his attempt "to get [the] attention" of the child brought to life between two worlds, and his spontaneous "singing out loud" of part of a joyful regional song (XXXIII). Both manifest a subconscious desire to continue to hold on to two essential realities in his life – his half-sister and his language – the living symbols of the two worlds that have already become part of the components of his and her identity; they are the links between what he earlier called "point of departure" and "destination," the "Valle del Sole" and "America" (XXI). They are the two points between which the psychological pendulum begins to swing more rapidly the moment Cristina announces her decision to emigrate: "'We're going to leave the village, Vittorio,' she whispered finally. 'In a few weeks we're going to America'" (XX).

It is this announcement regarding emigration that marks the pivotal point in the story and in the novel, psychologically and structurally (the psychological moment of transition is, in fact, reinforced by the structural division). The narrator's intervention, "she whispered finally," reveals Vittorio's sense of satisfaction for having been made part of the "secret" and a sense of relief that the decision has been "finally" reached. After months of "silence" and "estrangement" (IX), son and mother are suddenly drawn closer again by a common lot, by a shared dream to escape – but one that will, ironically, separate them forever.

The idea of passage from one point to another, or of the end of one part of their lives in "the village" and the beginning of another in "America," is also strengthened by the separation of the two parts of the announcement, by the narrator's comment, as well as by the appearance, side-by-side yet visibly separate, of the same word *America*: one "whispered" almost with anticipation (by Cristina at the end of chapter XX); the other instantly evoked almost like a foreboding image in the mind of the narrator (at the beginning of chapter XXI). The juxtaposition itself foreshadows the narrator's exposition of the contradictory "two Americas": "America. How many dreams and fears and contradictions were tied up in that single word, a word which conjured up a world, like a name uttered at the dawn of creation, even while it broke another, the one of village and home and family" (XXI). At this very point, emigration or "migration," in its various meanings, emerges as the central event in the characters' lives and in the story; and this part alone of the novel (XXI) as a "poetic" compendium of the main themes of the migration phenomenon, of its various socio-economic, historical, and mythological aspects.

The narrator reviews the highlights of the village migration story, and in almost alternating sequence reflects upon the causes and effects of migration: the ambivalence of America; the plight of the peasants and the persistence or the recreating of the myth through successive generations, despite the long-known "tales" about its ugly reality; the precarious condition of the immigrants and the visible degradation of the home situation, particularly after the postwar chain migration. The survey, while linking the particular undertaking of the two protagonists to the village – and thus to the Italian and Leamington – migration experience,[35] seems also to serve as a sort of ritual of propitiation for the two new migrants; it may even serve as a warning, not just for Vittorio and Cristina but for all prospective migrants. In fact, from Vittorio's comparison of previous departures with their own, and respective village "rituals of separation," emerges a contrast that seems ominous, even though it may bring a greater awareness of the reality of migration: "But my mother and I, it seemed, were being ripped untimely from our womb, without gestation" (XXI).

It is at this point, also, that Vittorio begins to sense, without fully understanding, the seriousness of their act, the violent nature of "one-way departures" (XXI), the irreversible displacement caused by migration, which he also compares later to the final human departure or going "off to the very bowels of hell" (XXVI). The changes that occur around him, even before departure, appear to him as dark portents, as signs of the sudden breakdown of life's cosmic order, affecting things, animals, as well as people: "our house ... a solid constant, unchangeable, infested ... with our lives and smells, our histories, became almost overnight an empty shell ... Our sheep and pigs, confused and stubborn, were chased out of their stable ... and my grandfather ... amidst groans and curses [was] moved ... back into the house where he'd spent his childhood" (XXI).

Vittorio himself, on seeing his "mother's packed trunk [sitting] alone in the middle of the kitchen floor," hovered around the still ungraspable "truth [of their leaving]," almost detached from his substantial self and from the familiar surroundings ("houses, faces, voices"); and "though [his] mind was filled with images of America ... [he] could not believe in the truth of them." Yet, at the end of the chapter (XXI), his look back at past migration experiences seemed to offer him some form of guide for the "future," suggesting in general terms that the "journey" of the migrant "into the [limitless] space" needs to take "direction not from its destination" (i.e., America, the "mythical place") "but from its point of departure, Valle del Sole, which somehow could not help but remain always visible on the receding shore" – that is, one's origins, the source of one's life can never be forgotten. Vittorio's "search" (i.e., Ricci's literary "invention") is a synthesis, an encapsulation, of the entire Leamington Italian community's struggle to recapture the best aspects of their ethnicity and thereby redefine identity (see chapter 12, "Ethnic Identity: Italian Canadians or Canadianized Italians?").

THE "MIGRATION" PARALLELS: FACT, FICTION, AND MEANING

The reasons for migration, as revealed also by the Leamington Italians (chapters 2, 3, 7), were as much economic need as a natural desire for adventure, or simply "necessity and curiosity."[36] In this sense, also, the novel's Valle del Sole recreates Villa Canale and other southern Italian villages: "Tales of America had been filtering into Valle del Sole for many years already" (XXI), just as they had been filtering into the Villa Canale area in the 1920s, according to Tony DiMenna (chapter 2); and clearly the same "tales" have also filtered first into Ricci's *Radici*[37] and then into *Lives of the Saints* through the Leamington Italian immigrants. The "tales" produced similar effects on both the real and fictional communities: the social and psychological condition of Valle del Sole's peasants, before and after immigration to America, corresponds to a situation generally described by the earlier Italian immigrants to the Leamington area. In essence, whether they never left the village or did go to find their fortune across the sea, their lot remained hard work, and "America" just "some vast village" or a longed-for dream yet unfulfilled:

> And for all the stories of America that had been filtering into the village for a hundred years … stories of sooty factories and back-breaking work and poor wages and tiny bug-infested shacks, America had remained a mythical place, as if there were two Americas, one which continued merely the mundane life which the peasants accepted as their lot, their fate, the daily grind of toil without respite, the other more a state of mind than a place, a paradise that shimmered just beneath the surface of the seen, one which even those who had been there, working their long hours, shoring up their meagre earnings, had never entered into, though it had loomed around them always as a possibility. And these two natures coexisted together without contradiction, just as goats were at once common animals and yet the locus of strange spirits, just as *la strega* of Belmonte was both a decrepit old woman and a witch, a sorceress. (XXI)

Views of America as "heaven-hell" or "siren-witch"; of migration as a "contagious disease" or "collective psychosis" and promise of renewal; and of migrants as "beasts of burden" or (in Ricci's term, *Radici*, 28) as "outsiders" have been traced to various late nineteenth- to early twentieth-century southern Italian political and literary works on peasant conditions and on the Italian migration phenomenon (chapters 1, 2, 3, 6). They can also be linked, as indicated in Pitto's *Al di là dell'emigrazione* (Beyond emigration), to more recent historical, sociological, and anthropological studies that present emigration as a process of "myth-making," and the emigrant-immigrant, in the words of Paolo Cinanni, as a "worker [who] goes out of the system that produced him, gives up specific rights which he enjoys in his own country as a member of the community, and [who] in the country of immigration remains only a *bearer of work capacities*, and as such is considered."[38]

Illusions or myths coupled with hard work appear as constant themes throughout the accounts of the Leamington Italians.[39] They are two equally necessary components in peasant-immigrants. If they need work to secure their material survival and progress, they also need to hold on to or create myths – the myth of the place they go to and the myth of the place they come from. They need the myths to protect their dream, for psychological and material self-preservation, even though in the process (as evidenced in both the fictional and real story) they often find "themselves trapped by the very tyranny they were trying to escape."[40] They become unwitting prisoners of the same needs and myths, at least until they can find a way to blend them into a new identity (chapters 12, 14).

The paradoxical situation of the migrants or immigrants, their exclusion from the "paradise [that] loomed around them always as a possibility" (XXI), may in time produce what Pitto calls an "existential crisis," resulting in a "[need to] return to the land of origin ... in order to rediscover one's own identity and cultural roots." Since "memory" is the sustainer of life, "the founder [and] supreme guarantor of cultural identity," of "the continuity of individual and group identity," the "return [often] takes form ... in the memory. It manifests itself as a search for an imaginary place from which to draw one's origins and to which one is drawn ... The search in the memory for a village, where we ideally place ourselves, is linked ... to that need to return to the past, which invests the minds of those who have lost the landscape of their own environment."[41]

The "search" and process were and are active among the Leamington Italian immigrants: in the "reconstruction" of their lives in Canada – of their family, traditions, community, and community centre; and especially in the recollection and recording of their experiences. They are, of course, visible in Vittorio, whose memories of his native village emerge, albeit involuntarily, more vivid and more idealized in the very last pages of *Lives of the Saints*: "the words of a song ... floating in [his] head, surfacing like sunken relics from a place ... no longer visible on the horizon" (XXXIII). Vittorio's spontaneous recalling of a significant part of his past (as the term "relic" suggests) represents Nino Ricci's own recovery of his traditions. His literary work represents also his "search as an intellectual who seeks," as Pitto phrases it, *"di 'appaesare' il suo spirito cosmopolita* – to restore his cosmopolitan spirit to its proper habitat – with the magical world of his imagined origins"; and, in Ricci's case, with the "magic" of his artistically reconstructed "real" origins, mostly drawn from both his own memory as a child of immigrants and from the memories of three generations of Leamington Italian immigrants. The novel – *Lives of the Saints* – is "his return" to the past, to his Italian-Canadian ethnocultural roots, to the base on which it is possible to recompose or "re-establish one's own identity."[42] Indeed indicative is the quotation, at the beginning of Ricci's novel, from Proust's *Remembrance of Things Past*.

The many-sidedness and ambivalence of migration presented in the literary mode in the novel find particular correspondence in Cesare

Pitto's collection of essays.[43] Though seemingly unrelated, the essays are tied together by "a research ... focused on [Italian migrant] groups which best manifest the development of a cultural identity process" (i.e., the disintegration and integrative process of migration). A number of essays, in fact, deal with southern Italian peasant immigration (and return migration) and with reference to Canada. Above all, the volume establishes a close link between empirical evidence (oral and written accounts) and intuitive evidence (analysis of poetic and literary texts by both Italian and Italian-Canadian writers). Pitto's work, like Ricci's novel, also bridges the socio-economic, psychological, and mythological reasons behind migration; and the overall aim is to seek a more comprehensive explanation (or meaning) of the "traumatic process of migration," which "can certainly be defined," writes Pitto, "as the most concrete act of the cultural apocalypses of contemporary society."[44]

At the same time, however, migration, as the novelist suggests and describes (mostly through Vittorio) and as the anthropologist discovers and explains, is both an end and a beginning. In fact, "this end of society" is seen by Ernesto DeMartino (whom Pitto quotes) "as a reforging of a new moral and social order, first in the 'new world,' but also in the 'paesi' [hometowns] cut in half by the great exodus. The end of 'one' world has nothing of the pathological: it is on the contrary a beneficial experience, connected to the historicity of the human condition. The world of infancy ends and that of maturity begins; the world of maturity ends and that of old age begins .... The end of 'one' world is therefore in the scheme of human cultural history." It is from this concept of "the end of the world" that Pitto's essays "have started out to trace the lines through which the cultural identity of the migrant people is progressively re-established." Pitto compares the volume, in fact, to a "diary of a journey," and the essays are simply "the description of these itineraries in their extreme diversity and in their common direction, the formation of a new type of human being."[45]

The story of Cristina and Vittorio, of the Innocente family and of their village, is also an unfolding of the double process of emigration-migration, of the simultaneous breakdown and, at least incipient, reconstruction of their world, individually and collectively. The process of change, evolution, or transformation (caused directly or influenced by emigration) is evident in particular episodes as well as in the overall action of the novel: in the general decline of the mountain villages (VI, VII, XI, XII) and the emergence of a new community overseas, in Canada (i.e., the "Sun Parlour" or the Leamington area) where Valle del Sole immigrants are not only working in factories and buying farms but some have also become rich (IX, XII, XXI); in the need itself to abandon old country inter-village hostilities (IX) in order to build a more closely knit group among immigrants from different villages (XXI); in the developing political changes in Valle del Sole, the decline of the old and rise of the new order (XX, XXIV); in the almost simultaneous death-birth event (XXXI), or the end of the "old" generation (Cristina) and the starting off of the "new" one (her daughter, Vittorio's half-sister); and, above all, in the series of Vittorio's displacements: from his mother's bed (IV), his grandfather's house (XXI), his native village and land (XXV, XXVII).

With Vittorio, influenced by both his father's emigration and by his own psychological and then physical migration, it is an ongoing process of change throughout the novel, from its very beginning with his being jolted ("awakened") from his blissful daydreaming or naïveté to a frightening reality ("a snake"), and to a pressing need to be aware, to understand, and "pick out ... the right response" (I), and then on through the slow and difficult development of his faculty to recall and, at the end, to ponder even "complicated schemes and theories" (XXXII). Vittorio's tortuous "journey" is almost an embodiment of the collective immigrant experience.

A TRUE STORY OF MIGRATION THOUGH NOT A WORK ABOUT EMIGRATION

Lives of the Saints is essentially the story of emigration-migration in its various manifestations simply because migration has long been, a way of life in the isolated, backward mountain villages: the "underlying world" from which emerges the story of Vittorio and Cristina, themselves migrants, "travellers" in the concrete and figurative sense. The migration phenomenon appears in its multiform connotation: not simply as the act of changing location (temporarily or permanently), but also as an attempt to initiate change, to free oneself from tyranny and exploitation as represented especially by the village leaders – mayor, priest, teacher, entrepreneurs, and gentry. Consequently, also present is migration in the socio-economic and political sense, as flight from poverty, rebellion against reactionary ideologies, and search for better material opportunities, as well as for self-fulfillment and freedom (the peasants, Cristina). Migration appears at the emotional and psychological level as escape from the overpowering evil forces, natural and supernatural – recurring droughts; human "envy" and "superstition," or the witch's curse (VI, XXI); and as a longing for, or lure of, an ideal "unfallen world," "a state of mind ... a paradise" (XXI; the villagers in general); it is "that desire for the Edenic paradise" that Ricci speaks of in reference to the Leamington Italians.[46] Migration appears even in the sense of being "transported" or "[drifting] into a dream [world]" of books, stories, storytelling – "suddenly filled with light" (XII, XVI; Vittorio; the villagers).

Migration appears also in the form of mental activity, intellectual search or research, an investigation of facts and fantasies, a search for clues to arrive at the causes of seemingly inexplicable phenomena (i.e., Cristina's "disease," "crime," or "misfortune" [XVIII]), at some "visible form of a truth" (XXI), or at "piecing out the truth" (XXXI; Vittorio). At the figurative or metaphorical level, migration presents itself also as a form of exile: the ostracism of the family; Cristina's isolation, withdrawal "into a shadowy silence" (VI, IX); the forced and self-imposed solitude and shunning of Vittorio (IX, XIII); and the general "estrangement," especially between mother and son (IX). But, at the same time, it presents itself as a pilgrimage, a passage from one stage or form of life to another: from the false and stifling security of the patriarchal family and deceiving pastoral setting to a freer, more independent, albeit riskier, type of life. Migration manifests itself as a physical and philosophical adventure and misadventure.

The novel traces a journey in space, time, and consciousness, a change in state and status. The story begins with a woman "bitten by a snake" (I) – the "snake bite" (IV, XIV, XX) – and a sudden loss of an Eden-like innocence (I–IV). It continues as a physical and mental struggle, as a quest for balance, truth, or simply as a "waiting for the [restoration] of the normalcy of things" (IX); and it ends in violence (the storm), sickness, death, separation – in tragedy; but also in birth, discovery, awareness (Vittorio of his half-sister and of some secrets), and reunion (Vittorio and his father) – in renewed hopes, especially in finding an affectionate father (XXIX–XXXIII). The story combines various meanings of "odyssey": "toilsome way back," "wayward travel," "journey of discovery" or "spiritual quest." It is almost a re-enactment of the human journey in general. At the same time, since that created "world" is derived mostly from the world of migration that shaped Ricci's early life, *Lives of the Saints* is also the story of the journey of the Leamington Italian community whose tri-generational immigrant experience represents various phases or aspects of migration: from the socio-economic hardships and cultural alienation to financial security (first generation); to increasing intercultural interaction, integration, and community consolidation (second generation); to greater independence, self-reliance, self-definition, and cultural growth, or balance of old and new (third generation).

Lives of the Saints proves to be an effective story of migration mostly because it is *not* a novel about emigration. Its main goal is not the gratification of immigrants' nostalgia, nor community glorification or condemnation, though all those elements may be implicitly present. Ricci's intent and achievement can again be made clearer by Umberto Eco's comments on the writing of his own novel, *The Name of the Rose* (and on its success). For Eco, "writing means constructing, through the text, one's own model reader"; not, however, by "constructing" books "according to a ... mass-production formula" or "a kind of market analysis." A writer who "plans something new, and conceives a different kind of reader ... wants to be ... not a market analyst, but, rather, a philosopher who senses the patterns of the Zeitgeist." When he "seeks to produce a new reader," a writer "wants to reveal to his reading public what it *should* want, even if it does not know it. He wants to reveal the reader to himself." In order to make the reader "the prey of the text," of its world and times, a text has to be "an experience of transformation for its reader," and what the text offers has to be "pleasurable." Since Eco in *The Name of the Rose* wanted his readers "to feel as pleasurable the one thing that frightens us – namely, the metaphysical shudder – [he] had only to choose (from among the model plots) the most metaphysical and philosophical: the detective novel." People, according to Eco, "like thrillers not because [of the] final ... triumph of order ... over the disorder of evil," but mostly because "the crime novel represents a kind of conjecture, pure and simple"; and the "space of conjecture is a rhizome space" or a "potentially infinite [labyrinth]." Above all, Eco "wanted the reader to enjoy himself ... In amusing himself, somehow, he [also learns]"; he becomes "another person"; he is transformed. "The reader should learn something either about the world or about language."[47]

Eco availed himself of his "direct knowledge of the Middle Ages," in order to create the setting for *The Name of the Rose* – his "crime novel" that enabled him to fulfill his aim to offer entertainment and knowledge. Similarly, Nino Ricci used his direct knowledge of the Leamington Italian community and their stories of emigration-migration to create the setting for *Lives of the Saints* – his own version of the detective novel; and though it is not a crime novel in the usual sense, it is indeed the story of a "crime – of Cristina's crime of infidelity, as Vittorio refers to it several times (VIII, XV, XVI, XVIII) – and a crime that is the direct result of an act of emigration (her husband's). In fact, the theme of emigration-migration is a thread running throughout the novel's mysteries, investigations, and conjectures; emigration-migration is particularly associated with the theme of the labyrinth: emigration-migration is a curse, a maze of contradictions whose effects are lifelong and mostly inescapable.

THE MIGRATION LABYRINTH: THE HARDSHIPS AND JOYS OF SELF-DISCOVERY

In his novel, Ricci also revisits the past and senses its inextricable connection to the present: the content, form, and purpose of his literary work reflect "the traumatic process of emigration," also defined as an "[apocalyptic act] of contemporary society"; and today, the "universal persistence and pervasiveness of major conflicts and strife" have been "related to issues of ethnicity."[48] And ethnicity is at the very base of self-identity. Ricci's text fuses those themes with the classical-humanistic theory of *utile-dulci*, usefulness and enjoyment, as well as with the modern plot of the "detective story." His novel is basically a mystery story, where Vittorio is the detective, involved in a series of inquiries, conjectures, guesswork (and not all successful, just as in Eco's work): Who is Cristina's lover? Will Vittorio ever be able to discover the truth about his mother? his father? his half-sister? himself? And above all: What will happen to him in Canada?

As a synthesis of the migration experience in its amplest sense, Ricci's story is a miniature representation of the flux of human life. Thus, Vittorio's inquiries cover a variety of fields: the metaphysical and philosophical – superstitions, curses, myths, miracles, secrets, dreams, oracles, riddles, witchcraft, religion, and the mystery of life and death; the historical-sociological – the origins and nature of the villages (I–IX, XII, XVI, XX–XXIII); the conditions of peasant communities (I, VI, VII, XI); the causes and effects of change, especially the effects of emigration (IV, VI, IX, X, XVII, XVIII, XX, XXI, XXIV); the linguistic-literary – the social role of dialect and standard Italian (III, V, X, XII, XIV, XXII, XXIII, XXVI–XXXI, XXXIII); the style and effects of sermons, speeches, stories, tales, poems, songs, metaphors, and rhetorical flourishes; the moral-ethical – his mother's or the women's "sin or crime" (VIII, XXVIII); virtues, vices, behaviour, sense of guilt of villagers (I–VIII, XVI, XVIII, XXV, XXVII, XXIX–XXXI); his paternal grandfather's rage (III); his own violence (XIII). There's even an attempt at a "medical diagnosis," which Eco lists among the "examples of conjecture":[49] Vittorio observes in two instances the symptoms of pregnancy – the "bluish-green vomit [resulting] from some pain in [a young woman's] stomach" (III), and "a pool of vomit, a pale unearthly blue" resulting from his mother's own pregnancy (XIV) – which Vittorio, unaware or unwilling to accept, keeps describing as "the swelling in her stomach" (XVI), "her disease" (XVIII), or "the bulge [in her belly]" (XX).

Ricci's novel, following Eco's analysis of his own novel, is analogously "a story of labyrinths, and not only of spatial labyrinths." Ricci's creation reflects Eco's "three kinds of labyrinth": the "Greek" or "classical labyrinth," which "does not allow anyone to get lost"; "the mannerist maze" or "the trial-and-error process" – "a structure with ... many blind alleys [and] only one exit, but you can get it wrong"; and "the net" or "rhizome" – the "potentially infinite" labyrinth.[50] In fact, in *Lives of the Saints*, the "forgotten ... sleepy peasant village" (I, IX) – hemmed in by steep, "rocky slopes," dark ravines and "woods ... full of thieves" (XI, XIII, XV, XIX), and nestled in "the hollow of stony mountains that cradled it" (XXI) – seems hidden away in the centre of a geographical labyrinth: the "trail" and the "roads," leading in or out of it, are "pitted and scarred," mostly "made for mules ... carved straight out of the mountainside ... between a solid rock wall ... and a steep slope" and full of "erratic curves, with little margin for error" (II). For those who chose emigration, the only way out was even more difficult and dangerous: "A bus ride down pitted, mountain-slung roads ... [l]ong switchbacked descents into rain-drenched valleys, then ... up another rise, up and up, into gloomy cypress forests and [snow-crusted] small stony villages," just to reach "after several hours of hard mountain" a more gently rolling "land" and the garbage-strewn, traffic-jammed streets of Naples. But at least they make it "to the sea" (XXVI) – they all get out, like those in the "classic labyrinth."

Above all, the village life and outlook, still locked within its "medieval" framework, "in the dark ages" (XII, XX), its pagan taboos and primeval fears and superstitions (VI, VII, XIV), resemble Eco's medieval "world in which William realizes he is living": an endless maze without exit ("the net" or "rhizome" type of labyrinth). All "the lore" of rituals against the evil eye – that Vittorio "had ever collected" from various village sources ("overheard conversations ... stories ... random horde of facts"), that "[now] seemed tangled in [his] head in a great muddled heap" (XIV) – may well be considered the village's "labyrinth of superstitions." It is escaping from the "psychological" or "cultural" labyrinth that is almost impossible. And this is quite evident in the villagers' various forms of evasion, including migration, that become themselves a sort of "labyrinth": their seeking refuge, each behind a "mask" (II, XII), and collectively behind hypocrisy, duplicity ("more than a single face" [XX]), or in supernatural, natural, and manufactured wonders or diversions. Particularly in the yearly "carnival[-like] festival" of the patron saint: "Three days of festivities – music, dancing, processions, fireworks" (IX) offered all the villagers some form of escape: "their shock," their awe before the "miracle," the "magic" of electricity; their state of "trance from the sudden rush of light and sound" and their "moving slowly towards the stage as towards an oracle ... as if ... transported into one of *la maestra*'s stories of the saints, the world suddenly filled with light, and all possibilities open again" (XII); the men's drunken stupor ("with beer and wine"), and their frenzied "whirling ... around the dance area ... with a kind of joyless intensity that bordered on violence, as if ... anxious to spend before the end of the evening some anger or resentment ... bottled up inside them." Dancers "churned around [Cristina and Vittorio] like the wheels of some great machine," and all "seemed suddenly infected by the crowd's strange energy" (XII). For the reader they are all enjoyable scenes, but they hardly help to solve Vittorio's or Cristina's problems. They are all "blind alleys" in the novel's ever-expanding maze.

Cristina also realizes she is living in a prison-like world of "stupid rules and superstitions" (XXV), which she tries to escape in her own unique way: mainly through her "tight-lipped aloofness" (XX) and her firm final stand "to be free and to make a choice" (XXV). She also attempts the other more conventional village forms of escape, but with little success. The village festival offers her also a moment of abandonment to its "light and noise": her dizzying "breathless" dance with Vittorio results either in their being temporarily "forgotten ... anonymous, invisible" in the "crush of bodies [churning around them]" or in their being "left alone [in the sudden darkness]" and silence that followed the end of the dance, as if the crowd had "faded away" or the village itself had vanished (XII). Her withdrawal into herself does not save Cristina from the villagers' mockery (XX). Her failed abortion attempt lands her in the hospital (XIV). Her belated offer of the expected "sign" of penance – attending Christmas mass (XVII) – produces only a false truce, "leaving the same air of desolation as the village square had after the festival ... its familiar heavy silence" (XVIII). Finally her migration attempt, which appears to be the best way out, leads instead into another "blind alley" or conundrum – especially for Vittorio.

Through Vittorio, the labyrinth theme is continuous and complex. The "trial-and-error process" is present in the increasingly entangled net of circumstances in which he finds himself as a result of the "snake bite" (IV, XIV, XX), and particularly in his attempts to find a way out of it: his "retreat" in "the silence of the house ... suspended in a pure, electric emptiness" (IX); his rather listless participation in the village festivities

(XI, XII); his resorting to physical violence, even against his friend (XIII); particularly his fruitless experiments with magic rituals – "the sacrifice [of the dead chicken]" – or his lucky charms in order to "calm the spirits" (XIV, XV); but also his "reform" from "troublemaker" to "teacher's favourite," which, however, "filled [him] with revulsion and self-hatred" (XV); and finally his escape into the dream-like "world" of books – of tales and stories (XVI).

Vittorio's attempts are mostly unsuccessful; they lead him at times "into a fitful sleep," into a maze of "[strange] images," including a threatening labyrinth-like form – "some great black jaw stretching open in front of me, ready to swallow me like the whale that swallowed Jonah" (XIV); or at times into a nonsensical "world ... abruptly changed into its opposite ... completely overturned." Vittorio seems "caught in a ... trap" or in certain "events ... beginning to distort and skew like objects in a curved mirror" or in a tangle of feelings – "anger ... hate ... shame," disappointment and remorse. Nevertheless, Vittorio, though "disoriented and lost," escapes from the "winding and twisting" physical labyrinth into which he was led by one of his young tormentors; and almost simultaneously he begins to see, though still unclear and frightening, the way out of the bewilderment caused him by his mother's act: "an awful truth was already forcing itself on me" (XV).

Vittorio's constant probing and pondering draw the readers into a mesh of "scraps of information" and "dim ... insubstantial" memories (IV), often intertwined with thoughts, sensations, images, and a chain of "riddles" (persons, objects, deeds, words): from the fateful "snake ... in [his] mother's garden" and the shadowy "figure [with the luminous blue eyes] swooping down on [him]" – the probable German "hero" (I, VII), which are partially solved (XXXI, XXXII), to the nature of "good luck" charms and "fortune" (VII), his "father's mysterious life across the sea" (XX), and the inscrutable, "final secret message" in the vanishing "lucky one *lira*" coin (XXXIII) which remain mostly a mystery. His emigrating may be, though not completely as it seems, an escape from the spatial and psychological village labyrinths and "into an endless freedom" (XXVII), but it appears also as an entry into the larger, more intricate, though intriguing world outside his native area: "the city [with its] billboards and ... smouldering heaps of garbage ... [narrow] streets hemmed in by ... buildings [or sentries-like *palazzi*] ... crammed with cars ... carts and people [and] an enormous square where the traffic formed almost a solid sea"; a world that spoke "in a ... thick ... dialect [he] couldn't understand"; the port [with] a great ship taller than ... buildings ... a leviathan ... half a mile [long]"; "the mile-long pier [with] the great

collective wailing of a thousand agonized goodbyes." It seems at times
a descent into "the very bowels of hell," into "an inferno," or simply "a
room [reeking of] perfume ... overlaying a faint whiff of mould and rot
[with a] table with an old brown map ... the countries and continents
all distorted from the shapes *la maestra* had taught [him]," and from
where "the sea ... looked not blue but murky green" (XXVI, XXVII);
or "the sea [around them stretched] away in every direction ... to the
very ends of the earth" (XXVIII): "Everything seemed ... on the edge
of some yawning chasm" (XXXI). It is the "journey" Vittorio imagined
earlier: "a journey into [the limitless space] that took shape in [his] head
as the sea" – the journey into his "future," into the uncertain world of
"America," of migration (XXI).

Frequently, the riddles or his mental confusion cause Vittorio and the
reader to slide back and forth between a dream-filled sleep and reveries, or into a phantasmagorical and finally delirious "world of dreams,"
which may produce moments of clarity and other foreboding puzzles (I,
IV, IX, XIV, XVI, XX, XXI, XXVI, XXXI, XXXII, XXXIII). In fact, the
spatial labyrinth image appears most vividly in "a familiar dream, one
[he has] had a hundred times before in Valle del Sole: my mother and
I were in a dark passageway, slowly feeling our way along the walls in
search of a way out, hoping to slip unseen past the hunch-backed guardian who inevitably barred our way. Tonight, though, the hunchback did
not come; but at some point, reaching out into the darkness, I realized
with sudden horror that my mother was no longer beside me" (XXVI).

Quite significantly, Vittorio relates his dream only when it recurs in
Naples on the morning after leaving the village and of the same day he
begins his sea voyage for Canada ("America"). The unhindered "dark
passageway" may offer an easier escape, but Vittorio is also more aware
that it may lead into a more horrible one: his having to face his journey and perhaps his future alone. Through Vittorio, migration clearly
emerges as a most complex labyrinth. A parallel can be seen between
Vittorio's situation and that of Umberto Eco's William: "the world in
which William realizes he is living ... has a rhizome structure: that is,
it can be structured but is never structured definitively."[51] Such is also
the world of migration that Vittorio becomes more aware of on the
day he begins his journey to Canada; it is particularly the world of that
"America" that he described earlier as the enigmatic place of "dreams
and fears and contradictions," where many villagers, including his father,
have gone to seek their fortune, but where they live mostly suspended
between its contradictory visions, between myth and reality (XXI). On
the other hand, both migration and the labyrinth represent also a journey

of self-discovery. Once again, life and art come together into a full circle: the real-life stories about the traumatic experience of emigration seem best come to life in the literary work that the stories helped produce.

THE "JOYFUL" REDISCOVERY OF THE PAST AND SELF-IDENTITY

Ricci, like Eco, wants as well "to tell the whole *storia* [story-history]" of his chosen southern Italian peasant world, which, however limited, has its own "mysteries, its political and theological events, its ambiguities," and Ricci tells his story also "through the voice of someone who experiences the events, records them all with the photographic fidelity of an adolescent, but does not understand them" (and perhaps Vittorio himself, like Eco's young narrator, Adso, "will not understand them fully even as an old[er] man, since he [himself] chooses a flight into [various forms of] nothingness"[52]). Through the eyes and voice of Vittorio "Innocente," Ricci's own "innocent" speaker, *Lives of the Saints* captures and presents the "rhythm and [the] innocence" of the world of the *contadini*, the southern Italian peasants; their raw frankness especially evident in their speech – proverbs, sayings, imprecations, names (I, VII, XII, XIV, XVIII). Yet the novel does not lose the memory of the wider cultural world of which the peasants are also part and by which they are deeply influenced, particularly by the legacy of the Second World War and Fascism, the German presence in Italy, the policy of neglect of the rural areas by the central authorities – both political and ecclesiastical – and above all the phenomenon of emigration (I, IV, VI, IX, XII, XX, XXIX).

Remembered, though only briefly, are also various Italian historical figures: Mussolini (VI, XXIV); "*Vittorio Emanuele III Re e Imp.*" – Victor Emmanuel III, King and Emperor (VII); Garibaldi (XII); San Francesco – St Francis of Assisi (XVI); Caesar (XXIX); and Dante (XII); while "Giambattista del Fiore" (XVI) clearly recalls the twelfth-century Calabrian reformer Gioacchino da Fiore – Joachim of Floris (ca 1135–1202). Various aspects of the actual geography, history, economy, politics, religion, beliefs, customs, and languages of the southern Italian mountain villages are integrated in the story, as well as references to nearby southern Italian cities (Campobasso, Termoli, Caserta, Naples). That Ricci's world of the novel "contains the recollection of the culture with which it is loaded (the echo of intertextuality)" can be further illustrated by the various echoes of Italian literary works in the novel: they range from reminiscences of a short story by Giovanni Boccaccio (1313–75), in Vittorio's "dream" in Naples (XXVI), to similarities with Carlo Levi's *Christ Stopped at Eboli*, especially in the description of the condition of Italian immigrants and their ambivalence toward "America" (XXI).[53]

The novel presents also an array of typical characters, with their particular physical traits, attitudes, modes of behaviour and of speaking that reflect and illustrate that Italian world and related social institutions and classes. The village leaders include *lu podestà*, the "Fascist" mayor – the decorated war veteran and cripple; the landowning pensioner and dictatorial head of the family, whose "things," position, and public image matter more to him than his daughter's fate; the local political boss who "had loomed large, who commanded respect" and who, "shrunken and small," felt "betrayed" by all "[his] people," including "[his] own daughter" (I, V, IX, X, XII, XIII, XVIII, XX, XXIV); "*Don Nicola*," the village priest, "Father Nick" – a sort of local inquisitor, rhetorical preacher, and raconteur of strange stories, mocked in private, revered in public, suspected of pocketing the collection money, nicknamed "*Zappa-la-vigna* ... hoer-of-the-vineyard" (apparently the nickname of a Leamington Italian) or "our fatted calf," and considered to be like other "priests ... no better than the rest of us" (V, X); *la maestra*, the schoolteacher (Gelsomina – Jasmine) – contrary to her name, "a big-boned woman ... whose body gave off a strong odour of garlic and perfumed soap," and who believed that miracles and saints were "an ever-present possibility" (I, V, XV, XVI, XXIII, XXXII). Typical of a class are the two opportunistic, petty entrepreneurs: the "bumbling DiLucci," the "balding, thick-waisted," self-important owner of the bar-grocery and "only car in [town]," well versed in prying, gossiping, cheating, and "snake lore," and a good example of "the villagers' instinct that beneath every simple event there lurked some dark scandal" (II, III, IV); and the "small, swarthy," greedy, and brazen owner-operator of the "bus" service – "Cazzingulo (a nickname meaning 'balls [literally, penis] in your ass' – what usually happened when you rode in his truck)" (VII, XXV).

Other realistic, representative figures include "Alfreddo [*sic*] Mastroantonio," the fawning "chairman of *il comitato della festa*" (festival committee), then "Fascist" candidate for mayor, and a sort of country gentleman who had attended "*la scuola superiore* [high school] in Rocca Secca [and] spoke ... in a careful, florid Italian" (X, XVIII, XX); "Silvio ... the village postman," regular drinker and festival poet-entertainer-fool, ridiculed by the villagers as their reminder of "the dangers of high educational aspirations" (XII, XVI); and thus partly also a reflection of the skeptical attitude of some Leamington Italians toward culture or the more cultured class (see chapter 12);

"Zia Lucia ... large and matronly" aunt Lucia, whose "continued dignified calm ... seemed the mark of a rare wisdom, but ... only ... the same commonplaces crossed her lips [the same ghost of a smile manifesting her stupidity or obstinacy] as if she ... had not noticed our household's agitation ... as if nothing had changed" (V, XVI); mysterious, "ageless" Marta, who "moved through a room like a shadow" and from "her dark silence ... watched over us all like a fate" or some sort of supernatural being (V, XVI, XXV, XVIII).

The village has also its typical school clown, Guido the *"buffone"* (XV); its young bullies, ringleaders of children's "gangs" (with their rustic initiation "test" [IX, X, XV]); as well as its habitual drinkers, professional gossipmongers, and curiosity seekers (I, II, V, XII, XIII, XVI, XVIII, XX, XXV). Well defined, above all, are the southern Italian peasant women and mothers who "formed a class" clearly distinguished by all their features: their physical appearance ("ruddy swollen hands ... hair short ... round bellies"); their movements ("slow, elephantine gait ... regal ... exquisitely poised"); their speech ("the most flattened form of the local dialect"); their chores ("wash the clothes, haul the water, make the bread, feed the goats"); their "small freedoms" and their love of gossip, especially about secret love affairs (V). The novel is indeed a most vivid and enjoyable representation of the rural and still basically feudal southern Italian world in the late 1950s and early 1960s, with all its basic characteristics, including its bureaucracy and corruption of small officials (III).

The readers of Ricci's novel, while discovering or rediscovering that world, will also and, above all, find enjoyment in the story as a whole (i.e., the plot) – in Vittorio's gradual coming to terms with the bitter truth about his "mother and the snake" (the curse of the evil eye), in his unwilling acceptance of what his friend Fabrizio tries to tell him in very clear terms, her "screwing in the stable" (her shameless infidelity), and in his pleasant discovery that the baby his mother gave birth to had all its human features and "it was not the snake-headed child" that he been warned about (XI, XIII, XXXI). In the midst of her struggle, Cristina offers many enjoyable moments with her open-minded, ironic, and occasionally suggestive banter (I, II, IV, V, VI, VIII, XII, XX, XXVII, XXVIII, XXIX, XXXII). Some pleasure may be found in the countless amusing scenes and episodes, or in the underlying rustic, raw, and sometimes mean and profane humour, often dealing with human sexuality (I, III, IV, V, VII, XI, XII, XIII, XIV, XV, XXI, XXII, XXVI, XXVII, XXVIII, XXIX). An example of rural humour is appropriately provided by the young village clown, Guido the *buffone*: he made "even the teacher's reproving face ... crack into a smile" when she asked him, "Why did Joseph and Mary have to stay in a stable ... in Bethlehem?" and he answered, "In those days all the hotels were owned by the Fascists" (XV). Readers may find pleasure in the riddles that challenge Vittorio – the riddle of the snakebite, the riddle of the evil eye and related superstitions and remedies, particularly the never-ending and insoluble riddle of emigration, the passage from a familiar environment to an uncertain "future across the sea" (XX; see also chapters I, II, IV, V, VI, XI, XIII–XVI, XXI, XXVI, XXVII, XXX–XXIII). And as they are being entertained, the readers will perhaps also "learn" or be transformed.[54] Both the enjoyment and the understanding are clearly meant to increase in proportion with the readers' familiarity, or willingness to familiarize themselves, with at least some of the historical figures; for example, who is this "Dante" whose works Silvio, as a university student, was forced to burn? (XII); and to become familiar especially with some of the many Italian and dialect terms and phrases present in the novel: not just their meanings, mostly given by the author himself, but their role in the context of the episode or the story as a whole, particularly their role in expressing or re-establishing identity.

THE REDISCOVERY OF ITALIAN HERITAGE: THE ROLE OF LANGUAGE AND CULTURE

"The reader," Eco states, "should learn something either about the world or about language."[55] *Lives of the Saints* offers all that to the readers. Ricci's novel includes over 375 distinct Italian words (over 2,280 with the repetitions). On almost every other page, the readers will encounter "familiar" or traditional standard Italian and southern dialect (Molisan) words, sayings, stanzas of a song, dialogue, and a variety of invocations and curses, including a most desecrating blasphemy (not translated [XII]). They will find also the term used often by the Leamington Italians themselves to define their own community – *invidia*, envy (III, VI, XXVII]) – as well as "new," constructed forms, particularly proper names – the "strange fellow ... *Dompietro*" (Fatherpeter or Reverendpeter [V]); the mythical "Giant ... *Gambelunghe*" (Longlegs [VI]), which recalls the name of an actual Molisan town, *Gambatesa*, Stretchedleg; the ship's unprofessional doctor, *"il dottor Cosabene"* (Dr Thingwell or Dr Tinkerswell [XXIX]); and nicknames, at times made up with vulgar terms referring to body parts – *Cazzingulo* (Dickinass [VII]); *Rompacazzo* (Dickbuster [XVI]); *Facciabrutta* (Uglyface [IX]). The quite transparent compound names depict the "inhabitants" of the novel's world.

But, in general, the purpose of the traditional Italian phraseology or the neologisms is more than to add an element of local colour or to enhance realism. Their role, in a way similar to the Latin quotations or the "long didactic passages" in Eco's novel (*The Name of the Rose*), is to impart pace, or rhythm, and mystery to the story, or even to present a sort of test – "a penance or an initiation" – for the readers (thus resulting also in greater enjoyment through effort and understanding).[56] The Italian words are all an integral part of the story; they serve to represent effectively and fully its world, almost every aspect or circumstance of life; in Eco's words, they help "construct a world, furnished as much as possible, down to the slightest detail."[57]

The villagers' beliefs or contradictory attitudes toward religion, the church, or the supernatural are essentially established through the frequent repetition of the most common invocations or imprecations, both in dialect and in Italian, and with great variation: *Gesù Crist' e Maria* (Jesus Christ and Mary [I, III, XXXI]); *Crist' e Maria* (Christ and Mary [XII, XXV]); *Gesù Bambino, Gesù e Maria, Dio mio* (Baby Jesus, Jesus and Mary, my God [XIII, XV]); *per l'amore di Cristo/Crist'/Dio* (for the love of Christ/God [II, III, V, XIII, XVIII, XIX, XXI, XXIV, XXV, XXX]); *Crist' e Giusepp'* (Christ and Joseph [XXVIII]); *madonna/Madonna* (holy mother [XI, XXVII, XXX, XXXI]); and, worst of all, the common Italian blasphemy *porca madonna* (the sow or filthy holy mother [XII]).

Their religious traditions and practices are manifested also through other Italian words or expressions: the names of saints – *San Camillo, Leonardo, Bartolomeo, Vittorio, Innocente*, and *Santa Cristina*, which appears sixteen times (V, XVI); the terms and phrases referring to special feast days or the village festival and the related committee and its work – *la festa della Madonna, la festa di san Giuseppe, lu comitato della Madonna, il comitato della festa*; *la questua* (door-to-door collection of money [III, IV, IX, X, XX]); the names of places – *Colle de' Santi, Colle di Papa* (Hill of the Saints/Pope [I, V, VI, VII, XIV, XV, XXI]); and the names of streets – *via San Giuseppe, Giovanni Battista* (St Joseph, John the Baptist [I, II, III, XI, XII, XIII, XIV, XX, XXII, XXV]). In fact, the Italian names of beings or things with special powers, *la strega di Belmonte, lu malocchiu, la serpe* (witch, evil eye, snake) sum up the villagers' basic fears and superstitions or their other "religion" (I, VI, XI, XIII, XV, XXI).

Their socio-political structures, institutions, or classes are essentially outlined by the professional, religious, social, and familial terms or titles, both in standard Italian and in dialect: *lu podestà, la maestra, Don, Dom* (the mayor, the teacher, the priest, or the civil, educational, and religious authorities [I, V, X, XII, XIII, XV, XVI, XIX, XXII, XXIII, XXVII,

XXXII]); *dottore/dottor* (Dr), used to mock, to banter, and to indicate mostly the physician, i.e., health (XIX, XXVIII, XXIX, XXX); *carabiniere* (policeman or soldier at the port in Naples); *Capitano* (captain of the ship *Saturnia* used to migrate [XXVI]): the last three terms appear mostly in situations away from the village. The titles *il signor, signore, la signora, signora, signó, signor' e signori* are used for Mr, sir, gentleman, Mrs, lady, madam, ma'am, ladies and gentlemen; *signora*, appearing over thirty times, most frequently refers to Cristina, but *Signora* (Lady) is also used to address the Blessed Virgin; the truncated dialect form *signó'*, refers to both genders and numbers, and without the truncation mark, *signó*, to the Lord (I, III, IV, VII, XII, XIV, XXIII, XXV–XXIX, XXXI); *contadini* (peasants) also indicates their miserable plight (VI); *lu forestier* (the foreigner) appears only in its dialect and singular form as it to enhance the closed-in nature of the village and the villagers' parochial outlook (II). *Americani* and *paesani* are the villagers residing overseas who maintain close ties with their place of birth (IX). Various Italian terms define the family unit: *Tatone, mamma, figlio, zia* (grandfather, mother, son, aunt [I, II, III, IV, V, VII, XII, XVI, XX, XXI, XXIII, XXIV, XXXI]); or the changing status of Vittorio: *citro di mamma, ragazz' giovanotto* (mama's boy, boy, kid, young man [XV, XXX]). But, indicatively, the term *il Padre* is used only in relation to God "the Father" (V): it is absent in the familiar context, as are absent Vittorio's father and most village fathers during the day or for longer periods (I, XVIII, XXI).

The villagers' friendly and hostile interaction, as well as general Italian manners and social behaviour, are also essentially reflected in a series of Italian salutations – words of greeting, farewell, well-wishing, and terms of politeness and insult that cover a variety of daily and other social occasions: *Ciao, Salve, Auguri, a/Addio* – hi, hello, hail, so long, (best) wishes, congratulations, goodbye, farewell. *Addio*, instead of the usual "O Dio" (O God) is also used to express surprise, regret, pain (III, VII, XXII, XXVII–XXX). Present are also *Buongiorno, Buonasera, Buonanotte* (good morning / day / evening / night [V, XII, XXIX]), as well as *Buon appetito, buon natale* [*sic*], *buon viaggio, Buona fortuna* (enjoy your meal, Merry Christmas, bon voyage / have a pleasant trip, good luck [XVIII, XXII, XXIII, XXVI, XXIX]). Quite frequent are the familiar and polite forms of "excuse me": *S/scusa, S/scusate, S/scusi* (II, III, XXIII, XXV, XXVI, XXVII, XXIX, XXX); and other expressions of courtesy: *per favore, Gr grazie, La ringrazio, Piacere, Tanto gentile* (please, thanks, thank you [polite], pleased to meet you, very kind [II, V, XII, XIV, XV, XVIII, XIX, XXII, XXIII, XVI, XXVII, XXIX]). The term *Saluti*, normally "greetings," is used instead of the more common *salute* or *alla salute* to propose a toast or to raise a glass to one's health (XXIX). The frequency of *Addio* (goodbye, in the sense of God be with you, as in a final farewell), and the absence of *arrivederci* (goodbye, in the sense of until we see each other again) seem to emphasize the themes of separation, separateness, emigration, particularly with respect to the two main protagonists: Vittorio and Cristina, at their departure from the village, do not even receive a last farewell – "no one raised a hand to wave goodbye to us, the way they did when other families left the village" (XXV).

Various epithets, often vulgar, are used mostly by the villagers, including the women and children, or generally the lower class – and the wine-loving, "drunken idiot" ship's physician (XXIX). The terms, in both dialect and Italian forms and in both genders, are used in an offensive way and to express a mockingly friendly attitude: *scimunit, scimunoit, scimunito/a* (idiot, stupid); *stronzo, che stronzo* (turd, what a turd); *Quella cagna! Quella strega! quella porca!* (that bitch/witch/sow); *Diavoli* (little devils or rascals [VIII, XII, XIII, XVI, XX, XXII, XXIII, XXVI, XXX]). Generally, the use of standard Italian and dialect, of polite and vulgar terms, also helps to distinguish the novel's social classes or the levels of social refinement, as well as enhance the change of setting from the village to the city, to Naples and to the Canada-bound ship (XXVI–XXX).

Italian and dialect terminology sums up a variety of other basic activities, situations, or practices. The villagers' level of education or type of schooling and school are indicated by *la terza media* or *media* (IV, V) and *la scuola superiore* (X) (third grade of middle school or senior elementary school, i.e., grade eight, and high school). While "university" appears only in English (XII), the titles of two of their basic books are in Italian – *Principi Matematici* [sic], *vocabolario* (mathematical principles or beginnings, vocabulary [I, XVI]), that is, arithmetic and language, the foundations of education. Italian is also used for most of a catechism oral test on God and the principal mystery of the Christian faith – the Trinity: "quante persone ci sono in Dio ... Tre persone" (how many persons are there in God ... Three persons). The question and answer represent in essence the villagers' traditional religious beliefs and instructions (V). But a parody of the same question, in Italian, is also used by one of the schoolchildren to ridicule the village teacher and to give vent to their frustration, even hostility, toward that repressive, dogmatic form of education and religion (XXII).

The Italian terms for foods, eating, and drinking can be presented as a sort of menu of a hearty Italian meal (see chapter 12): appetizers or *antipasto – prosciutto, provolone* (cured ham and cheese [XXIX]); main dishes – *pasta all'uovo, tortellini alla bolognese, trippa* (homemade egg pasta, stuffed pasta with bolognese meat sauce, tripe [I, VII, VIII]); salad – *sesse di vacca* (tomatoes, IX); desserts and fruit – *ostie, cancelle* (typical Molisan wafers, especially at Christmastime [XVIII]); *castagne* or *castà* (chestnuts, in Italian and in dialect [XXVI]); beverages – *acqua* (water [XXVII]), *gassosa* (a sparkling soft drink [XXIX]), *amaretto* (an after-meal almond liqueur [X, XVIII]). The term *bicchieri* (drinking glasses) suggests the ever-present wine, which appears only in English and is often linked to its negative effects (I, VII, VIII, XII, XXIX, XXX, XXXI). Even the term *provolone* (cheese) is used also to suggest an unpleasant situation (XXVI). But in general the menu suggests and may include the good wish *Buon appetito* (enjoy your meal [XXIX]).

Italian words also indicate diverse forms of recreation quite typical of rural areas – a well-known card game, *scopa* (I); traditional dances and a familiar local song – *tarantella, tarantelle, saltarelli, vola, vola, vola*, with folk music provided by a regional *Gruppo Folkloristico* (IV, XII, XXXIII). Some of the gathering places for their pastimes are the *Bar e Alimentari* (bar and grocery store [I]), *Hostaria del Cacciatore* (Hunter's Tavern/Inn/Wine Shop [VIII]); *Colle di Papa* (Hill of the Pope [I, V, XV]). The most complete form of enjoyment is provided by the carnival-like festival of the patron saint – *la festa* (IV, IX), with outdoor entertainment, in the *piazza* (square [XXIII]) and in the streets – *via San Giuseppe / Giovanni Battista* (XI, XII). The vernacular term *sesse di vacca* (Roman [i.e., Roma] tomatoes, cow's teats) is another example of concrete peasant speech that, while describing the shape of the fruit, provides also another source of humour (IX).

The term *tomolo* alone is employed by Ricci to depict levels of the world of the novel. It is first presented as "a hollowed-out stone [in the middle square] ... used to measure grain for rent and taxes." It was thus a traditional local standard of economic and social valuation. Then the stone assumed a significance beyond its material presence. The story of the *tomolo* was linked in the novel to the public declaration of bankruptcy by a member of "the most powerful family in the region." Thus the *tomolo* came to represent also the seat of public self-humiliation, a symbol of failure and shame. It stood as a constant reminder of the fall of the noble family: it was seen as a "curse" and at the same time "an oracle, the prediction of their own town's declining fortunes" (VII). But the place of the *tomolo* served also as a respectful point of reference: "The *tomolo* had recently been replaced by a stone obelisk, a memorial to the townspeople killed in the second war" (VIII). The town's main square became *Piazza del Tomolo*: a significant setting or meeting place in the novel – "the 'Hostaria del Cacciatore' [restaurant]"; and the address of one of its influential protagonists – the teacher (XXIII). The term *tombolo*, of Arabic origin, indicating a unit of measure of land and dry goods once used mainly in Central-Southern Italy, reinforces the setting and time of the story – its functions are manifold in the novel.[58]

Above all, other Italian and dialect terms and phrases provide an essential outline of the story, foreshadow key events, and establish parallels and contrasts that may reveal clues for solving some of the mysteries. Three statements, two proverbs, and one comment announce and sum up three basic themes and actions. The first saying, almost completely in standard Italian, appearing at the beginning of the novel, *"Do' l'orgoglio sta, la serpe se ne va"* (where pride is, the snake goes, I), recalls pride (hubris) as the cause of the human fall, and the snake as the agent or intermediary; it also foreshadows Cristina's inevitable tragedy (XXXI), as well as her main character trait and the village superstitions as her nemesis (V, VI, VII, XI, XIII, XX, XXV, XXX). The second aphorism, in dialect, appearing during the preparations to leave the village, *"Tutt' lu mond' è paes"* (life [is] the same all over the world [XXI]), summarizes the bitter truth that migration, leaving one's native land may change very little after all, just as "nothing much seemed to change as a result of people dying]" (III). And third, the children's comment in mockery of Vittorio, *"Na bella serpe verde"* ([a beautiful] green snake [XV]), contrasts with the earlier association of a "green"-coloured snake with "good" (I, II, III), since both Vittorio and his mother Cristina are already victims of "bad" luck, or the "curse" of the evil eye that causes everyone to fear and shun the family (V, VI, XI, XIII).

Contrast and foreshadowing are also produced by other Italian statements and terms, repeated three times or appearing in a series of three: Vittorio's cry of fear, "È morta! (My mother's dead!) at the beginning of the story (III); and his silence when the tragic reality is whispered like a secret to him: *"È morta tua mamma ... È morta"* (XXXI). The term *invidia* (envy) recurs in three chapters (III, VI, XXVII), and in the second of the three, which seems "dedicated" to envy, the term is repeated three times (VI). In the first instance, *invidia* is used to explain as a "curse" the death of dear ones, as well as the pregnancy of an unmarried, young peasant woman (III); in the central one, it is presented once as "the root of all the peasants' troubles," and (according to the legend of the giant *Gambelunghe*, Longlegs) as the result of their abuse of their "good fortune"; it appears a second time to explain the fragmentation of their farmlands; and a third time, to present "boasting" as the cause of envy and the accompanying "tremendous forces ... that found their incarnation in the evil eye"; and along with the dangers of envy, this chapter also presents a warning against the practice of "boasting" and a remedy against the evil eye – magic or witchcraft (VI). Finally, the term *invidia* is mentioned in a situation that links the word to a central theme of the novel – infidelity – the cause of the breakdown of marriage and the family and the source of general ill will (XXVII). The Italian word, said in three different settings – fear of evil forces, social and material misfortune, death – underlines the continuity of the theme of envy throughout the story (II, X, XXI). The novel again reflects the Leamington Italians' accounts of the presence of envy throughout life in general.

The progression of the story is pinpointed by three Italian exclamations that link three moments in Cristina's life: she lashes out at Alfreddo [*sic*] Pannunzio with *"Che cretino!"* (What an idiot!) (and uses the vulgar insult *stronzo*, turd) who's visiting his family after five years in Canada as she rebukes him for his warning that her husband in Canada will hear about her behaviour, and as she proudly rejects the money Mario sent her as an unacceptable substitute for human feelings (XII). *"Che figura!"* (What a shameful display!) is Cristina's angry reaction to the sight of Vittorio's blood-covered face after a fight with a schoolmate to defend her name (XIII). Yet shortly after, Cristina herself fights with the mother of Vittorio's opponent to defend their honour (XIII). More ironically, the phrase anticipates Cristina's father's condemnation of her behaving "like a common whore" or displaying her "shame in the streets" resulting in "disgrace upon [his] name," further emphasized by his Italian epithet for her, *"Disgraziata"* (Wretched woman [XVIII, XX]). Finally, the ship's physician exclaims *"Che spettacolo"* (What spectacle, what wonder) just after the risk-ridden delivery of Cristina's illegitimate child – or at the miracle of life itself – followed, shortly after, by Cristina's death (XXXI). The three similar Italian constructions summarize Cristina's drama: her rebellion against husband, father, and village; and her "sin" or "crime" that leads to her end at the bottom of the ocean (XXXII).

The endearing words *"figlio mio"* (my son) are said in reference to Vittorio by three people closest to him, mark a rise in the dramatic story of migration to evoke both joy and sorrow, life and death. The phrase is first used by Vittorio's teacher on his "last day of school" shortly before his departure for Canada: *la maestra*, not at all *"quella porca* [that bitch of] a few days before," but a woman who sobs like a baby and hugs him like a mother when she gives him as a parting gift her *Lives of the Saints* with the hope that he'll "live by it ... follow their example" (XXIII). Second, the phrase is used by Vittorio's grandfather on "the eve of [the boy's] departure" as he gives his grandson his three First World

War medals, including a bronze one "engraved with ... the inscription *Al valore militare*'" (For military valour). But in this case, the words of affection are spoken at the culmination of a monologue full of sadness, bitterness, and anger: the broken old patriarch rails against all traitors - daughter, villagers, and Italians in general. Thus, he tells his grandson, "You're lucky to leave this country ... a place of Judases and cowards," and to take with him his almost meaningless war decorations: "Take them, *figlio mio*," he urges Vittorio, adding a last note of regret: "I hope they bring you better fortune than they brought me." The grandfather's farewell makes separation and migration even more difficult; the words and the gift seem more a warning than a wish for the young migrant (XXIV). Finally, the two words are tenderly whispered by a weary Cristina as she "kissed [her son] on the forehead" just after she's informed of the birth of a baby girl and shortly before her death, leaving Vittorio with those tender last words and an infant half-sister as his only companions in a painful journey toward the unknown (XXXI).

The gifts that Vittorio and the other emigrants receive upon departure, are tangible representations of the affection expressed by the Italian phrases; they serve as concrete links between those left behind and those departing. For the migrants the "object-gifts" will, in time, turn into precious "object-myths" of the more familiar reality of their past, the embodiment of their dearest memories – a vital bond with the people and places they left behind: relatives, friends, and native village. The gift-giving is at times accompanied by wishes of good fortune. In two situations the wish is expressed to Vittorio in Italian – *Buona fortuna*. The American jackknife that Fabrizio gives to the departing Vittorio, as a symbol of his friendship and commitment to reunite with him in the future, is his "most prized possession ... a part of him ... as inseparable as a finger or toe." The value of the gift gives strength to the sincerity of his wish, *"Buona fortuna in America"* (Good luck in America [IX, XXII]). Vittorio's teacher also at the end of their farewell, after giving him her precious book, "planted a last silent kiss on [his] forehead," and said, *"Buona fortuna."* The gift and the wish are also accompanied by an address – expressed in Italian – that each one, Fabrizio and the teacher, gives to Vittorio, in the hopes of receiving news from him from America (IX, XXII, XXIII).

However, the Italian expression of good luck does not accompany the grandfather's farewell words and gift to Vittorio. The only luck that the bitter war hero is certain of is that at least his grandson is able to leave his land of traitors and fools. A heartfelt good luck cannot easily be wished by those who feel betrayed and abandoned: the old cripple has only tears left for his innocent grandson and curses for his ever-defian daughter. Good wishes, gifts, and memories are not deserved or offered if the separation from the native land is forced or violent, as in the case of Cristina and Vittorio. Usually, relatives and "well-wishers" would like to take "a few pictures … *Per ricordo*," to remember those who leave But the defiant Cristina objects: she prefers not to be remembered, no remember the village she has rejected. Similarly, she rejects villagers gifts for their relatives in Canada and refuses to serve as their messenge (XXV). And yet the wish *Buona fortuna* appears a third time and i directed to both Cristina and Vittorio just before boarding the ship a the port of Naples: it is the half-hearted wish of a stranger who's just a half-hearted in helping the two migrants – the pregnant woman and he young son. The wish seems to lose some of its meaning and sincerity a the travellers move farther away from their native soil (XXVI).

Clearly, Italian words and phrases are key to the novel, and most sig nificantly at the very end. The village festival, which is a highlight in the annual cycle of life in the village, ends with the singing in the square of "the verses of a familiar local song," in which the whole audience takes part, almost in a state of collective trance, as if the entire village has rediscovered a state of harmony. The singing out loud of the two four-line stanzas of their traditional Italian song underscores the role o singing, language, the recollection of happy times in the reconciliation o individuals, the community, and particularly of migrants. The repetition in the last chapter of the song, which expresses the desire to conjure up happy times, re-establishes the link to the land and language of birth especially in an unfamiliar and uncertain environment. The spontaneous recollection of the song safeguards and re-establishes the traveller's o migrant's language and traditions, his self-identity (XII, XXXIII).

UNDERSTANDING THE MANY CANADIAN TRADITIONS

The frequency of the three-time pattern in Italian forms – words or phrases including three *buon natale* (Merry Christmas [XVIII]) – while reflecting the trine or trinomial English constructions (I, XVIII, XXI), draws atten tion to the recurrence of the magical and mystical number *three* itself. The numeral *three* – as a word both in English and Italian, as the figure *3* or a the forms *triplets* and *third* (including the Roman numeral *III*) – appear well over thirty times, as if to suggest to the reader other "secrets" beside those mentioned (V, VI, XII, XIV, XX, XXII, XXXIII). The mystery-related number suggests the presence of other mysteries hidden in the story (itsel consisting of thirty-three chapters).

Most often the *three* is mentioned in relation to the main protagonists – Vittorio and Cristina – individually or together: it relates to Vittorio's age when his father emigrated; to his early indifference to school and books (I); and to his difficult birth (II, XXVI). *"Vittorio Emanuele III,"* Victor Emmanuel III, or the third (VII), is the king of Italy, whose name and profile appear on the dubiously "lucky one *lira,"* that his namesake Vittorio lost during his sea voyage to Canada (XXXIII). The unsuccessful magic ritual and witch's formula to "make a cure" or "calm the spirits," that both Cristina and Vittorio attempted, required the reciting of specific words "three times" and making "three full turns to the right, three to the left" (VI, XIV). Both the priest and the teacher use the number *three*, in Italian, to teach the children about God and the Trinity (V, XXII); after his fight, the teacher instructs Vittorio to "drink at least three glasses of water" (XIII); and her address, which Vittorio receives from her only before his leaving for Canada, is *"Piazza del Tomolo No. 3 "* (XXIII).

The three-pattern also relates to Cristina's life: she is the third and only surviving child whose mother died giving birth to her (IV); and the only village woman to have completed the third level of middle school – *"la terza media"* (V). She "survived her snake bite" with only "three days" in the hospital (IV). And she is held responsible for the death of three family members (XIII, XVIII). Her name saint, *Santa Cristina*, is brought before three magistrates, and on the "third morning ... the third magistrate ordered [her] to be cast into the sea" (as Cristina's body is later, XXXIII), but the saint is miraculously "led ... up into the heavens" (XVI).

The number *three* and derivatives appear also in relation to the geography of the village – "three thousand feet above the valley floor" (I); the fragmentation of the farmlands – "a third [piece] all the way down by the Valley of Pigs" (VI); the fertility-related tripe – helps "give birth to triplets" (VIII); the possible length of the snake – "Three feet long?" (XV); emigration from the village – "three departures since *la festa*" (XX); a woman "had left [for the Sun Parlour] with her parents and her three children" (XXI). The three-pattern is also associated also with the Canada-bound ship: the "third class" first assigned to Cristina and Vittorio; the "third mate" – the officer who becomes Cristina's friend; the "three large clocks" in the captain's quarters (XXVI); the "three-tiered arrangements of dishes [at the captain's table]"; the unfortunate birth on the ship "only three months ago" (XXIX); and the third month is suggested in the "mid-March" beginning of the sea voyage (XXVIII). The number is also implicit, with corresponding suggestions, in the vision of "the barren trees ... leaning toward us like silent magi" (XVII). The members of Vittorio's household – "only the three of us" (IV) – include Vittorio himself, his mother, and his grandfather; later the members of the family change – the grandfather is replaced by the child, and Cristina by Mario – but the family recomposes always into a unit of three – the number of the Holy Family!

The number *three* or a group of three (triangle, clover) has long been a symbol of the Trinity, the triune God, or divinity. The triad is linked to the mystical and the miraculous, to supernatural and mythological wonders, good and evil (the three worlds of the afterlife, the three fates, the three circles of angels, the three beasts) in the Christian, Judaic, Hindu, and other Western and Eastern traditions. According to the Italian poet-philosopher Dante (also mentioned in the novel), "The sole factor [maker] of miracles is three, that is, Father, Son and Holy Ghost, who are three and one" (*Vita Nuova, New Life* [XXIX]).[59]

In *Lives of the Saints* the number *three* or the sets of three seem to be associated mostly with unhappy circumstances or sad events about to happen. Or at least the situations appear unpleasant, as evidenced especially in the two references to God and the Trinity: "At school [the children] feared [the priest who came] to test [them] on [their] catechism, administering three thwacks to the buttocks with a short paddle for every incorrect answer, one for the Father, one for the Son, one for the Holy Ghost." And that was frequent, since no one knew the answer to the follow-up question: "How can it be that these three persons are one?" (V). For Vittorio's friend, who was forced to quit school, the catechism question became a bad memory and a source of mockery and hostility toward the teacher who also posed it: "'Tell me, Fabrizio, *ma chi sono le tre persone in Dio?' Addio, quella porca!*" (who are the three persons in God? Goodbye, that bitch! [XXII]).

But, at the same time, the one-God-three-persons mystery parallels Vittorio's attempt to understand human behaviour, human nature itself. The priest, who appearing suddenly like "a dark angel … never failed to crucify a scapegoat or two on his visits" to the school, after the test and punishment, would tell the children "stories [that] would make [Vittorio] forget his paddle." Vittorio's "mind could not understand how the Father Nick with the paddle and the Father Nick who told stories were one and the same person" (V). Similarly, he wondered how his teacher, "*la maestra* … had split before [his] eyes into two separate people: one who had babies that died, the other who appeared as if from nowhere every morning in our classroom" (XXIII). One lesson on the Trinity may serve as a means to think about the coexistence of "two natures" in such entities as America, goats, and the witch of Belmonte (XXI), and perhaps become more aware of the complex, often contradictory nature of every individual human being!

In general, both the "trinity" and the "three" seem to present opposite values: their meanings seem to be reversed or do not appear completely in accordance with what is expected in Christian terms (though even popularly, things, especially adverse ones, are said to come in threes). The three-patterns suggest mystery; they are basically linked to the nature of the miracle, that even quite recently has been defined in a widely read weekly as "a wonder, a beam of supernatural power injected into history"; or as an extremely remarkable, unexpected event or achievement that cannot be generally predicted or readily explained.[60] Yet it is this very awareness of the reversal of the ordinary (of a miracle at work) that can offer an interpretation key for the title and the story as a whole of *Lives of the Saints*.

The title itself, *Lives of the Saints* (perhaps suggested by Eco's *The Name of the Rose*, 237), is misleading. Ricci's novel is not a book or collection of saints' lives and legends, of Christian men and women who pursue sanctity and practise all the virtues. Though saints in the traditional Christian sense do appear in the novel (V, X, XVI), *Lives of the Saints* deals mainly with the lives of ordinary people who seem more sinners than saints – in fact, through them the major human faults, the deadly sins, are well represented in the story: pride, envy, greed, lust, violence or anger, drunkenness or gluttony, laziness or sloth. And yet there are parallels and resemblances between the novel's characters and the traditional saints, especially between the Innocente family (Cristina, Vittorio) and the Holy Family (Mary, Joseph, Christ).

The suggestion is that the novel's *real* saints are the villagers, all the ordinary people who struggle and make sacrifices to raise a family. They may be like Mary and Joseph who, according to the monsignor's homily, "underwent ... the same hardships we all face, the hardships of the poor"; they may be like Mary, "a woman filled with goodness and grace [but] also a woman of flesh and blood, the wife of a simple labourer [who had to endure] the shame ... from skeptics who did not believe in [her inner purity]"; a woman who felt a "mother's pain ... when her *first born son* was spit on by the crowds and nailed to the cross like a criminal" (X). Some of the villagers, particularly Cristina and Vittorio, may be compared to the saints whom Vittorio discovers in his teacher's book, the martyrs of the faith: those who suffer or die for their beliefs, their principles (like Cristina); all the victims of human ignorance, arrogance, prejudice, and general malevolence (XVI). They also resemble those saints who were originally sinners before their conversion and redemption, particularly "San Camillo de Lellis, founder of the Ministers of the Sick, a local saint who ... was a ruffian [when he was a young man]" (V). And these saints, like the saints of tradition, may be even performing "miracles," wonders or changes that for most are still unrecognizable or unacceptable.

Cristina, like Santa Cristina who (in the *Lives of the Saints* within the novel *Lives of the Saints*) "broke up all of the gold and silver images of the pagan gods in her father's house, selling the pieces to help the poor" (XVI) has also broken all the "stupid rules and superstitions" in her father's village (XXV) for the sake of freedom, equality, justice for herself, the village women, and the downtrodden "damn peasants" (as a village petty entrepreneur calls them [II, VII]). Cristina is indeed a sinner (guilty especially of what Petrarch called "the most grievous sin of pride"); but she may well be also a "saint" similar to her name saint or the other saints described in the teacher's book, but especially in accordance with the teacher's belief for her "the saints were not merely the ghosts of some mythical past but an ever-present possibility, the mundane and everyday verging always on the miraculous." In fact, Cristina's suffering and death, her rejection of abortion (i.e., murder in Catholic morality) make the teacher's belief and what she said about the saints appear not as humorously far-fetched as they first seem: "Who knows," she said once to her pupils before telling them the story of the former sinner San Camillo, "if there isn't a saint among us right now?" (V). The teacher's belief and statement seem to reinforce the theme of Cristina's own "redemption" or "sainthood," especially if linked, as they seem to be, to the monsignor's words about the suffering and shame of the Virgin Mary as a woman and as a mother (X). The link is further reinforced by the meanings of the Italian names of the protagonists and of the family: *Cristina*, "little female Christ"; *Vittorio*, "Victor," the "victorious one" or even "victory"; and *Innocente*, "Innocent." The names may be signs of moral integrity.

Awareness of the Italian used in the novel offers the readers added insights and thereby a more active role in the interpretation of the story. According to Eco, "A title, unfortunately, is in itself a key to interpretation" that sometimes "can represent an undue interference of the author"; a title can "mislead" its readers; and Ricci's title, *Lives of the Saints*, is also quite puzzling – who are the saints in the story? But Ricci's novel also offers its readers the means to reduce the author's influence and make the title an invaluable key to interpretation. As indicated, the various interconnections of the title with the parallel references, sequences of numbers, and meanings of Italian words expand the dimension of the novel's title: the term *saints* may well include both the ancient saints in the teacher's "stories of the saints" and the more modern "saints" in Ricci's story of a contemporary family. A very thin line seems to separate the "old" and "new" saints. There seems to be an attempt to renew, update the meaning f saint. In fact, Ricci's title does also what Eco suggests: "A title must muddle the reader's ideas, not regiment them."[61] And Ricci's title retains ts puzzling effect; the mystery remains – who are the saints? Ricci's novel may suggest another proof that "miracles [do] become mortal": they "are ike wonders of the storyteller's invention, full of surprise."[62]

The fusion of more than one linguistic and cultural tradition can also e observed in the recurrence, in three-fold form, of the symbolic *13* – a umber that evokes mystery and is also linked to sanctity-related suf-ering. The number first appearing as a word and in Italian – *"Numero redici, via Giovanni Battista"* (number thirteen, John the Baptist Street XXII]) – indicates the house number of Vittorio's "only friend" (XV), abrizio, who lived in "the poorer section of town, where [the] houses vere ramshackle [or] deserted, their owners gone to America" (XIII). he street is, of course, named after St John the Baptist, the forerunner nd baptizer of Christ, who was beheaded for preaching against the ypocrisy and immorality of the powerful. Earlier in the novel, Fabrizio imself had established a more explicit link between his suffering and his laim to some degree of sanctity. During one of the more severe beatings y his father Facciabrutta (Uglyface), Fabrizio relates to Vittorio, he told is father, "'Now I'm just like Christ,' because they hit him too" (IX). Because of the curse of the "evil eye" on his friend's family, Fabrizio is ot only forbidden to see Vittorio, but he is also "locked … in the house vith the goats" to prevent him from participation in the village festival XIII), taken out of school, "hired out to a farmer" away from the vil-age, and sent away to work at the ominous "Valley of the Bones" (XVI). Nevertheless, Fabrizio continues to see his friend Vittorio, defends him gainst the other boys, and gives him his most precious possession before e leaves for Canada (XI, XIII, XV, XXII).

Similar themes resonate in the other occurrences of the number *13*, hough the links are not as clear: The sign on the road that took Vittorio nd his mother Cristina to Naples and to the Canada-bound ship read Napoli 13." Vittorio saw the sign just after he noticed that his "moth-r's eyes melted slowly into runnels of quiet tears, which she hid by urning to the window [of the bus] and bringing a discreet hand up to vipe at her cheek" (XXVI). Cristina's silent tears of sorrow, perhaps f penance and certainly of joy for the anticipated "endless freedom," eappear just as the ship sails away (XXVII). Finally, the number appears nore than once embedded in "213," or more specifically "Room 213." he living quarters given to Cristina and Vittorio at the last minute may ave been a room associated with infidelity, envy, and intrigue, but that oom enabled them to avoid their assigned cabin in the hospital-like "third class" (XXVI, XXVII, XXIX). Indicatively, at the captain's dinner which included as guests Vittorio and Cristina, "There were twelve or thirteen ... in all"; and the "captain's quarters" where the dinner was held, had "a larger replica of the table in room 213, with the same old brown map" showing a "distorted" world (XXVII, XXIX). The evening dinner was, in fact, Cristina's "last supper," the same night of the storm, the birth of her premature baby, and her death (XXX, XXXI).

The use of 13 also presents some ambivalence,[63] which is the result of the fusion of the two traditions in the novel: Is the number 13 intended as an omen of bad luck in accordance with the Anglo-Canadian tradition? Or is it a symbol of good luck as often considered in the Italian one? Perhaps both or neither! After all, the outcome of Fabrizio's life and Vittorio's migration are still unknown (and in Ricci's subsequent novel much of the ambivalence remains). Room 213 becomes both the room of death (Cristina) and of life (her daughter): of both end and beginning. The two opposite associations seem to be reciprocally voided, leaving in doubt both traditions in this case, or suggesting also that, either way, some traditions and practices are, as Vittorio sadly discovers (XV) and as Cristina calls them, "*stupidaggini!* ... stupid ... superstitions ... stupidities" (VI, XXV). The ambivalence seems to suggest that some traditions are best left behind or at least challenged, especially in the emigration process.

Familiarity with Italian hand gestures can provide another key to better understand some central themes of the story, particularly the interconnection of adultery or infidelity, the snake and the evil eye (III, V, VII, XI, XIII, XVIII, XXVII, XXIX). The story, it is worth recalling, begins with a snakebite incurred by Cristina during her adulterous act in the stable (I), and results in the shunning of her family, since snakes in the local superstition "were agents of the evil eye, which the villagers feared far more than any mere Christian deity or devil" (I). Thus, they "avoided anyone or anything that had been touched by the evil eye as if there was a peril that the affliction might spread by contagion" (VI). Her son Vittorio was particularly affected: he was increasingly alone, especially after his "only regular friend" Fabrizio was forced to stay away from him and regularly beaten by his father for neglecting his chores in order to see Vittorio in secret. On one occasion, Fabrizio accompanies his explanation of their separation with an Italian hand gesture that is said "to mimic the evil eye" (XI); but, in fact, the gesture, for most Italians indicates cuckoldry, adultery. And the novel itself provides convincing, if not conclusive, evidence for the latter meaning of the gesture!

Hand gestures are used by Fabrizio on two occasions in order to help his younger and more naive friend understand and perhaps accept the sudden events that affect, disrupt one's life (IV, XI). The first gesture, clear and self-evident, highlights also a central motif – sexual intercourse or mating – that is closely linked to the adultery meaning of the second gesture. Vittorio, about to turn seven, is upset that he is no longer allowed to sleep with his mother: "I brooded over the meaning of these changes being forced on me." Fabrizio's explanation is quite straightforward and far-seeing: "'If your father was home he wouldn't let you sleep with your mother … He'd want to do the thing to make babies. Like the goats.' And he … made a circle with the thumb and index finger of one hand and passed a finger from the other through it, back and forth" (IV).

Early in the novel, with a crude simile and the simple sign of copulation – mainly drawn from his observation of life at home where "he and his family slept on one side of the curtain, the goats and sheep on the other" (IX) – Fabrizio not only sets forth key aspects of the story but also anticipates what will be clearer to Vittorio, and the readers, only later: briefly, the causes and effects of infidelity. More particularly, the absence of men, the separation of husbands and wives because of work, and especially emigration, can lead to the disruption, breakdown of the family. The non-fulfillment of the natural need to mate – basic to humans and animals alike – results in infidelity of both partners; it leads particularly to the men's fears of their wives' unfaithfulness; the fears that during their absence their women will seek other mating partners like the courtyard animals that their women are compared to in the men's proverbs about adultery or cuckoldry: "Guard your women like your chickens … or they'll make food for the neighbour's table" or "A woman is like a goat: she'll eat anything she sees in front of her" (XVIII, XX, XXVII, XXIX).

It is Fabrizio's second-hand gesture that is quite equivocal, perhaps purposely ambiguous. Fabrizio explains to Vittorio the reason for being kept away from him: "'It's not you … It's because of your mother and the snake. *Lu malocchiu*.' He twisted his face into a scowl and brought two fingers up to his head as horns, to mimic the evil eye" (XI). Fabrizio's words do indeed indicate snake and evil eye, which is expressed only in the southern Italian dialect term of the villagers, but his hand gesture, according to Italian practice, does not "mimic the evil eye," as Vittorio relates, but cuckoldry; it is the sign of the cuckold – a man whose wife has committed adultery: in the context of the novel, Vittorio's father, Mario, who is in Canada, and his mother, Cristina. The term *horns* with reference to the cuckold or "wronged man" appears a little later in association with goat that in Italian also means cuckold (XII).

As most Italians know, the sign of the evil eye, or to repel the curse of the evil eye, is slightly but significantly different: "two fingers … as horns" pointing downwards towards one's feet or the ground. Surely Fabrizio, "ready with facts on any subjects" (XXI), as Vittorio once described him, was aware of this subtle difference! Is he then purposely creating the ambiguity to humour Vittorio, to protect his sensitive friend from the harsh reality about his mother? And is the author allowing it to mislead the readers and make the story more intriguing? For the moment, it seems, the evil eye is allowed to be a cover-up or another metaphor (a term already used to allude to sexual activity [V]) for adultery or infidelity. But not for long: only a week later Fabrizio reacts to a sulky Vittorio with the bitter truth: "What's the matter with you? ... It's not your fault, it's your mother. Because she was screwing in the stable" (XIII).

Vittorio's violent reaction to Fabrizio's frankness makes his wiser friend recant in an attempt to appease Vittorio and protect his innocent illusion: "Oh ... have you gone crazy? It was the snake's fault, you stupid! You're just a stupid like your stupid father! Sí, sí [Yes], stop, it was only the snake, you're right, it was only the snake" (XIII). Clearly, Fabrizio's insistence on the exclusive fault of the snake and his binding of son and father in a common stupidity, but no mention of the evil eye, reinforce his original statement about his mother "screwing in the stable." The seeming recantation tends to emphasize the interconnection of snake and adultery or cuckoldry, and to confirm also that the hand gesture of the horns "to mimic the evil eye" meant, on the contrary, the horns of the cuckold, who, again in keeping with Italian custom, is usually so but doesn't know it or pretends not to know it, or is "stupid," i.e., lacks awareness, also to save face. In this light, the role of adultery or infidelity becomes much clearer.

In fact, the villagers fear the snake and the curse of the evil eye that Cristina may bring upon them as much as Cristina's adultery itself, of which she is not only unrepentant but proud! For this reason "it was the women of the village who had been hardest toward [her]" (XVIII). The women feared her shamelessness might expose their own secret affairs; after all, when people gossiped, as they were widely doing about Cristina, their husbands tended to "find out. They always [did]" (V). Her defiance, or her "[walking] around like a princess," as one of the women warned her, was turning people against her, might even become the cause of her downfall: in fact, that was the "curse" that Cristina would "bring ... on everyone around [her]" (VI). Her brazen attitude was also reinforcing the village men's fears of their wives' sexual infidelity, as evidenced in their proverbs: "If the cock is in the fields, the men ... said, the hen would lay her eggs in someone else's nest" (XVIII). The scandal, not the snake, made women avoid Cristina. Besides, the snake was considered

o be of secondary importance (V), even "a stupid mistake," according
o Cristina herself. She just feared that her lover might have made her
pregnant, because "he got very excited when he saw that snake" (VII).
The boys who mock Vittorio about the colour and length of the snake he
saw coming out of the stable where his mother "was screwing," continue
o ridicule him by establishing a similarity with "the colour, the length
and the thickness" of Vittorio's penis; and the whole deception of the
initiation ritual is based on references to the events at the beginning of
the story: Cristina's snakebite and her "[going] with another man" (XV).

Adultery, or sexual intercourse in general, emerges more clearly as an
underlying theme once the references and allusions to the snake and evil
eye are viewed in the larger context of the story. Fabrizio's two hand
gestures in relation to each other and to other episodes have provided
ample evidence, while showing quite clearly that the Italian hand gesture indicated cuckoldry (IV, XI). Further proof for the centrality of the
theme of adultery can be found also in Cristina's struggle for equality,
both for herself and for all women. Her vindication rests mainly on her
defiant adulterous act; on her challenge of the sexual double standard;
on her rejection of the label "whore" applied to women and to her in
particular, by both the men and the women of the village, including her
father-in-law (III, VI, XX).

Her first claim is directed toward her husband and her father: "He's
probably slept with every whore in America by now, but for me it's a
disgrace. Women have had their faces up their asses for too long, they
let their men run around like goats and then they're happy if they don't
come home and beat them!" (XX). The second target is the captain of
the ship *Saturnia*, who's been married for thirty years to a faithful wife,
but involved in a ten-year love affair (XXVII): "Tell me ... doesn't it
worry you to spend so much time at sea? What do you think your wife
does when you leave her alone like that?" (XXIX). The scolding is a
warning not only for the captain but for all men. Her challenge is also
emphasized by the reversal of a simile in the men's proverbs (XVIII):
here the men are likened to the goats!

The linking of goats to sexuality in the story presents another instance
where knowledge of Italian language and customs can further illustrate
the theme of adultery through the horns of cuckoldry. The Italian term for
the male goat – *becco* – also means figuratively *marito tradito* (betrayed
husband). Goats have horns; thus, instead of the word, Italians often use
the horns, formed with the index and small fingers of the hand, up against
one's forehead, to signify *becco* or *cornuto*, the man with horns, cuckold.
Fabrizio's gesture is the same (XI). Fabrizio also used a simile that likened

human mating to that of goats, just before his hand gesture for the sex act (IV). Again, the promiscuous behaviour of both men and women is indicated by a comparison with the indiscriminate eating and roaming practices of goats (XVIII, XX). Goats also appear in the story as quasi-anthropomorphic double-natured creatures, "at once ... animals and .. strange spirits," not unlike the local witch, "both a decrepit old woman and ... a sorceress," and both goats and witch reflecting the "two natures" of America, the beautifully dangerous seductress of many village men (XXI). Even America, i.e., emigration, can cuckold, betray people.

Above all, goats – more specifically the horns of goats – are mentioned with clear reference to the man betrayed by his woman. The situation is pivotal: at the village festival a man and a woman onstage entertain the villagers with jokes based on a widely familiar topic – women's infidelity. The man, who dared to ask his woman about the number of times she was unfaithful to him, was told as many times as the number of stars in the sky. He warns her to "be careful ... a wronged man can turn into a devil." She responds, "Not everything with horns is a devil. Goats have horns too" (XII). The reference appears in the chapter immediately following the one with the hand gesture with the horns. The association of goats with various entities – spirits, witch, devil – also recalls the satyrs, the mythological woodland deities, part man, part goat, with horns and fond of lechery.

The example of the Italian hand gesture, with all its associations and implications throughout the story, is ample evidence of the far-reaching significance of knowing the language and traditions that are reflected in the novel, that are part of the multicultural heritage of Canada. Familiarity in particular with Italian language and culture, so intrinsically part of the novel, can be the source of other intriguing puzzles and complications and simultaneously of other valuable insights and interpretations. The result is that the readers can better achieve the classical balance of learning and pleasure. And the greater the knowledge, the more complete the enjoyment: a fuller experience.

THE DEEPER ROOTS: LANGUAGES – DIALECT, ITALIAN ... AND ENGLISH

A significant legacy of Ricci's first novel is clearly the language of his cultural roots. The novel seems to be meant also as an introduction to Italian, arguably the unofficial third or fourth language of Canada. The stock of Italian words in the novel (over 375 distinct terms or over 2,280 with the repetitions) can be arranged to form a comprehensive Italian grammar with aspects of phonology, morphology, and syntax.

The phonological categories are quite varied: the Italian alphabet is complete – twenty-one letters, five vowels, sixteen consonants, including he open and closed sounds of *e* /*o* and six of the seven digraphs (*ch, i, gi, gl, gn, sc*) – or thirty-two of the thirty-five sounds of the Italian ystems – as well as *k* and *x*, two of the five "foreign" consonants borowed by Italian (XII, XXI). Syllabication or the division of Italian vords appears in both correct and incorrect forms, mostly for special ffects (V, XIV, XXI). Various diphthongs and semi-vowels appear: most ombinations of *i* and *u*, with each other or with any other vowel, in oth stressed and unstressed position (*più, malocchiu, Diàvoli, invìdia, ïióre, ringràzio, Bicchièri, òstie, Dài, nói, sèi, Guído, Aquilònia, quànto, cqua, uòvo, quèstua, Cinquecènto, Augùri*). The accent or stress posiion in words reflects its distribution in Italian: in approximate figures, ʼ7 per cent paroxytone (*amóre, appetíto, signóra, maèstra*), 6 per cent roparoxytone (*nùmero, matemàtica*), and 4 percent oxytone (*podestà, ʒesù*); also, the monosyllables, both tonic and atonic, make up about 3 per cent and represent every part of speech, including adverbial and ronominal atonic monosyllables in proclitic and enclitic position (*se ne a, sbrigati, Eccola*).

The graphic or written accents – both acute (´) and grave (`) accent narks – are widely used in the novel's Italian for various purposes: to listinguish homonyms and homophones (*è*, verb, "is," and *e*, conjuncion, "and"; *là*, adverb, "there," and *la*, definite article, "the"); to indicate pen *è*/*ò* or closed *é ó* sounds, and to show the fall of a vowel or a syllaile in dialect terms and proper names: *signó*', truncated dialect form of oth *signóra* (madam, lady) and *signóre* (sir, mister), and for both singular nd plural (VII, XXVI); *castà* for *castagne* (chestnuts), *saporí* for *saporite* tasty); *Andò* for Antonio, *Vittò* for Vittorio, *Silvó* for Silvio, *Marí* for Vlaria, *Cristí* for Cristina. At times the accent sign has a double purpose s in *Andò* and *Silvó* – to indicate truncation and the open or closed *o*.

Elision and apostrophe are also frequently used: to indicate the fall of vowel in articles, prepositions, adjectives, pronouns, and even nouns, articularly in dialect words appearing in proverbs or songs, or for synactic coupling and special effects: *l'orgoglio, l'amore, un'ora, Trent'anni,)'Amico, Do'* for *dove* (where); *i'* for *io* (I) in *i' ti coprivo* (I covered ou); *forestier'* for *forestiero* (foreigner); *signor' e signori* for *signore signori* (ladies and gentlemen); *ragazz'* instead of *ragazzo* in *Come ti hiami ragazz'?* (What's your name, boy?). Truncated or elided Italian vords without the elision mark are also frequent in accordance with he Italian pattern of dropping the final *e*/*o* preceded by a liquid (*l, r*) or asal (*m*/*n*) consonant: *quel, dottor, signor, far, provar; buon, san* and even *Don* (from *donno,* old form for "sir"). Other aspects of phonology are: all consonants, except *v,* appear in their double form (*Repubblica Bicchieri, gassosa, Piazza*); capital letter for every letter of the alphabet at times used for special effects (MARIA, SATURNIA); the abbreviation *Imp.* for *Imperatore* (emperor).

The morphological categories presented by the Italian words in *Live of the Saints* include all nine parts of speech or word classes: the five variable parts – article, noun, adjective, pronoun, verb; and the four invariable parts – adverb, preposition, conjunction, interjection. The variations reflect the Italian gender and number patterns as well as other classifications. Thus, the article appears in both forms – definite and indefinite (*il, lo, la, le, un*), and combined with some prepositions (*al, alla all', del, della*). The noun is present in a high degree of variations such as the three classes according to the singular endings of both genders, as well as some of the respective plural endings: –a >-i/-e; o/e > i (*Papa, lira* > lire, *giorno, anni, Cinquecento, signore* > *signori, luce, stupidaggini*) the six divisions of nouns according to the meaning: concrete/abstract common/proper; collective/individual (*acqua/amore; tarantella/Cristina gruppo/capo*); the four divisions according to form: primitive/derived altered/compound (*cagna/baldacchino; poveretto/malocchiu*). Creativity is particularly displayed by the new compound names formed by joining various parts of speech: two nouns (Dompietro < Don + Pietro); noun and adjective, modelled on the names of towns in Molise – Belmonte Campobasso, Capracotta (Fairmountain, Fieldlow or Lowfield Goatcooked or Cookedgoat) – *Facciabrutta* (Uglyface), *Gambelunghe* (Longlegs); two nouns joined by a preposition – *Cazzingulo* (Dick-in ass); a verb and a noun – *Girasole* (Turnsun, Sunflower), *Rompacazze* (Breakdick), *Tornamonde*; a verb and a noun joined by hyphens and an article – *Zappa-la-vigna*; a noun or a verb and an adverb – *Cosaben* (Thingwell or Tinkerswell). Versatility is displayed also in the transformation of a feminine common noun into a masculine proper name – "*signor Gallino*" (XIV), Mr He-hen, from *gallina* (hen).

The over fifty adjectives vary not only in gender and number, in agreement with the noun they refer to, as exemplified by some forms of both classes of adjectives – *Santo, Santi, Santa; militare* (masculine), *verd* (feminine), *Alimentari* (masculine plural) – but also in species and structure. The species consists of two classifications – qualifiers and indicative or limiting – with the former constituting the majority: *bello/a, bravo Brava, buono/Buona, stupido/Stupida, gentile, Matematici.* The indicative adjectives, though limited in number, represent various subdivisions possessive – *mio, tuo, tua;* demonstrative – *quel, quella, quest';* indefinit

– *Tutt'*; interrogative/exclamatory – *quante, che*; numerical, both cardinal and ordinal – *tre, tredici, Trent', terza*, including a Roman numeral *III*, "the third" (VII). The qualifiers represent also variations in morphological structure: primitive (*alta, nuda, giusta*); derived from other words through prefixes and suffixes (*Disgraziata < grazia, Bolognese < Bologna, Italiano < Italia, Folkloristico < folklóre*); compound (*Cinquecento*) or altered into the diminutive forms (*bambino < bambo, poveretto < povero*). The adjective *superiore* represents an irregular comparative degree. The adjectives also have various functions in the novel: as attributive and predicative (*alta voce, un'ora sola; Sí, è vero, è buono*), as a noun (*Alimentari, Americani, Calabrese*), and as an adverb (*Tanto gentile*). The position of Italian adjectives, before and after the noun, is also illustrated in the phrase "*Na bella serpe verde*" (A beautiful green snake) (XV).

The sixteen or so pronouns represent four types or categories: the demonstrative and the indefinite have one form each (*questa, Nessuno*); the interrogative has two forms (*chi, che*); and the rest are all personal pronouns, which display various functions: subject – first- and second-person singular (familiar and polite) and first plural (*i', tu, Lei, noi*); indirect object – first- and second-person singular (*me, ti*); direct object – second-person singular, familiar and polite (*ti, La*); and third-person singular, masculine and feminine (*lo, la*); reflexive – second-person singular and plural (*ti, vi*); and prepositional – first-person singular (*me*). Identifiable are also other characteristics of the personal pronouns: both the stressed and unstressed forms (*me* in *Venite con me*; *ti* in *Come ti chiami?*); both positions are present – preceding the verb and attached to the end of the verb (*L'* in *L'ammazzo*; *ti* in *alzati*) or to the end of certain exclamations (*la* in *Eccola*). Also, the combination of the unstressed indirect and direct object pronouns, with the appropriate change in the former, can be seen in a familiar imperative form – *mi > me* in *famme lu* [*sic*] *provar* (XII); and a similar pattern (*si > se* before *ne*) is found in an inflected form of the verb *andarsene*, used in a proverb – *se ne va* (I). Also noteworthy is the polite form of *you*, second-person singular, expressed in two ways: with the third-person feminine pronoun, subject and object, with a capital – *Lei, La*, and with the second-person plural, reflexive *vi* in *Calmatevi* (see syntax, below). The ample variety of the personal pronouns is also a reflection of the complexity of Italian in the novel.

The over twenty-five verb forms represent various categories: all three conjugations, both regular and irregular, with over half belonging to the first conjugation; all seven moods – indicative (most frequent); imperative (various examples); subjunctive and conditional (one example each); infinitive and gerund (only first conjugation); and past participle (two second-conjugation verbs). Only the indicative has three (of its eight) tenses – present (first-, second-, third-person singular; third-person plural) present perfect (*passato prossimo*, second- and third-person singular, and only with one of the two auxiliary verbs, *essere*, "to be"); and the imperfect (first-person singular). More particularly, the second-person plural appears only in the imperative mood, in familiar and polite address – *scusate, Ammazzatelo!* (excuse me, Kill him! [*you* plural]; II, XV); *Scusate, Cristina*; *Scusate, signora*; *Venite con me* (Excuse me, Cristina; Excuse me, madam; Come with me [*you* singular, polite], II, III, XXVI).

Other verbal characteristics presented include the type – both transitive (*coprire*, in *ti coprivo*, I covered you, XII); and intransitive (*andare* in *Come va?* How goes it?, IV); the form – active only, *La ringrazio* (I thank you, XXVII); the reflexive – both real and apparent – *sbrigarsi*, in *sbrigati* (hurry up, XXX); *alzarsi*, in *alzati* (stand up, V). Also present are the three functions of the verb: as predicate – *chiamarsi*, in *Come ti chiami?* (What's your name? XXXI); as copula – *essere*, in *Sei scimunita* (You're an idiot, XX), and as auxiliary with a modal verb, *volere* in *Vorrei far ritornare* (I would like to bring back, XII). Worthy of note are the three different functions of *essere* (to be): as auxiliary, *È morta* (She has died, XXXI); as copula, *chi e questa?* (who is this? XXVII); and as predicate or autonomous verb with the meaning of "exist" – *quante persone ci sono in Dio?* (how many persons are there in God? [V]). But totally absent is the verb *avere* (to have).

The four invariable parts of speech, so called because they do not change in gender and number as do the previous five parts, which vary in other ways – type, structure, form. The fewer than twenty adverbs and adverbial phrases reflect the two Italian classifications: qualifiers (*bene*, well; *alla bolognese*, as made in Bologna) and definite, which can be grouped into various types: to indicate quantity (*molto, Tanto*, a lot); place (*ci*, there; *Di là*, that way) and affirmation (*sí, certo*, yes, certainly); to introduce a direct question (*come...?*, how?) or an indirect relative clause (*Do'/Dove*, Where?). Also present are three other forms of the adverb: simple (*bene*), compound (*dappertutto*, everywhere) and derived (*finalmente*, finally), as well as the comparative and superlative degrees – *più vicino* (closer), *molto bene* (very well).

The prepositions, both simple and in combination with the definite articles, include *a, al, all', alla* (to, to the); *di, de, de', D', del, della* (of the); *in* (in); *con* (with); *per* (for). The preposition *da* appears only in the compound adverb of place *dappertutto* (< *da per tutto*), but not with the usual meaning of "from."

The coordinating copulative conjunction *e* (and) and the coordinating adversative conjunction *ma* (but) appear quite frequently in their usual functions, as well as in particular syntactical functions (see syntax below). The only subordinating conjunction appears twice in the same stanza of a song – *Quando che* (When [XII, XXXIII]).

The interjection – an interpolated sound, word or phrase – is, for some, a mere exclamation, an utterance of an immediate sensation or mood, and thus, according to some grammarians, not a real grammatical category, part of speech, or an essential part of the sentence or its sense.[64] And yet, the interjection constitutes a recurring linguistic and stylistic aspect of *Lives of the Saints*, in both English and Italian. In fact, the vocalic exclamations – *Ah, Eh, Oh* – appearing about forty times, are similar in structure and meaning in both languages. The numerous Italian interjections (both in standard and colloquial Italian) appear in all three forms: monosyllables (*Beh, Dai*), words (*addio, Salve*), and phrases (*che cretino! Viva il Duce!*). Various parts of speech function as interjections: nouns (*Auguri! Saluti*), adjectives (*bravo! bello!*), verbal forms (*basta! L'ammazzo!*), adverbs (*Bene, finalmente!*); including obscene, profane, and blasphemous words and imprecations (*stronzo, madonna! Gesù bambino! Crist' e Maria, per l'amore di Dio, porca madonna!*). The oaths or curses alone, numbering over twenty-five, are ample evidence of the key role of the everyday spoken language reflected in *Lives of the Saints*.

Italian syntax is well illustrated in the pieces of Italian text scattered throughout the novel: over thirty simple sentences, about eight compound and complex sentences (including a compound-complex one), and various elliptical sentences. The simple sentences are of four types listed in order of frequency): imperative (command) – *Antonio ... alzati* Anthony ... stand up [V]); interrogative (question) – *È vero?* (Is it true? VII[); declarative (statement) – *Sí, è vero* (Yes, it's true [XXVII]); exclamatory (exclamation) – *È morta!* (She has died! [III[). The compound and complex sentences consist of both structures: coordination (parataxis) – *Apri! Senti!* (Open up! Listen! [XXVII]), particularly the three independent sentences in the second stanza of the popular song *vola vola* (XII); and subordination (hypotaxis) – the relative clause indicating place, *Do' l'orgolgio sta* (where pride is [I]); and the clause indicating time in the first stanza of the same song (XII, XXIII).

The syntactic categories, besides subject and predicate, include the attributive – *il tempo bello* (the beautiful times [XII, XXXIII]); the appositive – *Giuseppe lu forestier* (Joseph the foreigner [II]); object – direct and indirect – *ti coprivo* (I covered you [XII, XXXIII]); *E buon viaggio alla signora!* (And [I wish] a pleasant journey to the lady! [XXIX]); as well as objects of prepositions indicating possession, place, manner, material company, and purpose. The categories usually omitted in the elliptical sentences are the subject and the predicate: *Dio mio, che figura!* (My God what a figure [we have cut]! [XIII]); *Ma come?* (But how [could it be possible / could I be wrong]? [XXVII]). The ellipsis occurs in phrases introduced by the adversative conjunction *Ma*, But (II, XIX, XXIX). This particular use of *Ma*, appearing also at the beginning of twelve simple sentences, serves to express opposition, contrast, disagreement, as well as impatience and good-natured irony and mockery, especially when *Ma* is followed by *che*: *Ma che sei, scimunoit* [*sic*]? (What are you, crazy? [XXII]).

The novel includes other Italian syntactic and stylistic peculiarities: syntactic coupling through elision – *signor' e signori* (XII) for *signore e signori* (ladies and gentlemen); it appears particularly in vernacular speech – *Cald' e saporí* (XXVI) for *Calde e saporite* (Hot and tasty). Syntactic gemination (or doubling of a consonant to fuse words together), quite common in the spoken language, is evidenced in the doubling of the *p* in *dappertutto* (XXVII) < *da per tutto* (everywhere). The copulative conjunction *e* (and) is used to link an antiphrastic or ironic wish to the preceding curse uttered in English – "Go to the devil then. *E buon viaggio alla signora!*" (And a pleasant journey to the lady [XXIX]). The omission of the singular, feminine article *la* (the) with a possessive adjective modifying the endearing form of a noun indicating a family member may be grammatically incorrect – *È scimunita tua mamma* (Your mother is an idiot [XXVI]); *È morta tua mamma* (Your mother has died [XXXI]), instead of *la tua mamma*. But the omission (which some may justify by the reversal of the regular subject-predicate syntactic order) may also be a useful stylistic device: it is another example of colloquial Italian, the living language of the common people of the novel, an imitation of a popular form of speech, or even an example of the quite common interference of English on the Italian spoken in Canada. *Lives of the Saints*, after all, is a Canadian novel.

Various aspects, then, of Italian phonology, morphology, and syntax constitute variants that reflect or imitate the world of the novel and the Italian-Canadian reality. The interference of English can be seen in other examples: in the spelling of some words – *communista*, with two *m*s (XX); *Alfreddo*, with two *d*s (but revised to *Alfredo* in a subsequent edition); in syllabication – *Pover-etta* (XXVII) for *Poveret-ta*, *Gi-useppe* (II) for *Giu-seppe*; in the capitalization of book titles – *Principi Matematici* (I) for *Principi matematici* (Mathematical principles or beginnings); in the use of terms, such as the masculine plural form *Saluti* (Greetings)

XXIX), instead of the feminine singular *Salute* (to your health), said while making a toast. The tendency to mix English and Italian in every-day speech is exemplified in the polite question "May I carry *la signora*'s luggage?" where the typical English genitive-possessive construction – final *'s* – is attached to an Italian noun (XXVI). The phonological, mor-hological, and syntactical variations are simultaneously a reflection of the author's creative freedom and of the living language of everyday communication of ordinary people, particularly evident in the southern Italian words, names, phrases, proverbs, and the two stanzas of a song.

But the significance of the presence of Italian in the novel is manifested only partly by a cold compilation of inert grammatical structures. The scattered words and phrases, when brought together, can also constitute a sort of small Italian primer, an elementary practical manual with real-istic live conversations ranging from the familiar to the formal level. Its beginning can be the usual introductory simple dialogue: *Buon giorno / Salve / ciao, come va?* (Good day / Hello / Hi, how are you?); *Bene, grazie, e tu / Lei* (Fine, thank you, and you) – familiar and formal; *Molto bene / Tanto gentile* (Very well / You're very kind); *Scusa, come ti chiami? Scusi, chi è Lei?* (Excuse me, what's your name? Excuse me, who are you?) – both familiar and formal; Beatrice / Dante ... *Piacere ... Piacere* (Pleased to meet you); *Buonasera signore e signori* (Good evening, ladies and gentlemen); *Buonanotte dottore* (Good night doctor).

One of the dialogues may be constructed to stress simple, useful commands (singular and plural imperative forms with and without pronouns); they can range from the quite common *Dai* (come on), to the friendly threat, *Ammazzatelo!* (Kill him!) and to the historical – as well as nostalgic or ironical – *Viva il Duce!* (Long live the Duce! i.e., Mussolini). The exhortations may include: *Avanti* (Come in); *sbrigati* (hurry up); *alzati* (get up or stand up); *Apri* (Open); *Senti* (Listen); *Basta* (Enough); *calmatevi* (calm down); *venite con me* (come with me); *più vicino* (closer); *Eccola* (There it is, or There she is).

Other dialogues may contain the various nouns, pronouns, adjectives, adverbs, or interjections expressing different feelings or moods. Consent, agreement, or approval are expressed by *Sì, sì* (Yes); *giusto* (correct); *Ah, bello!* (Ah, beautiful!); *Brava* (Well done); *perfetto* (perfect); *Ma certo* (Of course); *Sì, è vero* (Yes, it's true). Negation, uncertainty, or doubt is rendered by *Nessuno* (Nobody); *Ma come* (But how); *Ma chi sei tu?* (But who are you?); *Ma chi è questa?* (But who is this woman?), as well as the widely used colloquial monosyllabic exclamation, *Beh* (So). Compassion or pity is manifested by *Poveretto, Poveretta* (Poor man, Poor woman). And dislike, hostility, or insult is conveyed by various terms, some in both masculine and feminine forms: *stupido/a* (stupid); *scimunito/a* (idiot); *cretino* (cretin); *Disgraziata* (wretched); *strega* (witch); *cagna* (bitch); *porca* (pig, sow).

Life and culture components may be derived from a variety of term and expressions: *Repubblica Italiana* (the Italian Republic); *lire* (lira, th pre-euro Italian currency [VII]); "Cinquecento" (II) and "Seicentos" (X the 1950s/60s models of Italian Fiat cars, and *communista* [*sic*] (commun nist [XX]), provide topics for historical, political, economic, and ideolog ical discussion and debates. Expressions such as *ad alta voce* (out lou [V]) may recall singing or communal prayer, while *tutta nuda* (V), "utterl naked" woman (IV), may suggest on the one hand indecency, pornogra phy, sin (V), and on the other spontaneity, maturity, beauty (IV). Som words may help illustrate origin or nationality: *Americani* (Americans which also refers to Italian immigrants who have returned to their villag [IX]); *Molisana* (a woman from Molise [XXVI]); "Calabrese" (a man o woman from Calabria, two regions of Central-South Italy [XXIX]). Som words convey ampler characteristics: *giovanotto* (young man [XXXI] but also a young sailor responsible for minor duties on a ship; aptly use during a sea voyage); *Diavoli* (Devils, or mischievous children [VIII]). On particular phrase – *Quest' 'Alifax* (This Halifax [XXI]) – while specifyin the Canadian port of entry of many immigrants, may also help generat discussion on the use of the apostrophe, the elision of the vowel *o* or *a* (i *questo* or *questa*) because of the fall of the initial *H* which in Italian is mute letter, even though it has a role, which can be explored. The manua may even include a component for more advanced learners: the uses o some particular parts of speech, such as the definite article, the conjunc tions *e*, *ma* (and, but), and especially the particular Italian use of the polit address expressed by the pronoun *Lei*. They all will surely produce livel discussions on both language and culture.

A conversation may even be made to sound more spontaneous o approximate that of native speakers by including some of the dialecta terms and phrases: "*Oh, castà! Cald' e saporì! Venite signó' e signó'!*" O *castagne! Calde e saporite! Venite signore e signori!* (Here, chestnuts! Ho and tasty! Come ladies and gentlemen! [XXVI]). One small section ma even serve as an introduction to southern Italian dialectology: frequent i the typical shortening (apocopation) of forms and especially of first name which usually indicate familiarity and friendship as well as annoyanc and sarcasm: *Vittò* (Vittorio); *Cristí* (Cristina); *Giuseppì* (Giuseppina *Luí* (Luigi); and *Andò* (Antonio), which reflects another typical phonc logical trait (*t > d*), also noticed in the speech of the Leamington Italian especially in the name *Donino*, Tonino or Antonio DiMenna (chapter 2)

Additional exercises in both the spoken and written Italian (and dialect) can be provided by the two stanzas of the love song: for the oral-auditory practice, quite suitable is the stanza with the succession or repetition of the verb form *vola* ... *E vola lu pavone* (And so flies the peacock); and for a better understanding, the song can even be translated into English (not done by the author), especially the first stanza that appears twice (XII, XXXIII); in fact, by its very repetition, the stanza serves as a key to the story: it becomes a link to one's heritage, it is a sign of the effort itself to recover an aspect of one's culture and identity at a critical moment of one's migration:

I wish I could bring back for just one hour
The beautiful times of happiness
When we used to play at *vola vola* [fly, fly away]
And I covered you with kisses and caresses.

And in order to complete the translation "lesson," one can include Ricci's Italian translation of a verse of an English-language poem: *Acqua, acqua dappertutto* (Water, water, everywhere [XXVII]).[65]

Ricci's first novel presents two fundamental ways to learn Italian: the formal, grammatical method and the situational, conversational, or communicative approach. One integrates the other. The Italian presented in the novel is, of course, in written form: as such, phonology, the study of sounds, is less evident than the other two grammatical categories – morphology and syntax. And yet, the emphasis seems to lie on the sounds, in fact the sound of the language – the living, spoken word. The frequent use of interjections, exclamations, echoic or onomatopoeic sounds, in both in Italian and English – Poof! Pom! plop! (XII, XXII, XXIX) – is quite indicative of the role of spontaneous speech. The interjection, which is not even ranked by grammarians among the "real" parts of speech, is nevertheless defined as a most expressive form of speech; instinctive, immediate! A simple sound or cry – Ah, Oh, Eh – can evoke a gamut of emotions: pain, delight, regret, disgust, surprise, doubt, fear, enquiry, wonder, or others, according to the manner of expression.

The widespread stylistic evidence for the emphasis on the spoken language – Italian – parallels the young narrator's keen awareness of the Italian spoken by the various speakers. Vittorio describes the Standard Italian he hears with such terms as "burnished," "rounded and precise," "polished ... stripped clean of dialect," "florid," even "meticulous"; while he characterizes the various dialects as "flattened," having a "recogniz-able twang" or spoken in an incomprehensible "thick, rounded" accent

(III, V, X, XII, XX, XXVI). Through Vittorio, Ricci makes the reader aware of the spoken Italian.

Ricci's legacy is clear: Language is identity. The regional language, or dialect, is itself a direct link to the basic wisdom of one's origins (proverbs, songs, customs). But speaking good Italian is a sign of distinction and advancement: it smooths the peasant and regional aspects of one's origins (XXVI, XXIX); it easily sets apart the non-native speakers who often use "only broken Italian" (XXVII), which can be a source of ridicule. The ability to speak correct Italian (for which the novel provides formal and informal learning guidelines) not only helps establish a link to present-day Italy, but can also be a vehicle to rediscover the past achievements of Italian civilization, without intermediary translations. The Italian language, therefore, becomes the surest base of Italian identity, or more precisely of self-identity in a multicultural Canada.

Language is identity and strength: if the language or languages of one's roots need to be rediscovered and kept, the language or languages of the new country need to be learned early, as suggested also through Cristina, who is already learning English on the ship (XXVIII). The two linguistic, and thus cultural, traditions in the novel are distinct and yet integrated into an inseparable unity. Tradition and experience, life and history are indeed magically interwoven in the novel to create what has been called "a rich and wonderful tapestry [where] the gods make appearances on every page."[66] More concretely, the novel suggests a model for an ideal multicultural identity – basically Italian but at the same time very much Canadian!

LIVES OF THE SAINTS:
A LEGACY AND A GOAL FOR ALL CANADIANS

Lives of the Saints can be considered one of the most significant outcomes of the creative encounter of Old Country traditions and New World experiences. The "reality" of the three generations of Leamington Italians, and thus Ricci's own Italian-Canadian heritage, has thoroughly "filtered" into his "fictional" world; his literary creation is clearly an artistic "concentrate" of his and their world. If Eco's novel, *The Name of the Rose*, has been hailed as a work of fiction that has brought the world of the Middle Ages "successfully to life,"[67] then Nino Ricci's widely acclaimed first Canadian novel is the work of fiction that has brought "successfully to life" the world of migration, of an Italian Canadian community; a world that has been changed, above all, through and into a type of "art" that, according to Eco, "is an escape from personal emotion."[68]

Ricci's work, in fact, has reached far beyond what Sister Anne Leonard said about other Canadian novels related to the immigrant experience: "These novels reflect the need for the story to be told not only about the immigrants and the pioneers but about their children – those sons and daughters of smaller heroes – who have to find their identity, their purpose, their community."[69] The meaning and function of Ricci's story are expanded, amplified by the very qualities that characterize both his storytelling mode and the content or the "world" of his novel: the "wit ... compassion ... maturity ... power ... beauty"; that is, mainly Ricci's stylistic-imaginative force for which his work has won wide success and prestige.[70] This very fact alone is an immediate source of deep pride for all Italian Canadians, both in Leamington and throughout Canada.

In the long run, the novel cannot but help enhance the image other Canadians have of Italian Canadians and, most importantly, their own self-image. And such effects are profound and enduring – at least more so than those produced by, or derived from, any other Italian-Canadian enterprise or invention. This is due mainly to the fact that their particular ethnocultural past and the historical migration experience itself have been presented in a widely recognized product of language and culture – the basic moulders of individual and group identity. The novel, therefore, represents the highest point, the most advanced signpost in the immigrant community's journey toward a higher level of Italian-Canadian awareness. It provides a "cultural model" through which one can "recreate one's own identity"; or it can serve as a stage in the "formation of a new type of human being."[71]

The long-term, multiple significance of the novel, for both the community of origin and Canadian society at large, consists also in the fact that a particular Canadian ethnocultural reality, rediscovered and artistically recast, has been made universally appealing, a more "palatable product," a common Canadian property. Imported customs and old memories have been transferred through a refined text (i.e., aesthetic form) from the ethnic enclave into the public domain. Ethnicity itself has become art: ethnicity from a possible "straitjacket" has turned into a creative force. In effect, a concept of Canadian multiculturalism – the retention and sharing of cultural values – has been transformed into literature, by a delicate process that can be defined as "the sublimation of reality through linguistic images," or a process that seeks to balance, as Eco suggests, "art [i.e., beauty] and enjoyability."[72]

They are sufficient reasons for Ricci's work to also become a sort of guide for Canada's many "solitudes" or ethnicities in their search for that elusive link between ethnocultural loyalty-pride and full Canadian identity; for that difficult but attainable and aspired to intercultural and multicultural communication and understanding. The story – that is the young narrator's search for meaning and truth – can at least suggest a way toward a possible dénouement for the immigrant's lifelong drama (see chapter 12); or a possible solution to the conflict or duality present in any immigrant or migrant, and for that matter in all living beings, since life is change, and "the past," writes Eco, "cannot really be destroyed, because its destruction leads to silence." The immigrant state is a dreamy half-conscious state like that of the child-migrant Vittorio. But Vittorio seeks, at inevitably great pain, a more complete conscious state or maturity by reflecting on his experience, on his past, as all must do, for "not to know what took place before you were born," wrote Cicero, "is to be always a child."[73]

The past, then, "must be revisited," as both Vittorio and Ricci do, "but with irony, not innocently," as Eco suggests. The past must be rediscovered in a non-innocent way, or in a conscious manner, through memory, history, literature, or art in general. The past needs to be continually remoulded by each individual in order to give more meaning, more value to one's present life. One mode of rediscovery is the historical novel where, according to Eco at least, "the appearance of recognizable [i.e., historical] characters is not necessary." In fact, "What the [fictional] characters do serves to make history, what happened, more comprehensible. Events and characters are made up, yet they tell us things ... that history books have never told us so clearly."[74] It was "writing the *Lives of the Saints*," Ricci said, that "put him in touch with his cultural roots in a way that his upbringing never did."[75]

AN ITALIAN-CANADIAN HISTORICAL NOVEL?

In a sense Ricci's *Lives of the Saints* can also be considered an Italian-Canadian historical novel, and it is uniquely so because it is *not* strictly about, nor exclusively intended for, Italian Canadians, even though much of its world (characters, places, events) derives from his community. It is mainly Ricci's creations or recreations, or what has been called the novel's "quite cumulative power" that rivets the readers to the dramatic unfolding of "the history of a family" and generally of life in a southern Italian mountain area in the early 1960s. It is his own invention that makes the readers simultaneously enjoy and possibly become more aware of the unending human pursuit of a better life: the recurring struggle and rebellion against seemingly unchanging conditions and often inexplicable forces in the villages of origin; the need or desire to migrate and its unfortunate, if not tragic results; the difficult interaction among the generations, and the changes that inevitably take place in the passage from one to the other in the new land. Under the intriguingly pleasurable story the readers will eventually also discover Ricci's cultural roots, and consequently learn more about Italy and Canada, as well as the Sun Parlour, that is, Essex County and its towns, Leamington, and its Italian community and the author himself. The Leamington-born novelist gives new life and meaning to the Leamington Italian community and, through it, truth to his invented world: he makes them both equally represent a microcosm of humanity.[76]

Ricci himself, as a successful Canadian storyteller and interpreter of ethnic ways to a wider public, may very well be regarded as an embodiment of that hope with which the Leamington Italian immigrants looked ahead to the next generation for their self-fulfillment. Of course, a particular achievement, however singular, can hardly constitute the realization of the hopes and dreams of an entire community. Nevertheless, Ricci's undertaking itself is an extension of that dream, of that "immigrant experience" which he defined "such a vital part of Canada's culture and heritage."[77] His own endeavour is intended partly as a continuation of his community's search; to serve as a stepping stone toward, in Ricci's own concluding words in *Radici*, "that Eden which, years ago ... they thought of as only a dream." Ricci, above all, emerges as a master of that overwhelming obstacle to further advancement of all immigrants – language – the language of the new land; and its mastery (quite evident in the novel) does not at all diminish the knowledge of the language of the land of origin; on the contrary, it increases the desire to learn more about its literature and culture. In a way imitating Alessandro Manzoni, Nino Ricci himself, before writing *Lives of the Saints*, "completed a year of study in Italian literature at the University of Florence" (Italy).

CONCLUSION: A UNIQUE ITALIAN AGRICULTURAL COMMUNITY IN CANADA

"All migration," Brinley Thomas said, "is a flow of labour to capital." But for Harney, "That harsh and categorical economic determinism becomes more comprehensible if we say that all Italian immigration has been a flow of talent to opportunity – and that the need for work has made immigrants adopt [*sic*] the culture of their homeland to the opportunity for work."[78] For most Leamington-area Italian immigrants, economic need was initially a strong motivation, and subsequently an important factor was also the presence of relatives in the area. But the well-known psychological motives cannot be discounted or underestimated: the natural tendency to chase a dream; the contagion of the migration disease throughout southern Italy (as indicated by the Leamington pioneers as well as by studies); the vision of the wonders of America spread by the tales by boastful relatives and friends (a distorted image that Arturo Scotti tried in vain to correct in his 17 December 1957 Italian editorial about Canada),[79] an image that even in the 1960s continued to lure Italians away from their jobs, often only to find unemployment and a "woeful reality." In fact, at times, not even talent, industrial skills, opened the door of opportunity; at least that was the case in some parts of Canada more than in others (see chapter 12, "The View of Canada").

In the Leamington area, the farms and greenhouses made a difference for the Italian immigrants. Even so, their collective story – from the pioneers' vivid memories of their striving and hopes, to the younger generations' critical evaluation of their forerunners' legacy to the adopted land, as well as of their own aspirations – covers the gamut of the Italian immigrant experience in the twentieth century.

The journey of the Leamington-area Italian community has been long and tortuous. Nevertheless, in spite of the many physical, social, and psychological obstacles (climate, attitudes, language, fears), it has travelled far: from a handful of men (eight Molisani, two *Laziali*, one Sicilian) who less than a lifetime ago ventured into the unknown in search of fortune (*all'avventura*) and who landed in the Windsor-Leamington area mostly by chance, it has grown to an over 500-family strong community, commercially well-established, socially fairly integrated, and recognizably "Italian" or Italian Canadian. Even in the presence of a variety of frequently opposite views, generation clashes, the typical envy, and the increasing occupational differentiation, the community has remained a distinguishable entity, sharing some traditional and some developed common traits, in certain ways "unique."

The uniqueness of "Leamington's Italian community," for Ricci himself,[80] seemed to rest on his definition of them as "in a way [representing] a lost generation, a time capsule"; or at least his view of them seemed based more on what they *were not* than on what they *were* or had become: "Thus," he states, "the [Leamington] Italian immigrants have not evolved along the same lines as Italy's Italians. In one way, therefore, they miss their claim to be Italians ... But neither have they become assimilated into Canadian history ... They have not been subsumed by the collective mentality of their Canadian environment. In this respect, then, they miss their claim to be Canadians (if any such species exists)." They "are," said Ricci, "the image of an Italy now forgotten ... To a certain extent, they have kept the values, the ideas, and the mentality, [as well as the same dialect] which they had when they left Italy and entered Canada" (i.e., mostly 1950s, 1960s). Ricci's conclusion is that "to call these immigrants Italian-Canadians is merely to make a statement of what they are not. They are unique. They are the immigrants, whose history is shared only by the members of Leamington's Italian community."[81]

Nevertheless, these "Italian immigrants," as Ricci called them, have long been Canadian citizens; and at least on those grounds they can claim to be Canadians. Also on the basis of their Italian mentality, albeit more traditional and rural than modern and urban, they can still claim to be Italians: in this sense they are indeed "Italian Canadians." One thing is certain, however: they are definitely different from both the Italians in Italy and the other Canadians in Canada, including in many respects the "Italians" in other parts of Canada. Among the reasons for this difference or uniqueness is indeed – as Ricci noted) – their "common bond in having been a part of the Italian immigrant experience in the Leamington area [or their shared] history";[82] but clearly theirs is a history that has been shaped as much by their point of origin – mostly rural Central-Southern Italy – as by their final destination or their particular development over three generations in rural Southwestern Ontario.

More specifically, their uniqueness rests on or results from five facts or events: (1) their common southern Italian origin and similar heritage or customs; (2) the mostly sponsored chain migration of relatives and friends from limited areas or districts of mainly three Italian regions: (Abruzzo-) Molise (mostly Villa Canale–Agnone); Lazio (mostly *Ciociaria* or Frosinone province); and Sicily (mostly San Vito Lo Capo); (3) the "common bond" or linguistic-cultural affinity, particularly of the first two groups which together form over 82 per cent of the community; (4) the extended interfamily ties along with their uninterrupted policy and practice of reciprocal assistance; and above all, (5) the shaping and unfolding of a lifestyle and way of life within a determinate, palpable, rural framework and within or around relatively solid institutions – family, farm or family business, and community centre – as well as their long allegiance to one political party (Liberal) or local political figures. Moreover, the absence of a strictly Italian church or parish, in itself unique, may have further strengthened the "religion" of the family, the community bonds, and even the striving for commercial success.

They all contributed, each feature in its own way, to the evolution of a fairly compact, if not uniform, community. But the pivotal factor in this unique growth was the purchase of the parcels of land in the 1930s and 1940s by almost all the pioneer families. Farm ownership provided security for them and for the postwar immigrants they sponsored. Life and work began to rotate around the farming and greenhouse industries very early in the development of the community – today, and through the years, the only Italian-Canadian agricultural community in Canada.

Particularly because of its distinctive physical and cultural characteristics (size, composition, rural nature), the Leamington-area Italian community offers a clear overall view of the modern migration phenomenon. It is a mirror of the fortunes of Italy and Canada in the past century; it reflects the changing policies and attitudes toward emigration-immigration, and toward Italian immigrant communities in particular; it constitutes a *tessera* (a small stone) in the ever-changing Canadian ethnocultural or multicultural mosaic; it is a visible, concrete example of the possible outcomes of the clash and/or encounter of two or more traditions and lifestyles, of the forces of continuity and change at work within a migrant group, or of the increasing interaction of ethnicities with and within a dominant culture. The Leamington Italian community may indeed be one of the clearest examples of those "cultural models" that scholars have been exploring in order to more fully explain the complex phenomenon of migration – both the transformations that take place in the migrants themselves and the social (and political) effects on homeland and adopted country.

Finally, their collective journey, not unlike the entire human passage, especially in the later stages, has been more than a search for a material paradise (which was partly reached anyway). It has gradually become also a cultural and spiritual quest – as evidenced by clashes within the family and club (e.g., financial vs socio-cultural objectives) or by their sense of uneasiness about their "foolishness" (their internal conflicts). Or at least it was a journey of rediscovery, of renewed interest in what they had lost or were losing: their language and selected Old World values, particularly with respect to the family. However unconscious at first, their aim, at times, was to regain their lost self-identity, or at least rebuild it somehow, by becoming more aware of both Italy and Canada. The journey has also become a transition, equally painful at times, toward a new self-awareness.

Collectively, they give concrete form to the more philosophical or poetic sense of migration. Their odyssey to a hoped-for better destination brings to mind the "witless flight" of Dante's Ulysses, who was also spurred by "the restless itch to rove / And rummage through the world" even at the risk of breaking all affective bonds and of losing his own life. Their own, often perilous, journey was a sort of death, but at the same time a new beginning:[83] it allowed them to reach first a level of contentment and self-satisfaction; then achieve, at times, a better understanding of both themselves as products, if not yet sums, of two cultures, as well as of "the failings and felicities of mankind"; and eventually provide their descendants a solid economic base, if not the courage, necessary to continue the journey toward still higher goals; or, again in the words of Dante Alighieri, the father of the Italian language, to "press on toward [hu]manhood and recognition" or to "follow after knowledge and excellence."[84]

A cycle, if not the circle, reaches near completion through Nino Ricci and *Lives of the Saints*: while Cristina and Vittorio may represent the "witless flight," the earlier stages of the journey or transition – the more trying and tragic moments – their creator represents the latter part, the achievement of a high degree of maturity and excellence; and the novel itself, as a whole, is a crucible, a collector, and a transmitter of a renewed historical reality of life as well as of literary themes. The Leamington Italian community, in its relatively brief existence and microcosmic world, is a clear reflection of the human vicissitudes that especially come to the fore or to life through migration.

A "LIVING TESTAMENT":
THE FORGING OF A NEW IDENTITY

"In attempting to research the history of the Italian community in the Leamington area," wrote Ricci in his preface of *Radici*, "the Italian Historical Committee had two purposes in mind: they wished to provide a living testament to the experiences of the Italian immigrants in their area, both for present and future generations; and they wished to produce a volume of history which would shed light on the nature of the immigrant experience in Canada." The project was clearly worthwhile: the research generated not only a historical account but also a most enjoyable literary synthesis of their experiences. And the work of art by one of their descendants, as its success also indicates, will increasingly be the truly "living testament" to the collective experience of the Leamington-area Italian immigrants and community, as well as to other Canadian communities. *Lives of the Saints*, the poetic history of their stories, embodies the legacy of all the Italian migrants, of their long efforts to forge the heritage of their two homelands into a new identity, and renews the centuries-long creative links between Italy and Canada.

APPENDICES

Leamington Italians 1920s–1980, and Date of Entry in Canada

The over 560 names listed (mostly by the student-researchers) represent approximately 550 Leamington Italian families: perhaps not the entire Italian community (due mainly to the inevitable and involuntary omissions) but certainly the majority, since among them are many of the immigrant children who now have their own families.

About 120 individuals (or family units), according to the students' observations, were not able to participate in the study-project for a variety of reasons (e.g., some were deceased or otherwise unavailable, and others simply untraceable, i.e., no longer in the Leamington area).

The total number of interviews conducted was 446 (12 of which with Canadian-born people, who were excluded from certain statistics. Therefore, the study was based mostly on 434 family units, or over 75 per cent of the names listed.[1]

KEY: b. = born; h. = husband; w. = wife; L = Leamington area;
* pre–Second World War entries

Abbruzzese, Arduino (1953)

Abbruzzese, Eugenio (1956)

Abbruzzese, John (1956)

Abbruzzese, Luigi (1957)

Accardo, Antonio (1967)

Accardo, Steve (1972)

Adragna, (Vito?) Gaspare (1966)

Agosta, Girolamo (1962)

Aiello, Giuseppe (1965)

Aiuto, Frank (1958)

Aiuto, Nino (1957)

Aiuto, Rosario (1958)

Alongi, Benedict (1965)

Alongi, Pietro (1962)

Amicone, Lino (1966)

Amicone, Lucio (1961)

Amicone, Pat (1959)

Baldassare, Italo (1949)

Barraco, Carlos (1964)

Barraco, Diego (1953)

Barraco, Jim (Girolamo) (1950)

Barraco, John (1953)

Barraco, Nino (1954)

Barraco, Pietro (1954)

Battaglia, Franco (1970)

Battaglini, Antonio (1968)

Battisti, Franco (1965)

Belli, Dario (1968)

Belli, Edoardo (1955)

  (w. Pierina Grossi) (1955)

Belli, Venanzio (1970)

Bianchi, Francesco (1967)

Bileti, Frank (1961)

Bileti, Frank (1978)

Bileti, Paul (1966)

[Bommarito, Salvatore – no longer in

  L area]

Bonfiglio, Armando (1967)

Brindisi, Valerio (1955)

[Brunato, John – b. in Canada, L

  1939]

Butiniello, Pasquale (1971)

Cacciavillani, Corrado (1949)

Cacciavillani, Floyd (1948)

Cacciavillani, Gino (1951)

Capogna, Domenic (1951)

Capogna, Sam (1953)

Cappelli, Mario (1957)

Cappussi, Antonio (1967)

Capussi, Mario (1967)

Capussi, Tony (1949)

Caradonna, Joe (1970)

Carducci, Augusto (1949)

Carlini, Domenico (1966)

Carnevale, Luigi (1949)

Carnevale, Tony (1951)

Cascio, Paolo (1970)

Castiglione, Vito (1971)

Catalano, Michele (1966)

Catrini, Sam (Salvatore)

  (via Toronto / L 1968/69) (1965)

Causarano, Francesco (1973)

Causarano, John (USA 1972/73)

  (1972)

Cervini, Adriano (1958)

Cervini, Angelo (1958)

*Cervini, Antonio (Tony) (1927)

Cervini, Antonio (1962)

Cervini, Emilio (1954)

*Cervini, John (1939)

Cervini, John (1951)

Cervini, Natalino (1951)

Cervini, Pat (1950)

Cervini, Pat (1954)

Cervini, Quirino (1964)

Cervini, Stanley (1949)

Chiuchiolo, Mariano (1971)

Ciacelli, Frank (1955)

Ciacelli, John (1955)

Cianfarani, A. (Anthony/Tony) (1956)

Cianfarani, Pietro (1956)

Ciaravino, Salvatore (1968)

Cinicolo, Frank (1967)

Cioci, Bernardino (1969)

Cioci, Giovanni (moved to Italy, Lazio, mid-1980s) (1970)

Ciotoli, Frank (1975)

Ciotoli, Giuseppe (1968)

Cipolla, Antonio (moved to Sicily 1980s) (1968)

Clerici, Adamo (1959)

Colaizzi, Bruno (1968)

*Colasanti, Alex Sr (Eleuterio) (1924)

Colasanti, Andy (1955)

Colasanti, Cesare (1966)

Colasanti, Domenico (1949)

Colasanti, Filippo (1950)

Colasanti, Giacomo (1950)

Colasanti, Joe (1948)

Colasanti, John (1950)

Colasanti, John (1951)

Colasanti, Pasquale (1960)

Colasanti, Peter (1952)

Colasanti, Tony (1957)

Colasanti, Tony (1965)

Coppola, Alfonso (1968)

Coppola, Andrea (1968)

Coppola, Andrew (1965)

Coppola, Andy (1965)

Coppola, Cristoforo (1955)

Coppola, Francesco (1962)

Coppola, G.T. (1966)

Coppola, Girolamo (1956)

Coppola, Giuseppe (1957)

Coppola, Leonardo (1967)

Coppola, Tony (1968)

Coretti, Remo (1963)

Corpolongo, Umberto (1949)

Costanza, Milvo (1954)

Cristofari, Augusto (1969)

Cristofari, Giovanni (1968)

D'Agnillo, Enrico (1972)

D'Amelio, Tony (1961)

D'Aversa, Sante (1966)

DeBenedetti, S. (Saverio) (1956)

DeBenedetti, Tony (1955)

DeCamillis, Filippo (1966)

[DeCristofaro, Gino – moved to Toronto]

DelBrocco, Alex (1966)

DelBrocco, Rosa (h. Luigi) (1966)

DelCiancio, Cesare (1958)

DelCiancio, Corradino (1954)

DelCiancio, Ernesto (1960)

DelCiancio, Ron (1961)

DelCiancio, Tony (1961)

DelGreco, Angelo (1953)

DelGreco, Gino (1952)

DelGreco, Loreto (1952)

*DeLellis, Joseph (via USA) (1931)

*DeSantis, Amato (Tony) (1924)

*DeSantis, Fred (1926)

DeSantis, Mario (1959)

*DeSantis, Rocco (Roy) (1926)

DiCarlo, Luigi (1959)

DiCiocco, Biagio (1961)

DiCiocco, Carmen (son of Enrico) (1949)

DiCiocco, Enrico (1949)

DiCiocco, Fiorina (mother of Merceda Mastronardi) (1972) [h. Raffaele D'Agnillo, in Italy, never in L]

DiLaudo, Filippo (1965)

Dilullo, T. (Tony) (1965)

Dimaio, Giuseppe (1954)

DiMenna, Alfino (1952)

DiMenna, Alfred (1955)

DiMenna, Allen (Adelchi) (1949) (w. Carmela Mastronardi) (1954)

*DiMenna, Antonio (Tony) (1923)

DiMenna, Antonio (1959)

DiMenna, Bambina (Ingratta) (1951) (h. Pacifico) (1949)

DiMenna, Costantino (1956)
DiMenna, Dante (1950)
DiMenna, Domenico (1969)
DiMenna, Ercole (1957)
DiMenna, Erenia (Massanisso)
  (1957)
  (h. Gelserino, Gerry) (1954)
DiMenna, Ermenegildo (1957)
DiMenna, Felix (1955)
DiMenna, Genuino (1963)
*DiMenna, Gino (1936)
DiMenna, Guido (1961)
DiMenna, Joseph (1952)
DiMenna, Mario (1956)
DiMenna, Michael (1949)
DiMenna, Mike (1951)
DiMenna, Nick (1951)
DiMenna, Sam (via Argentina) (1960)
DiMenna, Tony (1957)
DiMenna, Tony (1966)
Dimicco, Antonio (1956)
DiMilo, Joseph (1958)
DiMilo, Vince (1955)
DiNiro, Alfonso (1959)
DiNiro, Nicola (1958)
DiPietro, Giuseppe (1969)
DiPrimio, Rolando (1965)
DiSchiavo, Rosato (1968)
Ercole, Aldo (1952)
Esposito, G. (1966)
Ferrante, Americo (1955)
Fiacco, Enrico (1963)
Figliomeni, A. (1967)
Finelli, Salvatore (1967)
Floreno, Francesco (1972)
Flores, Joe (1965)
Fornella, Giustino (1957)
Fornella, Mario (1965)
Foscarino, Ercolino (1971)
Fratarcangeli, D. (1956)
Fratarcangeli, Elio (1965)

Fratarcangeli, G.C. (1962)
Fratarcangeli, Julio (1968)
Fratarcangeli, John (1964)
Fratarcangeli, V. (Vittorio) (1965)
Gabriele, A. (1952)
Gabriele, Frank (1951)
Gabriele, Guido (1951)
Gabriele, Joseph (1956)
Gabriele, Loreto (1953)
Gabriele, Roberto (1957)
Gabriele, V. (Vittorio) (1953)
Gori, Tony (1964)
Giudice, G. (Giuseppe) (1966)
Graziano, Gaetano (1958)
Graziano, Santo (1962)
Graziano, Teresio (1964)
Graziano, Vito (b. Tunisia) (1961)
Grossi, Bruno (1952)
Grossi, Carl (via South America)
  (1959)
[Grossi, Cataldo]
  (w. Rosa D'Alessandris) (1959)
Grossi, Lorenzo (1951)
Grossi, Tony (via Argentina) (1959)
Gualdieri, Sante (1968)
Gualtieri, Alfredo (1967)
Gualtieri, Mario (Lina) (1967)
Guerrieri, Paul (1950)
Guerrieri, Vittorio (Gino) (1949)
[Iaciancio, Pat – no longer in L area]
Iacobelli, Angelo (1954)
Iacobelli, Onorio (1954)
Iacobelli, Vincenzo (1954)
Iarusso, Domenic (1954)
Imperioli, Gino (1966)
Incitti, Amadio (1957)
Incitti, Domenico (1968)
Incitti, Franco (1958)
Incitti, Joe (1967)
Incitti, Lino (1959)
Incitti, Mario (1954)

Incitti, Pasquale (1959)
Incitti, V. (Vincenzo) (1966)
Ingratta, Americo (1961)
Ingratta, Angelo (1951)
Ingratta, Antonietta (1954)
  (h. Frugolino) (1952)
Ingratta, Augie (Augustino) (1953)
Ingratta, Bruno (son of Antonietta)
  (1954)
Ingratta, Bruno (son of Ercolino)
  (1963)
Ingratta, C. (1961)
*Ingratta, Domenic (1930)
*Ingratta, Enrico (Henry) (1925)
Ingratta, Ercolino (1964)
Ingratta, Erminio (1952)
Ingratta, Felice (1962)
Ingratta, Fiorentino (1959)
Ingratta, Gasper (via Argentina)
  (1973)
Ingratta, Igino (1949)
Ingratta, Gino (1966)
Ingratta, H. (1968)
Ingratta, Mario (1959)
*Ingratta, Marius (1930)
Ingratta, Mike (Cottam) (1958)
Ingratta, Mike (Union) (1960)
Ingratta, Mike (1972)
Ingratta, Modestino (1956)
Ingratta, Moretto (1956)
Ingratta, Nick (1951)
Ingratta, Nicola (1953)
Ingratta, Philip (1960)
Ingratta, Pierino (1967)
*Ingratta, Raffaele (1923)
Ingratta, Raffaele (1974)
Ingratta, Ralph (1953)
Ingratta, Sam (Sabatino) (1953)
Ingratta, Tony (1969)
Ingratta, Tony (Fiorina) (1950)
Ingratta, Vincenzo (1964)

Ingratta, Vitantonio (1951)
Ippoliti, Andrew (1954)
Ippoliti, Frank (son of Pietro) (1954)
Ippoliti, Joe (son of Pietro) (1954)
Ippoliti, Pietro (1951)
Labbate, Dino (1958)
Labbate, Eric (1960)
Labbate, Fred (1957)
Labbate, Giovanni (1969)
La Sala, Joseph (1959)
La Sala, Vito (1965)
Latino, Giovanni (1966)
Leone, Gabriele (1949)
Leone, Reno (1949)
Ligori, John (1966)
Ligori, Vince (1966)
Ligotino, Giovanni (1974)
Ligotino, Salvatore (1971)
Longo, Bambino (1967)
Longo, Rinaldo (1967)
Lusetti, Peter (Belgium to London,
  Ontario / L 1972) (1956)
Luzzi, Guerino (1967)
Luzzi, Julio (1967)
*Macchio, Tony (via Toronto / L area
  1969) (1929)
*Magri, Dominic/Domenic (1927)
*Magri, Saveria (Sovie)
  (h. Michele) (1927)
Maiuri, Giuseppe (1953)
Maiuri, Lorenzo (1951)
Maiuri, Luigi (1953)
Maiuri, Mario (1967)
Maiuri, Natale (1951)
Mancini, Domenic (1976)
Maniaci, Salvatore (1950)
Marcoccia, E. (1962)
Marcovecchio, Alex (1959)
Marcovecchio, Joe (1950)
Marcovecchio, Luigi (1963)
Marcovecchio, Marco (1966)

Marcovecchio, V. (1970)

Marcovecchio, Victor (1961)

Massaccesi, C. (Claudio) (moved to
Italy, mid-1980s) (1970)

Mastrangelo, A. (Ascenzio) (1952)

Mastromattei, Armando (1954)

Mastromattei, Pete (1953)

Mastromatteo, Nick (1949)

Mastronardi, A. Ercole (1956)

Mastronardi, Agostino (1966)

Mastronardi, Alberico (1958)

Mastronardi, Alberino (1951)

Mastronardi, Amedeo (1966)

Mastronardi, Angelo (1966)

Mastronardi, Antonio (1957)

*Mastronardi, Armando (1925)

Mastronardi, Beato (1954)

Mastronardi, Bruno (1964)

Mastronardi, Carlo (1966)

Mastronardi, Ciro (1953)

Mastronardi, Costantino (1955)

Mastronardi, David (Villa Canale)
(1953)

Mastronardi, David (Poggio Sannita)
(1979)

Mastronardi, Diego (1959)

Mastronardi, Domenico (1963)

Mastronardi, Enrico (1956)

Mastronardi, Enrico Pierino (1968)

Mastronardi, Ercole (nephew of
Luigi, 1925) (1949)

Mastronardi, Ercole (brother of
Armando, 1925) (1949)

Mastronardi, Fernando (1951)

Mastronardi, Francescantonio
(Frank A.) (1949)

Mastronardi, Francesco (1955)

Mastronardi, Frank (1948)

Mastronardi, Frank F. (1960)

Mastronardi, Gaetano (1953)

Mastronardi, Gemino (1958)

Mastronardi, Gino (1957)

Mastronardi, Guido (1970)

Mastronardi, Gus (1953)

Mastronardi, Henry (1951)

Mastronardi, Igino (1953)

Mastronardi, Jim (1952)

Mastronardi, Joseph (1949)

Mastronardi, Joseph
(Giuseppe) (1953)

Mastronardi, Leonardo (1952)

Mastronardi, Leopardo (1954)

Mastronardi, Levino (1958)

Mastronardi, Levino (1969)

Mastronardi, Luca (1949)

*Mastronardi, Luigi (1925)

Mastronardi, Mario (1950)

*Mastronardi, Marius (1933)

Mastronardi, Mike (1951)

Mastronardi, Mike (1956)

Mastronardi, Mike (1957)

Mastronardi, Mike (1963)

Mastronardi, Miracolo (1970)

Mastronardi, Moretto
(via Argentina) (1953)

Mastronardi, Nick (1950)

Mastronardi, Nick (1953)

Mastronardi, Nick (1958)

Mastronardi, Olindo (1951)

Mastronardi, Ollie Jr. (1951)

*Mastronardi, Ollie (son of
Armando, 1925) (1930)

Mastronardi, Raffaele (Seacliff Drive)
(1952)

Mastronardi, Ralph (Long Beach
Drive) (1952)

Mastronardi, Ralph (Talbot W.)
(1952)

Mastronardi, Sal (w. Beatrice) (1954)

Mastronardi, Salvatore (1959)

Mastronardi, Sam (1952)

Mastronardi, T. (1951)

Mastronardi, Teodoro (1969)
Mastronardi, Tony (1950)
Mastronardi, Tony A. (1954)
Mastronardi, Tony G. (1955)
*Mastronardi, Umberto (1930)
Mastronardi, Vincenzo (3rd Con. Rd., Mersea) (1952)
Mastronardi, Vincenzo (Regent St., Ruthven) (1960)
Mastronardi, Vincenzo (Talbot W.) (1963)
Matassa, Attilio (1948)
Matassa, Bruno (1948)
Matassa, Lou (1949)
Matassa, Nello (1948)
Mattei, Edward M. (1959)
Mattei, Gus (1956)
Mattia, Clement (1961)
Mattia, John (1952)
Mattia, Loreto (1967)
Mattia, Pat (1953)
Mattia, Silvio (1966)
Melatti, Rino (Reno) (via Toronto / L 1972) (1956)
Milana, Vincenzo (1959)
Minaudo, Carlo (1964)
Minaudo, Joe (1972)
Minaudo, Tony (1955)
*Moauro, Angelo (1923)
*Moauro, Costantino (Gus) (1923)
[Moauro, Frank Jr b. in Canada] (w. Rina Marcovecchio) (1959)
*Moauro, Frank Sr (1936)
*Moauro, Rocco (1938)
Moavro, Giuseppe (via Argentina) (1963)
Molliconi, Mike (1954)
Monaco, Filippo (1967)
Monaco, Giuseppa (1969)
Monaco, Joe (1966)
Monaco, Nicola (1968)

Moracci, Ottavio (1951)
Mucci, Domenico (1966)
Mucci, Gino (1961)
Mucci, Tony (1961)
Norcini, Umberto (1966)
Orlando, Tony (1963)
Orsini, Andy (1952)
Orsini, Frank (1952)
Orsini, Remo (1952)
Pace, Vincenzo (1957)
Paglione, Angelo (1959)
Paglione, Giulio (moved to Capracotta, Molise) (1968)
Paglione, Italo (1957)
Paglione, Mario (1962)
Paglione, Mauro (1959)
Paglione, Vittorio (1955)
Palazzi, Natale (1957)
Paliani, Gino (1952)
Paliani, Italo (1952)
Paliani, Laurino (1951)
Paliani, Rolando (1954)
Paliani, Tony (1953)
Pallotta, Armando (1969)
Pallotta, Vittorio (1965)
Pallotto, Antonio (1969)
Pallotto, Giuseppe (1970)
Palomba, Amedeo (1970)
Palomba, Domenico (1960)
Palomba, Tony A. (1958)
Palomba, Umberto (1955)
Palombo, Ermete (1959)
Palombo, Eroi (1964)
Palombo, Flavio (1963)
Palombo, Italo (1965)
Pannunzio, Antonio (1948)
Pannunzio, Armando (1974)
Pannunzio, Austin (1952)
*Pannunzio, Domenico (1923)
Pannunzio, Frank (1949)
Pannunzio, Fred (Goffredo) (1949)

*Pannunzio, Gino (1931)
Pannunzio, Guido (1948)
Pannunzio, Henry (1948)
*Pannunzio, Joseph (1925)
Pannunzio, Luigi (1977)
Pannunzio, Perry (Pierino) (1950)
Paoletti, Mario (1968)
Paventi, Amedeo (1959)
Peraino, A. (1970)
Peraino, Vito (1965)
Peralta, Girolamo (Jerry)
   (since 1953 in USA) (1949)
Peralta, Nick (1952)
Peralta, Salvatore (Sal) (1950)
*Peralta, Vito (1927)
Peralta, Vito (grandson) (1952)
Perciballi, Gino (1967)
Perciballi, Henry (1968)
Perciballi, Pierino (1962)
Perciballi, Steve (1965)
Perciballi, Tony (1963)
Petrucci, Mario (1959)
Pezzotti, Giuseppe (1964)
Piroli, Andy (1955)
Piroli, Carlo (1966)
Piroli, Domenico (1955)
Piroli, Giovanni (1966)
Piroli, Guido (1957)
Piroli, Joe (1957)
Piroli, Vincenzo (1957)
Piroli, Walter (1953)
Policella, Harold (1958)
Policella, Joe (1958)
Policella, Luca (1956)
Policella, Mario (1954)
Policella, Nino (1956)
Puglia, Bernardo (1953)
Puglia, Domenico (1954)
Puglia, Donato (1951)
Quadrini, Joe (1962)
Quatrini, Domenic (1968)

Rauzino, Mike (1964)
Ricci, Domenic (1956)
Ricci, Domenico (1966)
Ricci, Edilio (1973)
Ricci, Gino (1969)
Ricci, Giocondino (1956)
Ricci, Giovanni (1966)
Ricci, Jack (1963)
Ricci, Rocco (1959)
Ricci, Rolando (1968)
Ricci, Tony (1965)
Ricci, Virginio (1954)
[Riggio, Frank – no longer in L area]
[Riggio, Rosario – no longer in L area]
Rinaldi, Mike (1966)
Rossi, Mario (1965)
Rossi, Tony (1972)
Rossi, Fr Ugo (via USA 1948 / L
   1967) (1960)
Rubino, Gaetano (1967)
Rubino, Nicola (1968)
Rubino, Salvatore (1951)
Sabelli, Angelo (1968)
Sabelli, Antonino (father of Angelo)
   (1957)
Sabelli, Antonio (son of Peppino)
   (1952) (w. Antonietta) (1968)
Sabelli, Antonio Leo (1956)
Sabelli, Claudio (1962)
Sabelli, Domenic (nephew of Gus
   Moauro, 1923) (1952)
Sabelli, Enrico (1966)
Sabelli, Giustino (1962)
Sabelli, John (1962)
Sabelli, M. (1968)
Sabelli, Michele (1956)
Sabelli, Pat (1953)
Sabelli, Paul (1954)
Sabelli, Ralph (1950)
Sabelli, Stefano (father of Domenic)
   (1949)

Sabelli, Tony (son of Angelo) (1957)
Saccucci, Gino (1967)
Saccucci, Vincenzo (1968)
Salvati, Neil (Nello) (1951)
Salvati, Nick (1959)
Santaniello, Lamberto (1951)
Santilli, Rinaldo (1955)
Sera, John (1965)
Serafini, P. (Pasquale) (1970)
Silvestri, Domenico (1972)
Simoni, Massimo (1970)
[Spampinato, V. – no longer in L area]
Spano, Isidoro (Sid) (via Toronto / L
    1973) (1952)
Spano, Vince (not related to Sid)
    (1959)
Sperduti, Luigi (1955)
Sperduti, Serafino (1954)
Spidalieri, Amelio (1950)
Spineti, Peter (1949)
Stramacchia, Matteo (1950)
Stravato, Pasquale (1961)
Taccone, Domenic (1975)
[Taglieri, John – no longer in L area]
Tannini, Frank (1966)
Testa, Joe (1957)
Testa, Umberto (1957)
Testani, Antonio (1964)

Testani, Elio (1965)
Testani, S. (1965)
Tomanelli, Pietro (1978)
[Tortorici, John – no longer in L area]
Totaro, Nick (1969)
Urbano, Valentino (1959)
[Valente, Antonio – no longer in L
    area]
Valeri, Albano (USA 1912 / L 1978)
    (1946)
Valeri, Giuseppe (1967)
Valeri, Orlando (1957)
Valeri, Romeo (1960)
Vernaroli, Celestino (1961)
Vernaroli, Ennio (1960)
Vernaroli, Germano (1966)
Vernaroli, Guido (1961)
Vespa, Eugene (1968)
Vespa, Giovanni (1970)
Vespa, Pat (1974)
Vilardi, Salvatore (1971)
Visca, Carlo (1957)
Visca, Gerardo (1957)
Visca, Tulliano (1954)
Zaccardi, Domenic (1956)
Zarlenga, Domenic (1963)
Zompanti, Antonio (1955)
Zompanti, Arduino (1961)

Italians in the Leamington Area, (Southeast Essax County): 1920s–1945

KEY
f. = family
b. = birth/born
bro. = brother
C. = arrived/settled in Canada
chldn. = children
dtr. = daughter
F. = immigrated as a family unit
gdchldn. = grandchildren
hb. = husband
I. = individual
L. + year = arrived/settled in Leamington, town or area
m. = married (to)/marriage
Nl/Nt/Nv + C/L = no longer/not/never in Canada/in Leamington, town or area
sn. = son
wf. = wife
W. = arrived/settled in Windsor, town or area

A. (ABRUZZO-) MOLISE: Molisani: 11

f.1. (C1923; W1924; L1928/29) Tony (Antonio) DIMENNA: wf.
(2nd m. 1936) Antonietta Appugliese & sn Gino [by 1st wf.
Prudenzina – also née DiMenna – Nv C] – (L1936) [chldn b.C:
Domenic, Ronald, Lina].

f.2. (C1923; W1924; L1928) Domenic PANNUNZIO: wf. Fenizia
(Finizia) Ingratta & chldn (L1931): sn Gino, dtrs Mary (m. John
Cervini, Tony's sn) & Fiorina (Florence) (m. Nicola Valentino
W1924).

f.3. (C1923; W/USA1924–38; L1938) Angelo MOAURO: wf.
Angelina Sabelli & dtr Esterina (m. Louis Ingratta, John's sn)
(L1939); sn Rocco (L1938) [other dtr Pasqualina & hb. Enrico
DiCiocco – L after WWII].

f.4. (C1923; W/USA1924–34; L1934) Costantino MOAURO: wf.
Paolina Sabelli (sister of Angelina, his bro. Angelo's wf.) &
sn Frank Sr (m. Ida Mastronardi, Luigi's dtr) – (L1936) [sn
Pasquale/Pat – b.C 1938].

I.5. (C1923; W1924–28; L1932) Raffaele (Ralph) INGRATTA:
[Rodney 1928–32 with bro. John & cousin Henry]: 1930s
back & forth L – Italy; war years Italy; end WWII – L1951 [wf.
Ernesta DiMenna NvC].

f.6. (C1923; W1924–28) Giovanni (John) INGRATTA: [1928
Rodney permanently: wf. Chiarina DiMenna & sns Louis (m.
Esterina Moauro, Angelo's dtr) & Mike – Rodney Sept. 1930;
eldest sn Vincenzo (Jim) – Rodney Feb. 1930, voyage with cousin
Domenic & six others.
[NB: Geremia Capussi and cousin Michele Capussi, the other two
members of the 1923 group, never settled in Leamington area: W/
USA 1924–33: deported, never returned to N. America].

Sponsored by 1923 Group: 7 to 10

f.7. (C/W1924–28; L1933) Enrico "Ricuccio" (Henry) INGRATTA
[Rodney 1928–33]: wf. Merceda (Maria/Mary) Mastronardi,
sn Marius (m. Clara Pannunzio, Joe's dtr) & dtr Mary (Dec.
1930); sn Domenic (Feb. 1930, voyage with aunt Luisa (Lisetta)
Mastronardi & cousin Jim) [other dtr Aquilina – m. Antonio
Pannunzio (L1948) bro. of Domenic & Joe – in Italy until
L1950].

f.8. (C/W1925; L1928) Armando MASTRONARDI: wf. Luisa (Elisa or Lisetta) DiMenna (Raffaele Ingratta's wf.'s half-sister) & sns Umberto (Bert) & Olindo (Ollie) – (L Feb. 1930).

f.9. (C/W1925; L1928) Giuseppe (Joe) PANNUNZIO: wf. Adorina (Audrey) Ingratta (L Feb. 1930) [chldn b.C: dtr Clara (m. Marius Ingratta, Henry's sn) & sn David].

f.10. (C/W1925; L1928) Luigi MASTRONARDI: wf. Paolina (also née) Mastronardi & 3 chldn (L1933): sn Marius; dtrs Florence (m. John Kasarda) & Ida (m. Frank Moauro Sr, Gus's sn); eldest sn Alfred (L Feb. 1930, voyage with Adorina Pannunzio & six others).

F.11. (C1927; L1940) Michele (Michael) MAGRI with wf. Saveria (Sovie) Carlone and sn Domenic (m. Loretta Cervini, Tony's dtr): "First" group to arrive as a family but via McGregor–Amherstburg–Essex Town (1927–40).

B.   LAZIO (Latium): Laziali (or Ciociari): 6

f.12. (C/W/L1924) Alex (Eleuterio) COLASANTI: wf. Emma Colagiovanni [b. in Ohio, same regional origins, Detroit resident] (L1932) [3 sns b.C: Joe, Ronald, Alex Jr].

f.13. (C/W/L1924) Tony (Amato, "Amatuccio") DESANTIS: wf. Gaetana ("Matuccia") Simonelli – probably first Italian immigrant woman in the area – & 2 sns (1926): Rocco (Roy) & Fred (former mayor of Kingsville) [2 chldn b.C: Mike, Mary].

I.14. (C/L1927 to USA1937) Loreto COLASANTI: Harrow–Kingsville 1927–29 (with bro. Alex); L1929–37 (1930–37 with bro. Frank) [1937 m. Mary Colagiovanni, sister of Emma – his bro. Alex's wf. – & settled in Detroit].

f.15. (C/W1927/L1938) Antonio (Tony) CERVINI: wf. Rosa Fratarcangeli & chldn (L1939): sn John (m. Mary Pannunzio, Domenic's dtr), sn Santuccio (Sandy) & dtr Loretta (m. Domenic Magri, Saveria's sn) [dtr Antonietta b.C].

f.16. (USA1922; C/L1930; back to USA) Frank COLASANTI (bro. of A. & L.): wf. Palmina (C/L 1930) & chldn in L1930–41 [year Frank & chldn returned to USA].

f.17. (C1918?; W/L1920s/30s?; L farm ownership 1942) Joe MATASSA & family: wf. Maria, probably the "Maria Matassa" that Saveria Magri mentioned working with her and Esterina Moauro in a L tobacco factory during WWII.

C. SICILY: one Sicilian

I.18. (C/W1927; L1943) Vito PERALTA: L first Sicilian; perhaps first downtown L resident (& only known WWII internee, 1940–42). [wf. Giuseppina (Josephine) Milana, chldn, gdchldn after WWII: L1948 wf. & sn Girolamo, Jerry (to USA1953); sn Salvatore (Sal) L1950; Sal's wf. (Pietra Adragna) & 3 chldn – L1952].

D. OTHERS

I.19. (C/L early 1920s?) Vittorio (Vic) DELZOTTI: considered "the first Italian to work on a [Mersea Twp or L] area farm"; early 1920s sponsored bro. Pete [Vic returned to Italy (Puglia region?): never part of L Italian colony].

I.20. (C/L early 1920s?) Pietro (Pete) DELZOTTI, Vic's bro. [1948: m. by proxy Isabella A. Catauro from Molise; 1948–63: "joint tenants" of L farm. No Delzotti descendants in L area].

f.21. (C/L1931 from USA) Joe DELELLIS (b. Lazio – L1964): wf. Maria (?) (b. Molise – L1977), sn Al (Alfonse) & dtrs Louise, Hazel (Isotta), Mary, & Lina.

f.22. (Cb./Guelph 1918; W1936; L1939) John BRUNATO: wf. Ines (Enes) Orlando (downtown L Shoe Repair). [chldn b. in C: sn Peter (L farmer); dtr Joanne (L resident); dtr Lynn (Toronto res.)] [also: Ines's stepfather and mother: Albano VALERI (b. Lazio – W1984) USA1912; W1946; m. 1940 W resident Giacomina Polano (b. Friuli – W1984) – L1978–83].

I.23. (C1911; W1923/24; L late 1930s) Louis (Luigi) BERNACHI (or BERNACCHI): Louis, 2 bros. & parents, from Gallarate, Varese, Lombardy, to C/Guelph 1911–21; all returned to Italy; Louis C/W1923–24 (m. Brunato's aunt, Canadina); late 1930s at Brunato's L Shoe Repair; 1940/early 1940s back in W owner of Humphries Shoe Repair (mid-1950s operated by son-in-law Mario Agnolin; 1957/58? sold to Nick CICCHINI) [1952 remarried, moved to Wyandotte, Michigan, USA].

f.24. (W1927; L1939–42) Nick CICCHINI: mgr Brunato's L Shoe Repair (before Vito Peralta); Canadian army (1942–47) [W1947; owner-operator Humphries Shoe Repair (1957/58?–late 1970s/early 1980s).

f.25. (C1927; W1920s–early 1940s; L1944) Fernando D.B. [DEL BEL] BELLUZ (Friuli-Venezia Giulia); m. Sonia Urkosky; 1944 settled on L farm (see appendix D).

f.26. (C late 1870s–early 1880s; Wheatley 1930s) Rocco ROMANELLI (?–1941).[1]

I./f.(?) 27 ... (1920s–40s W/rural Essex County): mentioned by L Italians: John BORIO (region of origin?C?); 1920s W Italian agency.

MECONI bros. (Lazio) (W based; farm/business in county).

– Clemente; C1924; W grocery dtore (wf. Gilda).

– Luigi; C1913; WWI veteran; W travel/service agency.

– Mariano; C1915/1916; W & Michigan winery.

Francesco LAROSA family (Puglia?C?); early 1930s county farm labourers.

Pasquale SASSO (region of origin?C?); late 1920s/early 1930s River Canard farm.

Mike TOTARO (Molise? Puglia?); C/W1923/24 (?); L1948/49; back to W.

See also Essex County Branch, Ontario Genealogical Society, *Evergreen Memorial Park Cemetery Leamington* (Windsor: OGS, 1983), which lists the tombstone transcriptions of the Leamington cemetery up to 1983.

Reproductions of Passports/ Military Discharge Papers

Domenico Pannunzio. Passport 1
Issued at Isernia, 5 June 1913; valid for three years with specific destination:
New York; at age sixteen travelled to United States with his brother-in-law,
Giuseppe Mastronardi, who served also as his garante (guarantor or guardian
(see passport 1, pp. 2–5). Name appears (p. 1) as "Domenicantonio," that is
Domenico-Antonio, Domenic-Anthony (see chapter 2, "The 'Right' America
and the 'Wrong' America" and note 34).

— 2 —

Connotati del Titolare del Passaporto

Statura m. *1-54*
Età anni *16 circa*
Fronte *regolare*
Occhi *castani*
Naso *giusto*
Bocca *id*
Capelli *castani*
Barba —
Baffi —
Colorito *bruno*
Capratura *regolare*
Segni particolari —

FIRMA DEL TITOLARE

— 3 —

Il presente passaporto è rilasciato per (1)
Newr. York

è valido (2) *per tre anni*

(3) *gratis*

Isernia 5 giugno 1913
Il sottoprefetto
Orioli

(1) Stato o Stati di destinazione.
(2) Per tre anni ovvero fino al 7° aprile (per gli iscritti di leva di terra, fino al 31° gennaio per gli iscritti di leva marittima) dell'anno ... (Art. 5, comma 2°, del regio decreto 31 gennaio 1901).
(3) Luogo per l'apposizione della marca speciale (o per la dichiarazione che il passaporto viene *rilasciato gratuitamente* a *norma dell'art. 6, comma 2°, del regio decreto 31 gennaio 1901*), bollo, data e firma dell'autorità che rilascia il passaporto. Se si tratta di passaporto rilasciato all'estero, in sostituzione della marca speciale l'autorità che lo rilascia annoterà, accanto al bollo, l'ammontare della tassa percetta.

— 4 —

Persone che accompagnano il Titolare

	COGNOME E NOME	Rapporto col Titolare	ETÀ
1	*Mastronardi Giuseppe*	*garante*	anni *35*
2			
3			
4			
5			
6			
7			

— 5 —

(Art. 4 del R. Decreto 31 gennaio 1901).

Luogo di nascita	Osservazioni
Agnone	*Isernia 5 giugno 1913* *Il sottoprefetto* *Orioli*

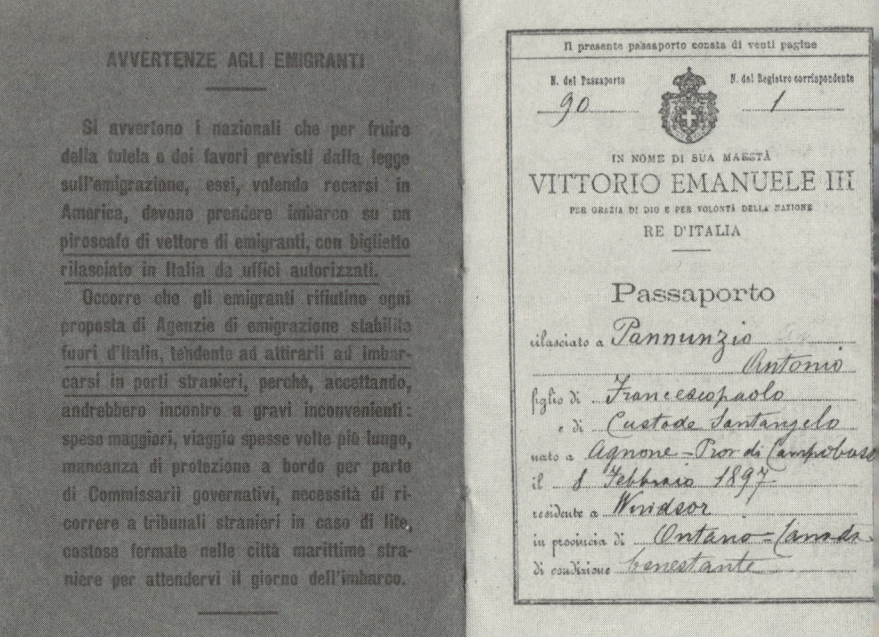

Domenico Pannunzio, Passport 2

Issued by the Italian Royal Office of Emigration for Canada, Ottawa, 14
November 1924 (a year after his arrival in Canada): valid for one year to
visit the United States and return (pp. 2, 7–9). Name shown on passport is
"Antonio" and place of residence, "Windsor" (pp. 1, 2).

The "Instructions" or "Advice to the Emigrants" (*Avvertenze agli Emigranti*)
state:

> Italian nationals are advised that in order to enjoy the protection and
> assistance provided by the law on emigration, when they intend to go to
> America, they must secure passage on a *ship carrying emigrants, with a
> ticket issued in Italy by authorized offices.*
>
> It is necessary that the emigrants refuse every offer, made by
> *emigration agencies established outside Italy, that aims to draw them to
> foreign ports for embarkation*, because, by accepting, they might incur
> serious inconveniences: higher expenses, often a longer journey, lack of
> protection on board by government commissioners, the need to appeal
> to foreign courts in case of litigation, costly stops in foreign sea towns to
> wait for departure day. (translation mine)

(See also chapter 3, "Could Some of the Risks Have Been Avoided?").

— 2 —

Connotati del Titolare del Passaporto

Statura m. _____

Età _Ventisette anni_

Fronte _alta_

Occhi _scuri_

Naso _regolare_

Bocca _regolare_

Capelli _neri_

Barba _rasa_

Baffi _rasi_

Colorito _sano_

Corporatura _giusta_

Segni particolari _____

FIRMA DEL TITOLARE

Tommasin Antonio

— 3 —

Il presente passaporto è rilasciato per (1) _gli
Stati Uniti e ritorno_

ed è valido (2) _per un anno_
Ottawa, 14 Novembre 1924

(3) _Al R. Console_

Percez. n° 90
Tassa Lit 25.00
Cod 56 T. C.

(1) Stato o Stati di destinazione.
(2) Per tre anni; ovvero fino al 1° aprile (per gli inscritti
di leva di terra, o 1° gennaio per gli inscritti di leva marittima) dell'anno .... (art. 5, comma 2°, del regio decreto
31 gennaio 1901).
(3) Luogo per l'apposizione della marca speciale (o per la
dichiarazione che il passaporto viene rilasciato gratuitamente
a norma dell'art. 6, comma 2°, del regio decreto 31 gennaio 1901),
bollo, data e firma dell'autorità che rilascia il passaporto,
se si tratta di passaporto rilasciato all'estero, in sostituzione della marca speciale l'ufficiale che lo rilascia annot-
terà, accanto al bollo, l'ammontare della tassa percetta.

— 4 —

Persone che accompagnano il Titolare

— 5 —

(Art. 4 del R. Decreto 31 gennaio 1901).

	COGNOME E NOME	Rapporto col Titolare	ETÀ	Luogo di nascita	Osservazioni
1					
2					
3					
4					
5					
6					
7					

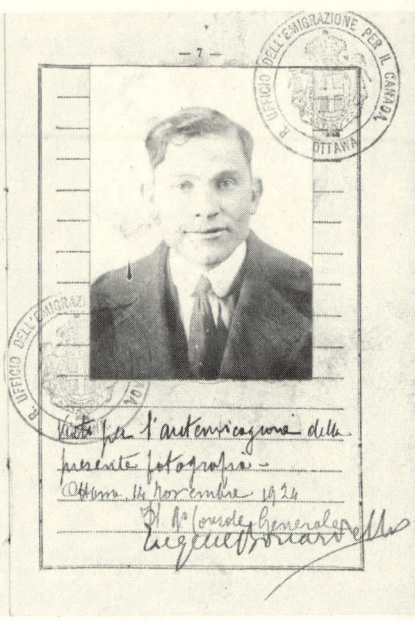

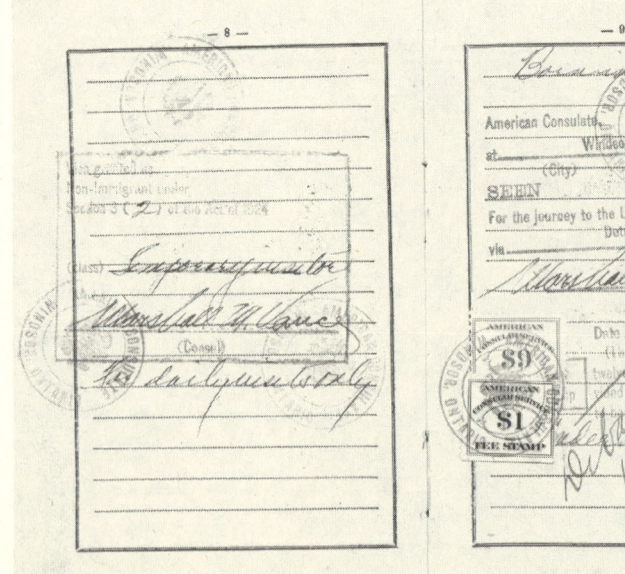

Domenico Pannunzio, Military Discharge Papers

Royal Italian Army: 11th Regiment Bersaglieri (Sharpshooters). Issued at Ancona, 11 April 1920; signed by the mayor of Agnone, his municipality of residence, 15 April 1920. Recognition of his "good conduct and of having served with loyalty and honour." The Molisani were required to bring the discharge papers with them in order to be able to leave from France (see chapter 2, "The Rewards of the 'Ugly War'").

A) Stato civile.

Figlio di *Francesco* c. d. *Santangelo Custode*
nato il *8 Febbraio 1897* 18 a *Agnone* Mandamento
di *id* circondario di *Isernia* distretto militare di *Campobasso*

B) Contrassegni personali.

Statura metri 1,*66* capelli *castagni* occhi *castagni* colorito *rosso* dentatura *sana*
segni particolari // sopracciglia *castagni* fronte *giusta*
naso *regolare* bocca *regolare* mento *ovale* viso *ovale*

C) Arte e grado d'istruzione.

Arte o professione *Contadino* Se sa leggere e scrivere *sì*

D) Arruolamento e prima venuta alle armi.

Arruolato di *leva* il *25 8 1916* 191 Estrasse il N.
nella leva della classe 18*97* mandamento di *Agnone* circondario di *Isernia*
Chiamato alle armi e giunto *5-10-1916*

E) Trasferimento di corpo durante il servizio e data dell'ultimo grado.

Dal *12° Regg.to* trasferito al *18° Bersaglieri*
il *31-1-1917* 191 Trasferito al *11° Bersaglio 24-?1* 1917
Trasferito al il 191 .

F) Intervento alle chiamate alle armi dal congedo illimitato.

Giunto alle armi per 191 Il Comandante
Rinviato in congedo illimitato 191 del

Giunto alle armi 191 Il Comandante
Rinviato in congedo illimitato 191 del

G) Campagne, ferite, decorazioni ed encomi.

Campagna di Guerra 1917
Campagna di Guerra 1918

H) Trasferimenti ed altre variazioni durante il congedo.

Il Relatore
(Ten. Col. ALFREDO BALZARINI)

Section C: Occupation – farmer. Ability to read and write – Yes
Section G: War Campaign 1917. War Campaign 1918.

INDENNITÀ DI VIAGGIO PAGATE.

a) — PER L'INVIO IN CONGEDO

Il titolare del presente parte da *Ancona* per recarsi in congedo a *Agnone* soddisfatto di soldo a tutto il _____ e di indennità di trasferta, per N. *una* giornate, come pure di indennità di trasporto:

per ferrovia { da *Ancona* a *Pescolanciano* in L. *9.80*
{ da _____ a _____ in L. _____

per mare — da _____ a *Ancona* addì *12 Aprile* _____ in L. _____

L'Aiutante maggiore

b) — PEL RINVIO IN CONGEDO DOPO IL PRIMO RICHIAMO

Il titolare del presente parte da _____ per _____ soddisfatto di soldo a tutto il _____ e di indennità di trasferta per N. _____ giornate, come pure di indennità di trasporto:

per ferrovia { da _____ a _____ in L. _____
{ da _____ a _____ in L. _____

per mare — da _____ a _____ in L. _____

A _____ addì _____ 191 L'Aiutante maggiore

c) — PEL RINVIO IN CONGEDO DOPO IL SECONDO RICHIAMO

Il titolare del presente parte da _____ per recarsi in congedo a _____ soddisfatto di soldo a tutto il _____ e di indennità di trasferta per N. _____ giornate, come pure di indennità di trasporto:

per ferrovia { da _____ a _____ in L. _____
{ da _____ a _____ in L. _____

per mare — da _____ a _____ in L. _____

A _____ addì _____ 191 L'Aiutante maggiore

ANNOTAZIONI.

(1) Corpo che rilascia il congedo.
(2) Per coloro che vanno in congedo per trasferimento alla 2ª o alla 3ª categoria, si indicherà la categoria alla quale vanno ad essere ascritti all'atto del congedo.
(3) Alla quale, o per arruolamento o per trasferimento, risulta ascritto al momento che va in congedo.
(4) Per coloro che nel momento del licenziamento, anziché essere trasferiti ad altro corpo, debbono essere ascritti alla milizia mobile o alla milizia territoriale, s'indicherà inoltre che sono ascritti alla *milizia mobile o territoriale del . reggimento ..... o del distretto di ......*
Poi trasferimenti successivi vedasi la casella 11 della 2ª pag.
(5) Indicare la causa per la quale si rilascia il congedo, e cioè per:
  a) fine di ferma;
  b) anticipazione;
  c) trasferimento alla 2ª o alla 3ª categoria per modificazioni sopraggiunte nello stato di famiglia;
  d) effettuata surrogazione di fratello per incambio di categoria;
  e) compiuta istruzione (se di 2ª o 3ª categoria);
  f) compiuta raiferma;
  g) collocamento a riposo prima dell'invio in congedo assoluto della classe cui appartiene.
Se il militare viene inviato in congedo illimitato per una causa qui non prevista, occorre sempre che sia indicata.
(6) Cognome e nome, grado ed impiego speciale e, se il corpo è suddiviso in specialità, indicare tra parentesi la specialità nella quale ha prestato servizio. Aggiungere inoltre le indicazioni che occorre aver presenti in caso di richiamo alle armi e che, a tale scopo, siano state apposte sul quadro 17 del mod. 59.
(7) Indicare il numero di matricola avuto nell'atto dell'iscrizione sul Ruolo N. 5, del distretto.
(8) Spazio per il giudizio sintetico sulla condotta (§ 942 e segg. Regolam. sul Reclutam.).

(9) Da apporsi quando nella casella «arte e grado d'istruzione» è dichiarato che sa leggere e scrivere.
(10) Apporre secondo i casi, in *tutte lettere* l'annotazione: «leggere e scrivere» — «sa leggere ma non sa scrivere» — «non sa nè leggere nè scrivere».
(11) Di leva in... categoria o volontario o surrogato di fratello.
(12) Se di leva o surrogato avanti il consiglio di leva, data dell'arruolamento al consiglio di leva. Se volontario o surrogato al corpo, data dell'arruolamento alle armi.
(13) Data, per gli arruolati di leva, nella presentazione al distretto.
Non occorrono, oltre la data, altre indicazioni, come ad esempio i motivi della ritardata presentazione, ecc.
(14) Corpo cui fu assegnato dal distretto di leva nella prima venuta sotto le armi.
(15) Grado rivestito al momento del congedo.
(16) Istruzione (o per rassegna, per mobilitazione od altra indicazione che fosse stabilita dal Ministero). Per ogni chiamata occorre sia apposta la firma del Comandante del distretto o del deposito, ecc. secondo i casi, e il bollo d'ufficio.
(17) Tanto prima del rilascio del presente congedo quanto in occasione di richiami alle armi.
(18) Quando il trasferimento è accompagnato da passaggio alla milizia territoriale dovrà farsene cenno. In questa casella si cranno registrare anche le più importanti modificazioni che potranno avvenire nella posizione del militare in congedo, cioè retrocessioni, rimozioni dal grado, ecc.

N.B. — Occorrendo di rilasciare un duplicato, il foglio porterà la data del rilascio nel duplicato stesso, ma al disopra della firma del Comandante del corpo si scriverà:
Per duplicato dell'altro smarrito che fu rilasciato in data................191....

Payment of Travel Allowance from Ancona to Agnone.
Train fare from Ancona to Pescolanciano: Lire 9.80

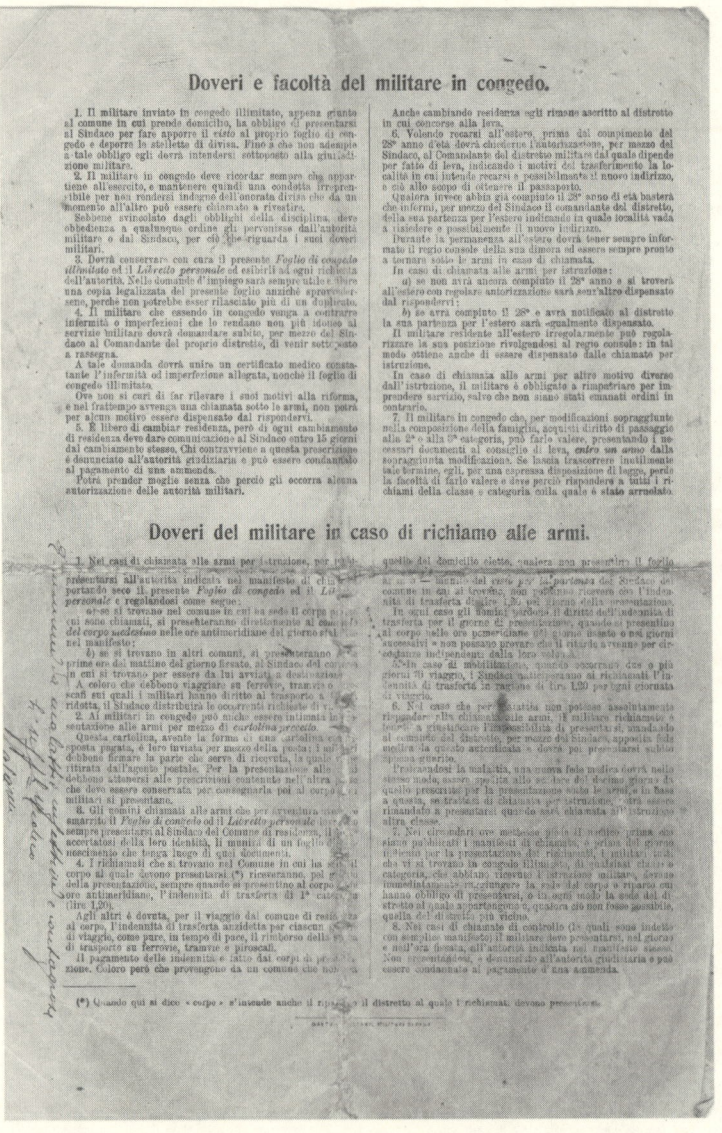

Top section: "Duties and Faculties of the Discharged Soldier."
Part 6. Instructions on the mode of obtaining a passport for travel outside Italy and duties of the discharged soldier, even if residing abroad in the event of a call to arms by Italy: Translated and quoted in chapter 3, "Could Some of the Risks Have Been Avoided?"
Bottom section: "Duties of the Soldier in the Event of a Recall to Arms."

Antonio DiMenna, Passport for the Interior
Issued by the mayor of Agnone, 6 October 1923 (apparently on the same day the second group of Molisani set out for "America"): Valid for One Year. DiMenna's age: twenty-five; occupation: farmer (see chapter 3, "The Eight Molisani's Destination – Somewhere, Canada").

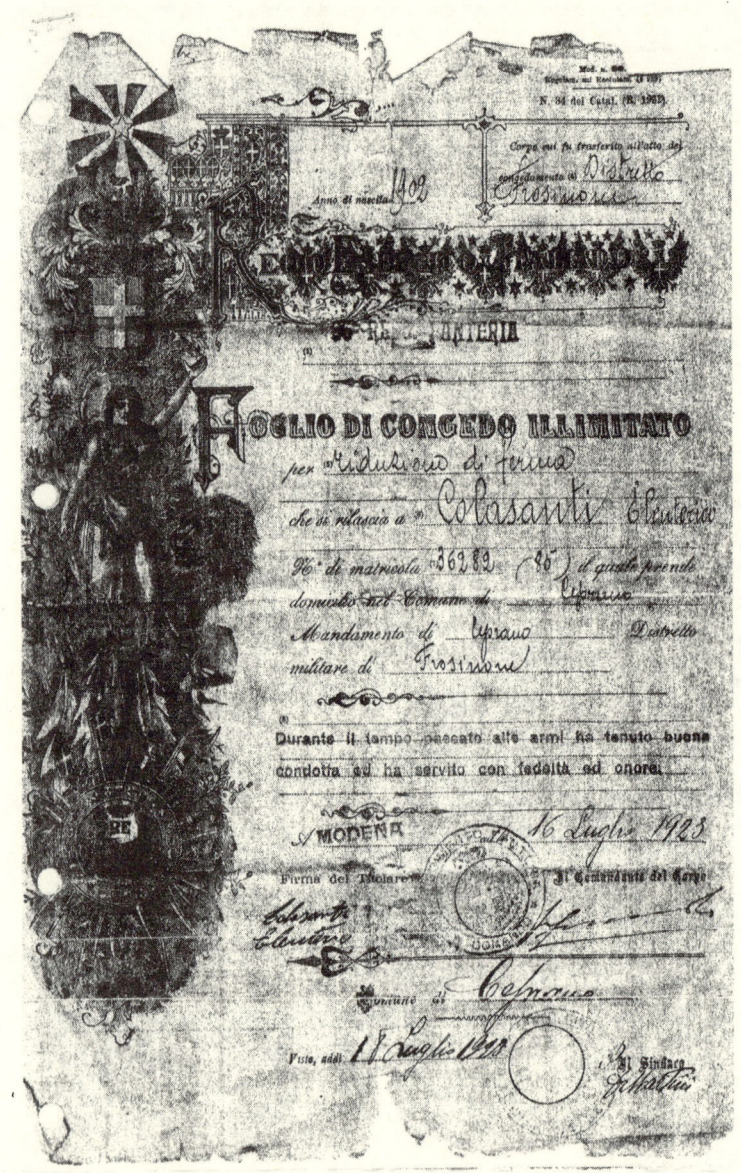

Eleuterio (Alex) Colasanti, Military Discharge Papers
Royal Italian Army: 36th Regiment Infantry. Issued at Modena, 16 July
1923; signed by the mayor of Ceprano, his municipality of residence, 18 July
1923: "During the time spent in the army, he maintained good conduct and
served with loyalty and honour."

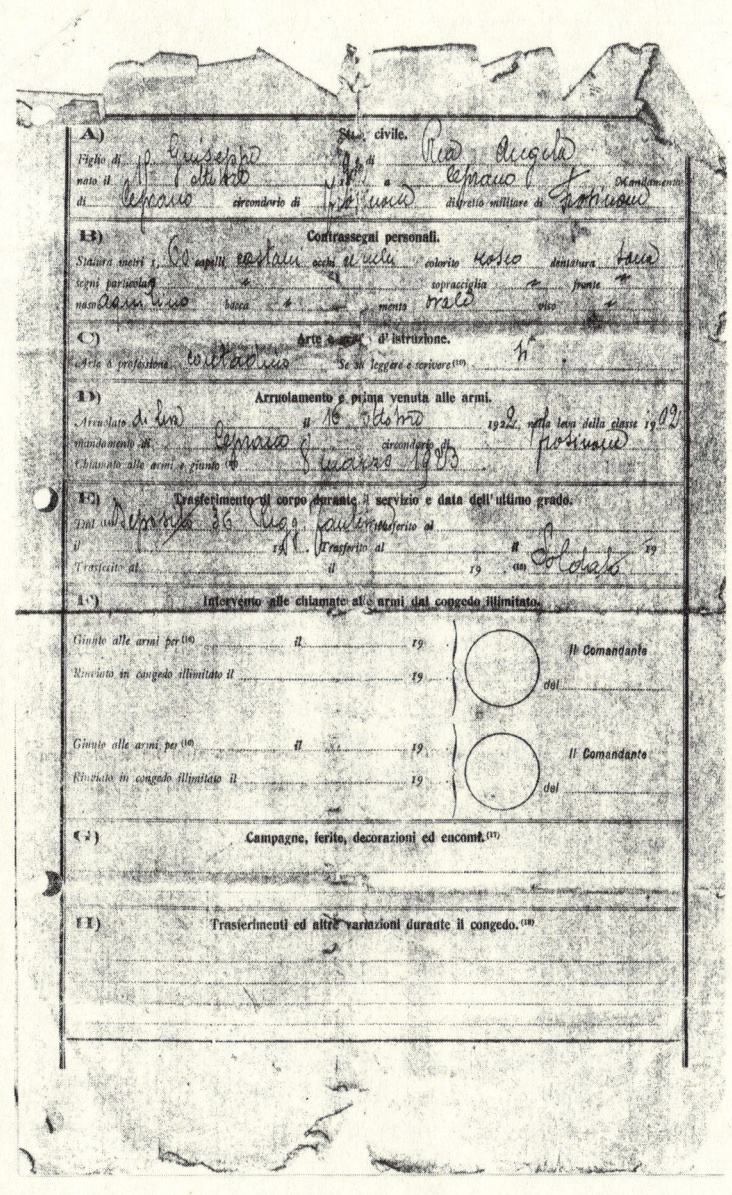

Section C: Occupation – farmer. Ability to read and write – Yes.
Section D: Drafted, 16 October 1922, at Ceprano.

Fenizia Ingratta, Passport

Issued by the Italian Ministry of Foreign Affairs through the Police Department of Campobasso (Molise), 24 April 1931, for specified destination – Ontario, Canada – and valid until 23 April 1932 (pp. 2, 5). Fenizia, wife of Domenico Pannunzio, and their children (also shown in passport photo on both sides of their mother, L. to R.: Gino, 26 January 1919; Maria Custode, 11 March 1922; Fiorina, 18 November 1916), travelled together to Canada in 1931: Departure, Naples, 13 June; arrival, New York, 22 June; entry in Canada at Bridgeburg Ontario, 23 June (pp. 7–10). Fenizia (occupation shown as farmer) was among the first few women to join their husbands in the Leamington area (see chapter 5, "Saveria Magri and the First Women").

Farm Purchases by Leamington
Italian Immigrants 1920s–1960s

Source: Deeds of land and other records (from respective families and Land Registry Offices, Windsor and Leamington)

KEY

Ac. = no. of acres
C = concession
Cty = county
Lt = lot
Lz = Lazio
M = (Abruzzo-)Molise
* = "Pioneer" families: 1920s/1930s, settlers from (Abruzzo-)Molise and Lazio directly related to development of Italian Community (see appendices A, B)
Pt = part
S = sponsors of immigrants, especially in post–WWII period
Twp = township
= descendants still in the area or on the same farm in 1980s
$ = total price paid (most often cash and mortgage)

I. "PIONEERS" AND OTHER PRE–SECOND WORLD WAR
ENTRIES

1928 (29 Feb.) [Only farm not in Essex County]
P/S* INGRATTA, Enrico (Henry, M 1925) and his cousins, Raffaele (Ralph, M 1923) and Giovanni (John, M 1923): partnership (until 1932; see Henry INGRATTA, below); Elgin Cty/ Aldborough Twp (near Rodney) C10/Lt A; 100 ac./$5,000 (vendor: A. Eastlake family and Mary Ross).

2. 1931 (30 Sept.) [Mersea Twp first recorded farm owned by Italians]
   S* DELELLIS, Joseph (Lz via USA 1931 with Molisan wf. and thei chldn) and Alfonse DeLellis: father and son partnership, Essex Cty. Mersea Twp/IC/West 1/2 Lt 2 (N. side IC Rd or Seacliff Dr. W); 37 ac./$12,000 (vendor: Agricultural Development Board).

3. 1934 (24 Dec.) and 1935 (5 Apr.)
   P/S* PANNUNZIO bros "Domenic," i.e., Domenico (M 1923) and Joseph (M 1925) &
   P/S* MASTRONARDI, Luigi (M 1925): partnership – three equal parts (until 5 Mar. 1942: sale to Pannunzio bros); Essex Cty/Mersea Twp/IC/East 1/4 Lt 5, West 1/8 Lt 6 (N. side IC Rd = Seacliff Dr W or Hwy 18 West of Leamington); 1934 purchase: 28 ac./$13,500 (vendor: James and Maude M. Bradford).
   [NB: Second Mersea farm owned by Italians, first greenhouse operation by Italians]

4. 1938 (15 Feb) [returned to USA; farm sold in 1941]
   COLASANTI, Frank (bro. of Alex) (Lz via USA 1930): sole "grantee"; Essex/Mersea [III C E. or North Talbot Rd Concession] South 3/5 of East 1/2 (or S.E. Pt) of Lt no. 240 (N. side of Talbot Rd E. or Hwy 3; S. of "Pere Marquette Rlwy," i.e., Chesapeake & Ohio Rlwy); 25 ac./$7,000 (vendor: Robert J. Grant).

5. 1940 (23 Sept.)
   P/S* MASTRONARDI, Armando and wf. Luisa (M 1925/1930): "joint tenants"; Essex/Mersea/IC/Pt of Lts 1, 2, 3, as per Reg'd Plan No. 440 (S. side II C Rd or Oak St W; N. of present Elliston St, formerly W.E. & L.S. Electric Rlwy or W.E. & L.S. Rapid Rlwy); 25.7 ac./$10,800 (vendor: Stanley Howard & Lila Pearl Ellis).

6. 1940 (18 Oct.) [one of 2 farms not in Mersea Twp; see DIMENNA, Antonio]
   P/S* COLASANTI, Eleuterio (Alex, Lz 1924) and wf. Emma (< USA 1930s): "joint tenants"; Essex/Gosfield S. Twp/III C/S.1/2 Lt 9 (N. side III C Rd; W. of Hwy 3); 19 3/4 ac./$11,950 (vendor: Almina E. Tapping).

7. 1941 (5 Apr.) [early 1960s sold to non-Italians]
   S* MATASSA, Giuseppe (Joseph, Lz 1918?; Montreal/W/L 1920s–30s) and Maria: "joint tenants"; Essex/Mersea Twp/IC/ Lt 13, northerly ten acres of West 1/2 of East 1/2 (S. side IIC Rd or Oak St E., E. of Noble or Bullock Rd); 10 ac./$1,600 (vendor: Reo Clyde and Margaret Williams).

8. 1942 (4 Feb.) [1946: wf. Paolina joint tenant; later sold to
    non-Italians]
    P/S* MOAURO, "Constantina" (i.e., Costantino), Gus Angelo's
    bro., M 1923): sole "grantee"; Essex/Mersea/II C/Lt 5 (N. of
    Talbot Rd; S. of Chesapeake & Ohio Rlwy at Hodgins St);
    approx. 4.5 ac./$3,000 (vendor: Russell J. and Anne Buchanan).
9. 1942 (25 Feb.)
    P/S* MASTRONARDI, Luigi (M 1925), wf. "Palina" (i.e.,
    Paolina) and sons Alfred and Marius (M 1930/1933): "joint ten-
    ants" (see below, C-11, Mastronardi: "transfer"); Essex/Mersea/
    II C/S.W. Pt Lt 2 (N. side II C Rd. = Talbot Rd W. or Hwy 3);
    approx. 12 ac./$12,000 (vendor: Robert and Grace Leslie).
10. 1942 (28 July)
    P/S* INGRATTA, Enrico (Henry, M 1925) and wf. Maria (M
    1930): "joint tenants"; Essex/Mersea/II C/S.W. Pt Lt 2 (N. side
    II C Rd = Talbot Rd W.; E. of L. Mastronardi); approx. 6 ac.
    (?)/$6,000 (vendor: Regina Stegman)
    (see below, C-2, 1950, 13 Oct., "transfer" to sons).
11. 1944 (15 Jan.)
    D.B. [DEL BEL] BELLUZ, Fernando (Fred Belluz, Friuli, via
    Windsor 1920s/1930s?) and wf. Sonia (Urkosky): "joint tenants";
    Essex/Mersea/Concession C/Pt of Lt 13 (S. of I C Rd or Hwy
    18 E., N. of Point Pelee National Park); 35 ac./$1,750 (vendor:
    Annie Urkosky, Sonia's mother).
12. 1944 (13 Oct.) [took possession 1 Mar. 1945; sold 1959]
    P/S* MAGRI, Michael and wf. "Savaria," Saveria (M 1927):
    "joint tenants"; Essex/Mersea [Border III–IV C E.], S. side IVC
    Rd; North Talbot Rd Concession)/Pt N. 1/3 Lt 243; approx. 30
    ac./$7,200 (vendor: Mike and Susan Udak).
13. 1944 (14 Dec.) [in 1970s sold to A. Mastrangelo (M 1952)]
    P/S* MOAURO, Angelo (Gus's bro., M 1923): sole "grantee";
    Essex/Mersea [III C/Lt 4 W. 1/2], i.e., Pt of Lts 3, 4, 5, 6, as per
    Reg'd Plan N. 615 (N. side of Wilkinson Dr. and W. side of
    Morse Ave. [Lane]); 17 ac./$18,700 (vendor: George and Susie
    Harrington).
14. 1945 (13 Mar.) [1950s: "grant" to son John and wf. Mary
    "jointly"]
    P/S* CERVINI, Antonio and wf. Rosa (Lz 1927/39): "joint ten-
    ants"; Essex/Mersea/III C/Pt of farm Lt no. 6 (N. of Wilkinson
    Dr., W. side of Hwy 77 or Erie St N.); 9.6 ac./$7,500 (vendor:
    Ellis Eldon and Olive Mae Scratch).

15. 1945 (20 Oct.) [first farm purchase by "Pioneer" children]
    P* MOAURO, Frank Sr (Gus's son, M 1936) and wf. Ida (M
    1933) (dtr of Luigi Mastronardi): "joint tenants"; Essex/partly
    in Mersea Twp, partly in Town of Leam./II C/Lt 5 (N. of Talbot
    Rd; W. of Michigan Central Rlwy; s. of his father's farm); 8.91
    ac./$4,000 (vendor: C. Hugh and Jenny Read)
    [eventually sold to Town for expansion of Leam. & District High
    School].

16. 1946 (23 Dec.) [2nd farm not in Mersea Twp; see COLASANTI,
    Alex above]
    P/S* DIMENNA, Antonio and wf. "Antionetta," i.e., Antonietta
    (M 1923/36): "joint tenants"; Essex/Gosfield S. Twp/I C Eastern
    Division/Pt Lt 10; Pt Lts 12, 13, 16, 17, 18, as per Reg'd Plan No.
    28 [or 30?]: both sides of Hwy 18 (at Union Ave. or Cty Rd 45);
    7.5 ac./$11,000 (vendor: Mary Alberta Jones).

17. 1948 (19 Oct) [1963: sold to Beato Mastronardi (M 1954) and
    wf. Maria (Gabriele, Lz 1957)]
    S/DELZOTTI (in deed DEL ZOTTI), Peter (region? L 1920s?)
    and wf. Isabella A. Catauro (M 1948/49): "joint tenants": Essex/
    Mersea/III C/farm Lt 6 (W. of Hwy 77 or Erie St N.; approx. 1/2
    km N. of CERVINI); 17 ac./$10,000 (vendor: A. Clarence and
    Gladys Lorraine Stewart).

B. SUMMARY 1928–1948

17 purchases – 16 in Essex Cty; 1 in Elgin Cty
14 of 16 in Mersea Twp; 2 in Gosfield S. Twp
10 of 17 by Molisani; 5 by Laziali; 2 by others
15 of 16 in Essex Cty purchased within 15-year period (1931–46)
11 of 15 by "Pioneer" families: 9 by Molisani; 2 by Laziali
9 of 15 were located in C I/II/III West of Leamington or Mersea Twp W.

C. 1950–1960S SELECTED PURCHASES AND/OR
   TRANSFERS

1. 1950 (12 Jan.) [later sold to non-Italians; see BRUNATO/
   MOAURO, no. 5 below]
   P* MOAURO, Rocco (Angelo's son/M 1938) and wf. Frances
   (b. USA): "joint tenants"; Essex/Mersea/II C/Pt Lt 5 (S. side of
   III C Rd or Wilkinson Dr., W. of "Hodgson," i.e., Hodgins St, N.

of Chesapeake & Ohio Rlwy, S.E. of his father and N. of uncle Gus); approx. 2 ac./$6,600 (vendor: Frank Dyck).

1950 (13 Oct.) (= transfer to sons)
P/S* INGRATTA, Enrico (Henry, M 1925) and wf. Maria (M 1930), "joint tenants": "grant" their farm (see A-10/C II/Lt 2) to sons Marius and Domenic (M 1930) = "joint tenants": mother, father, and sons; approx. 6 ac./$1.00 ("transfer for natural love and affection").

1952 (15 Nov.) [1958: transfer to son Dante and his wf. Lucy for $1.00]
*DIMENNA, Pacifico and wf. Bambina (M 1949/51): "joint tenants"; Essex/Mersea/II C/Lt 5 (S. of Rocco Moauro, N. of Gus Moauro, and N. of Chesapeake & Ohio Rlwy)/approx. 2ac./$7,350 (vendor: Henry and Kate Warkentin) [1991: Dante's widow, Lucy, still in house without land].

1952 (20 Nov.) [later sold to cousin Ralph Sabelli (M 1950); resold to Bruno Colaizzi (M 1968)]
(in deed "DICIOCCO"), Enrico and wf. Pasqualina MOAURO (dtr of Angelo; sister of Rocco) (M 1949): "joint tenants"; Essex/Mersea/II C/Lt 5 (E. of her bro. Rocco's land, see above); approx. 1 ac./$7,000 (?) (vendor: Edward and Margaret Millor or Miller).

1953 (25 Apr.)
*BRUNATO, John (b. Canada) and MOAURO, Rocco: partnership (till 25 May 1957: thereafter owned by Brunato); Essex/Mersea/III C/Pt Lt 1 (N. of III C Rd or Wilkinson Dr.; E. of Albuna Townline Rd or Cty Rd 31, boundary between Mersea and Gosfield S. Twps); 10.45 ac./$10,500 (vendor: Nelson LeRoy and Nora Cook).

1953 (1 Oct.) [formerly owned by C. Harvey Hilborn; original farm 25 ac.]
S* CACCIAVILLANI, Floyd (M 1948) with father Corrado CACCIAVILLANI (M 1949) and mother-in-law Fedela (née INGRATTA) MASTRONARDI (M 1950): "grantees"; Essex/Mersea/IIC/E. Pt Lt 3, Lt 4(?) (N. side of Talbot or Hwy 3 W.; N. and S. sides of Chesapeake & Ohio Rlwy); 39.5 ac./$39,000 (vendor: Ljubomir and Ljubica Rusnov).

1953 (19 Oct.) [took possession in early 1954; sold, less house, to son Gerald, 23 Mar. 1984]
P/S* PANNUNZIO, Gino (M 1931) (Domenic's son) and wf. Elaine (née Giuliano, in USA, of Molisan origin): "joint tenants";

Essex/Mersea/I C/Pt of Lt 5 (N. of I C Rd = Seacliff Dr. W. or Hwy 18 W.; W. of PANNUNZIO Bros farm (I C/Lt 5); 9.45 ac./$17,000 (vendor: Ivan E. and Margaret M. Kennedy) [NB: 1980s: covered greenhouse from 61,000 sq. ft. to 2.5 ac. with tomatoes].

8. 1955 (7 Nov.)
P* MAGRI, Dominic (son of Michael and Saveria, M 1927) and wf. Loretta (Lz 1939) (dtr of Antonio Cervini): "joint tenants"; Essex/Mersea/II C/W. Pt Lt 3 (S. side III C Rd or Wilkinson Dr.); 10 ac./$15,250 (vendor: Louis and Elizabeth Dragomir).

9. 1957 (30 July)
* SABELLI, Domenico (Gus Moauro's nephew, M 1952), his father Stefano and wf. Maria; Essex/Mersea/II C/Lt 5 (N. of uncle Gus, separated by Chesapeake & Ohio Rlwy & S. of Pacifico & Bambina DiMenna); 2.36 ac./$17,500 (vendor: Diedrich A. Froese).

10. 1957 (3 Oct.) [1991: covered greenhouse 57,000 sq. ft; tomatoes up to 1.5 ac.]
P/S* DIMENNA, Gino (M 1936) (son of Antonio/Tony, M 1923) and bro-in-law Joe MARCOVECCHIO (M 1950) [wives are sisters]; partnership (until 1978: bought by Gino) Essex/Gosfield S. Twp/I C Eastern Division/Pt Lt 9, 10 (N. of Hwy 18; E. of Union Ave. or Cty Rd 45; across from Gino's father); 7.5 ac./$17,000 (vendor: Frank and Marion Moody).

11. 1969 (5 Sept.) (= transfer)
P/S* Luigi MASTRONARDI (M 1925) transfers to son Mario (M 1933); 1/4 of his 1/3 interest in approx. 12 ac. farm (II C/ Lt 2; see A-9) bought in 1942 at $12,000; in 1969 valued at $127,512; ac.?/$NIL ("transfer for natural love and affection").

Notes

PREFACE

1 Vecoli, "Report on the Status of the Italian American Ethnic Group."

INTRODUCTION

1 Ricci, *Radici.*
2 One of the first immigrants, Domenic Pannunzio, passed away in 1983, shortly after the interview was recorded. See also Ricci, *Radici,* v.
3 Harney, *Topics for Discussion.*
4 The exact number of Italian families (or individuals) in the larger Leamington area could not be established with certainty, particularly for lack of continuity in the research (interviews and contacts). As a result, a discrepancy may have crept into the number of families listed among those not having participated in the interviews. In some cases, for example, because one adult member of the family was interviewed but not the other, the families appeared in the list of those non-participating. Nevertheless, whether the Italian families in the Leamington area total 550 or 560, as reported, and whether the number of those interviewed is over 430 or over 440, the ratio on which the study is based remains constant: about 78 per cent of the total. Ricci, *Radici,* i–ix, and appendices A, B.
5 The students' dedication may also be illustrated by their willingness to accept a cut in their allotment for travel expenses. Ricci, *Radici,* i, v.
6 Ricci, *Radici,* iii.
7 Harney, *Oral Testimony and Ethnic Studies,* 1.
8 All references to Braudel's work derive from Braudel, "The 'New History.'"

9   Streuver, *The Language of History in the Renaissance*, 3, 63, and front and
    back inside jackets.
10 Garin, *Medioevo e Rinascimento*, 206–8.
11 Tateo, *I centri culturali dell'Umanesimo*, 10–11, 59, note.
12 Panofsky, *Meaning in the Visual Arts*, 5.
13 Eco, *Postscript to The Name of the Rose*, 75. See also "Postille a 'il nome
    della rosa' 1983.
14 Proctor, Introduction, *Education's Great Amnesia*, xv, xviii.
15 McLuhan, *Understanding Media*), 300–11.
16 In one of his posthumously published essays, "If One Were to Write a
    History of Postwar Toronto Italia," Robert F. Harney discussed the difficulty
    in choosing a method or an approach common to "all historians asked to
    deal with a looming recent past [such as the immigrant experience] in which
    trends seem inchoate and random facts defiant of encodation in an interpret
    ative narrative." Harney was himself "in search of what Hayden White has
    called an emplotment, a particular and appropriate story form, in which to
    fit the facts ... so that they offer more than merely a chronicle and transform
    themselves into 'a comprehensible drama of development,' which [Harney
    referred] to as a narrative." Harney also pointed out "the allusion to Italo
    Calvino's *If on a Winter's Night a Traveller*" recognizable "in the style of the
    title for [his own] essay. From the title," Harney continued, "[one] should
    gather either that I believe that I have failed to find an emplotment that
    works, or that I am content to suggest some of the many narratives that
    seem possible, or that I have for myself a deeper narrative in my encounter
    with the chaotic mass of source material, memory culture and folk wisdom
    which exists." The traditional literary genres are recalled to explain certain
    historical events and views: "Of the four or five standard types of emplot-
    ment for narrative – romance, tragedy, comedy, epic and farce or satire,"
    Harney stated, "the one most appropriate to [a particular] view is tragedy."
    Even the title of the volume where Harney's essays appear "was inspired by
    the Pasolini poem 'Prophecy.'" *From the Shores of Hardships*, ix, xi, note 1,
    75–103. See also chapter 15, especially "*Lives of the Saints* as a 'Story of
    Emigration-Migration.'"
17 Pei, *The Story of Language*, 210–16. See also chapter 12, "Language
    Awareness, Education and Identity."
18 Sister Ann Leonard, "Language and Literature in a Multicultural
    Curriculum."
19 Tateo, *I centri culturali*, 59 and note 6; Braudel, "New History," 32; Taylor
    The Ethics of Authenticity, quoted in Alan Ryan, "Don't Think for
    Yourself Unless You Can," *New York Times Book Review*, 27 September
    1992; and Taylor, *Reconciling the Solitudes*, 200.

20 Craig, Graham, Kagan, Ozment, and Turner, "Preface," *The Heritage of World Civilizations*, xxvii–xxx.

21 Garin applies this phrase to the "virtue" or ability of the fifteenth-century Italian humanists, particularly Leon Battista Alberti (1404–72), who embodies "the serene certainty of the secure builder of his own world." For Garin, Alberti is "a *poet*, that is, a *creator* … quite aware of the whole risk that creating implies … of the transitoriness of all constructions," of the uncertainty of life or that life is change. But in the vortex of the river of life, continues Garin, "a serene and free spirit, with the help of the *bonae artes* [humanistic studies], will be able to keep himself within the limits, and thus hold on more firmly and longer." *Medioevo e Rinascimento*, 93–5.

22 Garin, ed., *L'uomo del Rinascimento*, 1–12. "For Leonardo Bruni [1370–1444]," Garin also states, "culture is *humanitas* and therefore community … Bruni's ideal was to use *humanae litterae* and *studia humanitatis* as a means for the education of the complete man." In conclusion, if humanism consisted in a renewed confidence in man and his possibilities and in an appreciation of man's activity in every possible sense [then] it is only fair to give Humanism credit for the new methods of scientific investigation, the renewed vision of the world and the new attitude towards objects." And recalling the words of Augustin Renaudet that "the Italy of the Renaissance unites in herself all manner of conflicts," Garin states that because of the new awareness the "man of the Renaissance was indeed a living synthesis, a meeting-point, a mediator" between the increasingly explored physical world and the still honoured divinity. "The Renaissance succeeded in bringing about a new harmony … the Renaissance was the dawn of modern thought and the whole of Europe in the 16th century was full of echoes of Italian culture." Garin, *L'umanesimo italiano*, 48, 257–8.

23 In 1392, Coluccio Salutati wrote a letter that Garin defines as "a distinguished monument of his thought." Salutati praised "history [as] the educator of humanity, the source of [concrete] knowledge … the true creator of the individual, for humanity consists, above all, in the recollection of human actions in this world and for this reason history is a kind of 'philanthropy,' an encounter and a dialogue with all human beings. Civilization takes shape and politics are defined through the dimensions of history … It cannot be a surprise," Garin adds, "that the first historian in the modern sense of the word was the great pupil and friend of Salutati, Leonardo Bruni … Poliziano wrote some pages that contain not only a grand lesson for mankind, but also define a method valid for any kind of research. In reading those pages one understands why the Renaissance was not only an age of artists, but also an age of scientists like Toscanelli and Galilei." In fact, Garin states, "The science of both Leonardo and Galilei originated

precisely in that age ... that Machiavelli wrote during that very age and that the whole critical ferment that led to Bacon and Telesio took place at that time ... neither Erasmus nor Montaigne could ever have been thought of without the specific mental climate of the 15th century ... And in view of this rigorous (one is tempted to say pitiless) critique [that emerged from these schools of philology], one can understand, finally, the doubt of Descartes. Garin, *L'umanesimo italiano*, 3–4, 9, 18–19; Garin, *Italian Humanism*, 3, 7–8, 17.

24 According to A. William Salomone,

The true innovator, the real founder of an epochal "new science" of history, was ... Giambattista Vico (1668–1744). And Vico's *Scienza Nuova* [*New Science*, 1725] ... is, first of all, a fascinating illustration of the real difference between mathematical and poetic truth – its parts add up to more than the whole! ... A key to Vico's method in the *Scienza Nuova* lives in his statement that, for the purposes of his investigation, he will assume that there are no more books in the world. This makes for an inversion of the Cartesian *tabula rasa*, and it alone can serve as a new beginning to reconstruct the origins and earliest developments of human history ... Vico reconstructs the three basic principles of all human societies ...: the sentiment or idea of divinity, or the gods or of God; the evolution of marriage-rites as consecration of the nuclear social group in the family; and the burial of the dead ... as the organic cord between the living and the dead ... In the *Scienza Nuova*, the history of mankind is the history of the rise, development and decay of societies and nations, of cultures and civilizations.

But Vico, who has a Renaissance humanistic view of humanity, also states that human beings "are not ... doomed [to a fatal spiral of course and recourse in their history] since history is really an intricate and infinite tragicomedy of errors in which ends and means are often confused and at variance or obscure. But history is never beyond the partial dominion of those who make it." Salomone, "From the Crisis of the Renaissance," 108–11. For Vico as a renewer of the humanistic tradition and method, including his opposition to Descartes, see Garin, *Medioevo e Rinascimento*, 8–12, 40–1, 78–9, 96–7, 100–1, and particularly 126–7. See also Croce, *La Filosofia di Giambattista Vico*, 135–43.

25 Feyerabend, "How to Defend Society against Science."

26 Braudel, "'New History,'" 31–2.

27 Nader, "End of the Old World."

28 Ibid., especially 794, and 504–25; Mignolo, "The Darker Side of the Renaissance." See also Braudel, "'New History,'" 30–2.

29 Struever, *Language of History*, 15, 17, 43, 151.

30 The testimonies of the migrants, their "accounts ... of minute and personal vicissitudes [become not only an epic narrative, a saga, but] also a source of great significance for that other alternative history that is gradually overturning the field of vision of traditional historiography ... Beyond any likely pathetic aspect [the] documents [serve also as] alternative sources of great importance for the 'reconstruction from the grassroots' of the history of our [Italian] emigration." Cresci and Guidobaldi, eds., *Partono i basti-menti*, jacket, 5, 17, translation mine.

31 A good example of the power of intuitive knowledge, though unfortu-nately referring to a hideous crime and practice, can be found in Tierney: A "noted biblical scholar Hyam Maccoby [concluded in his book *The Sacred Executioner*] that Cain was indeed the hero in the original telling of Genesis" and that his "killing of his brother was not a senseless homicide but the primeval sacrifice that secured the civilization of the human race. Intuitively, [the Aymara Indian shaman with the alias Maximo] Coa reached the same conclusion as [the scholar] Maccoby." Tierney, "Sacrificial Lam," 32, 67; Braudel, "'New History,'" 32; Struever, *Language of History*, 3, 12, 18.

32 "Since science has begun to distrust general explanations and solutions that are not sectorial and specialized, the grand challenge for literature is to be capable of weaving together the various branches of knowledge, the various 'codes,' into a manifold and multifaceted vision of the world." Italo Calvino, *Six Memos for the Next Millennium*, 112. "For better or worse, language always brings us back to literature" and "the road to the critical spirit of science is entangled, in the end, in the words of literature, which teach us how to see and how to understand the new, even when it seems old. That today's scientific knowledge cannot do without imagination is a precept that comes to us from the scientific community itself ... Indeed [as Octavio Paz stated], 'language is not only the man but also the world.'" Raimondi, "Language and the Hermeneutic Adventure"; see also chapter 12, especially note 42. For Northrop Frye, "Literature leads us ... towards the regaining of identity ... Literature ... is not a dream world: it's two kinds of dreams, a wish-fulfillment dream and an anxiety dream, that are focussed together, like a pair of glasses, and become a fully conscious vision." According to Borklund, that statement

leads directly to Frye's conception of the purpose or final cause of litera-ture. By imagining what we want – and don't want – we move closer to the goal of life, which for Frye is the free, humane community of men. The ethical goal of liberal education ... "is to liberate ... to make one capable of conceiving society as free, classless, and urbane. No such society exists, which is one reason why a liberal education must be deeply concerned with works of imagination" ... The myths of a given culture, including our own, are always incomplete and tend to make us intolerant of differing imaginative visions. Thus by teaching [or utilizing] imaginative works from the past and from different cultures we not only keep our students' [and our own] imaginations open and flexible, we also "teach [or increase] the ability to be aware of one's imaginative social vision, and so escape the prison of social conditioning." What we teach in the humanities, properly conceived of, is "some aspect of the freedom of man." No social vision is definitive, Frye concludes: "There is always more outside it." And therefore the proper experience of literature helps us to be "continually expanding and reshaping that vision." See Borklund, *Contemporary Literary Critics*, 216–17. See also Frye, "*Il Cortegiano*"; and "'Key to Education' Is Love of Learning," interview with Frye by Louise Browne and Bill Schiller, *Toronto Star* (*Sunday Star*), 10 May 1987, A1, A10.

33 "Widely regarded as the most brilliant theoretical physicist since Einstein," Stephen Hawking, author of the phenomenal bestseller *A Brief History of Time*, stated, "I rely on intuition a great deal. I try to guess a result, but then I have to prove it." Thus, by joining "intuition ... theory" and logical "proof," Hawking has been able "to reveal an extraordinary array of possibilities for our understanding of the universe." Hawking's method is not unlike that of literature as outlined by Italo Calvino, Ezio Raimondi, and Northrop Frye. See Hawking, *Black Holes and Baby Universes*, inside front jacket, 158, 171.

34 Struever, *Language of History*, 16–17, 77, 88. See also Temelini, review of *The Language of History*.

35 Eco, *Postscript to The Name of the Rose*, 59.

CHAPTER ONE

Partly presented as a paper at the Third Annual Symposium on Italian Canadiana (University of Toronto, 16 May 1986), and subsequently published as Walter Temelini, "Study of an Agricultural Community: The Italians of Leamington," Italian Canadiana 3, no. 1 (Spring 1987): 80–91.

1 Spada, *The Italians in Canada*, 301–3.

2 Ibid., 301–3.

3 Henceforth "South Italy," "the South of Italy," "the Italian South," or "southern Italy" will include Sicily, unless a clear distinction is necessary

between the continental regions of the South and the island region(s); and it will coincide with the "South Italy Investment Fund" designation of the general area, i.e., from Lower Lazio and Lower Marche (or the Marches) to and including Sicily and Sardinia; also, the form "(Abruzzo-) Molise" will be used to indicate that "Molise" was the area of origin of most of the 1920s to 1963 immigrants from "Abruzzo-Molise" (or "Abruzzi e Molise") which formed a single region until 1963. See *La Cassa per il Mezzogiorno*, documentazione per i partecipanti alla Conferenza Nazionale per l'Emigrazione, Rome, 24 February–1 March 1975, 4; Gambino, *Una finestra sul Mezzogiorno d'Italia*, 5–6; and "La Regione Molise," in *Vita italiana: documenti e informazioni* (Rome: Presidenza del Consiglio dei Ministri, 1984), 69–71. For the use of the form *Abruzzo* or *Abruzzi*, see chapter 2, note 32. See also chapter 7, "Post-Fascist Italy."

For a general overview, with statistics and charts of the Italian migration flux – expatriation, repatriation – between 1876 and 1976, and for more specific periods and related issues, see Rosoli, ed., *Un secolo di emigrazione italiana*, which includes French and English summaries for each of the various essays.

Even Spada – who boasted about the Italians' ability to transform any piece of land into "vineyards and orchards," of their control of the "best vineyards" in British Columbia and Ontario, and of their being "pioneers of wine making and fruit growing" in the Niagara Peninsula and the Leamington-Kingsville area – wrote, "No, the Italian is not a farmer ... The idea that the Italian is a farmer in Canada is not substantiated by facts. He is the enemy of the soil ... Of many who went west for gangwork, very few settled on the land, and even fewer remained on their homestead. Canadian farming there was not for Italians" (*Italians*, 80–1, 301–3).

Morrison, *Garden Gateway to Canada*, 1; *Leamington-Mersea Souvenir History*, 49; Essex County (Ontario) Tourist Association, *Essex County Sketches*, 5–6. See also chapters 5, 8 (especially notes 17, 18).

According to Spada, "The last failure in Italian farm settlement occurred in 1923 in the Trout Creek and Huntsville area in Ontario." While "Carlo Lamberti became a sponsor of the experiment," Carlo Allegretti of Huntsville "obtained a permit from the land settlement of Ontario" and contracts for fifty "farm hands from the rice fields of Lombardy" (northwest Italy). But when "those small contracts were over," the men "were released from obligations to settle the land" and left the area. "Some went to ... Montreal, others remained in Ontario; a few returned to Italy" (*Italians*, 82–3). In comparison, see the story of Tontitown and the "rebels of

Arkansas": At the end of the nineteenth century, Father Bandini and a group
of fifty Italian families left Sunny Side Company and moved to a northwest
area of Arkansas, bought 900 acres of land, and founded Tontitown, in honour of Enrico Tonti, called "the father of Arkansas." The experiment was a
complete success, as photos show: they built houses, stores, a school, and a
church; they developed a vegetable farm (with seeds from Italy) and a dairy
production centre to make "Tontitown a model agricultural community."
Cresci and Guidobaldi, *Partono i bastimenti*, 66–7.

8 *Campanilismo* (from *campanile*, bell tower, and *ismo*, ism), used also to
describe interregional rivalry and North-South hostility, refers mainly to
the attitude of Italian immigrants toward their *paese* or village of origin,
particularly manifested in their attempts to recreate its *ambiente* or hometown environment by grouping around a church, a club, or a patron saint
in specific areas of North American cities, the Little Italies. "*Campanilismo*
for the immigrants was a source of strength and comfort. By banding
together with their *paesani* they achieved a degree of security in a hostile
environment. But it is difficult to understand how a half century later their
children and grandchildren are still in the grip of such a parochial view of
the world." In other words, chronic *campanilismo* can be quite an obstacle
to the development of the individual and the community. It can generate
divisions in the community through the proliferation of regional and
hometown clubs and associations, prevent the establishment of a larger
Italian cultural and community centre, which can serve and speak for all
the community, especially in matters common to all, and in accordance
with the old principle of *divide et impera* – divide and rule – it can also
lead to exploitation. See Vecoli, "A Report on the Status of the Italian
American Ethnic Group"; W. Temelini, "Little Italies in North America";
Robert F. Harney, "Toronto's Little Italy, 1885–1945," in Harney and
Scarpaci, eds, *Little Italies in North America*, 44–5; and Harney, *Dalla
frontiera alle Little Italies*, 238–40. See also Romano, *Storia d'Italia dal
Risorgimento ai nostri giorni*, 38–9.

9 Windsor, with an Italian community of approximately 19,000 people (7.7
per cent of total population) in the 1980s, had five major Italian clubs:
Caboto, Calabria, Ciociaro, Fogolar Furlan, and Sicilia. Only the Caboto
Club, the largest and oldest (established 1925), has a pan-Italian membership. The Calabria Club, which was also open to all Italians, closed in the
1980s; and later so did the Sicilia Club. Other regional and provincial
groups have associations but not centres (Partenope-Campania, Puglia,
Vicentini, Trentini). In Essex County, besides the Leamington Roma Club,
there is also the Verdi Club in Amherstburg (eighteen kilometres from

Windsor). See Statistics Canada, *1981 Census*; and Temelini, "The Italians in Windsor."

10 Barzini, *The Italians*, 306–7; and Romano, *Storia d'Italia*, 21.

11 The "two cultures" of Italy came into full view soon after Italian unification (1860–3): "The Piedmontese armies ... came into contact with a social and cultural reality radically different from their own ... They were learning ... that Italy had been for centuries divided 'into two worlds, on one side [the North] the Germanic-Roman cycle, on the other [the South] the Byzantine-Islamic world,' in keeping with the words of the first Italian Marxist, Antonio Labriola." Romano, *Storia d'Italia*, 30–1; translation mine.

12 The North uses *terrone* and *cafone* (rube, ignorant peasant, boor) for the Southerners. The South uses *polentone* (*polenta* or corn mush eater, big lump of cornmeal) for the Northerners (see Cresci and Guidobaldi, *Partono i bastimenti*, 193). Twenty-five years or so after Barzini's comments on "the *Problema del Mezzogiorno*" (*Italians*, 244–61), the gap between North and South is far from being bridged: Italy is still "divided into two distinct countries ... two Italies," and the Italian South is "lagging behind in the process of European integration." Mattioli, "Italia del Nord"; Martino, "I ritardi del Mezzogiorno italiano" (translation mine). See also Villari, ed., *Il Sud*, 2:712–34; Tucci, *L'Italia dimezzata*, 3–4; Capecelatro, *Il linciaggio del mezzogiorno*, 20–2; and *Economist*, "North-South," 30–1.

13 Salvadori, "Italy as a Country of Regions"; Hearder and Waley, eds, *A Short History of Italy*, 8–12, 28–75, 153–5; Hearder, *Italy*, 66–82. "By the thirteenth century the glory of Amalfi was no more than a memory, and most of the trade of the southern ports had got into the hands of the Pisans, the Genoese and the Venetians." Procacci, *History of the Italian People*, 37, 17–22.

14 Valeri, ed., *Storia d'Italia*, 1:26–8; Hearder, *Italy*, 40.

15 On 18 February 1984 a new treaty was signed to replace one signed in 1929 when Mussolini, in order to secure support for his regime, guaranteed the church numerous privileges. As a result, among other stipulations, the "Catholic religion" ceased to be the "only religion of the Italian State"; matrimonial legislation was no longer an exclusive ecclesiastical jurisdiction; the teaching of religion in the schools was no longer compulsory; and church property on Italian soil not used as places of worship were subject to Italian fiscal policies. "La Regione Abruzzi," *Vita italiana*, Anno 34, nos 2–3 (February–March 1984): 3–16; "La Regione Sicilia," *Vita italiana*, Anno 34, no. 12 (December 1984): 35–59; and *La Gazzetta*, "La revisione del Concordato," 17 February 1984, 5; "Ansafoto," Agenzia Ansa, Rome, 18 February 1984.

16 Procacci, *History*, 324–5. For Sergio Romano, the official definition of the "first war of united Italy ... as a vast, necessary police operation" was as "partial and exaggerated" as the definition it provoked among "the democratic historians of this [twentieth] century" for whom "the war in the southern regions became ... a 'war of secession,' similar to the [American Civil War]" (*Storia d'Italia*, 24–8). Nevertheless, according to Rosario Villari, after the former Bourbon Kingdom of Naples (and Sicily) voted by plebiscite for union with the North (October 1860), the new Italian state, influenced by the oligarchic tendencies, reneged on the promises to grant "a real *self-government* to the [southern] regions and provinces," and by discrediting Giuseppe Garibaldi, the liberator of half of Italy, destroyed the good will of the southern population toward the North: "The break in the link between the *Mezzogiorno* and the [Garibaldian] democratic revolution [produced] a climate of resentment, hostility and hatred against the new administrators, and marked the beginning of perhaps the most tragic and painful page in our [Italian] national history." *Mezzogiorno e contadini nell'età moderna*, 250–9; translation mine. Similar ideas have been also reflected in southern literary works. The Sicilian writer Giovanni Verga (1840–1922) has the simple village people in one of his novels attribute many of their misfortunes to Italian unification and even to Garibaldi, who had become identified with the northern oppressors; others blamed the steamboats for the disappearance of fish in their waters, or the telegraph wires for carrying away all the rain. Though they may be viewed as anti-progress attitudes, the statements nevertheless indicate the feelings of simple folk toward a new distant lord whose policies were destroying their families and their traditional way of life. Verga, *I Malavoglia*, 41–2, 64–7; Verga, *The House by the Medlar Tree*, 18, 33–5. Even today one can still hear southern Italians say that Garibaldi should have proclaimed a separate independent state of "South Italy," rather than hand over the territories won by him and his thousand volunteers to Victor Emmanuel, king of Piedmont. See also chapter 3 and notes.

17 Villari, *Il Sud*, 2:516.

18 For the effects of emigration on the South, see Rosoli, *Un secolo*; especially Luigi Favero and Graziano Tassello, "Cent'anni di emigrazione italiana (1876–1976)," 9–64; Eugenia Malfatti, "L'emigrazione italiana e il Mezzogiorno," 97–116; Francesco P. Cerase, "Economia precaria ed emigrazione," 117–52; Antonio Golini, "Migrazioni interne, distribuzione della popolazione e urbanizzazione in Italia," 153–87, who points out that as a result of emigration, Molise by 1971 was left with half the population the region should have had in the most productive age bracket, twenty-five to thirty-four years (168); and Anna Maria Birindelli, G. Gesano, and E.

Sonnino, "Lo spopolamento in Italia nel quadro dell'evoluzione migratoria e demografica (1871–1971)," 189–251, who quote popular sayings and songs to illustrate southern Italy's loss of its "young men" and the depopulation phenomenon (230, 236 respectively):

Cristofiru Culumbu, chi facisti?
La megghiu giuvintù tu rruvinasti.
Christopher Columbus, what have you done?
You've destroyed the best of our young ones.
(Calabria)
Nebbi' a la valle e nebbi' a la muntagne
ne le campagne nun ce sta nesciune.
Fog in the valley and fog on the mountain
in the countryside there is no one left.
(Abruzzo)

In referring to the Italian migrant workers in Canada at the beginning of the twentieth century, Robert F. Harney also stated that "the bulk of these newcomers were young men." "Italians in Canada," 229.

19 Procacci, *History*, 326; Cerase, "Economia precaria ed emigrazione," 151–2; Tucci, *L'Italia dimezzata*, 94.

20 Rosoli, *Un secolo*, "Presentazione" (translation mine). See also Harney, "Italians in Canada," 226–9, 242–3; Sturino, "Italians," 2:1059–1100.

21 For lack of complex and consistent data, there are many discrepancies in the number of Italians or Italian Canadians present in Canada in the late twentieth century, and the rank they occupy as a group. According to the 1981 census, the Italian group consisted of 747,970 people (indicating "single" ethnic origin) or of 871,735 people (if included are the 123,765 who "combined 'Italian' with some 'other' origin"): the group thus represented 3.1 or 3.6 per cent of the Canadian population and the fourth-largest group after the British (40.2 per cent), the French (26.7 per cent), and the Germans (4.7 per cent). See Statistics Canada, "Population by Selected Ethnic Origins, Canada, Provinces and Territories (1981)," *Canada Update from the 1981 Census*, 26 April 1983, 1–2; see also Jansen, *Italians in a Multicultural Canada*, 1:113–15. According to Harney, "The Italians have recently taken their place as one of the largest ethnocultural groups after the British and French ... The most recent [1977] census seems to indicate that the Italian ethnic group will soon be the largest in the country except for the English and French." Harney, "Frozen Wastes," 115, and 129, note 1. "Official statistics put the number of Italian immigrants who came to Canada at 800 000. No one is sure how many Canadians today [in 1979] are of Italian ancestry. A conservative estimate is 2 500 000." Mastrangelo, *The Italian Canadians*, 57. For Bruti Liberati, the number of Italians in Canada is "più di un milione

[more than one million]." Bruti Liberati, "Gli Italiani in Canada," 12. Others
wrote, "Oggi gli italiani in Canada sono un milione [Today the Italians in
Canada are one million]." Di Michele and Pirone, "Album degli Italiani,"
164; and Clivio noted that by June 1982 "the population of Italian origin
residing in Canada was estimated – according to the latest Census data – at
1,049,600 units." Clivio, "Su alcune caratteristiche dell'italiese di Toronto,"
483. In the late 1980s Sturino wrote that Italian Canadians at "three-
quarters of a million [formed Canada's fourth-largest ethnic group follow-
ing] the British, French and Germans ... almost seventy per cent of the
Italian Canadians [were] post–WWII immigrants or their descendants."
Sturino, foreword to *Canadese*. One reason for the different figures and esti-
mates may be the different readings and interpretations of the census data.
The 1986 census statistics give the number of Italians in Canada, single origin: 709,950; number of Italians in Canada, multiple origin, 297,325, for a
total of the two figures of 1,007,275. "Statistics on migration are generally
unreliable and, for a number of reasons, the Canadian figures are particularly difficult to read." Harney, "Italians in Canada," 229; see also Rosoli,
"Presentazione," *Un secolo*, 5–8; and Jansen and LaCavera, *Fact-Book on
Italians in Canada*. See also chapter 2, "The Molisani: Flight from *Miseria* or
Search for *Fortuna*?"

22 By the time of the First World War, Italians were also to be found in
smaller Canadian centres across Canada: "in Sydney (NS), Welland, Sault
Ste Marie and Copper Cliff (ON) and Trail (BC)"; see Sturino, "Italians."
Today they are well established in all ten provinces of Canada and the
Northwest Territories. Sestieri Lee, "From Tuscany to the Northwest
Territories." See also Vangelisti, *Gli italiani in Canada*, 69–70.

23 See Harney and Scarpaci, eds, *Little Italies in North America*, particularly
introduction, and the articles on the Little Italies of Toronto, Montreal,
and some American cities. In 1981, according to census figures, "74 per
cent of Italians in Canada [lived in urban areas of 500,000 or more,
against 41 per cent of total population of Canada]. In all urban areas the
respective proportions were, total: 75 per cent, Italians: 95 per cent. In
Quebec, nearly all Italians (96 per cent) lived in Montreal, 61 per cent of
Ontario's Italians lived in Toronto with a further 34 per cent in other
urban areas and 58 per cent of British Columbia's Italians lived in
Vancouver with a further 32 per cent in other urban areas." Jansen,
Italians in a Multicultural Canada, 116.

24 Sturino referred to Italian "agricultural colonies ... established at Lorette,
Man, and Hylo, Alta." But he gave no indication of their present existence
("Italians"). See also Harney, "Italians in Canada," 229 and 237; Harney
and Troper, *Immigrants*, v. Helling, *A Socio-Economic History of*

German-Canadians, 34–48; and Lehr and Moodie, "The Polemics of Pioneer Settlement."

25   At the turn of the century, Anglo-Canadians ... fitted [Italian immigrants] into two basic occupational stereotypes: Italians were either gangs of migrant railway navvies or they were street vendors and entertainers. In Volume 7 of Shortt and Doughty's *Canada and Its Provinces*, the most magisterial social study of life in Canada produced before the First World War, the point was made baldly: "If we except the hand-organ man and the fruit-dealer practically all [Italians] are engaged at work as navies. In every city you see them digging drains; on railway construction from the Atlantic to the Pacific their services are eagerly sought."
      Harney, "Italians in Canada," 231–2.
      In the volume published in Italian, Harney offered a meaning for *navvy* (translation mine):
      Navvy is a Canadian [English] term borrowed from the motherland, which apparently did not become part of American usage. A *navvy* was a labourer employed in construction or in ditchdigging, usually on railroads, bridges and roads. The *navvy* was considered an emigrant, not a settler; an industrial not a rural worker; a necessity for the economy but not a desirable immigrant. The destiny and growth of Italian communities in Canada were inextricably tied to the *navvy* stereotype. Even if not all *navvies* were Italians, the majority of the new Italian immigrants were considered as such because [in the words of the superintendent of immigration in Ottawa, W.D. Scott]: "The Italian is a good navy. He obeys the orders of the boss. He is not anxious to go on strike ..." For this reason Canadian capitalists, in spite of the fact that the government showed preference for North Europeans, needed the Italian emigrant workers.
      Harney, *Dalla frontiera alle Little Italies*, 218 and 301, note 12. See also Harney, "Toronto's Little Italy, 1885–1945," in Harney and Scarpaci, *Little Italies*, 47–8; and Zucchi, *Italians in Toronto*, 68–73.

26   Procacci, *History*, 100–48. In spite of conflicts and rivalries, the wealth and learning accumulated by the Italian cities since the eleventh century had made Italy, between 1450 and 1550, the leader, innovator, "initiatrix," "the teacher of Europe" in letters, arts, and sciences; and the Italian *Quattrocento* (fifteenth century) in spite of "spiritual deterioration, moral turpitude and political corruption ... one of the most resplendent periods in the history of mankind." See Mandrou, *From Humanism to Science, 1480–1700*, 17–27; Hearder and Waley, *Short History of Italy*, 93; and Cantarella, *The Italian Heritage*, 74.

27   Procacci, *History*, 111–13, 122, 132–6.

28 Hale, ed., *Guicciardini*, 85–9; Machiavelli, *The Prince*, chap. 26; Skinner, *Machiavelli*, 31–47; Salomone, "From the Crisis of the Renaissance," 95–100; Roeder, *The Man of the Renaissance*, vii; and Cochrane, *Historians and Historiography*, especially book 3, "La Calamità d'Italia," 163ff.

29 Salomone, "From the Crisis of the Renaissance," 96–7; *Guicciardini*, xviii–xix. Besides the Florentines, "already early in the fourteenth century, we find a Genoese, Manuele Pessagno, as admiral of the king of Portugal, and another, Enrico Marchese, building ships on the Seine for Philippe Le Bel. They were the forbears of a Genoese progeny that includes Christopher Columbus, who discovered America for the King of Spain." Procacci, *History*, 46. See also Goldthwaite, *The Building of Renaissance Florence*, 31–5, 44–5; Lipinsky, *Giovanni da Verrazzano*, 5; Mann, *Petrarch*, 3–9; chapter 14, "Community Self-Identity," especially note 4; and chapter 1.

30 Giovanni Caboto, who in 1496 had obtained a "royal decree, with exclusive rights to sail west and north to search for new lands," but no royal funds for his first voyage in 1497, "prepared for [his great] expedition at his own expense or with the help of friends." Though the evidence is inconclusive, it seems that both Giovanni Caboto and one of his sons, Sante, met "a tragic end, in December 1498 [at Grates Cove near Grates Point, Newfoundland, between Conception Bay and Trinity Bay]." Menchini, *Giovanni Caboto*, 65, 112–14, 122–36. Others disagree or state simply that Caboto "is not heard of after March 1499." Langer, ed., *An Encyclopedia of World History: Ancient*, 367; and Vangelisti, *Gli italiani in Canada*, 14–17. Similarly Verrazzano, at least in the second voyage in 1526, "participates ... not only as [principal] helmsman but also as entrepreneur"; and he also meets a tragic end: during his third and last voyage, Verrazzano and six of his men were captured and eaten by cannibals on an island of the West Indies, probably Guadeloupe. Menchini, *Giovanni da Verrazzano*, 85, 196–7, 212–13. See also Lipinsky, *Verrazzano*, 5–6; Harney, "Italians in Canada," 225–6; and Migliorini, *The Italian Language*, 234–5.

31 Cantarella, *Italian Heritage*, 118–19. Procacci states, "Historians are now more cautious in speaking of a decline in Mediterranean trade during the sixteenth century," of a sudden decrease of "the role of mediators between East and West that the Mediterranean sailors had held for centuries," or of a drastic "decline of the Italian ports' trading activities" as a result of "the development of Atlantic and colonial trade." Procacci, *History*, 149–52. Yet Procacci also points out that "following a tendency that can already be traced in the fifteenth century, the Venetian nobility converted into land more of the wealth it had won by trade, and Venice's whole economy

increasingly withdrew from sea to land. As this happened, the conservative nature of the solution adopted after Agnadello [had] paralyzing results." Thus "the history of Venice after Agnadello [1509] is ... one of decline." Also, "Italy's political order" had completely changed in the years between the death of Lorenzo de' Medici (and the discovery of America, 1492) and the departure from Italy (1512) of King Louis XII, who, like his predecessor, Charles VIII, attempted "to get a firm foothold in Italy." Procacci, *History*, 74, 124–7, 169–70. In the economic sphere, the trend is similar: "In 1460 the most impressive business organization in Europe was the Medici Bank of Florence. By 1545, the Fugger Company of Augsburg was the largest firm." Rice, *The Foundations of Early Modern Europe*, 41. Yet "from the 1570s Genoa became ... the greatest western financial centre, and controller of the international exchange market [the same city that first sent its navigators to sail all the routes of the world] then became the home of one of the first international money markets in modern history." Procacci, *History*, 175–9.

32 Caboto, after his voyage of discovery, is no longer the "foreigner and poor man" hardly able to gain trust, support, or credit from the English, but "the grand admiral," honoured not only by King Henry VII, who grants him an annual stipend, but by many English merchants, now eager to participate in his next voyage to seek profits or titles. Menchini, *Giovanni Caboto*, 119–20. Verrazzano, who "never experienced difficulties resulting from his status as foreigner," even when Florence joined forces against Francis I in 1522, was always held in high esteem by the king and his ministers, who at first addressed him as the "Florentine merchant" and then with the title of "principal pilot" or "captain of the ships equipped for the voyages to the Indies." Menchini, *Giovanni de Verrazzano*, 163.

33 "The capitalist and commercial revolution dates from thirteenth-century Italy." Scaglione, "Italy in the Middle Ages," 54. See also Procacci, *History*, 44–50; and Hodgett, *A Social and Economic History of Medieval Europe*, 57–71. See also Lopez and Raymond, *Medieval Trade in the Mediterranean World*, 3–9.

34 Garin, *Scienza e vita civile*, v–viii. See also Garin, *L'uomo del Rinascimento*, 1–12, 167–201, 205–36; and Mandrou, *From Humanism to Science*, 17.

35 Caboto, described as a sort of visionary (a vain boaster like Columbus, with much "*fantasia*," wild fancy), was nevertheless a man of "great talent, most expert in navigation," with travel experience (Black Sea, Alexandria, Mecca), and a practical man who, as evidence of his "cosmogeophysical theories," had made himself, perhaps before leaving Venice, "a geographical chart and even a solid sphere" (a globe) with "the description of the

world"; thus, not simply a dreamer or a determined adventurer, but a convincing geographer and cosmographer. Menchini, *Giovanni Caboto*, 55–6, 61–2, 79–80, 88, 95–6, 111–13; and Langer, *Encyclopedia of World History*, 367. Verrazzano, whose classical-humanistic education and knowledge of geographical and mathematical sciences are well evidenced in the "Report" of his journey, was not simply put in command of the 1524 undertaking: he "was chosen by Francis I and his mother, Louise of Savoy, to be the *scientific leader of the expedition* across the unknown seas" (italics mine); Lipinsky, *Giovanni da Verrazzano*, 5; Menchini, *Giovanni da Verrazzano*, 159–70; and Menchini, *Giovanni Caboto*, 162.

36 Caboto's date of birth is uncertain (1440–50?), but documents are clear about his origin ("another Genoese like Columbus ... of equal genius, daring and courage"); his marriage in Venice (ca 1470); his Venetian citizenship (granted him "following the customary fifteen years of residence," 29 March 1476); and his three sons, Ludovico, Sebastiano, and Sante (if not all three Venetian-born, certainly Sebastiano who accompanied his father to Canada); as well as his immigration to England (after two or three years in Spain, where he probably met Columbus). In fact, during the first years in Bristol where he settled with his family (around 1494), Caboto was known as the "poor foreigner." Menchini, *Giovanni Caboto*, 99–111.

37 Since Verrazzano's "small diary" kept during the voyage and the "original letter" containing "a detailed account of his discoveries [dictated to a scribe upon his return on 8 July and] presumed to have been written in Latin or French ... have never been found," the only complete and authoritative copy, among the extant (and all in Italian), is the one discovered in a private library in Rome in 1908 or 1909: The "*Cellere Codex*" or Report is "a good, original duplicate, dictated by Verrazzano, and written in Italian with twenty-six marginal and interlineated notes in his own hand." Lipinsky, *Giovanni da Verrazzano*, 8; Menchini, *Giovanni da Verrazzano*, 17–20; and Migliorini, *Italian Language*, 234–5.

38 Menchini, *Giovanni Caboto*, 8, 45, 115. It even seems that, according to "documents in the archives of the over 1000-year-old ... Marinelli Foundry in Agnone, Molise, the bell of the *Niña* [one of Columbus's three ships] came from those ancient [bell] furnaces" – from the same town of origin of many Leamington Italians (see *La Gazzetta*, "Colombo: era italiana la campana della 'Nina,'" 26 June 1992; chapter 7, "Postwar Molise" and chapter 15, "The Novel's Other Villages."

39 Of the twenty-two names given to places Verrazzano discovered (according to the *Cellere Codex*), ten refer to French personalities; two are botanical and two other ethnological names; one refers to the characteristics of a place, one to religion, and one other to a classical-literary theme (the last

two with an Italian connection); and five place names refer to Italian personalities, including Verrazzano himself ("Isthmus Verrazano," today Pamlico and Albemarle Sounds, North Carolina); another Florentine friend, the historian Paolo Giovio ("Jovio Promontory," Sakonnet Point or Point Judith, Rhode Island); and an unpleasant person, the rapacious tax collector Cardinal Francesco Armellini ("The Shoals of Armellini," and the "Promontory Pallavicino," near Cape Cod); the religious place name recalls the Florentine feast day of the Annunciation, 25 March ("Annunciata," Virginia and North Carolina). Other brief Italian references are as curious as they are accurate: "The Sicilian Lamentation" in "The Country of Refugio ... situated in the parallel of Rome," today, Narragansett Bay, Rhode Island (Lipinsky, *Giovanni da Verrazzano*, 7–23; Menchini, *Giovanni da Verrazzano*, 25–75, 179–82). For other place names or coincidences related to Italy in the early years of Canadian history, see Lanctot, *Histoire du Canada*, quoted in Menchini, *Giovanni Caboto*, appendix 3, 161–5. See also Durnford, ed., *Heritage of Canada*, 85; *Enciclopedia Garzanti della letteratura*, 1972, 666.

40 Menchini, *Giovanni da Verrazzano*, 183–5; Menchini, *Giovanni Caboto*, 162–4, 171. The arbitrary division of the world between Portugal and Spain, as set out in the Treaty of Tordesillas (7 June 1494), also meant that "almost all the voyages of discovery by England and France were a violation of the rights of Spain." Menchini, *Giovanni Caboto*, 96–7, note 19, and 144.

41 Procacci, *History*, 108–9; Lipinsky, *Giovanni da Verrazzano*, 5.

42 Even Marco Polo two centuries earlier, whether "in the presence of the Khan of the Tartars, or in prison, never forgot that he was a citizen of Venice." Procacci, *History*, 46. See also Menchini, *Giovanni Caboto*, 104–5.

43 Not only were art and science, humanistic scholarship and scientific thought closely linked in the Renaissance, but a far-reaching connection was also established between "thought and experience," theory and application, as manifested not only by Leonardo da Vinci, but also by Filippo Brunelleschi, Leon Battista Alberti, Paolo Toscanelli (1397–1482) and others: "The circulation of ideas among technicians [engineers], artists and scientists [was] continuous." If, on the one hand, the studies and calculations of Toscanelli, the Florentine "scientist ... astronomer ... geographer, great mathematician and physician" constitute the premises of Columbus's voyage, on the other, Columbus's actual discovery of the New World, as well as the post-Columbian explorations, were linked to further "geographical research and calculations of the Earth's dimensions," which served also to "verify through actual observation a daring hypothesis" – Copernicus's proposal of a sun-centred universe. It was a convergence, a link of ideas and actions that had "revolutionary consequences in the

concept of the world ... a completely new human awareness and world outlook." Garin, *La cultura del Rinascimento*, 137–50. See also Procacci, *History*, 100–8; Dotti, *L'età dell'umanesimo*, 41–95; and Zhang, "In Celebration of Columbus Day."

44 Procacci, *History*, 104–5; Olga Zorzi Pugliese, "The Renaissance in Italy," in Chandler and Molinaro, *Culture of Italy*, 83–6; and Menchini, *Giovanni Caboto*, 47, 73–74.

45 In the 1790s, Pietro Verri, regretting that the ideas of the French Revolution had not been understood in Italy, commented bitterly, "We are immature ... Because of our desire to be cunning we are, like the Greeks, the rejected people of Europe, after having been its masters." Procacci, *History*, 255. See also Hale, ed., introduction, *Guicciardini*, xvii; Hearder and Waley, *Short History of Italy*, 94–120; Procacci, *History*, 193–214, 219–27; Salomone, "From the Crisis of the Renaissance," 94–116; Paolucci, *Storia per la scuola media*, 2:306–7; Scaglione, "Italy in the Middle Ages," 59; Cantarella, *Italian Heritage*, 212–18; and Valeri, *Storia d'Italia*, 3:398–401.

46 Valeri, *Storia d'Italia*, 3:497. Though historical speculations are normally inexcusable, some "ifs" can suggest some intriguing questions about the different course history might have taken had certain decisions or events occurred at a particular time. Thus, "if" the Italian princes of the late fifteenth century had been in a position to engage the early navigators and adventurers, and "if" Italy had not collapsed in the sixteenth century, it is quite possible that some form of Italian (Tuscan or Venetian or even Genoese) might have become one of the official languages, along with English, French, Spanish, and Portuguese, in some area of North or South America.

47 See Harney, *Italians*, 202, 226–7; Polidoro, *Tricolore in Canada*, 161; Re, *Michigan's Italian Community*, 1; Spada, *Italians*, 32–47; Vangelisti, *Gli Italiani in Canada*, 61–6; Ontario Ministry of Culture and Recreation, "Ontario Ethnocultural Profiles: Italians," 1979; Potestio, ed., *The Memoirs of Giovanni Veltri*.

48 "An original copy" of a 1657 map of New France, which Bressani promised to make "available separately," can be found in Library and Archives Canada (Ottawa) and reproduced with comments in Menchini, *Francesco Giuseppe Bressani*, 140–1.

49 Harney, "Italians in Canada," 225–7; Spada, *Italians*, 29–53; Vangelisti, *Gli italiani*, 23–70; Di Michele and Pirone, "Album degli Italiani," 156–62; Villata, "Piemontesi nella Nuova Francia."

50 Hearder and Waley, *Short History of Italy*, 94–102, 119–20; Romano, *Storia d'Italia*, 15–17; Procacci, *History*, 321–3; Spotts and Wieser, *Italy*, 222.

51 Pucci, "Canadian Industrialization."

52 Procacci, *History*, 325–8, 335–6, 341–3. Yet even in nineteenth-century Canada it was still possible to find Italians contributing to its exploration and development: "F.C. Capreol, for whom a town in northern Ontario was named" (Capreol, near Sudbury), in 1834 "was active in promoting the railway north from Toronto to Georgian Bay"; and in 1897, Prince Luigi Amedeo of Savoy, Duke of Abruzzi, led an expedition of Italian alpinists to the Saint Elias Mountains, Yukon, and thus became the first team to scale the second-highest Canadian peak, Mount Saint Elias. See Ontario Ministry of Culture and Recreation, "Ontario Ethnocultural Profiles: Italians"; Carletto Caccia, "Il Duca degli Abruzzi e il Monte S. Elia," *La Gazzetta*, 27 September, 4, 11 October 1985. See also Verna, "I nomi d'origine italiana nella toponomastica canadese."

53 Their situation was similar at departure and at arrival: They were "crammed … into the holds of transatlantic ships," and they were treated like "animals for slaughter." In Canada, "it was only as *bestie*, beasts of burden, that the Italians seemed acceptable to some Canadian immigration authorities." Procacci, *History*, 342; Cresci and Guidobaldi, *Partono i bastimenti*, 47; and Harney, "Italians in Canada," 231. See also Sacchetti, "Cento anni di 'Politica dell'Emigrazione'"; see also chapter 2, "Clandestine Emigration and the South," and chapter 3, "The Second Expedition."

54 Harney, "Italians in Canada," 233–6, 239–41. The popularity and support of Fascism among many Italian Canadians and their newfound Italian identity can be more easily understood, if not justified, in the light of the often copious praise of Mussolini from his contemporaries, both statesmen and intellectuals, such as George Bernard Shaw, George Sorel, G.K. Chesterton, Sigmund Freud, Oswald Spengler, John Gunther, Nicholas Murray Butler (president of Columbia University, 1902–45), David Lloyd George, Austen Chamberlain, as well as Mahatma Gandhi, F.D. Roosevelt, and Pope Pius XI who referred to Mussolini as "a man sent by Providence." Charles DeGaulle, even after the Second World War, declared Mussolini "a great man, a very great man." Mackenzie King, after visiting Mussolini in 1928, wrote in his diary (25 September) that he became full of admiration for the man and his work. See Mack Smith, *Mussolini*, 163; Bruti Liberati, "Fascismo, antifascismo e gli italiani in Canada"; Cappadocia, review of *Il Canada*. Perhaps the most indicative are Churchill's views:

> In 1927 Winston Churchill visited Rome and was widely reported as having said, "If I were an Italian I would don the Fascist Black Shirt." "I could not help being charmed," he said at a press conference reported by *The*

Times, 'like so many other people have been, by Signor Mussolini's gentle and simple bearing and by his calm and detached pose in spite of so many burdens and dangers ... If I had been an Italian I should have been wholeheartedly with you from start to finish in your triumphant struggle against the bestial appetites and passions of Leninism." The following day *The Times* congratulated Mr Churchill "on having understood the real spirit of the Fascist movement." Hibbert, *Benito Mussolini*, 95–6.

On 18 February 1933 at Queen's Hall, Churchill stated that Mussolini embodied the Roman genius: "He is the greatest living legislator." Bocca, *Mussolini socialfascista*, 113, 155, note 38, and 66–7. See also Fisher, "The Evolution of Marxism," 7–8, chapter 2, "The Ill-Fated First Trip," especially note 37, and chapter 6, "Vito Peralta ... Victim of Fascism and Canadian 'Justice'"; also "Fascist and Anti-Fascist Activities in Windsor," and notes 7–24.

55 Harney, "Italians in Canada," 241–3.

56 Procacci, *History*, 458–61. See also Finzi, "L'Italia che cambia"; W. Temelini, "Come va in Italia?"; Harvey, "Eppur si muove." In another article the *Economist* wrote, "Actually, 1987 is the year when Italy looks set to overtake Britain to become the fifth largest industrial economy" and become perhaps "the junior member of the world's top group of five – behind America, Japan, West Germany [and] France." *Economist*, "Italy's Vita Is Now More Dolce." In fact, however puzzling to many, including some Leamington Italians, Italy, in spite of its political situation, has been ranked second, after Denmark, among the countries of the world where living is most pleasant (at least according to a University of Pennsylvania study, reported by *Il Cittadino Canadese*, "L'Italia seconda in classifica," 24 September 1986, 3). Favero and Tassello, in their study of the total Italian expatriations and repatriations during 1876–1976, state, "In 1975 there were 132 repatriations against 100 expatriations." "Cent'anni di emigrazione italiana (1876–1976)," 55, 64.

57 "A policy of multiculturalism within a bilingual framework commends itself to the government as the most suitable means of assuring the cultural freedom of Canadians ... The government will support and encourage the various cultures and ethnic groups that give structure and vitality to our society. They will be encouraged to share their cultural expression and values with other Canadians and so contribute to a richer life for us all." P.E. Trudeau, prime minister, Announcement of Implementation of Policy of Multiculturalism within Bilingual Framework, House of Commons, 8 October 1971.

58 W. Temelini, "The Humanities and Multicultural Education"; and Temelini, "Literature and Culture in a Multicultural Society."

59 Harney, "Italians in Canada," 225–6.
60 Italian name changes, whether the result of distortions, phonetic transcriptions, or translations, seem to have occurred in every century, often with many variants: *John Cabotus*, 1496; *John Kabotto*, 1498; *Johanne Cabot*, 1512; even *Joan Caboto*, 1544; Verrazzano, or the older Italian form *Verrazano*, produced more than six versions, from *Verezan to Varacène* (see also *Culomb*, *Colon*, and *Columbus* from *Colombo*). Burlamacchi became *Bourlamaque*; Enrico Tonti, *Henri de Tonty*; and De Lieto (the Neapolitan name of Tonti's relatives) was changed to *Desliettes, Dulude,* and *Duluth*. The not uncommon name "Litalien" was clearly the term indicating origin, as in the eighteenth-century Milanese "Joseph Andre, dit *l'Italien*." In the more recent period, changes occurred through Anglicization by immigration officials or literal translation, especially during the Second World War, by the immigrants themselves (such as *Whitehead* for *Capobianco*, *Shepherd* for *Pecoraro* or *Pegoraro*, and *Ross* for *Rossini*). Some lists of name changes refer to the Italian soldiers who settled in Quebec, Ontario, as well Michigan in the seventeenth, eighteenth, and nineteenth centuries. See Harney, "Frozen Wastes," 115–16; Menchini, *Giovanni Caboto*, 124; Menchini, *Giovanni da Verrazzano*, 135–9; B. Villata, "Piemontesi nella Nuova Francia," 144–5; Spada, *Italians*, 52–3; Re, *Michigan's Italian Community*, 1–9; and Bagnell, *Canadese*, 101; Harney, "Italians," 226.
61 See Menchini, "Il Canada di Jacques Cartier"; Menchini, *Giovanni da Verrazzano*, 154, 190; Menchini, *Giovanni Caboto*, 98, note 22; 162. See also R.P. Pierre Biard, SJ, *Relation de la Nouvelle France (1616)*, quoted by Menchini, *Verrazzano*, 180, note 8; and 181. Some French and English historians in the last two centuries have made attempts to deny the discoveries by the Italian navigators, to discredit the authors who confirm them, even to prove the English origin of one of them. James A. Williamson quotes a nineteenth-century English historian who had reported to have found "what he [considered] documentary evidence of John Cabot's English origin, and of his never having come to Venice ... until the year 1461." Williamson, *The Voyages of the Cabots*, 21, quoted in Menchini, *Caboto*, 18, 60–1; and Menchini, *Verrazzano*, 182 and note 11.
62 Procacci, *History*, 50.
63 Migliorini, *Italian Language*, 197.
64 Barzini, *Italians*, 306–7 (italics mine).
65 Scaglione, "Italy in the Middle Ages," 51.
66 Scaglione, "Italy in the Middle Ages," 54; Procacci, *History*, 24–7, 41–3, 44–50, 56–63. See also chapter 1, note 33, and chapter 12, "*Italianità*."

67 Procacci, *History*, 324–8; Barzini, *Italians*, ix–xvi.
68 Bertoldi, *I nuovi italiani*, 47–9. Joseph LaPalombara, quoting Giacomo
   Leopardi, a nineteenth-century poet and thinker, wrote, "Italians not only
   lacked feelings for the nation as such; they were also devoid of any sense
   of society." But Leopardi suggests that Italians can also be "more flexible
   and more tolerant than [their] inflated rhetoric ... would lead one to
   believe." *Democracy, Italian Style*, 25–7.
69 Harney and Scarpaci, *Little Italies*, 1–2. See "Italy's historic disaster during
   the Cinquecento" (Salomone, "From the Crisis of the Renaissance," 96);
   the fifteenth- and sixteenth-centuries "calamities of Italy" (Guicciardini,
   History, 85).
70 Spada, *Italians*, 81–2.
71 The president of the University of Calabria, commenting on Italy's postwar
   economic success, on one occasion suggested, perhaps both in jest and in
   praise of all Italians outside Italy, that if to Italy's gross domestic product
   (GDP) were added the value of the product of all the Italian immigrants,
   Italy might even be able to reach "third" place among the world's top five
   industrial nations (Pietro Bucci, "Address to the Calabro-Canadian
   Confederation," Toronto, 23 January 1987).
72 The year within parentheses following a name usually indicates the time of
   arrival in Canada: e.g., Alex Colasanti (1924).

CHAPTER TWO

1 Villari, *Il Sud*, introduction, 1:v–viii.
2 Francesco P. Cerase, "Precarious Economy and Emigration" (English
   Summary), in Rosoli, *Un secolo*, 151–2.
3 Regarding the first period, Procacci wrote, "Italy's first modest industrial
   boom thus coincided with the beginning of the great agricultural crisis
   [resulting in] a typical 'scissors' situation ... The rise of prices of the industrial products that were protected by customs barriers tallied with the fall
   in agricultural prices, and the draining of capital from the country to the
   town, from south to north, steadily increased"; and for the second period,
   particularly after the 1950s "so-called 'economic miracle,'" he stated:
   "Following this sudden industrial expansion, millions of peasants left the
   countryside [and] about 3 million people [emigrated]." *History*, 348, and
   458–60. See also Villari, *Il Sud*, 1, s 6, "Il Mezzogiorno e l'industrializ-
   zazione italiana," especially Francesco Saverio Nitti, "Il Mezzogiorno e lo
   sviluppo economico italiano," 311–18.

4 According to Favero and Tassello the total number is over 25.8 million emigrants for the entire century, which they divide into three main periods: 1876–1914 (the "great exodus"): over 14 million departures or more than 54 per cent of the century's total; 1916–42: over 4.3 million or almost 17 per cent of total; 1946–76: almost 7.5 million, or 29 per cent of total. See "One Hundred Years of Italian Emigration" (English Summary), in Rosoli, *Un secolo*, 64; and Favero and Tassello, "Cent'anni," which includes charts and tables relating to origin, destination, composition of the migratory flux (expatriation and repatriation) for each period, and overview. See also chapter 4, "Restrictions and Immigration between the Wars."

5 Villari, *Il Sud*, 1:403. "Altogether in the period 1876–1915, 44% of the emigrants are directed toward Europe and 56% toward overseas countries." Favero and Tassello, "Cent'anni," 21.

6 See Rosoli, introduction, in *Un secolo*, 5–8; and essays by Eugenia Malfatti, "L'emigrazione italiana," 97–116; A.M. Birindelli, G. Gesano, and E. Sonnino, "Lo spopolamento in Italia nel quadro dell'evoluzione migratoria e demografica (1871–1971)," 189–251; and Sacchetti, "Cento anni di 'Politica dell'Emigrazione,'" 253–71; also de Rosa, *La rivoluzione industriale in Italia*, 107–17.

7 Villari, *Il Sud*, 1:172–3, 403–4.

8 Favero and Tassello, "Cent'anni," 16–20; especially tables 1 and 2, 19, 32–7, especially tables 10 and 11, 34; and 38–42, especially table 16, 40.

9 Antonio Golini, "Migrazioni interne, distribuzione della popolazione e urbanizzazione in Italia," in Rosoli, *Un secolo*, 153–5; tables 2 and 3, 156–7; and English Summary, 186–7.

10 Procacci, *History*, 409–10; Villari, *Il Sud*, 2:571–3.

11 Favero and Tassello, "Cent'anni," 32.

12 Sturino, "Italians." See chapter 1, note 20.

13 Villari, *Il Sud*, 1:176, 403–7.

14 The law on the "abolition of feudalism" in the Kingdom of Naples (South Italy) dated back to the Napoleonic era (2 August 1806): on this basis "all powers of feudal jurisdiction … were suppressed … But though this meant a revolution [legally and administratively], things did not greatly change in terms of social relations. The feudal lords may have ceased to be *signori*, but they had become owners of their land *pleno jure* [with full right of authority] … So the abolition of feudalism did not make very important changes in the existing distribution of land … Neither did any changes result from the sale of [the confiscated] ecclesiastical lands; [in fact] 65 per cent of the property sold fell into the hands of about two hundred and fifty buyers, almost all of them noblemen, high state officials, including many

Frenchmen, and the rich bourgeois." Nor did any significant change come from the subsequent "law on commune demesnes, which declared, among other things, that part of these lands should be apportioned to the peasants ... So the great estates of men of property and the tiny, subsistence holdings of the small landowners remained the two poles of a general backwardness, and there remained a social abyss between the privileged [*signori*] and the *cafoni* [rubes]." It was not very different at the end of the nineteenth century: "The south ... remained locked more tightly than ever within its backwardness and its subordinate position," while the "development of capitalism in Italy represented a widening of the already immense social and regional gaps in the country," which also contributed to the "formation of a popular opposition" and of the "socialist movement" in the 1880s. Procacci, *History*, 220–1, 266–7, 348–9, 360–1; Villari, *Il Sud*, especially Pasquale Villari, "Il Mezzogiorno e la questione sociale [1878]," 1:105–17, 128–30, 138–40, 161–3, 171–9, 216–17, 225–9, 236–40, 244–9, 291–307, 372–3, 405–7, 412–13; 416–17; Valeri, *Storia d'Italia: Da Camillo Cavour alla fine della 1ª guerra mondiale (1852–1918)*, 4:251.

15 The "reactionary alliance between the Southern landowners and the Northern industrialists, the *pactum sceleris* [the pact of wickedness], as it was later defined," may be traceable to Cavour's *connubio*, an alliance of parties, and to the 1870s attempt at a right-left coalition. But in the 1880s, the "alliance ... bound with much more complex political, economic and institutional ties" became "*trasformismo* ... a parliamentary practice [which] consisted of assuring the government an adequate majority in Parliament, either by a preliminary deal with the more prominent members of the opposition, and by eventually absorbing them into the government, or by means of favouritism, and by corrupting ... deputies ... or by a combination of these methods. [Briefly] it was a contract between the middle class of northern Italy and the *galantuomini* of the South, on the basis of a compromise, of which both groups reaped the advantages [at the expense of the working masses]." Villari, *Il Sud*, especially Sidney Sonnino, "La crisi agraria," 1:186 and 200; Procacci, *History*, 311, 337–9, Valeri, *Storia d'Italia*, 4:355. See also Sacchetti, "Cento anni di 'Politica dell'Emigrazione," 253–7.

16 The Government of the Right (1861–76), by concentrating on political and financial issues, may have succeeded in "completing Italian unification" (gained Venetia and Rome, defined state-church relations, balanced the budget), but with their indifference to the overwhelming social problems, aggravated the "Southern Question": high levels of poverty, illiteracy, and crime; miserable living standards; exploitation of workers (a crime to strike); emigration (35,000 in 1862; 143,000 in 1870; from the South, about 1,000 in 1862; 25,000 in 1871); excessive taxes and no voting rights

for majority of Italians (in 1861, of about 22 million people, less than half a million had the right to vote). In general, social problems were often seen as police matters; the budget was balanced without concern for the poorest taxpayers; civil and political liberties were not always respected; military intervention and arrests of adversaries were often used; and Italy inherited "a suffocating system of centralized government." Valeri, *Storia d'Italia*, 4:203–5, 346–8, 363–4.

17 The Government of the Left may have begun with a "parliamentary revolution" (March 1876) but "did not mark that radical change in direction that many had feared and some had hoped for. The set of reforms introduced during the first years of its government was not negligible, but neither was it outstanding": extension of franchise and free, compulsory education from six to nine years old; social welfare and services; workers' protection; even a limited "right to strike" and emigration measures. But some laws (education, employers' liability for accidents, emigration) were so poorly administered as to be ineffective. The electoral reform was limited – the electorate increased "from 2 to 7 per cent of the population. But … it was designed in such a way as to benefit the towns" more than the countryside, and North and Central Italy more than the South. The reform also reinforced *trasformismo*, as well as northern and southern established interests. With "the arrival in power of the Left the southern element in the government was considerably increased, and from that date on the growth of southern influence in public administration has been a characteristic of modern Italy. [But] southern politics remained dominated on the whole by deputies' cliques of supporters, and by the *galantuomini*." The exclusion of "the rural areas and more backward regions of Italy [from] the democratic advancement that was achieved in the cities and more advanced areas created conditions for an uneven development, and a heightening of the already existing conflict between town and country, between North and South." Procacci, *History*, 335–40; Valeri, *Storia d'Italia*, 4:371–2; Langer, *Encyclopedia*, 660–1.

18 "Mass protest … became a constant social and political feature of the new Italy"; in 1866 there was the "Palermo revolt." In 1869 in the North "there were violent and widespread uprisings … following the imposition of the much hated grist tax." Immediately after unification, the former Kingdom of Naples saw a sudden increase in banditry, which found new support among the southern peasants and lower classes to whom unification had also brought general conscription, unknown under Bourbon rule, and one that lasted "seven years!" Procacci, *History*, 326–7; Valeri, *Storia d'Italia*, 4:233–4, 251; Villari, *Il Sud*, especially Giuseppe Massari, "Il brigantaggio," 1:89–102.

19 Repression was not only legalized, but the 1863 "Pica law ... suspended constitutional liberties in the brigand-infested [southern] provinces, and made the most rigorous repression," as defined by Mack Smith, quoted by Villari "'not an exceptional measure, but a rule sanctioned by law.'" Often bloody, and as frequent as the (quite often justified) peasants' uprisings or demonstrations of their discontent and frustration, repression was used not only to combat brigandage but also in other situations: in the 1866 "Palermo revolt ... quelled by an expeditionary force"; in the 1890s against the "Sicilian *Fasci*" (a union and movement of socialist workers fighting for more equitable taxes, distribution of lands, as well as "regional autonomy"), when a fleet sent to the Port of Palermo placed the city in a "state of siege," and over ninety persons were killed in 1893–4; in the 1902 slaughter of farmers in Candela (Puglia), in Giarratana (Sicily), and in Matera (Basilicata). With Fascism, violence against peasants became systematic, and incidents of it appeared also after the Second World War. Villari, *Il Sud*, 1:89–90, 137–8, 161–3, 225–7, 245–9, 313; 2:491, note 1, 571; Procacci, *History*, 326–7, 361–2, 461; Valeri, *Storia d'Italia*, 4:252–3, 557–63, 591.

20 Procacci, *History*, 341–2; Villari, *Il Sud*, 1:183–6, 199–206, 299–300. According to the calculations by some southern reformers, which others doubted, at the turn of the century "Southern Italy, with a little more than a fourth of the national income ... paid almost one-third of the taxes." Villari, *Il Sud*, 1:355.

21 Villari, *Il Sud*, 1:162–3, 188–98.

22 Valeri, *Storia d'Italia*, 4:567–8; Villari, *Il Sud*, 1:199–200, 291–2, 311–14, 343–6; R. Villari, *Mezzogiorno e contadini nell'età moderna*, 264–5.

23 Villari, *Il Sud*, 1:227, 312; 320, especially Napoleone Colajanni, "Per la razza maledetta," 2:431–4; and Antonio Gramsci, "Il Mezzogiorno e la rivoluzione socialista," 2:535–43. Gramsci's text (in Villari, *Il sud*, 1:535–68) was first published as *Alcuni temi della quistione meridionale* [Some themes of the Southern Question] (in "Stato operaio," January 1930). One of these themes is the oppression and exploitation of the southern peasants and uneducated classes by the northern and southern middle class, including the southern intellectuals and the clergy.

24 Villari, *Il Sud*, 1:291, 296–7. Ettore Ciccotti, in a 1900 speech, "The Socialist Movement and the South," indicated that in Southern Italy "the proletariat, for more than nine-tenths illiterate, does not yet constitute an active political force." Villari, *Il Sud*, 2:452.

25 Procacci, *History*, 341–3; Villari, *Il Sud*, 1:196, 408; 2:516.

26 Francesco Coletti, "L'emigrazïone," in Villari, *Il Sud Nella Storia D'Italia*, 1:404n1.

27 Coletti, "L'emigrazione," 1:404n1.

28 Villari, *Il Sud*, especially Sydney Sonnino, "L'emigrazione e le classi diri-
genti," 1:171–9; and Francesco Coletti, "L'emigrazione [1911]," 1:403–22.
See also Leopoldo Franchetti, "Africa e Mezzogiorno" 1:213–22; Langer,
Encyclopedia, 835; Procacci, *History*, 352, 357, 366.

29 "La rivoluzione italiana sarà meridionale o non sarà [The Italian revolution will be a southern revolution or there won't be a revolution]." Guido
Dorso, "La rivoluzione meridionale [1925]," in Villari, *Il Sud*, 2:519–34.

30 Luigi Sturzo, "Il Partito popolare e la questione meridionale [1923] [The
Popular Party and the Southern Question]"; Giuseppe Di Vittorio, "Il
Fascismo contro i contadini [1929] [Fascism against the peasants]"; in
Villari, *Il Sud*, 2:501–4, 571–94. See also chapter 2, notes 44, 45, 46.

31 Villari, *Il Sud*, 1:32–7; 407–9. See also Carlomagno, *Agnone*, 237; Rosoli,
Un secolo.

32 "La Regione Molise," 69–71. *Abruzzo* instead of *Abruzzi* will be used
throughout the text, unless the latter appears in a quoted text: "Abruzzi is
the name used in the Italian Constitution and regularly by the Italian
Central Statistics Institute," as well as by most English texts. But modern
Italian usage prefers the singular *Abruzzo* to the plural form *Abruzzi*, since
there is no longer "the ancient distinction, dating back to the XIV century,
between [the Abruzzo above and the Abruzzo below the Pescara River]."
The "establishment of the regions into organic political-administrative
units led the [Abruzzo] regional government in 1974 to ask for a change of
the toponym in the text of the Constitution." "La Regione Abruzzi," 223,
note 1. See also chapter 1, especially note 3.

33 Carlomagno, *Agnone*, 236–7. According to Vangelisti, the majority of the
fifty-one families in the first "Little Italy" of Montreal (St Timothée Street)
at the end of the nineteenth century were Molisani from Campobasso. *Gli
italiani in Canada*, 85.

34 Domenico's passport, issued at Isernia 5 June 1913 (full name appearing as
"Domenicantonio," Domenic-Anthony), was valid for three years and for a
specific destination: New York. Since Domenic (born February 1897) was
only sixteen years old, his brother-in-law Giuseppe (Joseph) Mastronardi,
then twenty-five years old, had to be his *garante* (guarantor) (as indicated
on page 4 of his 1913 passport). According to Domenic's discharge papers,
he was called to arms and presented himself on 5 October 1916, served in
the *Bersaglieri* (Sharpshooters) Corps, and was in the war both years, 1917
and 1918 (see appendix C).

35 After the First World War and the Russian Revolution, "it became more
difficult for south Europeans to emigrate to North America." Harney,
"Italians in Canada," 238. And "from 1925 until the end of World War II,

Canadian immigration policy was similar to the American, Nazi, and Fascist policy – insomuch as it obstructed the free flow of immigrants." Spada, *Italians*, 122. "Right after the [First World] war, the American authorities had turned the tap off. Emigration continued just the same, the illegal way. Whoever intended to emigrate was forced to embark as a sea-man: in New York he got off as a clandestine and for a few years did odd jobs, without having the necessary permit." Carlo Cassola also wrote, "Emigranti/Emigrants," in Cresci and Guidobaldi, *Partono i bastimenti*, 201 (translation mine). See also Favero and Tassello, "Cent'anni," 30–1; and chapter 4, "Restrictions and Immigration between the Two World Wars," "The First Men from Lazio."

36 The first Marriage Register (9 February 1929–9 June 1956), Church of St Angela Merici, Windsor, lists the marriage at number 53, and includes the following information: "Contracting parties – Albano Valeri; residence: 13115 E. Jefferson, Detroit, Mich.; Date and Place of Baptism: Born at Fara Sabina [or Fara in Sabina], Rieti, Italy, 1908; Parents: Agostino, Adele Benedetti; – Giacomina Vitale (Wid.); residence: 891 Louis Ave., Windsor, Ont. [no date, place of birth, or baptism]; Parents: Nicola Polamo [*sic*], Irene Bridorli; Date of Marriage: April 13, 1940; Witnesses: Louis Andolini, Angelina Michelutti; Priest: C. DeSantis." The interview card shows Giacomina (née Polano), born in 1901 in San Daniele del Friuli, arrived in New York (Ellis Island) June 1920; died at age eighty-two on 18 November 1984 in Windsor. According to Gino Pannunzio's communica-tion, Albano was Ines Brunato's stepfather, her mother's second husband. After 1983 Albano (born 1893), lived in a Windsor senior citizens' resi-dence, where he died on 19 December 1984 at age ninety-one. *Windsor Star*, 19 November, 20 December 1984.

37 Mussolini thought of "leaving his sleeping car" and entering Rome "on horseback with a guard of blackshirts, but there was a risk of looking ridiculous, so he went the whole way by train." Mack Smith, *Mussolini*, 55. The myth of Mussolini's equestrian prowess was glorified even in a "gigantic fresco" on the vaulted ceiling behind the main altar in the Montreal Italian church Notre Dame de la Défense. Bruti Liberati, "Fascismo, antifascismo e gli italiani in Canada," 57; Vangelisti, *Gli italiani in Canada*, 168 and 200. See also chapter 1, "The Changing Fortunes of the Italians in Canada and in Leamington," especially note 54; and chapter 6, "Fascist and Anti-Fascist Activities in Windsor," and notes 7–17.

38 Tasca, *Nascita e avvento del Fascismo*, 2:397 and 479. As an anti-Fascist Tasca had to leave Italy and live in Belgium and France, where he also used the pseudonym A. Rossi. Tasca's work was published in France in 1938 with the title *Naissance du Fascisme*. The English and Czech translations

appeared almost at the same time, while the first Italian edition appeared in 1950. Renzo De Felice, "Premessa," *Nascita e avvento* by A. Tasca, 1:ix–xvi, 2:back cover.

39 Colloquially the Italian term has the same meaning as *masciata*: a message, information, or news brought to someone for a third party; a service to be performed; run an errand. See Pei, *The Italian Language*, 35–47; Devoto and Oli, *Nuovo vocabolario illustrato*. See also Nino Ricci's use of similar forms in *Lives of the Saints* (chapter 15).

40 In order to reach Pietrabbondante from Villa Canale, they must have walked for twenty to twenty-five kilometres southward past Poggio Sannita, then probably used the Agnone-Pescolanciano electric train. Carlomagno, *Agnone: dalle origini*, 286.

41 They most likely used the Rome-Genoa train route up the west coast of Italy, reaching Cuneo by way of Savona and Mondovì; and from Cuneo south through Borgo San Dalmazzo on the Italian side of the border and then to San Dalmazzo di Tenda (Saint Dalmas de Tende) on the French side.

42 "Marshal," or, in this case, a petty or warrant officer of the carabinieri; singular *carabinieri* (from *carabina*, *carabine*), a member of the Italian army corps, which is also a police force.

43 Francescopaolo Covitti was mayor from 1920 to 1923, and probably the last in Agnone to be democratically elected to that office prior to the first "Fascist terroristic offensive" against rural Italy, "October 1920–August/September 1922." Carlomagno, *Agnone: dalle origini*, 341; Villari, *Il Sud*, 2:582–3. See also chapter 2, 32.

44 Villari, *Il Sud*, 2:571–94. After 1925, Mussolini aimed "at the 'fascistisation' of every institution" by relying less on violence and more on legislation: "Local self-government was therefore abolished: district and town councils would no longer be elected, and a centrally nominated *podestà* would replace every elected mayor. The prefect would continue to act as the chief agent of the government in each province, but alongside him would be the local [Fascist] party-secretary or *federale* who ... was given a parallel and independent authority." Mack Smith, *Mussolini*, 39, 63, 101–4. "In all the rural municipalities, the *podestà* [was] usually a small land-owner, appointed by the government or by its prefects, upon recommendation of the landed bourgeoisie" (the *galantuomini*). "The laws on the *podestà*, which [completed] the regime of the Fascist dictatorship, [were] specifically directed against the peasants." In fact, the first law "(November 1925) established a *podestà* in municipalities with less than 5,000 people, that is, in all the Italian rural areas. The subsequent laws [1926/7 extended] the *podestà* to all municipalities." Villari, *Il Sud*, 2:585.

In Agnone, Covitti's successor, the lawyer Raffaele Sabelli, was a Commissario Prefettizio (1924–6), an official appointed by the prefect as temporary head of the municipal administration, while Sabelli's successor, Ulisse Tirone, also a lawyer, was first mayor (1926–7) then, in 1927, *podestà*. Carlomagno, *Agnone: dalle origini*, 341. See also chapter 2, 32.

45 Mack Smith, *Mussolini*, 39–77, 104; Salvemini, *The Fascist Dictatorship in Italy*, 103, 121–9.

46 At the January 1921 Congress of the Socialist Party at Livorno, "its more extreme wing defected to found a communist party." In February, "Communist and Fascist riots at Florence [inaugurated] a period of constant clashes which ultimately approximated civil war between the two factions." Mack Smith, *Mussolini*, 42; Langer, *Encyclopedia*, 987.

47 Valeri, *Storia d'Italia*, 4:784–901; Procacci, *History*, 403–7; Consonni, *Ponte nei secoli*, 3:307–27.

48 Langer, *Encyclopedia*, 930–1, 938–9; Palmer, *A History of the Modern World*, 685; Valeri, *Storia d'Italia*, 4:836; Wells, *The Outline of History*, 2:854, 862; Consonni, *Ponte*, 3:316–17.

49 Valeri, *Storia d'Italia*, 4:831–3, 838–40, 866; Langer, *Encyclopedia*, 932, 941.

50 Valeri, *Storia d'Italia*, 4:848–52; Langer, *Encyclopedia*, 938–44; Wells, *Outline*, 2:860–2; Procacci, *History*, 408–9; Manaresi, *Pantheon*, 3:256.

51 Langer, *Encyclopedia*, 944–5; Consonni, *Ponte*, 3:323–4 and note 1; Manaresi, *Pantheon*, 3:259; Bacci, *Viaggio nel tempo*, 3:215, 232–33; Quazza, *Corso di Storia*, 3:255.

52 Palmer, *History of the Modern World*, 687.

53 Langer, *Encyclopedia*, 763, 923–5, 932; Procacci, *History*, 400–1; Valeri, *Storia d'Italia*, 4:801, 807, 811–13, 824–5; Bacci, *Viaggio nel tempo*, 3:205–11; Consonni, *Ponte*, 3:304–12.

54 Valeri, *Storia*, 4:829–30; Langer, *Encyclopedia*, 921, 939, 948–9; Wells, *Outline*, 2:856; Palmer, *History of the Modern World*, 673, 681–2, 687; Bacci, *Viaggio*, 3:217.

55 Langer, *Encyclopedia*, 925, 951–2, 955, 987; Valeri, *Storia d'Italia*, 5:41–50, 69–73, 90–2, 115–16; Procacci, *History*, 388–419; "D'Annunzio, Gabriele," *Enciclopedia della letteratura Garzanti*, 1974 ed.; Bacci, *Viaggio nel tempo*, 3:216–20.

56 Procacci, *History*, 401–4; see also Langer, *Encyclopedia*, 941; Valeri, *Storia d'Italia*, 4:787–94, 799, 814, 827–33.

57 Villari, *Il Sud*, 2:571–2; Procacci, *History*, 406–7. See also chapter 2.

58 Langer, *Encyclopedia*, 941, 949; Manaresi, *Pantheon*, 3:274.

59 Palmer, *History of the Modern World*, 686–7.

60 Langer, *Encyclopedia*, 949, 951; Valeri, *Storia d'Italia*, 4:900–3; Wells, *Outline*, 2:866.

61 Procacci, *History*, 408–9.

62 Interviews with Tony DiMenna, 28 May 1979 and 26 August 1980 at Tony DiMenna's residence in Leamington.

63 Procacci, *History*, 424–5; Langer, *Encyclopedia* 987–8, 1021, 1095; Valeri, *Storia d'Italia*, 5:181; 204–10, 372, 441–3; Mack Smith, *Mussolini*, 43, 55–74, 89, 95–6, 124; Bocca, *Mussolini*, 31–51; Cantarelia, *Italian Heritage*, 261, 300–10; Beccaria, *Italiano*, 181. See also De Maria, ed., *Per conoscere Marinetti*, 6.

64 "The Fascist theory of restricted migration was based on contradiction; they favoured immigration as it extended the borders of their fatherland ... they were against emigration as it would reduce the economic and military efficiency of the *regime*." Spada, *Italians*, 122. "The Fascist government in Italy ... hindered emigration and encouraged either internal land reclamation schemes or settlement in Tripolitanian or Eritrean colonies." Harney, "Italians," 238. See also Valeri, *Storia d'Italia*, 5:348–51, 569–70; Tasca, *Nascita e avvento*, 567–8; and chapter 2, note 34. See also interviews with Tony DiMenna, 28 May 1979 and 26 August 1980.

CHAPTER THREE

1 "[The] investigation into the [extremely backward] conditions of the southern peasants ... conducted by [Leopoldo] Franchetti in 1874, and [the] one into the peasants of Sicily, by Franchetti and [Sidney] Sonnino, in 1876 ... were the first of a type of politico-social study that was to be known as *letteratura meridionalistica*, which was to have its famous exponents and devotees throughout contemporary Italian history. One of the most able of these students of the South was Giustino Fortunato." Procacci, *History*, 335–6. See also Villari, *Il Sud*, 1:105–38.

2 In *"Gli 'americani' di Gagliano* [The 'Americans' of Gagliano]," a chapter in Levi, *Cristo si è fermato a Eboli*, "America," in the eyes of the humble "people without hope," is the only "kingdom" of salvation; yet "even America, for the peasants, has a double nature. It is a land where one goes to work, where one sweats and toils, where the little money is saved with a thousand sacrifices and privations, where sometimes one dies, and no one remembers him anymore; but at the same time, and without contradiction, it is paradise, the promised land of the Kingdom." See Cantarella, ed., *Prosatori del Novecento*, 57–62. See also Slonim, afterword, *Bread and Wine*, 278–80; and chapter 15, especially note 53.

3 Villari, *Il Sud*, especially Antonio Genovesi, "Il problema della terra," 1:3–11; Gaetano Filangieri, "Città e campagna," 1:12–23; Giustino Fortunato, "Il problema demaniale," 1:161–70; Luigi Sturzo, "Il partito popolare e la questione meridionale," 2:501–18; Gramsci, "Il Mezzogiorno e la rivoluzione socialista," 2:535–68; and Giuseppe Di Vittorio, "Il Fascismo contro i contadini," 2:571–94. See also Spotts and Wieser, *Italy: A Difficult Democracy*, 230–3.

4 Carlomagno, *Agnone*, 196–9; Arduino and Arduino, *Le due valli del sole*, 20–2.

5 *Tomolo*, an old, agricultural, varying unit of liquid, dry, and land measure, used mostly in Central-Southern Italy before the adoption of the decimal system; as a liquid measure it was equal to about 45 litres and for dry goods to about 55 litres (comparable to a bushel, 35.239 litres). Mostly an arbitrary measure that varied from area to area (if not from person to person, since one measure depended on the length of the step), according to some immigrants who had worked the land in parts of Southern Italy (such as Guido Benvenuto of Windsor), a *tomolo* in Calabria was equal to the amount of land covered in sowing fifty kilograms of seed; it was usually about 3,300 square metres of land (equal to a field 100 by 33 metres). In the Agnone "System of Weights and Measures," according to a local historian, the *tomolo* as a weight varied from forty-two to forty-four kilograms and as a surface measure it was equal to 3,086 square metres (either way one *tomolo* is about an acre of land: 1 *tomolo* = 0.33 hectare; 1 acre = 0.4047 hectare). See "Tomolo," *Enciclopedia italiana "Treccani,"* 1937 ed.; Carlomagno, *Agnone*, 307–8; and chapter 15, "The Novel's Other Villages."

6 Villari, *Il Sud*, 2:547–8.

7 Ibid., 1:403–22; 2:612–24; Cantarella, *Prosatori*, 57–68; Slonim, afterword, 280. See also notes 5, 12, and chapter 2, "The Molisani."

8 Villari, *Il Sud*, 1:412–14.

9 Levi's "volume," "as hard to classify as is its author … is the cohesive portrait of a region [Lucania or Basilicata] seen through a homogeneous series of historical, socio-political, literary vignettes and frescoes done with the incisive yet humane clinical insight of a physician, the eye for colour and form of a painter, and the aptness of a politician." Cantarella, *Prosatori*, 57–8. The work has also been described as a "report [of a forced exile] elevated to a lyrical and meditative meaning." *Enciclopedia della letteratura Garzanti*, 1974 ed. See also Villari, *Il Sud*, 2:612–24, and notes 5 and 10.

10 Villari, *Il Sud*, 1:105–8.

11 Elisa A. Carrillo, "The Church in Italy," in Chandler and Molinaro, *Culture of Italy*, 194; Temelini, "Study of an Agricultural Community," 88–9.

12 Bartoli Perrault and Affron, eds., introduction to *Fontamara*, outside back cover, and vii–ix. "Silone," the authors point out "has often insisted that his fiction is autobiographical ... In a lengthy preface which establishes the relationship between the author and the tale and underscores the historical and aesthetic objectivity of the narration, Silone makes quite clear his intent. [*Fontamara's*] peasants, the *cafoni*, resemble all those who work the land and know hunger: 'coolies, peons, fellahs, muzhiks. They are joined in a family which knows no national, racial, or religious boundaries, the family of the impoverished peasant.' All Silone's works show a continuous commitment to the 'struggle [against] oppression [for] the awakening of a social conscience [for] liberty, freedom, and justice' ... Silone's search for truth [led him to] a belief in salvation based on individual action [in] [b] rotherhood and selflessness." Contemporary "novelists owe Silone a debt ... for the strengthened bonds between literature and society." Introduction, vii–xv. See also chapter 15, "The 'Migration' Parallels" especially note 53.

13 Rimanelli's life and works reflect and exemplify varied experiences of the Molisan people: born (in 1926) at Casacalenda (Campobasso), while at university he worked as a tutor, boxer, and labourer in order to finance his studies (which he was unable to complete). During the Second World War, at eighteen, he ran away to North Italy and "lived the terrible experience of the [Fascist] Salò adventure" (1943–45), which left him quite bitter but provided the inspiration for his 1953 novel *Tiro al piccione* (Pigeon shooting), from which a movie was made in 1961. After entering journalism (in 1948), he travelled around Europe, visited his family in Canada for almost a year, then moved to Rome where he continued to write. But, restless like all emigrants, he resumed his travels until he settled in the United States, where for some time he was a professor of Italian literature. The characters in his novels resemble the Molisani whose struggle against "*miseria* (poverty) and hunger" in their remote villages resulted in emigration. But in one case (in *Peccato originale*), "Seppe, the old peasant who has been to America seven times in order to provide for the needs of his family, reminds his wife of the hard work of the emigrant, but [his wife], who is full of bitterness and resentment because her life is spent among sacrifices and privations [in the small Molisan villages], speaks almost with envy about her neighbours who have been to Rome and [are now preparing for their departure for America]." Sardelli, ed., *Narratori Molisani*, 217–42. See also S. Martelli, "Foreword," and Sheryl Lynn Postman, "A Bridge to America: *Biglietto di terza* and *Tragica America*," in Mortelli, *Rimanelliana*.

14 Jovine (1902–1950) was the author of several works, including *Un uomo provvisorio* (1934), *Ladro di galline* (1940), *Signora Ava* (1942), *Il pastore*

sepolto (1945), and *Le terre del Sacramento* (1950). Sardelli, *Narratori Molisani*, 27–74. See also Sebastiano Martelli, "L'enciclopedia e il cruciverba: il primo romanzo di Jovine," in *Proposte Molisane*, 177–84.

15 *Gente in Aspromonte* by Alvaro (1895–1956) translated by Frances Frenaye as *Revolt in Aspromonte*, considered a classic of modern Italian literature, frequently compared to Verga's *House by the Medlar Tree*, was presented to the English-reading public as a "short but powerful novel of peasant life in Calabria ... the story of the shepherd Argiro and his family – of their struggle for survival, and some shred of dignity, against the degrading oppression of the feudal family which controls their village." Jacket summary in Frenaye's translation.

16 "Silone with *Fontamara*, Vittorini with *Conversazione in Sicilia* and Levi with *Cristo si è fermato a Eboli* not only focused a glaring white light on the tragic conditions of Southern Italian peasants but also gave fresh impetus to that veristic literary current which, interrupted by the Fascist dictatorship, had had in Giovanni Verga (1840–1922) its master and originator." Cantarella, *Prosatori*, 58. See also chapter 1, especially note 16.

17 Luigi Pirandello (1867–1936), best known for his cerebral theatrical works and his philosophical relativism, has also dealt with the adversities of the humble people of Sicily and the tragic results of emigration, especially in his short stories *Il fumo* (The smoke) and *L'altro figlio* (The other son). See *Novelle per un anno*, 1:96–131, 926–944. The short story "The Other Son" (which the Taviani brothers made into the 1985 film *Kaos*) is "the story of ... a small Sicilian village in the early twentieth century ... being daily emptied out of its inhabitants by emigration," and of a mother who, having no news of her two sons in America, "wastes away in her tears" and is near madness. Sebastiano Martelli, "Emigrazione e America nella letteratura del Sud d'Italia," in Candeloro, Gardaphe, and Giordano, eds., *Italian Ethnics*, xx, 73. See also Cantarella, *Italian Heritage*, 311–15, and notes 2, 22.

18 Cantarella, *Prosatori*, 57–8.

19 Napoleone Colajanni, "Le cause del movimento dei Fasci siciliani," in Villari, *Il Sud*, 1:229–30.

20 "Cavalleria Rusticana" (1880), one of Verga's best-known short stories, rewritten as a one-act tragedy (1883) and performed at the Teatro Carignano in Turin (1884), was the subject of at least four Italian operas (most famous the 1890 version, with libretto by Giovanni Targioni Tozzetti and music by Pietro Mascagni, considered, though Verga called it a travesty of his work, a cornerstone of Italian "veristic" opera); of various film versions (1911, 1939, 1953) and also of a ballet (*Racconto siciliano*, 1956)

set to music by Valentino Bucchi. See D. Maxwell White, ed., *Pane Nero and Other Stories* by Giovanni Verga, 88; Piero Nardi, ed., *Novelle* by G. Verga, 35–45; Nardi, ed., *I Malavoglia*, 89–93, 346; Mosbacher, trans., *House by the Medlar Tree*, 264; and Cantarella, *Italian Heritage*, 291–8. See also chapter 1, especially note 16.

21 Coletti, "Dell'emigrazione italiana," 418–19. See also chapter 5, "Saveria Magri and the First Women"; chapter 10, "*La Famiglia* [The family]" and "The 'Special' Role of the Woman."

22 The concept of emigration as a contradiction-producing phenomenon and of America as a dichotomous reality dates back to the late nineteenth-century emigration-inspired literary works, including *Cuore* (1886) and *In America* (1897) by E. De Amicis, as well as "Italy," G. Pascoli's unique poem on emigration. America, representing the new "civilization … of the city, of machines, of progress … of the future," is at times the antithesis of the old, "dying … agrarian civilization," while emigration described as the cause of "grief, disease, madness [and death]" is at times the juxtaposition to the "[health-restoring] … peasant civilization." According to Martelli, the "dichotomy America-*paese* [village of origin], myth of America – myth of the land of their origins, becomes … a central identeme [essential element of identity] of the literary imagination," that will reappear in certain post–Second World War literary works. The "suspended existence" that most "migrants" eventually experience is also a metaphor for the wider socio-psychological disruption and identity crisis in modern times. See Martelli, "Emigrazione e America," 71–8. See also notes 2, 17, and chapter 2, "The Ill-Fated First Trip"; chapter 5, "The Hardships" and note 17; chapter 15, "The 'Migration' Parallels," especially note 53; and "Conclusion," especially note 83.

23 Illusions or self-deception, a recurring theme in the works and thought of Giacomo Leopardi (1798–1836), are in his view inherent to human nature in order to "make life pleasant and bearable." Ferretti, ed., *Prose di Giacomo Leopardi*, 317–18, 354.

24 See chapter 7, "Chain Migration"; chapter 9, "The Significance of 'Farming.'"

25 "All along this *via dolorosa*, or *via commerciale* [commercial route], the Italian migrant was misled and exploited by steamship agents, labour bureaux, *padroni* and North American businessmen." Harney, "Italians in Canada," 230; see also Cresci and Guidobaldi, *Partono i bastimenti*, 10–17, 21–2, 30–3.

26 In the camp they earned over five dollars per day, but later the railroad job earned them only twenty-five cents per hour, and on the farm the pay was even less, one to two dollars per day. See "The Wages," chapter 9.

27 Bruno Ramirez and Michele Del Balzo [*sic*], "The Italians of Montreal: From Sojourning to Settlement, 1900–1921," in Harney and Scarpaci, *Little Italies*, 63–8.

28 *Bordanti* (sing. *bordante*), formed by crossing English *board / boarder* and the Italian present participle ending of first conjugation verbs, is often used in reference to early twentieth-century "Little Italies" to signify the male immigrants without wives or families who lived in the houses of relatives or of Italian families preferably of the same region or town, *paesani*. See Harney, "Italians," 233; Ramirez and Del Balzo, "Italians of Montreal," 80–1; and Danesi, *Loanwords and Phonological Methodology*, 3; and chapter 12, "Italian Language and *Italianità*."

29 Though in DiMenna's interview the name sounded like "Thematis" or "Tomatoi" Street, no doubt he meant St Timothée: the street runs in a north-south direction from Boulevard Maisonneuve (north) to Boulevard Dorchester (renamed René Levesque, south) and between Papineau Avenue (west) and Rue St Denis (east). See Ramirez and Del Balzo, "Italians of Montreal," 65; Ramirez, "Immigration et rapports familiaux"; Del Balso, "No, Sir, I Would Rather Starve..."; and Vangelisti, *Gli italiani in Canada*, 85.

30 Sacchetti, "Cento anni di 'Politica dell'emigrazione,'" 253–71.

31 See appendix C: D. Pannunzio, *Foglio di Congedo Illimitato*: "*Doveri e facoltà del militare in congedo*," especially part 6.

32 See appendix C: Passports issued to "Pannunzio Domenicantonio" [Domenico Antonio] or "Antonio," i.e., the same person: Domenico Pannunzio. See also Harney, "Italians in Canada," 229–30; Cresci and Guidobaldi, *Partono i bastimenti*, 64–5; Favero and Tassello, "Cent'anni," 9–10; Sacchetti, "Cento anni di 'Politica dell'emigrazione,'" 258–60; Zucchi, *Italians in Toronto*, 21, and chapter 12, "*Italianità*: 'The Feeling of Being Italian' without or outside Italy."

CHAPTER FOUR

1 Essex County (Ontario) Tourist Association, *Essex County Sketches*, 7–12; Morrison, *Garden Gateway*, 272–4; "Historical Essex '75," *Windsor Star*, 11 July 1975, 29–44.

2 "Windsor's Alien Immigrants," *Evening Record*, 1 June 1904.

3 By the turn of the century, because of Cauzillo's untimely death in 1898, his business was no longer in existence, but other Italian businesses were flourishing: Joseph Bova's Fruit Store and Confectionery at 39/63 Sandwich Street West, near Ouellette; and the Ferrari family's numerous enterprises: at the end of the nineteenth century "in Walkerville, L. Ferrari

[was] prominent in [the wine] industry"; Eugene and John, from 1903 to 1908, are listed in the *Windsor Business Directories* as grocers, wine manufacturers, wool and coal merchants in Walkerville (north side of Wyandotte at Susan Street); and in 1905/6, Eugene is listed as a fruit grower at 122 Lincoln Road. See Morrison, *Garden Gateway*, 159; and W. Temelini, "A History of the Italian Business Community."

4 Cancian and Dycha, *Windsor*, 12; and Temelini, "Italians in Windsor," 73–5.

5 Re, *Michigan's Italian Community*, 21. Montreal's Italian colony, the first to develop "into a socio-economic and cultural entity deserving the name of 'Little Italy,'" in 1905 had an "Italian population of four thousand souls, half [of whom] were 'workers without family,'" while Toronto's "Italian population stood at about 5,000" in 1906, but it too was a "fluid [population]": half or more of them had "gone home to Italy for the winter." See Ramirez and Del Balzo, "Italians of Montreal," 63–5; John E. Zucchi, "Italian Hometown Settlements and the Development of an Italian Community in Toronto, 1875–1935," in Harney, ed., *Gathering Place*, 123–4; and Zucchi, *Italians in Toronto*, 44.

6 The Michigan Central Railroad, an American corporation that owned a number of lines in western Ontario, had begun operations in 1838 in Detroit and by 1852 had reached Chicago. From 1873, when Canada Southern was built and became part of the New York Central–Michigan Central systems, until 1910, passengers and freight were carried across the Detroit River on car ferries (for freight still used by the Canadian National). The railroad tunnel under the river opened a new era for the area. See "Michigan Central Railroad," *Encyclopedia Canadiana*, 1977 ed.; Woodford and Woodford, *All Our Yesterdays*, 194–6; and Morrison, *Garden Gateway*, 236–8.

7 Re, *Michigan's Italian Community*, 4–6. Alessandro Gavazzi was a controversial figure whose ideas and attacks on the Catholic Church resulted in a riot, with fourteen (some say forty) dead, in Montreal in June 1853. Spada, *Italians*, 59–62; Polidoro, *Tricolore in Canada*, 161. See also Sylvain, *Clerc*, Vol. 1.

8 Interviews, documents, research on the Windsor Italians (Windsor Italo-Canadian Culture Centre Archives, 1985), quoted in Temelini, "Italians in Windsor," 75 (henceforth, WICCC Archives: Windsor Italians [1985]). See also Woodford and Woodford, *All Our Yesterdays*, 25–6, 35–6.

9 "Dante Alighieri Society Formed by Border Italians," *Border Cities Star*, 18 December 1920.

o Temelini, "History of the Italian Business Community"; Temelini, "Italians in Windsor," 73–9; Temelini, "The Growth of Sports Involvement"; and Whelan with Archbold, *Whelan*, 10.

11 Swift & Company, one of the largest American packing firms (founded by Gustavus Franklin Swift, 1839–1903) with processing plants, distributing units, and offices "throughout the Free World" (including a plant in Genoa Italy, after a 1967 joint venture), has several branches in Canada. In Windsor, the Swift Canadian Company Limited (meat packers) on Janette Street last appeared in the *Windsor Directory* in 1970. See *Swift & Company Annual Reports*, 1960, 1962, 1967, 1970; and "Swift, Gustavus Franklin," *Who Was Who in America*, vol. 1, 1897–1942, 1211.

12 The calculations are based on the figures appearing in the Appendice Statistica in Rosoli, *Un secolo*, table 3, 353–5. However, Rosoli's figures do not coincide with "Immigrants Admitted to Canada by Ethnic Origin, 1896–1961," 24 Statistical Tables by Employment and Immigration Canada, Immigration Statistics Division, Program Data Directorate, Hull, QC, 1985. For example, for the period 1916–45, Rosoli has 47,762 and Statistics Canada 33,939. Also, in comparing the figures in the above-cited documents and the chart in Mastrangelo, *Italians in Canada*, 57, similar variants and discrepancies appear in the data on Italians who entered Canada in the first five or six decades of the century. For example, see the following table:

Period	Rosoli	Statistics Canada	Mastrangelo
1911–20	83,630	62,700	45,000
1951–60	229,330	250,800	245,000

13 Harney, "Italians in Canada," 238. Rosoli has 7,783 entries for 1923 and 3,459 for 1924. In Rosoli's data for the period 1916–45, the 1923 entries form the second-largest yearly number (behind 1920 with almost 8,500).

14 Of the 4,355,240 Italians who left Italy in 1916–42, 51.5 per cent (2,245,660) went to Europe and 44 per cent (1,920,280) to North and South America; 60 per cent of the total number had already left Italy by 1926. Favero and Tassello, "Cent'anni," 30. See also chapter 2, especially note 4.

15 In 1926–45, according to Rosoli's "Statistical Appendix," 322,441 went to North America, of which 307,828 went to the United States and 14,613 to Canada. For this period Statistics Canada figures do not differ greatly: 13,267.

16 Morrison, *Garden Gateway*, 233 and 297.

17 Immigration Records (1925–1935), 1926, vol. 7, 115, RG76, Immigration, series C-1-e, Library and Archives Canada.

18 At least according to Armando Mastronardi's statements in *Leamington Post*, Larry A. Cornies, "*Our Town*: Italian Community," 2 March 1977.

19 *50th Anniversary Giovanni Caboto Club 1925–1975* (Windsor), 7 and 16.

20 Personal communication (1991) from Velma Meconi (Belle River, Ontario), Luigi Meconi's daughter-in-law. The letterhead of the Meconi Brothers & Company used by Luigi Meconi for a letter of reference (20 April 1927) to the Windsor chief of police in favour of an Italian (Nereo Brombal) seeking a position in the "Force," has address at 301–303 Wyandotte St East, and lists in Italian the following: "Notary Public; General and Special Legal Documents; Expatriation Documents; Work Contracts; Assistance to Emigrants Detained at the Battery [a U.S. immigration station, now Battery Park in New York City]; Money Remittances to All Parts of the World through *Credito Italiano* and *Banca Commerciale*; Post Office; Official Interpreter; Legal Counselling." See W. Temelini, "La Polizia di Windsor ricorda e onora Nereo Brombal," 3; Cresci and Guidobaldi, *Partono i bastimenti*, 41; and chapter 7, especially notes 38, 40.

21 Concession g/G or Gore, Colchester South Township, south of Highway 18, west of Ridge Road or east of the Harrow Research Station Agriculture Canada.

22 7th Concession, Mersea Township, and later probably in Colchester South Township, at the former Jack Noble farm bought by Conklin.

23 Records show that two of them – Enrico Ingratta and Armando Mastronardi – reached Halifax on 6 November 1925, and the other two – Luigi Mastronardi and Giuseppe Pannunzio – arrived on 5 December 1925: see chapter 5.

24 It is not unusual even more recently to see envelopes mailed from Italy addressed to *Windsor, Ontario, Canada, USA*. In this light, this writer's mother may have been forgiven for a similar error she made in 1952 during the medical visit at the Canadian Consulate in Rome. When she was asked where she was going, she answered, as most Italians would have: "America." "America is America and Canada is Canada," sternly replied the official. Feeling his mother had been unfairly reprimanded, her thirteen-year-old son, in an attempt to defend her, retorted quickly and sarcastically: "And where's Canada? In Africa?" The boy's impertinence was not kindly received and had the Canadian official wanted to be equally unkind he might have easily prevented us, or made it difficult for us, to come to Canada, even though my father had been here since 1950. See also chapter 2, "The 'Right' America and the 'Wrong' America," and chapter 15, "*Lives of the Saints* as a 'Story of Emigration-Migration.'"

25 *The 1929–30 Windsor City Directory* lists him as "Peralto [*sic*] Vito, shoe repr., h. 324 Tuscarora" Street.

26 Some of them played key roles while serving the North American colonial powers in this general area or elsewhere: the Jesuit Francesco Giuseppe Bressani (or Bresciani), first Italian missionary in Huronia (1642–50), whose Italian written "Brief Relation on New France" included a map with the outline of Lake Erie and the Southwest Ontario–Lower Michigan region; the Neapolitan Tonti brothers: Enrico, who as aide to LaSalle and explorer of the Great Lakes and Mississippi (1678–82), travelled through Lake Erie (later 1670s) and supervised the launching (Niagara River, 1679) of the first ship on the Great Lakes (the *Griffon*, which sailed with a multinational crew, including Italians, through this area and to its doom near Tobermory, 1680); and Alfonso, first Italian in what is now Detroit: captain at Mackinac, governor of Fort Frontenac (Kingston), Cadillac's second in command in the building of Fort Pontchartrain (Detroit, 1701, suggesting to some writers that "Italians can claim to have been among the city's founders"), and governor of Detroit (1704–06), the post he also held when he died in 1727. The list includes as well the Recollet friar and descendant of a noble Florentine family, Costantino Degli Agli (gallicized into Del Halle), first priest to live and die in Detroit (1704–06), who had reached the new settlement in 1702 also via the Lake Erie route. But their early presence and work in what is now the Windsor-Detroit area seems only to have helped strengthen the very systems that buried their Italian identity.

According to Giovanni Schiavo (*The Italians in America before the Civil War*, 1934, quoted in Vittorio Re, *Michigan's Italian Community*), the forty-five-ton *Griffon* had a "crew of thirty Frenchmen, Flemings, and Italians, all jealous, not quite satisfied with their lot, always threatening to mutiny"; and Alfonso Tonti, whose "daughter Teresa was the first European to be born in [Detroit], where she died in infancy," in 1702 predicted that the Detroit site was "very good for building eventually a large town." Alfonso, who also owned a farm on Belle Isle, must have been quite familiar with the whole region of the Great Lakes, particularly with both shores of the Detroit-Windsor Strait. See Re, *Michigan's Italian Community*, 1–7; Re, "In Defence of Alfonso Tonti,"; Almazan, "1679"; Durnford, ed., *Heritage of Canada*, 75, 81; *Leamington-Mersea Souvenir*, 3; Fuller, *Windsor Heritage*, 4–5, 8–9; and Woodford and Woodford, *All Our Yesterdays*, 35–8, 250.

27 Such as the Crisafi brothers, Sicilian noblemen: Antonio, commander of Fort Condanga and governor of Trois Rivières, and Tommaso, second in command to Count Frontenac and defender of Niagara (late seventeenth and early eighteenth century); Paolo Marini, commander of French forces

in the Ohio Valley (1700s), and his son who fought with Montcalm on the Plains of Abraham; Burlamacchi (or Burlamaque) from Lucca, defender of the New York border for the French (1700s); as well as marquis Alessandro Malaspina, officer in the Spanish navy, explorer (late 1700s) of Canadian areas now bearing his name (*Malaspina* Glacier, Saint Elias Mountains, Yukon/Alaska area, and *Malaspina* Strait, British Columbia); or even Bartolomeo Galoina of Bernozzo (Bernezzo? Cuneo) of the "Italian Legion" that, along with the numerous Italian soldiers in the DeMeuron and Watteville regiments, defended Canada and the British Crown in the War of 1812, and then became farmers in Quebec and southern Ontario.

.8 The Bruschesi, Donegani, and Rusconi families in Montreal; Captain Filippo (Philip) DeGrassi, the first Toronto Italian, whose daughters served as British "spies" against the rebels (1837); Giacomo (James) Forneri, professor and promoter of a Modern Languages Department at the University of Toronto (1853–66); or Father Luigi da Lavagna, the Capuchin Missionary in Toronto (1856–57).

.9 Harney, "Italians in Canada," 227–8; Spada, *Italians*, 56–9; Kuitunen, "L'italianistica e l'emigrazione italiana"; and Kuitunen, "Italian and Italians in Educational Institutions"; Principe, "Italiani a Toronto prima del 1861"; Pautasso, *Il Santo cappuccino di Toronto*, 91–117; Zucchi, *Italians in Toronto*, 44, and chapter 1, "The Centuries-Old Italy-Canada Link," especially notes 46–52.

,0 Fuller, *Windsor Heritage*, 15–16; Re, *Michigan's Italian Community*, 2.

,1 Whelan with Archbold, *Whelan*, 10–14. According to Paul Marra of Windsor, his grandfather Nicola Antonio Marra (1888–1949) in 1897 emigrated with his family from Terreti (Calabria) to the United States, lived in Buffalo and St Catharines (where Nicola was employed as a foreman on the Niagara power lines), and in 1919 settled in Amherstburg, where he opened a small grocery store, which in a short time he transformed into Marra's Bread Company. Nicola, who served on the Amherstburg Town Council, Public Utilities Commission (for seventeen years), and as mayor for at least twelve years, was also "personally responsible for bringing over at least seventy-five families from Italy, the majority from Abruzzo" (personal communication, March 1991).

2 Emigration from the Puglia Region, particularly from the Foggia area, started to become more intense, according to Coletti, at the beginning of the twentieth century. Villari, *Il Sud*, 1:409–10. During the period 1916–42, 155,632 people emigrated from Puglia, but half (77,864) went back home; and between 1946 and 1976, out of the 856,503 emigrants, 573,876 repatriated. Favero and Tassello, "Cent'anni di emigrazione," 34–5, tables 11, 13; 40, tables 16, 17. The family name "Totaro" also

appears in the Molise region and among the Leamington Italians from that
region: Nick Totaro, from Villa Canale (1969), married Rosie Mastronardi
also from Villa Canale (1959); and Maria V. Totaro, from Villa Canale
(1953), married Alberino Mastronardi, also from Villa Canale (1951) (see
appendix A). In fact, the Totaro family appears in the list of those who first
settled in Villa Canale. Arduino and Arduino, *Le due valli del sole*, 21.

33 *1929–30 Windsor City Directory* has Joe and wife Mary at 800 Tecumseh
Road W.

34 Gino Pannunzio's information on Italian immigrant individuals and families
in the Leamington area after the First World War has provided a more complete view of the early community. For the information about Costanzo
Carlone, Mike Totaro, and Francesco LaRosa, see Gino Pannunzio's personal notes and communications (July 1988). See also Ramirez and Del
Balzo, "Italians in Montreal," 64–5.

CHAPTER FIVE

1 Cresci and Guidobaldi, *Partono i bastimenti*, 10–11, 190–3.

2 The hiring of Mexican workers for the Amherstburg and Leamington
farms sparked at least one controversy that involved the local member of
Parliament, who was also the minister of agriculture. See Kemp and
Martindale, "Whelan Explains 'Why' of Using Migrant Workers." In the
Windsor area there are also many domestic workers from the Caribbean
Islands; and, quite ironically, in Italy, once the land of emigrants, already
by the 1970s there were more than one million immigrants from the developing countries brought in (many of them illegally) as domestic "assistants" and for other unpopular jobs. For an explanation of
"tobacco-picking," see note 19 below.

3 Villari, *Il Sud*, 1:422.

4 Cresci and Guidobaldi, *Partono i bastimenti*, 42, 47, 87, 190.

5 Villari, *Il Sud*, 1:183; Cresci and Guidobaldi, *Partono i bastimenti*, 159.

6 In 1925, Domenic Pannunzio sponsored both his brother, Giuseppe (Joe),
and Luigi Mastronardi, a brother of his brother-in-law (that is, of the
same Giuseppe Mastronardi, the late husband, killed in WWI, of his sister
Rosina, and the same man who had been a "guarantor" for his passport in
1913 when the young Domenic travelled with him to America). At the
same time, the Ingrattas – most likely not Giovanni (John) but Raffaele
(Ralph), as indicated also by his grandson Ralph Ingratta of Leamington –
"called over" (sponsored) their cousin Enrico "Ricuccio" (Henry) Ingratta,
and Armando Mastronardi (no relation to Luigi, but related to Raffaele,
through their wives: Armando's wife Lisetta DiMenna and Raffaele's wife

Ernesta DiMenna – no relation to Tony DiMenna – were half sisters through their father). In October 1926, Tony (Amato) DeSantis, then most likely working in Kingsville, sponsored his wife (Gaetana Simonelli, 1902–44) and their two sons (Roy, 1923–91; and Fred, 1924–88, Mayor of Kingsville, 1966–74). In 1927, Alex Colasanti sponsored his brother Loreto who went to live with him and most likely to work on the same Jack Noble farm in Harrow.

7 Such as in Armando Mastronardi's case: in both his interview and in Cornies, "*Our Town*," he referred to an "agreement" with Canadian immigration authorities (refund of his "$200 bond" after two years of farm work). In his interview, however, he remembered, a bit reluctantly, Luigi Meconi ("who worked with immigration"); and he quickly alluded to a "brother-in-law who had been here" but "skipped the country," but he did not mention Raffaele Ingratta at all. Nevertheless, according to Raffaele's grandson, Ralph, after Armando and his wife Lisetta visited Villa Canale in 1950, Armando "sponsored Tony Ingratta, Raffaele's son, and Costantino Ingratta (of Windsor), Raffaele's grandson, as a favour to Raffaele [1923] for having sponsored him to Canada" in 1925.

8 Armando Mastronardi sponsored his wife Luisa (Lisetta or Elizabeth) DiMenna and their two sons, Umberto ("Bert," who died in 1973 at age fifty-one) and the five-year-old Olindo (Ollie); Luigi Mastronardi sponsored his eldest son Alfredo (who died in 1955 in a truck accident); and Joe Pannunzio, his wife Adorina (Audrey) Ingratta. Audrey guaranteed three underage immigrants from her area: fifteen-year-old Alfredo (Al) Mastronardi (Luigi's son), and the two Ingratta cousins, fifteen-year-old Jim (John's son) and sixteen-year-old Domenic (Henry's son), both sponsored also by their respective fathers. The group of seven travelled together to the New World and joined their respective families in Rodney (Jim and Domenic) and in Leamington in February 1930.

9 Nicola Valentino (b. 1908, Carpineto Sinello, Chieti, Abruzzo) emigrated to Canada with his family in 1920, and after four years in London (Ontario) moved to Windsor. Nicola and Fiorina Pannunzio may be considered, as Nicola claimed (personal communication, June 1991), "the first Italians married in Leamington, St Michael's Church, January 1938." In fact, the three pioneer couples recorded as being married in the same church before 1938 were already legally married: the civil and/or religious marriage, outside Canada, was followed by a church marriage or ceremony in Leamington: Giuseppe (Joe) Pannunzio (1925) and Adorina Ingratta (1930), first in Italy before his departure, then in Leamington (after her arrival), 28 July 1930; Eleuterio (Alex) Colasanti (1924) and Emma Colagiovanni, first in Detroit, March 1932, then in Leamington, 24 August

1935; while Antonino (Antonio or Tony) DiMenna (1923) and Antonietta Appugliese (1936), who had contracted civil and religious marriage by proxy upon her arrival in Leamington, repeated (for unclear, if not strange reasons) the church ceremony, 11 June 1936 (see certificate of marriage obtained from St Michael's Church and from Agnone, Italy). See also chapter 10: "The Proxy Marriage," and "Old and New Marriage Practices."

10 Many Italian women were in demand, even in France, for this type of work and were well remunerated: "A nurse ... could earn even three times as much as a labourer and [their work], the *baliatico*, made a considerable contribution to the flow into Italy of hard currency, which supported and almost saved for decades the almost non-existent Italian economy of the time." Cresci and Guidobaldi, *Partono i bastimenti*, 36–9.

11 The wife of Tony DeSantis is Gaetana, but Saveria in her interview often uses the name Matuccia. Apparently Tony, whose name was Amato, was also known as Amatuccio or Matuccio. Saveria must have just used the feminine form of Tony's popular name. Gino Pannunzio, personal communication, July 1986.

12 Saveria Magri, interview.

13 The interviews also presented some confusion; nevertheless, whether a "thirteen-acre farm with vineyards," as Saveria described it, or a "five-acre vineyard," as her son Domenic stated, it was most likely owned by Mariano Meconi, who also operated a winery in the Windsor area; the one "at 5th Concession," mentioned by Alex Colasanti, was in farm lot 11, 5th Concession, Gosfield South Township, and clearly owned by Mariano's brother, Luigi, but not until 23 September 1924, as indicated in the deed of land. See chapter 4, "The First Men from Lazio" and note 20; and "Truly Pioneers."

14 For the significance of the *compare-comare* tradition within the Southern Italian immigrant family and community, see chapter 10, "The Extended Family: The *Comparatico* or *Compare-Comare* 'Network'"; also chapter 11, "The Home Visit."

15 Villari, *Il Sud*, 1:419–22. See also chapter 3, "The Southern Italian 'Dream of America' – Reality and Fiction"; chapter 10, "*La Famiglia* – The Family."

16 In reality, as reported by Gino Pannunzio, they did not "have" a farm: the three of them and Joe Pannunzio worked as sharecroppers for Jack Noble in the Harrow area (see chapter 4).

17 Martelli, "Per un viaggio senza ritorno," 6, 489. See also chapter 3, "The Southern Italian 'Dream of America' – Reality and Fiction," especially note 22; and chapter 15, "Conclusion," and note 83.

18 "The one large room ... had a big old potbellied stove in the corner and no electricity, so on dark winter days we worked by the light of kerosene lamps ... There was no running water – no bathroom – just two outhouses, one for girls and one for boys, in two corners of the schoolyard. Around behind the outhouses was one of the places where we kids fought" and at times "we gave [the Italian] quarry kids quite a hard time. [They] had a little bit of a rough reception when they arrived." Whelan with Archbold, *Whelan*, 12, 14.

19 The immigrants used the term *pick* to mean *sucker* tobacco: breaking the shoots that grew between the leaves and stem of the plant in order to produce a bigger and healthier leaf; also used was the term to *prime* tobacco: "picking off two or three leaves from the bottom of the plant as they became yellow, making an armful, placing it in a cart-like vehicle pulled by a horse and taken to the kiln to be made ready for curing"; and in the 1920s and 1930s tobacco was generally "flue-cured" (cured or dried by hot air passed through flues). Gino Pannunzio, personal communication, March 1992. See also chapter 6, "The War Bonanza and the 'New Landowners': From Tobacco to Vegetables."

20 The Model T with a crank (fifteen million made between 1908 and 1927) had too many problems: the Ts were very hard to start ("often the back wheels had to be jacked up to allow for more power – the transmission and engine were all in one, everything turned at once"); the oil was too thick (#30 regular grade); good gasoline was unavailable (not as refined as today); the batteries were very weak (the engine could be "turned over" only once, so there wasn't enough power in the six-volt battery to do it again). "Antifreeze existed, but not in the form we know today ... Ethylglycol in those days ... would have eaten the paint off the car. Their antifreeze consisted of an alcohol base," and in the summer only water was used. Bob Gault, curator of the Canadiana and Auto Museum, LaSalle, ON, personal communication, 15 February 1991. See also Woodford and Woodford, *All Our Yesterdays*, 285–6.

21 Gervais, *The Rumrunners*, 8–11, 17, 23, 27, 50–2, 56, 67, 71, 131–3, 142–3; Woodford and Woodford, *All Our Yesterdays*, 303–10.

22 Interview by student-researchers, 1981.

CHAPTER SIX

1 Interview with Leamington Italian immigrant Domenic Magri.
2 Macaluso, "'Enemy Alien' Stigma Leaves Scars," A10.
3 Procacci, *History*, 442–5; Mack Smith, *Mussolini*, 262–77.
4 Finlay and Sprague, *The Structure of Canadian History*, 369–72, 386–87.

5 Gino DiMenna and Gino Pannunzio provided most of the information on
the gradual change from tobacco to vegetable growing and the reasons for
it. See also Essex County (Ontario) Tourist Association, *Essex County
Sketches*, 31; and articles in "Historical Essex '75," *Windsor Star*, 11 July
1975, 29–44, especially Rennie:

> In the 1920s the soils of Norfolk County were found to be ideal for
> tobacco. A new belt of flue-cured tobacco developed in that area and
> declined in Essex and Kent Counties. Burley tobacco remained import-
> ant in Essex and Kent Counties however, but all flue-cured tobacco
> research eventually went to Delhi … Since the 1920s the burley industry
> has gone through difficult times as overproduction and a failure to
> develop foreign markets caused prices to sag. Peak acreage was probably
> reached in 1947 when 13,200 acres were planted but this declined to
> 1,096 in 1953. In 1960 no burley was grown at all.

Rennie, "Harrow Ends as Tobacco Research Hub," 38.

But "of the 26 research stations across Canada [run by the federal
Department of Agriculture], Harrow's is one of the largest in terms of
staff size [of 102 people, 32 are research personel – mostly PhDs].
Offices at the station are also provided for staff of the Ontario Ministry
of Agriculture and food, fruit and vegetable extension services, and the
Western Ontario Fruit Testing Association." Rennie, "Harrow Research
Program One of the Most Diversified," *Windsor Star*, "Historical Essex
'75," 11 July 1975, 42. In "Essex, Kent Counties Look Ahead to Bumper
Crops," in the same issue of the *Star*, 38, Essex County was described as
"one of the most productive agricultural areas in Canada, second only
to neighbouring Kent," particularly in the acreage of corn and soybeans
(Essex 75,000 and 65,000 acres – Kent 200,000 and 140,000 acres); but
in winter wheat, "Essex with 55,000 to 65,000 acres seeded" surpassed
"Kent with 50,000" in 1975. In 1974, also according to the article,
"farmers from both Essex and Kent were estimated to have earned gross
incomes totalling $250 million, placing agriculture in competition with
all other heavy industry in the area." Though the greenhouse industry
was not mentioned, the conversion from tobacco to vegetables in the
1940s proved to be quite remunerative also for the Leamington Italian
growers in the following decades.

6 Procacci, *History*, 11, 28, 68–69, 74, 86–8, 127, 151, 162–3, 171–3, 202–
3, 220.

7 Fascism was seen (and misunderstood) by the emigrants as a sort of
Italian rebirth … Observed from far away it did not fail to bolster
patriotism; Mussolini's own career, from a blacksmith's son, labourer
and socialist interventionist to government leader, typified the rise of the

"self-made man," an idea that was esteemed and respected in the two Americas. Italo Balbo's transatlantic flights finally exported an organizational and civic heroism that erased the memory of the destruction of democracy by the Fascist Regime. The Italian-American colonies were split apart: the traditionally socialist and libertarian emigrants remained anti-Fascist; the most well-to-do, the most ignorant and the most naive became Fascists. Since the Italian newspapers published and printed by the communities were mostly funded by small and big businessmen, almost all took a Fascist colour. (Cresci and Guidobaldi, *Partono i bastimenti*, 200; translation mine)

Since 1931 Mussolini viewed "imperialism as the supreme test of a nation's vitality," and he "provided the core of Fascist political education" with the "endless repetition of ... ominous or comical phrases ... To the Fascist youth movement, he gave the watchword 'believe, obey, fight'; to army conscripts ... 'better one day as a lion than a hundred years as a sheep'; to the party ... 'the more enemies, the greater the honour.'" Mack Smith, *Mussolini*, 173. See also chapter 1, especially note 54; chapter 2, "The Ill-Fated First Trip," and note 37; chapter 9, note 9.

8 Harney, "Italians in Canada," 240–3; Spada, *Italians*, 125–7; Restaldi, "Memoriale sugli Italiani," 5–8; Helling, *Socio-Economic History*, 80–1.

9 Windsor Italo Canadian Culture Centre Archives, wiccc Archives: Interviews, Documents, Research: The Windsor Italians 1985 Project No. 7893 (which contains interview with Gilda Meconi).

0 "Italians Here Having 'Hell on Earth,' Says Mayor," *Windsor Daily Star*, 20 January 1941; "Reopen Issue of Enemy Aliens in City Service," *Windsor Daily Star*, 29 March 1941.

1 Hull, "Scores of Windsor Italians Arrested."

2 Ibid.

3 "200 Italian-Born Here Affected by New Ottawa Ruling," *Windsor Daily Star*, 24 August 1940.

4 Claiming to present "absolutely unprejudiced ... views" based on "a very deep study of Fascism," both doctrine and system, Artico declared that "its aim is the subjugation of the working class," the elimination of "freedom and liberty," as events had shown since the ascent of Hitler and Mussolini. "The Italian workers realized too late their mistake ... and 25,000 of them have been killed since 1921, while from February 1927 to June 1930, 1,558 anti-Fascists were given jail terms aggregating 10,100 years." Artico "charged that 'one of the chief leaders of Fascism in the Border Cities is an Italian who has never done an honest day's work in his life but has exploited the poor, ignorant Italian immigrant. This gentleman, also, has attempted to start the Black Shirt movement but he was stopped by other

Italians.' The speaker said the rank-and-file of the Blue Shirt movement does not understand the aims of that organization, 'but join it blindly, thinking they will better themselves.'" "John Artico Will Speak on Fascism," *Border Cities Star*, 25 October 1933, 3; "Blue Shirts of Canada Attacked," *Border Cities Star*, 27 October 1933, 5. Again, at the October 1933 meeting of the Windsor Italian Liberal Association, John Artico asked Major James H. Clark, speaker at the event, about "the Liberal Party's probable reaction to the recently organized Blue Shirts, a suspected Fascist organization 'negative of liberty.'" "Major Clark [and] Mr Henry," *Border Cities Star*, 28 October 1933, 9. In fact, the president of the Windsor Italian Canadian Political Club did not recognize the Italian Liberal Association, "On Italian Clubs in Border Cities," *Border Cities Star*, 31 October 1933, 7, claiming that its "so-called leader" P.C. Scarpelli was not only "not popular with the [Italian] people" but was also the "mouthpiece of the Italian Blue Shirts of Windsor." J. Palmieri, letter to the editor, *Border Cities Star*, 31 October 1933. The "fight against the sup-posed growth of Fascism in Canada" was causing many divisions; it had also split the Windsor Workers' Ex-Servicemen League into "right and left wings." "Veterans Will Decide Policy at Rally Tonight," *Border Cities Star*, 27, 30 October 1933. "Beware of Fascism, Says This Writer," *Border Cities Star*, 30 October 1933, 7.

15 When Luigi Meconi, president of the Dante Alighieri Society and organizer of the Italian school, was "unable to confirm or deny the report [of his appointment as director of the 'Fascist section' in Windsor] he was con-fronted 'with a copy of an Italian paper containing his picture and the announcement of his appointment." "Meconi [Luigi] Vague on Role as Head of City's 'Fascist Section,'" 18 May 1938, *Windsor Daily Star*, 8. The Toronto *Bollettino Italo-Canadese* "stated that 'The Secretary of the Toronto Fascists, Mr M.J. Magi has announced the formation of a Fascist section in Windsor giving the trustworthy direction (or full leadership) to Mr Luigi Meconi ... a very active element, well known and influential in Windsor' ... That was on April 9, 1937. Yesterday – the *Star* reported – Mr Meconi flatly declined to make any comment on the report." "Secretary Quenneville Rebuked by Trustees in Stand on Fascism: Meconi Vague on Role as Head of City's 'Fascist Section,'" *Windsor Star*, 18 May 1938. Luigi Meconi "denied being a Fascist, but there was much documentation against him. Indignant at the result of the investigation, he resigned from the Order of the Sons of Italy where he was grand officer, on the grounds that the brothers of Windsor failed to support him during the inquiry." Principe, "The Italo-Canadian Anti-Fascist Press," 129.

16 Hull, "Scores of Windsor Italians Arrested."

7 The photo of Sergeant James Wilkinson with two organizers of the event at his side – Luigi Meconi and Joseph Falsetto, president of the Legion – appeared in the *Windsor Daily Star* on 26 May 1936.

8 "Local Italians Donate Gold to Help Il Duce," *Windsor Daily Star*, 27 January 1936.

9 "Windsor Italians Fight Plan to Aid Duce," *Windsor Daily Star*, 25 January 1936.

0 Ibid.

1 "Fascist Teachings in Windsor Probed: Classes Stay Closed until Their Purpose Subjected to Scrutiny," *Windsor Daily Star*, 14 May 1938; "Meconi [Luigi] Vague on Role as Head of City's 'Fascist Section,'" 18 May 1938.

2 "Fascism Is Glorified in Italian Readers," *Windsor Daily Star*, 19 May 1938. One of the "Fascist texts" used in Windsor was *Storia e geografia per la IV classe elementare* (Verona: A. Mondadori, 1937–XV). On the front cover under the main title (History and geography for the fourth grade) appears also *Scuole Italiane all' Estero* (Italian schools abroad). No author is given. But the 237 pages, with many illustrations and covering a period from "The First Inhabitants of Italy" to "The Italian (i.e., Fascist) Empire" (222–37), contain an endless exaltation of Italian and Fascist achievements.

3 "Ottawa Probes Windsor Fascist Class: Two Italian Teachers Barred from Canada by Immigration Law," *Windsor Daily Star*, 16 May 1938.

4 The Fascist consuls' frequent use of moral blackmail against the Italian Canadian anti-Fascists and the threat of reprisals against their relatives in Italy made life even more difficult for the immigrants whose emotional lifeline with their land of origin was suddenly cut; and the post-1940 period was "the most sorrowful page in the history of the Italians in Canada also because of a split that opened during those years within the immigrant community, and that would take many years to resolve" since hatred and resentment was kept alive by a widespread "atmosphere of suspicion." Bruti Liberati, "Fascismo, antifascismo," 53, 61. See also chapter 1, "The Changing Fortunes of the Italians in Canada and in Leamington"; chapter 2, "The Ill-Fated First Trip."

5 See Macaluso, "'Enemy Alien' Stigma Leaves Scars."

6 "More Arrested in Drive against Enemy Alien Suspects," *Windsor Daily Star*, 12 June 1940.

7 Windsor Italo-Canadian Culture Centre, *The Windsor Italians*, sponsored by Employment and Immigration Canada, 1985. "The four-day purge netted about 40 'heads of households,' including one housewife.'" "[Constable Nero/Nereo Brombal] Suspended [from Windsor Police Force]," *Windsor Daily Star*, 13 June 1940, 5.

28 Macaluso, "'Enemy Alien' Stigma Leaves Scars."

29 "More Arrested in Drive against Enemy Alien Suspects," *Windsor Daily Star.*

30 "Airman Asks Aid for Dad," *Windsor Daily Star*, 21 March 1941.

31 Macaluso, "One Man's Story of Internment."

32 "More Arrested in Drive against Enemy Alien Suspects," *Windsor Daily Star*; Macaluso, "Mystery Surrounds Cruel Wartime Raids."

33 "Reopen Issue of Enemy Aliens in City Service," *Windsor Daily Star*, 24 March 1941.

34 Macaluso, "One Man's Story of Internment."

35 "Send Enemy Aliens Home," *Windsor Daily Star*, 14 June 1940.

36 "Italian Vote Calls for Aid, but Once Great Voice Not Heard by Members of Ottawa," *Windsor Daily Star*, 12 June 1940.

37 "Italian Liberals Elect Officers," *Windsor Daily Star*, 10 February 1940.

38 "Italian Vote Calls for Aid," *Windsor Daily Star.*

39 Windsor Italo-Canadian Culture Centre, *The Windsor Italians.* Similarly, after his return to Windsor, when a neighbour afraid to associate with a former internee refused to acknowledge his greeting, Angelo Dominato was left with sadness and tears in his eyes. Macaluso, "'Enemy Alien' Stigma Leaves Scars."

40 "Border Italians Have Ceremony at Cenotaph: Italians Pay Deep Tribute. Initiation of Local Lodge Impressive [Loggia Generale Umberto Nobile of the Ordine Figli d'Italia]," *Border Cities Star*, 25 May 1927. The Ontario Order of the Sons of Italy, which received its provincial charter in 1926, in order to avoid the split into the pro- and anti-Fascist factions experienced by the Quebec Order, "steered away from direct propaganda," even though "the Fascists … held most of the important positions in the Grand Lodge." Principe, "The Difficult Years." Among the officers of the Windsor Lodge were listed Louis A. Merlo, *venerabile*; Luigi Cennamo, assistant *venerabile*; Clemente Meconi, *oratore*; A. Sorrentino, *Segr. di finanza*; Mariano Meconi, *Segr. archivista*; A. Fenech, *tesoriere*, and several others as *curatori*; while "Luigi Meconi is grand deputy representing the grand lodge in Ontario."

41 "Airman Asks Aid for Dad," *Windsor Daily Star.* On that occasion Angelo Zamparo declared, "Italians haven't caused any trouble to Canada; there hasn't been an Italian arrested for espionage or sabotage from coast to coast since the beginning of the war. We are loyal today as those born in Canada or in the British Isles," and "industrialists had been wrong in denying jobs to Italians thereby doubting their loyalty to Canada." "Italians Here Give $1,200: Money Handed Over to Red Cross; Yearning for Axis Defeat," *Windsor Daily Star*, 20 March 1942. See also Harney, "Italians in

Canada," 242; Temelini, "Italians in Windsor," 76–8; and chapter 9, "The Factory..." especially note 9.

42 Several Italians known to the writer who lived in Windsor through the war years referred to the presence of RCMP informers within the Windsor Italian community. But it was done only in private and without disclosing names, in spite of the assurance given them of their anonymity. "Paid informants played a big role in the raid against Italians," according to Luigi Pennacchio, a research fellow at the Toronto-based Multicultural History Society of Ontario" (interviewed in 1989). "Documents Pennacchio obtained through the Freedom of Information Act show the RCMP established a national network of civilian informants. They relied heavily on information provided by an Italian consular employee for $60 a month." Macaluso, "Mystery Surrounds Cruel Wartime Raids."

43 Clearly meant to promote patriotism and sacrifice among the young, since it derived from the nickname given to G.B. Perasso, the boy who in 1746 initiated the revolt of the Genoese against Austrian forces.

44 Mack Smith, *Mussolini*, 176. See also Macaluso, "One Man's [Vito Peralta's] Story of Internment"; *Windsor Daily Star*, "Police Raid in Windsor [on the City's Italian Community]," 12 June 1940; and Gino DiMenna and Salvatore Peralta, personal communication, 1991.

45 See Finlay and Sprague, *Structure of Canadian History*, 385–6.

46 Luigi Meconi was the only one of the three Meconi brothers to be interned: Clemente had died in 1934 and Mariano, though involved in the Windsor Chapter of the Order of Sons of Italy, managed to avoid it. Velma Meconi, personal communication, 1991.

See also *Border Cities Star*, "Border Italians Have Ceremony"; "Blue Shirts of Canada Attacked: Anti-Fascist [John Artico] Warns of Troubles Experienced in Italy," 27 October 1933, 5; "Major Clark [and] Mr Henry." And see *Windsor Daily Star*, "Windsor Italians Fight Plan to Aid Duce: Fascist Help Is Opposed. Soliciting Funds by Vice-Consuls Brings Protest," 25 January 1936, 3, 8; "Fascist Teachings in Windsor Probed: Classes Stay Closed until Their Purpose Subjected to Scrutiny. Separate School Board Chairman Orders Inquiry: 125 Children Attending Saturday Courses at St Alphonsus," 14 May 1938, 3, 8; "Ottawa Probes Windsor Fascist Class. Two Italian Teachers Barred from Canada by Immigration Law: 'Loyal Canadian' Charges Other Text Books Used by Organizer also Contain Obvious Propaganda," 16 May 1938, 3, 8; "Fascism Is Glorified in Italian Readers: Excerpts from Books Used in Canada Belie Claim No Propaganda Contained in Them," 19 May 1938, 5; "Scores of Windsor Italians Arrested in Fascist Purge."

47 See Windsor Italo-Canadian Culture Centre, *Windsor Italians*; Macaluso, *Windsor Star*, "'Enemy Alien' Stigma"; "Mystery Surrounds Cruel Wartime Raids"; "One Man's Story"; "Redress Sought for 'Injustices,'" 24 January 1989, A1, A9; "Repetition of Violations Can Be Avoided," 24 January 1989, B1; "Righting 47-Year-Old Wrongs," 23 January 1989, B1; Castrilli, "Remarks to the 9th Biennial Convention"; and Mulroney, "Notes for an Address"; Vincent Della Noce, House of Commons Debates, Monday, 5 November 1990; Allen, "Mulroney Apologizes to Italian Internees"; Beltrame, "'Unfair, Illegal, Abusive'."

48 "We Are Sorry: To Right the Wrongs of 1940," *Ottawa Citizen*, 9 November 1990, A12; Dunn, "Five Decades Later"; Bernier, "Antonio Capobianco affirme qu'il n'oubliera jamais 1940." See also Macaluso, "'Enemy Alien' Stigma," "Righting 47-Year-Old Wrongs"; Beltrame, "Italians Get Apology"; Della-Mattia, "Words Come Too Late" Temelini, "Le scuse di Mulroney agli Italiani."

49 Peralta and Peralta, letter to the editor, *La Gazzetta*, 7 January 1991, 3.

50 The Board of Police Commissioners for the City of Windsor presented the plaque on 5 December 1990, during a ceremony attended by Brombal's son and granddaughter as well as representatives of the Windsor Italian Canadian associations. The inscription "to the memory of Constable Nereo Brombal ... whose 12 years of service ... [were] unjustly terminated in ... June 1940 because of his [Italian] birth," also stated that the police "acknowledge with gratitude the work of Constable Brombal and their due regret for the injustice done him and others of the Italian community at a time when reason and humanity had been abandoned." The translation of the inscription and Walter Temelini, "La Polizia di Windsor," prompted Helen McCrory's letter to the editor, *La Gazzetta*, 6 May 1991.

51 "We Are Sorry."

52 McLuhan, *Understanding Media*, 306.

53 Villari, *Il Sud*, 1:415–17. With respect to the Southern Italian family in general, in "1904 ... Adolfo Rossi, head of the *Commissariato Generale dell'Emigrazione*, an Italian governmental agency responsible for overseeing the condition of emigrants at the time of departure from Italy, those in transit, and those already living abroad, observed that the family ties of the Southern Italian 'are deep and tenacious; in their hearts they develop an attachment to the fellow townsman along with affection for the family.'" Zucchi, *Italians in Toronto*, 5–6. See also chapter 10, "Marriage and the Family," especially section "The Extended Family ..."

54 Leonardo Sciascia, "... per terre assai lontane," and Maria Messina, "La Merica," in Cresci and Guidobaldi, *Partono i bastimenti*, 7 and 42.

5 See Alighieri, *The Divine Comedy, I: Hell*, XXVI, 94 ff.; also chapter 3, "The Lessons of the Ill-Fated First Attempt"; and chapter 15, "Conclusion."

6 Harney, *Dalla Frontiera alle Little Italies*, 218; Spada, *Italians*, 80–3; and Romano, *Storia d'Italia*, 94.

CHAPTER SEVEN

1 Sturino, "Italians."

2 Procacci, *History*, 457–9; Valeri, *Storia d'Italia*, 5:492–3.

3 Villari, *Il Sud*, 2:630.

4 Hapgood and Richardson, *Monte Cassino*, 25–6.

5 Procacci, *History*, 452–8; Norman Kogan, "Italy in the Modern World," in Chandler and Molinaro, *Culture of Italy*, 159–60.

6 Procacci, *History*, 409, 441–52; Valeri, *Storia d'Italia*, 5:493–4, 500–14; Consonni, *Ponte nei secoli*, 3:424–8; Bacci, *Viaggio nel tempo*, 3:255–9; Langer, *Encyclopedia*, 1162–3; Hapgood and Richardson, *Monte Cassino*, 4–5, 9–11, 21–3, 27–9, 78–9, 121–2, 256–60.

7 "The horrible and destructive avalanche" of the Second World War ravaged Agnone also and brought through it "soldiers of every colour, of every race and of every continent." In fact, the Agnone-Pescolanciano railroad, in operation since 1915, was destroyed during the German retreat in 1943. The resulting lack of any means of transportation caused many hardships, especially to students who wished to pursue higher education. But it also led to the opening in 1945 of two schools that still exist: the Scientific Lyceum and the Technical School. Carlomagno *Agnone*, 286–7, 294. See also Marrocco, *La guerra nel Medio Volturno nel 1943*, 13–18, 34–5, 220–4.

8 Valeri, *Storia d'Italia*, 5:505; Langer, *Encyclopedia*, 1162.

9 Procacci, *History*, 452–8; Kogan, "Italy in the Modern World," 159–60.

10 Procacci, *History*, 452–8; Kogan, "Italy in the Modern World," 159–60.

11 Consonni, *Ponte nei secoli*, 3:491.

12 Also referred to as Cassa del Mezzogiorno, the fund was allotted "one thousand billion lire" by the government to not only create "a new economic environment for the development of the Mezzogiorno" but also to end "the theoretical and historical debate around the 'Southern Question.'" Consonni, *Ponte nei secoli*, 3:491. From 1950 to 1975 the "fund's programs have required a global commitment of about 14,500 billion lire, with a capacity to generate investments for over 25,000 billion lire." *La Cassa per il Mezzogiorno*, 5. See also chapter 1, especially note 3.

13 Villari, ed., *Il Sud*, 2, chapter 10, "La nuova democrazia," introduction, 627–32; and Giorgio Amendola, "Contro la istituzione della Cassa per il Mezzogiorno," 2:633–46; Pasquale Saraceno, "L'industria del Nord e la spesa pubblica nel Mezzogiorno," 2:647–59; Manlio Rossi-Doria, "La riforma agraria," 2:660–80; Emilio Sereni, "Vecchio e nuovo nelle campagne italiane," 2:681–711; "Bilancio di dieci anni [Relazione Pastore, 1960]," 712–34; and Antonio Giolitti, "La questione meridionale e il socialismo in Italia," 2:735–54.

14 Procacci, *History*, 348, 455–6, 460–1.

15 Rocco Scotellaro, the young peasant-poet, socialist intellectual, and mayor of his town in Lucania, was imprisoned for leading the peasants' struggle for land after the war. For Martelli, "the Scotellaro 'case' became and still is today a central passageway" in "the history of Southern Italian culture in the last thirty years," in "the clash between, on the one hand, the capital istic, colonizing and consumeristic civilization [of the North] and, on the other, the peasant civilization [of the South]." Scotellaro represents the "final defeat of the Mezzogiorno, of its culture, of its peasant civilization," or of the Southern Italian peasant class, in postwar Italy. See Martelli, "Due casi di critica senza 'distanza'"; and Santeramo, "La lingua di Rocco Scotellaro."

16 *Questa è l'Italia* (Rome: Istituto Poligrafico e Zecca della Stoto, 1979), 163.

17 Procacci, *History*, 349, 459–61.

18 Procacci, *History*, 349, 459–61. See also Procacci, *Storia degli italiani*, 553–9; Romano, *Storia d'Italia*, 31; Valeri, *Storia*, 4:695.

19 Villari, *Il Sud*, 2:727–31 (especially table 5 and 729n1); 735–8.

20 According to 1983 CENSIS calculations based on data from Istituto Nazionale Previdenza Sociale (National Social Security Benefits Institute), Molise had the "highest ratio between, on the one hand, the number of people receiving Disability Pensions and, on the other, those receiving Old Age Pensions, the work force and the number of inhabitants." Also, "the improvement in living conditions in the last thirty years [since early 1950s] has been partly the result of immigrant remittances (Molise with Abruzzi receives the most consistent flux of money that is directed to the Italian Regions from abroad)." One problem also mentioned was insufficient "development of intensive agriculture," partly because of "the fragmentation of farmlands" and partly because of "the flight of young energies from the farms." "La Regione Molise," 74–7.

21 Labanca, "Agnone ... da quarant'anni in qua!" According to the statistics in "La Regione Molise," 74, "one-eighth of the funds invested in the South between 1951 and 1971 ... in the road building program" was absorbed

by Molise. But in the same issue of the Agnone newspaper (*L'eco dell'alto Molise*, 20 June 1986) there were complaints against the "inconceivable delays" in receiving funds for public works (Costantino Mastronardi, "Ai lettori – Lavori pubblici: ritardi inconcepibili"); while Labanca in another issue poses a series of "why's" about money for work projects never reaching the outlying areas … such as "Upper Molise" (20 May 1987).

22 Salvadori, "Italy as a Country of Regions," 16.

23 Mastronardi, "Vogliono che disertiamo?"; also Lanciano, "La questione meridionale"; and Delli Quadri, "Considerazioni sul futuro di Agnone." The "Mountain Community" or "Community of Upper Molise" includes the municipalities of Agnone, Capracotta, Pescopennataro, S. Angelo del Pesco, Pescolanciano, Pietrabbondante, Carovilli, Vastogirardi, Castel del Giudice, and Belmonte del Sannio. Carlomagno, *Agnone*, 52. See also chapter 15, "The Novel's Other Villages."

24 Nice, *Questo nostro mondo*, 1:151–4; "La Regione Molise," 69–82; Carlomagno, *Agnone*, 275–9; Lanciano, "Agnone industriale"; see also Maiorino, "Agnone's Bells That Ring Round the World"; and *Le Regioni in cifre* (Rome: Istituto centrale di statistica, 1988), 18–20, 37, 58–9. See also chapter 1, especially note 38; chapter 15, especially note 11.

25 Santoro, "Il parco come ultima spiaggia?" *L'eco dell' alto Molise*, 20 May 1987 (in the same issue: "L'artigianato: fatti non promesse"); and Mastronardi, "Ai lettori."

26 Frequent earthquakes (recorded since the year 847), landslides, as well as the plague (which in the early 1500s decimated Agnone's population) also contributed to the exodus and slow growth of Agnone and area. Carlomagno, *Agnone*, 283. See also chapter 2.

27 Personal communication from Luigi Mastronardi, a teacher in Villa Canale, 30 May 1985. In 1961, population of the village and outlying area was 752, while the village alone was 532. Touring Club Italiano, *Annuario generale*, 1070. Arduino and Arduino recorded 962 people for 1901 and "about 400 people" in 1988. *Le due valli del sole*, 28.

28 The 1961 figure derives from Touring Club Italiano, *Annuario generale*, 9; while Lanciano, "Agnone industriale," gives the population as of 28 February 1988. In 1951 the population of Agnone by itself was 4,462 and 4,232 in 1961. Touring Club Italiano, *Guida rapida*, 35; and *Annuario generale*, 9, respectively.

29 Villari, *Il Sud*, 2:633–6, 703–4 (esp. table, 704: "Mechanization of Agriculture and Agrarian Reform in South Italy," 1949–55); 721–3 (esp. table 4: "Investments in Manufacturing Industry in the South to 1959"), 730–4, 745–54. See also "Disoccupazione e Pil pro-capite in Italia nel periodo 85–90," *GRTV Press* (Rome, 1991), reprint in *La Gazzetta*, 3 June

1991, 4; Martino, "I ritardi del Mezzogiorno..."; Mattioli, "Italia del Nord, Italia del Sud..."; and *Economist*, "*North-South: Italy*"; see also Procacci, *History*, note 16.

30 Guido Fink, arguing against Dominique "Fernandez's 1950 *terminus-ad-quem* ... of the 'American myth' among Italian intellectuals" (e.g., Cesare Pavese's 1950 novel *La luna e i falò*), states that it "is very hard to eradicate a myth, especially if (as in Pavese's case) one happens to share a good deal of the responsibility for its creation and diffusion. Also, this particular myth, Phoenix-like, never seems to be so alive and well as when it is officially put to death – which means it never dies, it only changes." With examples ranging from Mario Soldati's 1941 novella *La verità sul caso Motta*, set in the 1930s "when American cinema is indeed a giant screen, and America dominates the imagination of film-goers, film-makers and would-be film-makers," to DeSica's *Ladri di biciclette*, manifesting still in the forties the American films' "pervading presence," to Bertolucci's magnification of Marilyn Monroe in *La luna* and to "Umberto Eco's ... analysis of three different generations of Italian boys ... all variously affected by more or less unconscious '*Americanismo*,'" Fink concludes that "America," whether enlarged or attacked, has been "an essential part of what we nowadays are." Fink, "The Other Side of the Moon."

31 Some satirical aspects of the Italian "cult" of American films in pre– and post–Second World War Italy have also been captured in both Federico Fellini's *Amarcord* (I remember, 1973) – in which one character tries to imitate Ronald Colman – and in Giuseppe Tornatore's *Nuovo cinema Paradiso* (late 1980s) – an *Amarcord* in a Sicilian context, and the first Italian film since *Amarcord* to win the Oscar for best foreign film, in 1990. See Grazzini, *Gli anni Settanta in cento film*, 223–6; and Silvestri, "Un Oscar e un nuovo film."

32 First published in 1947 by the Ministry of Foreign Affairs of Canada, the second edition (Ministry of Citizenship and Immigration, Ottawa, 1951) contained "revisions of the text in the light of recent events and was illustrated with a completely new series of photographs and maps," 2 (translation mine).

33 "Italians," *Canadian Encyclopedia*, 1988 ed.

34 Spada, *Italians*, 128–9.

35 See Cellino Temelini, "Garanzia per Espatrio [Sponsorship declaration]" for Antonino (Antonio) Temelini, 6–8 February 1950 [copy], WICCC Archives (translation mine).

36 Joe Dziver, "Italian Pioneers Aid Newcomers: Industrious Immigrants Take Key Business Roles," *Windsor Daily Star*, 18 July 1959.

37 McKinnon, "Italian Farmworkers Enjoy Canada Freedom."

8 In a letter of 15 November 1948, written in Italian, addressed to Corpolongo Umberto (Pastena, Frosinone) and signed by L. Meconi, Meconi (Luigi no doubt) "officially" informs Corpolongo of the Canadian authorization for his "entry in this Dominion," enclosing in the letter both the "Official Document No. C.8881 ... as well as an Order for a pre-paid ticket No. 29677 from Naples to Windsor via New York and for $8.00 that will be given you at debarkation ... to be used during the train journey to Windsor." Corpolongo is also told to follow closely both the instructions in the letter that he will soon receive from the Canadian Immigration Office in Rome, as well as those in Meconi's letter: For passage reservation on the ship *Sobieski* and date of departure, he should contact the Cosulich Brothers in Naples (address given) and for other information he should write to his "uncle Giuseppe DeLellis ... at R.R. #2, Leamington, Province Ontario, Canada." *Documents and Photographs*, 1920s–1970s, binder by student-researchers, 1979–1981, WICCC Archives. See also chapter 4, especially note 20.

9 Spada, *Italians*, 129.

o Most likely Luigi Meconi, of the Meconi Brothers Company, who continued to find farmers in Essex County also for the postwar immigrants as he had done twenty-five years earlier for Alex Colasanti.

1 Between 1946 and 1976, 44,454 Italians, or about 10 per cent of Italian immigrants to Canada returned to Italy. Favero and Tassello, "Cent'anni," 38–40, especially tables 15 and 17. See also chapter 2, "The *Molisani*: 'Flight from *Miseria*' or 'Search for *Fortuna*'?"; and chapter 12, "'Outsiders,' 'Prisoners' or Simply Living between Two Worlds?" especially note 33.

2 "Italians," *Canadian Encyclopedia*, 1988, ed.

3 Personal communication, 1 February 1991.

4 Personal communication from G. DiMenna and G. Pannunzio, February–April 2000.

5 Personal communication from Alfio Golini, 20 January 1986. "Canada was the dream of many Italians who at that time were leaving their homeland to find a new future," according to Alfio Golini, founder and director for almost three decades of the Italian radio program at CHYR Radio (Leamington). That dream "may have inspired the authors Mascheroni (music) and Panzeri (lyrics)" to write the song; and though it was not entered in the yearly San Remo Festival of Italian Song, in 1957 it became the most popular. The second stanza said:

Lui fece un'altra casa piccolina in Canadà
con vasche e pesciolini e tanti fiori di lillà
e tutte le ragazze che passavano di là

dicevano che bella la casetta in Canadà.
He built another little house in Canada
with pools and little fishes and many lilac flowers
and all the girls that went by would say:
How lovely the little house in Canada.

46 Sturino, "Italians," 1099–1100.

CHAPTER EIGHT

1 "In 1835 … [the] closest [school] to what was to become Leamington was located … on the south side of Concession 1 roughly half a mile west of Erie street south." In "1846 … a school was built on the northeast corner of Erie street south and Concession 1," which is Seacliff Drive today. In 1850, one year after the Western District was divided into separate counties, "Peter Conover came to Leamington and developed 170 acres along the Lake Erie shoreline as Sea Cliff Park Farm [and] set aside 20 acres of his property as a park" ("Seacliffe Park … a popular and celebrated picnic resort," as it was described in 1890 and still considered so in the 1950s); and where, in 1886–87, "the Michigan Central Railway built [for its spur line between Leamington and Comber] a station … called Sea Cliff Park." *Leamington-Mersea Souvenir History*, 4, 6–7, 20, 64. As early as 1825, the Mersea Township lots along today's Seacliff Drive were already owned and/or assessed, and by 1851–52, of the total 166 Mersea Township lots, 102 were occupied and 24 cultivated. Pryke and Kulisek, eds., *The Western District*, 89, figure 11; and 127, table 3. In the first part of the twentieth century a good portion of the Seacliff area was owned by Americans.

2 As quoted by Leonard, "Language and Literature in a Multicultural Curriculum," 51.

3 For the Mersea Assessment Rolls, see Mersea Township Office (Leamington). Copies of deeds of land were made available partly by some of the families themselves (through Gino DiMenna and Gino Pannunzio) and obtained partly from the Land Registry Office for the County of Essex in Windsor (with the kind assistance of Keith Ouellette).

4 The deed lists "*Ferdando D.B.* Belluz," but clearly the first name is *Fernando* and the full surname (apparently changed during the war) was "*Del-Bel* Belluz" or Del-Bel-Belluz, like that of several Windsor families, including a distant relative originally from Azzano Decimo (Friuli-Venezia Giulia Region). Fernando (in Canada since 1927 from Rivarotta, Udine) and his Ukrainian Canadian wife, Sonia Urkosky, moved to Leamington in 1944 when they bought the thirty-five-acre farm from Anna Urkosky to raise chickens. Though acquainted with some of the Leamington Italian

pioneers, Fernando's association with the community and eventually the Roma Club was marginal (as communicated by Gino Pannunzio).

5 The Township of Mersea, excluding the southern triangular section from First Concession Road to Point Pelee (about nine miles), is almost a perfect nine miles square. The northern section, from First Concession Road (or Seacliff Drive) to the northern boundary (County Road 18), is divided into eleven concessions (I–XI); and the southern section, from First Concession Road to the boundary of Pelee National Park, into four (A–D). Also, each concession, from the western boundary line of the township (Albuna Road or County Road 31), is subdivided, in ascending order from west to east, into farm lots (1–22 in Concession I, and 1–24 in Concession XI). Though not consistent, the depth of a farm lot (and thus the distance, more or less, from one concession to another) is approximately seven-eighths of a mile (or 1.4 kilometres) and its width about 1,980 feet (or about 600 metres). Leamington is in the southwest corner of Mersea Township, with present irregular boundaries from Lake Erie, south, to mid-Concession III, north; on the west reaching out to Lot 4, and on the east to Lot 10 (based on calculations made following the Township of Mersea map, scale 1 inch = 1 mile). See also Fuller, *Windsor Heritage*, 47–9.

6 Harney, "Italians," 243.

7 As recorded in the Master Seniority List, 12 August 1954.

8 An influx of Belgian families during World War I greatly increased the number of Roman Catholics in the district and led to the elevation of Leamington as a parish under the patronage of St Michael in 1919. Latecomers to the Sun Parlor [*sic*] scene were the Mennonites, who came here in 1925. About 30 families formed the vanguard of hundreds of immigrants from Russia who settled in the Leamington area during the 1920's and 1930's. Most had been farmers and they chose employment on farms as laborers or share-growers ... A second influx of Mennonites before and after World War 2 led to the expansion of the church building in 1937 and again in 1948. *Leamington-Mersea Souvenir History*, 13.

9 *Leamington-Mersea Souvenir History*, 45–6.

10 Statistics Canada, *1971 Census of Canada*, Population: Specified Ethnic Groups, Census Divisions and Subdivisions, special bulletin (SP-4), 2-66, table 2: "Population by Specified Ethnic Groups." Statistics Canada, May 1974.The ratio does not change with the slightly different figures for the 1971 population of Leamington Town and the Leamington Italians: 10,440 and 1,040, respectively, as given in table 5: "Population by Ethnic Group and Sex, for Incorporated Cities or Towns and Other Municipal

Subdivisions of 10,000 Population and Over, 1971." Population, vol. 1, part 3, bulletin 1.3-2, 5-9, and 5-10.

11 Ontario Ministry of Citizenship and Culture, "Leamington Census Agglomeration, 1981: Distribution and Percent of Ethnic Origin Groups," received by the Windsor Italo-Canadian Culture Centre, 31 August 1984. The 1981 census also recorded 1,505 Italians, of which 900 were Italian-born, representing 4.3 per cent of the population of Leamington Town and Mersea Township. "Leamington Census Agglomeration, 1981: Distribution and Percent of Population by Place of Birth."

12 Este, "Leamington."

13 *Leamington-Mersea Souvenir History*, 6–15, 18–20, 43, 52–3; Essex County (Ontario) Tourist Association, *Essex County Sketches*, 29–31.

14 The notes in the document quoted explain that "Leamington Census Agglomeration, 1981" "includes Leamington Town and Mersea Township," that ethnic origin "includes counts of single and multiple origins," and that the total population of 20,870 "excludes inmates." That figure differs from the total population number of 21,369, obtained by adding the figure for Leamington Town (12,528) and Mersea Township (8,841) recorded in the *1981 Census of Canada*, vol. 3, profile series B, 1-352 and 1-362, table 1: "Selected Population, Dwelling, Household and Family Distributions, Showing Selected Social and Economic Characteristics for Census Subdivisions of 5,000 Population and Over."

15 "Leamington Census Agglomeration, 1981: Distribution and Percent of Mother Tongue Groups" WICCC Archives.

16 *Leamington-Mersea Souvenir History*, 14.

17 Perhaps Leamington preserved some of the pristine and pure aspect for which the first Europeans praised this entire area: "Father Louis Hennepin ... the historian of the ... *Griffon*'s western voyage ... the first sailing [ship to enter] the Detroit River [August 1679] ... left a promised-land description of the strait ... In 1700 Robert Livingstone, Secretary for Indian Affairs at Albany, wrote to the Earl of Bellemont, Governor of New York" to encourage the English "to build a fort" in the area "'called by the French DeTroett the most beautiful and plentiful inland place in America by all relations, where there is arable land for thousands of people'"; and Antoine Laumet Sieur de Lamothe Cadillac, founder and first governor of Detroit, described Detroit and area in a letter of 25 September 1702: "This country, so temperate, so fertile, and so beautiful that it may justly be called the earthly paradise of North America." Lajeunesse, ed., *The Windsor Border Region*, xxxv–xl, and 21. See also chapter 9, "The Significance of 'Farming' and the 'Search for Eden.'"

18 *Canadian* (*Toronto Daily Star*), "The Big Move...," 22 January 1966, 10–13.

9 The 1975 Leamington Centennial Italian Fountain Project was truly a collective effort of the Italian community. The Roma Club and its president, Armando Masciotra, responding to a Leamington City Council invitation to ethnocultural groups and clubs to participate in the Centennial Celebration and thereby also beautify the city-owned piece of land in front of the Library, formed a Centennial Committee (with Milvo Costanza, chairperson, Victor Paglione, treasurer, and including Fr Ugo Rossi). With City Council approval of the Italian project, the committee collected almost $26,000, or a $50 average donation, from "approximately 90% of the [Leamington-area] Italians." At least three worthy project designs were submitted to the committee by three Italian families (Peralta Brothers, Bruno Matassa, Carl Grossi). The Fountain Project was chosen; its construction was carried out by a local builder, T. Grossi & Son Construction; and its inauguration took place on 28 June 1975, with a festival at the Roma Club. Victor Paglione interview, 1981.

CHAPTER NINE

1 On 3 February 1912 Samuele Turri left Italy to join his friends in Canada, what he called *"la terra dei $3 dollari* [the land of $3]," because he was told one could earn "$3 for 9 hours of work" and he thought, and later ironically wrote, that his "fortune was imminent." Cresci and Guidobaldi, *Partono i bastimenti*, 24–7.

2 Domenico Porzio describes the early immigrants as "mostly illiterates" whose only possession was the "culture of poverty, their only defence against the 'foreign-ness' of the countries they were absorbed into ... That grieving, patient and tenacious flood of people," played an important role in the Americas; many "succumbed [or] disillusioned ... went back home," but many others became "protagonists of a new social and economic history." Domenico Porzio, introduction to *Partono i bastimenti*, 5 and 65.

3 Some people disagreed with such a view of postwar Canada, though less inappropriate for the early days, especially during the Depression (see chapter 5, below, especially Saveria Magri's story; "The Hardships"; and Gus Moauro's interview). Nevertheless, the fact that even one had such an experience demonstrates the difficulty of immigration, even to a country as rich as Canada, even after the Second World War.

4 "The recommendation of the Rowell-Sirois Commission regarding unemployment compensation ... went through the Canadian Parliament without controversy in the summer of 1940." Finlay and Sprague, *Structure of Canadian History*, 370–1.

5 Strati, "Calabria contadina ed emigrazione," 60–6 (translation mine).

6 According to an advertising brochure by Omstead Fisheries/Foods Limited, *The Omstead Story*, n.d.

7 Lambert, *Ontario's Lake Erie Commercial Fishery*, 25.

8 Este, "Leamington"; see also *Wheatley Journal*, "Wheatley-Mersea-Romney Salute L.R. Omstead," special edition, 16 May 1976; Omstead Fisheries/Foods Limited, *Omstead Story*; and Jake Omstead interview, 1981, WICCC Archives.

9 Some Leamington Italians disagreed, but that was the impression among several who were interviewed; and also what had happened, at least to a former Ford foreman, Angelo Dominato of Windsor, after his return from internment camp. In 1942, Angelo Zamparo, president of the Italian Mutual Benefit Society of Windsor, referred to persistent suspicions that Italians were barred from factory jobs. *Windsor Daily Star*, "Italians Here Give," 20 March 1942; Macaluso, "'Enemy Alien' Stigma"; and chapter 6, "Fascist ... Activities in Windsor," especially notes 14, 16.

10 "One Italian man lost his finger during work and Bill tried to persuade him to collect compensation for the rest of his life but the man wanted to buy a car so he only took $400 cash. So Bill went to talk to the *patrone* to help convince this guy to take compensation. Bill LaMarsh interview, 1979–80. In the interview, however, no name was ever mentioned.

11 Pyramid Canners, started in the mid-1950s, averaged ninety to one hundred employees, including numerous Italians (but no records were available). The Italian farmers, who held some of its shares, grew crops (tomatoes and other vegetables) for Pyramid, which was owned by the Sun Parlour Co-operative between 1963 and 1967 (also widely supported by the Italian farmers). Later taken over by Nabisco, Pyramid was shut down and its operation transferred elsewhere. Gino DiMenna and Gino Pannunzio, personal communication, August 1995.

12 Gino DiMenna and Gino Pannunzio, personal communication, August 1995.

13 Vansickle, "Growing Financial Problems."

14 Widick, *Detroit*, 55–6; see also chapter 4, note 10.

15 Finlay and Sprague, *Structure of Canadian History*, 371.

16 Lazio was also favoured by Fascist policies: the 1926–39 draining of the Pontine marshes gave the south of Rome one of the two or three larger plains in its territory. Though Lazio itself is 54 per cent hilly, the altitude of most towns of origin of the Molisani is two and even three times that of the towns of origin of the Laziali. See *Vita italiana*, "La Regione Lazio," Anno 34, no. 1 (January 1984): 97–134; Nice, *Questo nostro mondo* (1966): 163–74; Alonzi, "L'agricoltura e la risurrezione".

17 *Vita italiana*, "La Regione Sicilia"; Nice, *Questo nostro mondo*, 235–6.

18 Alaimo, Fiasconaro, Licata, Lo Castro, and Rapisarda, eds, *Tante Sicilie*, 131–4.

19 See Salomone, "From the Crisis of the Renaissance," 108–11; and introduction in this text, especially note 23.

20 "In an alien culture, people try to create a 'safe' environment for themselves so that they can continue to thrive. Much of this 'safe environment' is formed through the mass media ... They acculturate the newcomers to their new cultural environment and also help them retain the security of their cultural roots by giving them information about the environment they have just left." Surlin and Romanow, "The Uses and Gratification of Heritage Language Newspapers." See also W. Temelini, "Media and Multiculturalism"; and Grohovaz, "Toronto's Italian Press."

21 In one example, the initial words of the anthem are made to rhyme with Italian words that portray a Canadian reality – the climate: "O Canadà, che freddo fa [O Canada, how cold you are!]." See also chapter 11, "The Home Visit: Stories, Jokes and Gossip"; chapter 13, "Group Interaction and Intercultural Prejudice."

22 Spicer, "His Strike Is Food for Thought."

23 In an editorial entitled "Take It Easy," Arturo Scotti warned that the Italian translation – *Prendetela con comodo* – does not convey its real meaning, especially when "used in reference to the newcomer and particularly to the Italians." "Take it easy," far from being an invitation to take it with leisure, is an admonition from the foreman or employer to the worker to listen carefully to the order given, understand it, and then carry it out quickly and accurately. The Italian worker, too often, in order to impress the boss, scurried off without fully understanding what he had been told and ended up complaining about the English language and the way the foreman spoke it, tight-lipped. If understood properly, the English phrase is not at all opposite, as Italians then thought, to the other English-American phrase "Time is money." Knowing this, Italian newcomers would not feel caught in a dilemma or the doubt often heard, "If time is money, how can I take it easy?"

24 The First Article of the Italian Constitution (1948) reads, "Italy is a democratic republic, founded on work."

25 The student-researchers warned that the percentages in the employment figures that they presented were "not the most reliable," since they were based only on the information provided in the written interviews, rather than on the more detailed recorded interviews, the main source prepared by the writer with the assistance of Nevi Rusich (executive director, Windsor Italo-Canadian Culture Centre).

26 The co-op's Italian presidents from 1957 to the early 1980s included: John Brunato (1958–60); Gino Pannunzio (1962–7); Augustino Ingratta (1972–3); Domenic Magri (1977–80, 1984); and T. Mastronardi (1982–3). Among the vice-presidents were: John Brunato (1957–8); Marius Ingratta (1960–2);

Floyd Cacciavillani (1972); Domenic Magri (1973–7); and H. Mastronardi (1985). The above mentioned, as well as others (Joe Colasanti, Frank Pannunzio), also held positions of secretary or treasurer, as well as being directors along with several others (John Cervini, Rocco Moauro, Frank Moauro, Gus DiMenna, Virginio Ricci, Gino Mucci, and other Mastronardis); they are for the most part members of the prewar immigrant families. "Co-op Officers List" provided by Gino DiMenna and Gino Pannunzio; also Gino Pannunzio interview, 13, 17 July 1981, WICCC Archives.

27 The 1980 list of the Ontario Greenhouse Growers Marketing Board members for the Leamington area consisted of 160 farmers, seventy-eight (or 48 per cent) of whom were Italian families (e.g., eight DiMennas, six Ingrattas, one Magri, over thirty Mastronardis, one Moauro, four Pannunzios, and one Totaro). Since the list did not include field-crops growers, the number of Italian families operating farms in the area may very likely have been close to one hundred. In that case, if the total number of Leamington Italian families can be estimated between 450 and 550, then the families in the farming industries made up 15–20 per cent of the Italian Canadian families (and even close to 25 per cent if the children's families are not counted as part of the original families; i.e., considered as separate units).

28 Once known as a tobacco-growing centre, and now as a producer of a very large variety of vegetables and fruits (apples, peaches, pears, lemons), Leamington has been increasingly identified with the tomato.

29 Hazan, *The Classic Italian Cook Book*, 5.

30 Artusi, *La Scienza in cucina*, title page.

31 Anthony Montello immigrated to Canada in 1914 and moved to Windsor in 1924. He operated the Paradiso restaurant on Mercer Street (near Wyandotte Street East) for over forty years. In its heyday, it was frequented by NHL teams and sports celebrities visiting the Windsor-Detroit area, including Joe Louis and Jake LaMotta, and during the Second World War it was a favourite spot of members of Canada's armed forces, especially because there was no charge for members of the military in uniform. His son Frank Montello of Windsor was for years a renowned criminal lawyer. See Temelini, "Italians in Windsor," 75 and 80, note 18; "Restaurateur Dead at Age 90," *Windsor Star*, 16 December 1985; *Windsor Business Directory*, 1937–40.

32 Hornberger, "A Fine Kettle of Fish."

33 Some of the jokes, even the uncouth ones, are not limited to the factories, bars, or docks, but crop up also where one would least expect them, given the institution and the purported higher level of education of the people in it. Not long ago, slipped under my office door at the University of Windsor, I found several typed sheets of these jokes. One of them read:

Q. How do you recognize an Italian at a wedding?

A. He's the one with the cement-covered T-shirt!

An acquaintance of mine seemed to find a distorted sort of pleasure in posing the same question to me every time he saw me: "Do you have your trowel with you?"

34 A 1975 description of the Lake Erie "Fishing Fleet" stated, "Four out of every five boats (79%) were in the 'forty foot plus' category, 13% were in the 20'–39' range, and a small group of 8% were under 20' in length … The average original boat purchase price was $18,556." Lambert, *Ontario's Lake Erie Commercial Fishery*, 19.

35 Coleman, "Fishing Quota Dispute Facing Supreme Test."

36 Cairns and Coleman, " Showdown with the Law."

37 Hornberger, "Fine Kettle of Fish."

38 See Cairns and Coleman, "Showdown with the Law"; Hornberger, "Fine Kettle of Fish"; and Coleman, "Fishing Quota Dispute Facing Supreme Test," for all quotations related to Vito Peralta and the fish quota controversy.

39 See Cairns and Coleman, "Showdown with the Law"; Hornberger, "Fine Kettle of Fish"; and Coleman, "Fishing Quota Dispute Facing Supreme Test," for all quotations related to Vito Peralta and the fish quota controversy.

40 See Bauch, "Nino Ricci"; and "Ricci's Novel 'Beautifully Paced': Times," *Windsor Star*, 12 June 1991, which quotes Barbara Grizzuti Harrison in the *New York Times Book Review* to define Ricci's *Lives of the Saints*. Ricci's second novel, *In a Glass House* (1993), received mixed reviews. The immigration trilogy came to a close with the 1997 novel *Where She Has Gone*. See chapter 15, note 20.

41 See Bauch, "Nino Ricci"; and "Ricci's Novel 'Beautifully Paced': Times," *Windsor Star*.

42 The *indovinello veronese* (Veronese riddle) is "a metaphor of the act of writing" using images of ploughing a field. In the metaphor, the fingers (*boves*, oxen) guide the pen (*albo versorio*, the white plough or the quill) over white parchment (*alba pratalia*, white fields or the page), writing in black ink (*negro semen*). The riddle relating writing and ploughing was widely known throughout Italy and Europe and dates back to ancient times. See Clivio, "The Development of the Italian Language," 29–30; Pei, *Italian Language*, 177; Dionisotti and Grayson, eds, *Early Italian Texts*, 1–3; Lazzeri, *Antologia dei primi secoli*, 1–3. See also chapter 12, "Language."

43 Spada, *Italians*, 80, 301–3.

44 See Whelan with Archbold, *Whelan*, 256–61. The visit to Leamington, the Roma Club, and Gino Pannunzio's greenhouse is described in chapter 13, "Political Views and Behaviour."

45 Lambert, *Ontario's Lake Erie Commercial Fishery*, 15.

46 Lovelock, *The Ages of Gaia*.

47 Ibid., xiii–xvi, jacket, 15–41, 203–23. See also Grant, *The Founders of the Western World*, for the ancient belief in Earth Mothers, Great Goddess, or Great Mother (11, 45, 182); the belief (Heraclitus, sixth–fifth centuries BCE) that "the individual soul [consists] of the same material as the macrocosm of the universe" (43); and the four basic primary elements – fire, air, water, and earth – by the fifth-century BCE philosopher-poet Empedocles of Acragas (Agrigento) in Sicily (88–9).

48 Lajeunesse, *Windsor Border Region*, xxxv–xl, and 21; see also chapter 8, note 17.

49 Essex County (Ontario) Tourist Association, *Essex County Sketches*, 26–35. For the French voyageurs and missionaries who "paddled along the north shore of Lake Erie from Niagara … Point Pelee was a prominent landfall." To them, the point appeared "bare"; thus, the name *pelée*, the feminine form of the French *pelé* – "skinned, peeled or bare." *Leamington-Mersea Souvenir History*, 3.

50 "The Big Move … " *Canadian (Toronto Daily Star)*, 22 January 1966.

51 Ibid.; see also "Tourism Abounds Here," "Historical Essex '75," *Windsor Star*, 11 July 1975, 42; and chapter 8, "Growing Together: The Italians and Leamington."

52 The longer version reads: *omne tulit punctum qui miscuit utile dulci* (he has won universal approval who has combined the useful with the agreeable; Horace, *Ars Poetica* 1.343). See also *The New Century Dictionary of the English Language*, 2:2460.

53 *Windsor Star*, "Ontario Chamber Award Goes to Colasanti Farms," 30 September 1986; Temelini, "Study of an Agricultural Community," 91, especially note 13.

CHAPTER TEN

1 *Dictionary of Colorful Italian Idioms*, 121.

2 In the version recently heard at the Italian American Cultural Society in Warren, Michigan,

> A young Italian American, on one of his first visits home from university reported, "Papa, I found a nice German girl."
>
> To his surprise his father did not disapprove! "German, *tedesca*, American, no matter nowadays."
>
> Some time later the young man announced, "Papa, I have a new girl; she's a fine Jewish girl!"
>
> Again his father calmly accepted and commented, "Jewish, English, *giudea*, Protestant, what's the difference so long as she's a nice woman."

On another visit home the boy came with another surprise: "Papa," he said, "I found a beautiful Black girl."

But his father again agreeably answered: "*Bianca*, *nera*, Black, white, we're all the same, son."

With the last girl the young man did not wait for a special occasion to come home and report. He was very proud to have found an Italian girl and wanted to tell his father immediately: "Papa, I found the most wonderful Italian girl; oh papa, I'm so happy!"

This time his father looked at his son in silence then after a moment inquired worriedly, "What part of Italy is she from?" (See also chapter 11, "The Pastor's Views on Italian 'Religiosity'" and note 38).

3 Cresci and Guidobaldi, *Partono i bastimenti*, 126–8.

4 Barzini, *Italians*, 198.

5 Francesco Coletti, "L'emigrazione," in Rosario Villari, *Il Sud nella Storia d'Italia*, 1:403–22.

6 Barzini, *Italians*, 190. In Roman law, the *paterfamilias*, the "oldest male ancestor" (literally the father of the family), had "complete control over the persons of his descendants," before and after their marriage (*patria potestas*), "even to the extent of inflicting the death penalty on them. This … was not, however, an arbitrary power," but was subject to a family council decision. Also, no subordinate member could own property; and acquisitions made went straight to the *pater*. Jolowicz and Nicholas, *Historical Introduction to the Study of Roman Law*, 114–20, 238–9; Balsdon, *Life and Leisure in Ancient Rome*, 115–16; and Paoli, *Vita romana*, 103.

7 Ricci, *Radici*, 33–4; and chapter 15.

8 A similar idea was expressed in a sixteenth-century Italian book of manners. Castiglione, *The Book of the Courtier*, 107.

9 *Tu*, second-person singular subject pronoun (you), and the plural form, *voi*, are normally used in addressing people the speaker knows very well: members of the family, children, and close friends (and also animals). The polite forms for "you" are *Lei* (singular), *Loro* (plural), normally written with a capital *L* to distinguish them from the subject and object third-person singular and third-person plural pronouns respectively: she/her; they/them. In rural Italy, particularly in the South, a generation or so ago, *voi* was also used as a form of respect to address only one person who was familiar to, but not of the same age or social status as, the speaker: i.e., for a grandparent, an uncle, an aunt or even mother or father. *Voi* in this sense stands between *tu*, the familiar form of address, and *Lei*, the very formal form of address. Today *voi* is hardly ever used in the formal sense because of its suggestion that the person addressed is old; *Lei* is used only among

strangers but also among people who, though acquainted, wish to keep a certain distance in order to avoid possibly dangerous familiarity (between in-laws, neighbours, and so on). Before the *Lei* form is dropped there have to be sound bases of friendship established: the English to be on first-name basis is rendered in Italian with the expression *darsi del tu*, literally "give each other *tu*; address each other with the *tu* form." *Signore* and *Signora* are the Italian terms for Mister or Sir and Mrs or Madam.

10 Recent statistics show that the Italian family in Italy has not only been changing in the last decades, its present portrait is not a comforting one: 42 per cent of those polled defined it as an "institution in crisis," and 23 per cent judged it not as solid as it once was. The same research also indicates that Italians are having fewer children: 35 per cent of those who do not want many children stated that they are worried about the future, and 29 per cent that it is necessary for the woman to work today. In general, the majority of Italians still think that matrimony is necessary for happiness, but they don't think as they did perhaps only a few decades ago that happiness comes from having children. The goal of the modern Italian family is not to make sacrifices for children. See Simonetta Annibali, "Noi: gli italiani." *La Gazzetta*, 29 July 1988.

11 Ciongoli, "Origins of American Values," 27, 32, 34.

12 Ibid.

13 Ibid. See also Paoli, *Vita romana*, 101–6; Ricci, *Radici*, 32–6.

14 Devoto and Oli, *Dizionario della lingua italiana*.

15 Bertoldi, *I nuovi italiani*, 53. See also Zucchi, *Italians in Toronto*, 5–6, quoted partly in chapter 6, note 25; and chapter 11, especially note 47.

CHAPTER ELEVEN

1 In a 1960s song entitled "Casa mia [My home]," the seasonal or "commuter" immigrant (*il pendolare*), while still on the train during one of his visits home, which he hopes always to be the last, sings, "*Torno a casa* [I'm going home]" and looking forward to embracing his wife and to a period of well-deserved rest, he observes happily, "I'll hear my own language, I'll understand what I say."

2 The "system" is explained in chapter 10, "The Extended Family: The *Comparatico* or *Compare-Comare* 'Network'"; see also chapter 13, "Interaction within the Community."

3 An attempt has been made to write skits making use of some of these words to create laughter: such words as *key* with a sound exactly like the Italian interrogative pronoun *chi* ("kee") and *hurry up*, which to an Italian ear sounds like *arriop*, an expression used to exhort an animal or someone

inferior, can produce confusingly comic situations. This type of humour is proper to Italian immigrant communities where in general all have some knowledge of English and/or French, besides knowing Italian or a dialect. In a situation where only one language is known, there would be no laughter. The skits, performed several times in the Windsor-Detroit area during the 1970s, achieved their intent. See W. Temelini, "Le avventure di Peppino l'emigrante."

4 In some dialects the standard Italian word for fire – *fuoco* – is *foc* (*fok*, pronounced with an open *o*); roof – *tetto* – is *tet* (*e* pronounced very closed or like the *i* in the English word *bit*). The others are *basta* (*a* pronounced very open as in *father*); *facchino, fa caldo,* and *canti* have two parts: the first is pronounced like the very familiar four-letter words, the second part sounding like *eeno, aldo*, and *ee* respectively.

5 *Cool* sounds like the Italian dialect and vulgar word for "rear"; *bye bye* seems to reproduce the sound of a barking dog (or part of the verb that means "to bark" – *abbaiare > baia*. In fact, the usual comments after one said "bye, bye" were *"baia baia, basta che non mordi"* (bark as long as you wish but as long as you don't bite); *talk* sounds like the dialect form of *tocco* (< *toccare*, to touch). Therefore "You don't talk English" may sound like "You don't 'touch' English people"; and the Italian obliges: "I won't 'touch' English people as long as they don't 'touch' Italian people." *I'll see you* sounds like *alsio* or *altsio*, "to" or "for the uncle." (Shortly after an uncle of the writer arrived in Canada in the 1950s, he happened to hear the phrase several times during a stroll together, in Sudbury. He was pleased to hear it especially from the writer's friends to whom he smiled graciously as they went on their way. Later he told his nephew that he appreciated the warm welcome but all that attention was not really necessary. When I told him what it meant he couldn't stop laughing and he laughed every time he recalled the incident.) See also chapter 9, "Italian and Non-Italian Employees and Employers" and note 21.

6 The words *the mass* in some dialects look, if not exactly sound, like "I'll kill you": *the* = *te*, personal pronoun object; *mass* < *(am)maz(zo)* < *ammazzare*, "to kill"; thus, *Christmas* – "Christ-kill." See W. Temelini, "1950: La prima cartolina di 'Christmas' dal Canada."

7 Arturo Scotti, in welcoming the news of an Italian government plan to open halls or centres "where Italian immigrants can get together after working hours and feel less lonely in the foreign lands," hoped that the Italian authorities and those in Rome in charge of "public relations" would avoid opening *"Dopolavori [sic]* in Canada and the United States ... particularly in Canada [where] this name is definitely disliked by the Italian Canadians since a large number of them spent years in concentration

camps for having been members of such clubs." Even though "tomorrow's *Dopolavoro* will not have any political significance, it is natural and human to understand the hostility of those who on a purely psychological reflex become nervous just on hearing that name." "A proposito di 'Dopolavoro'" (translation mine). See also Mack Smith, *Mussolini*, 120.

8 In a letter to Arturo Scotti a reader complained about Canada: "Liberty here is an illusion that I do not wish to compare to Russia since I know nothing about Russia. But I am speaking about the freedom to go out in a group of four friends (maximum number) and stop on the sidewalk to talk. The police come and evict us, that is, force us to move on and break up the group. Is this freedom?" Scotti defended the Canadian police whose main "duty is to protect the citizen." But, while admitting that Italians were sometimes "loud," he thought it unjustified to be denied the freedom to engage in sidewalk conversations. "Abituarsi alla libertà d'essere liberi" (translation mine). The copy of By-Law 2640 in part reads, "The said Municipal Council is empowered to pass by-laws for the health, safety, morality and welfare of the inhabitants of the municipality." The by-law states specifically, "No person shall lounge, loaf, loiter or stand as an idler in any public place so as to obstruct the due and proper use thereof.

9 Ben Giglio, a prominent Windsor businessman who was active for many years in the Windsor Italian community, the Multicultural Council of Windsor and Essex County, as well as in the Calabria Club and other clubs, met an unfortunate and untimely death in January 1986.

10 See Leamington Roma Club Italian Community: By-Law Number 1 and Amendment, August 1978; *Introduction*, i.

11 "The Big Move," *Canadian*, 22 January 1966.

12 "Introduction," By-law Number 1 and Amendment, August 1978.

13 Compare with another general observation about Italians: "Alone an Italian is a genius; two Italians play cards; three quarrel." According to Claudio Antonelli, the Italians have also imported "envy" into Canada, their (but not exclusively) "worst defect." "Il peggior difetto degli italiani." In the early 1970s the Italian journalist-author Silvio Bertoldi was not certain whether Italians were "a people of envious or simply unsatisfied individuals." Is what they feel "envy or a craving" for everything that others have? "Perhaps, in our [the Italians'] parabola of former poor people, we are getting rid of ancient epidermal and corporate envies." *I nuovi italiani*, 120–1.

14 For the effects and a definition of *campanilismo* see chapter 1, especially note 8; see also Harney, "Italians," 243; Arturo Scotti's 1957 editorials in *Corriere Canadese*: "Porte Aperte," 15 January; "Promemoria per l'On. De Martino," 20 August; and chapter 13, "Interaction within the Community."

15 Presidents of the Leamington Roma Club, 1960–1992 (with period of arrival in Canada)

Name	Pre-war arrival	Postwar arrival	Years	Term
Gino DiMenna	x		1960–7	first
Donato Puglia		x	1967–9	first
Virginio Ricci		x	1969–1	first
Rolando Paliani		x	1971–2	first
			1972–3	second
Armando Masciotra		x	1973–4	first
Filippo DeCamillis		x	1974–5	first
Tony DiMenna (not the pioneer)		x	1975–6	first
Tony D'Amelio		x	1976–7	first
			1977–8	second
Gino Pannunzio	x		1978–9	first
Virginio Ricci		x	1979–80	second
Gino DiMenna	x		1980–3	second
John Abbruzzese		x	1983–4	first
Erminio Ingratta		x	1984–5	first
John Cristofari		x	1985–6	first
			1986–7	second
Gino DiMenna	x		1987–8	third
Domenic DiMenna	(x born in Canada)		1988–9	first
Frank Gabriele		x	1989–92	(3 terms)
Margaret Ingratta		x	1992–	

16 "The founders of the Italian community in Essex County were honored at a special banquet at the Roma Club, Saturday evening" (30 April 1977). "Founders of Italian Community Honored," *Leamington Post*, 4 May 1977.

17 It may just be a reflection of the centuries-old Italian dislike for and distrust of authority for which Indro Montanelli has given an interesting

explanation: The Italian, though "by nature kind ... lacks a social sense and respect for others. When the Italian excels, he immediately slides into excess [i.e., in a position of leadership he tends to be arrogant]. When he rises above others a little, he expects others to visibly recognize him for it." At the same time, the Italians, for centuries a poor people subjected by powerful lords and by a sort of dutiful deference ["the worst Italian defect," according to Montanelli], "have always hated the sight of those who rule [i.e., all leaders]. No one in Italy loves those in power. The face of authority, in Italy, has been for centuries hateful." Bertoldi, "I difetti: Intervista con Indro Montanelli," 47–55.

18 *Leamington-Mersea Souvenir History*, 30–1.

19 See Barzini, *Italians*, 306–7; and chapter 1, "The Changing Fortunes of the Italians in Canada."

20 Boni, *Il talismano della felicità*.

21 Ricci, *Radici*, 23.

22 Pasta, the Italian contribution to international cuisine, has been defined by Hazan as "one of the most miraculous creations of all gastronomy," and Thelma Dickman, quoting Hazan, states, "In the course of civilization's long and erratic march, no other discovery has done more than, or possibly as much as, pasta has to promote man's happiness." "Pasta Perfect," 14; and also chapter 9, "The First 'Italian Grocery' Store."

23 See Principessa, Chiarilli, and Amati, "Qui Roma ... Per difendere Roma," 4; and Carli, "Diario italiano," 5. On the other hand, Frank L. Holt, professor of ancient history at the University of Houston (Texas), does not consider this invasion of Rome by the McDonald's hamburger chain a grave danger to Rome's legacy and civilization. In fact, this event is one of many in its multi-millennial history and it will again manifest Roman genius to merge past and present, to create

> a single civilization out of many peoples and places, an eclectic culture out of many contributors ... Even the latest lament of Italian fashion designer Valentino has an ancient echo in the works of Nero's tutor, Lucius Annaeus Seneca. In the words of Valentino, McDonald's has introduced into his neighbourhood "a significant and constant noise and an unbearable smell of fried food fouling the air." Such a "degradation of the ancient Roman streets" is nothing new, for as Seneca said in the first century A.D.: "It is disgusting for me to list the varied cries of the sausage sellers and confectioners and all the restaurant peddlers, each hawking his foods in foreign accents."

"The Forum," 96.

24 "It would probably occur to very few people ... to regard Italian cooking as the source of every other Western cuisine ... Indeed, the Larousse

gastronomic encyclopedia, the bible of the French kitchen, goes so far as to concede that 'Italian cooking can be considered, for all countries of Latin Europe, as a veritable mother cuisine.'" Waverly Root and the editors of Time-Life Books, *The Cooking of Italy*, 9.

25 *Windsor Star*, "Dieting? Just Eat Italian," 25 June 1986. The June 1986 issue of the *Runner*, in "Oil's Well," 11, recommended olive oil against heart disease. Dr Scott Grundy showed that "the high monounsaturated fat diet was at least as effective in reducing cholesterol as the low-fat diet … Found in olive oil and peanut oil, monounsaturated fat contains no cholesterol."

26 Camillo Carli, journalist, novelist and editor (1960s/1970s) of the prestigious Italian-language weekly *La tribuna italiana*, in Montreal (where he lived for about three decades), after his return to his native Tuscany continued to contribute insightful articles on Italian life and culture to Italian-language newspapers in Canada (including the Windsor Italian weekly *La Gazzetta*), for "his" Italian-Canadian readers (as he often called them). Carli relates oenology and gastronomy to the development of civilization: "The temptation to accelerate wine making [with particular reference to the wine so produced containing the poisonous methyl alcohol which caused about twenty deaths in Italy] is not new. Because time is money. But today, the particularly 'wild' nature of certain wine producers conceals perhaps a deterioration of Italian civilized living which is echoing the penetration [into Italy] of 'fast food' and the disquieting subculture of the *'paninari'* sandwich peddlers." "Cibo veloce morte precoce" (translation mine).

27 "Canadians' Nutrition Poor, Food Meet Told," *Windsor Star*, 22 February 1978, A7.

28 "Agriculture and fisheries would benefit through increased demand for their products if the diet guide were more rigorously adhered to, Begin said." The conference, attended by 400 delegates, including "health professionals, producers, consumers and other groups in the food system [who were] trying to make the public more aware of nutritional needs … was weakened by the failure of any of the ministers to say what are future plans for the food strategy." See Bégin, "Notes for an Address"; and "Canadians' Nutrition Poor, Food Meet Told."

29 Giuseppe Arcimboldi or Arcimboldo, for many years at the Hapsburg court (1560–87), became known for his allegorical portraits composed of fruits, flowers, fish, vegetables, and game animals, symbolizing the seasons, in a way anticipating the surrealists and depicting "the concept of people being what they eat." See *Enciclopedia Garzanti*, 1967 ed.

30 See Hazan, *Classic Italian Cook Book*, 5. The close link between "food" and "culture," or lifestyle was highlighted by a group of high school

students from Quebec after a three-month stay in Windsor, "as part of an inter-provincial exchange program ... Language aside, the Quebec students say our [Ontario's/Windsor's] eating habits are a major difference. In Quebec, there is home-cooked meals and lavish desserts, they say, but here there is fast food. 'Your junk food is just awful,' said [one of them]. 'I hate to say it, but that's the way it is.'" *Windsor Star*, "Problems in Language, Fast Food," 29 November 1984, C16.

31 Hazan, *Classic Italian Cook Book*, 5.

32 Comparing French and Italian cuisine, Luigi Barzini explains their fundamental difference in ingredients: the French blend them, transform them to give French dishes "a mysterious, vague, wonderful, all-pervading taste ... Italians obviously believe that the pleasure of eating (and living) is enhanced by preserving the characteristic tastes of separate ingredients (and the personalities of individuals), more than by blending them artistically." "A Robust Cuisine Based on People's Character," in Root and the editors of Time-Life Books, *The Cooking of Italy*, vii–xv.

33 Carrillo, "Church in Italy," 179.

34 There was at least one Leamington Italian from Villa Canale whose former family members were not all Catholics: Paolina Mastronardi's father (according to Gino Pannunzio) had become a Protestant, the only one in the Villa Canale area. Paolina Mastronardi was Luigi Mastronardi's wife (same last name but unrelated). Apparently, at least one member of the Leamington pioneer group had converted to Protestantism (i.e., Jehovah's Witnesses).

35 Lorenzo Perosi (1872–1956), Italian secular priest and composer; music director, St Mark's, Venice (1894) and Sistine Chapel, the Vatican, Rome (1897–1915). *Webster's Biographical Dictionary*, 1972 ed. The *Prima Pontificalis* is a solemn mass for four voices for the major feasts (Christmas and Easter). The church choir was started in the fall of 1961 by Fr Ugo Rossi and Gino Del Col. Fr Rossi interview, June 1981, WICC Archives.

36 See "St Michael's Parish: A Brief History," WICCC Archives.

37 As for the North-South prejudice, it still exists in various forms, including violence, as evidenced by at least one publicized physical assault against Southern Italians "Vittima di uno violenza razzista," in *LaRepubblica*, 14 July 1989; and yet Montanelli thought that Italians are "the least racist people of all." Silvio Bertoldi, *I Nuovi italiani*, – "I difetti-Intervista con Indro Montanelli," 47–59. Also, the recent resurgence in Central and Northern Italy of pre–United Italy loyalties seems to indicate separatist tendencies and therefore indifference (if not hostility) toward the less developed areas (the South): in Tuscany people flaunt the old emblem of the Grand Duchy of Tuscany when it was ruled by the House of Lorraine (eighteenth century); Milan and Province look back to the times the area

was an independent city state (eleventh to thirteenth centuries); and with
the North (Lombard) League Party, which won over 8 per cent of the
popular vote in the 1992 election, they seem in a stronger position to
advocate an Italian federal system. Well known are also the traditional
Italian self-deprecation, lack of patriotism, and incorrigible *esterofilia* or
xenomania, a love for anything foreign and critical of anything their own,
while proclaiming the "Made in Italy" product among the best in the
world. Barzini, *Italians*, 294. As for their reciprocal envy, Italians (as
Montanelli pointed out) can be spontaneously kind, even to the point of
appearing obsequious (especially with the powerful) and at the same time
ill-mannered to the point of being offensive.

38 Many Italian defects, including parochial views, seem to be well spread
throughout North America: in Canada, it often seems that the Italians
make a special effort to exhibit all their kindness and obsequiousness for
non-Italians (especially those in positions of power from whom they think
they can obtain favour); while for other Italians (especially for those from
other regions) they seem to deploy mistrust, criticism, and even malicious
gossip (and yet they can't stay away from one another and congregate in
clubs and in specific city areas).

39 Vito Peralta (arr. 1927) was certain that a cause of his misfortunes – the
accusation of his being a Fascist sympathizer, his arrest and internment –
was "*il segno del malocchio italiano*" (the curse of the Italian evil eye). See
chapter 6, "Peralta's 'Boarding School Term'").

40 Carlomagno states, "Technical and scientific progress is not able to eliminate superstition, it only transforms it because it is rooted in the human psyche ... Superstition presents itself as a means of defence against the obscure
forces of evil and as self-projection toward the future" (translation mine).
The author quotes Paolo Beccari's *Folklore of Molise*, with a list of the
"superstitions most in vogue and still in use." Carlomagno, *Agnone: usi
costumi*, 131–8.

41 "People say Italians are Catholics. But they are so out of convenience, by
custom, by tradition, because they have a Catholic mentality; however, it is
not that they have a Catholic conscience. As for God, Italians do not make
it an issue. What Italian makes an issue of the transcendental?" Bertoldi, *I
nuovi italiani*, 47.

42 Antonio Gramsci, "Il Mezzogiorno e la rivoluzione socialista," in Villari, *Il
Sud*, 2:559.

43 Cresci and Guidobaldi, *Partono i bastimenti*, 84 and 144.

44 Faccioli, ed., *Il teatro italiano*, 1:vii–xxx.

45 Villa Canale's only church remained a dependency of the parish of Saint
Emidio in Agnone until 1855, when it was "decreed" an independent

parish "dedicated to St Michael the Archangel, who was also the patron saint of the village." Carlomangno, *Agnone*, 240. In fact, the "patron saint of Villa Canale is San Giocondino, honoured yearly on the first Sunday in July"; but the "most characteristic feast is that of St Michael, celebrated yearly on 29 September." Luigi Mastronardi, personal communication, Villa Canale, 30 May 1985. Records of Leamington St Michael's Church from the 1930s list the first baptism and burial services held for Italians, as well as the marriage dates of three Italian pioneer couples.

46 Gramsci gives historical reasons for development of that southern attitude:
In the North, the separation of Church and State and the expropriation of ecclesiastical lands was more radical than in the *Mezzogiorno* [South], where the parishes and the convents have either conserved or restored considerable personal and real property. In the *Mezzogiorno* the priest appeared to the peasant: 1) as a land administrator with whom the peasant enters into conflict over the rent issues; 2) as a usurer who demands very high interest rates and plays on the religious element in order to make sure he collects either the rent or the usury; 3) as a man subject to common human passions (women and money) and who therefore spiritually inspires no confidence with respect to discretion or impartiality. Confession therefore exercises a very limited controlling power, and the southern peasant, though often superstitious in a pagan sense, is not a clericalist.
Gramsci, "Il Mezzogiorno e la rivoluzione socialista," in Villari, *Il Sud*, 2:559. See also chapter 12, "Level of Education," especially note 47.

47 Procacci, *History*, 52–3.

48 According to the *St Joseph Daily Missal*, "participation in the Holy Sacrifice of the Mass is the greatest and most sublime act of religion" (1–4).

49 Scotti, editorials, *Corriere Canadese*: "Porte aperte," 15 January 1957; "La vostra collaborazione," 16 April 1957; "A proposito di 'Dopolavoro,'" 9 July 1957; and "Promemoria," 20 August 1957.

50 According to Indro Montanelli, the only "society" the Italian recognizes is "the family, and that is all"; and "the Italian is an *apolide*," a stateless individual; consequently his "lack of a social sense [of civism]." Bertoldi, *I nuovi italiani*, 47–53. See chapter 10, "The Extended Family."

CHAPTER TWELVE

1 Bissell, introduction to *Two Solitudes*, xvii.
2 Ibid.
3 Ibid.

4 Ibid.

5 The *Report of the [Ontario] Provincial Advisory Committee on Race Relations: The Development of a Policy on Race and Ethnocultural Equity* (September 1987), defines *ethnic* as "an adjective used to describe groups which share a common language, race, religion, or national group. Everyone belongs to an ethnic group. The term is often confused with racial 'minority,'" 42. The term (*ethnic* and *ethnicity* from the Greek *ethnos*, "nation") has been used in a positive way to signify awareness of, or belonging to, a particular group, and in a more negative sense to indicate someone or something peculiar, odd, different, and even inferior, or at least belonging to a "subculture" and not part of the Canadian mainstream, as are often considered to be those of French or Anglo-Saxon origin. See Royal Commission on Bilingualism and Biculturalism, *Book 4* (Ottawa: Queen's Printer, 1970), introduction; special issue, *History and Social Science Teacher* 17, no. 1 (Fall 1981); Bienvenue and Goldstein, eds, *Ethnicity and Ethnic Relations in Canada*, 7 17; Bouraoui, ed., *The Canadian Alternative*, introduction and 104–10; Buchignani and Engel, *Cultures in Canada*, especially chapter 8, "Living with Our Differences"; Driedger, ed., *The Canadian Ethnic Mosaic*, 29–39; Elliott, ed., *Two Nations, Many Cultures*, preface, and 220–36; Friesen, *When Cultures Clash*, 21–3; Gardner and Kalin, eds., *A Canadian Social Psychology of Ethnic Relations*, 37–54; Isajiw, ed., *Identities*, 109–31.

6 Bissell, introduction, xix.

7 See the poem "Canada: Case History." The Calgary-born Earl Birney (1904–95), Diltz, *New Horizons*, 73 and 288; *The Canadian Encyclopedia*, 1988 ed.; and Bissell, introduction, xviii–xix.

8 Luigi Barzini pinpoints a specific time and place at which the Italians lost control of their history and destiny: 6 July 1495, at the Battle of Fornovo. The defeat of the heterogeneous "army of the Italian league" by the "dim-witted and deformed king" Charles VIII of France not only "opened the way for a long period of foreign interventions, bloody conflicts, civil wars and revolts," but also "showed the world," among other things, "*the passive weakness of the over-civilized inhabitants,* their incapacity to work in cohesive and coherent bodies, their readiness to resign themselves pliantly to the ways of rough, brutal and resolute invaders." Above all, the "sack of Rome [1527], the distant consequence of the defeat at Fornovo, was the catastrophe from which Italians never recovered, the *trauma which left its indelible marks in their national character.*" In fact, Emperor Charles V emerging as "the sole winner ... imposed on Italy a heavy Pax Hispanica ... In 1530 he was also elected Emperor of the Holy Roman Empire at the same time Emperor and King of Italy [in a] ceremony [that]

inaugurated a new era, a period of more than three centuries of subjection to foreign rulers, during which it can be said that *Italy had no history of her own." Italians*, 287–310 (italics mine).

9 Harney, *Italians*, 225–6.

10 Hazan, *Grande dizionario*.

11 Palazzi, *Noviscimo dizionario della ligua italiano*.

12 Devoto and Oli, *Dizionario della lingua italiana*.

13 Especially in the "Canzone di Legnano," a poem celebrating the victory of the Lombard Communes over the German Holy Roman Emperor, Barbarossa (Legnano, 29 May 1176), Carducci exalts the medieval Italian communes or free city states as expressions of the "purest and most perfect *italianità*, almost antithetic to Germanism." Bernini and Bianchi, eds., *Carducci, Pascoli e D'Annunzio*, 195–7. See also Procacci, *History*, chapter 1, "The Years around 1000," 13–43, and 353–4; Heichelheim and Yeo, *History of the Roman People*, 54–97, 195, 248–9, 433–4; Ferguson and Bruun, *A Survey of European Civilization*, 103–14, 138–57, 158–70; Langer, *Encyclopedia*, 223; Salvadori, "Italy as a Country of Regions," 3–22; Scaglione, "Italy in the Middle Ages," 45–9; Cantarella, *Italian Heritage*, 4–6; and Volpe, *L'Italia che nasce*, 7–13; see also Procacci, *History*, 44–50.

14 Migliorini, *Storia della lingua Italiana*, 169–71; see also Migliorini, *Italian Language*, 117–18.

15 Mann, *Petrarch*, 113; Petrarca, *Canzoniere*, sonnet CXLVI: "... *il bel paese / ch'Appennin parte, e 'l mar circonda et l'Alpe.*" Particularly his poem "*Italia mia*" (CXXVIII), which Machiavelli quotes at the end of his *Prince*, as well as his letters to Italian princes, expresses a "deeply felt ideal ... of the Motherland [Italy], once again enjoying peace and on the road to ancient greatness," as in the letter to the Doge of Venice, Andrea Dandolo, whom he exhorts to make peace with the Genoese for the sake of Italian brotherhood: "If you have some respect for the Latin name, think that those people you wish to conquer are your brothers." Petrarca, *Le Familiari*, 133–47, 234–5. Though famous for his *Canzoniere*, or love poems for Laura, which was imitated throughout Europe, he wrote many Latin works (for which he was offered the crown of poet by both the University of Paris and the Senate of Rome, but he chose the latter): one of them, *Invectiva contra eum qui maledixit Italiae)* (Invective against him who spoke ill of Italy) was directed against the French who opposed the return of the Papal Court from Avignon to Rome. For Francesco De Sanctis, Petrarch was a man "without homeland, without family, without a social centre." While "Dante [feels] Italian and has all the passions of one ... [what] on the contrary strikes one in Petrarch's personal and lonely

world is the absence of reality" including the reality of his faraway, albeit beloved Italy: "Petrarch is forced to demonstrate his *italianità*." *Storia della letteratura Italiana*, 1:249–50; Procacci, *History*, 60.

16 Migliorini, *Storia*, 235–55, 291–3, 409; see also Migliorini, *Italian Language*, 155–169 ff. (particularly "vernacular humanism"), 196–200, 260; Procacci, *History*, 100–13, 185; Barzini, *Italians*, 294, 301–2.

17 Bergin, "Italy and the English-Speaking World."

18 Procacci, *History*, 222–9; Romano, *Storia*, 13–18.

19 See Peter C. Newman's 1987 series of four "columns on Italy's dramatic economic recovery" in *Maclean's*, especially "Italy's Daredevil Entrepreneurs" (9 November, 40); "Mussolini's Corporate Legacy" (23 November, 31); and "Olivetti's Global Deal Maker" (30 November, 51). Raul Gardini, president of Montedison, "Italy's biggest private chemical firm," which became part of Gardini's Ferruzzi Group, was involved in two major industrial events of international scope: Montedison and another Italian chemical corporation, Enichem, part of the giant state-owned ENI group, "along with a third partner, Occidental Petroleum, made a six-billion-dollar deal with the former Soviet government for the exploitation of the Russians' Caspian Sea gas and oil fields," which, according to "Armand Hammer, Occidental's chairman, is 'the world's biggest joint venture.'" Gardini and Franco Reviglio, president of Enichem, also signed an agreement in 1988 to join forces and create Enimont, which will rank "among the world's top ten chemical companies, alongside the likes of Dow Chemical, Hoechst and ICI." See *Economist*, "Italy's New Chemistry set," 13 August 1988, 60; ITALY *Italy*, "World's Biggest Joint Venture ...," 15 April–15 May 1988, 70–1; *La Gazzetta*, "Un 'polo' che vale 13 mila miliardi," 10 June 1988, 1. See also *Economist*, "*Mediobanca*: New Boys' Club," 12 December 1987, 92; Mario La Feria, "Raul d'Inghilterra," *L'Espresso*, 22 June 1986, 183, 185; and articles by Peter Nichols in ITALY *Italy*, particularly "The Worldwide Farmer," 15 October–15 November 1986, 44–7; "[Gardini's] Ferruzzi: Greater Agro-Industry for a Bio-Based Future," 15 May–15 June 1987, 58–61; and "In His [Gardini's] View Big Is Better and Giant Is Best," 15 September–15 October 1988, 50–2. Gardini's suicide on 23 July 1993, explained by some as a result of the "Clean Hands" investigations, shocked the political and business world in Italy and abroad. *La Gazzetta*, "Un'altra vittima di un certo metodo," 26 July 1993, 1, 5.

20 "Perennial Energy of an Anarchist: Kate Kellaway Meets Dario Fo, Master of Elegance and Political Farce," *Observer* (London, UK), 30 September 1990, 63.

21 While the *Maclean's* headline is "A National Contempt for the Law," 7 December 1987, 40, in the column itself Peter C. Newman emphasizes

"disregard for authority" or distrust of political leaders: "Unlike Canadians, who spend their lives deferring to authority, Italians have nothing but contempt for governments and official pronouncements." The 1992–3 "Clean Hands" investigations into political corruption, headed by the Milan judge Antonio Di Pietro and resulting in the ousting of over 100 parliamentarians, received general support from the Italian population. "Tutti I numeri di 'Tangentopoli,'" *La Gazzetta,* 9 July 1993, 1; "La corruzione? Tangentopoli? Tutto il mondo è Paese," *La Gazzetta,* 1 October 1993, 4. On the other hand, La Palombara questions the extent and role of this "Italian" attitude: "Italians are invariably reported to be somewhat less satisfied than are other Europeans with their democracy – and much more distrustful of their national government. [But] no one has yet shown what difference it makes that Italy's distrust-of-government index is 3.4 while the average for the European Community is 2.8 ... In the case of Italy, postwar history suggests that distrust of government ... if it relates to politics at all, has positive, not negative effects." La Palombara, *Democracy, Italian Style,* 1–3, 21–5, 259–61. See also Spotts and Wieser, *Italy: A Difficult Democracy,* 2–4.

22 Thomas G. Bergin, "Italy and the English-Speaking World," in Chandler and Molinaro, *Culture of Italy,* ix. See also Spotts and Wieser, *Italy: A Difficult Democracy,* 46–7.

23 See Scaglione, "Italy in the Middle Ages," 51; and Temelini, "Literature and Culture in a Multicultural Society," 42–57.

24 At the turn of the sixteenth century, "the powerful Medici banking house and [the] Genoese bankers ... in spite of competition from their northern colleagues, the Fuggers of Austria and the Artaveldes of Antwerp, were still the major financial forces of Europe, in whose eyes they seemed the very personification of Italian wealth and industriousness." Florence did not cease "to be a great financial and productive power" until "the end of the sixteenth century"; that same century "was a period of decline for Venice. But it was also a period of ... greatness in the economic sphere ... above all, it was a time of cultural and artistic greatness." The Venetians refused Philip II's offer of "the monopoly of the trade in the spices that arrived at Lisbon" because of "their prevalently eastern interests ... Not until the early years of the seventeenth century were spices classified as goods from the West rather than from the East." It was by the beginning of that century that Venice ceased to be "a great Mediterranean power." Genoa, in the 1570s, "took over the place of Lyons and Antwerp as the greatest western financial centre, and controller of the international exchange market." Procacci, *History,* 110–11, 161, 170–4, and 177.

25 Re, "In Defence of Alfonso Tonti." There seems to be no doubt about the Tonti brothers' Neapolitan origins. But W.J. Eccles refers to Enrico Tonti as "the Sicilian soldier of fortune, Henri Tonty." See *Frontenac*, 83. And an Italian-American newspaper referred to him as the "Florentine." *Il popolo italiano*, "Tonti, Henry [Enrico]," March 1987, 5. See also chapter 1, esp. "The Centuries-Old Italy-Canada Link: Early 'Exporters' of *Italianità*" and notes 26–48.

26 Harney, "Italians," 225–6.

27 Romano, *Storia*, 14–15. Carlo Goldoni (b. Venice 1707, d. Paris 1793), author of 120 comedies, studied law at Pavia, from where he was expelled for having written a satire against women, graduated in Padua, practised law in Venice then in Milan and was also Genoese consul in Venice. After Pisa he left the legal profession, joined a Venetian acting company, and all his activity was centred on the theatre, first in Venice then in France, where he was invited by the actors of the Théâtre-Italien. He became tutor of Louis XV's daughter and lived at Versailles until he was given a pension, which was cancelled by the Revolution. One of his plays, *Il teatro comico* (Comic theatre) is a sort of program of all Goldoni's art. Giovanni Giacomo Casanova (b. Venice 1725, d. Dux in Bohemia, 1798), author of *Histoire de ma vie* or *Mémoires* and of a novel also in French, *Icosameron*, travelled throughout Europe, and though a gambler and swindler, was befriended by kings, artists, philosophers, and scientists; his escape from the Venetian prison of Piombi is legendary, as are his love affairs and adventures. His work is a fresco of seventeenth-century life and mores. *Enciclopedia della letteratura Garzanti*, 1974 ed.

28 "The historians of united Italy have purposely ignored the more or less servile relations of collaboration that tied the subordinate classes to the ruling powers in the Lombardy-Venetia area (administrators, police) and the profoundly anti-unification sentiment of the aristocracy and of the middle class in most of the Italian regions." Romano, *Storia*, 16–17. See also La Palombara, *Democracy*, 8–9; Harney, "Italians in Canada," 226; and chapter 4, "Truly Pioneers."

29 See especially chapter 2, "Tony Di Menna's War Memories ..."; and for a list of illustrious Italians remembered by the immigrants, see chapter 14, especially note 4.

30 Temelini, "Study of an Agricultural Community," 90, note 4. See also chapter 9, "The Quest for the 'Steady Job.'"

31 According to official Italian statistics gathered by Istituto centrale di statistica (ISTAT) for 1951–81, the socio-economic portrait of Italy in those three decades completely changed: in 1951 over 42 per cent of the Italian

population were employed in farming and mining; less than a third (32.1 per cent) were involved in the industrial sector; and one-quarter of the population (25.7 per cent) worked in service-related jobs. The transformation, begun in the 1950s, accelerated in the following decades to bring a total reversal: by 1971, those employed in the industrial sector constituted over 44 per cent of the total population, larger than the agricultural workers of twenty years earlier. Even though the industrial sector, by 1981, constituted a lower figure (almost 37 per cent), the agricultural sector continued to decrease: 17.2 per cent in 1971, 13 per cent in 1981. In less than a generation, therefore, Italy changed from a mainly agricultural to an industrial country. Two books published in 1982 dealt with this phenomenon and referred to Italy as a kind of "mystery": Enzo Biagi – in his *Il buon paese: Vale ancora la pena di vivere in Italia?* – after searching all over Italy for an answer to whether it is "still worth living in Italy" or "the good land" (as in the title), discovers an Italy that few know: the Italy of thousand-year-old traditions fused with twentieth-century needs; and convinces himself and the reader of the positive answer. Giorgio Bocca – in his book *In che cosa credono gli italiani* (What do Italians believe in?) – after a journey among the contradictions of Italy, reaches the same conclusion: in 1982, Italy remains a mystery, but "the Italian miracle in the last 20 years has been phenomenal, perhaps unique in the world." See Temelini, "Come va in Italia?" 1, 3, 4. See also "Italy's Vita Is Now More Dolce," 51–2; and "Sorpresa: siamo ricchi," *L'Espresso,* 7 December 1986, 270–3.

32 Silvio Berlusconi, a Milan entrepreneur, often called the "king of Italian commercial television," has built a European television empire since deregulation of broadcasting in the late 1970s. Berlusconi's challenge to the Italian state television company, RAI, has transformed, if not revolutionized, the basic structure of electronic mass media in Italy. He has turned television in Italy into big business, and he is trying to do the same in France and in other parts of Europe. See "Editoriale: Guerre dell'etere e guerre di carta," *L'Espresso,* 9 September 1984, 5–12; "Lottizzazione televisiva: Le mani sul video," *L'Espresso,* 29 June 1986, 6–9; Carlo De Benedetti, as Olivetti's chairman in 1986 (then fifty-one), was defined by Richard l. Kirkland Jr as "a world-class entrepreneur" who "epitomizes Italy's industrial revival. When De Benedetti took the helm in 1978, Olivetti was a barely profitable typewriter company sinking rapidly under a $1-billion debt load ... he turned Olivetti into one of the world's leading manufacturers of personal computers and one of Europe's most profitable companies." Kirkland, "Competition," 98. Peter Nichols wrote, "Italians regard themselves as second to none in technological ingenuity, and Olivetti is one of the world's leaders in information

science." After his attempt to take "partial control of the leviathan of Belgian business, Société Générale de Belgique," De Benedetti was "dubbed the *condottiere* (soldier of fortune) by the Belgian and French Press." Nichols, "A Summit Made in Italy," 54. The *Economist,* in its usual way, refers to his vast European holdings (ranging from Yves St Laurent to the *Financial Times*, which has a stake in the *Economist* itself) and his international transactions as "spaghetti-like activities" ("Carlo De Benedetti: In the steps of Carlos V," *Economist*, 23 January 1988, 60–1); while *Time*, recalling the Belgian protest against his "financial piracy," presented De Benedetti as a sort of modern-day conquering Caesar: "I Came, I Saw, I Gained Control … Italy's De Benedetti Stages a Daring Raid on Belgium Inc.," 1 February 1988. See also "Il Manager: La'Fortune' di DeBenedetti," *L'Espresso*, 20 April 1986, 217; "Il patto elettronico," 27 April 1986, 215–16; "Olivetti in altesa," 31 August 1986, 154; "Nella rete dell'ingegnere," 2 November 1986, 295–8; "Parla De Benedetti," 14 December 1986, 40–50; and Newman, "Olivetti's Global Deal Maker." For Italy's aerospace industry and telecommunications, in particular, see Pilati, "Appalti stellari," 229–30; Di Rienzo, "Il socio americano," 187–8; Brady, "Into Space Together," 65–9; and "Who's Ahead in the Space Race," *Omni,* July 1988, 72.

33 In 1946–76, 248,344 people left Molise and 117,827 went back. Italian immigrants to Canada in the same period numbered 440,796, and those who went back 44,454. See Favero and Tassello, "Cent'anni," 39–40, tables 14–17. See also chapter 2, "The *Molisani:* 'Flight from *Miseria*' or 'Search for *Fortuna*'?"; chapter 7, "Relationship and 'Quest for Sponsors'"; and Kaihla, "Destination Europe," 20–1.

34 Candelora, Gardaphe, and Giordana, eds, *Italian Ethnics*, 78.

35 "With Abruzzi, Molise received the highest amount of money remitted from abroad to the Italian regions"; and, according to Social Welfare Statistics (INPS), in 1983 Molise had "the highest ratio between, on the one hand, the recipients of disability pension and, on the other, the recipients of old age pensions, the work force and number of inhabitants." "La Regione Molise," *Vita Italiana* 34, no. 4 (April 1984): 74. The comments of visiting immigrants echoed what others had observed: depopulation of the villages as a result of emigration and the trend among the young people to go to the larger cities in search of employment. See Carlomagno, *Agnone*, 283; Mastronardi, "Ai lettori: Vogliono che disertiamo?" 1; and chapter 7, "Postwar Molise." For the effect of depopulation on the country as a whole and on the hinterland in particular, see Antonio Golini, "Migrazioni interne, distribuzione della popolazione e urbanizzazione in Italia [Internal migration, population distribution and urbanization in Italy]," in Rosoli,

Un secolo, 153–87; and Birindelli, Gesano, and Sonnino, "Lo spopolamento in Italia ..." 189–251. In 1971 the Italian Touring Club launched an appeal to "defend the hill towns ... a serious problem that concerns all of Italy: from the Monferrato to Abruzzo, ancient towns have been abandoned and neglected." Bazzoni, "Difendiamo le 'Terre Alte.'"

36 Adriano Celentano, *Il ragazzo della via Gluck* (1965–66). See Perboni, *Dizionario della musica pop-leggera italiana,* 72–3.

37 Prof. Enzo Battaglia, former mayor of San Vito Lo Capo, Trapani, Sicily, visited Windsor as representative of the Council of Mayors of the towns on the Gulf of Castellammare. See W. Temelini, "Colloquio con il prof. Enzo Battaglia."

38 In 1957, following an article about the Italians in the Toronto area, published in the Milan based *Tempo,* Arturo Scotti, editor-in-chief of the *Corriere Canadese,* received "numerous letters from various parts of Italy," requesting help or advice on how to reach the "'Milan' of Canada, Toronto ..." or Canada "this earthly 'Paradise.'" In an attempt to set the record straight, Scotti answered with an editorial:

> And so, while in Italy the desire to emigrate to Canada intensifies ... here [in Canada] thousands of immigrants, since the very first act of their tragedy, clench their teeth and some other thing to resist the first inevitable clash [of reality and mirage]. It is from this clash that will then be formed the mental armour plate that will permit [the immigrant] to get through the discrimination (real and imaginary) and all sorts of complexes that will cause him to see enemies in every comer and, above all, a strange world that will make him pour out tears of sorrow and of anger.

If Italians continue to arrive in Canada with "two ships – the one that carries them and the other behind it full of dreams and illusion," the responsibility falls also on the immigrants themselves and their numerous letters [to Italy] describing the wonders of America"; and those who return to Italy for a visit, after "the period of incubation" and after shedding the no-longer needed "armour plate," often tell "their friends and relatives the story of how they have 'conquered' Canada. They make no mention of the first months and first years of suffering and privations, material and spiritual; the only aim is to impress the *paesani* with a portrait of Canada that has little resemblance with reality." "La voce della verità," *Corriere Canadese,* 17 December 1957 (translation mine).

39 In the late 1960s few Italian immigrants to the Toronto area shared that hope: "Metro Toronto, mecca of 'the land of opportunity' [that] immigrants read about back home, has become the pinnacle of bitterness for hundreds of newcomers to Canada. Throughout Metro, hundreds of skilled and professional immigrants are either unemployed or working at

jobs far below their abilities and qualifications. Hundreds of others have given up in despair and returned home. Many more are trying to save enough money to follow them." Barnes, "We Promised Jobs." Another article in the same issue lists more than ten Italians, ranging from eighteen to fifty-four years of age and holding diplomas and degrees (including law, electronics, and chemistry) and with a knowledge of English, who had already left or were planning to leave. "The Disenchanted – And Why They're Leaving."

o Alighieri, *La divina commedia*; Alighieri, *The Divine Comedy*. Dante Alighieri, in his treatise on the Italian vernacular, *De Vulgari Eloquentia*, "the first European treatise on historical linguistics," anticipating humanistic thought, considered language not only as natural to humankind but also as an essential vehicle of thought: "Language is as necessary an instrument of our thought as the horse is to the rider." This idea of language as the specifically human act is a fundamental point in Dante's works, especially in the *Divine Comedy*, where "over and over again the Dantean characters say to us: *Loquor, ergo sum"* (I speak, therefore I am). Dante's complex drama, and thus his identity, states Cambon, come to the fore not so much in his relation with Latin, but in his attitude to his beloved Italian language, not to the "learned" tongue, but to the native tongue, the language that nourished him as a child, the language of everyday life, "the language of the common people" which for Dante was more noble than Latin, and which he heralded as "a new light, a new sun." Glauco Cambon, "Dante and the Drama of Language." Alighieri, *La lingua volgare*, 25–82; also Alighieri, *Convivio*, particularly book 1, chapters 7–8; Chandler and Molinaro, eds., *The World of Dante*, 3–24.

1 Curtius, *European Literature and the Latin Middle Ages*, 16, note 11.

2 Ezio Raimondi used the quotation, along with Wittgenstein's "language is a labyrinth of paths" to introduce and conclude his 1983 lecture "Landscape and Language in the Modern Novel." With numerous references Raimondi points out the similarities of the literary and scientific modes of exploring or explaining reality, as well as the role of language as the basic link among all the protagonists: if the reader is

> aware of his own moment and [of] his own role as a 'performing self,' as an executor and interpreter of himself ... the classroom becomes the theater and laboratory of a literature which, in addition to being an end for knowledge, constitutes an energy field for exploring in the code of the possible and of memory the liberating force of language, from the sphere of the everyday to that of the science and study of man with its various finite regions of meaning ... Just as forms always have origin in time, the anthropological structure of understanding presupposes the dialectic

between past and present, the encounter with the multiple and the different, the comparison between us and the other ... Wittgenstein ... said
... that when one reads out loud ... the words are accompanied by very
vivid acts of the imagination. Perhaps things should be done in a way ...
that [readers] discover that the road to the critical spirit of science is
entangled, in the end, in the words of literature, which teach us how to
see and how to understand the new, even when it seems old. That
today's scientific knowledge cannot do without imagination is a precept
that comes to us from the scientific community itself ... [W]hat literature
proves and perhaps risks, should it continue to exist, is always a dialogic
imagination in the spoken environment of an open system. Indeed, "language is not only the man but also the world."
Raimondi, "Language and the Hermeneutic Adventure in Literature." See
also introduction, especially note 32.

43 Pei, *Story of Language,* 209–16, and 421–5. See also Hoy and Somer, eds,
The Language Experience, xiii–xix, 17–28; Hall, *Linguistics and Your
Language*, 244: "All of our thinking, as such, involves the use of language,
and if we have no clear notion of the nature of language and our use of it,
we are bound to get confused on the nature of our thinking itself"; and
Danesi, "Language Learning and Mental Flexibility," 20–1.

44 Prof. Battaglia seemed familiar with the discomfort of the immigrant going
home after some years abroad. Though he agreed that the immigrant struggle was heroic, he also felt that upon his return, the immigrant was "like a
fish out of water ... out of the cultural context what will become of the
emigrant?" he asked. And he quickly proposed a cultural exchange program as one response to this alienation. Temelini, "Colloquio con il prof.
Enzo Battaglia." See also Temelini and Bison, "Servizio Speciale," 1, 4–5.

45 See McLeod, "Multiculturalism and Multicultural Education"; and
Multiculturalism and Citizenship, *Multiculturalism*, 8, 27, 35–8.

46 "Most immigrants were unschooled, which is *not* to say that they lacked
intelligence." Vecoli, "A Report on the Status of the Italian American
Ethnic Group."

47 A view that echoes some of the observations made by Antonio Gramsci
and other Italians: "Once again," wrote Gramsci in reference to the posi-
tivistic writings that declared the southern Italians an inferior race, "the
aim of 'science' was to crush the wretched and exploited masses." For
Gramsci, both Giustino Fortunato, the southern reformer, and Benedetto
Croce, the idealist philosopher, were "the two greatest figures of Italian
reaction ... Southern intellectuals are one of the most interesting and most
important social classes in Italian national life. To be convinced just consider that more than 3/5 of the state bureaucracy is formed by

southerners." But unlike the new type of intellectual introduced by capitalism and industry, i.e., "the technical organizer, the specialist in applied sciences … with all their characteristics of order and discipline," the traditional rural intellectual of an agricultural society, the type that "prevails in South Italy," functions as "an intermediary between peasant and the ruling class," and is characteristically double-faced "a democratic face for the peasant, a reactionary face for the big landowner and the government" – as well as

> a petty politician, corrupt and disloyal … The southern intellectual derives mostly from a class still quite notable in the *Meridione*: the rural middle class; that is, the small and median landowner who is not a farmer, does not work the land and would be ashamed to be a farmer, but who, from the little land that he owns and has rented or contracted out on a sharecropping basis, wants to earn what he needs in order to: live comfortably; send his children to university or a seminary; provide a dowry for his daughters who have to marry an officer or a civil servant. From this class the intellectuals receive a deep aversion for the working peasant, viewed as a working machine that must be exploited down to the bone and which can easily be replaced given the overpopulation of workers.

From it "they also derive their ancestral and instinctive feeling of mad fear of the peasant … and consequently an attitude of refined hypocrisy and a most refined art of deception and control of the peasant masses … The southern peasant is tied to the great landowner through the intellectual." Gramsci, "Il Mezzogiorno e la rivoluzione socialista," 543, 557–9. According to Montanelli the "treachery of the intellectuals in Italy has always been a shameful matter. Italian intellectuals have always been at the service of power." Bertoldi, *I nuovi italiani*, 57 (translation mine). See also chapter 2, "The *Molisani*: 'Flight from *Miseria*' or 'Search for *Fortuna*'?"; chapter 11, "The Patron Saint Festival," especially note 46; and chapter 15, "Cristina and the 'Breakdown' of the Old Patriarchal Institutions."

48 Battaglia and Pernicone, *Grammatica italiana*, 5 (translation mine).
49 Procacci, *History*, 60.
50 Migliorini, *Storia*, 569–75.
51 Ibid., 293–306, 314–42, 359–61, 434–5, 492–9; Migliorini, *Italian Language*, 212–25, 234–5, 274–5, 306–10, 359–66, 413–18, 470–5; Romano, *Storia*, 32–9. "From the fourteenth century on, English poets visited Italy in steady succession, returning, as their poetry shows, with a constantly renewed familiarity with Italian literature, both old and new." Corrigan, *Italian Poets and English Critics*, 1; Clivio, "Development of the Italian Language and Its Dialects," 38.

52 Romano, *Storia,* 33–4.

53 "Italy Ponders Switching to Use of English," *Detroit Free Press,* 13 September 1978.

54 See Magister, "La Multilingua."

55 Burnet, "Multiculturalism Ten Years Later," 3 (emphasis mine).

56 Burnet, "Multiculturalism," 5. According to Paul A. Kolers's theory, reported in the *Scientific American,* "Bilingual [People] May Have 3 Memory Banks." *Toronto Daily Star,* 21 March 1968.

57 Even though a critic, at least in reference to the movie *Film d'amore e d'anarchia,* said that "only half the dialogue is comprehensible." See Grazzini, *Gli anni Settanta in cento film,* 185–7.

58 McLuhan, *Understanding Media,* 83.

59 Clivio, "Development of the Italian Language and Its Dialects," 39–40.

60 Strickland, *The Language Arts in the Elementary Schools,* 58.

61 Pei, *Story of Language,* 210–11.

62 Struever, *Language of History in the Renaissance,* 43.

63 Hazan, *Classic Italian Cook Book,* 1.

64 In fact language, or mother tongue, out of the "bewildering variety" of factors that identify ethnic groups in Canada, was placed among the "four principal components of ethnic identity":

1 *ethnic origin,* largely determined – according to Canadian census specifications – by the mother tongue spoken by an individual or his patrilinear predecessor upon immigration to North America; or referring to patrilinear descent from a forefather claiming membership in a certain ethnic group in a region from which he emigrated (not necessarily in the mother country), with this descent represented in a family name typical of the group (unless changed, e.g., Anglicized);

2 *mother tongue,* i.e., a language traditionally spoken by members of a particular ethnic group;

3 *ethnic-oriented religion,* i.e., participation or membership in a religious affiliation recognized as the traditional religion of a particular ethnic group;

4 *folkways,* i.e., the practice of certain customs unique to the group. In short, ideally the typical tradition bound ethnic group member may (a) value his ethnic origin, (b) fluently and primarily speak his traditional mother tongue, (c) attend an ethnic-oriented church as regularly as possible, and (d) follow various customs particular to his group. Conversely, ethnic identity change may refer not only to (a) de-emphasis of an ethnic origin, but also to (b) loss of mother tongue, (c) conversion from or loss of interest in an ethnic-oriented religion, and (d) failure to practise various folkways. See Anderson and Frideres, *Ethnicity in Canada,* 36–7.

5 Inscription at the entrance of the Northwest Territories Pavilion, Expo '86. Whether it is a Canadian official language, a non-official heritage language of a more recent immigrant group, or an ancient ancestral language of a Native people, language is "among our most intimate and precious possessions or associations." Language is closely linked to heritage and culture, and without these there is no survival of the individual or of the group. See Yalden, "The Ambivalence of Language," 1.

6 Cambon establishes a symmetry between "the contemporary agony of European culture" and "the growth crisis of Dante's world ... For Dante, as for the experimental moderns, there was a language to repossess ... He had a culture to create, we have a culture to save or to reject (depending on how we feel about our massive heritage)." This symmetry can also be extended to the modem world of immigrant communities. In fact, the parallels even assume more socially intense and dramatic aspects. Dante's attitude to language and his artistic and human search are comparable to the immigrants' search for an identity, of which language is an essential part. The complex nature of Dante's relation to his native language (Italian) is not unlike the complex attitude of the Italian immigrant communities toward their native language and simultaneously to the official language(s) of power and culture (Latin in Dante's case, English in the immigrants' case). Perhaps even more than for the modern Europeans or for the Italians in Italy, for the immigrants, who often came speaking only a dialect, there is a standard language to repossess, especially for their children, if they wish to repossess their culture, their heritage, and therefore their sense of identity. The search becomes even more pressing in an atmosphere of multiculturalism. See Cambon, "Dante and the Drama of Language," 4–24.

7 The type of society and individual proposed by multicultural education whose goals are not unlike those of humanistic education: "the synthesis of all the best aspects of our culture and of our technology" (see Temelini, "Humanities and Multicultural Education," 62–3; and Temelini, "The Multicultural Person").

CHAPTER THIRTEEN

1 See editorials by Arturo Scotti in *Corriere Canadese*, 1957: "La vostra collaborazione," 16 April; "Il nostro capitale," 7 May; "L'immigrazione continua," 13 August; "Promemoria per l'On. DeMartino sottosegretario agli Esteri," 20 August. The 7 May editorial commented on a speech by J. Pickersgill, minister of citizenship and immigration, who stated that Italians have not yet been successful in the political arena for "lack of cohesion in the community."

2 See also chapter 11, "The Home Visit ..." especially note 2.

3 Leopardi, *Prose di Giacomo Leopardi*, 355.

4 At a 1976 forum focusing "primarily on the problems of prejudice in the educational system," some of the speakers stated, "Immigrant children ... may be suffering academically because their problems are being treated strictly as cultural differences by educators ... there is 'a general crisis in academic progress' among immigrant children ... language barriers pose both short- and long-term problems ... Children of immigrant families whose mother tongue is not English 'may take up to 10 or 11 years to catch up with other students in academic skills ... 'the first priority of the school system ... must be to help them achieve self-esteem. 'A weak self-image can be absolutely devastating for a child's academic achievement' [and if racial problems in education weren't dealt with properly, immigrant children could be stranded at the bottom of the economic ladder, lacking a proper education." Watson, "Educators Blamed for Hurting Education".

5 Scotti, "La Discriminazione c'è ma non si vede."

6 Scotti, "L'abito non-fa il monaco, però!"

7 Scotti, "Lavoro, non beneficenza"; Scotti, "Labour Day"; Scotti, "Un'arma a doppio taglio."

8 Scotti, "Le Amazzoni Calabresi."

9 Scotti, "Povera, ma generosa l'Italia."

10 Scotti, "Gli Orangisti vedono rosso."

11 Scotti, "Il Circolo Fascista del Consigliere Comunale.".

12 Scotti, "Un povero giudice."

13 Scotti, "Gli occhi neri dei poliziotti."

14 Scotti, "Sono tutti emigranti."

15 Scotti, "Il 'mosaico' canadese non ha un nome inglese."

16 Scotti, "Non siamo criminali."

17 Scotti, "Il 'mosaico' canadese non ha un nome inglese."

18 Translation mine of the portions of Scotti's Italian-language editorials. For an effect of the multiculturalism policy and an excerpt of it, see chapter 1, "The Changing Fortunes of the Italians in Canada" and note 57. For anti-Italian discrimination in the United States, see La Gumina, ed., *wop!*

19 Marchand, *Marshall McLuhan*, 209.

20 Scotti often urged Italian immigrants to learn English if they wanted to progress and be respected by Canadians ("Bisogna tornare a scuola"); to become better acquainted with the laws and local customs in order to avoid exploitation and unfair treatment ("Labour Day"); and not to blame the "English" foreman for his "incomprehensible" English, and not to fall into the error of doing work quickly without thinking in order to win the respect of the employer ("Take It Easy").

21 Interview with Indro Montanelli, in Bertoldi, *I nuovoi italiani*, 50.

22 Gorbachev's visit to Canada in May 1983, as a result of Whelan's invitation, "was his only major trip to a Western country before becoming General Secretary of the Communist Party." "Whelan's account of travelling with Gorbachev and of Gorbachev as houseguest gives a fascinating insight into the personality of the man who [has changed] the face of the Kremlin." One of the most memorable moments of the trip was the visit to a Leamington greenhouse owned and operated by the son of an Italian pioneer and a major force behind this history of the community, Gino Pannunzio. As Whelan described the visit,

> One particular event in the Ontario part of his trip seemed to stick in Gorbachev's mind, because he referred to it several times afterwards. It happened when we visited Gino Penunzio's [Pannunzio] greenhouse near Leamington. As Gorbachev was leaving Mr Penunzio [Pannunzio] shook his hand and said, "I'm just a little tomato farmer, and I know you're from a big country, but I don't think my wishes are any different from yours or those of your people. I hope and pray for peace for you and your people." It was one of the nicest speeches I heard from anyone on the trip – politicians included – and I think Gorbachev was quite moved by it.

Whelan with Archbold, *Whelan*, 255–61, and book jacket.

23 See the *Windsor Star* 1978, particularly Fox, "[Leamington Italian] Roma Club to Boycott Luncheon for the PM"; Sandre, letter to the editor; "Boycott Denied by Roma Club," 17 January, 3; Cacciavillani, letter to the editor. See also chapter 11.

24 In May 1979, the Conservatives, under the leadership of Joe Clark, formed a short-lived government: by February 1980, Trudeau and the Liberals were back in Ottawa, but the party lost again after Trudeau retired from politics in 1984.

25 In the 1957 federal elections (when Diefenbaker won a majority government) and when Quinto Martini of Hamilton was elected MP, Scotti was asked whether "the Italian Canadians," known to be traditionally Liberal supporters, had instead voted, "against all expectations, for the Conservative Party." Scotti felt that the "Italian Canadians [had] become so well integrated in Canadian life, to behave like the [other Canadians] even in the political field." Nevertheless, he also recognized that more than embracing one party or another, the Italian-Canadian "voters were guided by their preferences for the candidate in their own riding." Scotti, "Un Italo-Canadese al Parlamento di Ottawa." In his 13 August 1957 editorial, "L'immigrazione continua," Scotti refers to the restrictions on immigration announced by the new minister of immigration, E.D. Fulton.

26 A poll analysis may show strong Italian support for the Liberal candidates in a particular election, but not necessarily Italian commitment to the Liberal party or a decisive influence on the voting patterns in that area, since two non-Liberal candidates were able to win seats in subsequent elections. Could it mean that Italians were changing voting patterns? The only information available on the Federal Electoral District of Essex-Kent, where Leamington is located, is that 1,480 people – out of a population of 76,525 – listed Italian as their mother tongue (1986 census). However, this gives no indication of voting patterns. The only example is that provided by Poll 26, Anderdon Township (Amherstburg), Essex-Windsor Federal Electoral District, which includes Texas Road, an area with an identifiable Italian constituent base. According to the figures received from the office of Steven Langdon (MP, Essex-Windsor), in the 1984 federal election the vote, based on 252 ballots cast out of 319 eligible voters (78.9 per cent), was:

Liberal	98 (38.8%)
New Democrat	61 (24.2%)
Progressive Conservative	90 (35.7%)

27 "Friends Mourn the Loss of Fred DeSantis," *Kingsville Reporter*, 23 February 1988, 1, 3; and personal communications from Gino DiMenna and Gino Pannunzio, 16 July 1992.

28 After Whelan's withdrawal, Steven Langdon won his riding of Essex-Windsor for the NDP; while Jim Caldwell, the PC candidate, won Essex-Kent, formerly held by the Liberal Bob Daudlin.

29 Again Montanelli, in his depiction of the Italian character, states, "The Italian remains what he has always been, without offending, an adventurer. The Italian goes abroad, places himself at the service of a powerful master, gives him good advice, guides him well and robs him. See Mazzarino, Alberoni, Casanova, Cagliostro ... The Italian is without a state, ready to set down roots in any country as long as he can profit from it. Metastasio becomes the court poet in Vienna, Goldoni settles down in Paris." Bertoldi, *I nuovi italiani*, 53–4.

CHAPTER FOURTEEN

1 Scotti in his 1957 *Corriere Canadese* editorials referred to Italy with the terms that the immigrants themselves used, especially when related to the conservation of their links with the land of origin: "*i legami con la Patria non si mantengono esclusivamente tramite le rimesse bancarie!*" (the bonds

with the Motherland are not conserved exclusively through bank remittances); "The Italian immigrant in Canada ... lives in an Italian-Canadian community, where from a material point of view he finds what he needs to live as he lived in *Patria* (in the Motherland). *Ma non si vive di solo pane!*" (But one does not live by bread alone). He needs the "presence of that *Patria* (that Motherland), that he may have cursed many times, but which nevertheless remains the *Grande Madre* (the Great Mother), that he loves and will defend always at any cost" ("A proposito di 'Dopolavoro,'" 9 July 1957).

2 See Heimler, *Mental Illness and Social Work*: "It is difficult to assess whether or not immigrants are more prone to mental ill health because of the tensions, conflicts, and prejudices set up by living in an alien society, but it is known that it is extremely difficult to help those who do break down unless one has an intimate knowledge of their background, culture, and history ... We have yet to learn the subtle interactions between emotional and cultural stability and instability" (104–6). See also chapter 12, "The View of Canada."

3 Harney, "Italians in Canada," 239.

4 Cristoforo Colombo (Christopher Columbus, or in Spanish, Cristobal Colon, 1451–1506) is the "discoverer of America." Because he lived for many years in Portugal and Spain and sailed under the Spanish flag, his origin has always been a source of controversy. However, "Paolo Emilio Taviani, one of the world's leading Christopher Columbus scholars, puts to rest the rival claims, summoning the documentation that shows that Columbus was indeed Genoese. His case has been recognized as airtight and thus irrefutable." Fant, review of *La Genovesità di Colombo*; see also *Webster's Biographical Dictionary*, 1972 ed.; and chapter 1, especially notes 29, 43, 60.

Guglielmo Marconi shared (with Karl Ferdinand Braun) the 1909 Nobel Prize for physics, the development of wireless telegraphy. *Webster's Biographical Dictionary*. The first museum dedicated to Marconi was built in Glace Bay, Nova Scotia, from where Marconi sent his first transatlantic message, and where Marconi established the first radiotelegraphic station in North America. The museum was cosponsored and financed by the governments of Italy and Canada with the participation of many Italian Canadians (see "Glace Bay, Nova Scotia: Il primo museo al mondo dedicato [all'opera] di Guglielmo Marconi," *La Gazzetta*, 19 July 1985).

Galileo Galilei, commonly known as Galileo (1564–1642), astronomer and physicist (born in Pisa), is considered by many the founder of modem physics. In 1613, after the publication of his *Letters on the Solar Spots* in which he advocated the Copernican system, he was denounced for propounding heretical views (sun-centred vs earth-centred system). After the

publication of the *Dialogo dei due Massimi Sistemi del Mondo* (1632), he
was summoned to Rome, tried by the Inquisition, and forced to abjure belie
that the sun is the central body around which earth and planets revolve.
Webster's Biographical Dictionary; Stillman Drake, "Italy, Science and
Modern Culture," in Chandler and Molinaro, *Culture of Italy*, 143–55. See
also chapter 12, "*Italianità*: 'The Feeling of Being Italian.'"

   Giuseppe Garibaldi (1807–1882), was a patriot and hero of the
Risorgimento, and in a way himself an "immigrant" in the United States,
where he became naturalized and worked as a candle-maker (Staten Island
early 1850s). After 1854 he was back in Italy as commander of the corps
known as Cacciatori delle Alpi (Hunters of the Alps) in the Sardinian army
But he became especially popular for leading the expedition of 1,000 men
(the famous Redshirts) against the Bourbons of Sicily and Southern Italy.
He attacked Sicily (May 1860), crossed the mainland of Italy, and expelled
Francis II from Naples, thus defeating the so-called Kingdom of the Two
Sicilies. Instead of proclaiming himself king of Southern Italy, as he could
have easily done, Garibaldi met Victor Emmanuel of Sardinia and gave the
conquered territory to the king, who, as a result, was proclaimed also king
of Italy (17 March 1861). *Webster's Biographical Dictionary*; Cantarella,
Italian Heritage, 270–8; Trevelyan, *Garibaldi and the Thousand*; Salvatore
Mondello, "Italians in the United States," in Chandler and Molinaro,
Culture of Italy, 204. See also Nese and Nicotra, *Antonio Meucci, 1808–
1889*; chapter 1, "A Colony with Common Ties," especially note 16, and
chapter 15, "The 'Joyful' Rediscovery of the Past."

   Totò, pseudonym of Antonio De Curtis (1898–1967), born in Naples, was
a film and theatre actor whose originality as a comedian make him comparable to Fernandel and Charlie Chaplin. (*Enciclopedia Garzanti*, 1967 ed.).

   Giuseppe Verdi (1813–1901) was a master of dramatic composition and
outstanding figure of nineteenth-century Italian opera, born in Roncole,
Parma. From Shakespeare, in whom he found a kindred soul, he drew the
plots of his greatest operas. Like Shakespeare, he wrote not for the select
few or for his own country alone, but for humankind. Cantarella, *Italian
Heritage*, 279–82; Ewen, *Encyclopedia of the Opera*, 529–31; *Webster's
Biographical Dictionary*. See also Erasmi, "'Norma' ed 'Aida': Momenti
estremi della concezione romantica."

   Enrico Toti (1882–1916) was a hero of the First World War. During an
attack he was gravely wounded. Just before dying he threw his crutch at the
enemy. See chapter 13, and chapter 2, "Di Menna's War Memories."

5 Hall, *Linguistics and Your Language*, 28; see also chapter 12, especially
   "Attitudes toward Italy," "Language Awareness," "Level of Education,"
   and "Italian Language"; as well as Ricci, *Radici*, 38–9.

6 In a sense unfortunate, since the loss of a dialect represents also the loss of a linguistic and cultural patrimony; dialects in Italy are slowly being abandoned for the standard Italian on social and economic grounds. According to national surveys conducted in 1974 and 1982, the use of standard Italian was first under and then over 50 per cent of the population, "both in public and in the home." The standard Italian, therefore, once the language of culture and academia, even with all its regional varieties and traits, is becoming the language of the Italian masses. One key reading of the entire survey is "the passage from dialect to Italian as an upward step in the social scale." Magister, "La Multilingua."

7 "Perhaps long association with the area would permit some sort of differentiation but only in the area of economics. In all other fields they consider themselves equal." Spada, *Italians*, 302; see chapter 1, "Distinctive Features."

8 See chapter 12, "Italian Language and *Italianità.*"

9 Scotti repeatedly urged the Toronto-area Italians to do so, not just to avoid "exploitation" but to become more fully part of the political process and have a greater voice in Canadian affairs. Quoting an old proverb "*Carta canta ... e villan dorme*" (Paper sings ... and peasant sleeps), Scotti warns newcomers against signing any document, especially when buying something on instalment, unless they have read and understood even the small print: the agreement in writing is a legal document, and their protests and claims after the fact are useless. "Canada 1980," *Corriere Canadese*, 12 March 1957; see also *Dictionary of Colorful Italian Idioms*, 42. In "Maturità politica," 22 April 1957, Scotti questions the poorly timed trip to Ottawa by a delegation of Italian Canadian businessmen to present to the prime minister a petition to appoint an Italian Canadian to the Senate just when Parliament was about to be dissolved in view of the upcoming election for which all ministers and MPs were hurriedly getting ready; the petition itself, Scotti thought, was untimely; suggesting to him that, in spite of the success of many Italians in Canada, not one for the moment had a long enough history of political, cultural, or economic activity to be eligible for or deserving of such an appointment. In fact, the first Italian Canadian senators were appointed almost ten years later: Pietro Rizzuto of Montreal in 1976; and Peter Bosa of Toronto in 1977. The first Italian Canadian to be elected to Parliament was the conservative Quinto Martini of Hamilton in the 1957 election (see Scotti's June 18 editorial), followed by the Italian-born Carletto Caccia in the ranks of the Liberal Party in 1968 (subsequently re-elected in every election including 1993; and for a period minister of the environment). In 1993 a record number of fifteen Italian Canadian MPs were elected, including three women: one in BC, twelve in Ontario, two in Quebec, and all Liberal.

10 "Generally speaking, southerners [i.e., Italian] tend to make money in order to rule, northerners to rule in order to make money. The difference may not be identifiable in every individual but is always discernible in the two societies. It permeates every detail. It strengthens the contrasting characteristics of the Two Italies." Barzini, *Italians,* 248–9.

11 Ricci, *Radici,* 8–9, 40–2.

12 See Temelini, "Humanities and Multicultural Education," 62–3; and chapter 13, "Political Sheep."

13 Frye, *The Bush Garden,* 226, quoted by Leonard, "Language and Literature in a Multicultural Curriculum," 52. See also chapter 11, "Roma Club."

14 Ciongoli, "Origins of American Values."

15 Gian Luigi Beccaria, in Bonanate, "Questo è l'italiano"; translation mine. See also Beccaria, *Italiano,* 7–10.

CHAPTER FIFTEEN

1 Ricci, *Radici,* i–iii.

2 Ricci, *Radici,* 42.

3 Eco, "Postille," 512–20; *Postscript,* 19–41.

4 Robey, introduction to *The Open Work,* vii.

5 Eco, "Postille," 507–9; and Eco, *Postscript,* 1–5.

6 Alighieri, *La Vita Nuova (Poems of Youth),* I, 1, p. 29.

7 "*Lives of the Saints* snares the reader with its quiet cumulative power. We are drawn into luminous moments in the history of a family ... A rich and wonderful tapestry. Haunting." Janette Turner Hospital, in Ricci, *Lives of the Saints,* back cover.

8 While the patron saint is St Giocondino, the "most characteristic feast is that of St Michael, celebrated yearly on September 29 when the Walnut Festival is also held. This precious fruit is offered and eaten with a good glass of wine in the company of friends and acquaintances along the village streets. During the evening in St Giocondino Square, a small band plays music until late at night for the pleasure of all those who on this day come to Villa Canale from the nearby villages to spend an evening ... without worries. The feast ends with impressive fireworks." Luigi Mastronardi, personal communication, Villa Canale, 30 May 1985. See also chapter 11, especially "The Patron Saint Festival" and note 45; and *Saint Joseph Daily Missal* (1959), 960 and 1074.

9 "Agnone was no doubt a Samnite nucleus; it is not equally certain whether it corresponded to the ancient Roman city Aquilonia." In the novel the "imposing cities, Aquilonia, Bovianum, Cominium," said to be

built by the Samnites and "levelled by the Romans" (VII), recall three major Samnite cities, Aquilonia, Bovianum, and Cominium, conquered by the Romans after more than fifty years of fierce struggle against the powerful Samnite people (Three Samnite Wars, 343–290 BCE). Today, Aquilonia is the name of a town in Avellino province, Campania; Bovianum is the town of Boiano, southeast of Isernia, Molise; and Cominium is only part of the name of a village northeast of Frosinone, Lazio – San Donato Val di Comino. The archaelogical area near the town of Pietrabbondante (south of Agnone) is also believed to be the "Ancient Bovianum" or *Bovianum Vetus* (see chapter 15, note 14). The references to the Samnite cities recall as well the ancient Italic city of Corfinium, today Corfinio (L'Aquila province, Abruzzo) and the ancient Roman city of Saepinum, today Sepino (Altilia), south of Boiano (Bovianum) in Molise. Santini, *Il Molise*), 18, 26, 38–44; *Almanacco del Molise 1989*, II, 7; Carlomagno, *Agnone*, 37–9, 41–56, 69–72, 85–6; Kinder and Hilgemann, *Penguin Atlas of World History*, 1:78–9. See also Touring Club Italiano, *Annuario generale*.

10 For the list of the twelve municipalities see chapter 7, note 23. See also Carlomagno, *Agnone: usi costumi,* especially "Agriculture and the Mountain Community," 49–52; "The Monastic Orders," particularly St Francis Caracciolo, 69–72; "The Emblems" of Agnone's noble or illustrious families, 81–5; "Craftsmanship," 87–9; "The Arts and Their Masterpieces," (91–8); and a brief outline of "Goldsmithing in Agnone," its origins in the "eleventh century," its famous goldsmith Giovanni di Agnone, and the works still present in Agnone's churches, 117–30. For the reaction of the people of Agnone against the bureaucrats in the regional and national capitals, see the Agnone newspaper, *L'eco dell'alto Molise*, in the 1980s (chapter 7, "Postwar Molise" and notes 20–8).

11 "Bell casting is perhaps the most renowned and important aspect of Agnone. This art dates back to the Middle Ages and the fact that it is still alive bears witness to the skill of the local masters and to the beauty of these bells that are now spread all over the world, in the bell-towers of hundreds of churches," including "Exeter, Pennsylvania, Calgary, Alberta, Simcoe, Ontario, and Sherbrooke, Quebec." Santini, *Il Molise*, 29; Maiorino, "Agnone's Bells": and Marinelli, *Arte e Fuoco*, 27–30, 47–9, 112–13, 142–9. See also chapter 1; and chapter 7, "Postwar Molise." Tomolo is also mentioned in this copy of chapter 15 in the section titled "The Rediscovery of Italian Heritage: The Role of Language and Culture."

12 Carlomagno, *Agnone: dalle origini*, 307–8. See also chapter 3, "The Fragmented Unproductive Farmlands."

13 Carlomagno, *Agnone: usi costume*, 28, 31, 47, and 240; see also Touring Club Italiano, *Annuario generale*, 218–19; and *Telephone Directory for the Provinces of Campobasso-Isernia* (1983–4), 105.

14 Pietrabbondante has an "archaeological area [*Bovianum Vetus*] with some religious buildings (2 temples), besides a theatre well set in a complex of the sacred area" perhaps "dating back to the Italic civilization, particularly to the age of the Samnites." Santini, *Il Molise*, 30. The "monumental complexes at Pietrabbondante and Vastogirardi, in the Samnite heartland [belong also to the late second century BCE]." Crawford, *The Roman Republic*, 130. See also note 9, above; and "Isernia: carta della provincia" – Pietrabbondante/Bovianum Vetus.

15 Arduino, *Le due valli del sole*, Prefazione, by Giovanni Labbate; and pp. 20–22; Santini, *Il Molise*, 3. See also chapter 7, "Postwar Molise."

16 Ricci, *Radici*, 33.

17 Ricci, *Radici*, 33.

18 Eco, "Postille," 510. In Ricci's discussion of the family and marriage, besides the reference to Karl Marx, there may be also echoes of earlier Italian works. In *The Courtier* (1528), certain speakers refer to the infidelity or "the incontinence of women" as the source of "countless evils"; thus, they argue, women ought to "devote all their resources to preserving that one virtue of chastity," because without it "there would be doubts about one's children and the bond which binds the whole world on account of blood, and of each man's natural love for his offspring, would be dissolved." Castiglione, *Book of the Courtier*, III, 241. Similarly, in the *Scienza Nuova* (New Science, 1744), one of the "three basic principles of all human societies – of humanity through the ages" that Giambattista Vico "discovered" in the study of human history is "the evolution of marriage-rites as consecration of the nuclear social group in the family." Salomone, "From the Crisis of the Renaissance," 109–10. See also introduction, especially note 24; chapter 10, "*La Famiglia* – The Family"; "The Generation Gap and the Family."

19 Carlomagno, *Agnone: usi costumi*, 51–2.

20 Ricci, *Radici*, 5–6, 8–9, 12–16, 34–6.

21 See Carlomagno, *Agnone: usi costumi*, 51, 138; particularly the sections: "La Superstizione," 131–5; and "Il Malocchio," 137–8. Also for the effects of the Second World War and the presence of the Germans in the Agnone–Upper Molise area, see chapter 7, "The War and Its Effects on Southern Italy"; and Carlomagno, *Agnone: dalle origini*, 287; *Agnone: usi costumi*, 46. For the ambivalence of emigration-immigration (well-being – hardships) or America as Heaven-Hell (i.e., progress; the shock of uprooting; disruption in home and village life), see chapter 2, especially "The Ill-Fated

First Trip"; chapter 3, especially "The Southern Italian 'Dream of America' – Reality and Fiction" and notes 22, 23; chapter 5, especially "The First Links of the Sponsorship Chain"; "The Hardships"; chapter 6, especially "The Peraltas and Early Sicilian Immigration"; chapter 7, "Reasons for Emigrating (1948–1970s)"; and "Canada: 'Land of Opportunity.'" For the younger generations' reactions, see chapter 10, especially "The Young People's Confused Values"; and chapter 14, especially "The Uncertain Legacy."

22 Ricci, *Radici*, 33.

23 "The peasant's attitude toward the clergy is summed up in the popular saying: 'The priest is a priest at the altar; outside he is a man like all the others.'" Gramsci, "Alcuni temi," 559. See also chapter 11, "From Social Life to Community Spirit" and note 46.

24 Graves, *The Greek Myths*, I: III–15.

25 Eco, *Six Walks in the Fictional Woods*, 30.

26 Ibid., 117.

27 The second novel, *In a Glass House*, has been described as "a vivid portrait of self-discovery" (inside front jacket, 1993 ed.); similarly, his third novel, *Where She Has Gone*, as "a beautifully crafted story of self-discovery" (inside front jacket, 1997 ed.); and also as he stated during a reading of a section of his second novel at the conference titled "The Future of Your Past." See Nino Ricci, "Going to the Moon," 56: "Windsor seemed a kind of purgatory to me, a temporary stop between whatever hell my parents had left behind in Italy and the vague promise of the skyline that opened up beyond the Detroit River." "His second book called *In a Glass House* and set in a fictional village modelled on Ricci's hometown of Leamington, Ont., picks up the story of [*Lives of the Saints*]." Wallace, "Nino Ricci: Novelist," 53. See also Dodge, review of *In a Glass House*.

28 See Bertoldi, *I nuovi italiani*, 47–58, especially 49.

29 Ricci, *Radici*, 24, 28.

30 Pearson, "The Gospels According to Ricci."

31 Ricci, *Radici*, 3.

32 Carlomagno, *Agnone*, 79.

33 And that Ricci recorded in *Radici*, 8–9, 12–13, 24.

34 Ricci, *Radici*, 14.

35 Ricci, *Radici*, 8–12.

36 Pitto, *Al di là dell'emigrazione*, 129.

37 Ricci, *Radici*, 12.

38 Pitto, *Al di là dell'emigrazione*, 129; 41 (quotation from Cinanni, *Emigrazione e imperialismo*, 14); also Pitto, *Al di là*, 49; and chapter 3, "The Lessons of the Ill-Fated First Trip," especially note 1.

39 As pointed out also in *Radici*, 8, 30, 31.

40 Ricci, *Radici*, 24.

41 Pitto, *Al di Là*, 87, 101–2.

42 Ibid., 87, 101–2. See also Martelli, "Emigrazione e America," chapter 3, note 22.

43 Pitto, *Al di Là dell'emigrazione*.

44 Ibid., 10, 11.

45 Ibid., 7–12, which includes a list of topics and the author's introduction; and 129–41, which deals with Italian presence in Canada (translation mine).

46 Ricci, *Radici*, 8.

47 Eco, "Postille," 521–8; and *Postscript*, 48–59. See also Macrone, *It's Greek to Me!*, 11.

48 Pitto, *Al di là dell'emigrazione*, 11; and "International Colloquium on Ethnicity: Conflict and Cooperation," Detroit (Michigan)-Windsor (Ontario), 24–6 October 1991, information brochure, 3.

49 Eco, *Postscript*, 54.

50 Eco, "Postille," 524–5; also, Eco, *Postscript*, 58.

51 Eco, "Postille," 525; also, Eco, *Postscript*, 58.

52 Eco, "Postille," 518; and Eco, *Postscript*, 33–4. In his Toronto reading of an excerpt from his second novel, Ricci provided a glimpse of an older Vittorio, a university student still searching for a meaning, for an identity, in books, ideas, as well as, for a while, drugs or rebellion. See *In a Glass House*, XVIII.

53 The "dark passageway" and "the hunch-backed guardian" (XXVI) bring to mind Boccaccio's novella about Andreuccio da Perugia who, during a night of "three serious misfortunes" in a quarter of Naples of ill fame, finds himself "in a narrow alleyway" threatened by *Buttafuoco* (Belchfire), the horrible guardian of the brothel or The Fleshpots. Boccaccio, *The Decameron*, 141–55. The "village rivalries" over the patron saints (IX) recalls Giovanni Verga's short story "Guerra di Santi" (War of saints). Vittorio's father, Mario, "on furlough from his army service, dressed in his khakis and soldier's cap, and all the young women ... trying to catch his eye" (IV), echoes "Turiddu" in Verga's *Cavalleria rusticana* (Rustic chivalry), while the village priest calls to mind another short story by Verga, "Il Reverendo" (The Reverend). Verga, *Tutte le novella*, 1:205–13, 139–44, 243–50. The peasant-immigrants' view of "America" as a place of "dreams and fears ... of ... back-breaking work and poor wages" and yet remaining "a mythical place [a paradise] as if there were two Americas [whose] two natures coexisted together without contradiction" (XXI) retraces almost verbatim Carlo Levi's *Christ Stopped at*

Eboli, particularly the chapter entitled "Gli 'americani' di Gagliano" (The "Americans" of Gagliano): "Even America, for the peasants, has a double nature. It is a land where one goes to work, where one sweats and toils, where the little money is saved with a thousand sacrifices and privations ... but at the same time, and without contradiction, it is paradise, the promised land of the Kingdom." Their attitudes toward the "two Americas" are also similar, and almost the same is the name of a character: Ricci's *Facciabrutta* (Uglyface) (IX) seems to derive from Levi's *Faccialorda* (Dirtyface). Cantarella, *Prosatori del Novecento*, 59–68. Also, Ricci's "forgotten and unsung ... Valle del Sole" (I) recalls aspects (isolation, backwardness, exploitation, emigration) of the villages depicted by both Carlo Levi (i.e., "Gagliano") and Ignazio Silone (i.e., "Fontamara"). As already mentioned, Cristina herself resembles 'Ntoni in Verga's *Malavoglia* (both outsiders, even before their flight from the village); and her comment and attitude toward priests (V) parallel Antonio Gramsci's words (see note 19). They all reflect and strengthen Eco's idea that "books talk among themselves." "Postille," 510 and 533; and *Postscript,* 11–12, 81. See also chapter 3, "The Southern Italian 'Dream of America,'" and notes; and chapter 15, note 18.

54 As Eco suggests, *Postscript,* 53, 59.

55 Eco, *Postscript,* 59.

56 Eco, "Postille," 520–6; Eco, *Postscript,* 41–61.

57 Eco, *Postscript,* 23.

58 Carlomagno, *Agnone: dalle origini,* 307–8. See chapter 3, note 5.

59 See also *The Encyclopedia of World Faiths,* 9–10, 32–51, 54–65, 73, 186–208, 229–40; and Mercatante, *The Facts on File Encyclopedia,* xiii–xviii, 4–5, 152, 190, 207–8, 269. The three-in-one concept may be well illustrated by the widespread three persons in grammar and therefore in the human sphere: *I, you, he/she* (or corresponding plural forms *we/you/they*): the same person can be identified by, or simply be, all three persons according to the situation *I,* when speaking; *you,* when spoken to or directly addressed; *he/she,* when spoken about or referred to.

60 "How to Believe in Miracles," *Time,* 30 December 1991.

61 Eco, *Postscript,* 2–3, 47.

62 "How to Believe in Miracles," *Time.*

63 *La Vita Nuova* [Poems of youth], 80. In Sumerian literature, as "in so many world mythologies, 13 is the number of death ... the unlucky, fateful number." But it also suggests the opposite, as do the triad, the "three-part parallelism" and the "snake": particularly the snake's "imprisoning aspects" and its suggestion of "rebirth and sexuality." Wolkstein and Kramer, *Inanna,* 136–46.

64 Sensini, *Le parole e il testo.*

65 Verses 119 and 121 from Coleridge, "The Rime of the Ancient Mariner," 145.

66 Comments by Janette Turner Hospital and Timothy Findley appearing in the back cover of the 1990 Cormorant edition of Ricci's *Lives of the Saints.*

67 Robey, introduction to *Open Work,* vii.

68 Eco, "Postille," 518; Eco, *Postscript,* 34.

69 Leonard, "Language and Literature in a Multicultural Curriculum," 53.

70 See back cover of the 1990 Cormorant edition of *Lives of the Saints.* See also Bausch, "Nino Ricci"; and "Ricci's Novel," *Windsor Star,* 12 June 1991. By October 1993 *Lives of the Saints* had been "published to acclaim in the U.S. and the U.K., and [had] appeared in translation in France, Spain, Denmark, Sweden, and Germany, with editions forthcoming in Italy and Holland." See "Nino Ricci," *Maclean's,* 5 July 1993; and Ricci, *In a Glass House,* book jacket.

71 Pitto, *Al di là dell'emigrazione,* 10–12.

72 Eco, "Postille," 531; Eco, *Postscript,* 72; see also Temelini, "Literature and Culture in a Multicultural Society," 42.

73 "Nescire autem quid ante quam natus sis acciderit, id est semper esse puerum. Quid enim est aetas hominis, nisi ea memoria rerum veterum cum superiorum aetate contexitur?" (To be ignorant of what occurred before you were born is to remain always a child. For what is the worth of human life, unless it is woven into the life of our ancestors by the records of history?). *Cicero, Orator,* 395.

74 Eco, "Postille," 529–32; Eco, *Postscript,* 67–75.

75 Hubert Bauch, "Nino Ricci: From Guinea Pig to Winning Governor-General Award," *Gazette,* 26 January 1991.

76 That Ricci was able "to invent freely," while bound by what Eco called "the constraints [of] the surrounding world" (*Postscript,* 25), is also evident in specific aspects of *Lives of the Saints.* The novel's setting, for example, is not an exact duplicate of the Upper Molise area in the 1960s; thus, "Valle del Sole [which] did not have any electrical service" (XII) is unlike Villa Canale, where such service dates back to 1928; similarly, while the fictional village "church had no organ" (X), the church of Villa Canale had an "antique and characteristic ... organ." "Tornamonde" (V), apparently the name of a village or a locality, is a pure invention. But compare the invention to the actual name of a town in Abruzzo: *Tornimparte.* Also, with respect to traditional signs or gestures: the "two fingers [brought] up to his head as horns, to mimic the evil eye" (XI) do not usually refer to the "evil eye" but to indicate the horns of a cuckold or cuckoldry. According

to Andrea de Iorio, "Index and little fingers extended, the remaining middle and ring fingers folded and pressed on the thumb [is called] the *mano cornuta* (horned hand). The *mano cornuta* carried to the forehead denotes ... true [conjugal] infidelity [and] in this way has this meaning only." The same gesture, with the hand extended away from the body and toward others, can be used both as a curse and as protection against it. It may be "used as an amulet against a spell produced by evil spirits"; it is an antidote against the evil eye or bad luck in general. With respect to the novel's village, it seems partly based more on those depicted by such writers as Carlo Levi and Ignazio Silone or on the memories of the 1920s pioneers than on the actual 1960s town. See Arduino and Arduino, *Le due valli del sole*, 19; de Jorio, *Gesture in Naples*, 141–3, 147, 152; and Munari, *Speak Italian*, 26–7, 58–61, and chapter 15.

77 Letter to the Ministry of Culture and Recreation-Heritage Division, 4 June 1979. See Ricci, *Radici*.

78 Harney, "Italian Immigration and the Frontiers of Western Civilization," 5.

79 Scotti, "La voce della verità."

80 Ricci, *Radici*, 38–9.

81 Ibid., 39.

82 Ibid., 1.

83 See Pitto, *Al di là dell'emigrazione*, 10–12; Pitto also states that "in rural communities, the migrant comes to be represented, at the symbolic level, in the same manner that has always been followed to celebrate the passing of the deceased"; and for additional information on "emigration as a death experience" he refers to Lombardi Sartriani, *Intervista sulla Calabria*, 46; see *Al di là*, 129, 134, 139, note 7. See also chapter 2, "The Ill-Fated First Trip"; chapter 3, "The Southern Italian 'Dream of America': Reality and Fiction" and note 22; and chapter 5, "The Hardships."

84 Migliorini, *Storia*, 169; see chapter 12, note 11; Alighieri, *The Inferno*, XXVI, 89–93, III; and Alighieri, *The Comedy of Dante Alighieri: Cantica I, Hell*," XXVI, 94–142.

APPENDIX A

1 Almost 100 per cent of the Leamington Italians trace their origins to South Italy, or to seven of the nine regions (equivalent to provinces in Canadian terms) of the peninsular and insular South (or *Mezzogiorno*). The home regions most represented (at least according to those who participated in the project) are (Abruzzo-)Molise (47 per cent); Lazio (or Latium, 35.3 per cent) and the island region of Sicily (13.1 per cent) for a total of 95.4 per cent. The other four regions – Abruzzo, Puglia, Calabria, Campania – together

formed 3.91 per cent. The two not represented were Basilicata (or Lucania) and the island region of Sardinia.

Four other regions – two in Central Italy, two in North Italy – also appeared, but rarely: Le Marche (or The Marches, specifically Ascoli Piceno or the southernmost district of the region), Emilia-Romagna and Veneto (or Venetia) together made up 0.69 per cent of the interviewed immigrants; while Friuli-Venezia Giulia (or Friuli-Julian Venetia in the Northeast) was indicated by only one person (F. Belluz, who had moved from Windsor to Leamington in 1944). Lombardy (in the North) was excluded, since Leamington was a temporary residence for the immigrant from that region.

Other regions or areas may have been excluded because of the inadvertent omission of certain families from the list. Such was the case of a family from that area around Trieste (Julian Venetia) which, after the Second World War, was assigned to then Yugoslavia: classified as "displaced persons" (DPs), Silvano and Anna Giurissevich, "rather than live under Communist rule," chose to emigrate to Canada (1949/50). They, and perhaps others, may have been overlooked by the student-researchers because of their atypical Italian surname (see Introduction). But in fact, the Giurissevich couple, at least when they arrived in Canada, spoke no other language (nor dialect) except "Standard Italian" (Gino Pannunzio, personal communication, July 1988).

APPENDIX B

1   An Italian musician of some renown, according to a 1938 *Windsor Star* article, "Romanelli the Great Now Lives on Pension ... Was Once with Caruso, But Is Now Practically Penniless ... from a family of musicians ... Rocco ... came to Canada with his brother Joe [father of] Luigi and Leone [who] have one of the most popular dance orchestras in Canada ... met [on one of his appearances in Detroit] a Wheatley girl, Sarah Shaw [1876–1943] ... married [her] and retained the Shaw farm [as] permanent residence ... The Italian violinist who claims to have met ... [in a saloon in Toronto and] accompanied the famous Enrico Caruso and to have played with Madam Melba, now lives retired and forgotten on an almost destitute farm near here." (Communication to student-researchers from Rita Lobzun, Wheatley, 21 August 1981; and to Gino Pannunzio, 5 October 1993.)

Bibliography

ARCHIVAL MATERIAL, DOCUMENTS, RECORDS

Leamington Area

H.J. Heinz Co. Ltd
Italian Community Centre/Leamington Roma Club (1960s–80s)
Mersea Township Office (Leamington)
Omstead Fisheries/Foods Limited (Wheatley)
St Angela Merici (Italian Church)
St Michael's Church/Parish7
Sun Parlour Greenhouse Growers Co-operative / Marketing Board
Windsor Italo-Canadian Culture Centre Archives

Italy

Costituzione della Repubblica Italiana (1948). Art. I.
A Glimpse at Italy. 4th ed. Rome: Istituto Poligrafico dello Stato, 1974.
La Cassa per il Mezzogiorno. Documentazione per i partecipanti alla
   Conferenza Nazionale per l'Emigrazione. Rome, 24 February–1 March
   1975. Introd. Giulio Andreotti, Ministro per gli Interventi Straordinari nel
   Mezzogiorno. Rome, 1975.
Le Regioni in cifre. Rome: Istituto centrale di statistica, 1988.
ISTAT. *Istituto Centrale di Statistica*. Rome. "Espatriati e rimpatriati – Anni
   1876–1973." Estratto da ISTAT, *Bollettino Mensile di Statistica,* no. 1 (gen-
   naio 1975), Appendice II, 253–65.
Presidenza del Consiglio dei Ministri. Direzione Generale delle informazioni,
   dell'editoria e della proprietà letteraria, artistica e scientifica [Presidency of
   the Council of Ministers, Information and Copyright Services].

Questa è l'Italia. Rome: Istituto Poligrafico e Zecca dello Stato, 1979.

Ufficio Stampa della Cassa per il Mezzogiorno.

Vita italiana: documenti e informazioni.

"Il nuovo Concordato: enti e beni ecclesiastici. Il 'Protocollo di approvazione' firmato il 15 novembre 1984 dal presidente Craxi e dal segretario di Stato della S. Sede cardinale Casaroli." 34, no. 12 (December 1984), 35–59.

"Il nuovo Concordato: Il testo dell'Accordo tra la S. Sede e l'Italia che modifica il Concordato lateranense del 1929." 34, nos 2–3 (February–March 1984), 3–16.

"La Regione Abruzzi." 34, nos 2–3 (February–March 1984), 223–48.

"La Regione Basilicata." 34, no. 5–6 (May–June 1984), 116–28.

"La Regione Calabria." 34, nos 7–8 (July–August 1984), 86–95.

"La Regione Lazio." 34, no. 1 (January 1984), 97–134.

"La Regione Molise." 34, no. 4 (April 1984), 69–82.

"La Regione Puglia." 34, no. 9 (September 1984), 162–72.

"La Regione Sardegna." 34, no. 11 (November 1984), 73–82.

"La Regione Sicilia." 34, no. 12 (December 1984), 153–65.

GENERAL BIBLIOGRAPHY
(Books, Journals, Newspapers, Magazines, Periodicals, Press Agencies, Reference Works, and Other Sources)

Acme Windsor City Directory, 1943–60.

Alaimo, Roberto, Paolo Fiasconaro, Salvo Licata, Giuseppe Lo Castro, and Carmelo Rapisarda, eds. *Tante Sicilie: L'emigrazione nei Comuni dei Golfi [del Golfo].* Palermo: Edizioni Centro Kolbe, 1988.

Alighieri, Dante. *Convivio.* Milan: Rizzoli, 1952.

– *La Divina Commedia.* Edited by Natalino Sapegno. Florence: "La Nuova Italia" Editrice, 1957.

– *The Comedy of Dante Alighieri: Cantica I, Hell (L'Inferno).* Translated by Dorothy Sayers. Harmondworth: Penguin Books, 1972.

– *The Inferno.* Translated by John Ciardi. New York: New American Library, Mentor Books, 1954.

– *La lingua volgare.* Translated by Massimo Felisatti. In Dante Alighieri, *Opere latine,* 23–82. Milan: Rizzoli, 1965.

– *The Paradiso.* Translated by John Ciardi. New York: New American Library, Mentor Books, 1970.

– *La Vita Nuova.* Edited by Kenneth McKenzie. Boston: Heath, 1922.

– *La Vita Nuova.* Translated by Barbara Reynolds. Harmondworth: Penguin Books, 1969.

Allen, Gene. "Mulroney Apologizes to Italian Internees: No Financial Deal Pledged to Victims." *Globe and Mail*, 5 November 1990, A1, A5.

Almanacco del Molise 1989. 21st ed. A cura di Enzo Nocera. Vol. 2. Edizioni Enne, 1989.

Almazan, Vincenzo. "1679: Il primo italiano nella nostra regione: Enrico de Tonti." *La Gazzetta* (Windsor, Ontario), 29 February 1980, 12; 7 March 1980, 12; 14 March 1980, 12.

Alonzi, Luigi. "L'agricoltura e la risurrezione commerciale e industriale." In *La Ciociaria: Storia arte costume*, 205–26. Rome: Editalia, 1972.

Alvaro, Corrado. *Revolt in Aspromonte*. Translated by Frances Frenaye. New York: New Directions Books, 1962.

Amendola, Giorgio. "Contro la istituzione di una Cassa per il Mezzogiorno (20 giugno 1950)." In *La democrazia nel Mezzogiorno*, 265–8, 280–7, 288–94. Rome: Editori Riuniti, 1957. Reprinted in Villari, *Il Sud nella storia d'Italia*, 2:627–32, 633–46.

Anderson, Alan B., and James S. Frideres. *Ethnicity in Canada: Theoretical Perspectives*. Toronto: Butterworths, 1981.

Annibali, Simonetta. "Noi: gli italiani." *La Gazzetta*, 29 July 1988, 3.

Annuario Generale: Comuni e frazioni d'Italia. Milan: Touring Club Italiano, 1968.

Antonelli, Claudio. "Il peggior difetto degli italiani." *Il Cittadino Canadese*, 7 January 1987, 3.

"Arcimboldi, Giuseppe." *Enciclopedia Garzanti*. 15th ed. 1967.

Arduino, Anna Claudia, and Antonio Arduino. *Le due valli del sole: Villacanale – Leamington*. Agnone: Arti Grafiche "San Giorgio," 1988.

Artusi, Pellegrino. *La scienza in cucina e l'arte del mangiar bene*. Florence: Adriano Salani Editore, 1907.

Avvertenze per l'Emigrante. Rome: Commissariato Generale dell'Emigrazione, 1901–27. Reprint in Cresci and Guidobaldi, *Partono i bastimenti*, 64–5.

Babson, Steve. *Working Detroit: The Making of a Union Town*. New York: Adama Books, 1984.

Bacci, Marsilio. *Viaggio nel tempo: Corso di storia per la scuola media*. Vol. 3. Bologne: Sansoni, 1966.

Bagnell, Kenneth. *Canadese: A Portrait of the Italian Canadians*. Toronto: Macmillan, 1989.

Balsdon, J.P.V.D. *Life and Leisure in Ancient Rome*. London: Bodley Head, 1969.

Baretti, Giuseppe. *An Account of the Manners and Customs of Italy*. London, 1768–9.

Barnes, Sally. "We Promised Jobs but These Men Found Despair in Canada." *Toronto Daily Star*, 14 March 1968, 7.

Bartoli Perrault, Cecilia, and Mirella Jona Affron, eds. Introduction to Silone, *Fontamara*, vii–xv.

Barzini, Luigi. *The Italians: A Full-Length Portrait Featuring Their Manners and Morals*. Toronto: Bantam Books, 1965.

– "A Robust Cuisine Based on People's Character." In Root and the editors of Time-Life Books, *Cooking of Italy*, vii–xv.

Battaglia, S., and V. Pernicone. *Grammatica italiana*. Turin: Loescher editore, 1975.

Bauch, Hubert. "Nino Ricci: From Guinea Pig to Winning Governor-General's Award." *Gazette* (Montreal), 26 January 1991, F2.

Bavington, Jack. *Cultures in Canada*. Toronto: Maclean-Hunter, 1976.

Bazzoni, Renato. "Difendiamo le 'Terre Alte.'" *Qui Touring: Periodico quindicinale del Touring Club Italiano*, March 1971, 17–22.

Beccari, Paolo. *Il folklore molisano*. Rome, 1929. Quoted in Carlomagno, *Agnone: usi costumi tradizioni*, 133–5.

Beccaria, Gian Luigi. *Italiano: Antico e Nuovo*. Milan: Garzanti, 1988.

Bégin, Monique. "Notes for an Address by the Honourable Monique Bégin at the Food Strategy Conference on the Health Element in Canada's Food Strategy." Ottawa, 22 February 1978.

Beltrame, Julian. "Italians Get Apology for Wartime Treatment." *Windsor Star*, 5 November 1990.

– "'Unfair, Illegal, Abusive': PM [Mulroney] Apologizes to Italians for Treatment during War." *Ottawa Citizen, Gazette* (Montreal), and *Windsor Star*, 5 November 1990, A1.

Bergin, Thomas G. "Italy and the English-Speaking World." In Chandler and Molinaro, *Culture of Italy*, ix–xii.

Bernier, Conrad. "Antonio Capobianco affirme qu'il n'oubliera jamais 1940." *La Presse* (Montreal), 12 November 1990.

Bertoldi, Silvio. *I nuovi italiani*. Milan: Rizzoli, 1972.

Bertolini, Daria, ed. *L'Italia nel mondo*. Rome: AVE, 1969.

Biagi, Enzo. *Il Buon Paese: Vale ancora la pena di vivere in Italia?* Milan: L. Longanesi, 1981. Quoted in *La Gazzetta*, "Come va in Italia?," 10 September 1982, 1, 3–4.

Biard, Pierre, S.J. *Relation de la Nouvelle France ... 1616*. Quoted in Menchini, *Giovanni da Verrazzano*, 7, 179–80, 245.

Bienvenue, Rita M., and Jay E. Goldstein, eds. *Ethnicity and Ethnic Relations in Canada: A Book of Readings*. 2nd ed. Toronto: Butterworths, 1985.

"Bilancio di dieci anni (Relazione Pastore, 1960)." In Villari, *Il Sud nella storia d'Italia*, 2:712–34.

Birindelli, A.M., G. Gesano, and E. Sonnino. "Lo spopolamento in Italia nel quadro dell'evoluzione migratoria e demografica (1871–1971) [Depopulation in Italy in the framework of demographic and migratory evolution]. In Rosoli, *Un Secolo di emigrazione italiana*, 189–251.

Birney, Earle. "Canada: Case History." In Diltz, *New Horizons*, 73.

Bissell, Claude T. Introduction to *Two Solitudes*, by MacLennan, vii–xxiii.

Bocca, Giorgio. *In che cosa credono gli italiani?* Milan: Longanesi, 1982. Quoted in *La Gazzetta*, "Come va in Italia?," 10 September 1982, 1, 3–4.

– *Mussolini socialfascista: Il socialismo reale non è fascismo ma come gli somiglia*. Milan: Garzanti, 1983.

Boccaccio, Giovanni. *Decameron*. 8th ed. Milan: Hoepli, 1960.

– *The Decameron*. Translated by G.H. McWilliam. Harmondsworth: Penguin Books, 1972.

Bonanate, Mariapia. "Questo è l'italiano. Parola mia." *Famiglia Cristiana*, 29 June 1988, 62–3.

Boni, Ada. *Il talismano della felicità*. Rome: Casa Editrice Colombo, 1972.

Border Cities Star. "Beware of Fascism, Says This Writer," 30 October 1933, 7.

– "Blue Shirts of Canada Attacked: Anti-Fascist [John Artico] Warns of Troubles Experienced in Italy," 27 October 1933, 5.

– "Border Italians Have Ceremony at Cenotaph: Italians Pay Deep Tribute. Initiation of Local Lodge Impressive [Loggia Generale Umberto Nobile of the Ordine Figli d'Italia]," 25 May 1927, 3, 5.

– "Dante Alighieri Society Formed by Border Italians," *Border Cities Star*, 18 December 1920.

– "Italians to Hear Liberal Speakers" ["Italian Liberal Association"]. 27 October 1933, 5.

– "John Artico Will Speak on Fascism," 25 October 1933, 3.

– "Major Clark [and] Mr Henry," 28 October 1933, 9.

– "On Italian Clubs in Border Cities," 31 October 1933, 7.

– "Veterans Will Decide Policy at Rally Tonight," 27, 30 October 1933.

Borklund, Elmer. *Contemporary Literary Critics*. New York: St Martin's, 1977.

Bosco, Umberto. *Francesco Petrarca*. Bari: Laterza, 1968.

Bouraoui, Hédi, ed. *The Canadian Alternative: Cultural Pluralism and Canadian Unity*. Downsview, ON: ECW, 1980.

Brady, Clift. "Into Space Together." *ITALY Italy*, 15 November–15 December 1986, 65–9.

Braudel, Fernand. "The End of the Old World." *Renaissance Quarterly* 45, no. 4 (Winter 1992): 791–807.

– "The 'New History': Musings on an 'Interscientific' Quest for Truth." Interview by François Ewald and Jean-Jacques Brochier. "Magazine

Littéraire" (Paris). Excerpts quoted in *World Press Review*, March 1985, 30–2.

Bruti Liberati, Luigi. "Fascismo, antifascismo e gli italiani in Canada." *Italian Canadiana* 2, no. 1 (Spring 1986): 50–62.

– "Gli italiani in Canada: Studi e interpretazioni." Introduction to *Dalla frontiera alle Little Italies: Gli italiani in Canada, 1800–1945* by Robert F. Harney, 11–37. Rome: Bonacci, 1984.

Bucci, Pietro. "Address to the Calabro-Canadian Confederation." Toronto, 23 January 1987.

Buchignani, Norman, and Joan Engel. *Cultures in Canada: Strength in Diversity*. Edmonton: Weigl Educational Publishers, 1983.

Burnet, Jean. "Multiculturalism Ten Years Later." Special issue, *History and Social Science Teacher* 17, no. 1 (Fall 1981): 1–6.

Burton, Clarence M., William Stocking, and Gordon K. Miller, eds. *The City of Detroit, Michigan, 1701–1922*. Detroit: S.J. Clarke Publishing, 1922.

Buttitta, Ignazio. "Un populu" [A people]." Quoted in Leydi, *I canti popolari italiani*, 8.

Caccia, Carletto. "Il Duca degli Abruzzi e il monte S. Elia." *La Gazzetta*, 27 September, 2; 4 October, 3; 11 October 1985, 2.

Cacciavillani, Floyd. Letter to the editor, *Windsor Star*, 20 January 1978, 11.

Cairns, Alan, and John Coleman. "Showdown with the Law: Court Orders 'Hands Off Tugs.'" *Windsor Star*, 27 October 1984, A3, A4.

Calvino, Italo. *Six Memos for the Next Millennium*. Cambridge, MA: Harvard University Press, 1988.

Cambon, Glauco. "Dante and the Drama of Language." In *The World of Dante: Six Studies in Language and Thought*, edited by S. Bernard Chandler and J.A. Molinaro, 3–24. Toronto: University of Toronto Press, 1968.

Campobasso-Isernia. 1983–84. Elenco ufficiale alfabetico e pagine gialle degli abbonati al telefono aggiornato all'8 giugno 1983.

Canadian (Toronto Daily Star). "The Big Move ..." 22 January 1966, 10–13.

The Canadian Encyclopedia. 2nd ed. (1988).

Cancian, Robert, and Karol F. Dycha. *Windsor: A Statistical Package (1851–1983)*. Windsor: Essex County Historical Society, 1984.

Candeloro, Dominic, Fred L. Gardaphe, and Paolo A. Giordano, eds. *Italian Ethnics: Their Languages, Literatures and Lives*. Vol. 20. Proceedings of the 20th Annual Conference of the American Italian Historical Association, Chicago, 11–13 November 1987. Staten Island, NY: American Italian Historical Association, 1990.

Cantarella, Michele. *The Italian Heritage*. New York: Holt, Rinehart and Winston, 1959.

– ed. *Prosatori del Novecento*. New York: Holt, Rinehart and Winston, 1967.

Capecelatro, Ennio. *Il linciaggio del Mezzogiorno*. Cosenza: Lerici, 1978.

Cappadocia, Ezio. Review of *Il Canada, l'Italia e il Fascismo, 1919–1945*, by Luigi Bruti Liberati. *Italian Canadiana* 2, no. 1 (Spring 1986): 111–12.

Carducci, Giosuè. "Canzone di Legnano (1876–79)." In *Carducci, Pascoli e D'Annunzio: Antologia poetica per uso delle scuole medie*, edited by F. Bernini and L. Bianchi, 195–205. Reprint. Bologne: Zanichelli, 1955.

Carli, Camillo. "Cibo veloce morte precoce: Dal fast wine al fast food?" *Vice Versa* 15 (May–August 1986): 47–9.

– "Diario italiano: I 'fast-food' alle corde, in Italia ..." *La Gazzetta*, 28 November 1986, 5.

Carlomagno, Custode. *Agnone: dalle origini ai nostri giorni*. Campobasso: Tipografia Lampo, 1965.

– *Agnone: usi costumi tradizioni*. Campobasso: Casa Editrice Lampo, 1984.

Caroli, Betty Boyd, Robert F. Harney, and Lydio F. Tomasi, eds. *The Italian Immigrant Woman in North America*. Proceedings of the Tenth Annual Conference of the American Italian Historical Association, Toronto, 28 and 29 October 1977 in Conjunction with the Canadian Italian Historical Association. Toronto: Multicultural History Society of Ontario, 1978.

Carrillo, Elisa A. "The Church in Italy." In Chandler and Molinaro, *Culture of Italy*, 178–97.

Casa Mia [My home]. Equipe 84 in "I Complessi." P.I. Records (MCPP-4001). Italy, n.d., side 1.

"Casanova, Giovanni Giacomo" (1725–1798). *Histoire de ma vie [Mémoires]* (1822). Quoted in Romano, *Storia d'Italia*, 14–15n, and 33.

Cassola, Carlo. "Emigranti." In Cresci and Guidobaldi, *Partono i bastimenti*, 201–6.

Castiglione, Baldesar. *The Book of the Courtier*. Translation, introduction by George Bull. Harmondsworth: Penguin Books, 1967.

Castrilli, Annamarie P. "Remarks to the 9th Biennial Convention ...," Congresso Nazionale degli Italo Canadesi, June 1990.

Cerase, Francesco P. "Economia precaria ed emigrazione [Precarious economy and emigration]." In Rosoli, *Un secolo di emigrazione italiana*, 117–52.

Chandler, S. Bernard, and J.A. Molinaro, eds. *The Culture of Italy: Mediaeval to Modern*. Toronto: Griffin House, 1979.

– *The World of Dante: Six Studies in Language and Thought*. Toronto: University of Toronto Press, 1968.

Chiarilli, Giovanna, Nazzareno Principessa, and Patrizia Amati. "Qui Roma ... Per difendere Roma." GRTV Press (Rome, 1986). Reprinted in *La Gazzetta*, 30 May 1986, 4.

Ciccotti, Ettore. "Il movimento socialista e il Mezzogiorno. Discorso tenuto a Brindisi l'11 novembre 1900." In *Sulla questione meridionale*. Milan, 1904, 149–54. Reprinted in Villari, *Il Sud nella storia d'Italia*, 2:452–7.

– "Mezzogiorno e Settentrione d'Italia." Milan-Rome, 1898, 79–80, 81–4, 85–7, 89–101. Reprinted as "Il Mezzogiorno alla fine dell'Ottocento," in Villari, *Il Sud nella storia d'Italia*, 1:291–307.

Cicero. *Orator*, xxxiv. 120. In *Cicero: Brutus, Orator*. Translated by G.L. Hendrickson and H.M. Hubbell. Loeb Classical Library. Edited by T.E. Page, W.H.D Rouse, and Edward Capps, 394–5. Cambridge, MA: Harvard University Press, 1962.

Cinanni, Paolo. *Emigrazione e imperialismo*. Rome: Ed. Riuniti, 1975. Quoted in Pitto, *Al di là dell'emigrazione*, 41, 52.

Ciongoli, A. Kenneth. "Origins of American Values." *Fra Noi: A Monthly Journal of Italian American Life*, March 1988, 27, 32, 34.

Citizenship and Immigration. *Il CANADA: dall'Atlantico al Pacifico*. Edito a cura del Ministero degli Affari Esteri Canada, Ottawa, 1950. 1st ed. 1947. 2nd rev. ed. Citizenship and Immigration. Ottawa: Stampatore Reale e Controllore della Cartoleria [King's Printer and Controller of Stationery], 1951.

Clark, W.L. "Send Enemy Aliens Home … Instead of Keeping [Them] in Internment Camps in Canada." Part of "As We See It," *Windsor Daily Star*, 14 June 1940, p. 2.

Clivio, Gianrenzo P. "Competing Loanwords and Loanshifts in Toronto's *italiese*." In *ALTRO POLO: Italian Abroad*. Studies on Language Contact in English-Speaking Countries. Edited by Camilla Bettoni, 129–46. Sydney: Frederick May Foundation for Italian Studies, University of Sydney, 1986.

– "The Development of the Italian Language and Its Dialects." In Chandler and Molinaro, *Culture of Italy*, 24–41.

– "Su alcune caratteristiche dell'italiese di Toronto." *Il Veltro: Rivista della civiltà italiana*, Anno 29, nos 3–4 (May–August 1985): 483–93.

Cochrane, Eric. *Historians and Historiography in the Italian Renaissance*. Chicago: University of Chicago Press, 1985.

Colajanni, Napoleone. "Gli avvenimenti di Sicilia e le loro cause." Palermo, 1894, 111–16, 118–24, 125–40, 142–6. Reprinted as "Le cause del movimento dei Fasci siciliani" in Villari, *Il Sud nella storia d'Italia*, 1:225–45.

– "Per la razza maledetta." Palermo-Rome, 1898, 1–14, 16–19, 31–8. Reprinted in Villari, *Il Sud nella storia d'Italia*, 2:431–44.

"Colasanti's Cactus and Tropical Gardens." In *Welcome to Windsor and Essex County: Experience Canada's Most Southern Hospitality*, 21. Visitor's brochure. Windsor: Tourist & Convention Bureau of Windsor & Essex County, n.d., 21.

Coleman, John. "Fishing Quota Dispute Facing Supreme Test." *Windsor Star*, 23 February 1985, B5.

Coleridge, Samuel Taylor. "The Rime of the Ancient Mariner." In *Poems, Chiefly Narrative*, edited by W.L. Macdonald and F.C Walker, 141–61. Toronto: J.M. Dent and Sons, 1952.

Coletti, Francesco. "Dell'emigrazione italiana." In *Cinquant'anni di vita italiana*. Rome, 1911, 3:138–47, 269–73. Reprinted as "L'emigrazione" in Villari, *Il Sud nella storia d'Italia*, 1:403–22.

"Columbus, Christopher. *Ital.* Cristoforo Colombo. 1451–1506." *Webster's Biographical Dictionary*. 1972 ed.

Consonni, Domenico. *Ponte nei secoli: corso di storia per il triennio degli istituti tecnici*. Turin: Società Editrice Internazionale, 1972.

Cornies, Larry A. "*Our Town*: Italian Community." *Leamington Post*, 2 March 1977, 1.

Corrigan, Beatrice. *Italian Poets and English Critics, 1755–1859*. Toronto: University of Toronto Press, 1969.

County of Essex Gazetteer and General and Business Directory for 1866–7. Windsor: Southerland.

Craig, Albert M., William A. Graham, Donald Kagan, Steven Ozment, and Frank M. Turner. *The Heritage of World Civilizations*. 4th ed. New York: Macmillan Publishing, 1997.

Crawford, Michael. *The Roman Republic*. Glasgow: Fontana/Collins, 1978.

Cresci, Paolo, and Luciano Guidobaldi, eds. *Partono i bastimenti*. Milan: Mondadori, 1980.

Croce, Benedetto. *La filosofia di Giambattista Vico*. 3rd ed. Bari: Laterza, 1973.

Currie, A.W. *The Grand Trunk Railway of Canada*. Toronto: University of Toronto Press, 1957.

Curtius, Ernest Robert. *European Literature and the Latin Middle Ages*. Translated by Willard R. Trask. New York: Harper & Row, 1963.

Danesi, Marcel. "Language Learning and Mental Flexibility." *Graduate: The University of Toronto Alumni Magazine* 12, no. 4 (March/April 1985): 20–1.

– *Loanwords and Phonological Methodology*. Ville LaSalle, QC: Didier, 1985.

"D'Annunzio, Gabriele." *Enciclopedia della letteratura Garzanti*. 2nd ed. (1974).

Da Ponte, Lorenzo [Emanuele Conegliano]. *Memorie* [Autobiography]. New York [1807, 1823–27; 1829–30]. Quoted in Romano, *Storia d'Italia*, 34.

De Amicis, Edmondo. *Cuore* (1886). Quoted in Martelli, "Emigrazione e America," 71–2.

– *In America* (1897). Quoted in Martelli, "Emigrazione e America," 71–2.

De Felice, Renzo. "Premessa." In *Nascita e avvento del fascismo: L'Italia dal 1918 al 1922*, by Angelo Tasca. Bari: Laterza, 1976, 1:ix–xvi.

de Jorio, Andrea. *Gesture in Naples and Gesture in Classical Antiquity.* Translated by Adam Kendon. Bloomington: Indiana University Press, 2000.

Del Balso, Michael. "No, Sir, I Would Rather Starve..." *Quaderni Culturali dell'Associazione di Cultura Popolare Italo-Quebecchese* 2, no. 1 (1982): 25–9.

Della-Mattia, Elaine. "Words Come Too Late." *Windsor Star*, 5 November 1990, A1, A11.

Delli Quadri, Giuseppe. "Considerazioni sul futuro di Agnone." *L'eco dell'alto Molise*, 20 May 1987, 4.

De Maria, Luciano, ed. *Per conoscere Marinetti e il Futurismo.* Milan: Oscar Mondadori, 1973.

De Martino, Ernesto. *La fine del mondo.* Turin: Einaudi, 1977. Quoted in Pitto, *Al di là dell'emigrazione*, 11–12, 97–8, 114, 116.

"Democracy." Letter to the editor, *Border Cities Star*, 30 October 1933, 7.

de Rosa, Luigi. *La rivoluzione industriale in Italia.* Bari: Laterza, 1980.

De Sanctis, Francesco. *Storia della letteratura italiana.* 2 vols. Rome: Cremonese, 1957.

Detroit Free Press. "Italy Ponders Switching to Use of English," 13 September 1978, 16A.

De Viti De Marco, Antonio. "Gli effetti del protezionismo" [1891]. In Villari, *Il Sud nella storia d'Italia,* 1:199–206.

– "Il Mezzogiorno 'mercato coloniale'" [1929]. In Villari, *Il Sud nella storia d'Italia,* 1:343–53.

Devoto, Giacomo. *La Ciociaria: Storia arte costume.* Rome: Editalia, 1972.

Devoto, Giacomo, and Gian Carlo Oli. *Dizionario della lingua italiana.* Florence: Le Monnier, 1971.

– *Nuovo Vocabolario Illustrato della Lingua Italiana* [Dictionary of the Italian language]. Edited by Gian Carlo Oli and Lorenzo Magini. 2 vols. Florence: Le Monnier/Milan: Selezione del Reader's Digest, 1987.

Dewar, Gordon, Jr. "Immigrants Posing Problem in Canada: Many Disillusioned by False Promises Made in Europe." *Windsor Daily Star*, 1 February 1952, 3, 8.

Dewlin. E.W. "The Leamington ... Colony of Italians." Radio Canada. Reprinted in *Il Cittadino Canadese*, 23 December 1966. Quoted in Spada, *Italians in Canada*, 301–2.

Dickman, Thelma. "Pasta Perfect." *Leisure Ways*, June 1987, 14.

Diltz, Bert Case. *New Horizons: An Anthology of Short Poems for Senior Students.* Toronto: McClelland & Stewart, 1956.

Di Michele, Carmine, and Michele Pirone. "Album degli Italiani." In *Tricolore in Canada*, by Nicola Polidoro. Montecarlo: Edizioni "Il Gabbiano," 1977, 164.

Dionisotti, C., and C. Grayson, eds. *Early Italian Texts*. 2nd ed. Oxford: Basil Blackwell, 1965.

Di Rienzo, Renzo. "Il socio Americano" [The American partner]. *L'Espresso*, 24 July 1988, 187–8.

– "Mass Media: Va in onda il terremoto." *L'Espresso*, 9 September 1984, 5–12.

"Disoccupazione e Pil pro-capite in Italia nel period [19]85–90." GRTV *Press* (Rome 1991). Reprinted in *La Gazzetta*, 3 June 1991, 4.

Di Tommaso, Carla. "Da Milano a Wall Street: Nel futuro di Silvio Berlusconi c'è l'America." GRTV *Press* (Rome 1991). Reprinted in *La Gazzetta*, 18 February 1991, 5–6.

Di Vittorio, Giuseppe [M. Nicoletti, pseud.]. "Le fascisme contre le paysan: L'expérience italienne." Paris, 1929, 8–18, 22–4, 26–8, 59–62. Reprinted as "Il fascismo contro i contadini," in Villari, *Il Sud nella storia d'Italia*, 2:571–94.

Dodge, Bill. Review of *In a Glass House* by Nino Ricci. *Globe and Mail*, 2 October 1993.

Domnick Pierre, Karin. "Health beyond Medicine: Acting Together for Individual Well-being." *University of Toronto Magazine* 19, no. 3 (Spring 1992): 11–13.

"Donnaconna." *Encyclopedia Canadiana*. 1966 ed.

"Donnaconna." *The Encyclopedia of Canada*. 1935 ed.

Dorso, Guido. "La rivoluzione meridionale." Turin: ed. Gobetti, 1925, 220–37 (2nd ed. Turin: Einaudi, 1945). Reprinted in Villari, *Il Sud nella storia d'Italia*, 2:519–34.

Dotti, Ugo. *L'età dell'umanesimo*. Palermo: Palumbo Editore, 1978.

Drake, Stillman. "Italy, Science and Modern Culture." In Chandler and Molinaro, *Culture of Italy*, 143–55.

Driedger, Leo, ed. *The Canadian Ethnic Mosaic: A Quest for Identity*. Canadian Ethnic Studies Association Series. Vol. 6. Toronto: McClelland & Stewart, 1978.

Durnford, Hugh, ed. *Heritage of Canada*. Canadian Automobile Association in conjunction with Reader's Digest Association (Canada), 1978.

Dunn, Kate. "Five Decades Later, the Pain Lingers: Italian Canadians Recall Horror of Wartime Internment." *Gazette* (Montreal), 11 November 1990.

Dziver, Joe. "Italian Pioneers Aid Newcomers: Industrious Immigrants Take Key Business Roles." *Windsor Daily Star*, 18 July 1959, 3, 6.

Eccles, W.J. *Frontenac: The Courtier Governor*. Toronto: McClelland & Stewart, 1959.

Eco, Umberto. "Postille a 'Il nome della rosa' 1983." In *Il nome della rosa*, by Umberto Eco, 532. Milan: Fabbri, 1980.

– *Postscript to The Name of the Rose.* Translated by William Weaver. New York: Harcourt, Brace, Jovanovich, 1984.
– *Six Walks in the Fictional Woods.* Cambridge, MA: Harvard University Press, 1994.
Economist. "Carlo De Benedetti: In the Steps of Carlos V," 23 January 1988, 60–1.
– "Italy's Capitalist Capital [Milan]," 9 March 1988, 75.
– "Italy's New Chemistry Set." 13 August 1988, 60.
– "Italy's Vita Is Now More Dolce." 24 January 1987, 51–2.
– "*Mediobanca*: New Boys' Club," 12 December 1987, 88, 92.
– "North-South: Italy: The Mending of the Mezzogiorno." 16 August 1986, 30–1.
– Review of *Agnelli and the Network of Italian Power*, by Alan Friedman. 6 October 1988, 90–1.
"Eh compare." Italian American popular song, by Julius LaRosa. 1950s.
Elliott, Jean Leonard, ed. *Two Nations, Many Cultures: Ethnic Groups in Canada.* Scarborough, ON: Prentice-Hall of Canada, 1979.
"Ellis Island, an Immigration Center from 1892 to 1954." In *I Love New York.* New York: Visitors Guide and Map.
Employment and Immigration Canada. Immigration Statistics, 1896–1961. Immigration Statistics Division. Program Data Directorate. Hull, QC.
Enciclopedia della letteratura Garzanti. 2nd ed. (1974).
Enciclopedia Garzanti. 2 vols. 15th ed. (1967).
Enciclopedia italiana "Treccani." 1937 ed.
Encyclopedia Canadiana. 1966 ed., and 1977 ed.
The Encyclopedia of Canada. 1935 ed.
The Encyclopedia of World Faiths. Edited by Peter Bishop and Michael Darton. New York: Facts on File Publications, 1989.
Erasmi, Gabriele. "'Norma' ed 'Aida': Momenti estremi della concezione romantica." *Studi Verdiani* 5 (Parma: Istituto Nazionale di Studi Verdiani, 1989): 85–108.
Essex Branch of the Ontario Genealogical Society. *Evergreen Memorial Park Cemetery, Leamington.* Windsor: Essex Branch of the Ontario Genealogical Society, 1983.
Essex County (Ontario) Tourist Association. *Essex County Sketches.* Windsor: Herald, 1947.
Este, Jim. "Leamington: Is There Any Place You'd Rather Be?" *Windsor Star*, "Historical Essex '75," 43.
Ewen, David. *Encyclopedia of the Opera.* New York: Hill and Wang, 1955.
Faccioli, Emilio, ed. *Il teatro italiano: Dalle origini al Quattrocento.* Turin: Einaudi, 1975.

Fant, Maureen B. Review of *La Genovesità di Colombo* by Paolo Emilio Taviani. *ITALY Italy*, September 1987, 30–4.

[Fascist Text]. *Storia e geografia per la IV classe elementare. Scuole Italiane all'Estero*. Verona: A. Mondadori, 1937 – XV. A copy of the text used in Windsor Italian classes, in the writer's possession, has the name "Mary Valenti" handprinted on the inside page.

Favero, Luigi, and Graziano Tassello. "Cent'anni di emigrazione italiana (1876–1976) [One hundred years of Italian emigration]." In Rosoli, *Un secolo di emigrazione italiana: 1876–1976*, 9–64.

Ferguson, Jonathan. "Italians Get PM's Apology for Wartime Internment." *Toronto Star*, 5 November 1990.

Ferguson, Wallace K., and Geoffrey Bruun. *A Survey of European Civilization*. Part 1, to 1660. 3rd ed. Boston: Houghton Mifflin, 1958.

Ferraris, Maggiorino. "La 'felice armonia' [1902]." In Villari, *Il Sud nella storia d'Italia*, 1:371–87.

Feyerabend, Paul. "How to Defend Society against Science." In *Scientific Revolutions*, edited by Ian Hacking, 157–67. Don Mills, ON: Oxford University Press, 1983.

Filangieri, Gaetano. "La scienza della legislazione." Naples, 1781–3. Reprinted as "Città e campagna," in Villari, *Il Sud nella storia d'Italia*, 1:12–23.

Film d'amore e d'anarchia. Direction/screenplay by Lina Wertmüller. Euro International; Italia, 1972.

Findley, Timothy. "*Lives of the Saints* [by] Nino Ricci ... a novel of remarkable beauty and unforgettable power..." As quoted on the back cover of the 1990 Cormorant edition of *Lives of the Saints*.

Fink, Guido. "The Other Side of the Moon: Myth and Images of America in Italian Cinema." *Forum Italicum* 19, no. 1 (Spring 1985): 3–17.

Finlay, J.L., and D.N. Sprague. *The Structure of Canadian History*. 2nd ed. Scarborough, ON: Prentice-Hall Canada, 1984.

Finzi, Enrico. "L'Italia che cambia: il censimento ci ha fotografato così." Reprinted in *La Gazzetta*, 10 September 1982, 1, 4.

Fisher, Robert V. "The Evolution of Marxism in the Early Intellectual Development of Benito Mussolini: The First Elements of Fascist Doctrine." Senior honours thesis, University of Michigan, Ann Arbor, 1983.

Fortunato, Giustino. "La questione demaniale nell'Italia meridionale, 1879." In *Il Mezzogiorno e lo Stato italiano*. Bari, 1911, 1:88–95. Reprinted as "Il problema demaniale," in Villari, *Il Sud nella storia d'Italia*, 1:161–70.

– "La questione meridionale e la riforma tributaria (1904)." In *Il Mezzogiorno e lo Stato italiano*, 2:332–6, 366–73. Reprinted as "La riforma tributaria" in Villari, *Il Sud nella storia d'Italia*, 1:354–70.

Fox, Brian. "[Leamington Italian] Roma Club to Boycott Luncheon for the PM [Trudeau]." *Windsor Star*, 10 January 1978, 3, 4.

Franchetti, Leopoldo. "L'Italia e la sua colonia africana (1891)." Reprinted as "Africa e Mezzogiorno," in Villari, *Il Sud nella storia d'Italia*, 1:213–22.

Friesen, John W. *When Cultures Clash: Case Studies in Multiculturalism*. Calgary: Detselig Enterprises, 1985.

Frye, Northrop. *The Bush Garden*. Toronto: Anansi, 1971.

– "*Il Cortegiano*" [The courtier. By B. Castiglione]. *Quaderni d'italianistica* 1, no. 1 (Spring 1980): 1–14.

– "'Key to Education' Is Love of Learning." Interview by Louise Browne and Bill Schiller. *Toronto Star (Sunday Star)*, 10 May 1987, A1, A10.

Fuller, Robert M. *Windsor Heritage*. Windsor: Herald, 1972.

"Galilei, Galileo, 1564–1642." *Webster's Biographical Dictionary*. 1972 ed.

Gambino, Enzo. *Una finestra sul Mezzogiorno d'Italia*. Ufficio Stampa della Cassa per il Mezzogiorno, n.d.

Gambino, Richard. *Blood of My Blood*. Quoted in Ciongoli, "Origins of American Values," 32.

Gardner, Robert C., and Rudolf Kalin, eds. *A Canadian Social Psychology of Ethnic Relations*. Toronto: Methuen Publications, 1981.

"Garibaldi, Giuseppe. 1807–1882." *Webster's Biographical Dictionary*. 1972 ed.

Garin, Eugenio. *Italian Humanism: Philosophy and Civic Life in the Renaissance*. Translated by Peter Munz. Westport, CT: Greenwood, 1975.

– *La cultura del Rinascimento*. Bari: Laterza, 1967.

– *L'umanesimo italiano*. Bari: Laterza, 1958.

– ed. *L'uomo del Rinascimento*. Bari: Laterza, 1988.

– *Medioevo e Rinascimento*. Bari: Laterza, 1966.

– *Scienza e vita civile nel Rinascimento italiano*. Bari: Laterza, 1965.

Genovesi, Antonio. Introdroduction to *L'agricoltore sperimentato*, by C. Trinci. Naples, 1769, i–vi, x–vi. Reprinted as "Ragionamento intorno all'agricoltura con applicazione al Regno di Napoli," in *Scrittori classici italiani di economia politica*, vol. 9, Milan, 1803. Reprinted as "Il problema della terra" in Villari, *Il Sud nella storia d'Italia*, 1:3–11.

Gervais, C.H. *The Rumrunners: A Prohibition Scrapbook*. Scarborough, ON: Firefly Books, 1984.

Giolitti, Antonio. "Un dibattito alla Camera sulla politica per il Mezzogiorno." *Mondo Economico*, 18 February 1961. Reprinted as "La questione meridionale e il socialismo in Italia" in Villari, *Il Sud nella storia d'Italia*, 2:735–54.

Giovanni Caboto Club, 1925–1975: "50th Anniversary." Windsor, 1975.

The Godfather. Dir. Francis Ford Coppola. Screenplay Mario Puzo and Francis Ford Coppola. Prod. Albert S. Ruddy and Gray Frederickson. Alfran Productions. United States, 1971.

Goldoni, Carlo. *Mémoires de M. Goldoni pour servir à l'histoire de sa vie et* à celle de son *theatre*. Paris, 1787. Quoted in Romano, *Storia d'Italia*, 14–15n33.

Goldthwaite, Richard A. *The Building of Renaissance Florence: An Economic and Social History*. Baltimore: Johns Hopkins University Press, 1982.

Golini, Antonio. "Migrazioni interne, distribuzione della popolazione e urbanizzazione in Italia [Internal migration, population distribution and urbanization in Italy]." In Rosoli, *Un secolo di emigrazione italiana: 1876–1976*, 153–87.

Gramsci, Antonio. "Alcuni temi della quistione meridionale." In *Stato operaio*, January 1930. Reprinted as "Antonio Gramsci: Il Mezzogiorno e la rivoluzione socialista," in Villari, *Il Sud nella storia d'Italia*, 2:535–68.

– *Selections from Cultural Writings*. Edited by David Forgacs and Geoffrey Nowell-Smith. Translated by William Boelhower. London: Lawrence and Wishart, 1985.

"Grand Trunk Railway." *Encyclopedia Canadiana*. 1977 ed.

Grant, Michael. *The Founders of the Western World: A History of Greece and Rome*. New York: Macmillan, 1991.

Graves, Robert. *The Greek Myths*. I. London: Penguin Books, 1960.

Grazzini, Giovanni. *Gli anni Settanta in cento film*. Bari: Laterza, 1976.

Grohovaz, Gianni. "Toronto's Italian Press after the Second World War." *Polyphony* 4, no. 1 (Spring/Summer 1982): 105–13.

Hale, John R., ed., introd. *Guicciardini: History of Italy and History of Florence*. Translated by Cecil Grayson. New York: Washington Square, 1964.

Hall, Robert A., Jr. *Linguistics and Your Language*. Garden City, NY: Doubleday, 1960.

Hapgood, David, and David Richardson. *Monte Cassino: The True Story of the Most Controversial Battle of World War II*. New York: Berkley Books, 1986.

Harney, Robert F. *Dalla Frontiera alle Little Italies: Gli italiani in Canada, 1800–1945*. Rome: Bonacci, 1984.

– *From the Shores of Hardships: Italians in Canada*. Edited by Nicholas DeMaria Harney. Toronto: Centro canadese scuola e cultura italiana, 1993.

– "Frozen Wastes: The State of Italian Canadian Studies." In *Perspectives in Italian Immigration and Ethnicity*, ed. S.M. Tomasi, 115–31. Staten Island, NY: Center for Migration Studies, 1977.

– ed. *Gathering Place: Peoples and Neighbourhoods of Toronto, 1834–1945*. Toronto: MHSO, 1985.
– "Homo Ludens and Ethnicity." *Polyphony* 7, no. 1 (Spring/Summer 1985): 1–12.
– "Introduction" and "The Ethnic Press in Ontario." *Polyphony* 4, no. 1 (Spring/ Summer 1982): 1–14.
– "Italian Immigration and the Frontiers of Western Civilization." In *The Italian Immigrant Experience*, edited by John Potestio and Antonio Pucci, 1–28. Thunder Bay, ON: Canadian Italian Historical Association, 1988.
– "Italians in Canada." In Chandler and Molinaro, *Culture of Italy*, 225–46.
– *Oral Testimony and Ethnic Studies*. Toronto: MHSO, n.d.
Harney, Robert F., and J. Vincenza Scarpaci, eds. *Little Italies in North America*. Toronto: MHSO, 1981.
Harney, Robert F., and Harold Troper. *Immigrants: A Portrait of the Urban Experience, 1890–1930*. Toronto: Van Nostrand Reinhold, 1975.
Harrison, R.M. "Now [Reaction against] Influx of European DP's." *Windsor Daily Star*, 16 April 1952, 21.
Harvey, Robert. "Eppur si muove: A Survey of Italy." *Economist*, 23 July 1983, 46–94.
Hawking, Stephen. *Black Holes and Baby Universes and Other Essays*. New York: Bantam Books, 1993.
Hazan, Marcella. *The Classic Italian Cook Book: The Art of Italian Cooking and the Italian Art of Eating*. New York: Alfred A. Knopf, 1978.
Hazan, Mario. *Grande dizionario: inglese–italiano / italiano–inglese*. Milan: Garzanti, 1963.
Hearder, H. *Italy: A Short History*. Cambridge: Cambridge University Press, 1990.
Hearder, H., and D.P. Waley, eds. *A Short History of Italy: From Classical Times to the Present Day*. Cambridge: Cambridge University Press, 1979.
Heichelheim, Fritz M., and Cedric A. Yeo. *History of the Roman People*. Englewood Cliffs, CA: Prentice Hall, 1962.
Heimler, Eugene. *Mental Illness and Social Work*. Harmondsworth: Pelican Books, 1967.
Helling, Rudolf A. *A Socio-Economic History of German-Canadians: They, Too, Founded Canada*. Edited by Bernd Hamm. Wiesbaden: Franz Steiner Verlag, 1984.
Helling, Rudolf A., and Edward Boyce. *A Demographic Study of Essex County and Metropolitan Windsor*. Department of Sociology and Anthropology, University of Windsor and The General Mission Centre, Windsor, 1965.

Henley, Richard, and Jonathan Young. "Multicultural Education: Contemporary Variations on a Historical Theme." Special issue, *History and Social Science Teacher* 17, no. 1 (Fall 1981): 7–16.

Hibbert, Christopher. *Benito Mussolini: The Rise and Fall of Il Duce.* Harmondsworth: Penguin Books, 1965.

"Historical Essex '75." *Windsor Star*, 11 July 1975, 29–44.

Hodgett, Gerald A.J. *A Social and Economic History of Medieval Europe.* New York: Harper Torchbooks, 1974.

Holt, Frank L. "The Forum: French Fries and the Fall of Rome." *Archaeology* 40, no. 5 (September/October 1987): 96.

Horace. *Ars Poetica*, 1. 343. In *The Ars Poetica of Horace*, edited by Augustus S. Wilkins, 72–3. London: Macmillan, 1964.

Hornberger, Rob. "A Fine Kettle of Fish." *Windsor Star*, 17 November 1984, B5.

House of Commons Debates. 28th Parliament, 3rd Session, No. 8 (8 October 1971) 8545–48 (Right Hon. P.E. Trudeau).

House of Commons Debates. 33rd Parliament, 2nd Session (14 July 1988). (Vincent Della Noce).

House of Commons Debates. 34th Parliament, 2nd Session, Vol. 131, No. 243 (5 November 1990). (Vincent Della Noce and Sergio Marchi).

Hoy, James F., and John Somer, eds. *The Language Experience.* New York: Dell Publishing, Delta Book, 1974.

Hull, Norman. "Scores of Windsor Italians Arrested in Fascist Purge. Police Move Quickly to Check Suspected Anti-British Elements. Largest Raiding Squad in City's History Seizes Men, Firearms, Ammunition and Literature in General Round Up." *Windsor Daily Star*, 12 June 1940, 3, 8.

Il Cittadino Canadese. "L'Italia seconda in classifica." 24 September 1986, 3.

Illustrative Documents. Translated with introduction and notes. New York: Columbia University Press, 1990.

Il popolo italiano. "Tonti, Henry [Enrico]," March 1987, 5.

International Colloquium on Ethnicity: Conflict and Cooperation. Detroit – Windsor, 24–6 October 1991. Information brochure.

Isajiw, Wsevolod W., ed. *Identities: The Impact of Ethnicity on Canadian Society.* Canadian Ethnic Studies Association Series. Vol. 5. Toronto: Peter Martin Associates, 1977.

– Introduction to "How to Understand Today's Ethnic Group." In "Ukrainians in the Canadian City." Special issue, *Canadian Ethnic Studies* 12, no. 2 (1980): v–ix.

Italia centrale, seconda parte, e Sardegna: Nuova guida rapida. Milan: TCI, 1975.

ITALY *Italy.* "World's Biggest Joint Venture Will Exploit Russia's Gas and Oil," 15 April–15 May 1988, 70–1.

Jansen, Clifford J. *Italians in a Multicultural Canada*. Canadian Studies. Vol. 1. Lewiston, NY: Edwin Mellen, 1988.

Jansen, Clifford J., and Lee R. LaCavera. *Fact-Book on Italians in Canada*. Toronto: York University Press, 1981.

Johnson, Leo A. "The State of Agricultural Development in the Western District to 1851." In Pryke and Kulisek, *Western District*, 113–45.

Jolowicz, H.F., and Barry Nicholas. *Historical Introduction to the Study of Roman Law*. 3rd ed. Cambridge: Cambridge University Press, 1972.

Jovine, Francesco. *Il pastore sepolto*. Rome: Tumminelli, 1945; *Racconti*. Turin: Einaudi, 1960; *Le terre del Sacramento*. Turin: Einaudi, 1950. Quoted in Sardelli, *Narratori Molisani*, 31–7, 49–74.

Kaihla, Paul. "Destination Europe: Canadians Are Returning to the Old Countries." *Maclean's*, 6 April 1992, 20–1.

Kalin, Rudolf. "The Development of Ethnic Attitudes." In Samuda, Berry, and Laferriere, *Multiculturalism in Canada*, 114–27.

Kappler, Brian. "Star Checks Migrants: Their Suffering Is Not Imagined." *Windsor Star*, 16 August 1973, 1, 4.

Kemp, Lloyd. "One Migrant Says Life in a Garage 'Not That Hard.'" *Windsor Star*, 17 August 1973, 1, 4.

– "'Political Gesture': 'Inhumane' Tag Angers Farms." *Windsor Star*, 17 August 1973, 5.

Kemp, Lloyd, and Diahne Martindale. "Ottawa Won't Name Offending Farmers." *Windsor Star*, 18 August 1973, 1, 4.

– "Whelan Explains 'Why' of Using Migrant Workers." *Windsor Star*, 21 August 1973, 1, 4.

Kinder, H., and W. Hilgemann. *The Penguin Atlas of World History*. Vol. 1. Translated by E.A. Menze. London: Penguin Books, 1978.

Kingsville Reporter. "Friends Mourn the Loss of Fred De Santis," 23 February 1988, 1, 3.

Kirkland, Richard I., Jr. "Competition: A New Dose of Capitalism Turns Italy Around." *Fortune*, 14 April 1986, 98–102.

Kogan, Norman. "Italy in the Modern World." In Chandler and Molinaro, *Culture of Italy*, 158–77.

Kuitunen, Maddalena. "Italian and Italians in Educational Institutions of English-Speaking Canada (1840–1887)." *Italian Canadiana* 2, no. 1 (Spring 1986): 1–13.

– "L'italianistica e l'emigrazione italiana a Toronto (1853–1984)." *Italian Canadiana* 1, no. 1 (Spring 1985): 38–50.

Labanca, Sergio. "Agnone ... da quarant'anni in qua! (5): 1946–1986." *L'eco dell'alto Molise*, 20 June 1986, 7.

Labbate, Giovanni. Introduction to *Le due valli del sole: Villacanale – Leamington*, by Anna Claudia Arduino and Antonio Arduino. Agnone: Arti Grafiche "San Giorgio," 1988.

Labriola, Antonio. *Scritti varii di letteratura e filosofia*. Bari: Laterza, 1906, 487. Quoted in Romano, *Storia d'Italia dal Risorgimento ai nostri giorni*, 31.

"La casetta in Canada." Italian popular song, by Mascheroni (music) and Panzeri (lyrics), 1957.

La Ciociaria. Storia arte costume. Presentazione di Giulio Andreotti. Rome: Editalia, 1972.

La Feria, Mario. "Raul d'Inghilterra." *L'Espresso*, 22 June 1986, 183, 185.

La Gazzetta. "Colombo: era italiana la campana della 'Nina,'" 26 June 1992.

– "Ellis Island: 'Isola di speranza, isola di lacrime,'" 3 June 1988, 4, 5.

– "Glace Bay, Nova Scotia: Il primo museo al mondo dedicato [all'opera] di Guglielmo Marconi," 19 July 1985, 1, 3.

– "La corruzione? Tangentopoli? Tutto il mondo & Paese," 1 October 1993, 4.

– "La revisione del Concordato," 17 February 1984, 5.

– "Little Italies in North America" [Summary of the Toronto Conference]. 8 June 1979, 1, 5.

– "Tutti I numeri di 'Tangentopoli'," 9 July 1993, 1.

– "Un'altra vittima di un certo metodo," 26 July 1993, 1, 5.

– "Un 'polo' che vale 13 mila miliardi," 10 June 1988, 1.

La Gumina, Salvatore J., ed. *WOP!: A Documentary History of Anti-Italian Discrimination in the United States*. San Francisco: Straight Arrow Books, 1973.

Lajeunesse, Ernst J., ed. *The Windsor Border Region: Canada's Southernmost Frontier: A Collection of Documents*. Champlain Society for the Government of Ontario. Toronto: University of Toronto Press, 1960.

Lambert, L. *Ontario's Lake Erie Commercial Fishery: A Social and Economic Profile*. Toronto: Commercial Fish and Fur Branch. Division of Fish and Wildlife, Ontario Ministry of Natural Resources. 1975.

La mogliera. Italian popular song, 1954. Sung by the Neapolitan Aurelio Fierro (heard by Walter Temelini on Italian radio programs in Canada in the 1950s–60s).

Lanciano, Domenico. "Agnone industriale: il turismo residenziale." *L'eco dell'alto Molise*, 20 March 1988, 7.

– "La questione meridionale." *L'eco dell'alto Molise*, 20 November 1986, 3.

Lanctot, Gustave. *Histoire du Canada*. Montreal: Beauchemin, 1967. Quoted in Menchini, *Giovanni Caboto*, appendix 3, 161–5.

Langer, William L., ed. *An Encyclopedia of World History: Ancient, Medieval, and Modern, Chronologically Arranged*. Boston: Houghton Mifflin, 1960.

La Palombara, Joseph. *Democracy, Italian Style*. New Haven, CT: Yale University Press, 1987.

"La questione siciliana." 1896. In Villari, *Il Sud nella storia d'Italia*, 1:246–69.

Lazzeri, Gerolamo. *Antologia dei primi secoli della letteratura italiana*. Reprint. Milan: Editore Ulrico Hoepli, 1954.

Leamington-Mersea Souvenir History and Centennial Program, 1867–1967. n.p. 1966.

Leamington Post. "Founders of Italian Community Honored," 4 May 1977, 1.

L'eco dell'alto Molise. "L'artigianato: fatti e non promesse," 20 May 1987, 3.

Lehr, John C., and D. Wayne Moodie. "The Polemics of Pioneer Settlement: Ukrainian Immigration and the Winnipeg Press." In "Ukrainians in the Canadian City." Special issue, *Canadian Ethnic Studies / Études Ethniques au Canada*, 12, no. 2 (1980): 88–101.

Leonard, Sister Anne. "Language and Literature in a Multicultural Curriculum." *Education and Canadian Multiculturalism: Some Problems and Some Solutions*. Canadian Society for the Study of Education: Eighth Yearbook, Faculty of Education, University of Saskatchewan, 1981, 49–59.

Leopardi, Giacomo. *Prose di Giacomo Leopardi*. Volume secondo delle *Opere*, edited by Giovanni Ferretti. Turin: UTET, 1964.

L'Espresso. "Editoriale: Guerre dell'etere e guerre di carta," 9 September 1984, 5–12.

– "Gli italiani e il nuovo boom economico [Sondaggio]." 5 October 1986, 6–11; and 7 December 1986, 270–3.

– "Il Manager: La 'Fortune' di DeBenedetti," 20 April 1986, 217.

– "Il patto elettronico," 27 April 1986, 215–16.

– "Lottizzazione televisiva: Le mani sul video," 29 June 1986, 6–9.

– "Nella rete dell'ingegnere," 2 November 1986, 295–8.

– "Olivetti in attesa," 31 August 1986, 154.

– "Parla De Benedetti," 14 December 1986, 40–50.

– "Sorpresa: siamo ricchi," 7 December 1986, 270–3.

Levi, Carlo. *Cristo si è fermato a Eboli*. Turin: Einaudi, 1946. Quoted in Cantarella, *Prosatori del Novecento*, 57–68; and in Villari, *Il Sud nella storia d'Italia*, 2:612–24.

– *Enciclopedia della letteratura Garzanti*. 2nd ed. (1974).

Leydi, Roberto. *I canti popolari italiani: 120 testi e musiche*. Milan: Mondadori, 1973.

Lipinsky, Lino S. *Giovanni da Verrazzano: The Discoverer of New York Bay, 1524*. New York: Museum of the City of New York and Istituto Italiano di Cultura in New York City, 1964.

Lodge, John C. *I Remember Detroit*. Detroit: Wayne State University Press, 1949.

Lombardi Satriani, L.M. *Intervista sulla Calabria.* Edited by Pasquale Falco. Cosenza: Edizioni Periferia, 1985. Quoted in Pitto, *Al di là dell'emigrazione,* 129, 134, 139n1.

Lombardi Satriani, L.M., and M. Meligrana. *Il Ponte di San Giacomo.* Milan: Rizzoli, 1982. Quoted in Pitto, *Al di là dell'emigrazione,* 101, 109n12, 109n18.

Lopez, Robert S., and Irving W. Raymond. *Medieval Trade in the Mediterranean World:* New York: Columbia University Press 1990.

Io sono Americano. Italian popular song, 1957/58 [author/singer uncertain; remembered by some Windsor Italian immigrants; frequently heard by Walter Temelini on Italian Radio Programs in Canada in the 1950s–1960s].

Lovelock, James. *The Ages of Gaia: A Biography of Our Living Earth.* New York: W.W. Norton, 1988.

Macaluso, Grace. "'Enemy Alien' Stigma Leaves Scars." *Windsor Star,* 23 January 1989, A1, A10.

– "Mystery Surrounds Cruel Wartime Raids." *Windsor Star,* 21 January 1989, A1, A4.

– "One Man's [Vito Peralta's] Story of Internment: Police Based Arrest on Photograph." *Windsor Star,* 21 January 1989, E1.

– "Redress Sought for 'Injustices.'" *Windsor Star,* 24 January 1989, A1, A9.

– "Repetition of Violations Can Be Avoided." *Windsor Star,* 24 January 1989, B1.

– "Righting 47-Year-Old Wrongs." *Windsor Star,* 23 January 1989, B1.

Machiavelli, Niccolò. *The Prince.* Translated by George Bull. Harmondsworth: Penguin Books, 1967.

Mack Smith, Denis. *Mussolini.* New York: Alfred A. Knopf, 1982.

MacLennan, Hugh. *Two Solitudes.* Toronto: MacMillan Canada, 1951.

MacPherson, H.L. "Public Attitude on Immigration Often in Fair-Weather Class." *Windsor Daily Star,* 21 May 1952, 4.

Macrone, Michael. *It's Greek to Me! Brush Up Your Classics.* New York: Cader Books, 1991.

Magister, Sandro. "La Multilingua [Come si parla in Italia]." *L'Espresso,* 9 September 1984, 58–63.

Maiorino, Tarquinio. "Agnone's Bells That Ring Round the World." ITALY *Italy,* 15 May–15 June 1988, 52–5.

Malfatti, Eugenia. "L'emigrazione italiana e il Mezzogiorno [The Italian migration and the 'Mezzogiorno']. In Rosoli, *Un secolo di emigrazione italiana: 1876–1976,* 97–116.

Manaresi, Alfonso. *Pantheon: corso di storia per la scuola media.* Vol. 3. Bologna: Casa Editrice "Poseidonia," 1952.

Mandrou, Robert. *From Humanism to Science, 1480–1700.* Translated by Brian Pearce. Harmondsworth: Penguin Books, 1978.

Mann, Nicholas. *Petrarch*. Past Masters Series. Oxford: Oxford University Press, 1987.

Manzoni, Alessandro. *I promessi sposi*. 1825–7. Quoted in Romano, *Storia d'Italia*, 33–5.

Marchand, Philip. *Marshall McLuhan: The Medium and the Messenger*. Toronto: Random House, 1989.

"Marconi, Guglielmo: 1874–1937." *Webster's Biographical Dictionary*. 1972 ed.

Marinelli, Gioconda. *Arte e fuoco: Campane di Agnone (Art and Fire: Bells of Agnone)*. Campobasso: Edizioni Enne, 1980.

Marrocco, Dante B. *La guerra nel Medio Volturno nel 1943*. Naples: Tipografia Laurenziana, 1974.

Martelli, Sebastiano. "Due casi di critica senza 'distanza': Scotellaro e Pasolini." *Misure critiche* 48 (1983): 69–79.

– "Emigrazione e America nella letteratura del Sud d'Italia." In *Italian Ethnics: Their Languages, Literatures and Lives*, edited by Dominic Candeloro, Fred L. Gardaphe, and Paolo A. Giordano, 20:71–8. Proceedings of the 20th Annual Conference of the American Italian Historical Association, Chicago, 11–13 November 1987. Staten Island, NY: American Italian Historical Association, 1990.

– "L'enciclopedia e il cruciverba: il primo romanzo di Jovine." In *Proposte Molisane: Quaderni di studi & ricerche sul Molise e sul Mezzogiorno*, 117–84. Campobasso: 82/2 Edizioni Enne, 1982.

– "Per un viaggio senza ritorno: 'Emigranti' di Francesco Perri." In *La cultura italiana negli anni '30–'45* (Omaggio ad Alfonso Gatto). Atti del Convegno – Salerno, 21–24 aprile 1980. Pubblicazioni dell'Università degli Studi di Salerno: Sezione Atti, Convegni, Miscellanee. 6. Vol. 1. Edizioni Scientifiche Italiane, 471–504.

– ed. *Rimanelliana: Studi su Giose Rimanelli / Studies on Giose Rimanelli*. Stony Brook, NY: Forum Italicum Publishing, 2000.

Martino, Giuseppe. "I ritardi del Mezzogiorno italiano nel processo di integrazione europea." GRTV *Press*, Anno 8 (Rome 1991). Reprinted in *La Gazzetta*, 3 June 1991, 4.

Masi, Ralph. "Multiculturalism in Health Care: Understanding and Implementation." *Journal of Ethno-Development* (Michigan Ethnic Heritage Studies Centre) 1, no. 2 (1992): 85–93.

Massa, Gaetano. *Italian Idioms and Proverbs*. New York: Las Americas Publishing, 1940.

Massari, Giuseppe. "Il brigantaggio." 1863. In Villari, *Il Sud nella storia d'Italia*, 1:89–102.

Mastrangelo, Rocco. *The Italian Canadians*. Multicultural Canada Series. Toronto: Van Nostrand Reinhold, 1979.

Mastronardi, Costantino. "Ai lettori – Lavori pubblici: ritardi inconcepibili." Editorial. *L'eco dell'alto Molise,* 20 June 1986, 1.

– "Ai lettori: Natura ed esigenze umane." Editorial. *L'eco dell'alto Molise,* 20 March 1988, 1.

– "Ai lettori: Vogliono che disertiamo?" Editorial. *L'eco dell'alto Molise,* 20 December 1986, 1.

Mattioli, Silvia. "Italia del Nord, Italia del Sud: Due realtà differenti." GRTV *Press,* Anno 7 (Rome 1991). Reprinted in *La Gazzetta,* 27 May 1991, 4.

McKinnon, Blair. "Italian Farm Workers Enjoy Canada Freedom." *Windsor Daily Star,* 14 September 1951, 16.

McLeod, Keith A. "Multiculturalism and Multicultural Education: Policy and Practice." In *Education and Canadian Multiculturalism: Some Problems and Some Solutions.* Canadian Society for the Study of Education. Eighth Yearbook, Faculty of Education, University of Saskatchewan, 1981, 12–26.

– ed. "Statement Adopted by the Canadian Council for Multicultural and Intercultural Education." *Multiculturalism/Multiculturalisme* 8, no. 1 (1984): inside cover.

McLuhan, Marshall. *Understanding Media: The Extension of Man.* New York: New American Library, 1964.

– *War and Peace in the Global Village.* New York, 1968. As quoted in Marchand, *Marshall McLuhan,* 209–301.

McNamara, Eugene. "An Ode to the Tomato." (Part of "In praise of the tomato..." by Mike Dunnell). *Windsor Star,* 18 September 1986, A9.

Meligrana, M., and L.M. Lombardi Satriani. *Un villaggio nella memoria.* Reggio Calabria / Rome: Gangemi Editore, 1984. Quoted in Pitto, *Al di là dell'emigrazione,* 59.

Menchini, Camillo. *Francesco Giuseppe Bressani: primo missionario italiano in Canada.* Montreal: Edizioni Insieme, 1980.

– *Giovanni Caboto: scopritore del Canada.* Montreal: Edizioni Riviera, 1974.

– *Giovanni da Verrazzano e la Nuova Francia.* Montreal: Edizioni Simposium, 1977.

– "Il Canada di Jacques Cartier e di Giovanni da Verrazzano." *Il Veltro,* Anno 29, nos 1–2 (January–April 1985): 115–23.

Mercatante, Anthony S. *The Facts on File Encyclopedia of World Mythology and Legend.* New York: Facts on File, 1988.

Messina, Maria. "La Mèrica." In Cresci and Guidobaldi, *Partono i bastimenti,* 42–3.

"Michigan Central Railroad." *Encyclopedia Canadiana.* 1977 ed.

Might's [Metropolitan/Greater Windsor] City Directory, 1961–87.

Migliorini, Bruno. *The Italian Language.* Translated by T. Gwynfor Griffith. London: Faber and Faber, 1984.

– *Storia della lingua italiana*. Florence: Sansoni, 1966.

Mignolo, Walter D. "The Darker Side of the Renaissance: Colonization and the Discontinuity of the Classical Tradition." *Renaissance Quarterly* 45, no. 4 (Winter 1992): 808–28.

Mondello, Salvatore. "Italians in the United States." In Chandler and Molinaro, *Culture of Italy*, 201–22.

Montanelli, Indro. Interview. In Bertoldi, *I nuovi italiani*. 47–55.

Morettin, Clara, and Rosa Rinaldi. "A Study of the Italian Immigrants in Windsor." Supervised by Walter Temelini and Rita Bison. Windsor: La Gazzetta Publishing, 1977.

Morrison, Neil F. *Garden Gateway to Canada: One Hundred Years of Windsor and Essex County 1854–1954*. Windsor: Herald, 1954.

Morrow, Lance. "How to Believe in Miracles." *Time*, 30 December 1991, 57–8.

Multiculturalism and Citizenship. *Multiculturalism: What Is It Really About/Le Point Sur le Multiculturalisme*. Ottawa: Minister of Supply and Services, 1991.

Mulroney, Brian. "Notes for an Address by Prime Minister Brian Mulroney." National Congress of Italian Canadians and the Canadian Italian Business Professional Association. Toronto, 4 November 1990. "Revue de Presse," *La Gazzetta* Archives.

Munari, Bruno. *Speak Italian: The Fine Art of the Gesture*. San Francisco: Chronicle Books, 2005.

Munro, Angus. "Windsor Co-operates to Help New Canadians Learn English, Prepare for Citizenship" / and "Educational Programs Make Good Citizens." *Windsor Daily Star*, 28 February 1953, 36.

Nader, Helen. "The End of the Old World." *Renaissance Quarterly* 45, no. 4 (Winter 1992): 791–807.

Nese, Marco, and Francesco Nicotra. *Antonio Meucci, 1808–1889*. Rome: Editrice ITALY Italy Magazine Publisher, 1989.

Newman, Peter C. "Italy's Daredevil Entrepreneurs." *Maclean's*, 9 November 1987, 40.

– "Mussolini's Corporate Legacy." *Maclean's*, 23 November 1987, 31.

– "A National Contempt for the Law." *Maclean's*, 7 December 1987, 40.

– "Olivetti's Global Deal Maker [Carlo De Benedetti]." *Maclean's*, 30 November 1987, 51.

Nice, Bruno. *Questo nostro mondo: Come conoscere l'Italia*. Novara: Istituto Geografico De Agostini, 1966.

Nichols, Peter. "[Gardini's] Ferruzzi: Greater Agro-Industry for a Bio-Based Future." ITALY *Italy*, 15 May–15 June 1987, 58–61.

– "In His [Gardini's] View Big Is Better and Great Is Best." ITALY *Italy*, 15 September–15 October 1988, 50–2.

– "A Summit Made in Italy: Olivetti's De Benedetti and the Economic Summit in Venice," ITALY *Italy*, 15 May–15 June 1987, 54–7.

– "The Worldwide Farmer [Raul Gardini]." ITALY *Italy*, 15 October–15 November 1986, 44–7.

Nitti, Francesco Saverio. "Nord e Sud." Turin, 1900. Reprinted as "Il Mezzogiorno e lo sviluppo economico italiano," in Villari, *Il Sud nella storia d'Italia*, 1:311–29.

Observer (London, UK). "Perennial Energy of an Anarchist: Kate Kellaway Meets Dario Fo," 30 September 1990, 63.

Omni. "Who's Ahead in the Space Race," July 1988, 72.

Omstead Fisheries/Foods Limited. *The Omstead Story.* n.d.

Ontario Advisory Committee on Race Relations. *The Development of a Policy on Race and Ethnocultural Equity.* September 1987.

Ontario Ministry of Citizenship and Culture. "Leamington Census Agglomeration, 1981." Received by the Windsor Italo-Canadian Culture Centre, 31 August 1984, WICCC Archives.

Ontario Ministry of Culture and Recreation. "Ontario Ethnocultural Profiles: ITALIANS." One of a series of articles on ethnocultural groups in Ontario [1979].

Ontario Ministry of Labour. Ontario Human Rights Commission. Race Relations Division. *Towards a Policy ... Race and Ethnic Relations in the Education System* [1984?].

Ottawa Citizen. "We Are Sorry: To Right the Wrongs of 1940." 9 November 1990, A12.

Palazzi, Fernando. *Novissimo dizionario della lingua italiana.* Milan: Casa editrice Ceschina, 1950.

Palmer, R.R. *A History of the Modern World.* 2nd ed. New York: Alfred A. Knopf, 1960.

Palmieri, J. Letter to the editor. *Border Cities Star,* 31 October 1933, 7.

Panofsky, Erwin. *Meaning in the Visual Arts: Papers in and on Art History.* Garden City, NY: Doubleday Anchor Books, 1955.

Paoli, Ugo Enrico. *Vita romana.* Milan: Mondadori, 1976.

Paolucci, Silvio. *Storia per la scuola media: Da Maometto alla Rivoluzione francese.* Vol. 2. Bologne: Zanichelli, 1969.

Pascoli, Giovanni. "Italy [1904]." In *Giovanni Pascoli: Antologia lirica con una scelta di prose.* 3rd edition, edited by Augusto Cicinelli, 251–78. Milan: Mondadori, 1962.

Pautasso, Luigi. *Il Santo cappuccino di Toronto: La vita di P. Luigi da Lavagna.* Toronto: Pal's Books, 1990.

Pavese, Cesare. *La luna e i falò* (1950). Quoted in Guido Fink, "The Other Side of the Moon." *Forum Italicum* 19, no. 1 (Spring 1985): 3–17.

Pearson, Craig. "The Gospels According to Ricci." *Windsor Star*, 4 May 2002, A1–A2.

Pekelis, Carla. *A Dictionary of Colorful Italian Idioms*. New York: Dutton, 1967.

Pei, Mario. *The Italian Language*. New York: S.F. Vanni, 1954.

– *The Story of Language*. Rev. ed. New York: New American Library, Mentor Book, 1966.

Peralta, Jerry, and Salvatore Peralta. Letter to the editor. *La Gazzetta*, 7 January 1991, 3.

Perboni, Elia. *Dizionario della musica pop-leggera italiana*. Milan: Gammalibri, 1984.

"Perosi, Lorenzo. 1872–1956." *Webster's Biographical Dictionary*. 1972 ed.

Petrarca, Francesco. *Canzoniere*. Edited by Gianfranco Contini. Turin: Einaudi, 1974.

– *Invectiva contra Gallum: Invectiva contra eum qui maledixit Italie*. In *Opere*, II, 1153–253. Quoted in Mann, *Petrarch*, 41–42, 116.

– *Le Familiari, scelta*. Edited by Enrico Bianchi. Introduction by Guido Martellotti. Milan: Giulio Einaudi Editore, 1977.

Pietropaolo, Domenico. "Aspects of English Interference on the Italian Language in Toronto." *Canadian Modern Language Review* 30, no. 3 (March 1974): 234–41.

Pilati, Paola. "Appalti stellari." *L'Espresso*, 12 October 1986, 229–30.

Pirandello, Luigi. "Il 'fumo'"/"L'altro figlio." In *Novelle per un anno*, 1:96–131, 926–44. Introduction by Corrado Alvaro. 2 vols. 8th edition. Milan: Mondadori, 1969. First edition 1956.

Pitto, Cesare. *Al di là dell'emigrazione: Elementi per un'antropologia dei processi migratori* [Beyond emigration: Elements for an anthropology of the migratory process]. Cosenza: Ionica Editirice, 1988.

Polidoro, Nicola. *Tricolore in Canada*. Montecarlo: Edizioni "Il Gabbiano," 1977.

Porzio, Domenico. Introduction to *Partono i bastimenti*. Edited by Cresci and Guidobaldi, 5.

Potestio, John, ed. *The Memoirs of Giovanni Veltri*. Toronto: Multicultural History Society of Ontario and the Ontario Heritage Foundation, 1987.

Potestio, John, and Antonio Pucci, eds. *The Italian Immigrant Experience*. Thunder Bay, ON: Canadian Italian Historical Association, 1988.

Potter, Simeon. *Our Language*. Harmondsworth: Penguin Books, 1963.

Principe, Angelo. "The Difficult Years of the Order of the Sons of Italy: 1920–1926." *Italian Canadiana* 5 (1989): 104–16.

– "Italiani a Toronto prima del 1861." *Italian Canadiana* 7 (1991): 98–120.

– "The Italo-Canadian Anti-Fascist Press in Toronto: 1922–1940." *Nemla Italian Studies* 4 (1980): 119–37.

Principessa, Nazzareno. "ITALIA – Consuntivi di fine anno: Riaffiora il 'caso Italia.'" *La Gazzetta*, 23 January 1987, 1.

Principessa, Nazzareno, Giovanna Chiarilli, and Patrizia Amati. "Qui Roma ... Per difendere Roma." *La Gazzetta*, 30 May 1986, 4.

Procacci, Giuliano. *History of the Italian People.* Translated by Anthony Paul. Harmondsworth: Penguin Books, 1986.

– *Storia degli italiani.* Bari: Laterza, 1978.

Proctor, Robert E. *Education's Great Amnesia: Reconsidering the Humanities from Petrarch Freud – With a Curriculum for Today's Students.* Bloomington: Indiana University Press, 1988.

Provincial Advisory Committee on Race Relations. *Report of the [Ontario] Provincial Advisory Committee on Race Relations: The Development of a Policy on Race and Ethnocultural Equity.* September 1987.

Pryke, K.G., and L.L. Kulisek, eds. *The Western District: Papers from the Western District Conference.* Essex County Historical Society and the Western District Council, 1983.

Pucci, A. "Canadian Industrialization versus the Italian *Contadini* in a Decade of Brutality, 1902–1912." In Harney and Scarpaci, *Little Italies in North America*, 183–207.

Quazza, Guido. *Corso di storia per i Licei e gli Istituti Magistrali.* Vol. 3. Ottava edizione. Turin: G.B. Petrini, 1973.

Raimondi, Ezio. "Language and the Hermeneutic Adventure in Literature." Translated by Albert Sbragia. *Forum Italicum* 18, no. 1 (Spring 1984): 3–25.

Ramirez, Bruno. "Immigration et rapports familiaux chez les Italiens du Québec." *Quaderni Culturali* 2, no. 1 (1982): 17–23.

Ramirez, Bruno, and Michele Del Balzo [Balso]. "The Italians of Montreal: From Sojourning to Settlement, 1900–1921." In Harney and Scarpaci, *Little Italies in North America*, 63–84.

Re, Vittorio. "In Defence of Alfonso Tonti." *La Gazzetta*, 7 December 1984, 4.

– *Michigan's Italian Community: A Historical Perspective.* First in a series of monographs in international and ethnic studies. Edited by Malvina Hauk Abonyi. Detroit: Office of International Exchanges and Ethnic Programs, Wayne State University, 1981.

Rennie, Gary. "Harrow Ends as Tobacco Research Hub." *Windsor Star*, "Historical Essex '75," 11 July 1975, 38.

Restaldi, Vittorio V. "Memoriale sugli italiani nei campi di internamento (1940–1942)." *Quaderni Canadesi: Rivista di storia, letteratura e politica italo-canadese* 2, no. 2 (January–February 1978): 5–8.

Ricci, Nino. "The Future of Your Past." Multicultural History Society of Ontario. Victoria College, University of Toronto, 7–10 November 1991.

– "Going to the Moon." *Saturday Night*, September 1990, 56–9.

– *In a Glass House*. Toronto: McClelland & Stewart, 1993.

– *Lives of the Saints*. Dunvegan, ON: Cormorant Books, 1990.

– *Radici – A Study of the Italian Immigrants in Leamington: A Report on the Research Completed through a Young Canada Works Grant in the Summer of 1979*. Submitted to the Leamington Roma Club Historical Book Committee, 1979.

Rice, Eugene F., Jr. *The Foundations of Early Modern Europe 1460–1559*. New York: W.W. Norton, 1970.

Rimanelli, Giose. *Peccato originale*. Milan: Mondadori, 1954. Quoted with introduction in T. Sardelli, ed., *Narratori Molisani*, 217–35.

– *Tiro al piccione*. Milan: Mondadori, 1961. Quoted in Sardelli, *Narratori Molisani*, 237–42.

Robey, David. Introduction to *The Open Work*, by Umberto Eco. Translated by Anna Cancogni, vii–xxxii. Cambridge, MA: Harvard University Press, 1989.

Roeder, Ralph. *The Man of the Renaissance – Four Lawgivers: Savonarola, Machiavelli, Castiglione, Aretino*. New York: Viking, 1933.

Romano, Sergio. *Storia d'Italia dal Risorgimento ai nostri giorni*. Milan: Mondadori, 1978.

Root, Waverly, and the editors of Time-Life Books. "The Mother Cuisine." In *The Cooking of Italy*, 9–32. New York: Time-Life Books, 1968.

Rosoli, Gianfausto (G.F.), ed. *Un secolo di emigrazione italiana: 1876–1976*. Rome: Centro Studi Emigrazione, 1978.

Rossi-Doria, Manlio. "La riforma anno due (8 giugno 1951)." In *Dieci anni di politica agrarian nel Mezzogiorno*. Bari, 1958, 89–95, 100–11, 114–20. Reprinted as "La riforma agraria," in Villari, *Il Sud nella storia d'Italia*, 2:660–80.

Royal Commission on Bilingualism and Biculturalism. *Book 4: The Cultural Contribution of the Other Ethnic Groups*. Ottawa: Queen's Printer, 1970.

Runner. "Oil's Well." June 1986, 11.

Sacchetti, Gian Battista. "Cento anni di 'Politica dell'emigrazione': L'incerta presenza dello Stato di fronte alla realtà migratoria italiana [One hundred years of emigration policy]. In Rosoli, *Un secolo di emigrazione italiana: 1876–1976*, 253–71.

St Joseph Daily Missal. New York: Catholic Book Publishing, 1959.

"St Michael the Archangel." In *St Joseph Daily Missal*, 1074.

Salandra, Antonio. "La questione sociale in Italia," 1878. In Villari, *Il Sud nella storia d'Italia*, 1:139–60.

Salomone, A. William. "From the Crisis of the Renaissance to the Cultural Revolution of the Risorgimento." In Chandler and Molinaro, *Culture of Italy*, 94–117.

Salvadori, Max. "Italy as a Country of Regions." In Chandler and Molinaro, *Culture of Italy*, 2–22.

Salvemini, Gaetano. *The Fascist Dictatorship in Italy*. New York: Henry Holt, 1927.

Samuda, Ronald J., John W. Berry, and Michel Laferriere, eds. *Multiculturalism in Canada: Social and Educational Perspectives*. Toronto: Allyn and Bacon, 1984.

Sandre, Loris. Letter to the editor. *Windsor Star*, 16 January 1978, 11.

Santeramo, Donato. "La lingua di Rocco Scotellaro." Paper presented at the Learned Societies Conference, Queen's University, 1 June 1991.

Santini, Loretta. *Il Molise: guida fotografica a colori*. Narni, Terni: Edizioni plurigraf, 1983.

Santoro, Enrico. "Il parco come ultima spiaggia." *L'eco dell'alto Molise*, 20 May 1987, 3.

Sapegno, Natalino. *Compendio di storia della letteratura italiana: Cinquecento, Seicento, Settecento*. Vol. 2, 16th ed. Florence: "La Nuova Italia," 1961.

Saraceno, Pasquale. "La mancata unificazione economica italiana a cento anni dall'unificazione politica." In *L'economia italiana dal 1861 al 1961. Studi nel I° centenario dell'Unità*. Milan, 1961. Quoted in Villari, *Il Sud nella storia d'Italia*, 2:631.

– "Lo sviluppo economico dei paesi sovrapopolati." Rome, 1952, 137–43, 145–54. Reprinted as "L'industria del Nord e la spesa pubblica nel Mezzogiorno," Villari, *Il Sud nella storia d'Italia*, 2:647–59.

Sardelli, Titina, ed. *Narratori Molisani*. Isernia: Libreria Editrice Marinelli, 1975.

Scaglione, Aldo. "Italy in the Middle Ages." In Chandler and Molinaro, *Culture of Italy*, 45–67.

Schiavo, Giovanni. *The Italians in America before the Civil War*. New York: Vigo, 1934. Quoted in Re, *Michigan's Italian Community*, 1.

Sciascia, Leonardo. "… per terre assai lontane." In Cresci and Guidobaldi, *Partono i bastimenti*, 7.

Scotti, Arturo.

– "Abituarsi alla libertà d'essere liberi." Editorial, *Corriere Canadese*, 28 May 1957.

– "A proposito di 'Dopolavoro.'" Editorial, *Corriere Canadese*, 9 July 1957.

– "Bisogna tornare a scuola." Editorial, *Corriere Canadese*, 10 September 1957.

– "Canada 1980." Editorial, *Corriere Canadese*, 12 February 1957.

– "'Carta canta ... e villan dorme!'" Editorial, *Corriere Canadese*, 12 March 1957.
– "Gli occhi neri dei poliziotti." Editorial, *Corriere Canadese*, 17 September 1957.
– "Gli Orangisti vedono rosso." Editorial, *Corriere Canadese*, 16 July 1957.
– "Gli occhi neri dei poliziotti." Editorial, *Corriere Canadese*, 17 September 1957.
– "Il nostro capitale." Editorial, *Corriere Canadese*, 7 May 1957.
– "Il Circolo Fascista del Consigliere Comunale." Editorial, *Corriere Canadese*, 27 August 1957.
– "Il 'mosaico' canadese non ha un nome inglese." Editorial, *Corriere Canadese*, 26 November 1957.
– "L'abito non fa il monaco, però!" Editorial, *Corriere Canadese*, 23 July 1957.
– "*Labour Day.*" Editorial, *Corriere Canadese*, 3 September 1957.
– "La Discriminazione c'è ma non si vede." Editorial, *Corriere Canadese*, 2 April 1957.
– "'La voce della verità.'" Editorial, *Corriere Canadese*, 17 December 1957.
– "Lavoro, non beneficenza." Editorial, *Corriere Canadese*, 19 March 1957.
– "'La vostra collaborazione.'" Editorial, *Corriere Canadese*, 16 April 1957.
– "Le Amazzoni Calabresi." Editorial, *Corriere Canadese*, 14 May 1957.
– "Le cose più serie si dicono scherzando." Editorial, *Corriere Canadese*, 8 January 1957.
– "L'immigrazione continua." Editorial, *Corriere Canadese*, 13 August 1957.
– "Maturità politica." Editorial, *Corriere Canadese*, 22 April 1957.
– "Non siamo criminali." Editorial, *Corriere Canadese*, 3 December 1957.
– "Porte aperte." Editorial, *Corriere Canadese*, 15 January 1957.
– "Povera, ma generosa l'Italia." Editorial, *Corriere Canadese*, 25 June 1957.
– "Promemoria per l'On. De Martino Sottosegretario agli Esteri." Editorial, *Corriere Canadese*, 20 August 1957.
– "Sono tutti emigranti." Editorial, *Corriere Canadese*, 19 November 1957.
– "Take It Easy." Editorial, *Corriere Canadese*, 19 February 1957.
– "Un'arma a doppio taglio." Editorial, *Corriere Canadese*, 10 December 1957.
– "Un Italo-Canadese al Parlamento di Ottawa." Editorial, *Corriere Canadese*, 18 June 1957.
– "Un povero giudice." Editorial, *Corriere Canadese*, 24 September 1957.
Sensini, Marcello. *Le parole e il testo: Teoria e pratica della comunicazione linguistica*. Milan: Mondadori, 1989.
Sereni, Emilio. *Vecchio e nuovo nelle campagne italiane*. Rome: Editori Riuniti, 1956. Reprinted in Villari, *Il Sud nella storia d'Italia*, 2:681–711.

Sestieri Lee, Valeria. "From Tuscany to the Northwest Territories: The Italian Community of Yellowknife." *Canadian Ethnic Studies/Études Ethniques au Canada* 19, no. 1 (1987): 77–86.

Sgarbossa, Mario, and Luigi Giovannini. *Il Santo del giorno*. Rome: Edizioni Paoline, 1978.

Shakespeare, William. *The Merchant of Venice*.

Sicoli, Florence. "ITALESE Spoken Here: Italian-Canadians Are Creating Their Own Lilting New Language." *Spectator* (Hamilton), 6 December 1980, 74.

Silone, Ignazio. *Fontamara*. Translated by Harvey Ferguson II. Foreword by Malcom Cowley. New York: Dell Publishing, 1961.

– *Vino e pane*. Milan: Mondadori, 1955. As quoted in Cantarella, *Prosatori del Novecento*, 33–44.

Silvestri. Sandra. "Un Oscar e un nuovo film per Giuseppe Tornatore, il regista di 'Nuovo Cinema Paradiso.'" GRTV *Press* (Rome 1990). Reprinted in *La Gazzetta*, 23 April 1990, 4.

Skinner, Quentin. *Machiavelli*. Past Masters Series. Oxford: Oxford University Press, 1986.

Slonim, Marc. Afterword in *Bread and Wine*, by Ignazio Silone. Translated by Harvey Ferguson II, 278–86. New York: New American Library, Signet Classics, 1963.

Soldati, Mario. *La verità sul caso Motta*. 1941. As quoted in G. Fink, "The Other Side of the Moon." *Forum Italicum*, 19, no. 1 (Spring 1985): 3–17.

Sonnino, Sidney. "Discorsi parlamentari [1880s agricultural crisis]." Rome, 1925, 1:148–50, 152–5, 156–7, 165–7. Reprinted as "La crisi agraria," in Villari, *Il Sud nella storia d'Italia*, 1:183–98.

– "I contadini in Sicilia." Florence, 1877. Reprinted as "Proprietari e contadini," in Villari, *Il Sud nella storia d'Italia*, 1:128–38.

– "L'emigrazione e le classi dirigenti." 1879. In Villari, *Il Sud nella storia d'Italia*, 1:171–9.

Spada, A.V. *The Italians in Canada*. Vol. 6 of *Canada Ethnica*. Ottawa: Riviera Printers and Publishers, 1969.

Spicer, Keith. "His Strike Is Food for Thought." *Windsor Star*, 13 March 1986, A8.

Spotts, Frederic, and Theodor Wieser. *Italy: A Difficult Democracy – A Survey of Italian Politics*. Cambridge: Cambridge University Press, 1986.

Statistics Canada. "Population by Selected Ethnic Origins, Canada, Provinces and Territories (1981)." *Canada Update from the 1981 Census*, 26 April 1983.

– *1901 Fourth Census of Canada*. Vol. 1. Table 11: Origins of the People, 320–1.

– *1911 Fifth Census of Canada.* Vol. 2. Table 7: Origins of the People by Sub-districts, 212–15.
– *1921 Sixth Census of Canada.* Vol. 1. Table 27: Population Classified According to Principal Origins of the People by Counties and Their Subdivisions, 1921, 456–9.
– *1931 Seventh Census of Canada.* Vol. 2. Table 33: Population Classified According to Principal Origins for Municipalities etc., 402–3.
– *1941 Eighth Census of Canada.* Vol. 2. Table 32: Population by Principal Origins, for Census Subdivision, 410–11.
– *1951 Ninth Census of Canada.* Vol. 1. Table 34: Population by Origin and Sex, for Counties and Census Divisions, 34-13 and 34-14; Table 47: Population by Birthplace and Sex, for Counties and Census Divisions, 47-13 and 47-14.
– *1951 Ninth Census of Canada.* Vol. 2. Table 6: Population by Origin, Specified Age Groups and Sex, for Cities of 30,000 and Over, 6–33; Table 61: Immigrant Population by Mother Tongue, Period of Immigration and Sex, for Cities of 30,000 and Over, 61-33.
– *1961 Census of Canada.* Population: Ethnic Groups. Counties and Subdivisions. Series SP. Bulletin SP-2. Catalogue 92-526. Population by Specified Ethnic Groups, for Census Subdivisions, 54.
– *1971 Census of Canada.* Vol. 1, part 3, bulletin 1.3-2, catalogue 92-723. Table 5: Populations by Ethnic Group and Sex, for Incorporated Cities or Towns and Other Municipal Subdivisions of 10,000 and Over, 5-9 and 5-10.
– *1971 Census of Canada.* Population: Specified Ethnic Groups. Census Divisions and Subdivisions. Special bulletin (SP-4), catalogue 92-774. Table 2: Population by Specified Ethnic Groups, for Census Subdivisions, 2-66.
– *1976 Census of Canada.* Vol. 2, bulletin 2.2, catalogue 92-821. Table 7: Population by Mother Tongue and Sex, for Municipalities of 5,000 Population and Over, 7-15.
– *1981 Census of Canada.* Vol. 1. National series, catalogue 92-911. Table 1: Population by Ethnic Origin and Sex for Canada and Provinces, 1981, 1-5 and 1-6.
– *1981 Census of Canada.* Vol. 3, profile series B, catalogue 95-945. Table 1: Selected Population, Dwelling, Household and Family Distributions, Showing Selected Social and Economic Characteristics, for Census Subdivisions of 5,000 Population and Over, 1-352 and 1-362.
– *1986 Census of Canada.* Part 2, catalogue 94-112. Selected Characteristics for Census Divisions and Census Subdivisions, 1986: 20% Sample Data, 121-2.
– *1986 Census of Canada.* Profile of Ethnic Groups. Dimensions, catalogue 93-154. Table 2: Characteristics of Selected Ethnic Groups, Showing Single

and Multiple Origins by Sex, for Canada, 1986 sample: 20% Sample Data, 2-9 and 2-10.

Stevens, G.R. *History of the Canadian National Railways.* New York: Macmillan, 1973.

Storia e geografia per la IV classe elementare. Scuole Italiane all'Estero. Verona: A. Mondadori, 1937–XV. See [Fascist Text].

Strati, Saverio. "Calabria contadina ed emigrazione." *La Regione Calabria, Supplemento "emigrazione": Rivista della Giunta Regionale della Calabria,* nos 4–5 (April–May 1990): 60–6.

Strickland, R.G. *The Language Arts in the Elementary School.* Lexington, MA: D.C. Heath, 1969.

Struever, Nancy. *The Language of History in the Renaissance: Rhetoric and Historical Consciousness in Florentine Humanism.* Princeton: Princeton University Press, 1970.

Sturino, Franc. Foreword to *Canadese: A Portrait of the Italian Canadians,* by Kenneth Bagnell, v–vi. Toronto: Macmillan, 1989.

– "Italians." *The Canadian Encyclopedia.* 2nd ed. (1988).

Sturzo, Luigi. "La Regione. Relazione letta a Venezia al III Congresso nazionale del Partito Popolare italiano il 23 ottobre 1921 / Il Mezzogiorno e la politica italiana. Discorso tenuto a Napoli il 18 gennaio 1923." In *Riforma statale e indirizzi politici,* Florence, 1923, 135–42, 149–50, 277–81; and Sturzo, review of *La Rivoluzione meridionale* by Guido Dorso, *Bollettino bibliografico di scienze sociali e politiche* 3, no. 1. Reprinted as "Il Partito popolare e la questione meridionale," in Villari, *Il Sud nella storia d'Italia,* 2:501–18.

Surlin, Stuart H., and Walter I. Romanow. "The Uses and Gratification of Heritage Language Newspapers and General Canadian Mass Media by Five Heritage Language Groups." *Multiculturalism/Multiculturalisme* 8, no. 2 (1985): 21–7.

"Swift, Gustavus Franklin." *Who Was Who in America,* 1:1211.

Swift & Company Annual Reports. 1960, 1962, 1967, 1970.

Sylvain, Robert. *Clerc, Garibaldien, Prédicant des Deux Mondes: Alessandro Gavazzi (1809–1889).* Vol. 1. Quebec: Le Centre Pédagogique, Place de l'Institut Canadien, 1962.

Tasca, Angelo [A. Rossi, pseud]. *Nascita e avvento del fascismo: L'Italia dal 1918 al 1922.* 2 vols. Bari: Laterza, 1976.

Tateo, Francesco. *I centri culturali dell'Umanesimo.* Bari: Laterza, 1980.

Taviani, Paolo Emilio. *La Genovesità di Colombo.* Genoa: ICIG, 1987.

Taylor, Charles. *The Ethics of Authenticity.* Cambridge: Cambridge University Press, 1992. Quoted in Alan Ryan, "Don't Think for Yourself Unless You Can," *New York Times Book Review,* 27 September 1992, 16.

– *Multiculturalism and "The Politics of Recognition."* Princeton, NJ: Princeton University Press, 1992.

– *Reconciling the Solitudes: Essays on Canadian Federalism and Nationalism.* Edited by Guy Laforest. Montreal and Kingston: McGill-Queen's University Press, 1993.

Telephone Directory(ies). Windsor (Ontario) and surrounding area/et les environs (1980–1990).

Temelini, Cellino. "Garanzia per Espatrio [Sponsorship declaration]" for Antonino (Antonio) Temelini, 6–8 February 1950 [copy], WICCC Archives.

Temelini, Walter. "Colloquio con il prof. Enzo Battaglia." *La Gazzetta,* 14 February 1986, 2–3.

– "Come va in Italia?" *La Gazzetta,* 10 September 1982, 1, 3–4.

– "The Growth of Sports Involvement in the Windsor Area." *Polyphony* 7, no. 1 (Spring/Summer 1985): 21–6.

– "A History of the Italian Business Community of Windsor, 1880–1930." *La Gazzetta,* 13 February 1987, 4, 5, 8.

– "The Humanities and Multicultural Education." In *Multicultural Education: A Partnership,* edited by Keith A. McLeod, 53–64. Toronto: Canadian Council for Multicultural and Intercultural Education, 1987.

– "The Italians in Windsor." *Polyphony* 7, no. 2 (Fall/Winter 1985): 73–80.

– "La Polizia di Windsor ricorda e onora Nereo Brombal." *La Gazzetta,* 18 February 1991, 1–3.

– "Le avventure di Peppino l'emigrante." Unpublished skits written for the Windsor Dante Alighieri Society Drama Group, December 1973 Festival. Also in videocassette. University of Windsor Media Centre, Q6-164.

– "Le scuse di Mulroney agli Italiani: Bastano?" *La Gazzetta,* 5 November 1990, 1, 4.

– "Literature and Culture in a Multicultural Society." In *Italian Literature in North America: Pedagogical Strategies,* edited by John Picchione and Laura Pietropaolo, 42–57. Proceedings of the International Conference at York University, 11–12 March 1989. Canadian Society for Italian Studies: Biblioteca di Quaderni d'italianistica, 9, 1990.

– "Little Italies in North America: 'Prominentismo,' 'cafonismo' e 'campanilismo' nelle comunità italiane in America." *La Gazzetta,* 8 June 1979, 4.

– "Media and Multiculturalism: Public and Ethnic or Heritage Language Media – Canadian Strategies in a Global Society." In *International Colloquium Reader,* 1:75–87. Detroit: Michigan Ethnic Heritage Studies Center, 1991.

– "The Multicultural Person: A Sum of the Best of Past Civilizations and the Best of Our Modern Technology." *Journal of Ethno-Development* (Michigan Ethnic Heritage Studies Center) 1, no. 1 (1992): 61–72.

– "1950: La prima cartolina di 'Christmas' dal Canada." *La Gazzetta*, 19 December 1986, 3.

– Review of *The Language of History in the Renaissance: Rhetoric and Historical Consciousness in Florentine Humanism*, by Nancy S. Struever. *Renaissance and Reformation* 8, no. 3 (1972): 121–2.

– "Study of an Agricultural Community: The Italians of Leamington." *Italian Canadiana* 3, no. 1 (Spring 1987): 80–91.

Temelini, Walter, and Rita Bison. "Servizio Speciale: Le Regioni italiane riscoprono i loro figli all'estero." *La Gazzetta*, 8 January 1988, 1, 4–5.

Terence [Publius Terentius Afer]. *Phormio*. Translated by Douglas Parker. In *The Complete Comedies of Terence*, edited by Palmer Bovie, 227–300. New Brunswick, NJ: Rutgers University Press, 1974.

Terzani, Tiziano. "Behind Japanese Superiority: A Tough View from Germany." *Der Spiegel*, 12 January 1987. Reprinted in *World Press Review*, March 1987, 27–8.

Tierney, Patrick. "Explorations." *Omni* 12, no. 5 (February 1990): 32, 67.

Time. "I Came, I Saw, I Gained Control ... Italy's De Benedetti Stages a Daring Raid on Belgium Inc.," 1 February 1988.

Tomasi, S.M., ed. *Perspectives in Italian Immigration and Ethnicity*. Staten Island, NY: Centre for Migration Studies, 1977.

"Tomolo." *Enciclopedia italiana "Treccani."* 1937 ed.

Toronto Daily Star. "Canadian Women 'Frivolous': He Writes for Nice Italian Girl." 2 September 1969.

– "The Disenchanted: And Why They're Leaving." 14 March 1968, 7.

"Toti, Enrico (1882–1916)." *Enciclopedia Garzanti*. 15th ed. (1967).

"Totò [Antonio De Curtis] (1898–1967)." *Enciclopedia Garzanti*. 15th ed. (1967).

Touring Club Italiano. *Annuario generale: Comuni e frazioni d'Italia*. Milan: TCI, 1988.

– *Guida rapida: Italia centrale*. Milan: TCI, 1966.

Trevelyan, G.M. *Garibaldi and the Thousand*. Harmondsworth: Penguin Books, 1965.

Tucci, Bruno. *L'Italia dimezzata: viaggio nelle regioni subalterne*. Cosenza: Lerici, 1978.

"Tu vo' [vuoi] far l'Americano." Italian popular song, 1950s, by Renato Carosone.

Union ... Windsor Directory, Including Sandwich and Walkerville, 1888–1911.

Vacanze ad Agnone. Videocassette, 1989.

Valeri, Nino, ed. *Storia d'Italia*. 2nd ed. 5 vols. Turin: Unione Tipografica-Editrice Torinese, UTET, 1965.

Vandall, Paul E., ed. *Atlas of Essex County: Its Cultural, Economic and Physical Characteristics Graphically Presented*. Windsor: Essex County Historical Association, 1965.

Vangelisti, Guglielmo. *Gli italiani in Canada*. Montreal: Chiesa Italiana di N.S. della Difesa, 1956.

Vansickle, Janice. "Growing Financial Problems." *Windsor Star*, 16 February 1985, C9.

Vecoli, Rudolph J. "A Report on the Status of the Italian American Ethnic Group." Presented at the Italian Canadian Club, Toronto, 1 June 1979.

"Verdi, Giuseppe. 1813–1901." *Webster's Biographical Dictionary*. 1972 ed.

Verducci, Carlo. *Proverbi marchigiani commentati*. Palermo: "Il Vespro," 1980.

Verga, Giovanni. "Cavalleria rusticana" (1880). In *Pane Nero and Other Stories*, edited by D. Maxwell White, 19–25, 88–91.

– *The House by the Medlar Tree*. Translated by Eric Mosbacher. Garden City, NY: Doubleday, 1955.

– *I Malavoglia*. Edited by Piero Nardi. Milan: Mondadori, 1963.

– *Novelle*. Edited by Piero Nardi. Milan: Mondadori, 1968.

– *Novelle rusticane*: "Libertà." Quoted by Napoleone Colajanni in Villari, *Il Sud nella storia d'Italia*, 1:229–30.

– *Pane Nero and Other Stories*. Edited by Maxwell White. Manchester: Manchester University Press, 1962.

– *Tutte le novella*. Vol. 1. Milan: Mondadori, 1969.

Verna, Anthony. "I nomi di origine italiana nella toponomastica canadese." *Il Veltro*, Anno 29, nos 3–4 (May–August 1985): 495–502.

Vernon's City of Windsor [Ojibway, Sandwich, Walkerville, Ford and Riverside] Directory. 1912–42.

Vico, Giambattista. *Scienza nuova*. 1744. Quoted in Salomone, "From the Crisis of the Renaissance," 108–11.

Villari, Pasquale. *Le Lettere meridionali ed altri scritti sulla questione sociale in Italia*. Florence, 1878, 39–42, 44–8, 62–3, 74–76. Reprinted as "Il Mezzogiorno e la questione sociale," Villari, *Il Sud nella storia d'Italia*, 1:105–17.

Villari, Rosario, ed. *Il Sud nella storia d'Italia: antologia della questione meridionale*. 2 vols. Bari: Laterza, 1972.

– *Mezzogiorno e contadini nell'età moderna*. Bari: Laterza, 1977.

Villata, Bruno. "Piemontesi nella Nuova Francia con il Reggimento 'Carignano.'" *Il Veltro*, Anno 29, nos 1–2 (January–April 1985): 137–50.

Visser, Margaret. Interview by Peter Gzowski. CBC Morningside, 1991.

Viti, Gorizio. *Conoscere 'I promessi sposi'*. Florence: Le Monnier, 1981.

Vittorini, Elio. *Conversazioni in Sicilia*. Milan: Bompiani, 1958. As quoted in Cantarella, *Prosatori del Novecento*, 45–6.

Volpe, Gioacchino. *L'Italia che nasce*. Florence: Vallecchi, 1969.

Wallace, Bruce. "Nino Ricci: Novelist." In "100 Canadians to Watch," *Maclean's*, 5 July 1993, 53.

Wangenheim, Elizabeth D. "Introduction." *Multiculturalism: Ethnicity and Aging* 4, no. 1 (1980): 3–6.

Watson, Greg. "Educators Blamed for Hurting Education of Immigrant Children." *Toronto Star*, 4 February 1976, B1.

Watson, Russel. Review of *Kissinger: A Biography*, by Walter Isaacson. *Newsweek*, 7 September 1992, 56.

Webster's Biographical Dictionary. 1972 ed.

Wells, H.G. *The Outline of History*. Vol. 2. Garden City, NY: Garden City Books, 1961.

Wheatley Journal. "Wheatley – Mersea – Romney Salute L.R. Omstead, Citizen of the Year." Special edition, 16 May 1976.

Whelan, Eugene, with Rick Archbold. *Whelan*. Toronto: Irwin Publishing, 1986.

Widick, B.J. *Detroit: City of Race and Class Violence*. Chicago: Quadrangle Books, 1972.

Williamson, James A. *The Voyages of the Cabots*. London: Argonauts, 1929. Quoted in Menchini, *Caboto*, 18, 60–1.

Windsor and Essex County Tourist and Convention Bureau. *Welcome to Windsor and Essex County*. n.d.

Windsor Daily Star. "Airman [E.A. Diodati] Asks Aid for Dad: Native Italian Was Fired [from Windsor Public Works Department] When His Country [Italy] Entered War [June 1940]," 21 March 1941, 3.

– "[Constable Nero/Nereo Brombal] Suspended [from Windsor Police Force]," 13 June 1940, 5.

– "Fascism Is Glorified in Italian Readers: Excerpts from Books Used in Canada Belie Claim No Propaganda Contained in Them," 19 May 1938, 5.

– "Fascist Teachings in Windsor Probed: Classes Stay Closed until Their Purpose Subjected to Scrutiny. Separate School Board Chairman Orders Inquiry: 125 Children Attending Saturday Courses at St Alphonsus," 14 May 1938, 3, 8.

– "Italians Here Give $1,200: Money Handed Over to Red Cross; Yearning for Axis Defeat"; and "Windsor Italians Give to Red Cross," 20 March 1942, 5, 6.

– "Italians Here Having 'Hell on Earth,' Says Mayor. Tolerance Plea Made. Reaume Declares Those in Windsor Have No Use for Fascism. But Jobs Are Gone," 20 January 1941, 3.

– "Italians [in Canada] Are Rounded Up: Several Hundred Taken in Coast-to-Coast Police Raid." / "Disorders Break Out: Demonstrations against Italian in Toronto District," 12 June 1940, 3, 6, 8.

- "Italian Liberals Elect Officers," 10 February 1940.
- "Italian Vote Calls for Aid, But Once Great Voice Not Heard by Members at Ottawa," 12 June 1940, 3, 10.
- "Italian Women of Windsor Hand Over Their Jewelry. Local Italians Donate Gold to Help Il Duce: Wedding Rings Included in Collection as 300 Hear Toronto Vice-Consul Give Version of War [in Ethiopia]." 27 January 1936, 3, 12.
- "Local Italians Donate Gold to Help Il Duce," 27 January 1936.
- "Mark Dinner by Endorsing Il Duce's Actions," 26 May 1936, 22.
- "Meconi [Luigi] Vague on Role as Head of City's 'Fascist Section.'" 18 May 1938, 3, 8.
- "More Arrested in Drive against Enemy Alien Suspects," 12 June 1940.
- "Ottawa Probes Windsor Fascist Class. Two Italian Teachers Barred from Canada by Immigration Law: 'Loyal Canadian' Charges Other Text Books Used by Organizer also Contain Obvious Propaganda," 16 May 1938, 3, 8.
- "Police Raid in Windsor [on the City's Italian community]," 12 June 1940.
- "Reopen Issue of Enemy Aliens in City Service. Adjustment Is Sought ... Mayor Maintains Grave Injustice Done Workers," 29 March 1941, 3.
- "Romanelli [Rocco] the Great Now Lives on Pension [in Wheatley]: Uncle of Luigi and Leone Was Once with Caruso but Is Now Practically Penniless," 25 August 1938, 7.
- "[School] Official Reprimanded: Secretary [Charles] Quenneville Rebuked by Trustees in Stand on Fascism. [Luigi] Meconi Vague on Role as Head of City's 'Fascist Section' ... Bar Italians from Rooms: Trustees Confirm Action by Separate School Chairman," 18 May 1938, 3, 8.
- "Send Enemy Aliens Home," 14 June 1940.
- "200 Italian-Born Here Affected by New Ottawa Ruling. Regulation Extended: All Naturalized since 1922 Must Register and Report [to Police]. Formerly since 1929." 24 August 1940, 3.
- "Windsor Italians Fight Plan to Aid Duce: Fascist Help Is Opposed. Soliciting Funds by Vice-Consuls Brings Protest." 25 January 1936, 3, 8.
Windsor Italo-Canadian Culture Centre. *The Windsor Italians.* Sponsored by Employment and Immigration Canada, 1985.
"Windsor's Alien Immigrants." *Evening Record* (Windsor), 1 June 1904, 8.
Windsor Star. "Boycott Denied by Roma Club," 17 January 1978, 3.
- "Canadians' Nutrition Poor, Food Meet Told," 22 February 1978, A7.
- "Dieting? Just Eat Italian." 25 June 1986, C11.
- "Essex, Kent Counties Look Ahead to Bumper Crops." In "Historical Essex '75," 38.
- "Harrow Research One of the Most Diversified." "Historical Essex '75," 11 July 1975, 42.

– *Historical Essex '75.* 11 July 1975.
– "Ontario Chamber Award Goes to Colasanti Farms," 30 September 1986, C6.
– "Problems in Language, Fast Food," 29 November 1984, C16.
– "Restaurateur Dead at Age 90," 16 December 1985.
– "Ricci's Novel 'Beautifully Paced': Times," 12 June 1991.
– "Secretary Quenneville Rebuked by Trustees in Stand on Fascism: Meconi Vague on Role as Head of City's 'Fascist Section,'" 18 May 1938.
– "Tourism Abounds Here." "Historical Essex '75," 11 July 1975, 42.
Wolkstein, Diane, and Samuel Noah Kramer. *Inanna: Queen of Heaven and Earth. Her Stories and Hymns from Sumer.* New York: Harper and Row, 1983.
Wood, Dean. "Social Studies Textbooks in a Multicultural Society." Special issue, *History and Social Science Teacher* 17, no. 1 (Fall 1981): 21–9.
Woodford, Frank B., and Arthur M. Woodford. *All Our Yesterdays: A Brief History of Detroit.* Detroit: Wayne State University Press, 1969.
Yalden, Max. "The Ambivalence of Language: Excerpts from Language Ethnicity and Community. Notes from an Address by the Commissioner of Official Languages, to the Conference on Heritage Language Education." Saskatoon, 16 June 1981. *Il Mercurio Culturale / The Cultural Mercury,* 10 September 1982, 1.
Zhang, Shishan. "In Celebration of Columbus Day, 1990: Columbus and China." *China Today* 39, no. 10 (October 1990): 54–8.
Zorzi Pugliese, Olga. "The Renaissance in Italy." In Chandler and Molinaro, *Culture of Italy,* 83–6.
Zucchi, John E. "Italian Hometown Settlements and the Development of an Italian Community in Toronto, 1975–1935." In Harney, *Gathering Place,* 123–4.
– *Italians in Toronto: Development of a National Identity, 1875–1935.* Montreal and Kingston: McGill-Queen's University Press, 1988.

Index